A God So Near

Patrick D. Miller
Charles T. Haley Professor of Old Testament Theology
Princeton Theological Seminary

A God So Near

Essays on Old Testament Theology in Honor of Patrick D. Miller

Edited by

BRENT A. STRAWN AND NANCY R. BOWEN

Winona Lake, Indiana
EISENBRAUNS
2003

Cataloging in Publication Data

A God so near : essays on Old Testament theology in honor of Patrick
  D. Miller / edited by Brent A. Strawn and Nancy R. Bowen.
      p.   cm.
  "Bibliography of the works of Patrick D. Miller, 1964–2001": p.
  Includes bibliographical references and indexes.
  ISBN 1-57506-067-1
    1. Bible. O.T.—Theology.   2. Miller, Patrick D.—Bibliography.
  I. Miller, Patrick D.   II. Strawn, Brent A.   III. Bowen, Nancy R.,
  1956–.
  BS1192.5.G63   2003
  230′.0411—dc21
                                                         2002154073

The paper used in this publication meets the minimum requirements of the
American National Standard for Information Sciences—Permanence of Paper
for Printed Library Materials, ANSI Z39.48-1984.⊚™

Contents

———◆———

v

Part II

"As Just as This Entire Law"
God's Nearness in the Torah
(Deuteronomy and Beyond)

Preface

"For what other great nation has a god so near to it as the LORD our God is whenever we call to him? And what other great nation has statutes and ordinances as just as this entire law that I am setting before you today?" (Deut 4:7–8)

This volume takes its name from the text above, one of Patrick D. Miller's favorites in the book of Deuteronomy, which, in turn, is one of his favorite biblical books.[1] The title is therefore quite appropriate for a volume intended to honor this gifted scholar and teacher. But the title is even more appropriate insofar as this volume focuses primarily on two of Miller's central interests — Deuteronomy and the Psalms[2] — and uses these as text bases to get at the larger topics of Old Testament Theology and Biblical Theology, both of which are also central topics in Miller's research, writing, and teaching. In this light, the Deuteronomic text is an apt entrée into these issues as it highlights that Israel's God is near to it — indeed, near*er* to it than *any* other deity to *any* other nation — in two primary ways, each of which highlight a different aspect and a different subject:

- In *the calling out (qr')* of Israel to its God; and
- In *the just law (tôrâ)* of God given to Israel.[3]

Put this way, the whole of Israel's life with God, perhaps even the whole of the Old Testament, can be seen as an outworking of this schema — God giving just Torah to Israel, becoming manifest in the righteous life of the

---

1. One might note, for instance, that Miller utilizes this text in the titles of the first and second chapters in his book, *They Cried to the Lord: The Form and Theology of Biblical Prayer* (Minneapolis: Fortress, 1994). Those students who have studied Deuteronomy under Miller will also recall the emphasis he places on this text in his always-memorable lectures.

2. See the bibliography of Miller's works at the end of this volume and note, especially, the following items: *Interpreting the Psalms* (Philadelphia: Fortress, 1986), *Deuteronomy* (Interpretation; Louisville: John Knox, 1990), *They Cried to the Lord*, and "Deuteronomy and Psalms: Evoking a Biblical Conversation," *JBL* 118 (1999): 3–18.

3. For an extensive treatment of Deut 4:5–8, see Georg Braulik, "Wisdom, Divine Presence and Law: Reflections on the Kerygma of Deut 4:5–8," in idem, *The Theology of Deuteronomy: Collected Essays of Georg Braulik, O.S.B.* (trans. Ulrika Lindlbad; North Richland Hills, Tex.: BIBAL, 1994) 1–25. For Miller's own treatment, see his *Deuteronomy*, 53–63, esp. 54–57.

community of faith, as it were (so, especially, Deuteronomy); and God near to Israel whenever it cries out to its Lord, be it in praise, lament, or repentance (so, especially, the Psalms). Each of the essays in this collection speaks, in its own way, to these issues and these broader rubrics of prayer and praxis, Torah and Tehillah.

In addition, many of the essays speak to several tributaries that stem from these topics and that have also defined Miller's scholarly and ecclesial work. So, even while considering prayer and praxis, the essays also focus their attention on women's contributions to the life of ancient Israel and life today; the world, texts, and history of Israel and the ancient Near East; and the use of Scripture in the worship of faith communities, both ancient and modern. They also extend outward—as every theological endeavor must—to touch still other topics and themes that lie outside of Deuteronomy and the Psalms, even outside of the biblical text proper for that matter. This, too, is fitting in a volume intended to honor a scholar who, though a specialist in the Old Testament and its ancient Near Eastern environment, is also well-known for his work as the editor of the journal *Theology Today*.

The depths of Miller's contributions to church and academy are reflected in the depth of his relationships with family, friends, and colleagues. One of the most difficult editorial tasks in this project was to narrow down the huge list of potential contributors. A "steering committee" of sorts, comprising Nancy Bowen, Walter Brueggemann, James Limburg, Richard Nelson, Carolyn Pressler, Katharine Doob Sakenfeld, and Brent Strawn, convened in Orlando at the Annual Meeting of the Society of Biblical Literature (November 1998) to work on this very task. We express our thanks to this group for its helpful input and for assisting us in the initial stages of delimiting the potential contributor pool.

It became immediately apparent that we would be unable to invite everyone who could (and should) have been invited to contribute to this volume. Of the scholars that were finally invited to contribute, not one declined. And many of them suggested to us still others who should "definitely" be included in the tribute. This is, on the one hand, a confession and apology on our part to the many who are not included here, as well as—and this is more important than the confession—a testimony to the deep and wide appreciation for Miller and his work in the world of biblical and theological scholarship. A line from one of the persons involved in this project captures the mood quite well, when he wrote that he considered Miller "one of the finest scholars I know, both in terms of his academic achievements and his humanity." Such sentiments were commonplace in our correspondence with persons about this volume. Certainly an individual who receives such praise deserves a much longer (and perhaps even multiple) *Festschrift(en)*!

That is now out of our hands, however. So, on behalf of our fellow contributors and the many others not included here but who nevertheless join us in congratulating and appreciating Miller and his work, we offer the following collection as a small token of our deep appreciation and admiration of him. If it is true that our God is so near, that fact has been demonstrated—at least in part—by Miller's work and way among us.

Finally, we would be remiss if we did not acknowledge the help and labor of the many who helped make this volume possible. Our thanks go, first, to President Thomas W. Gillespie of Princeton Theological Seminary, whose generous help made this publication possible. We also thank each of the contributors for their outstanding work. We are also grateful to Jim Eisenbraun and Beverly Fields of Eisenbrauns for their professional and helpful assistance and for including this volume in Eisenbrauns' long and distinguished history of *Festschrift* publication. Finally, bouquets and praise to Mary Ann Miller who joyfully assisted us in making sure that this tribute came to be and that it would come to be unbeknownst to Pat!

BRENT A. STRAWN
NANCY R. BOWEN

Abbreviations

———◆———

AB	Anchor Bible
ABD	*Anchor Bible Dictionary* (ed. D. N. Freedman et al.; 6 vols.; New York: Doubleday, 1992)
AEL	M. Lichteim, *Ancient Egyptian Literature* (3 vols.; Berkeley: University of California Press, 1971–1980)
AEM	Archives épistolaires de Mari
AJBI	*Annual of the Japanese Biblical Institute*
AnBib	Analecta biblica
ANET	J. B. Pritchard, ed., *Ancient Near Eastern Texts Relating to the Old Testament* (3rd ed.; Princeton: Princeton University Press, 1969)
ANF	*Ante-Nicene Fathers*
ARM	Archives royales de Mari
ASNU	Acta seminarii neotestamentici upsaliensis
AUSS	*Andrews University Seminary Studies*
AV	Authorized Version
BASOR	*Bulletin of the American Schools of Oriental Research*
BDB	F. Brown, S. R. Driver, and C. A. Briggs, *A Hebrew and English Lexicon of the Old Testament* (Oxford: Oxford University Press, 1907)
BETL	Bibliotheca ephemeridum theologicarum lovaniensium
Bib	*Biblica*
BibInt	*Biblical Interpretation*
BKAT	Biblischer Kommentar, Altes Testament
BN	*Biblische Notizen*
BRev	*Bible Review*
BWANT	Beiträge zur Wissenschaft vom Alten und Neuen Testament
BZ	*Biblische Zeitschrift*
BZAW	Beihefte zur Zeitschrift für die alttestamentliche Wissenschaft
CAD	*The Assyrian Dictionary of the Oriental Institute of the University of Chicago*
CahRB	Cahiers de la Revue biblique
CBQ	*Catholic Biblical Quarterly*
CBQMS	Catholic Biblical Quarterly Monograph Series
CurTM	*Currents in Theology and Mission*
DDD	*Dictionary of Deities and Demons in the Bible* (ed. K. van der Toorn, B. Becking, and P. W. van der Horst; Leiden: E. J. Brill, 1995; 2d ed. = 1999)
DJD	Discoveries in the Judaean Desert
EvT	*Evangelische Theologie*

FOTL	Forms of the Old Testament Literature
FRLANT	Forschungen zur Religion und Literatur des Alten und Neuen Testaments
GBS	Guides to Biblical Scholarship
GKC	*Gesenius' Hebrew Grammar* (ed. E. Kautzsch; trans. A. E. Cowley; 2d ed.; Oxford: Oxford University Press, 1910)
HALOT	L. Koehler, W. Baumgartner, and J. J. Stamm, *The Hebrew and Aramaic Lexicon of the Old Testament* (trans. and ed. M. E. J. Richardson; 5 vols.; Leiden: E. J. Brill, 1994–2000)
HAR	*Hebrew Annual Review*
HAT	Handbuch zum Alten Testament
Hen	*Henoch*
HKAT	Handkommentar zum Alten Testament
HSM	Harvard Semitic Monographs
HSS	Harvard Semitic Studies
HTKAT	Herders theologischer Kommentar zum Alten Testament
HTR	*Harvard Theological Review*
IBT	Interpreting Biblical Texts
ICC	International Critical Commentary
Int	*Interpretation*
IRT	Issues in Religion and Theology
ITC	International Theological Commentary
ITQ	*Irish Theological Quarterly*
JAOS	*Journal of the American Oriental Society*
JBL	*Journal of Biblical Literature*
JHNES	Johns Hopkins Near Eastern Studies
JNES	*Journal of Near Eastern Studies*
JNSL	*Journal of Northwest Semitic Languages*
JPOS	*Journal of the Palestine Oriental Society*
JSNT	*Journal for the Study of the New Testament*
JSOT	*Journal for the Study of the Old Testament*
JSOTSup	Journal for the Study of the Old Testament: Supplement Series
JTS	*Journal of Theological Studies*
KatBl	*Katholische Blätter*
KD	Karl Barth, *Die kirchliche Dogmatik* (4 vols. in 13; Zollikon: Verlag der Evangelischen Buchhandlung, 1932-1970)
KJV	King James Version
KTU	*The Cuneiform Alphabetic Texts from Ugarit, Ras Ibn Hani, and Other Places* (ed. M. Dietrich, O. Loretz, and J. Sanmartín; Münster: Ugarit-Verlag, 1995)
LCBI	Literary Currents in Biblical Interpretation
LXX	Septuagint
MSU	Mitteilungen des Septuaginta-Unternehmens
MT	Masoretic Text
NAB	New American Bible
NAC	New American Commentary

NCB	New Century Bible
NEchtB	Neue Echter Bibel
NIB	*The New Interpreter's Bible*
NICOT	New International Commentary on the Old Testament
NJPSV	New Jewish Publication Society Version (Tanakh)
NPNF	*Nicene and Post-Nicene Fathers*
NRSV	New Revised Standard Version
NRTh	*La nouvelle revue théologique*
OBO	Orbis biblicus et orientalis
ÖBS	Österreichische biblische Studien
OBT	Overtures to Biblical Theology
OG	Old Greek
Or	*Orientalia*
OT	Old Testament
OTG	Old Testament Guides
OTL	Old Testament Library
OTS	Old Testament Studies
PG	Patrologia graeca (ed. J.-P. Migne; 162 vols.; Paris, 1857–1886)
PL	Patrologia latina (ed. J.-P. Migne; 217 vols.; Paris, 1844–1864)
PSB	*The Princeton Seminary Bulletin*
QD	Quaestiones disputatae
RB	*Revue biblique*
REB	Revised English Bible
ResQ	*Restoration Quarterly*
REV	Revised English Version
RevQ	*Revue de Qumran*
RSV	Revised Standard Version
SamP	Samaritan Pentateuch
SBAB	Stuttgarter biblische Aufsatzbände
SBLDS	Society of Biblical Literature Dissertation Series
SBLMS	Society of Biblical Literature Monograph Series
SBLSCS	Society of Biblical Literature Septuagint and Cognate Studies
SBTS	Sources for Biblical and Theological Study
SEL	*Studi epigrafici e linguistici*
TAPA	*Transactions of the American Philological Association*
TAPS	Transactions of the American Philosophical Society
TBT	*The Bible Today*
TDOT	*Theological Dictionary of the Old Testament* (ed. G. J. Botterweck and H. Ringgren; trans. J. T. Willis et al.; Grand Rapids: Eerdmans, 1974–)
TLOT	*Theological Lexicon of the Old Testament* (ed. E. Jenni and C. Westermann; 3 vols.; trans. M. E. Biddle; Peabody: Hendrickson, 1997)
TOTC	Tyndale Old Testament Commentaries
TT	*Theology Today*
TWAT	*Theologisches Wörterbuch zum Alten Testament* (ed. G. J. Botterweck and H. Ringgren; Stuttgart: W. Kohlhammer, 1973–)
UF	*Ugarit-Forschungen*

VT	*Vetus Testamentum*
VTSup	Supplements to Vetus Testamentum
WBC	Word Biblical Commentary
WMANT	Wissenschaftliche Monographien zum Alten und Neuen Testament
WW	*Word and World*
ZABR	*Zeitschrift für altorientalische und biblische Rechtgeschichte*
ZAW	*Zeitschrift für die alttestamentliche Wissenschaft*

Sigla

‖	is parallel to/paralleled by
/	used to separate lines of poetry

Additionally, note that: (a) versification follows the English text unless otherwise indicated, and (b) English translations follow the NRSV unless otherwise indicated.

Contributors

NANCY R. BOWEN
Associate Professor of Old Testament
Earlham School of Religion

WALTER BRUEGGEMANN
William Marcellus McPheeters Professor of Old Testament
Columbia Theological Seminary

FRANK MOORE CROSS
Hancock Professor of Hebrew and Other Oriental Languages, Emeritus
Harvard University

TERENCE E. FRETHEIM
Elva B. Lovell Professor of Old Testament
Luther Seminary

FRANK-LOTHAR HOSSFELD
Professor of Old Testament
Rheinische Friedrich-Wilhelms-Universität Bonn

J. GERALD JANZEN
MacAllister-Petticrew Professor of Old Testament, Emeritus
Christian Theological Seminary

WERNER E. LEMKE
Baptist Missionary Training School Professor of Biblical Interpretation
Colgate Rochester Crozer Divinity School

JAMES LIMBURG
Professor of Old Testament
Luther Seminary

NORBERT LOHFINK
Professor of Old Testament Emeritus
Philosophisch-theologische Hochschule Sankt Georgen Frankfurt am Main

JAMES LUTHER MAYS
Cyrus McCormick Professor Emeritus of Hebrew and the Old Testament
Union Theological Seminary and Presbyterian School of Christian Education

RICHARD D. NELSON
W. J. A. Power Professor of Biblical Hebrew and Old Testament Interpretation
Perkins School of Theology, Southern Methodist University

KATHLEEN O'CONNOR
   Professor of Old Testament Language, Literature, and Exegesis
   Columbia Theological Seminary

DENNIS T. OLSON
   Professor of Old Testament
   Princeton Theological Seminary

CAROLYN PRESSLER
   Harry C. Piper Jr. Professor of Biblical Interpretation
   United Theological Seminary of the Twin Cities

J. J. M. ROBERTS
   William Henry Green Professor of Old Testament Literature
   Princeton Theological Seminary

KATHARINE DOOB SAKENFELD
   W. A. Eisenberger Professor of Old Testament Literature and Exegesis
   Princeton Theological Seminary

GERHARD SAUTER
   Professor Emeritus of Systematic and Ecumenical Theology
   Rheinische Friedrich-Wilhelms-Universität Bonn

CHOON-LEONG SEOW
   Henry Snyder Gehman Professor of Old Testament Language and Literature
   Princeton Theological Seminary

BRENT A. STRAWN
   Assistant Professor of Old Testament
   Candler School of Theology, Emory University

MARK A. THRONTVEIT
   Professor of Old Testament
   Luther Seminary

W. SIBLEY TOWNER
   Professor Emeritus of Biblical Interpretation
   Union Theological Seminary and Presbyterian School of Christian Education

RENITA J. WEEMS
   Associate Professor of Hebrew Bible
   Vanderbilt University Divinity School

MICHAEL WELKER
   Professor of Systematic Theology
   Ruprecht-Karls-Universität Heidelberg

H. G. M. WILLIAMSON
   Regius Professor of Hebrew
   University of Oxford

ERICH ZENGER
   Professor of Old Testament
   Westfälische Wilhelms-Universität Münster

———◆———

Part I

"Near Whenever We Call"

God's Nearness in Israel's Crying Out (The Psalms and Beyond)

Reading the Lament Psalms Backwards

H. G. M. WILLIAMSON

The psalms of lament have long presented interpreters of the Old Testament with a crop of difficulties that have evoked a variety of widely diverging proposals and hypotheses. In his many publications on the Psalter, Patrick D. Miller has done much to advance our understanding of the issues involved, and he has naturally done so from the perspective of a well-informed and sensitive expert. In the present essay, I should like to consider an aspect of the lament psalms that arises from a sense of frustration with the standard proposal, experienced since my undergraduate days, that the lament psalms are to be read from the setting of the psalmist's own suffering. Although aspects of my proposal have been anticipated by others, the argument presented here is not generally acknowledged in mainstream literature, and, therefore, it may be worth opening up the topic once again. It is my experience of Miller's friendship, collegial openness, and warm hospitality that has emboldened me to do this within a volume designed so appropriately to honor him.

In order to clear the ground of any possible misunderstanding, let me start by affirming a couple of points that are now widely accepted and that I fully endorse. First, it is obvious that much of the language in the psalms of lament is metaphorical or pictorial, and that it makes use of stereotypical phraseology to give this expression, particularly in those sections where the psalmists describe their actual suffering.[1] There have been many attempts to identify the psalmist's situation(s) more precisely, and the cogency of these proposals varies.[2] It is probable, however, that whatever situations lie behind the present language, they are already at least one step

---

1. It is not my intention in this somewhat schematic essay to attempt full documentation of every possible opinion. For this particular matter, see, for instance, Patrick D. Miller, *Interpreting the Psalms* (Philadelphia: Fortress, 1986).

2. For a helpful overview, see John Day, *Psalms* (OTG; Sheffield: Sheffield Academic Press, 1990) 19–38, with further bibliography.

3

removed from the present text. To give a standard example, it may have been the case that there were occasions when individuals were falsely accused and that they turned to prayer before their trial. It is far less certain, however, whether there were standard psalms "on tap" for them to use in such situations. It is more likely that what we have now are imaginative poetic uses of these occasions to give expression to a much wider range of experiences of injustice.

Second, in any search for "original" purposes and settings for the psalms, there should be no claim that this is definitive for interpretation or that alternative uses are therefore in any way illegitimate. I know, for instance, that I am not alone in having found Walter Brueggemann's essay "Psalms and the Life of Faith: A Suggested Typology of Function" to be a shaft of light, penetrating the darkness that had settled over the responsible use of the psalms in personal and pastoral practice after the pall cast by the overly wooden and historicist application of some form-critical approaches.[3] Indeed, such use and reuse must have already been taking place within the long period covered by the composition and collection of the Psalter itself. Nothing that follows in this essay is at odds with this observation, even though it will be suggested that a better appreciation of the "original setting" of the psalms has positive theological implications of its own.

With these two points stated, I turn now to the issue at hand, namely, the situation underlying the composition and use of the psalms of lament.[4] The overwhelming majority of commentators assume this to be *the actual time of suffering*. The lament gives expression to a variety of deeply painful situations, such as sickness, social exclusion, false accusation, and so on; indeed, as already mentioned, the language is such that it is capable of serving to articulate an almost infinite number of such experiences, and this no doubt accounts for the enduring value that is set upon them. Furthermore, the very process of articulation is the first step in the healing process: a net of familiarity is thereby cast over the initially disorienting experience of suffering, and so serves rather like a medical diagnosis in the modern world. The frighteningly unfamiliar is found to have been traveled by others beforehand, and this may give rise to hope that deliverance will come, as it has

3. Walter Brueggemann, "Psalms and the Life of Faith: A Suggested Typology of Function," *JSOT* 17 (1980) 3–32, reprinted in idem, *The Psalms and the Life of Faith* (ed. Patrick D. Miller; Minneapolis: Fortress, 1995) 3–32.

4. In this connection, Erhard Gerstenberger's comment is apposite: "while formal analysis in many instances has reached a final stage, the exploration of settings is still very much a task of the future" ("Psalms," in *Old Testament Form Criticism* [ed. John H. Hayes; San Antonio: Trinity University Press, 1974] 179–223; citation from 221). Although Gerstenberger's comment is concerned primarily with social settings, it can equally well be referred to the setting for reading.

in the past. It thus follows that many of the psalms of lament conclude with a "certainty of hearing," in which the psalmists express confidence that their prayers will be heard and that they will again join the congregation of the faithful in worship at the sanctuary.

How convincing is this reconstruction of the psalmists' situation? Several questions remain that give one reason to doubt this reconstruction. Some of these may be obvious and pedantic, but they will not go away on that account alone. In the first place, it is difficult to see how such a situation can be accommodated with the widespread view that the majority of the psalms as we have them are closely associated with cultic usage, if not origin. Most of the material in the laments describes situations that render a cultic setting impossible. Sometimes, that is, the psalmists—at the time of their suffering—would have been physically unable to be present in the cult, and at other times they would have been excluded from the cultic community on ritual or quasi-ritual grounds, whether justifiably or not. It is thus no surprise that the laments frequently mention a period of separation or alienation from the sanctuary or a desire to rejoin the community at worship (e.g., Pss 27:4; 28:2; 35:18; 42:2, 4; 43:3–4; 61:4; 69:9).[5]

Second, this disjuncture would be particularly acute were it true that the change of mood in the laments was due to the (unrecorded) delivery of a priestly salvation oracle. Though by no means universally adopted, this explanation for the change of mood in most of the psalms of lament has been understandably popular ever since it was first proposed by Begrich.[6] The experience of Hannah in 1 Samuel 1 provides a fine example. It is clear, however, that the situation of most of the psalmists, in the usual understanding, would not have permitted them to imitate Hannah in attending the sanctuary.

Third, attention has not been sufficiently focused on the distinction in this regard between individual and communal laments. If, for the moment, we may accept the usual view that communal laments were used in times of national crisis, it is surely most peculiar that they never finish with the expression of a certainty of hearing. By definition, these laments must have been public—that is, cultic—performances, whether led by the king or by the priests. If ever there was an occasion in which we should expect an oracle of salvation to be delivered, it would be then, and indeed there is

---

5. The force of this point would still hold even if Gerstenberger's minority opinion were adopted that for "sanctuary" and "community" we should substitute something like "the small, organic group of family, neighborhood, or community." See Erhard S. Gerstenberger, *Psalms, Part 1: With an Introduction to Cultic Poetry* (FOTL 14; Grand Rapids: Eerdmans, 1988) 33; and Rainer Albertz, *Persönliche Frömmigkeit und offizielle Religion: Religionsinterner Pluralismus in Israel und Babylon* (Stuttgart: Calwer, 1978) esp. 25–27.

6. Joachim Begrich, "Das priesterliche Heilsorakel," *ZAW* 52 (1934) 81–92.

indirect evidence to suggest that this was in fact the case.[7] Nevertheless, oracles of salvation are rarely recorded in the Psalter,[8] nor do communal lament psalms even once give evidence for the change of mood that might have followed from their delivery. Certainly, there are expressions of hope that the community will survive to praise God in the future (e.g., Pss 79:13; 80:18; 85:6), but never the kind of confident statements with which so many of the individual laments conclude. This strict distinction would seem to argue that the situation of the psalmists was not identical in the two cases, if one of the basic premises of the form-critical method is to be believed.

Fourth, a similar distinction is to be observed between the lament psalms of the Psalter and the prose prayers for help elsewhere in the Old Testament.[9] Were it the case that expressions of confidence regularly accompanied such prayers at the time of distress itself, we might have expected there to be examples of this in the narrative contexts that characterize the use of such prayers outside the Psalter. The fact that this is not so suggests that we should, perhaps, look for some alternative setting for the laments that include this element within the Psalter.

Finally, there is something unrealistic, even faintly ludicrous (or macabre), about the suggestion that the suffering psalmist could give voice to the kind of optimistic sentiments that we find in many of the assurances of a hearing. In making this point, it should again be stressed that we are no doubt dealing with the imaginative world of the poet. The problem does not arise only if the psalm was literally written by someone during their suffering; indeed, in many cases it is difficult to see how they could have been physically capable of such writing. In the world of the text, however, which may in many cases have been informed by the memory of past distress, it is psychologically and pastorally difficult to imagine that anyone could have

---

7. An excellent example is provided by the oracle given in response to the uttering of a communal lament in 2 Chr 20:5–17. See my *1 and 2 Chronicles* (NCB; Grand Rapids: Eerdmans, 1982) 295–98, with further bibliography, to which add Mark A. Throntveit, *When Kings Speak: Royal Speech and Royal Prayer in Chronicles* (SBLDS 93; Atlanta: Scholars Press, 1987) 67–72.

8. Ps 12:5 is the only clear example. It is sometimes suggested that oracles of salvation have also been recorded in, or lie behind, Pss 60:6–8 and 85:8–13, but these are less certain. Ps 60:6–8, for instance, may be more plausibly read as a recollection of a past promise, used now as a basis for the prayer that follows. See Aubrey R. Johnson, *The Cultic Prophet and Israel's Psalmody* (Cardiff: University of Wales Press, 1979) 165–75; Graham S. Ogden, "Psalm 60: Its Rhetoric, Form, and Function," *JSOT* 31 (1985) 83–94; Marvin E. Tate, *Psalms 51–100* (WBC 20; Dallas: Word, 1990) 99–109 (note also p. 370 for Tate's comments on Ps 85:8–13).

9. Patrick D. Miller, *They Cried to the Lord: The Form and Theology of Biblical Prayer* (Minneapolis: Fortress, 1994) 127–33.

been so insensitive as to have believed that encouraging someone staring into, if not actually slipping into, the Pit to affirm with assurance that they would soon be enjoying a banquet with their friends and family in the temple would be helpful or realistic. That these poets were sensitive is beyond question; only that can explain the enduring help that generations of the faithful and not-so-faithful have derived from their articulation of the pain that distressed readers are incapable of putting into words for themselves. But being so sensitive, they were also aware of the limits of hope. Alongside angry accusation, it is realistic to find, as we do, a variety of attempts to cajole God into delivering them, including, as we have already seen, expressions of the wish to be restored socially and religiously. [10] I submit, however, that to attribute to such moments the kind of sentiments that we find, for instance, towards the end of Psalm 22, goes beyond the limits of even the horizon-changing power of poetry. From a literary perspective it empties the expression of lament in the first half of the psalm of its power, and from a pastoral perspective it invites contempt. [11] To express hope is one thing, but to rejoice in its realization is quite another. These poets were obviously capable of knowing the difference.

For reasons such as these, it seems that it is necessary to look for an alternative situation within which these psalms originally functioned. There are, of course, a few psalms (e.g., Pss 25; 70; 88; 141; 143) which are what might be called pure lament and petition, and for these a setting in the life of the psalmist comparable to that with regard to the community in the communal laments is appropriate; the same applies to those in which future praise is anticipated as something promised or hoped for (e.g., Pss 5; 7; 109; 140; 142). For the remainder, however, an alternative proposal seems preferable.

The problem has arisen in the first place because of the assumption, for which detailed justification is never forthcoming, that we should identify the psalmists' situation with their position at the *start* of the psalm. If that is not satisfactory, however, then it follows that we might consider reading these psalms from the situation that seems to be presupposed at their *end*.

There are analogies within the Psalter that indicate that this is not as far-fetched a proposal as might at first appear. Psalm 2, for instance, is often categorized as a psalm for a coronation, because of the oracles that

---

10. Ibid., 114–26.

11. This may lie behind the conjectures of an earlier generation of commentators to the effect that many of these psalms are composite. Nowadays, those commentators who remain uneasy about an original unity tend to argue in terms of the later development of a single psalm rather than the joining of two initially separate ones. This latter approach actually underlines the force of my point, which concerns the predominantly cultic, or at least public, setting of the psalms as we have them.

clearly refer to such an occasion in vv. 6–9. John T. Willis, however, has
argued convincingly that this is incorrect.[12] The psalm as a whole presupposes a different setting, namely a situation prior to a battle against rebellious vassals, in which the coronation ritual is recalled as an argument for
why the rebels should submit to the Jerusalem king. There are many analogies, both within Israel and Judah and beyond, for such a "cry of defiance"
before a conflict, and only this can do justice to vv. 1–3 and especially 10–11;
it is the latter, at the very end of the psalm, which make the setting clear
(note the introductory *w'th* in v. 10, which serves, as frequently in letters,
to mark the shift from background information to the substance of the
matter in hand).[13] Whether this situation follows closely after the coronation or after the passage of a greater length of time is immaterial.

In my opinion, this same approach may help resolve the puzzle that
Psalm 23 has posed to generations of interpreters.[14] In this familiar psalm,
two images—those of the good shepherd and of the gracious host—seem
to be juxtaposed in an uneasy manner, and attempts to conflate them
have not proved convincing. The last line of the psalm, however, gives us
a firm indication that a cultic setting is presupposed, and that (assuming
the MT is sound)[15] the psalmist is now leaving the sanctuary.[16] Verse 5 may

---

12. John T. Willis, "A Cry of Defiance: Psalm 2," *JSOT* 47 (1990) 33–50.

13. For discussion of this, see the works cited by Samuel E. Balentine, *Prayer in the Hebrew Bible: The Drama of Divine-Human Dialogue* (OBT; Minneapolis: Fortress, 1993) 58 n. 21.

14. For a recent helpful survey, with discussion, see Jörg V. Sandberger, "Herme-neutische Aspekte der Psalmeninterpretation dargestellt an Psalm 23," in *Neue Wege der Psalmenforschung* (ed. Klaus Seybold and Erich Zenger; Freiburg: Herder, 1994) 317–44.

15. Literally, "and I will return to the house of the Lord throughout a long life." See Hans Schmidt, *Die Psalmen* (HAT 15; Tübingen: Mohr, 1934) 40–41. The principal diffi-culty with this approach is, of course, the use of the preposition *b* following the verb *šwb*, though Hos 12:7 may give some support, and *'lh + b* in Ps 24:3 could be compared. Alternatively, it may be noted that there are many examples of the pregnant use of a preposition (cf. GKC §119ee); usually, it is the sense of a verb of motion that must be supplied, so that here *šwb* might be construed as an auxiliary, to produce something like "and I will come again." See Franz Delitzsch, *Biblical Commentary on the Psalms* (London: Hodder and Stoughton, 1887 [5th German edition: 1894]) 407; Peter C. Craigie, *Psalms 1–50* (WBC 19; Waco: Word, 1983) 204. Despite these two possibilities, commentators generally prefer either to revocalize as an infinitive construct of *yšb* (with appeal to the LXX and the identical phrase in Ps 27:4) or to emend to *wyšbty* (with appeal to Jerome), both giving rise to the familiar "and I shall dwell in." Even if one of these easier readings were to be preferred, my chief point would still stand, namely that the last verse of the psalm provides clear indication that the psalmist is participating in a cultic celebration.

16. The suggestion that "house" is here used figuratively in the sense of "household," referring to the community of God's people, seems less probable and, indeed, unneces-sary, especially as it depends upon the uncertain emendation of the previous word. See Aubrey R. Johnson, "Psalm 23 and the Household of Faith," in *Proclamation and Presence:*

be coupled with this as descriptive of the joyful meal which accompanied sacrifices of thanksgiving, and in that setting vv. 1–4 embody the testimony that the psalmist recited in praise for past mercies. In other words, if the psalm is read from the standpoint of its ending, the whole may be construed as a unity without difficulty.[17]

In view of the difficulties which seem to confront the normal view regarding the situation of the psalmists in the individual laments, it may be proposed by analogy that here too they may be more naturally understood as located in the situation envisaged *at the end* of many of these psalms, namely in a context of thanksgiving and celebration from which they look back and recall in words the time of trial from which they have been delivered. In particular, there are several examples that suggest the even more specific context of the payment of the vows that the psalmists may have promised at that earlier time.[18]

A clear example of the kind of thing I have in mind is furnished by Hezekiah's prayer in Isa 38:10–20. There has been some dispute as to whether this psalm should be classified as an individual lament or as a thanksgiving.[19] The fact that there can be such a discussion is itself revealing, and it arises because the psalm does not fit either category without qualification. If the initial "I said" is pressed as a strong argument in favor

Old Testament Essays in Honour of Gwynne Henton Davies (ed. John I. Durham and J. Roy Porter; London: SCM, 1970) 255–71. Alternative symbolic or mystical interpretations are dismissed by Ronald E. Clements, *God and Temple* (Oxford: Blackwell, 1965) 74.

17. Cf. Ernst Vogt, "The 'Place in Life' of Ps 23," *Bib* 34 (1953) 195–211 (though he presses the point further than is necessary); Walter Beyerlin, *Die Rettung der Bedrängten in den Feindpsalmen der Einzelnen auf institutionelle Zusammenhänge untersucht* (FRLANT 99; Göttingen: Vandenhoeck & Ruprecht, 1970) 111–16; Hans-Joachim Kraus, *Psalms 1–59: A Commentary* (Minneapolis: Augsburg, 1988) 305–6; and Klaus Seybold, *Die Psalmen* (HAT I/15; Tübingen: Mohr, 1996) 101: "Insofern ist der Text vom Ende her aufzuschlüsseln."

18. I find that this suggestion has been anticipated with regard to at least some of the psalms in question by Artur Weiser, *The Psalms: A Commentary* (OTL; London: SCM, 1962 [5th German ed.: 1959]); and Klaus Seybold, *Introducing the Psalms* (Edinburgh: T. & T. Clark, 1990 [German original: 1986]) 42 and 117–18; see too his earlier *Das Gebet des Kranken im Alten Testament: Untersuchungen zur Bestimmung und Zuordnung der Krankheits- und Heilungspsalmen* (BWANT 99; Stuttgart: Kohlhammer, 1973).

19. See the surveys in Hans Wildberger, *Jesaja 3: Jesaja 28–39. Das Buch, der Prophet und seine Botschaft* (BKAT 10/3; Neukirchen-Vluyn: Neukirchener Verlag, 1982) 1455–56; James W. Watts, *Psalm and Story: Inset Hymns in Hebrew Narrative* (JSOTSup 139; Sheffield: Sheffield Academic Press, 1992) 120–21; Marvin A. Sweeney, *Isaiah 1–39: With an Introduction to Prophetic Literature* (FOTL 16; Grand Rapids and Cambridge: Eerdmans, 1996) 494–96. The most influential analysis has been that of Joachim Begrich, *Der Psalm des Hiskia: Ein Beitrag zum Verständnis von Jesaja 38, 10–20* (FRLANT 42; Göttingen: Vandenhoeck & Ruprecht, 1926), who used the introductory "I said" in particular to argue that it must be a thanksgiving.

of the psalm being a thanksgiving, the concluding affirmation of confidence (v. 20) is equally an element which is primarily at home in the lament. It is difficult not to suppose that, had this psalm reached us independently of its present narrative context, it would have been generally labeled as a lament. Its initial *'ny 'mrty* could then be compared with the initial *'mrty* of Ps 39:1 (cf. *dbrty* in 39:3), which no one could possibly deny introduces a lament![20] As it is, however, the introduction in v. 9 makes clear that it was written (*mktb*) *after* Hezekiah "had been sick and recovered from his sickness." While many would understandably question the straightforwardly "historical" nature of this verse, it nevertheless provides powerful testimony to what an editor from the biblical period simply assumed (or knew) about the circumstances in which lament psalms were composed and used: they followed the period of restoration and reflected on the psalmist's suffering retrospectively.[21]

It is the nature of the case that my proposal concerning the situation presupposed by the psalmists in the laments can never be definitively established. A fuller study, with exegesis of each psalm, including attention to such matters as those cases where the lament appears to be cast in the past and where there are particular connections between the description of the suffering and the praise offered for deliverance, would clearly be desirable, but would exceed the limits of the present essay. The psalms as a whole lack the kind of contemporary rubrics that fix their setting, so that the familiar move from form to *Sitz im Leben* is inevitably conjectural. The normal view is as prone to this difficulty as any alternative proposal, and its authority derives only from the scholarly consensus which has developed and been adopted without due regard for such alternative possibilities.[22] At the end of the day, the interpreter can only propose the solution that seems to do greatest justice to the text regarded as a whole. In that case, it becomes necessary to demonstrate that one approach is freer of difficulties than another. What objections, then, might be raised against this alternative, and admittedly minority, approach?

---

20. It is noteworthy that none of the parallels that Begrich cites stand at the start of their respective psalms. One might contrast Jonah 2:2, where, however, the elements of thanksgiving are far more apparent. Interestingly, the passage in Jonah is a good counter-example: a thanksgiving psalm uttered *before* deliverance!

21. I have discussed some of the wider concerns of the editor in introducing this psalm (contrast 2 Kgs 20:1–11) in my *The Book Called Isaiah: Deutero-Isaiah's Role in Composition and Redaction* (Oxford: Clarendon, 1994) 202–7.

22. This is especially the case if it is assumed that the change of mood is brought about by the delivery of an oracle of salvation, for in this case not only the rubrics, but even the words used in the liturgy, have to be imaginatively supplied.

In the first place, it has been suggested that in the thanksgiving psalms (to which I shall return) the recall of the lament is explicit. Since that is not the case in the individual laments, the approach suggested here is less probable.[23] This objection is not serious, however, for there are, in fact, examples of thanksgivings where this shift is equally unmarked. The most telling example of this is undoubtedly Psalm 40, which from a formal point of view is simply the mirror image of an individual lament. In the first half of the psalm (vv. 1–10), the psalmist offers thanks for past deliverance and stresses more than once that he has done so in the context of "the great congregation" (vv. 9 and 10). In the second half, without any transitional rubric, the tone passes over into lament and petition, and of course the striking fact here is that part of this section (vv. 13–17) actually reappears as a separate psalm, Psalm 70, which nobody doubts is an individual lament. Moreover, the two verses which precede this, vv. 11–12, are as clear an example of an element of the lament as could be wished. If the psalm had been composed in the reverse order, that is to say vv. 11–17 followed by vv. 1–10, it would be classified as an individual lament including a certainty of a hearing. The basis for positing a completely different *Sitz im Leben* on this ground alone seems, therefore, weak.

The situation with regard to Psalm 40 is closely paralleled in Psalms 9–10.[24] There too thanksgiving and praise (9:1–12) are followed by the recall of an earlier lament. Although the transition is not quite so abrupt as in Psalm 40, because the praise concludes in v. 12 by stating that God "does not forget the cry of the afflicted," nevertheless it is not formally marked. It is also noteworthy that the balance between the two parts is the opposite of Psalm 40, the lament (9:13–10:18) being far more extensive.

A second, and more serious, objection is that my proposal runs into the difficulty that there is then an overlap in setting with the psalms of thanksgiving.[25] The implication behind the objection is that forms and settings are "rationed" to one apiece; my proposal would make the setting of thanksgiving greedy in claiming two forms. Several observations may be made by way of response.

The example of Psalm 40, already discussed, suggests that we are not dealing in every case with completely different forms, but rather with the

---

23. See, for instance, Day, *Psalms*, 30.

24. For a summary of the reasons for treating these two psalms together as one, see Arnold A. Anderson, *The Book of Psalms* (2 vols.; NCB; London: Oliphants, 1972) 1:104. In fact, the main point for my present purpose would stand even if Psalm 9 were treated in isolation.

25. When I once floated my idea in an unstructured way over the lunch table at Pat Miller's home, this was the substance of his immediate response.

different order in which the shared elements are presented. Now it is true that in form-critical study generally, the order of the constituent parts is often significant, but this is not always so, and this applies particularly to the laments. In his classic study of this genre, for instance, Westermann distinguished three main elements of the lament proper—the complaint against God, the lament over personal suffering, and the complaint about the enemy—but he also emphasized that they do not appear according to a fixed sequence.[26]

In development of this observation, it should further be noted that in both thanksgivings and laments the order in which the principal elements occur is also less stable than some textbooks imply.[27] In the laments, for instance, although it is usually implied that there is a two-part structure of lament followed by a certainty of hearing, we in fact find that in Psalm 86 this pattern is followed by the return of lament in vv. 14–17.[28] Psalm 55 is similar (cf. vv. 20–21), while Psalm 59 seems to alternate between lament and praise. Similarly, in the thanksgivings the reference back to the lament may be embedded within praise at the start and the finish (e.g., Pss 18:4–5; 30:8–10; 41:4–10; 116:3–4, 8–11) or it may come at the end, with no return to praise. This pattern has already been noted above on Psalms 9–10 and 40. Psalm 120 is a particularly striking example. Assuming, against the NRSV, that the perfect + *waw*-consecutive in v. 1 refers to the past ("In my distress I *cried* to the Lord and he *answered* me"),[29] then the whole of the remainder of the psalm is a recollection of the lament that the psalmist offered in his "distress." In the light of these and other examples, some of which are even more mixed, it therefore begins to look as though the distinction between the psalms of individual thanksgiving and some of the laments that conclude on a note of thanksgiving and praise rests on a shaky foundation, amounting to little more than the order in which the elements are pre-

---

26. Claus Westermann, "The Structure and History of the Lament in the Old Testament," in idem, *Praise and Lament in the Psalms* (Edinburgh: T. & T. Clark, 1981 [German original: 1954, repr. 1964]) 165–213.

27. I am grateful to my colleague Dr. Susan E. Gillingham for stressing to me the importance of this point, as well as for kindly commenting on an initial draft of this article (as did Dr. Walter Moberly). In Gillingham's book, *The Poems and Psalms of the Hebrew Bible* (Oxford: Oxford University Press, 1994) 214–19 and 222–24, she draws particular attention to the many variations that exist within the individual psalms of lament and of thanksgiving.

28. This conclusion is not affected by the uncertainty whether vv. 12–13 look back to past deliverance or constitute a vow with respect to future deliverance; see the careful discussion in Tate, *Psalms 51–100*, 374–84. The hymnic affirmation in vv. 8–10 already indicates a move in worship beyond the point of lament.

29. Cf. GKC §111a.

sented.[30] Indeed, there are even occasions when commentators are unable to agree whether to categorize a particular psalm as a lament or a thanksgiving in the first place![31]

Finally, even if it were true that each *Sitz im Leben* could only be associated with one single form, it would not, in fact, be difficult to imagine more than one setting where praise and thanksgiving would be appropriate. Lev 22:21–30, to go no further, distinguishes between the *zbḥ-šlmym* (v. 21) offered in payment of a vow and the *zbḥ-twdh* (v. 29) offered as a general thanksgiving. There can be little doubt that other sacrifices were also accompanied by worship and praise for past mercies or for forgiveness. For those who are wedded to a rigid association of form and setting, there are more than enough situations in which the varying types of psalm discussed here could be accommodated.

Before drawing any conclusions, it is necessary to enter some caveats. It should be clear from what has already been said that there is no intention here of denying that there were occasions when psalms might be used to give voice to lament at the time of suffering. We have already noted that there are a number that lack the certainty of a hearing, for instance, so that for these a different setting has to be presupposed. In actual practice, it is, of course, probable that the words of a sufferer's cry of lament and petition will not have been recorded; indeed, they may hardly have been articulated. "In my distress I cried to the Lord" (Ps 120:1) is as telling as a detailed lament. Where such psalms may have been used, however, the example of the reuse of Ps 40:13–17 as a separate psalm (Psalm 70) suggests that it may have been precisely in the form of material which had first been learned in happier times in the context of the psalmist's own, or someone else's, expression of thanksgiving. The long history of the use of the psalms since is similar. That which has become familiar from cultic—or, in more recent times, private—recitation may be used as a resource on which to draw at times when the individual needs help in articulating his or her distress in the midst of disorientation. The flexibility of the psalms' imagery, already noted, is, of course, a great facilitator for such reuse.

---

30. This need not detract from the positive assessment of Brueggemann's work mentioned above (n. 3). Although he builds on the usual form-critical distinctions that I am questioning here, Brueggemann's real concerns relate more to the experience of the psalmists as expressed in the psalms than to historical questions of the circumstances of original composition and setting. Nothing in what I am saying detracts from the reality of those experiences, whether actual, remembered, or imagined.

31. See, for instance, the discussion of the variety of opinion with regard to Psalms 9–10 in William H. Bellinger, *Psalmody and Prophecy* (JSOTSup 27; Sheffield: JSOT Press, 1984) 39–42.

Furthermore, in discussing the psalmists' situation, it should be made clear that it goes beyond the nature of the evidence at our disposal to determine in any given case whether this is to be taken at face value (i.e., that the psalm was written specifically for, and actually used at, thanksgivings and the like at the sanctuary) or whether it is a poetic composition which imaginatively makes use of that kind of setting. This is immaterial, however. My concern for the present purpose is to establish the standpoint from which the psalm is meant to be read, whether as poem or as liturgy.

Two broader consequences follow from my proposal that the majority of the psalms of individual lament should be read in the light of their conclusion rather than their opening. First, it reminds us that the broader outlook of the psalmists, as indeed of most biblical literature, is ultimately one of praise for deliverance experienced.[32] This is not in any way to downplay the reality with which the writers face the darker sides of human existence; their recall of the past in the lament elements remains as expressive as ever, and they testify to having lived through, not skated round, those situations. But, if the language of Christian theology may be introduced, the passion narrative is read in the light of resurrection. However imaginatively we seek to recreate the events and atmosphere of Holy Week and Good Friday, we cannot avoid the fact that the testimony on which we rely reaches us from witnesses who are already convinced of the reality of a risen Lord.

Finally, these considerations may have some bearing on the current discussion about the appropriate use of lament in contemporary liturgy.[33] To the extent that we might wish to use the psalms as a model, the distinctions between individual and communal expressions of lament should be considered. As we have seen, in times of national emergency, the communal laments gave voice to the shared concerns of the society or congregation, and that surely continues to be legitimate. Individual lament, however, appears generally not to have been given liturgical voice. It remained private,

---

32. As a broad generalization, laments become less frequent and hymns more frequent through the course of the Psalter. For more specific considerations, see Walter Brueggemann, "Bounded by Obedience and Praise: The Psalms as Canon," *JSOT* 50 (1991) 63–92, reprinted in idem, *The Psalms and the Life of Faith*, 189–213.

33. See, for instance, William L. Holladay, *The Psalms through Three Thousand Years: Prayerbook of a Cloud of Witnesses* (Minneapolis: Fortress, 1993) 293–99, with reference also to Robert Davidson, *The Courage to Doubt: Exploring an Old Testament Theme* (London: SCM, 1983) 12–15; and Walter Brueggemann, *The Message of the Psalms: A Theological Commentary* (Minneapolis: Augsburg, 1984) 51–52. See also Balentine, *Prayer in the Hebrew Bible*, 196–98 and 277–79. For the importance of lament in broader perspective, see Walter Brueggemann, "The Costly Loss of Lament," *JSOT* 36 (1986) 57–71, reprinted in idem, *The Psalms and the Life of Faith*, 98–111; and Kathleen D. Billman and Daniel L. Migliore, *Rachel's Cry: Prayer of Lament and Rebirth of Hope* (Cleveland: United Church Press, 1999).

individual: "In *my* distress *I* cried to the Lord." Where it became the property of the congregation's liturgy, however, was subsequently in the context of testimony leading to worship. And in that setting, it remains not just appropriate, but imperative:

> I will tell of your name to my brothers and sisters;
>> in the midst of the congregation I will praise you:
> You who fear the LORD, praise him! . . .
> For he did not despise or abhor the affliction of the afflicted;
> he did not hide his face from me,
>> but heard when I cried to him. (Ps 22:22–24)

"Without Our Aid He Did Us Make": Singing the Meaning of the Psalms

W. Sibley Towner

———◆———

I. Introduction

Two of Patrick Miller's many admirable qualities are his love of the Psalter and his love of music. Anyone who has stood next to him in church knows that he sings the hymns robustly! To me it seemed that one good way to honor him for his career of distinguished scholarship and his faithful collegiality would be to examine the conjunction of these two loves of his.

In religion, music plays an important role in communicating both essential ideas and appropriate passions. In the three western monotheistic faiths, chants, plainsongs, and hymns have been a central part in worship since the very beginning, as the very existence of the Hebrew Psalter itself attests. In Protestant Christianity, hymns have always been important vehicles for the teaching of Scripture and the conveyance of doctrine. At the heart of the canon of hymnody cluster the paraphrases of the psalms— poetic re-presentations of Scripture's own hymns. By this means, people acculturated in Protestant worship unfailingly take deep into their memories beloved metrical settings of some of their favorite psalms.

What shall we say, then, if the time-honored and vital theological medium of hymnody turns out to be conveying messages somewhat at variance with the very texts of Scripture that it purports to transmit? The fact is that the hymnic psalter, intended by the church that created it to be a faithful mediator of the biblical Psalter, is an interpreter and expositor of the Psalter as well as a transmitter. Like religious painting and sculpture, like stained glass, like preaching, yes, like Scripture itself, psalm-hymns[1]

---

1. The term "psalm-hymn" refers to those musical re-presentations of the biblical psalms that intend to convey meaning of the biblical text without being bound by the strict conventions of simple versification or even of paraphrase. These tend to be more recent (18th–20th centuries) than the traditional paraphrases and to emanate—in Britain and North America, at least—from the musical vitality of Wesleyan and other evangelical traditions.

sometimes expand upon their sources. Sometimes they redirect or subvert their sources' original intentions; sometimes they distort them altogether. This is true even of the paraphrases, though they attempt to reproduce the original more faithfully than the later, freely-composed hymns. The truth is, we have in the hymnal a second canon of accepted teaching, less authoritative than the canon of Scripture to be sure, and less theologically diverse, but widely accepted, meaningful, and useful in the theological enterprise of the church. It supplements the biblical canon, and, in the case of sung psalms, records how the Psalter has been appropriated and re-appropriated in the liturgical life of the church over the past four centuries. Anyone who doubts that hymns have that kind of status, in the Protestant churches at least, can mess with the hymnal and see what happens!

On the face of it, it appears that the hymnal carries out this mediatorial task in three ways.

1. The hymn *tunes* themselves are suggestive of meaning. Is a tune lyrical, written in a major key and with a quick tempo? Then it will support the theme of thanksgiving. Is the melody quiet and gentle? How reinforcing for a song of trust! Perhaps it has the 4/4 march beat of a band of pilgrims or the minor melancholy and largo tempo appropriate to lament.

2. The hymnbook also interprets the canonical Psalter by the *selections* that it makes among the 150 psalms available there. The liturgical churches — Roman Catholic, Eastern Orthodox, Anglican, Lutheran — have traditionally chanted the received texts of the psalms exactly as they are found in the Bible.[2] (While orally interpretive, chants are not textually interpretive devices; interpretation by selection is not operative if every psalm is appointed for use.) Even in other wings of Protestantism, loyalty to the Psalter has often resulted in a systematic, ideologically-driven creation of hymnic paraphrases for every one of the psalms.[3] For my purposes, however, I have set aside all but one of these systematic psalter hymnals in order to discern in the hymnals of the Protestant mainstream a principle of selection. The psalms that make the cut belong, I take it, to the contemporary "canon within the canon" of the Psalter.

---

2. In the Jewish tradition, the Great Hallel (all or part of Psalms 120–136) and other psalms used in the daily morning service, and the "Egyptian Hallel" (Psalms 113–118) appointed for Passover and other feasts, also employ the Hebrew text or its translation without interpretive alteration.

3. E.g., the *Genevan Psalter* (1539–1562); the first English-language book printed in America, the *Bay Psalm Book* (1640); the *Scottish Psalter* (1650); *The Psalter* published by the United Presbyterian Church Board of Publications (1912); and the *Psalter Hymnal* of the Christian Reformed Church.

3. The *texts* of the hymns themselves serve the primary interpretive function, and are therefore the real grist for the mill of this paper.

II. Thesis and Method

In this paper I will argue that the Psalter sung in paraphrase and hymn is both selective and interpretive. In its overall scope as well as in its re-presentation of individual psalms it offers theological communications somewhat at variance with the biblical psalms themselves. This is acceptable as long as no one claims that the two communications are the same.

The obvious way to elaborate this thesis is to set down some psalm texts alongside their cognate hymnic paraphrases, do some comparative exegesis, and then move from the resulting details to more encompassing principles. But deciding where to begin (and end) among the 150 psalms and the hundreds of sung paraphrases and hymns that append to them is no easy matter.

I began by collecting 211 psalm-hymns and paraphrases[4] from five hymnals from the American Protestant mainstream, all published since 1985.[5]

---

4. Only hymns that are identified as entire re-presentations of entire biblical psalms or at least very substantial parts of them were included in this analysis. Hymns that simply allude to a psalm, quote a verse or a phrase, or show thematic similarities were not. No hymn is counted more than once in the total of 211, even though a few appear in all five hymnals and many appear in two or three. Letter symbols given in n. 5 below are used to locate hymns that are cited.

5. The following sigla are used:

C = Emily R. Brink, ed., *Psalter Hymnal*, for the Christian Reformed Church (Grand Rapids: CRC Publications, 1987). The first section, hymns 1–150, offers one hymn for each canonical psalm. Thirty-one of these are taken from *The Psalter* (1912). Another thirty-five hymns are also taken from this source. Twenty-seven of the 150 psalm-hymns are taken from Calvin's *Genevan Psalter* (1539–1562). In America, it seems, the Dutch sing the songs of the Scots. In Holland and in Hungary, the first 150 hymns in the best-known current Reformed hymnals are the 150 psalms set to the tunes of the *Genevan Psalter*.

M = Carlton R. Young, ed., *The United Methodist Hymnal* (Nashville: The United Methodist Publishing House, 1989). In addition to hymns listed above, this hymnal includes a Psalter of 100 psalms set as chants with sung responses. The chants are only slightly altered from the NRSV. This hymnal is accompanied by Carlton R. Young, *Companion to the United Methodist Hymnal* (Nashville: Abingdon Press, 1993).

P = LindaJo McKim, ed., *The Presbyterian Hymnal* (Louisville: Westminster/John Knox Press, 1990).

R = Erik Routley, ed., *Rejoice in the Lord*, for the Reformed Church in America (Grand Rapids: Eerdmans, 1985).

U = Arthur C. Clyde, ed., *The New Century Hymnal*, for the United Church of Christ (Cleveland: The Pilgrim Press, 1995). In addition to psalm-hymns, this hymnal includes 107+ psalms set as chants and canticles, with texts only lightly altered from

Four of the five hymnals in the sample are published by denominations in the Reformed tradition. (The current United Methodist hymnal served as a kind of control but revealed no consistent differences from the others.) I took this approach because psalm- and paraphrase-singing have always been a hallmark of Reformed piety. From the beginning Lutherans enjoyed full hymnody, thanks in large part to Luther's own musical proclivities. "The Reformed branch of the Reformation (in contrast to Lutherans) restricted church music to unison (no harmony) congregational singing (no choirs) of the psalms (no hymns) in meter (no chant), and sung unaccompanied (no instruments)."[6]

III. Outcomes I: Selection

I set aside the interpretive function of the tunes of the paraphrases and psalm-hymns as a matter that lies beyond the competency of this essay (published, as it is, without an accompanying CD!). So we begin with the question of selectivity—that is, the "canon within the canon." This issue has two aspects:

(a) Which of the *genres* of psalms resonate more vigorously with the contemporary singing church?

(b) Do certain *individual psalms* emerge as most meaningful to the contemporary believing community, judged by the number of different settings for each one that our hymnals offer for congregational use?

1. The *genre/hymn ratio question* is amenable to a statistical analysis. The table that follows employs my own modified version of Gunkel's psalm

---

NRSV. This hymnal is accompanied by Kristen L. Forman, ed., *The New Century Hymnal Companion* (Cleveland: The Pilgrim Press, 1998). See esp. 83–94.

Other hymnals noted that systematically offer at least one chant or hymn for each of the 150 psalms are:

E = *The Hymnal 1982*, for The Episcopal Church (New York: The Church Hymnal Corporation, 1982).

L = *Lutheran Book of Worship* (Minneapolis: Augsburg, 1978).

6. Forman, *The New Century Hymnal Companion*, 85. The Genevan (or French) Psalter of 1562 survived intact until recent times. "Its treasured importance was second only to the Bible in the Reformed movement, a phenomenon seen in the fact that 225 editions were printed during the first century of its existence (exceeding a million copies)" (James R. Davidson, *A Dictionary of Protestant Church Music* [Metuchen, NJ: Scarecrow Press, 1975] 258). The most important early English psalter, written by Geneva-influenced Thomas Sternhold and John Hopkins (1549–1551), was often bound with editions of the King James Version after the publication of the latter in 1611.

classifications.[7] I have assigned every one of the 150 psalms to one or another of fourteen genres, even though some are mixed forms and some challenge any classification at all. Broad strokes are all we need in order to determine where the preponderance of hymnic interpretation lies, and thus the functional psalter of today's worshiping Christian community.[8]

Psalm Genre	No. of Psalms (total = 150)	No. of Hymns (total = 211)	Average Hymns/Psalm	Psalms with the Highest Number of Hymns (#)
Individual Lament (including Penitential Psalms	45	33	0.73	Ps 130 (6) Ps 51 (5)
Hymn (not including Songs of Zion and Enthronement Hymns; see below)	22	70	3.18	Ps 103 (12) Pss 148, 150 (10 each)
Communal Lament	16	10	0.63	Ps 90 (5) Ps 89 (3)
Individual Thanksgiving	11	15	1.36	Ps 118 (5)
Royal Psalm	9	7	0.78	Ps 72 (6)
Instruction (Wisdom)	9	13	1.44	Pss 1, 91, 119, 139 (3 each)
Song of Trust	8	21	2.6	Ps 23 (12) Ps 121 (4)
Prophetic Oracle of Judgment	7	3	0.33	Ps 95 (3)
Song of Zion	6	12	2.0	Ps 46 (5) Ps 84 (4)
Enthronement Hymn	5	7	1.4	Ps 96 (3)
Blessing	3	4	1.33	Ps 133 (2)
Communal Thanksgiving	3	4	1.33	Ps 67 (3)
Historical Psalm	3	2	0.67	Ps 105 (2)
Liturgy	3	10	3.33	Ps 24 (7)

This analysis is slightly skewed by the fact that genres with few exemplars can appear to be more popular in hymnody than they actually are. This

---

7. Hermann Gunkel, *The Psalms: A Form-Critical Introduction* (Philadelphia: Fortress, 1967). Gunkel's even more foundational 1933 work, completed by Joachim Begrich and recently translated by James D. Nogalski, is *Introduction to Psalms: The Genres of the Religious Lyric of Israel* (Macon: Mercer University Press, 1998).

8. In the sample I have taken, 64 of the 150 psalms (43%) have no cognate hymns at all, except, of course, in the programmatic *Psalter Hymnal* of the Christian Reformed Church.

occurs if one psalm in the classification is very frequently re-presented in song (e.g., Psalm 23 in the genre "Song of Trust"; the Entrance Liturgy, Psalm 24). However, the general lines of the "canon within the canon" readily emerge. We can sum up the result with a sentence of the wicked witch Evillene in *The Wiz*, that Broadway "re-presentation" in the Motown idiom of *The Wizard of Oz*: "Don't bring me no bad news!" Clearly, contemporary mainstream American Protestants want to praise God when they sing in worship, not to complain and lament.[9]

Of course, one might argue that the biblical hymns and songs of trust are by their nature more lyrical, singable, and communal than are the much more numerous Individual Laments. With their emphasis on the theme of joy (and "joyful noise"), their reiteration of the euphonic cry, Hallelujah!, and their use of the repertoire of music and musical instruments, Hymns like Psalms 146–150 practically beg to be sung in public worship. Moreover, we have every reason to believe they were in fact sung in Second Temple worship from the very beginning. But so also, we must assume, were the Individual and Communal Laments. Their preponderance in the Psalter and their connection with intercessory prayer, sacrificial offerings, and healing suggest that worship and chant in biblical times may have been substantially devoted to lament and intercession. We cannot explain the sharp preference for hymnic praise in our own worship by arguing that lament was meant only to be a prayer whispered in private. No, that preference surely also has something to do with the spirit of our times.[10]

2. Genre preference aside, *certain individual psalms emerge as most meaningful* to the contemporary believing community, if we take the number of different hymns based on each one as a clue. That Psalm 23 should stand at the top with 12 psalm-hymns and paraphrases depending on it comes as no surprise, though the psalm actually belongs to one of the less commonly-attested genres.[11] That Psalm 103 should draw an equal amount of hymnic

---

9. It should be noted that almost half of the psalm-hymns based on the canonical "Hymns" that appear in the modern hymnals surveyed have been written within the past 30 years.

10. Walter Brueggemann has argued this. He addressed the loss of lament from the functioning canon of the contemporary church in his 1986 essay, "The Costly Loss of Lament," reprinted in idem, *The Psalms and the Life of Faith* (ed. Patrick D. Miller; Minneapolis: Fortress, 1995) 98–111. "In the absence of lament," Brueggemann argues, "we may be engaged in uncritical history-stifling praise. Both *psychological inauthenticity* and *social immobility* may be derived from the loss of these texts" (111; emphasis his). See also Gerald T. Sheppard's article, "'Enemies' and the Politics of Prayer in the Book of Psalms," in *The Bible and the Politics of Exegesis: Essays in Honor of Norman K. Gottwald on his Sixty-Fifth Birthday* (ed. David Jobling, Peggy L. Day, and Gerald T. Sheppard; Cleveland: Pilgrim Press, 1991) 61–82.

11. James L. Mays, *Psalms* (Interpretation; Louisville: John Knox, 1994) 22 lists Psalm 23 in his category of "The Prayer for Help of an Individual" (i.e., Individual Lament). He

attention is perhaps slightly more surprising, given its 22–verse length. Its first five verses have, however, widespread liturgical use. The short, joyous hymns found in Psalms 148 and 150 and the familiar Entrance Liturgy, Psalm 24, fill out the roster of the five psalm texts most frequently represented in the hymnody of contemporary mainstream Protestant worship. Only when we drop to the second tier do we encounter the Individual Lament most frequently set to music, Psalm 130, *De profundis*.

Only two musical settings of psalms occur in all of the hymnals that I surveyed. They are "The Lord's My Shepherd, I'll Not Want" (Scottish Psalter, 1650), on the Song of Trust, Psalm 23; and "All People That on Earth Do Dwell" (Kethe, 1560), on the Hymn, Psalm 100. Their almost universal use recommends them for closer study below. In addition, I will discuss the hymnody based on the Lament, Psalm 130, thus sampling psalm-hymns and paraphrases from three very different psalm genres.

IV. Outcomes II: Texts

Psalm 23	*"The Lord's My Shepherd, I'll Not Want"* (1650)
[1] The Lord is my shepherd, I shall not *want*.[a]	1. The Lord's my shepherd, I'll not want; He makes me down to lie in pastures green; He leadeth me The quiet waters by.
[2] He makes me lie down in green pastures; he leads me beside still waters;	
[3] he restores my soul. He leads me in *right paths* for his name's sake.	2. My soul He doth restore again; And me to walk doth make Within the paths of righteousness, E'en for His own name's sake.
[4] Even though I walk through the *darkest valley*, I fear no evil; for you are with me; your rod and your staff – they comfort me.	3. Yea, though I walk in death's dark vale, Yet will I fear none ill; For Thou art with me; and Thy rod And staff me comfort still.
[5] You prepare a table before me in the presence of my enemies;	4. My table Thou hast furnished in presence of my foes;

[a] Italics mark words or phrases that receive special attention in the discussion that follows.

---

notes, however, that "[i]n some of the prayers the confession of confidence in God is so extensive that it shifts the emphasis in tone away from desperate need to trusting reliance (e.g., 4, 16, 23, 27, 56, 62)." I prefer to use a related but separate category, Songs of Trust, consisting of Psalms 4, 11, 16, 23, (27?), 52, 62, 121, 131.

you anoint my head with oil; my cup overflows. ⁶Surely goodness and mercy shall follow me all the days of my life, and I shall dwell in the house of the Lord *my* *whole life long.*	My head Thou dost with oil anoint, And my cup overflows. 5. Goodness and mercy all my life Shall surely follow me; And in God's house forevermore My dwelling place shall be.

Verse 1. The semantic repertoire of this best known psalm, the proto-typical Song of Trust, is pastoral in verses 1–4, then priestly in verses 5–6. Verbs and nouns alike convey notions of security, comfort, plenitude, and peace. As Miller notes, the absolute (without any object) construction of the verb "want" (*ḥasar*) "is comprehensive, all-inclusive. With the Lord as shepherd, nothing is lacking for life."¹²

Verse 3. As usual, the King James Version (KJV) renders the familiar Hebrew genitive construction in which the governing noun is possessed by another noun woodenly: "paths of righteousness." In recent years translators have captured the adjectival force of the genitive noun in this construction; hence, the "right paths" preferred by the NRSV. The latter rendering suggests a less metaphorical use of "paths." In this reading, the singer testifies that the Lord points out ways to proceed that are "safe and correct" (Miller), rather than announcing a moral judgment.¹³

Verse 4. The strange Hebrew compound word *ṣalmāwet* (apparently "shadow" [*ṣēl*] + "death" [*māwet*]), found only 18 times in the Old Testament (10 in Job), actually seems to convey a superlative sense of the notion of "shadow"; hence, NRSV's preferred "darkest valley."¹⁴ In this perspective, the term no longer leads to understanding Psalm 23 as a meditation on death and new life. However, it still strongly prepares the reader for the "Immanuel" affirmation of v. 4b. Even in the most ominous darkness—that is, in extreme danger—the psalmist is not afraid "for you are with me."

Verse 6. Had the psalmist wanted to close the poem with the word "for-ever," a perfectly good Hebrew word, *lĕʿôlām*, was available. Instead, the choice was made to use the phrase *lĕʾōrek yāmîm*, "for a length of days" or

12. Patrick D. Miller, Jr., *Interpreting the Psalms* (Philadelphia: Fortress Press, 1986) 114.

13. In his later book, *They Cried to the Lord: The Form and Theology of Biblical Prayer* (Minneapolis: Fortress, 1994) 391 n. 199, Miller takes a more neutral position between "paths of righteousness" as Torah-keeping vs. as the proper way to reach deliverance: "The ambiguity is not to be dissolved."

14. Cf. Jer 2:6; Amos 5:8; Ps 44:19; only in Job 10:21–22; 38:17 does it unambiguously refer to death and the underworld.

even, perhaps, "for a long time." NRSV renders the phrase paraphrastically, "my whole life long" (guided by the synonymous expression in v. 6a, *kōl yěmê ḥayyāy*, "all the days of my life"), but avoids introducing the theme of eternity. No evidence suggests that ancient Israel had any concept of life after death until the very end of the canonical period (see Isa 26:19; Dan 12:3). Some might wish to argue that Psalm 23 provides such evidence; however, the plain meaning of the Hebrew phrase with which it closes carries us no further than this life at most. The psalmist simply hopes to be near God always.

Mays rightly observes that "Psalm 23 has had a regular place in the liturgy of funeral services. That is a proper setting for its use. It gives the congregation poignant words of trust to say in the face of the enemy who is not yet destroyed (1 Cor 15:26)."[15] The operative word should be "trust," however, and not "forever."

The form in which many people know Psalm 23 best is the Scottish paraphrase "The Lord's My Shepherd, I'll Not Want" (1650).[16] Without egregious alterations, the anonymous poet succeeded in turning the six verses of the unrhymed, non-metrical KJV text (1611) into five quatrains with alternating lines of iambic tetrameter and iambic trimeter rhyming on lines 2 and 4. It is a classical example of the versified Scripture that was sung almost exclusively in the English-speaking churches prior to the introduction of true hymnody in the 18th century.

The paraphrase retains the absoluteness of "want." It does not refine the understanding of "paths of righteousness" nor "shadow of death" beyond the linguistic wisdom of its time, but follows the KJV readings. The only interpretive tendency visible in the paraphrase is the tilt toward the hope of life eternal in its fifth stanza. In this, it only reproduces the interpretive direction already manifest in the KJV text itself. While one may argue that "forevermore" is simply a logical and necessary extension of the trust that "Thou art with me," that would be an argument more typical of a Christian reader than of an ancient Hebrew writer. At any rate, as already noted, that tendency is based on a questionable reading of the concluding phrase of the psalm, *lě'ōrek yāmîm*.[17]

Congregationalist clergyman Isaac Watts (1674–1748) led the move in the English-speaking churches from psalmody toward true hymnody. His 1719 "imitation" of Psalm 23, "My Shepherd Will Supply My Need," shows

---

15. Mays, *Psalms*, 119.

16. Hymns 161C, 451L, 136M, 479U, 170P, 89R, 90R. A variant called "The Lord My God My Shepherd Is" appears in 663E.

17. The Scottish text was adapted by Lavon Baylor in 1992 for use in *The New Century Hymnal*. Part of the aim was to eliminate generic language, e.g., "The Lord . . . He." Part

the beginnings of this move, largely with not-very-tendentious expansions.[18] For example, a moralizing element, often retained in the subsequent tradition, is introduced to explain the biblical phrase "he restores my soul":

He brings my wandering spirit back,
   When I forsake his ways;
And leads me, for His mercy's sake,
   In paths of truth and grace.[19]

One is not surprised that Watts, the low church non-conformist, eschews the introduction of any sacramental or sacerdotal elements into his re-presentation of Psalm 23. One is a little surprised, though, that he also minimizes the eternal life theme that others extrapolate from Ps 23:6b. His handling of the phrase *lĕ'ōrek yāmîm*, "for a length of days" or "my whole life long" or "forever," invokes the vision of a child embraced by God in an intimate and tender relationship of unspecified location and duration (but with echoes of John 14:2–4):

The sure provisions of my God
   Attend me all my days;
O may your house be my abode,
   And all my work be praise.
There would I find a settled rest,
   While others go and come;
No more a stranger, or a guest,
   But like a child at home.

High church Anglican clergyman Henry Baker's beloved 1868 hymn, "The King of Love My Shepherd Is," is based on an earlier paraphrase by

---

of the aim was to fit the paraphrase text to Brother James' Air, a different tune than the more familiar Crimond. The result is not very felicitous, in my opinion. Although the NRSV was available in 1992, Baylor retains the eternal life motif even while introducing completely new material such as the manna in the wilderness. David Noel Freedman has argued forcefully that the language of Psalm 23 is deeply rooted in the Exodus imagery of Yahweh as shepherd of the flock, Israel, in the wilderness ("The Twenty-Third Psalm," in *Michigan Oriental Studies in Honor of George G. Cameron* [ed. Louis L. Orlin; Ann Arbor: Department of Near Eastern Studies, 1976] 139–66). However, manna and quails are lying on the table at v. 5 only implicitly at best. In Psalm 78 the question of the people, "Can God spread a table in the wilderness?" (v. 19) is answered with a forceful and deadly "Yes." Here the priestly Host simply sets the table and pours the wine, no questions asked and no doubts expressed.

18. Hymns 550C, 664E, 172P. A variant on this hymn called "My Shepherd Is the Living Lord" appears as 91R, 247U.

19. Emphasis mine; cf. Ps 23:3.

the English poet and cleric, George Herbert (1593–1633).[20] Now "The
Lord" has become "The King of Love." The absolute "not want" of the KJV
is now qualified with a conditional clause that heightens the motif of eternal life: "I nothing lack *if* I am His and He is mine forever." In fact, the
theme of eternal life now permeates the entire hymn, coupled with a move
away from the simple shepherd imagery toward a more priestly picture.
"Still waters" becomes "streams of living waters" (an allusion to the heavenly river of life in Rev 21:1–5; see also, among others, Ps 46:4; Ezek 47:1–12;
as well as Ps 1:3). "My soul" becomes "my ransomed soul"; "green pastures"
becomes "verdant pastures . . . with food celestial feedeth." Like Watts,
Baker introduces a moral judgment about human culpability where none
exists in the original: "perverse and foolish oft I strayed." God's "goodness
and mercy" (v. 6) are now no longer completely self-motivated, but are
manifested in response to human sin. The "shepherd" now engages in the
sacramental functions enumerated in v. 5:

> Thou spreadest a table in my sight;
> > Thy *unction* grace bestoweth;
> And O what transport of delight
> > From Thy pure *chalice* floweth!

Lest the singer question the identity of the shepherd, the fourth stanza
clears it up: "Thy rod and staff my comfort still, Thy cross before to guide
me." The hymnist anticipates an eternal relationship with the shepherd in
a fifth stanza that retains the Hebrew "length of days" but in a context of
eternity:

> And so through all the length of days
> > Thy goodness faileth never;
> Good Shepherd, may I sing Thy praise
> > Within Thy house forever.

In this hymn, the psalm has been moralized, sacramentalized, and Chris-
tianized, and its transcendent vision has been amplified.

Jane Parker Huber's "The Lord's My Shepherd" (1988)[21] was published
before the NRSV, but may have taken direction from RSV's note to Ps 23:6,
"for ever [or: *as long as I live*]." Hers is the only one of the several recently
composed paraphrases or hymns unambiguously to avoid the theme of
eternal life:

---

20. Hymns 645, 646E, 456L, 138M, 171P, 248U.
21. Hymn 174P.

> My cup is full, and more than full,
>   Such lavish love outpouring
> That I will live each night and day
>   My Shepherd Lord adoring.

She also neither moralizes, sacramentalizes, nor Christianizes the psalm. She proves that a hymnic re-presentation of a psalm can clarify and vivify without abandoning the canonical communication.

To summarize this brief review of the interpretation of Psalm 23 in hymnody, it can be said that semantic polyvalence and syntactical peculiarity in the Hebrew text led the KJV and many of its successors to give us "paths of righteousness," "the valley of the shadow of death," and "forever." The paraphrases and later hymns elaborated these translation choices in the directions of moral failure, priestly ministration, Christ as the Good Shepherd, and especially eternal life. Very little hymnic shift has happened since the translation was improved by the NRSV. We are left with two different messages: the message of trust conveyed by the beloved canonical psalm, and the message of hope for life beyond death through the ministration and in the presence of Christ, the Good Shepherd, conveyed by several beloved and authoritative (if not quite canonical) hymns.[22]

Psalm 100	*"All People That on Earth Do Dwell"* (1560)
[1]Make a joyful noise to the LORD, all the earth.	1. All people that on earth do dwell, Sing to the Lord with cheerful voice; Him serve with mirth, His praise forth tell, Come ye before Him and rejoice.
[2]Worship the LORD with gladness; come into his presence with singing. [3]Know that the LORD is God. *It is he that made us, and we are his;* we are his people, and the sheep of his pasture.	2. Know that the Lord is God indeed; Without our aid He did us make; We are His folk, he doth us feed, And for his sheep He doth us take.
[4]Enter his gates with thanksgiving, and his courts with praise.	3. O enter then His gates with praise, Approach with joy His courts unto;

---

22. William L. Holladay offers an interesting Epilogue, "How the Twenty-Third Psalm Became an American Secular Icon," in his rich study of the history of the interpretation of the Psalter, *The Psalms through Three Thousand Years: Prayerbook of a Cloud of Witnesses* (Minneapolis: Fortress, 1993) 359–69. Hymnody played a surprisingly small role in the post–Civil War development of the use of Psalm 23, as he reports it.

Give thanks to him,
bless his name.

5 For the LORD is good; his
steadfast love endures
forever, and his
faithfulness to all
generations.

Praise, laud, and bless
His name always,
For it is seemly so to do.
4. For why? The Lord our God is good,
His mercy is forever sure;
His truth at all times
firmly stood.
And shall from age to age endure.

Although uneven in strophic structure, the Hebrew of Psalm 100 is quite straightforward semantically and syntactically. As is typical of the Hymn genre to which it belongs, it is built around a series of imperative verbs (with the single indicative "he made us" in v. 3b), which exhort the worshiper to engage in all the practices of joyous and melodious praise. These are followed in v. 5 by a second feature typical of the Hymn genre, a motivation for the praise, rooted in Yahweh's own character, introduced by "for" (*kî*).[23] The only significant semantic alternatives taken by the NRSV (following the RSV) over against the KJV are the words "steadfast love" (*ḥesed*) and "faithfulness" (*ʾĕmûnâ*) in v. 5. In the psalms these virtues are frequently attributed in tandem to God, often in laments but also in hymns.[24] The modern translations stick even more consistently to "steadfast love and faithfulness" than the KJV and the older versions, which adhered to "mercy and truth."

Verse 3. The only significant improvement over the KJV is that the NRSV reads: "It is he that made us, and we are his," whereas the KJV reads for the final clause "and not we ourselves." Early in their careers many students of the Old Testament are referred to this passage as a prime example of *Kethib* and *Qere*. The ancient Masoretic scribes considered the written consonantal text to be in error here. Evidently two similar-sounding words got confused in the scribal process, perhaps as a scribe was dictating to a copyist. Someone wrote *lōʾ*, "not," when the word was really *lô* ("his"). Unwilling to alter the sacred consonantal text (*Kethib*), the scribes (as was their custom in many places) indicated the error with the marginal note "Read (*Qere*): *lô*." Either the KJV and its predecessors were ignorant of this ancient correction, or else they chose to ignore it. They attempted the literal, but essentially absurd, "it is he that hath made us, and not we ourselves."

---

23. James L. Mays, *The Lord Reigns: A Theological Handbook to the Psalms* (Louisville: Westminster John Knox, 1994) 74–75, sees the psalm as a composite of two short hymns, the second of which, vv. 4–5, is a *tôdâ*-hymn in the regular "praise . . . for" form.

24. Among others, Pss 25:10; 36:5; 57:3, 10; 61:7; 85:10; 86:15; 89:14; 108:4 (all laments); 40:10–11; 138:2 (thanksgivings); 115:1 (liturgy); 98:3; 117:2 (hymns). Also see Gen 24:27; Exod 34:6; 2 Sam 2:6; 15:20. Only seldom (Gen 32:10) does the cliché apply to human behavior.

We turn now to the beloved paraphrase by which Psalm 100 has been mediated to many generations of English-speaking Protestant worshipers, "All People That on Earth Do Dwell."[25] The Scottish clergyman, William Kethe (died 1608?), probably wrote this paraphrase while he was in Geneva where he had fled during the persecutions of Queen Mary. It is the oldest English-language psalm paraphrase still widely sung in churches today. It predates the KJV itself by more than half a century.

The older renderings of *ḥesed* and *'ĕmûnâ* as "mercy" and "truth," respectively, are in place in v. 5, but they do not betray any interpretive tendency. Neither does Kethe's adoption of the textual error in v. 3. Nevertheless, his perpetuation of the KJV flaw has been sung by congregations for centuries. Most of the singers probably failed to notice that they were singing nonsense—"Without our aid He did us make"—or else they thought the psalm and its paraphrase were driving home the point that the Creator's powers are infinitely superior to our own.

In my sample, I found only four other hymns based on Psalm 100. Two are chants, one based on the KJV and one the NRSV.[26] The third is a free expansion of just one motif of the psalm.[27] Another, "All the Earth, Proclaim the Lord," by Lucien Deiss (1965),[28] handles the corrected text of Ps 100:3 very nicely:

Know that the Lord is our Creator.
Yes, he is our Father; we are his own.

To sum up, we can say that little was at stake other than the meaningfulness of v. 3 and perhaps a nuance thrown on the God-human relationship by the traditional, but erroneous, "It is He that hath made us, and not we ourselves." Nevertheless, we have to ask: Are we content that one of the most beloved of all church songs should perpetuate a textual error?

Psalm 130:1–4	*"Out of the Depths"* (1524) (stanzas 1–2)
[1]Out of the depths I cry to you, O LORD. [2]Lord, hear my voice! Let your ears be attentive to the voice of my supplications!	1. Out of the depths to Thee I raise The voice of lamentation; Lord, turn a gracious ear to me, And hear my supplication.

25. Hymns 377E, 378E, 245L, 100C, 75M, 220P, 120R, 7U.
26. Hymns 74M, 821M.
27. Hymn 73U.
28. Hymn 176C.

3If you, O LORD, should
  mark iniquities, Lord,
  who could stand?
4But there is forgiveness
  with you, so that you may
  be revered.

If Thou shouldst count our every sin,
Each evil deed or thought within,
O who could stand before Thee?
2. To wash away the crimson stain
  Grace, grace alone prevaileth.
  Our works, alas! are all in vain;
  In much the best life faileth.
  For none can glory in Thy sight,
  All must alike confess Thy might
  And live alone by mercy.

This beautiful and beloved psalm belongs to the sub-genre of Penitential Psalms, within the larger genre of Individual Laments.[29] Like other laments, it opens with a cry of despair from one who feels totally cut off from God, derelict, and drowning (vv. 1–2). The cause of this despair comes from within; it arises from the psalmist's sense of personal iniquity and imperfection. All human beings may well share such a sense, for no one's record can stand God's scrutiny (v. 3). However, this psalmist captures the utter poignancy of the sense of alienation by crying out from the "depths" (*ma'ămaqqîm*). Other uses of this word, twice in another Individual Lament (Ps 69:2, 15), in Isa 51:10, and Ezek 27:34, make clear that the psalmist is conjuring the chaotic, watery abyss of the sea. The situation can thus be compared to that of Jonah in the belly of the fish at the bottom of the sea (Jonah 2:4–6).

Like Jonah, however, this psalmist also has good news. The good news is not quite the turn-around that lamenters often report—"You have been my help" (Ps 63:7); "Let your heart revive . . . for the Lord hears the needy" (Ps 69:33).[30] Instead, this psalmist makes a profound affirmation about God and our duty: "But there is forgiveness with you, *so that* you may be revered" (v. 4). God does not forgive for nothing; as Miller puts it, "[t]he forgiveness of God that delivers from the depths of despair, guilt, and anxiety is not an end in itself but makes possible that glorification of God that is the primary end of all human life."[31] God does forgive, not because of any merit of ours or because of any prayer we utter, but because God is God. Where God is there also are steadfast love (*ḥesed*) and the power to redeem (v. 7). The psalmist relies upon God's character for salvation from the "depths."

---

29. The Christian liturgical tradition recognizes seven Penitential Psalms (Psalms 6, 32, 38, 51, 102, 130, 143).

30. Claus Westermann, in his *Praise and Lament in the Psalms* (Atlanta: John Knox Press, 1981) and elsewhere, has defined the discussion on the lament psalms and established the unbreakable connection between petition and praise.

31. Miller, *Interpreting the Psalms*, 142–43.

In the second half of the psalm (not reproduced above), the recollection of God's forgiveness in v. 4 leads the psalmist to speak of hope and of waiting in trust "more than those who watch for the morning" (vv. 5–6). The psalm concludes with a collective appeal to all Israel to hope for the Lord's redemption (vv. 7–8).

As will be noted, Ps 130:1–4 has no textual or even semantic issues that are likely to lead to wide divergence among the English translations that hymnists use, or within the hymnic tradition itself. In this case, the single re-interpretation of the text in church song that I have chosen (by way of illustration of another type of subversion of the plain meaning of the text) has strictly to do with the ideas that it conveys.

That example is Martin Luther's 1524 hymn (not a paraphrase), "Out of the Depths."[32] It was among Luther's first hymns. Its long association with funeral services goes back to Luther himself: it was sung at Halle over Luther's own body in 1546. The first stanza freely but recognizably follows the language and thought of Ps 130:1–2. Only when the idea of God's gracious forgiveness of transgressors emerges in vv. 3–4 does Luther expand the idea through most of his second stanza. Now the psalm becomes a precursor of the Pauline, and quintessentially Lutheran, doctrine of justification by faith alone. Is this really the direction in which the psalm is going: "Our works, alas! are all in vain"? The psalm does not address itself to "our works," nor does it develop the faith vs. works antithesis. On the other hand, Luther's clause "For none can glory in Thy sight" seems to capture the sense of Ps 130:3. Furthermore, v. 4 and the appeal to Israel to hope in God's steadfast love and power to redeem in v. 8 can rightly be summed up in Luther's words, "All must alike confess Thy might / And live alone by mercy."

A Christianization of Psalm 130 has taken place in Luther's hymnic representation of it. For Christians, the psalm has a prototypical quality that places it on a continuum with other scriptural expressions of unmerited divine forgiveness, and as such we can understand and endorse Luther's expansion of this idea in his hymn. Miller emphasizes this in his remark that Luther "found in it [Psalm 130] the expression of that unmerited grace and forgiveness that are at the heart of the gospel and without which—*even as the psalm so clearly declares*—existence before God is not possible."[33] If so, perhaps our only reservation needs to be to question the headers or the footers in our hymnals that say in effect, "This hymn is the very Psalm 130."

---

32. Hymns 295L, 515M, 240P, 134R. The text reproduced above is Richard Massie's 1854 translation, with alterations, as it appears in *The Presbyterian Hymnal*.
33. Miller, *Interpreting the Psalms*, 138; emphasis mine.

V. Conclusions

All of our learnings from this study of the musical mediation of the psalms in the church point to the need for mindfulness about the niche that psalmody should fill in Protestant worship. First, as is shown by my survey of the selection of which psalms will be sung—the "canon within the canon" in hymnody—our sung psalters do not offer us a range of concept and emotion as wide as that of the biblical Psalter. Except for denominations committed to singing every psalm in chant, paraphrase, or hymn, contemporary hymnists and hymnals prefer to celebrate God as creator and thank God as liberator rather than to lament to the God who listens. To this end, they more often take as their texts the canonical Hymns and Psalms of Trust. Yet, perhaps this is to be expected—singing about sin and suffering sounds like an oxymoron, especially in the communal context of a congregation. Perhaps this selection also says something about the theological climate in the mainstream churches in recent decades. Put in commercial terms, in the competitive denominational marketplace of the twenty-first century, somber doesn't sell. We prefer to sin and repent, lament and die in silent privacy.[34]

In our study of the tiny sample of three individual psalms and the hymns and paraphrases that accompany them, we discern other types of subversions that occur between Hebrew text and hymnal. Of course, some recasting is inevitable whenever a biblical text is re-presented and not simply repeated. Easy to observe are earlier generations' imperfect understandings of the Hebrew text. Such homiletical or "midrashic" expansions as can be observed, at least in my small sample, have mostly to do with the Christianization of the Old Testament text (e.g., the Shepherd of Psalm 23 becomes the Good Shepherd of the New Testament; distinctively Christian emphases are placed on justification by faith alone and on blessed immortality).

I shared the gist of this essay with my neighbor, a devout laywoman in the church. She said, "What difference does it make?" She has a point. After all, when a painter or a composer or a novelist redoes an older theme, we rejoice at the value added. When the re-casting and transformation of Scripture goes on in the New Testament itself, in preaching, in pious reflection (midrash), and personal Bible study, are we gainers or losers thereby?

---

34. In my opinion, a persistent preference for praise in psalm-singing impoverishes the emotional range of worship, depriving worshipers of access to a source of hope that grows out of suffering. See Kathleen D. Billman and Daniel L. Migliore, *Rachel's Cry: Prayer of Lament and Rebirth of Hope* (Cleveland: United Church Press, 1999). See also Brueggemann's essay, "The Costly Loss of Lament," cited in n. 10 above.

Most would say we gain, as long as the transformation stays within recognizable parameters. However, the distinction between what is canonical, quasi-canonical, and ephemeral has to be maintained. Preaching is ephemeral, but liturgy and hymnody belong in the second category. The hymnists have loosed the moorings that bound the psalms to their various original cultic and historical settings and have let them float down into this newer, larger extended canon of the music of the church.[35] People learn their hymns by heart in church and then draw on them in prison camps and hospitals, while driving in the car and lying in bed, for guidance and consolation in their daily lives.[36] Well and good, and may the tradition continue and grow, as new outbursts of hymnody enrich the life of the church! The only questions is: How do we know when the float has gone too far?

Here are parting admonitions to the churches: Recognize that the canonical Psalter and the hymnic psalter frequently do not convey quite the same message. Print nothing in your hymnals nor say anything in church to imply that they do. Do not count on hymns and paraphrases to give the "plain meaning" of the canonical text, that meaning that exegetes pursue and prize and with which preachers should begin. Recognize that, like the poets that they are, the paraphrasers and the hymnists are in business to explore the "fuller meaning." Then, when everybody is clear about these things, go right on honoring the biblical text by extending its authority and elaborating its ideas in song.

---

35. Loosening the moorings of the psalms has been done, of course, since time immemorial, even within the Psalter itself. Witness the superscriptions of the Psalms, which sometimes suggest occasions for their use quite removed from their original settings (e.g., the Individual Thanksgiving Psalm 30 seems to have become a song for Hanukkah; the Individual Lament Psalms 57 and 142 have been placed with David in the cave of Adullam where he took refuge from Saul [1 Sam 22:1–2]).

36. See the contribution by Sauter in this volume.

The So-Called Elohistic Psalter: A New Solution for an Old Problem

Frank-Lothar Hossfeld and Erich Zenger

I. The Problem with the "Elohistic Psalter"

Since W. Gesenius, H. Ewald, and F. Delitzsch first called attention to the conspicuous differences in the use of *yhwh* (Yahweh) and *'lhym* (Elohim) in the Psalter, it has been debated how the virtually exclusive use of *'lhym* in Psalms 42–83 should be understood, because *yhwh* appears hardly ever—or not at all—in this section.[1] While F. Delitzsch was of the opinion that this characteristic of these psalms, which he called "Elohimic," was originally connected to their "specific kind of poetry,"[2] H. Ewald held the view that the Elohistic permeation of Psalms 42–83 was explained by redactional work that replaced the original name of God, *yhwh*, with *'lhym*.[3] Ewald's view has largely prevailed up to the present day;[4] subsequently, the

---

Authors' note: We first met our friend Patrick D. Miller at the 1993 International SBL meeting in Münster, where he gave a fascinating presentation on Psalms 15–24. Miller's work on the Psalms has provided impetus to and been exceedingly important for our own research on the Psalter. We are thankful for both of these things. In particular, Miller's outstanding monograph, *They Cried to the Lord: The Form and Theology of Biblical Prayer* (Minneapolis: Fortress, 1994), has proved to be (and still is) a valuable companion to us in our work. We always have it at the ready.

1. W. Gesenius, *Thesaurus Philologicus Criticus Linguae Hebraeae et Chaldaeae Veteris Testamenti* (3 vols.; Lipsiae: Fr. Chr. Guil. Vogelii, 1835) 1:97–98; H. Ewald, *Die Psalmen* (Die Dichter des Alten Bundes 2; Göttingen: Vandenhoeck & Ruprecht, 1839) 191–92; and F. Delitzsch, *Symbolae ad psalmos illustrandos isagogicae* (Leipzig, 1846) 2ff.

2. F. Delitzsch, *Die Psalmen* (BKAT 1; Leipzig: Dörffling und Franke, 1867) 16.

3. H. Ewald, *Allgemeines über die Hebräische Poesie und über das Psalmenbuch* (Die Dichter des Alten Bundes 1; Göttingen: Vandenhoeck & Ruprecht, 1835).

4. Moreover, most introductions to the Old Testament give the impression that an *additional* Elohistic redaction of Psalms 42–83 is an assured thesis. See, among others, Otto Eissfeldt, *The Old Testament: An Introduction* (trans. P. R. Ackroyd; New York: Harper & Row, 1965) 449; O. Kaiser, *Einleitung in das Alte Testament* (Gütersloh: Mohr, 1984) 352; Rolf Rendtorff, *The Old Testament: An Introduction* (Philadelphia: Fortress, 1986) 248; W. H. Schmidt, *Einführung in das Alte Testament* (Berlin: de Gruyter, 1995) 304–5; and R. Smend, *Die Entstehung des Alten Testaments* (Berlin: de Gruyter, 1989) 190–91.

occurrences of *yhwh* that cannot be overlooked in the so-called Elohistic psalms are usually explained as a later redaction that is supposed to have inserted *yhwh*. At the same time, there is, of course, the thesis that the Elohistic redactors worked so superficially in editing that they overlooked the occurrences of *yhwh*. Finally, the *yhwh*-passages are also sometimes explained as a later incorporation of "Yahwistic" psalms to an already existing and purely Elohistic collection, and as having been re-edited in the Elohistic sense only partially.

Ewald's thesis of an Elohistic redaction of original "Yahwistic" psalms has been taken for granted in many, especially German, commentaries in such a way that even the traditional Hebrew text has been adjusted to correspond to it. The translations printed in such commentaries frequently insert the Tetragrammaton in Psalms 42–83 where, text-critically, there is no doubt that *'lhym* is in the traditional text. This practice has almost become dogma in critical commentaries and in many Psalms monographs, especially via the influential work of H. Gunkel.[5]

H.-J. Kraus's commentary on the Psalms is a typical example of this scenario. In the "Introduction" to this commentary, the problem of why *yhwh* also occurs in the so-called Elohistic Psalter seems not even to exist. Kraus says simply:

> In Psalms 42–83 the *consistent* use of אלהים as the name for God is striking. . . .
> If we think of the "Elohistic Psalter" as a separate component, a partial compilation within the chief collection of the Psalter, then it becomes apparent:
> (a) that the "Elohistic Psalter" is put together from three sources; and (b) that
> it was the compiler of the Elohistic part of the Psalter who undertook the *consistent* use of אלהים as the name of God.[6]

Accordingly, in the commentary on Psalms 42–83, *yhwh* is substituted for *'lhym*. Consequently, the problem of why the Tetragrammaton nevertheless appears in the *traditional* Hebrew text in numerous psalms of the so-called Elohistic Psalter goes unexpressed and unexplained. Moreover, in the notes to the translation of these psalms, Kraus is content with a stereotypically repeated formulation: "Transpositions of אלהים to יהוה in the Elohistically revised part of the Psalter are mandatory."[7] This hypothesis

---

5. H. Gunkel, *Die Psalmen* (HKAT II/4; Göttingen: Vandenhoeck & Ruprecht, 1926). Gunkel's exegetical reasoning is not found in the commentary itself, but in his *Introduction to Psalms: The Genres of the Religious Lyric of Israel* (completed by Joachim Begrich, trans. James D. Nogalski; Macon: Mercer University Press, 1998) that was first published in 1933 (cf. there 343–45 [German edition = 447–49]).

6. Hans-Joachim Kraus, *Psalms 1–59: A Commentary* (Minneapolis: Augsburg, 1988) 17 (emphasis added).

7. See, e.g., ibid., 436 n. b.

can even appear as an argument when, for example, in Ps 47:5, the sequence of *'lhym* and *yhwh* that appears in parallelism is destroyed by the (in our opinion unjustified) substitution of *yhwh* for *'lhym*. In addition, *yhwh* is substituted for *'lhym* in Ps 47:1, where Kraus writes in the text-critical note, "In the Elohistically edited part of the Psalter יהוה is to be inserted as the original reading."[8] Still further, Kraus says of the change of the text of 47:5 only "Cf. note a."[9]

How strong the "dogma" of a so-called Elohistic redaction and the resulting pressure to "correct" the traditional (!) text are, is shown in a monograph by H. Spieckermann. He, too, changes the traditional text of Ps 74:1, 10, and 12, with the short remark, "In vv. 10, 12, 22 the appellation 'God' has probably replaced the name Yahweh due to the incorporation of the text into the Elohistic Psalter."[10] Nonetheless, Spieckermann sees the problematic nature of the "dogma" of an additional Elohistic redaction when examining Psalms 78 and 48. With regard to the first, he writes

> Although Psalm 78 is part of the Elohistic Psalter, the divine name Elohim was not exchanged for Yahweh in what follows [i.e., the translation] for it would be, in view of the accumulation of different names for God in this Psalm—among them El is almost as frequent as Elohim—without any real support: Elohim (vv. 7, 10, 19, 22, 31, 35, 56, 59), El (vv. 7, 8, 18, 19, 34, 41), Elyon (vv. 17, 56), El Elyon (v. 35), Yahweh (vv. 4, 21), the Holy One of Israel (v. 41), Adonai (v. 65). Of course, it cannot be ruled out that the Elohim passages go back to redactional influence (cf., especially, v. 31a with the pattern in Num 11:33); however, it would then be hard to explain why the name Yahweh remained in the prominent place of v. 4, which after all, states the theme with its first mention of God's name.[11]

Essentially, with these accurate and important observations the often uncritically accepted thesis of an *additional* Elohistic redaction of Psalms 42–83 is fundamentally shaken. The dubiousness of the position finally becomes evident when Spieckermann comments on his translation of Psalm 48, where he again substitutes "Yahweh" for "Elohim" even though the Tetragrammaton, already existing in the Hebrew text of vv. 2a and 9a, creates a problem for him: "Because the psalm belongs to the Elohistic Psalter, Elohim has been exchanged for Yahweh in vv. 4, 9–11, 15 [Eng. vv. 3, 8–10, 14]. Since v. 2 [Eng. v. 1] obviously refers to a fixed liturgical formula (cf.

---

8. Ibid., 466 n. a.

9. Ibid., n. 5d; cf. the German original: "Die Einsetzung von יהוה statt אלהים scheint unter den unter a [= zu v. 1 (= MT v. 2)] *dargelegten Gründen* wahrscheinlich zu sein" (emphasis added).

10. H. Spieckermann, *Heilsgegenwart: Eine Theologie der Psalmen* (FRLANT 148; Göttingen: Vandenhoeck & Ruprecht, 1989) 122 n. 1.

11. Ibid., 133 n. 1.

Ps 96:4a), the Tetragrammaton was not redactionally changed in it. The same applies to the combination Yahweh Sabaoth in v. 9 [Eng. v. 8]."[12] Here we see the whole inconsistency of the traditional "Elohistic-thesis": a consistent redaction that does not always redact (Psalm 78) or that cannot redact (Psalm 48) is, to say the least, not a "consistent" redaction!

That the assumption of an Elohistic redaction of Psalms 42–83 belies a more complex problem than many commentaries and monographs realize was pointed out already by B. Jacob in 1898 (!):

> For, if the "redactor" really had the intention to avoid the name of God altogether, he would have also accomplished this—since it is truly easy to do so—and he would not have let it stand 43 [*sic!*] times. Certainly, one should not always imagine redactors to be as incredibly and unreasonably maladroit and careless workers as they are often supposed to be. . . . Finally, statements like "nevertheless" has the other name for God "asserted" itself more often . . . are nothing more than mythological veilings of our ignorance, by which one introduces the insidiousness of the object into the critique. We would like to know how a word or verse was able to "assert itself" despite the redactor. . . .[13]

Looking to non-German research on the Psalms, one finds more reserve and methodological sobriety *vis-à-vis* the "Elohistic dogma." As one example among many, the following citation from the first volume of the voluminous commentary on the Psalms by G. Ravasi may suffice. He begins his analysis of Psalm 42, the first of the "Elohistic" Psalms, as follows,

> The so-called *Elohistic Psalter*, which extends from 42–83 and which is characterized by the systematic substitution of the sacred Tetragrammaton YHWH with the more generic term *'Elohîm*, "God" (a word common to the whole Semitic world for defining the divinity), begins with the psalms that we will treat in a moment [i.e., Psalm 42]. A decisive explanation has not yet been found for this redactional work that sometimes creates problems (*'Elohîm Ṣeba'ôt* in 80:5!), which often results in difficulties (45:8; 63:2; 68:9; 80:4, 8, 20), and for which the artificiality is documented from the duplicates, Psalm 53 (a re-edition of Psalm 14) and Psalm 70 (a re-edition of Ps 40:14–18). According to some scholars, the correction would be due to reverential and pietistic motives from more recent epochs, a relic of which would remain in this section of the Psalter. For others, it would be an *escamotage*, a disguise, contrived by the Hebrews in the diaspora for hiding the true identity of Israel's God from the pagans, preventing the magic and blasphemous use of his true name. For still others, it would be evidence of diverse editions of the Psalter, according to different geographic-cultural areas (perhaps that of

---

12. Ibid., 186 n. 2.
13. B. Jacob, "Beiträge zu einer Einleitung in die Psalmen IV," *ZAW* 18 (1898) 100–101 n. 1.

Mesopotamia). For others, it would be a kind of sophisticated reduction of biblical prayer to produce a more general and abstract invocation suitable for diverse believers or a less familiar and personal, more sacerodotal and ritualized type of prayer. It is better to conclude by declaring our ignorance about the origins of the phenomenon, remembering among other things, that the third book of Psalms (Psalms 73–89) turns out, in the end, to be "Yahwistic": Psalms 84–89, called "the Yahwistic supplement," have a proportion of 3 to 1 for the name YHWH in comparison with *'Elohîm*.[14]

Here it is clearly stated that we are far from having a convincing solution for *the problem* of the so-called Elohistic Psalms.

The skepticism expressed above toward the reigning hypothesis explaining the dominance of *'lhym* in Psalms 42–83 in comparison with the dominance of *yhwh* in Psalms 1–41 and 84–150, also obtains for the exact opposite perspective that posits a Yahwistic redaction of Psalms 1–41 and 81–150 that was not carried out consistently in Psalms 42–83. This latter thesis is considered, at least as a possibility, by G. H. Wilson and E. S. Gerstenberger. Wilson summarizes his deliberations on the genesis of the Psalter in his pioneering study *The Editing of the Hebrew Psalter* as follows:

> It is a matter of common knowledge that the name of the deity plays a role in the grouping of the pss in MT 150. The group of 42 pss from Ps 42 through Ps 83 has been designated the "Elohistic Psalter" because here the regular designation of the deity is *'lhym* "*Elohîm*," in contrast to the predominance of the name YHWH in the remaining 108 pss. The figures are quite impressive. In the 42 pss of the "Elohistic Psalter" *'lhym* occurs 197 times as the divine name. In the 108 pss outside this collection. . . . *'lhym* occurs *as a name* on only 19 occasions. Of these 19, nine occur in the speech of or in relation to unbelievers (and reflect the unbeliever's terminology); four occur in duplicate portions of two pss from the "Elohistic Psalter" (Ps 108 = Pss 57:8–12 + 60:7–14). This leaves only *six* occurrences in which *'lhym* appears to have a force equivalent to that of YHWH.
>
> The really striking feature of these data is not so much the reduced occurrence of the name YHWH in the "Elohistic Psalter" as it is the *almost complete elimination* of *'lhym* as a designation for the God of Israel elsewhere. Could this be evidence of a concerted effort to eradicate the more ambiguous term in favor of the more particularistic YHWH?[15]

E. S. Gerstenberger makes a similar proposition in the introduction to his commentary on the Psalms, after having introduced the traditional thesis

---

14. G. Ravasi, *Il libro die Salmi* (3 vols.; Collana Lettura Pastorale della Biblica 12; Bologna: EDB, 1981) 1:757.

15. G. H. Wilson, *The Editing of the Hebrew Psalter* (SBLDS 76; Chico: Scholars, 1987) 196–97.

of an "Elohistic redaction" of Psalms 42–83: "One should, however, be aware of the other possibility. Perhaps this collection preserved a fairly original mode of naming the deity, while the rest of the Psalter suffered a Yahwistic redactional revision."[16]

Even this rough sketch should have made it plain: the evidence in the so-called Elohistic Psalter is contrary to the impression that many commentaries and even famous "Introductions to the Old Testament" give.[17] This is, in fact, an unresolved problem that is hardly dealt with in a serious way in the scholarly literature. Only recently have two different works attempted to reflect on the problem in greater detail.[18] We would like to draw on some of this recent work in order to then give our own proposal that flows from the work on our commentary on the Psalms.[19] Obviously, space limitations prevent us from presenting our proposal in full detail. Hence, for at least some further treatment of the texts discussed here we refer the reader to both of our previously published commentaries on Psalms 1–50 and Psalms 51–100.[20]

II. New Possibilities for Solving the Problem

Both of the recent studies by Millard and Rösel on the Elohistic Psalter have clearly shown that Psalms 42–83 stand out from the remaining psalms by their specific usage of *'lhym* and *yhwh* and that this difference, by no means fortuitously, begins with Psalm 42—the beginning of the second book of Psalms and the opening of the Korahite collection of Psalms 42–49. Moreover, Psalm 83—the final psalm of the Asaph collection (Psalms 73–83)[21]—is the end of the collection. These data provide important indications of the structure and growth of the book of Psalms.

16. E. S. Gerstenberger, *Psalms, Part 1: With an Introduction to Cultic Poetry* (FOTL 14; Grand Rapids: Eerdmans, 1988) 37.

17. Cf. also the informative presentation of this problem by J.-M. Auwers, *La composition littéraire du Psautier: Un état de la question* (CahRB 46; Paris: J. Gabalda, 2000) 70–76. Important reflections with a beginning toward an independent solution can also be found in D. C. Mitchell, *The Message of the Psalter: An Eschatological Programme in the Book of Psalms* (JSOTSup 252; Sheffield: Sheffield Academic Press, 1997) 69–73, 302–3.

18. M. Millard, "Zum Problem des elohistischen Psalters: Überlegungen zum Gebrauch von יהוה und אלהים im Psalter," in *Der Psalter in Judentum und Christentum* (ed. E. Zenger; Herders Biblische Studien 18; Freiburg: Herder, 1998) 75–110; C. Rösel, *Die messianische Redaktion des Psalters: Studien zu Entstehung und Theologie der Sammlung 2–89** (Stuttgart: Calwer, 1999) 21–38.

19. F.-L. Hossfeld and E. Zenger, *Psalmen 51–100* (HTKAT; Freiburg: Herder, 2000); the commentary will be published in English in the series Hermeneia.

20. F.-L. Hossfeld and E. Zenger, *Die Psalmen I: 1–50* (NEchtB 29; Würzburg: Echter Verlag, 1993). For Psalms 51–100, see the previous note.

21. For the history of the origin of Psalms 42–83, see Hossfeld and Zenger, *Psalmen 51–100*, 26–32.

Both studies come up with the following result in light of the statistics emerging from the history of research. Thus Millard:

> Although Psalms 42–83, with 740 of 1527 verses, constitute nearly half (ca. 48.5%) of the entire Psalter, only 45 of the 695 occurrences (ca. 6.5%) of the Divine Name [יהוה] within the Psalter are found in these psalms. Accordingly, many examples can be found within Psalms 42–83 where formulations with אלהים are comparable to the corresponding Yahwistic use of language outside these psalms. Typical for these psalms, however, is not the total avoidance of the Divine Name in Psalms 42–83, but its receding in comparison with אלהים [22]

and Rösel:

> The table shows a significant concentration of the instances of אלהים as a proper name in Psalms 42–83, in connection with a clear decrease of the instances of יהוה in the same section. The existence of an Elohistic Psalter comprising Psalms 42–83 is therefore obvious and has to be taken into account as a structural element whenever one reflects on the Psalter. [23]

Despite this similarity, both scholars interpret the same phenomenon differently. Millard opts for a composition-critical explanation:

> The significant preference for the absolute אלהים in Psalms 42–83 and the Name Theology, especially in the Asaph Psalm collection closing this collection, are obvious indications of a literary composition; however, both of these characteristics refer to the environment of the entire Psalter. Therefore, Psalms 42–83 cannot be described as the source. Moreover, no reasons for assuming an Elohistic redaction were revealed. [24]

Rösel prefers a redaction-critical solution,

> The use of אלהים as the designation for God can therefore be explained best through redactional activity. A consistent redaction originally substituted אלהים for יהוה in a single operation in the Psalms. In turn, the first unequivocal evidence of the redaction was blurred only later through the interpolation of יהוה. [25]

One can note positively for both analyses that they approach this complex phenomenon by paying increased attention to the individual cases. We will follow them in this fashion when we, utilizing our redaction- and composition-critical concepts, [26] consider the occurrences of *yhwh* sorted

---

22. Millard, "Zum Problem," 85–86.
23. Rösel, *Die messianische Redaktion*, 25.
24. Millard, "Zum Problem," 97.
25. Rösel, *Die messianische Redaktion*, 35.
26. See Hossfeld and Zenger, *Psalmen 51–100*, as well as our individual research listed there in the general bibliography.

according to psalm-groups in the order of their historical development.[27] In this way, the attempt to interpret the occurrences of *yhwh* in a particular psalm will be grounded in style and content and this will have methodological priority over literary- and redaction-critical, or even text-critical, solutions.

Of course, the total of 45 occurrences of *yhwh* within Psalms 42–83, provided by Millard and Rösel and their predecessors, has to be rounded out by the four passages that employ the short form *yh* (Pss 68:4, 18; 77:11; 81:5) and in the passage (Ps 81:5) where the Tetragrammaton appears in the unique spelling of the name Joseph as יהוסף (note the theophoric element *yh-* in first position).

III. *Yhwh in the "Second Davidic Psalter":* Psalms 51–72

After the exclusively Elohistic Psalms 51–53,[28] Ps 54:6 offers the first occurrence of *yhwh* in the second collection of Davidic Psalms (Psalms 51–72). The vow to praise in v. 6b refers especially to the praise of the name *yhwh* so that here the Name Theology suggests the mentioning of *yhwh*. A reference to v. 1a, with its introductory plea for help through the divine name without mentioning *yhwh*, is not an argument against an original *yhwh* in v. 6b, because the plea of v. 1a and the promise of thanksgiving of v. 6b could be deliberate as a varying *inclusio*; if so, from the beginning, the Elohistic psalm had the concluding mention of the proper name in view. The confession of trust in Ps 52:9b, related to the promise of thanksgiving in Ps 54:6b, refers to the attitude of trust in the Divine Name and can therefore dispense with explicitly mentioning it. However, the promise of thanksgiving in Ps 54:6b remains oriented toward the act of praise—that is, toward the proclamation of God's name.

The first instance of parallel use of divine appellation and proper name can be found in Ps 55:16. This is intentional, particularly since the expectation of salvation requires the intimate closeness of the saving *yhwh*. The use of the Tetragrammaton later in the same psalm (Ps 55:22) can be ex-

---

27. The limited space of this essay allows only this methodological step; additionally it would be *both* necessary *and* profitable to discuss also the *'lhym* occurrences as well as all *šm* references (i.e., the "Name Theology") in detail.

28. Psalm 53 is renowned for being a chief witness for the Elohistic Psalter hypothesis. We agree; however, we do not agree that Psalm 53 was originally "Yahwistic" in its actual literary context and *then, only later*, was Elohistically edited in that context. Rather, we believe the psalm received its "Elohistic" structure when it was inserted into the context of Psalms 51–72. For the comparison of Psalm 14 with Psalm 53, see Hossfeld and Zenger, *Psalmen 51–100*, 75–79.

plained analogously. The pious pray-er stands in a special relationship to *yhwh*, whereas *'lhym* will execute judgment upon the evil-doers.

In Ps 56:10, *'lhym* and *yhwh* are also in parallel so that, even with the Elohistic tendency, the proper name is not only included, it is intentionally put in second position.

After the Elohistic Psalm 57, *'lhym* and *yhwh* can again be found in parallel in Ps 58:6. Verse 6 contains the Psalm's central plea that contrasts the designation for God (*'lhym*) and the proper name for God (*yhwh*) in chiastic form.

Psalm 59 mentions *yhwh* three times in vv. 3, 5, 8, whereas *'lhym* follows in vv. 9, 10, 13, 17. Verse 3 mentions *yhwh* in the context of a confession of innocence, perhaps in consideration of the statements of confession in vv. 5 and 8. Moreover, v. 5 stands out with its accumulation of titles—"Yhwh," "God of hosts," and "Israel's God." Here the old title "Yhwh of hosts," linked to the Ark of the Covenant, is expanded or rather burst open by the generic name "God" (in the *status absolutus!*).[29] This procedure demonstrates that the Elohistic tendency does not always replace God's name, but respects it, even if it does not prefer it.

Following Psalms 60–63 that utilize only *'lhym*, the next use of the Tetragrammaton is in Ps 64:10. Verses 9–10 describe responses to God's punishment of the psalmist's enemies; in addition they distinguish between the people's reaction to Elohim's act and the righteous' reaction to Yhwh's work. One and the same God has a distant relationship as Elohim to "all people" in distinction from the righteous who stand in a close relationship to Yhwh (cf. Pss 5:10–12, 32:10, and above on 55:22).

After the exclusively Elohistic Psalms 65–67,[30] Psalms 68 and 69 represent two special cases. Both psalms are prominent in the Elohistic Psalter, with each containing five occurrences of *yhwh*; both have the same scope, the same importance, and the same complexity. In the context of the first Davidic Psalter, it is the concurrent preexilic portions—Pss 68:7–31 and 69:1–4, 13–18, 30—that are of special interest here.[31]

Both of the framing strophes of Psalm 68 (vv. 7–10, 28–31) show a definite Elohistic tendency that avoids the proper name. The four instances of

---

29. Cf., among others, the connection *yhwh 'lhy ṣb'wt* in Amos 4:13; 5:14–16; and Ps 89:9 (*'lhym* in construct).

30. Psalm 67, especially, shows that the different occurrences of *'lhym* were placed deliberately, not that an *additional* Elohistic redactor had worked on the psalm. Instead, from the beginning, the psalm was an "Elohistic" transformation of the Yahwistic blessing formula handed down in Num 6:24–26. See Hossfeld and Zenger, *Psalmen 51–100*, 228–41.

31. On these literary-critical positions, see Hossfeld and Zenger, *Psalmen 51–100*, 246–50, 265–69.

yhwh can be found only in the body of the psalm: vv. 16, 18, 20, 26. The frequency of the occurrences of *yhwh* alongside other names for God like "Lord," "Almighty," and "El" has raised the question of whether this psalm has been Elohistically redacted at all.[32] Verse 16 is a clear case of intentional parallelism. God's mountain (Zion) is the mountain Elohim desired, and on which Yhwh lives. The stanza of vv. 15–18 culminates in addressing "Yh, God" (v. 18), whereby *'lhym* takes on the function of a complement "Yh (is, or rather, as) God." In v. 20, *yhwh* is combined with the title *'dny*, "Lord," which then dominates the pertinent stanza (vv. 19–23; see vv. 19, 20, 22). In this combination of proper name + title, the order is reversed when compared to Pss 69:6; 71:5, 16; 73:28. Here, "Lord" is most likely to be emphatically identified with *yhwh*. In v. 26, the praised "God" (*'lhym*) is in parallel with "the Lord, O you who are of Israel's fountain!"

The original portion of Psalm 69 has an occurrence of *yhwh* in v. 16, which is an urgent plea to Yhwh to act according to his goodness and mercy. The original portion of the psalm prefers the generic divine designation in vv. 1, 13, 30, but allows the proper name to come forward in central pleas framed in vv. 16–18 because Yhwh's self-assertion, or better, the creed of Exod 34:6 shows up. The tradition of the Jerusalem cult thus becomes present here. Contrary to expectations, the praise of the divine name in v. 30 is not connected with the proper name *yhwh*.

In the markedly Elohistic Psalm 70 (note *'lhym* in vv. 1, 4, 5), *'lhym* and *yhwh* are nevertheless found in parallel in vv. 1 and 5. Thus, a framing of the psalm (*inclusio*) develops at the same time.[33]

The three occurrences of *yhwh* in Psalm 71 (vv. 1, 5, 16) can be explained as follows: v. 1 belongs to the paragraph (vv. 1–3) that adopts and edits Ps 31:1–3. The use of *yhwh* here, then, is taken from Ps 31:1. In vv. 5 and 16, one finds the well-known combination "Lord Yhwh" (see Pss 69:6; 73:28). This is not surprising, because Psalm 71 is formally an anthology and uses several names for God (e.g., "Holy One of Israel" in v. 22 [repeated only in Pss 78:41 and 89:18]; "my God" in vv. 4, 22; *'lhym* six times in vv. 11, 12, 17–19).

Within the Elohistic Psalm 72, *'lhym* is mentioned only once in the address at the beginning of the psalm. The second Davidic Psalter closes with this psalm.

---

32. Cf. J. P. Fokkelmann, "The Structure of Psalm LXIII," in *In Quest of the Past: Studies on Israelite Religion* (ed. A. S. van der Woude; OTS 26; Leiden: Brill, 1990) 77: "Now older commentaries sometimes wondered whether this poem had undergone an Elohistic redaction. I don't think so."

33. For a comparison of Psalm 70 with Ps 40:14–18, see Hossfeld and Zenger, *Psalmen 51–100*, 282–85.

This investigation of the second Davidic Psalter brought to light *several regularities* that can explain the occurrence of *yhwh* despite the existing Elohistic tendency throughout this section. *First*, we discovered the intentional parallel, *yhwh* ‖ *'lhym*, in Pss 55:16; 56:10; 58:6; 68:16, 26; 70:1, 5. This parallel maintains the memory of *yhwh*, and ensures that Elohim's connection to the proper name does not get lost. *Second*, related to this intentional parallel is the interest in the proclaimed name *yhwh*, as we have come upon it in Ps 54:6b. *Third*, there is the differentiation in the perspective of or relationship to God: *'lhym* for those far away, the enemies, and transgressors; but *yhwh* for those who are near and righteous (see Pss 5:10–12 [a corroborating parallel from the first Davidic Psalter]; 55:22; 64:10). *Fourth*, various combinations of God's name occur with other terms for God, whereby old terms are taken over and are adapted to the Elohistic tendency (Pss 59:5; [68:20]; 71:5, 16). In the case of Ps 71:1, we have become aware of the intertwining with non-Elohistically-oriented psalms that has caused the infiltration of the Tetragrammaton into the Elohistic Psalter.

IV. Yhwh in the Asaph Psalms: Psalms 50, 73–83

The otherwise decidedly Elohistic Asaph Psalm 50 (see especially v. 7 with its Elohistic formula of self-introduction) begins in v. 1 with a rare triad of names for God (*'l 'lhym yhwh*), which is a programmatic and increasing expression of confession. The psalm intends to stress the final term in the triad, Yhwh, and relate the others to it.[34]

Ps 73:28 introduces the combination "Lord Yhwh" in the last line. It serves as a parallel to Elohim in the sense that God's closeness, given as a

---

34. Between Psalms 50 and 83—the two book-end psalms of the Asaph-David-Asaph composition (Psalms 50–83)—there are important semantic and thematic references. There is the theophany of Yhwh, announced in Psalm 50 as "God of gods" (50:1) and "Most High" (50:14), who is revealed in a tempest and fire (50:3). This revelation is also found and proclaimed in Psalm 83 (cf. the analogous motifs in vv. 13–15 and v. 18), but no longer as judgment on the people, or rather, on Zion (as announced in Psalm 50 and lamented in the popular lamentations of Psalms 73–80), but in the eschatological judgment on all world powers that threaten Israel. The connection from Psalm 83 back to Psalm 50 is enhanced by the redactional note in Ps 50:3a, "Our God comes and *does not keep silence*." It is in the light of this statement, that one has to understand Ps 83:2. Psalm 83 claims the completion of Yhwh's "coming" that started at Sinai or, as the case may be, at Zion, for the purpose of being the Deliverer—as announced in Psalm 50. Thus, the Asaph collection, as a whole, is a composition of lamentation and plea toward Yhwh that stands under the promise of Ps 50:15: "Call on me in the day of trouble; I will deliver you!"

gift by God and for the well-being of the supplicant, corresponds to the psalmist's trust in Yʜᴡʜ.[35]

Ps 74:18 is also evidence for the Name Theology that is also extant in this psalm. "Ps 74:10 [reminds one of] the disrepute of the Divine Name. . . . This passage is to be seen together with v. 18, which is parallel to its content, where the absolute אלהים of v. 10 is replaced by יהוה. . . . The dwelling place of the name of God is desecrated (Ps 74:7), and the psalm's perspective of its purpose is the praise of God's name (74:21)."[36]

In Ps 75:8, the expression "a cup in Yʜᴡʜ's hand" is conspicuous. It is imparted through the incorporation of the motif of the cup of wrath and judgment found in Yʜᴡʜ's hand elsewhere (see Isa 51:17; Jer 25:15; Hab 2:16).

In Ps 76:11, the mention of "Yʜᴡʜ, your God" stands out from its Elohistic context (see vv. 1, 9). But in connection with concrete cultic obligations, the inclusion of the proper name is a self-evident duty; it belongs to the spectrum of God's concrete manifestations after vv. 1–2.

As in Ps 75:8, the term "Yʜ's deeds" stands out in Ps 77:11 since it appears in an otherwise Elohistic context. Perhaps one has to think of this as a deliberate incorporation of a *terminus technicus* in the style of Exod 15:2 ("Yʜ's song") and Exod 17:16 ("Yʜ's ensign").

Psalm 78 generally uses *'lhym* save for two exceptions: vv. 4 and 21. Verse 4 belongs to the passages in the Elohistic Psalter "for which no immediate evidence of a redaction can be traced."[37] This verse is the indispensable programmatic statement of the theme of the entire historical psalm. The proper name is thus intentionally placed in front, analogous to Ps 50:1. God's history, narrated in Psalm 78, is, of course, Yʜᴡʜ's history with his people. Verse 21 is, like Ps 71:1, a redacted adoption of a text from another context outside the Elohistic Psalter, here even from outside the book of Psalms—namely, Num 11:1–10.

In the case of Ps 79:5, the invocation of God with the proper name sets a counterpoint to the invocation to Elohim in v. 1. "The invocation of God by name (v. 5) is in contrast with the plea against those who do not appeal to God's name (v. 6). With this plea the honor of God's name is at stake (v. 9)."[38]

---

35. Describing the theological profile of Psalms 42–83 would necessitate a detailed discussion of the occurrences of *'dny* especially since 23 of the 63 instances in the Psalter are found within Psalms 42–83 alone. They, too, hardly originate in an *additional* redaction of the already existing collection (Psalms 42–83), but are connected with the original program of the collection itself.

36. Millard, "Zum Problem," 92.

37. Rösel, *Die messianische Redaktion*, 34.

38. Millard, "Zum Problem," 92.

Psalm 80 presents a differentiated picture in relation to the designations for God. First, the "system" of the refrains in vv. 3, 7, 19 needs to be considered. Each of the introductory appeals to God are systematically intensified: God (v. 3); God of hosts (v. 7); Yʜwʜ, God of hosts (v. 19). The climax lies in the last refrain that stands in a matter-of-fact relation to the Name Theology in v. 18. "The appeal to God's name is the perspective of those who survived the catastrophe (v. 18)."[39] In the redactional refrains, Asaphite theology can be recognized without any difficulty. In v. 4, the pre-exilic original portion of the psalm anticipates the extended appeal to God that appears again in the final refrain. It presents an important accent at the beginning of the lamentation. As is the case in Ps 59:5, it describes an Elohistic variant of the old title "Yʜwʜ of hosts" which is copied outside the Elohistic Psalter in the Korahite Psalm 84 (v. 8). At the beginning of the supplicatory passage in Ps 80:14, the variant is taken up in the shortened form "God of hosts." Thus, the designations for God in the Elohistic original portions of the psalm in vv. 4, 14 get converted to the Asaphite "system" in vv. 3, 7, 19.

Psalm 81 has two characteristics that are germane to our investigation: (1) it incorporates an Elohistic fragment from the northern kingdom in vv. 2–5; and (2) it contains more instances of Yʜ/Yʜwʜ than of Elohim (three in vv. 5, 10, 15), which is unique in the context of the Elohistic Psalter. Verse 5 conceals the occurrence of the short form Yʜ as the theophoric element in the unique writing of Joseph's name already mentioned above. This is not subtle, but against the background of the reflective practices of the Asaphites, it must surely be a signal for the proper name of the God of the Exodus who is remembered in this psalm and whose own word is presented here. The self-introduction of v. 10 does without the Elohistic change *à la* Ps 50:7 and evokes the topic of the First Commandment. Verse 15 takes up the Yahwistic orientation of the entire psalm.

Millard has noted the crucial thing about both of the last occurrences of *yhwh* in the Asaph Psalter (Ps 83:16, 18):

> The Asaph Psalms have thereby a characteristic Name Theology that builds to a crescendo in the last psalm of the Elohistic Psalter, Psalm 83—the final perspective of the individual psalms, of the collection of Asaph Psalms, and the collection of Psalms 42–83, which is dominated by the Asaph Psalms— "Fill their faces with shame, so that they may seek your name, Yʜwʜ!" (83:16). Thus, God's name is definitely known within the Elohistic Psalter, but it is nevertheless concealed. There is a secret about God's name. One has to search for this name. The recognition of God's name lies in Psalm 83, as it does in Ezekiel, in a future that is identified by God's intervention, "Let

39. Ibid.

them know that you alone, whose name is the Lord, are the Most High over all the earth" (83:18). Coming, as this does, from the Name Theology—which becomes clear at the end of the Elohistic Psalter and which has its nearest parallel in Ezekiel—both the exilic origin of the composition of the Elohistic Psalter and its formation/shaping in the postexilic period, as in the book of Ezekiel, can be established."[40]

While corrections are necessary with regard to Millard's hypothesis on the origin of the composition of the Elohistic Psalter, both of his other points—the nature of the composition and the Asaphite Name Theology—are to be emphasized. Reading through the relevant passages in the twelve Asaph psalms reveals that despite provable Elohistic tendencies, each Asaph psalm mentions the name Yhwh at least once, even be it "only" in the short form; this must be intentional, not merely coincidental. The only exception, Psalm 82, actually proves the rule, since the setting of this psalm takes place in the trial of the gods in heaven. Psalm 82 is not about the historical revelation of Yhwh to his people, but about his superior divinity in comparison with the other doomed gods. The other Asaph psalms adhere deliberately to the proper name of Yhwh: they recall Yhwh in confession (Pss 50:1; 73:28); point to his working in the past, present, and future (Pss 75:8, 76:12, 77:11, 78:4, 81:5, 10, 16); and represent, like their predecessors in the second Davidic Psalter, a distinct Name Theology (Pss 74:18; 79:6; 80:18; 83:16, 18). From this perspective, one can revisit the specifically Asaphite parts of Psalm 68, namely, the outer ring of the vv. 4–6, 32–35.[41] These verses corroborate the Elohistic tendency and prove again in v. 4 the specific Asaphite Name Theology.

The subordinate second paragraph of the lamentation in Ps 69:5–13ab makes the move from *'lhym* (v. 5) to *yhwh* (v. 13b) in its introductory and closing invocations to God; in so doing it reminds one of Pss 79:1, 5; 80:3, 19. In v. 6, the psalmist amasses a number of important honorary titles. The psalmist combines "Lord" and "Yhwh" (cf. [68:20]; 71:5, 16; 73:28) with the title "(Yhwh) of hosts," which recalls Pss 59:5; 80:4, 19 (all with *'lhym*). Furthermore, the psalmist applies the honorary title "God of Israel," which was previously mentioned in Pss 59:5 and 68:8 (cf. the closing doxologies in Pss 41:13 and 73:18). In this fashion, traditional credal titles for belief in Yhwh are utilized in connection with the in-group—the supporters of the psalmist. In the final text at hand, Ps 69:13 (without the break after v. 13ab), there is again the typical paralleling of proper name and generic appelation name, however in an unusual order (*yhwh* ‖ *'lhym*).

---

40. Ibid., 92–93.
41. See Hossfeld and Zenger, *Psalmen 51–100,* 249–50.

The subordinate continuation of the praise in Ps 69:31–33 mentions *yhwh* in v. 31, speaks of those "who seek God" (cf. Ps 34:10: "who seek Yhwh") in v. 32, and comes back to *yhwh* in v. 33. The first mentioning of *yhwh* in v. 31 may have been instigated by the praise of God's name in v. 30 at the end of the original portion of the psalm. Thus, this praise would have challenged the Asaphite Name Theology, which immediately takes up the name of Yhwh in its own way. The change from *ʾlhym* to *yhwh* in vv. 32–33 corresponds to the common parallelism in the Elohistic Psalter. The four *yhwh* occurrences in Ps 69:6, 13ab, 31, 33 can be easily explained within the scope of Asaphite theology.

V. *Yhwh in the First Collection of Korahite Psalms: Psalms 42–49*

Within the solely Elohistic Psalms, 42–45 only Ps 42:8 is out of place in its use of the Tetragrammaton. According to broad consensus among exegetes, this verse is redactional, which in its own way transforms the "law" of parallelism, and connects the proper name with a variation on the Korahite divine appellation "Living God" (Pss 42:2; 84:2), namely, "God of my life." The solely Elohistic Psalm 49 closes this first collection of Korahite Psalms. The remaining seven instances of *yhwh* are only found in the so-called hymnic part of the collection (Psalms 46–48).

In Ps 46:7, both of the old northern kingdom titles for God, "Yhwh of hosts" and "God of Jacob" are found in chiastic arrangement. Here, an additional redaction can be ruled out, especially because this verse, according to the evidence of Ps 46:11, functions simultaneously as a refrain. Moreover, the declarations that begin in v. 1 with *ʾlhym* and end in v. 8 with traditional titles for God by employing the Tetragrammaton are the climax of vv. 1–7. The original preexilic portion of the psalm preserves an old tradition here. Verse 8, with its "deed of Yhwh," is Yahwistic in contrast to its near-by Elohistic parallel in Ps 66:5.[42]

Psalm 47:2a belongs to the original preexilic portion of Psalm 47; hence, it should not be excised.[43] It reflects the Jerusalemite tradition in which Yhwh is the Most High, the awesome God of peoples and kings. Psalm 47:5 also belongs to this original portion and shows a clear example of the intentional parallel *yhwh* ‖ *ʾlhym*.

The original preexilic portion of Psalm 48 consists of vv. 1–8, 12–14. That this is a psalm with Elohistic tendencies becomes evident in vv. 3, 8,

---

42. The discussion about the scope of the original, preexilic portion(s) of Psalm 46 cannot be dealt with at this point (in our judgment, only vv. 9–11 *or* v. 10 are postexilic).

43. Rösel, *Die messianische Redaktion*, 29–30.

and especially v. 14 ("that is God, our God"). The mention of *yhwh* at the
beginning of the psalm (v. 1) is indispensable. Both v. 1 and v. 8 ("in the city
of Yнwн of hosts") take up an old tradition (see Ps 46:7, 11). The preference
of *'lhym* in vv. 12–14 can be connected with the fact that the imperatives of
vv. 12–13 "exhort the inimical kings to expose themselves seriously to what
has happened to them and to act accordingly,"[44] and thus to accept *yhwh*
as God.

A short glance at the seven *yhwh* occurrences (excluding Ps 42:8) in the
preceding section of Korahite Psalms reveals that they are concentrated
within the so-called hymns and thus present the preexilic tradition, which,
just as in the second Davidic Psalter, couples an Elohistic tendency and a
consideration for the Yнwн tradition throughout the collection.

VI. Conclusions

We have examined the so-called Elohistic Psalter according to its constituent groups of psalms in their assumed chronological order (second Davidic Psalter [Psalms 51–72], Asaph Psalms [Psalms 50, 73–83], the first
collection of Korahite Psalms [Psalms 42–49]). This analysis has produced
the following insights:

1. The 49 occurrences of *yhwh* are distributed among all three groups.
The sheer quantity of these occurrences as well as their dispersion throughout this material should dictate that simplistic explanatory models for
the Elohistic Psalter—such as the substitution of the generic term Elohim
for the original proper name Yнwн with occasional re-infiltration of the
proper name—or the model of a consistent avoidance of Yнwн through a
particular group of psalms are best avoided. The frequent use of the generic term Elohim along with the less frequent, but purposefully-used
name for God, Yнwн, is not indicative of a secondary redaction, but an expression of theological thinking that typically reveals itself only as a theological tendency in these texts.

2. This theological tendency has a preexilic beginning and a postexilic
ending; between these points are specific metamorphoses of its imple-
mentation in the texts at hand. Its beginning can be grasped in the older
preexilic psalms of the second Davidic Psalter (Psalms 51–72) and in the
preexilic hymnic texts of the first collection of Korahite Psalms (Psalms
42–49). Certain regularities when using the proper name can be consistently observed throughout. These include: the intentional paralleling of
yhwh and *'lhym*; the inclusion of established divine titles and combined
terms for God; the differentiation in use *vis-à-vis* the perspective on God

44. Hossfeld and Zenger, *Die Psalmen 1–50*, 45.

(Yhwh for the ones who are close, Elohim for those who are far away); as well as credal-type reminders of the revealed proper name. The theologians responsible for the Asaph Psalms gave the Elohistic tendency a distinctive expression in that they propagated their theology of God's name and introduced the proper name Yhwh in an "all-encompassing manner." In the group of Korahite Psalms (Psalms 42–49) the proper name was accepted, or rather, tolerated chiefly as traditional material. The Elohistic tendency does not recur in the Korahite Psalms 84–88.

3. Chronologically, it is possible that the Elohistic tendency with its respective concerns is related to the so-called Elohistic texts of the Pentateuch, which, in our opinion, do not constitute a distinct literary entity or source. The northern kingdom traditions, known in the exegesis of the psalms in the Elohistic Psalter especially, do not speak against this. The Elohistic tendency should be clearly separated from the fear of misusing or pronouncing the Tetragrammaton, which only began later. This is shown by the fact that the use of *'lhym* markedly declines, whereas *yhwh* is ubiquitously used throughout the rest of the Psalter. "The fact that *yhwh* remained in the texts also speaks against a direct connection with the fear known from Judaism. Moreover, *'dny*, not *'lhym*, was chosen as the substitute word."[45]

4. Motivations for the Elohistic tendency arise from classical connotations of speech about "Elohim" in connection with Old Testament beliefs about Yhwh. The preference for "Elohim" presupposes a gravitation toward monotheism by which the generic term becomes the proper name. Moreover, as already indicated, the use of "Elohim" emphasizes God's distance and transcendence; the distant, dark, mysterious God is accentuated. Finally, "Elohim" is preferred when God's universality ought to be extolled (so, similarly the Priestly writings in Gen 1–11); such speech is suggested in the Psalms when the nations are included in prayer.[46]

---

45. Rösel, *Die messianische Redaktion*, 35–36 n. 104.

46. We thank Michael Zipser for translating this essay and the editors for their assistance with the English translation.

A Fairy Tale Wedding?
A Feminist Intertextual Reading of Psalm 45

NANCY R. BOWEN

I. Introduction

Nearly every study of Psalm 45 contains some variation on the statement "Psalm 45 is unique." There are many reasons for ascribing uniqueness to this psalm. Although often classified thematically as one of the many royal psalms, it is itself a unique genre, a wedding song for the king. Many words and word usages are unique to this psalm.[1] It is also the only psalm where women occupy a central place. Although this psalm has received extensive scholarly attention it is also unique in having so far escaped attention from feminist biblical interpreters. It is not mentioned at all in the entry on the Psalms in *The Women's Bible Commentary*.[2] Moreover, the only reference by a feminist interpreter that I am aware of suggests that we may be better off if Psalm 45 retains its uniqueness: "Certainly it is not the faint-of-heart feminist that dares to tread here in the Psalms. Women are rarely mentioned specifically, and one reading of Psalm 45 could make women think the cause is hopeless."[3] However, as a strong-of-heart feminist, my intent here is to engage in a reexamination of Psalm 45. If one reads this psalm with a feminist hermeneutic, what will he or she find? Does this psalm articulate the liberating experiences and visions of

---

Author's note: I am pleased to write this essay in honor of Patrick D. Miller and his commitment to including the voices of women in the church and the academy.

1. See Johannes Mulder, *Studies in Psalm 45* (Nijmegen: Karmel Doddendaal, 1972) 113–42.

2. Kathleen A. Farmer, "Psalms," in *The Women's Bible Commentary* (ed. Carol A. Newsom and Sharon H. Ringe; Louisville: Westminster/John Knox, 1992) 137–44.

3. Beth LaNeel Tanner, "Hearing the Cries Unspoken: An Intertextual-Feminist Reading of Psalm 109," in *A Feminist Companion to Wisdom and Psalms* (2nd series; ed. Athalya Brenner; Sheffield: Sheffield Academic Press, 1998) 295.

53

the people of God? Or is this a psalm that is only to be read *in memoriam*[4] or that cannot be accorded revelatory authority?[5]

Because the primary aim of this essay is to read Psalm 45 with a feminist hermeneutic, the focus will not be on the traditional historical-critical questions that have been addressed to this psalm.[6] Instead, the focus will be on the questions that have *not* been asked: How does this psalm engage the lives of women? What are the assumptions about gender relations in this psalm? What are the images the psalm provides of king/consort and husband/wife?

This essay will also explore this psalm using an intertextual methodology.[7] Intertextuality relates various "texts" to one another in a way that is not concerned with issues of priority or dependence.[8] Instead, it is concerned with the way a text acquires different meanings when it is situated in relationship to other texts. I am primarily interested in intertextuality as a means of having a "dialogue among several writings."[9] The purpose of this dialogue will be to see the effect it has on our understanding of the gender issues raised by Psalm 45. Will a dialogue partner support the discourse of Psalm 45 or reject it, decenter it, or transform it? The decision of which dialogue partners to include is my own.[10] The choices were determined, at least in part, by my own history and cultural context, by repetitions of words, and by similarities in themes. I have primarily limited myself to the canonical scriptures but such a restriction is not required.[11] Even so, I have

4. See Phyllis Trible, *Texts of Terror: Literary-Feminist Readings of Biblical Narratives* (OBT; Philadelphia: Fortress, 1984) 3.

5. Elisabeth Schüssler Fiorenza, *In Memory of Her: A Feminist Theological Reconstruction of Christian Origins* (New York: Crossroad, 1983) 33.

6. E.g., is *'ĕlōhîm* in v. 6a to be translated as a vocative? What does this say about Israelite kingship? Does it reflect a possible cultic enthronement ceremony? For which historical king was it written?

7. Detailed discussions of intertextuality and biblical interpretation can be found in the essays in Danna Nolan Fewell, ed., *Reading Between Texts: Intertextuality and the Hebrew Bible* (LCBI; Louisville: Westminster/John Knox, 1992); and George Aichele and Gary A. Phillips, ed., "Intertextuality and the Bible," *Semeia* 69/70 (1995).

8. Within theoretical and methodological discussions of intertextuality, "text" is not limited to something written. It may include other media such as art and television or even more broadly may include all of language and culture.

9. This expression is from Julia Kristeva, *Desire in Language: A Semiotic Approach to Literature and Art* (trans. Leon S. Roudiez; Chicago: University of Chicago Press, 1980) 65.

10. On the ideological considerations of the reader's determination of intertextual relationships, see Timothy K. Beal, "Ideology and Intertextuality: Surplus of Meaning and Controlling the Means of Production," in Fewell, ed., *Reading Between Texts*, 27–39.

11. E.g., in personal conversation, Dr. Archie C. C. Lee of the Chinese University of Hong Kong suggested that a fruitful dialogue might occur between Psalm 45 and the pre-Confucian Chinese poems *The Book of Odes* (the Chinese title of this work is variously transliterated as *Shijing* or *Shih Ching*).

excluded traditional intertextual readings that focus on the dependence or influence of ancient Near Eastern literature on the psalm. The dialogue partners I have chosen are romantic fairy tales, Abigail, Esther, Ezekiel 16, and the Song of Songs.

Before proceeding, it might be pointed out that there is yet another way in which this psalm is unique. Patrick Miller, quoting Walter Brueggemann, speaks about the liturgical, devotional, and pastoral ways that the Psalms have functioned in the community of faith.[12] Miller adds that there is also a theological-homiletical dimension to the way the Psalms function.[13] And yet, when I look around, Psalm 45 is unique in that it seems to have *no* function of *any* kind in contemporary communities of faith. In my own tradition, it can be noted that the Psalter in *The United Methodist Hymnal* skips from Psalm 44 to Psalm 46. I could not locate any hymn or other liturgical use of Psalm 45 in United Methodist, Presbyterian, Disciples of Christ, Lutheran, Religious Society of Friends, or Church of the Brethren worship resources. It does appear twice in the Revised Common Lectionary, but in one edition of the Lectionary it occurs with the statement "or Psalm 72," which may hint that Psalm 45 is thought to be a less desirable or easily replaced psalm.[14] Therefore, another concern of this essay will be with what may be the most critical question: What are the possibilities for the use of this psalm in contemporary faith communities?

II. A Fairy Tale Wedding

When I read Psalm 45 one song I hear echoes of is "Someday My Prince Will Come" from Walt Disney's animated movie *Snow White*. This echo presents itself because the gender relations in *Snow White* or *Cinderella* (or any other fairy tale where there is a Prince Charming and his Princess Bride) are similar to those found in Psalm 45. This genre of fairy tale can lead us to meditate on Psalm 45 as a song that celebrates a fairy tale wedding.

Just as in a fairy tale, Prince Charming (the king) is oh, so handsome! "You are beautiful [i.e., handsome] more so than all other human men" (v. 2aα).[15] And he is, in fact, charming. "Graciousness is poured out from your lips" (v. 2aβ). And the reason this king is so charming is because he is blessed by God (v. 2b). But this Prince is not just handsome; he is also strong and masculine. He is both a noble warrior and a virtuous ruler (vv. 3–7a).

---

12. Patrick D. Miller, Jr., *Interpreting the Psalms* (Philadelphia: Fortress, 1986) 20.

13. Ibid.

14. Year A, Sunday between July 3–9: Gen 24:34–38, 42–49, 58–67; Ps 45:10–17 or Psalm 72; Rom 7:15–25a; Matt 11:16–19, 25–30; Year B, Sunday between August 28–September 3: Song 2:8–13; Ps 45:1–2, 6–9 or Psalm 72; Jas 1:17–27; Mark 7:1–8, 14–15, 21–23.

15. Translations of Psalm 45 are my own.

The princess our prince marries is the fairest of them all. All it takes is one look for Prince Charming to know *she* is the one (v. 11a). She is indeed fit to be his queen (vv. 12–14). As with most fairy tale princesses, she will leave behind her family and people (v. 10). She will pay homage to her prince and recognize that he is her lord and master (v. 11b). Her prince has come and she will be his forever. They will have many children and will live happily ever after (vv. 16–17).

Like most fairy tales, Psalm 45 presupposes asymmetry in its gender relationships. The groom/king is on top of the sexual hierarchy. He is the dominant partner. The bride is clearly subordinate to him as indicated by the exhortation in v. 11b, "He is your lord, bow down to him!" In addition, the fairy-tale world of Psalm 45 presupposes particular concerns that may or may not be those of modern fairy tales. Some of those concerns are expressed in the dichotomy between what is required of the bride and groom. The central concern for the groom/king is expanding and maintaining his kingdom. The emphasis on military prowess points to the issue of expansion. Maintaining the kingdom will come through the king's concerns for justice and also through the perpetuation of his dynasty through his sons.

The central concerns for the woman/bride are two-fold. One is her loyalty to her new husband's household. The second is to bear sons for her husband. The bride's loyalty and fecundity can also be seen as functioning to support the kingdom. Artur Weiser expresses this clearly, if somewhat romantically.

> In this way the poet unites the young couple in their joint task and in the purpose of their matrimony, so that the queen will feel herself tied to her new homeland in her sons and by the strong bonds of her own blood. And the king and with him the whole nation will be proud of such a strengthening and safeguarding of his rule.[16]

In short, it is easy to conclude that that psalm is a song of, by, and for patriarchy. This is, after all, a song *for the king*. It is *his* concerns and purposes that are the central focus. The bride is present not for what *she* might seek from or bring to (beyond children) the marriage but is present only to enable the king to fulfill his mandate regarding the kingdom. We have no idea what concerns the bride may have had or what her song may have been. Were loyalty, beauty, submission, and fertility what she cared about or *all* that she cared about? We cannot say. Her voice and perspective are totally absent from this song.

Both Psalm 45 and fairy tales represent a certain idyllic wish about how gender relationships and marriage are to be constructed. But contempo-

---

16. Artur Weiser, *The Psalms* (OTL; Philadelphia: Westminster, 1962) 364.

rary feminist interpretation has shown how the wishful ideals of fairy tales have functioned in ways that have been and continue to be damaging for women.[17] So, what problems are encountered within the "fairy tale" world of Psalm 45? How well is the poetic wish of Psalm 45 fulfilled in the Bible? Are there texts that critique this world? Is there a text that might "hear into speech" the wishes and desires of the bride? I will now look at some biblical stories of royal brides to carry forth our dialogue around these questions.

III. Biblical Brides

The first stop along our intertextual pathway will be with two biblical brides. What evokes these texts initially is that they both involve a woman and her marriage to a king.

Abigail

The story of Abigail and David can be linked with Psalm 45 in two ways. The first link is in terms of plot. 1 Samuel 25 has been described as "a traditional plot of love and marriage."[18] It can be seen as a narrative of the fairy tale romance leading to the fairy tale wedding that Psalm 45 celebrates. The second link is linguistic. A common vocabulary binds the named and unnamed brides together.

1 Samuel 25 is the story of Abigail and how she ends up rescued by and married to her prince. In this case, there is no wicked stepmother, but there is a foolish husband who puts her in peril. Fortunately, Prince Charming, that is, David, is there to save her. Like the groom of Psalm 45, we know that David is handsome (1 Sam 16:12). And, like the bride of Psalm 45, Abigail is beautiful (1 Sam 25:3).[19] And as in the psalm, 1 Samuel 25 is concerned with issues of kingship. David has been anointed but Saul is still king. In this in-between time, David seeks to consolidate his power, which he accomplishes by various displays of military prowess. Thus, in the face of a new enemy, Nabal, David must demonstrate his military might. In Ps 45:3 the king is commanded to strap on his sword (*ḥăgôr-ḥarbĕkā*). Similarly, David commands his men to each strap on his sword (*ḥigrû ʾîš ʾet-ḥarbô*) and

---

17. Colette Dowling, *The Cinderella Complex: Women's Hidden Fear of Independence* (New York: Summit Books, 1981); Madonna Kolbenschlag, *Kiss Sleeping Beauty Good-Bye* (New York: Bantam Books, 1979).

18. Alice Bach, "The Pleasure of Her Text," in *The Feminist Companion to Samuel–Kings* (ed. Athalya Brenner; Sheffield: Sheffield Academic Press, 1994) 107.

19. The descriptions of David and Abigail, like the king and bride in Ps 45:2, 11 are based upon the Hebrew root *yph*. There is even a Hebrew pun that connects Abigail with Psalm 45. In Ps 45:15 we are told that the bride and her companions are led in "gladness and rejoicing" (*wgyl*); in Hebrew Abigail is *ʾbgyl* or *ʾbygyl*.

David does the same (*wayyaḥgōr gam-dāwīd 'et-ḥarbô*; 1 Sam 25:13). Now David doesn't actually have to use his sword in this story. But just the same the text signals his success. Instead of the king's enemies falling (*yippĕlû*) beneath him (Ps 45:5), Abigail falls (*wattippōl*) before David (1 Sam 25:23). In her speech to David, Abigail exalts his military superiority and acknowledges that David will defeat all his enemies (1 Sam 25:29, cf. Ps 45:5). In addition, as with Psalm 45, the bride/Abigail is expected to acknowledge male power. In Ps 45:11, the bride is admonished to display reverence to her new husband, "For he is your lord, bow to him!" (*kî-hû' 'ădōnayik wĕhištaḥăwî*). Abigail does exactly this when she goes to entreat David. She bows (*wattištaḥû*) and calls him lord (*'ădōnî*) (1 Sam 25:23–24). She does this not once, but twice (1 Sam 25:41)! In fact, throughout her speech she calls David "lord" (1 Sam 25:26–31). In the end, David rescues the fair maid from her wicked and foolish husband and takes Abigail as his wife (1 Sam 25:39–42). And they lived happily every after.

One can easily imagine Psalm 45 being sung at their wedding. One can also easily conclude that 1 Samuel 25 presupposes the same gender dynamics as Psalm 45. In both cases, there is a difference in power where the woman is understood to be subordinate to the man. It is David's/the groom's splendor, both physically and militarily, that is celebrated. The role of Abigail/the bride is to be submissive. It is this recognition of male power that makes for a good wife, and, traditionally, Abigail is described as a model wife whose good sense is advantageous for David.

This reading of the story of Abigail and David shows how it supports and reinforces the gender dynamics of Psalm 45. But another reading will show that there are also tensions within the story that undermine the poetic wish of the psalm. What are the possibilities for happily ever after? We know Abigail fulfills her obligation of being beautiful, but what of her other responsibilities? What of loyalty, submissiveness, and fertility? It turns out that this may not quite be the fairy tale romance that it seemed at first.

Alice Bach has argued that although the text supports the view of Abigail as a proper, deferential wife, the text also resists this reading, for Abigail is not only deferential. Although she appears as submissive and compliant, she is also a woman who is in control of her circumstances. She exercises power and speaks in her own voice. She seeks out David. The first speech is hers. She issues orders. "While her actions show that she is accustomed to controlling situations, her words assure David that she is handing over power to him."[20] There is almost a duplicitness to her character. On the one hand, she speaks soothing words of submission to the future king. On

---

20. Bach, "Pleasure of Her Text," 109.

the other hand, she is controlling and manipulating events, averting disaster for both her and David. You could say that it is the Princess who ultimately rescues the Prince![21]

There is also the matter of loyalty to consider with Abigail. The exhortation to the bride in Ps 45:10 to "forget your people and the house of your father," essentially admonishes the bride to forsake all others and be faithful to her husband as long as they both shall live. But we have to wonder how faithful a wife Abigail might have been. "Model wife? She refers to her husband as fool, sides with his enemy, and does not even mourn his death."[22]

The story of David and Abigail sends mixed signals concerning the fairy tale world of Psalm 45. On the one hand, Abigail fulfills the wish of the psalm by being submissive and loyal to David/the groom. On the other hand, she asserts her own authority in going to David and is disloyal to Nabal. Ultimately, although her loyalty to David/the groom is celebrated in 1 Samuel 25, that loyalty is not rewarded as the psalm promises. It is not her son who will end up appointed as a prince over all the earth. One may wonder whether this is a "punishment" for the other aspects of her character that do not quite make up a fairy tale bride.

Esther

Another bride that Psalm 45 calls to mind is Esther. Although there are very few textual links between Esther and Psalm 45,[23] what binds them is their interest in royal marriage. The story of Esther also calls into question the fairy tale world of Psalm 45. It does so by decentering the imperative of loyalty. The story of Esther is about what can happen when the glass slipper is on the other foot.

In Psalm 45, the question of loyalty is raised at the point of the exhortation to the bride in vv. 10–11. She is commanded to do two things. First, she is commanded to forget her people and the house of her father. Second, although it doesn't exactly say that she is to "love, honor, and obey," such sentiments are expressed in the commands that she show deference and subservience to her husband and king. Both commands function to bind the bride to the king and the king's house.

In 45:10 the bride is told to forget/deny any attachments to her people and to the lineage of her father. The use of *bêt 'āb*, "father's house," in 45:10 is significant in that, along with v. 16, it betrays a central concern for Psalm

---

21. She "rescues" David by preventing David from committing bloodguilt by killing her husband.

22. Bach, "Pleasure of Her Text," 119.

23. Note the reference to myrrh as a spice with sexual overtones (Ps 45:8; Esth 2:12) and the use of *śāśôn* and *śimḥâ* (Ps 45:7, 15; Esth 8:16–17). See Mulder, *Studies*, 125.

45: the concern for lineage. This normal masculine-oriented terminology for family and household derives from lineage concerns and the concerns of descent and property transmission that are reckoned along patrilineal lines.[24] Hidden within this concern for lineage is a concern for the loyalty and faithfulness of the bride to her husband. Such loyalty is usually expressed by sexual fidelity. It is the sexual faithfulness of the wife that ensures that offspring are in fact the descendants of the husband. Such insurance provides for the continuity of descent and therefore of property transmission within the family.

But in the Bible the concern for *sexual* loyalty can at the same time be a concern for *theological* loyalty. It is not clear from Psalm 45 if the bride is Israelite or not.[25] Perhaps it might be presumed, but it is clear that Israelite kings did marry non-Israelite women.[26] It is also clear that, for some writers/editors, non-Israelite brides are a problem. And they are a problem precisely for theological reasons.[27] The writer of Psalm 45 seems to agree with this. Anxious about the influence a foreign bride might have on the heart of the king, the admonition to the bride is, as Weiser bluntly states it, a warning against bringing to her husband's house foreign—that is, non-Israelite—ways, customs, and deities.[28] In other words, the psalmist insists that when an Israelite king marries a foreign woman, the foreign woman is commanded to forsake all the political and religious loyalties of her people and give her loyalty to Israel and to Yhwh alone.

---

24. C. J. H. Wright, "Family," *ABD* 2:762–66; Carol Meyers, "'To Her Mother's House': Considering a Counterpart to the Israelite *Bêt 'āb*," in *The Bible and the Politics of Exegesis: Essays in Honor of Norman K. Gottwald on His Sixty-Fifth Birthday* (ed. David Jobling et al.; Cleveland: Pilgrim, 1991) 40–42; and Lawrence E. Stager, "The Archaeology of the Family in Ancient Israel," *BASOR* 260 (1985) 20–23.

25. The crux of the issue is the phrase "daughter (of) Tyre" in v. 12. Many have understood this phrase to be in parallel with "king's daughter" in v. 13 and thus refer to the bride. However, F. W. Dobbs-Allsopp ("The Syntagma of *bat* Followed by a Geographical Name in the Hebrew Bible: A Reconsideration of its Meaning and Grammar," *CBQ* 57 [1995] 451–70) has argued that the expression "*bat* GN" in the Old Testament is a literary metaphor of the personified city. The translation of the NRSV expresses this with its phrase "the people of Tyre." Although "daughter of Tyre" does not refer to the bride herself, the fact that the city of Tyre pays her homage may reflect that Tyre is her hometown. Moreover, R. Tournay ("Les Affinités du Ps. XLV avec le Cantique des Cantiques et leur Interprétation Messianique," *Congress Volume: Bonn, 1962* [VTSup 9; Leiden: E. J. Brill, 1963] 195–96) sees in the use of *šēgal* (45:9), an Akkadian loan word, an indication of the foreign origin of the bride. Additionally, several scholars have argued that the exhortation to forget her "people" also indicates the bride's foreign origins.

26. I am using "Israel" to signify the United Monarchy and both the northern and southern kingdoms of the Divided Monarchy.

27. For example, Deut 7:1–4; 1 Kgs 11:1–4; Ezra 10:1–17; Neh 13:23–27.

28. Weiser, *Psalms*, 364.

Commentators usually approve of this exhortation and consider it an appropriate charge to the bride to ensure that she "will be able to belong from now on wholly to her husband and master."[29] This way an obedient bride will be faithful sexually to the king, politically to Israel, and theologically to Yhwh. But there is a sharp edge to this command to the bride. It is one thing simply to leave family and country (Ruth 1:16–19; 2:11); it is quite another thing to *forget* them. The verb *škḥ*, "forget," is what is said of a mother that forgets her infant (Isa 49:14–15), of lovers who forget Daughter Zion (Jer 30:14), of the friends who forget Job (Job 19:14), and of the people who have forgotten Yhwh (Hos 2:13). This word implies a rupture, a total detachment, which is why Israel is commanded *not* to forget the covenant with Yhwh (Deut 4:23; 6:12; 8:11, 14).[30] The use of *škḥ* in Ps 45:10, therefore, suggests that the bride should similarly rupture the bonds with her family and country. Whereas this exhortation might make some sense theologically, particularly from a Deuteronomistic viewpoint, how realistic is such an expectation? Would foreign kings really expect their daughters to practically become traitors to their people upon their marriage? More importantly, what happens when an Israelite bride marries a foreign king?

This is Esther's situation. She is a Jew who ends up married to a foreign king. We might imagine that a Persian version of Psalm 45 was sung for Esther when she was brought to Ahasuerus.[31] Hers is, after all, a fairy tale wedding. Here is poor Hadassah, an orphan and refugee. But because she is beautiful she wins the Miss Persia contest and ends up loved by the king more than any other woman. According to the conventions of Psalm 45, Esther's obligations would be to remain: (a) sexually faithful to Ahasuerus, (b) politically loyal to Persia, and (c) theologically loyal to Persian deities! That is, Esther would be expected to forget/forsake her obligations and loyalties to the family from whence she came and give her loyalty and service to her new husband, King Ahasuerus, his kingdom, and his gods. We would expect Esther to be a faithful, obedient, and subservient wife. And in some ways she is. She is called throughout the story by her Persian name indicating, if not loyalty to Persia, at least accommodation to Persian sensibilities. She worries about violating court etiquette (Esth 4:11). And she abides by Persian law. She knows that Ahasuerus' decree cannot be revoked, so she must ask for another decree to be issued to counteract the decree for destruction that Haman requested.

---

29. Ibid.

30. Tournay, "Les Affinités," 197.

31. Cristoph Schroeder, "'A Love Song': Psalm 45 in the Light of Ancient Near Eastern Marriage Texts," *CBQ* 58 (1996) 426–31, argues that Ps 45:7–15 describes a ritual for the consummation of the royal marriage depicted in the psalm.

And yet, the point of the story of Esther is that her ultimate loyalty is precisely to her father's house and her people and *not* to her husband's. Like Abigail, for all her appearance as an obedient and faithful Persian wife, Esther also transgresses that expectation. At the beginning, she hides her loyalty to Mordechai and the Jewish people (Esth 2:10, 20). But when the Jewish people are threatened by Haman's plot to destroy the Jews, Esther does not forget *her people* or her father's house. "For how can I bear to see the calamity that is coming on *my people* [cf. Ps 45:10]? Or how can I bear to see the destruction of my kindred" (Esth 8:6; emphasis added)? Instead, she works actively to save them including risking the violation of court etiquette which she has heretofore strictly obeyed.

Thus, it appears that there is loyalty and then there is *loyalty*. Esther and Psalm 45 display a hideous tension. Psalm 45 expects the bride to forsake what Esther says she will die to defend—her people.[32]

In fact, throughout Esther, the loyalty and obedience of wives is a problem in that they aren't loyal and obedient. Vashti is the prime example of the woman who refuses to be totally submissive and obedient. Her refusal calls the whole premise of obedience into question. In any hierarchical system, the primary definition of a "problem" is a subordinate who acts contrary to the system. Vashti's refusal to obey Ahasuerus' command to appear before him is so troubling to the men that a decree must be issued that women are to give honor to their husbands and that every man should be master in his own house (Esth 1:10–22). For our purposes, another problem arises in that the story at the same time condemns Vashti's rebellion and rewards Esther's. I think, as a bride, reading Psalm 45 and reading Esther, I would feel caught in a catch-22. Clearly, from the perspective of Psalm 45 and the men's reaction to Vashti, I am expected to be loyal and obedient to my husband. At the same time, Esther suggests that there are circumstances that call for loyalty to some higher cause. But this leaves me with questions. What will happen when I act contrary to the system? What will be the consequences? Will I be rewarded or punished? Esther and Vashti raise troubling questions about Psalm 45's exhortation to the bride.

The problem of the absolute loyalty demanded by Psalm 45 could be further decentered when read in the context of contemporary society. From a feminist perspective, such a demand is clearly countermanded by an abusive spouse. No woman (or man) should be asked to put loyalty to a spouse above their physical and emotional safety. A marriage across cultures or re-

---

32. The focus in Esther is whether she will be loyal to her husband's house and people or her father's house and people. The issue of theological loyalty is not directly addressed but must be assumed since theological language is never directly invoked in the book of Esther with the possible exception of the debated passage in Esth 4:14.

ligions will ask that the partners make a commitment to another people, but does that mean that one has to abandon one's own identity? Will one partner or another be called to "forget" her/his people? In our day and age of globalization and diversity, the question of one's racial and ethnic particularities are especially troubling. What happens when a Serb marries a Croat? Or a Palestinian an Israeli? Must immigrants settling in the U.S. become "American"?[33] In fact, in a world of increasing cross-cultural and interreligious commitments the question of loyalties is becoming ever more urgent. At what point is absolute loyalty called for and at what point must I abandon one loyalty in favor of another? Psalm 45 gives a clear answer to the question—for the bride at least. Her loyalty must be to her husband and his people. Esther tarnishes the glitter of the fairy tale world of Psalm 45 by suggesting that there are other loyalties that one must consider as well.

IV. Divorce Court

Psalm 45 is not only a song for a royal wedding. As a song of marriage it is a willing participant in the general view of marriage within the Old Testament. Within this system, a husband has exclusive rights to his wife's sexuality. The wife's sexual activity is restricted to marriage and she is expected to be sexually faithful within the marriage. The sexual faithfulness of the wife is the primary sign of a woman's loyalty to her husband. Any deviation from that norm is considered to be an offense and to bring dishonor to the woman's husband.[34] But a wife's sexual infidelity is more than that. As David Carr notes, "[a] woman of unruly sexual initiative symbolizes the subordinate person getting out of control, not knowing her place."[35] Thus a great deal of biblical energy is directed toward ensuring both women's sexual abstinence *before* marriage and fidelity *within* it.

With women's sexuality so tightly controlled, we might expect Psalm 45 to address this issue. Interestingly, it does not. Psalm 45 does not speak overtly of sexual fidelity. However, as already noted, the loyalty and fidelity of the bride *is* a key issue in the psalm. In particular, exclusive political and

---

33. On some of the tensions raised by cross-cultural and interreligious commitments, see Katharine Doob Sakenfeld, *Ruth* (Interpretation; Louisville: John Knox, 1999) 30–35.

34. David Carr, "Gender and the Shaping of Desire in the Song of Songs and Its Interpretations," *JBL* 119 (2000) 237–38; Carolyn Pressler, *The View of Women Found in the Deuteronomic Family Laws* (BZAW 216; Berlin: Walter de Gruyter, 1993) 90–92, 96–102; and Renita Weems, *Battered Love: Marriage, Sex, and Violence in the Hebrew Prophets* (OBT; Minneapolis: Fortress, 1995) 25–33.

35. Carr, "Gender," 240.

theological fidelity is demanded of the bride. As it turns out, the twin issues of sexual and theological fidelity are inextricably intertwined.

Alongside this human matrix of ideals for marriage, David Carr argues
that there exists a "theological marriage matrix":

> Many theological streams in Israel included God in this sexual system. . . . In
> this matrix the believing community is depicted as the female spouse of the
> male god—called on to love God with the exclusive love of a wife and pun-
> ished for failure to do so.[36]

Within the prophetic literature, the "exclusive love" of the marriage matrix is the focus. For the prophets, the absolute requirement for sexual
fidelity for a woman within marriage becomes the trope by which the
theological infidelity of the covenant people is judged. Thus within the
theological marriage matrix it is hard to separate sexual loyalty from other
kinds of loyalty.

This overlap between human and divine sexual relationships encourages
us to read Psalm 45 alongside Ezekiel 16, one of the primary prophetic texts
that employs the imagery of this matrix. Ezekiel 16 describes the history of
Israel and YHWH using the metaphor of God as husband and Jerusalem as
"his" spouse. Ezek 16:8–14, in particular, describe what God has done for
the abandoned female child, Jerusalem. In addition to the common theme
of marriage there are an amazing number of linguistic connections between these verses and Psalm 45. The NRSV of Ezek 16:8–14 follows; words
within brackets are also found in Psalm 45.

> I passed by you again and looked on you; you were at the age for love. I
> spread the edge of my cloak over you, and covered your nakedness: I pledged
> myself to you and entered into a covenant with you, says the Lord God, and
> you became mine. Then I bathed you with water and washed off the blood
> from you, and anointed you with oil. I clothed you with embroidered cloth
> [*riqmâ*; cf. *lirqāmôt* in Ps 45:14] and with sandals of fine leather; I bound you
> in fine linen and covered you with rich fabric. I adorned you with ornaments:
> I put bracelets on your arms, a chain on your neck, a ring on your nose, ear-
> rings in your ears, and a beautiful crown upon your head. You were adorned
> with gold [*zāhāb*; Ps 45:13] and silver, while your clothing [*ûmalbûšēk*; cf.
> *lěbûšāh* in Ps 45:13] was of fine linen, rich fabric, and embroidered cloth
> [*riqmâ*; cf. *lirqāmôt* in Ps 45:14]. You had choice flour and honey and oil for
> food. You grew exceedingly beautiful [*wattîpî*; cf. *yāpyāpîtā* in Ps 45:2 and
> *yāpyēk* in 45:11], fit [*wattiṣlěḥî*; cf. *ṣělaḥ* in Ps 45:4] to be a queen.[37] Your fame

---

36. Ibid., 238–39.

37. The phrase in the NRSV, "fit to be a queen," reads in Hebrew *wattiṣlěḥî limlûkâ*,
which can be translated something like "you were successful as royalty." There is no
exact connection here with Psalm 45 where the bride is never referred to as a "queen."

[*šēm*; cf. *šimkā* in Ps 45:17] spread among the nations on account of your beauty [*běyāpyēk*; cf. *yāpyāpîtā* in Ps 45:2 and *yāpyēk* in 45:11], for it was perfect because of my splendor [*bahădārî*; cf. *wahădārekā* in Ps 45:3 and *wahădārěkā* in 45:4] that I had bestowed on you, says the Lord GOD.

The beginning of Ezekiel 16 bears all the hallmarks of our fairy tale wedding. Instead of a wicked stepmother or foolish husband, this time our damsel in distress (Jerusalem) is an abandoned baby girl (Ezek 16:4–5). Along rides Prince Charming (God) who rescues her from her fate worse than death (Ezek 16:6–7). Ezek 16:8–14 describes the subsequent covenanting together in marriage of the prince and, now, fair maid. This passage in Ezekiel evokes the same image of a lavish wedding found in Psalm 45. As with Psalm 45, the bride is beautiful and clothed in gold and in colorfully woven/embroidered garments.[38] One could imagine a song such as Psalm 45 being sung on this festive occasion.

However, in Ezekiel 16 instead of living happily ever after, we hear of a fairy tale marriage that has gone horribly awry. The circumstance that derails this marriage is the "problem" of the disloyalty of the wife exhibited in her lack of sexual (i.e., theological) fidelity to her husband. The wife who seeks out other lovers is just like Jerusalem who has sought out other gods (Ezek 16:15–34). After v. 14, the rest of the chapter is YHWH's justification for violently punishing Jerusalem. YHWH's justification is that, just as a husband is obligated to humiliate and punish an unfaithful wife in order to (re)gain control and power over her, so is YHWH obligated to humiliate and punish unfaithful Jerusalem in order to (re)gain control and power over (Ezek 16:38, 42–43, 59).

Much has been written from a feminist perspective critiquing the prophetic portrayal of marriage, particularly the manner in which it mirrors situations of domestic violence.[39] Linda Day has argued that this is especially true in Ezekiel 16.[40] She notes that among the characteristics of an

---

There is debate about the meaning of *šēgal* in 45:9 as a title and whether it refers to the bride or to the mother of the king. Schroeder, "A Love Song," 428–29; and A. Caquot, "Cinq observations sur le Psaume 45," in *Ascribe to the Lord: Biblical and Other Studies in Memory of P. C. Craigie* (JSOTSup 67; ed. L. Eslinger and G. Taylor; Sheffield: Sheffield Academic Press, 1988) 258–61 believe that it refers to the king's mother. Others read it in parallel with the vocative "daughter" in v. 10 and understand it to refer to the bride. Whether or not the bride is ever given a title signifying royalty, it is certain that as the bride of the king she would of necessity be one who would be "successful as royalty."

38. *riqmâ*, "embroidered/colorfully woven cloth," occurs only in Ezekiel 16 and Psalm 45.

39. Weems, *Battered Love*; Athalya Brenner, ed., *A Feminist Companion to the Latter Prophets* (Sheffield: Sheffield Academic Press, 1995).

40. Linda Day, "Rhetoric and Domestic Violence in Ezekiel 16," *BibInt* 8 (2000) 205–30.

abuser is an obsessive need to control his woman and, in particular, her relationships with others. This arises out of the abuser's distorted sense of gender relationships. The batterer has the need to be dominant in the relationship and feels that he has the "right" to physically control anyone with lesser status, especially his wife. In most cases of abuse, the man will exhibit extreme jealousy towards any relationship the woman has apart from him. He can become suspicious of even the most innocent of relationships, so much so that even making eye-contact with the young man bagging groceries can lead to an accusation of infidelity.[41] Clearly in any covenanted relationship, transgressions of the covenant are to be taken with utmost seriousness. The problem is that in abusive relationships the accusation of infidelity can be leveled, with the inevitable result of assault for the infidelity, *even if no such infidelity exists*! Day argues that this is exactly the case in Ezekiel 16: "As woman batterers suffer from distorted presumptions about their woman's infidelity, one might ask the same of YHWH. Can we trust that YHWH's lurid description of Jerusalem's behavior is really true?"[42] Perhaps just as a batterer imagines his wife is having an affair with the grocery clerk, YHWH has imagined Jerusalem's infidelities, with the inevitable result of assault for the "alleged" infidelity.

Reading Ezekiel suggests that we question whether Psalm 45 also participates in violence against women. Like Ezekiel 16, Psalm 45 can be read as both a tale of human marriage as well as a story of divine-human marriage. Traditionally, Psalm 45 has been interpreted allegorically as the marriage between God and the people of Israel (in Judaism) and between Christ and the Church (in Christianity). And, as with the theological marriage matrix in the prophetic literature, the theological loyalty of the bride is emphasized in such allegorical interpretation.

The emphasis on theological loyalty is seen in the interpretation of the exhortation to "forget your people and your father's house." John Calvin provides a typical interpretation. He sees the marriage of Psalm 45 as the marriage between Christ and the Gentiles. "But in order to conduct into Christ's presence his bride chaste and undefiled, the prophet exhorts the Church gathered from the Gentiles to forget her former manner of living, and to devote herself wholly to her husband." Calvin recognizes that the bride/Church may not always be willing to make such a sacrifice. The psalmist must "gently and sweetly soothe the new Church" in order to induce her to "willingly despise and forsake whatever she made account of heretofore." Calvin's reading agrees with the biblical view of marriage that gives the hus-

---

41. Ibid., 218–20.
42. Ibid, 222.

band absolute authority over his wife. "If the Church refuses to devote herself wholly to Christ, she casts off his due and lawful authority."[43]

When read in this fashion—as a metaphor of divine-human marriage—Psalm 45 commits the same violence against women that Ezekiel 16 does. As the abuser has an obsessive need to be dominant in the relationship and to control his woman and her relationships to others, so Christ must dominate and claim the "right" to control the Church. One assumes that transgressions of that "lawful authority" will result inevitably in punishment.

It is this assumption of control that feminists have questioned. A man has no "right" to control his wife nor beat her, whether the infractions are real or imagined. If we believe that infidelity is inimical to covenant relationship, we should also believe that violence against one's wife is inimical to covenant relationship. Unfortunately, violence within marriages and within the Church still happens. Witness, for example, the backlash by various church authorities and governing bodies against women who attended the Re-Imagining Conference in 1993. It was like seeing Ezekiel 16 lived out. The accusations were made. We had gone after the goddess and refused to devote ourselves only to Christ. How dare we! Clearly we were not submitting to the power and authority of *The Church* nor were we demonstrating loyalty thereto. Unfortunately, as with batterers, many of the accusations were imagined. And even more unfortunately, the accusations led inevitably to violence. Attendees were fired from their jobs and threatened with being "stripped" of their clergy status and rights. Such actions toward clergywomen who participated in Re-Imagining is nothing more than the Groom attempting to (re)assert power over the Bride.

Our fairy tale world of Psalm 45 and Ezekiel 16 is a fantasy world of desire for obedience, power, and control. Unfortunately, the cost of living in this world for the bride can often be her life.

V. The Mother of All Love Songs

At first glance, Psalm 45 and the Song of Songs bear striking similarities. Both share the language of song (*šîr*; superscription to Psalm 45; Song 1:1) and lovemaking (*yĕdîdōt* in the superscription to Psalm 45; *dōdêkā* in Song 1:2).[44] They both sing of the relationship between king and consort. There

---

43. John Calvin, *Commentary on the Book of Psalms* (5 vols.; trans. James Anderson; Grand Rapids: Eerdmans, 1949) 2:188–89.

44. Calvin, *Commentary on the Book of Psalms*, 2:173: "But the context, in my opinion, requires that this term ידידות, *yedidoth*, that is to say, *loves*, be understood as referring to the mutual love which husband and wife ought to cherish towards each other. But as the word *loves* is sometimes taken in a bad sense, and as even conjugal affection itself, however well regulated, has always some irregularity of the flesh mingled with it; this song is,

are numerous linguistic connections between the two texts.[45] Both have traditionally been interpreted messianically in both Jewish and Christian traditions. In fact, Tournay argues they both partake of the same social milieu and must be interpreted in an analogous sense.[46] However, a closer look reveals that when these two texts are put in close proximity to one another a jarring culture clash occurs.

The culture of Psalm 45, and most of the other texts with which we have engaged in dialogue, is one of silent women, reproductively-focused sexuality, hierarchies, male rights, and vilified sexually-proactive women. In sharp contrast is the culture of the Song of Songs. Within the Song, the woman's voice and presence dominates. There is no secret of her passion for her lover; she vigorously pursues him, and assumes it is her right to initiate love. Although there is desire of the one for the other, there is none of the language of Psalm 45 requiring the woman to forget or submit. In fact, no forms of *škḥ* ("forget"), *ḥwh* ("bow down, worship"), or *'ādôn* ("lord") appear in the Song.[47] There is no clear indication in the Song that the lovers are married; their relationship, moreover, seems to directly counter cultural norms.[48] For example, there is no talk of children, nor typical use of fertility imagery. In Ezekiel, such a woman is the embodiment of the disobedient, adulterous community. In the Song, she is celebrated. As Carr notes, the Song clearly "presents an atypical view of premarital sexuality and non-productively focused female sexual initiative. Moreover, the often overpowering male of Israel's legal and prophetic texts is replaced here with a male passionately bound to the woman who loves him."[49]

Carr suggests that the vastly different world of the Song of Songs represents an alternative discourse to the dominant sexual discourse of the Old

---

at the same time, called משכיל, *maskil*, to teach us, that the subject here treated of is not some obscene or unchaste amours, but that, under what is here said of Solomon as a type, the holy and divine union of Christ and his Church is described and set forth." Cf. Carr, "Gender," 240 n. 24: "Though most translations render the plural of דוד here simply as 'love,' the word typically refers to actualized sexual relations of some sort. . . . Hence, I follow the Blochs in translating the term here as 'lovemaking.'" Carr is citing Marvin Pope, *The Song of Songs: A New Translation with Introduction and Commentary* (AB 7C: Garden City: Doubleday, 1977) 299; and Ariel Bloch and Chana Bloch, *The Song of Songs: A New Translation with an Introduction and Commentary* (New York: Random House) 137.

45. Specific word and thematic parallels are identified in Mulder, *Studies*, 101–42; Tournay, "Les Affinités," 168–212. See especially Song 1:7; 3:8; 14:11, 14.
46. Tournay, "Les Affinités," 172.
47. Mulder, *Studies*, 130.
48. For example, see Renita Weems, "Song of Songs," in Newsom and Ringe, ed., *The Women's Bible Commentary*, 156–60.
49. Carr, "Gender," 242.

Testament. The Song is therefore similar to songs sung at weddings by contemporary women of Mediterranean and Middle Eastern societies.[50] These present-day songs also stand in sharp contrast to their larger culture. Carr argues that the existence of such alternative passionate poetry indicates that multiple discourses can coexist within the same culture. Furthermore, such alternative poetry may inscribe sexual subjects somewhat different from those of more public discourses.[51]

Carol Meyers also argues that the Song of Songs presents an alternative discourse within the biblical world. Meyers comments on the repeated use of *bêt 'ēm* within the Song, as opposed to the *bêt 'āb* of Psalm 45. As noted above, *bêt 'āb* is the normal, masculine-oriented terminology for family and household derived from lineage concerns and the concerns of descent and property transmission that is reckoned along patrilineal lines. It is precisely these concerns that are lacking in the Song. Meyers suggests that in a text where the usual patriarchal concerns of lineage and property transmission are absent, the text turns away from the public functional aspect of family and instead turns inward toward the internal functional aspect of family and home life. These concerns are more rightly expressed by "mother's house" rather than by "father's house."[52]

Furthermore, the settings and imagery of the speeches in the Song come primarily from the rural/pastoral and domestic realms. Meyers argues that precisely because the Song is set apart from the national and institutional settings of most of the biblical corpus, such as Psalm 45, this allows for more of a balance between male and female and depicts that aspect of life in which the female role was primary: the domestic sphere. It is here where women exercised strong and authoritative positions.[53] In this light, it is not surprising that when Meyers examines all the uses of *bêt 'ēm* she discovers that in each case the story is of a woman, the setting is domestic, and the woman is an agent in her own right.[54]

The Song of Songs thus comes as close as we can get to imagining what kind of song a bride of the king may have sung on her wedding day and

---

50. Carr makes use of the work of various Middle Eastern ethnographers such as Lila Abu-Lughod, *Veiled Sentiments: Honor and Poetry in a Bedouin Society* (Berkeley: University of California Press, 1986) esp. 171–232.

51. Carr, "Gender," 242–44.

52. Carol Meyers, "Gender Imagery in the Song of Songs," in *A Feminist Companion to the Song of Songs* (ed. Athalya Brenner; Sheffield: Sheffield Academic Press, 1993) 209.

53. Ibid., 211–12.

54. Meyers, "Her Mother's House," 49. Meyers also argues that in each case marriage is involved but that it is implicit in the Song. The texts containing *bêt 'ēm* are the story of Rebekah (Gen 24:28), the book of Ruth (Ruth 1:8), and the Song of Songs (Song 3:4; 8:2).

presents us with an alternative fairy tale to tell. In this latter fairy tale, the woman is able to celebrate her choice, her passion, and her sexual initiative. Her concern is not with kingdoms or offspring but with the personal relationship she has with her beloved. Instead of a hierarchy there is mutual concern and desire.

The Song of Songs thus allows us to imagine the love relationship differently than Psalm 45 construes it.[55] It permits us to speak alternative discourses—to tell other fairy tales—that counter, that challenge, and that might one day overcome damaging and violent discourses. But this is not quite "happily ever after." The Song, like the other texts we have examined, is thoroughly heterosexual. Yet to follow the trajectory of the Song would indicate that we have a need for yet another alternative discourse—one that will allow a woman to choose to whom she will freely offer her love and loyalty, even another woman.

VI. Conclusions

These are but some of the intertextual readings possible between Psalm 45 and other texts. But there are still other possible dialogue partners. There is Isaiah 5, another text that shares the language of song and love-making. "Let me sing for my beloved my love-song" (ʾāšîrâ nāʾ lîdîdî šîrat dôdî; Isa 5:1). As another song of love gone wrong after the initial fairy tale romance and wedding, would a reading of Isaiah 5 in concert with Psalm 45 raise the same issues and problems encountered with Ezekiel 16?

Another intertextual possibility is Judges 11, the story of Jephthah's daughter. It is only in Ps 45:1 and Judg 11:37–38 that the feminine plural of "friend" (rēʿôt) is used.[56] Jephthah's daughter asks that she and her "companions" be permitted to go away and bewail her virginity. The "companions" of the bride in Psalm 45 accompany her as she is brought to the king. What might Jephthah's daughter have to say to the bride of Psalm 45 and vice versa?

But even from the few intertexts considered here some conclusions may be drawn. First, it cannot be said that Psalm 45 articulates the liberating experiences and visions of the people of God. It places women in a subservient and subordinate role and gives no voice to what a woman's choices, desires, and concerns may be within marriage. My work with this psalm leads me to suggest that it may be appropriate to omit Psalm 45 from our

---

55. Carr, "Gender," 245 suggests that we also use this to imagine the divine-human love relationship differently.

56. This is reading of the Qere at Judg 11:37, which has the support of the analogous form in Judg 11:38. The Kethib reading is probably from raʿyâ, a term that occurs throughout the Song of Songs.

acts of corporate worship. Regardless of the reasons this psalm may have originally been included in the canon, it is difficult to see what the liturgical, devotional, pastoral, or theological-homiletical dimensions of this might be for contemporary faith communities. Robert Davidson suggests that it is appropriate to have in the canon "an ode to marriage with its joyful celebration of sexuality."[57] I would agree with him if that were what this psalm actually portrayed. However, it does not, for all the reasons I have described.

The problem with Psalm 45 is that the gendered world it wishes for is the very world that feminists critique. To that extent, Psalm 45 is a song we might sing *in memoriam*, in memory of the damage done to women and men by this fairy tale world. The Song of Songs suggests that we need to sing songs that resist the fairy tale world of Psalm 45. We need to develop alternative discourses that celebrate egalitarian, mutual, and just relationships, both homosexual and heterosexual. These are the songs we will need to sing in our worship.

---

57. Robert Davidson, *The Vitality of Worship: A Commentary on the Book of Psalms* (Grand Rapids: Eerdmans, 1998) 151.

Notes on Psalm 93:
A Fragment of a Liturgical Poem
Affirming Yahweh's Kingship

Frank Moore Cross

Psalm 93:1–4,[1] when edited and arranged stichometrically, reads as follows:

²[4:4::4:4] ³(b:b::b:b) עז התאזר   לבש יהוה   גאות לבש   יהוה מלך .1

[4:3::5:4] (b:b::b:b) אתה < > מאז   נכון כסאך   בל תמוט   תכן תבל < > .2⁴

[8:8:8] (l:l:l) ישאו נהרות דכים⁵   נשאו נהרות קולם   נשאו נהרות יהוה .3

[7:7:7] (l:l:l) אדיר במרום יהוה   אדיר <מ>משברי ים   מקלות מים רבים .4

This can then be translated as follows:

1. Yahweh is king,
He is robed in majesty,
Robed is Yahweh
With might he is girded.

2. He has ordered the world,
It can not be altered;
Established is your throne,
You are of old.

3. The Deeps sounded, Yahweh,
The Deeps sounded their roar,
The Deeps sounded their pounding.

Author's note: This brief paper is offered in homage to Patrick D. Miller. Its brief proportions are in inverse ratio to the measure of my admiration for him personally, and of my appreciation for his scholarship.
    1. Versification follows the Hebrew text.
    2. The numbers in brackets are syllable counts.
    3. The letters in parentheses indicate short (b = *breve*) or long (l = *longum*) cola. See below.
    4. The MT begins v. 2 at נכון, a division that ignores the poetic structure.
    5. Note the structure: abc:abd:a₁be.

4. More than the roar of cosmic Waters,
More awesome than the breakers of Sea
Awesome in heaven's height is Yahweh.

I. Notes to the Text

Line 1. According to traditional stress counting, the first two lines of the text can be given the following notation: 2+2::2+2 ‖ 2+2::2+2.[6] Alternately, since there is parallelism not only between the elements labeled 2+2::2+2, but also between the pairs of cola labeled 2+2, we can scan 4+4::4+4. Against this analysis, however, is the internal parallelism—indeed, repetitive parallelism—especially in the second and third bicola of line 1. There is the repetition of לבש and יהוה in a chiastic pattern: *yhwh––lbš* ‖ *lbš––yhwh*.[7] I prefer a notation in which the basic building blocks of early poetry, short cola and long cola, are labeled b and l, *breve* and *longum*, symmetrical units in which the question of stress meter, or quantitative meter, is left unanswered.[8] In fact, I prefer an analysis that permits the oral poet to compose freely, using oral formulae. Thus the first (and indeed the second line) have the structure b:b::b:b.

Line 2. The particle אף is suspect. Like the conjunction introducing a colon, it is a rare element in old poetry. It may have arisen in anticipation of אף in the identical colon in Ps 96:10.

I follow most commentators in reading תכן for the MT's תכון. This reading ת[כ]ן is attested 11QPs[a] (11Q5) as well as in other important witnesses.[9]

I have emended the end of the line. מאז and מעולם, with virtually the same meaning, are evidently a doublet—ancient variants. If we preserve both with the traditional text, the meter is marred.[10]

---

6. Oswald Loretz in his *Ugarit-Texte und Thronbesteigungspsalmen* (Münster: Ugarit-Verlag, 1988) 277–79 records the attempts of a long series of scholars who have failed to reach consensus as to the structure of the hymn. This chaotic situation results in part by the failure of scholars to recognize mixed meter, and by a reluctance of many scholars to make even the most minor or obvious emendation to the MT.

7. The en-dashes indicate the position of elements in a colon: for example, *yhwh–* (first element) *–lbš* (last element) *–nhrwt–* (middle element in a long colon). The dashes should not be taken as indicating *immediate* proximity.

8. See Frank Moore Cross, "The Prosody of Lamentations 1 and the Psalm of Jonah," in idem, *From Epic to Canon: History and Literature in Ancient Israel* (Baltimore: The Johns Hopkins University Press, 1998) 99–134.

9. See J. A. Sanders, *The Psalms Scroll of Qumrân Cave 11 (11QPsᵃ)* (DJD 4; Oxford: Clarendon Press, 1965) 43 and Pl. XIV. This reading is reflected also in the Old Greek, the Syriac, the Targum, and the Vulgate; cf. Pss 75:4 [Eng v. 3] and 24:1–2. In Ps 96:10, the MT again reads נכון and the versions read תכן.

10. Compare the similar proposal of Loretz, *Ugarit-Texte*, 283 and the references there. Note that 11QPsᵃ does preserve both terms, but in a very broken context.

Line 3. The relation of *dkym* in Psalm 93 and *dkym* or *dk ym* in Ugaritic[11] remains problematic. I have chosen a meaning from the context, "pounding."[12]

Lines 3 and 4. The quatrain of short bicola, 4 (b:b), in the first two lines is followed by two tricola, 2 (l:l:l). This is an archaic prosodic style that we have labeled and described elsewhere as mixed meter.[13] It marks such ancient poems as David's Lament (2 Sam 1:19–27), the Song of Deborah (Judges 5), and the Song of the Sea (Exod 15:1–18). The first tricolon exhibits a pattern of repetitive (or climactic) parallelism. This was a prosodic pattern that was observed in Ugaritic poetry by H. L. Ginsberg, and elaborated especially in archaic biblical psalmody by W. F. Albright.[14] The most systematic analysis of parallelism in Psalm 93 is found in a study of Dennis Pardee.[15]

Line 4. In the second colon I have followed many scholars who have corrected the MT's אדירים משברי ים to אדיר ממשברי ים. The Masoretic reading arises in wrong division of the first two words. In Old Hebrew script and in Palaeo-Hebrew script no distinction is made between medial and final forms of *mem*.[16] Indeed in some Qumran manuscripts in the Jewish hand, the one form of *mem* is leveled through. This correction makes sense

---

11. See *KTU* 1.6 V 3.

12. For a full discussion and listing of the literature, see Loretz, *Ugarit-Texte*, 297–99.

13. See, for example, Frank Moore Cross, Jr. and David Noel Freedman, *Studies in Ancient Yahwistic Poetry* (Grand Rapids: Eerdmans, 1997) 8–18.

14. W. F. Albright, "The Psalm of Habakkuk," in *Studies in Old Testament Prophecy: Presented to Theodore H. Robinson on His Sixty-Fifth Birthday, August 9th, 1946* (ed. H. H. Rowley; Edinburgh: T. & T. Clark, 1950) 1–18. It is interesting that the first verse of Psalm 94 also exhibits climactic parallelism.

15. Dennis Pardee, "The Poetic Structure of Psalm 93," *SEL* 5 (1988) 163–70.

16. I follow here the distinctions set out in my essay "The Development of the Jewish Scripts," in *The Bible and the Ancient Near East: Essays in Honor of William Foxwell Albright* (ed. G. E. Wright; Garden City: Doubleday, 1965) 246–47 nn. 4–5. The script used in Israel in the preexilic period is properly labeled the Old Hebrew script. Palaeo-Hebrew script should be reserved for the archaizing descendant of the Old Hebrew script in use especially in the Hasmonean and Roman periods. However, there is now evidence that it never died out and was used sporadically throughout the postexilic era. An example is the fourth century B.C.E. seal of Sanballat inscribed in the Palaeo-Hebrew script. In the early centuries of the postexilic period in Israel and Judah—that is, the fifth to the beginning of the third century—the dominant script was the official Aramaic cursive. However, with the end of Persian hegemony, local scripts evolved from the imperial Persian cursive. In Judah by the mid-third century a distinct Jewish script had emerged and continued in use through out the Hellenistic and Roman times, indeed surviving in Modern Hebrew book hands. This Jewish script has been labeled "square" and "Aramaic" (or *mirabile dictu*, "Assyrian"). However, it is just as fully a local Jewish script as is Nabatean or Palmyrene, both of which are descendants of the standard Aramaic script of the end of the Persian period.

of the colon; moreover, it supplies a desirable continuation of the repetitive parallelism found in the preceding tricolon.

The repetition of אדיר at the beginning of the second and third cola of the tricolon is to be noted (a figure the Greeks called *anadiplosis*). We observe also the repetition of the element *mem* (*m*–, –*m*–, –*m*–, –*m* in the first colon; –*m*–, –*m*–, –*m* in the second colon; and –*m*–, –*m*– in the third colon) — a remarkable example of *parechēsis*.

II. Discussion

Verses 1–4 of Psalm 93 have a strong mythological color as well as an archaic poetic style. Verse 5, however, is pedestrian in content, an unsymmetrical tricolon, and apparently a pious addition to the vigorous, archaic first four verses. It exhibits no internal parallelism, no repetition of elements, and no chiasm. These verses remind us of other archaic passages in hymns that are then succeeded at the end by a pious phrase or two.[17] An example is the end of the Psalm of Jonah (Jonah 2:3–10 [Eng vv. 2–9]). Verses 8–10 [Eng vv. 7–9] have been described as "a stock cultic ending of later date welded on to the older traditional verses."[18]

The kingship of Yahweh, his creation of cosmos and his ascendancy or victory over the chaotic primeval waters, and finally his appearance (or theophany) in his heavenly precinct (מרום)[19] are mythological themes with which I have dealt at length in my chapter on "The Song of the Sea and Canaanite Myth."[20] These themes have also been treated by a number of other scholars; major examples include Sigmund Mowinckel, T. H. Gaster, Hermann Gunkel, E. Lipiński, Oswald Loretz, Mitchell Dahood, and John Day.[21]

---

17. Compare Loretz, *Ugarit-Texte*, 291 and the references there.

18. See Cross, "The Prosody of Lamentations 1 and the Psalm of Jonah," 134.

19. On מרום as the heavenly precinct where the deity dwells, see Ps 18:17 [Eng v. 16] (= 2 Sam 22:17). Ugaritic *mrym* has a similar meaning.

20. Frank Moore Cross, *Canaanite Myth and Hebrew Epic: Essays in the History of the Religion of Israel* (Cambridge: Harvard University Press, 1973) 112–43.

21. See Sigmund Mowinckel, *The Psalms in Israel's Worship* (2 vols.; trans. D. R. Ap-Thomas; Oxford: Basil Blackwell, 1962) esp. 1:106–92 (chapter 5: "Psalms at the Enthronement Festival of Yahweh"; his primary study is found in idem, *Psalmenstudien II: Das Thronbesteigungsfest Jahwäs und der Ursprung der Eschatologie* [Amsterdam: Schippers, 1961 (original: 1921)]); T. H. Gaster, *Thespis: Ritual, Myth, and Drama in the Ancient Near East* (2d ed.; New York: Harper & Row, 1961) 443–61; Hermann Gunkel, *Einleitung in die Psalmen* (2d ed.; Göttingen: Vandenhoeck & Ruprecht, 1966) 94–116; E. Lipiński, *La royauté de Yahwé dans la poésie et le culte de l'ancien Israël* (Brussel: Paleis de Academien, 1965); Loretz, *Ugarit-Texte* (Loretz provides full bibliography up to 1988 for treatments of Psalm 93 [pp. 274–303, esp. 300–303]; see more recently F.-L. Hossfeld and E. Zenger, *Psalmen 51–100* [HTKAT; Freiburg: Herder, 2000] 643–49); Mitchell Dahood, *Psalms II:*

This psalm as well as Pss 47:8; 96:10; 97:1; and 99:1 begins with the colon יהוה מלך, which I have translated "Yahweh is king." The expression is also found in a bicolon of Ps 96:10, reminiscent of parts of Ps 93:1. Sigmund Mowinckel, in his groundbreaking discussion of "Psalms at the Enthronement Festival of Yahweh," translated the phrase "Yahweh has become King."[22] Hermann Gunkel also so understands the expression in his distinguished *Einleitung in die Psalmen*: "Er ist König geworden."[23] Mowinckel and Gunkel have been followed by many, if not most, modern commentators.

My translation "Yahweh is king" is meant to place the events in vv. 1–4 in mythic time as opposed to the time of *epos* or history (past, present, or future). Yahweh assumes kingship and appears robed in glory in his victory over the unordered forces of watery chaos that surround the now-ordered cosmos. In short, the verses describe creation. However, they also describe events being enacted in the cult. Creation is being actualized anew in the cultic "Now." This cyclical or mythic time also dissolves into the future. In the epic traditions of Israel, creation is truly of old, the victory at the sea a definitive though still "datable" time in Israel's history. In such a prophet as Second Isaiah there are the old mighty acts of Yahweh and the new mighty acts of Yahweh that are imminent in the future. One may term this *historical time*. However, in the prophetic understanding of Israel's history there is retained an *epic dimension*. Its events do not consist of a frozen, unchanging cycle, but a spiral movement, events going forward toward a goal. However, the new *magnalia Dei* are recognizable as types of the old epic events: an old exodus from slavery, a new exodus from captivity, an old way through the desert, a new way through the desert.

The mythic character of vv. 1–4 of Psalm 93 points to its early date in the rituals of kingship. A tenth-century date has been suggested by some, and I should agree that a date in the early years of the First Temple is quite likely.[24] Like Psalm 29, it stands very close to its Canaanite forbears.

51–100 (AB 17; Garden City: Doubleday, 1968) 339–44; and John Day, *God's Conflict with the Dragon and the Sea: Echoes of a Canaanite Myth in the Old Testament* (New York: Cambridge University Press, 1985).

22. Mowinckel, *The Psalms in Israel's Worship*, 107. See also his *Psalmenstudien II*, 3ff. where he translates "Yahwä ist König geworden," and "Yahwä ward König."

23. Gunkel, *Einleitung*, 97.

24. Among the scholars arguing for a tenth-century date, see E. Lipiński, *La royauté de Yahwé*, 163–72; and Dahood, *Psalms II*, 339. However, I cannot base a tenth-century dating on 93:5, *pace* J. D. Shenkel, "An Interpretation of Ps 93,5," *Bib* 46 (1965) 401–16.

There the Blessing:
An Exposition of Psalm 133

James Luther Mays

———◆———

I. Introduction

Psalm 133 may seem too slight a text for an expository interpretation to honor Patrick D. Miller, especially in the light of our long relationship. He has been a memorable student, a valued colleague in teaching and publication, and a cherished friend over the course of most of our lives. But there is something about this little psalm that signals a quality of our relationship that makes the choice of the psalm appropriate. Note, for instance, that one possible rendering of the second colon of v. 1 is "when brothers live in harmony." But there are also more particular reasons for the choice. An illuminating interpretive context for elements of Psalm 133 can be found in the book of Deuteronomy, thus connecting two biblical books that have been a special occupation of Miller's.[1] The exposition draws on associations out of a personal history that he shares and will recognize. And finally, attention here to the use of the psalm in the continuing community of faith recognizes Miller's emphatic concern with the role of psalmody in the Church.

II. The Interaction of Text and Context in the Psalms

Years ago, Darby Fulton, who was the executive of the Board of World Missions of the then Presbyterian Church in the U.S., told about an experience he had in Korea just after the Second World War. He was on a long slow trip in a crowded train; the passengers pressed together in facing benches. He spoke not a word of Korean and could not share in the conversation of his fellow travelers. To redeem the time, he got out a Bible and

---

[1]. In addition to his published works on Deuteronomy and the Psalms (consult the Bibliography in this volume), see especially Miller's presidential address to the Society of Biblical Literature: "Deuteronomy and Psalms: Evoking a Biblical Conversation," *JBL* 118 (1999) 3–18.

began to read. The passenger who faced him broke into smiles, began to say something, and also produced a Bible. They recognized each other as brothers in the faith, but they could not exchange a meaningful word. After a long awkward pause, the Korean opened his Bible and pointed to a passage. Darby recognized the Psalms and by counting back from the end in the Korean Bible he came to the one that begins, "Behold how good and how pleasant it is for brethren to dwell together in unity!" (Ps 133:1; AV). The psalm said for the two what they felt in the encounter and could not say to each other. Its text interpreted the occasion and its words were reread by the occasion. Text and context together created a moment of meaning.

This little story captures one personal intimate minute in the long history of psalmody. But it illustrates the transition whose endless repetition composes the course of psalmody through the centuries. Wherever a psalm was used as the language of prayer and praise, its text proposed a reading of people and occasion. And its words were reread in light of the people and occasion. Notwithstanding its translation into many languages, the unchanging psalm and changing setting have interacted to create ever-new meanings.

This interaction of text and context holds true, of course, for the process of interpretation in general. But it is significant for psalmody in a special way because the texts of the psalms are not only interpreted as is the case with other Scripture. The psalms are also used as our language in praise and prayer. The interaction between text and context happens in the use of a psalm; it is enacted in the activities of praise and prayer. The psalm reads the reader as the reader reads the psalm.

It has long been an axiom of contemporary hermeneutical discussion that "a text has a life of its own." The force of the axiom is ambiguous, and one must deal with it carefully in the case of psalmody. It is possible to err on either side of the ambiguity. On the one hand, the axiom argues that a text has a capacity for meaning that is not bound to the intention of its author or the circumstances of its composition. The history of psalmody is a massive illustration of the truth of that argument. Any dogmatic historicism that will allow validity alone to an "original meaning" is forced to deny truthfulness to the practice of psalmody. On the other hand, the axiom has also been used to claim that a text is a blank formula to which readers and interpretation bring and create the meaning. But this is seriously to underestimate the effect and efficiency of the vocabulary, syntax, and structure of the text. The use of a psalm is not only an occasion for thought. The psalm proposes an agenda, a direction, and a stance for thought.

For instance, Ps 118:17 says, "I shall not die, but I shall live, and recount the deeds of the LORD." The sentence is a fundamental expression of faith that the prospect of life instead of death has been created by the saving work of the LORD. This is its agenda, direction, and stance. When that line was sung by the faithful in Israel, its words interpreted the situation created by the return from exile. The community had been given life instead of death. When that line was shouted by Christians celebrating Easter, its words interpreted the situation created by the death and resurrection of Christ. The contexts provided different construals of the words and their reference. But in both the verse provides the language that interprets the existence of those who sing it as a possibility created by the salvation of God.

III. Text and Contemporary Context in Psalm 133

Psalm 133 is a veritable fabric of semantic possibilities: its vocabulary and syntax are threads that can be woven into several constructions. Its literary structure is comprised of an exclamation (v. 1) whose content is elaborated by two (or three) similes (vv. 2–3a) and supported by a declaration (v. 3b).

The exclamation is a value statement: "Behold, how good and pleasant it is when brothers dwell in unity" (v. 1; REV). All the words in the subordinate clause have more than one possible sense. "Brothers" can mean children of common parents, "kin" in an extended family, or "kindred" (NRSV) in an extended sense in a larger social unit. "Dwell" can mean "sit," "remain," or "reside." "In unity" translates a Hebrew adverb that can mean simply "in proximity," but often means "in harmony."

The similes draw comparisons in order to evoke associations that actualize the value-adjectives "good and pleasant." (v. 1). The effect of "the precious oil on the head" (v. 2a) and "the dew of Hermon . . . on the mountains of Zion" (v. 3a) is clear enough in Israel's aesthetic experience. The connotation of "the beard of Aaron, running down over the collar of his robes" (v. 2b) is puzzling in the context. Is it an appositional phrase used to identify the beard in the first simile, or intended to be a second simile on its own? And how does the reference to the high priest's beard fit with the two similes that call on general experience? All three phrases employ the participle "coming/running down" (*yōrēd*), which seems to anticipate the final declaration and its "blessing" that comes down from God, thus functioning in relation to the end of the psalm as well as its beginning.

The concluding clause is a theological statement: "For there the LORD has commanded the blessing, life for evermore."[2] Contemporary translations render "commanded" as "ordained" (NRSV) or "bestows" (REB) to avoid the problem of "the blessing" as the direct object of a verb usually addressed to a person. To what place does the emphatic adverb "there"

---

2. The translation is my own.

(*šām*) refer? If it refers to Zion, the most proximate locale in the psalm's syntax, then how does the theological statement support the opening observation—unless Zion is the place where the brothers/kindred sit/dwell together?

My interest in Psalm 133, and the reason for selecting it as an illustration, grows out of my own personal experience. I was nurtured and reared in a small communion that originated in one of the early splits in the Church of Scotland—the Associate Reformed Presbyterian Church. And, mind you, "Reformed" added on to Presbyterian meant that our fathers and mothers in the faith had thought that the rest of the Church of Scotland was not reformed enough! One of our doctrines was an exclusive psalmody; we sang no hymns—only the very songs of Scripture would do for the praise of the Lord. When we celebrated the Lord's Supper, we always used Psalm 133. A long table was set up across the front of the church. After the words of institution had been read, an elder would stand up, strike a tuning fork, and begin to sing the metrical version of the Psalm: "Behold, how good a thing it is / And how becoming well / Together such as brethren are / In unity to dwell." The congregation would take up the verses, and to their rhythm we would assemble at the table as one family.

I can still, without the slightest difficulty, hear the sounds and remember the scene. In the years before I was admitted to the Lord's Supper as a communicant, and had to wait in the pew while the rest of the congregation was at the table, I used to ponder the strange language of the psalm, and wonder what it was all about—those words about Herman's dew, and precious ointment on the head, the beard of Aaron. Childlike, I dreamed up my own associations. In those years, "Brilliantine" and other hair oils were in, and beards were out.

I think it was in the midst of such ruminations that one of the questions with which I am concerned began to form. Because the psalm did, after all, grow on one. In spite of its comic strangeness, I began to ask, "What gave the psalm a place in our celebration of the Lord's Supper?" There was—and is—in its chiseled brevity a poignancy and a promise, a depth and power that made of our gathering and actions something that they would not have been without its language. What is there in the language of the poem that made it appropriate in the context of our celebration—and even more, gave it the capacity to appropriate and redefine our situation in line with a past out of which it came and a future toward which it tends? Here is a text that could easily be more than two and a half millennia old. It has a history of use that reaches through innumerable phases of cultural change. What has made it endure? What constant of the human condition is captured in its words? What need and possibility are evoked by its lines to be addressed by the reality of which faith speaks?

IV. Text and Ancient Context in Psalm 133

The clue to the first stage of the psalm's history lies in a tension in the psalm itself. Within its brief movement there is an incongruity in the genre of its language. It begins with the idiom, vocabulary, and values of folk wisdom and concludes with those of the cultic community of Israel. The title given to the Psalms in the collection to which Psalm 133 belongs is "song of ascents," literally "a song for the goings-up," or more freely, "a song to be sung on the pilgrim's way up to Jerusalem to celebrate one of the annual festivals." But judged by form-critical criteria the opening sentence does not fit that definition as it does not belong to any of the genres of expression at home in the life of praise, prayer, and liturgy.

"How very good and pleasant it is when kindred live together in unity! It is like the precious oil on the head, running down upon the beard." In style and intention such an exclamation belongs to old folk wisdom, the didactic tradition cultivated by most people especially during the early stages of their cultural history. It was the business of old wisdom to observe the course of life, to perceive how things worked, to discern the better ways to steer living through with its manifold problems and possibilities. The product of such folk wisdom was the basic proverb which expressed the wisdom of many and the wit of one, a saying like "One reaps what one sows," and "A penny saved is a penny earned." One form in which such proverbs were cast was an observation about what is good. Many sentences of this particular kind are collected in the book of Proverbs. But they are also found in collections of sayings from both Egyptian and Babylonian origins. Like folk wisdom itself, the pattern and purpose of these sentences belongs to human culture generally, and is not restricted to any one ethnic or religious tradition. Old proverbs were coined and taught and repeated as the common instrument for discerning the possibilities of living and knowing the values inherent in choices of conduct.

The simile or comparison is a frequent element of proverbial style. By putting one thing that is known in experience alongside that which needs to be understood, the latter is illuminated and perception is aided. Incidentally, "the best oil on the head" seems to be a motif from the rituals of host and guest in the biblical world.[3] The guest who received the best oil for his head in such quantity that it ran down on the beard had the pleasure of knowing that his host meant to do him the highest honor. That is how good it is when brothers live together.

It is possible to know what the social reference of this saying was. The clause, "when brothers live together" occurs in only one other place in

---

3. Note the assumption behind the language of Pss 23:5; 92:10; 141:5; and Luke 7:46.

classical Hebrew literature, Deut 25:5. It introduces the legal tradition that defines and regulates the early institution generally called Levirate marriage. In that context, the phrase refers to the arrangement in a clan or kinship culture in which the sons and grandsons of a father continued to live as a social unit, occupying and tending the same inheritance.[4] The saying speaks of this kinship community and observes that, when its members dwell in unity, that is good. And "good," the favorite value term in such sayings, characterizes those things that support and enrich life instead of diminishing it. It involves no more and no less than what we speak of as "the common welfare." The members of such a community were bound to one another by a mutual ethic, a tradition of obligations that were inherent in the kinship relationship. When they lived up to and fulfilled that mutuality, life was more secure and whole.

When marauding brigands raided their territory, the entire clan would gather for common defense. Their unity meant strength for the protection of life. Or when lions ravaged the flock of Uncle Jedidiah, all the kinsmen would together furnish him with a ram and flock of ewes for a fresh start. Unity meant the will to bear one another's burdens. When sorrow and death came unto some family in the clan, the entire kinship group would rally in sympathy and succor. In the presence of death, life was supported by the fellowship of concern and help. Those who grew up in rural settings have experienced themselves how the society of the larger family makes for a more abundant and durable life. And, of course, the larger family can also create problems.

The very fact that the saying should be transmitted as instruction about life is an explicit recognition that kindred did not always live in life-enhancing solidarity. The early Hebrews had the primal paradigm of Cain and Abel to instruct them about the other possibility. When brothers acted out of self-interest instead of community-interest, that made for death. But how very good it is when the living of all is woven in a fabric of unity. For each it meant having a place of honor in the community like the guest who was honored with the best oil.

The recognition of the social reference of the saying uncovers, I think, the first dimension of Psalm 133 that gives it an abiding vitality and makes it resonate in other times and circumstances. The subject of the saying is the relation between human interdependence and life, and obversely, the relation between human selfishness and death. It articulates in the simplest way a perception that is valid for every social unit in human history from

---

4. Gen 13:6 ("they [Abram and Lot] could not live together") and 36:7 ("their [Esau and Jacob's] possessions were too great for them to live together") illustrate the social arrangement and its problems.

the smallest to the largest and most complex: life is of value, so the very fact of life obligates. Actions diminish or increase the life of others. So you can live up to life only by a unity composed of awareness of the other and commitment to the other. This is true for the old kinship clan and true for the global village. It is something we all know—and yet still have to learn. The perception is accessible to any thoughtful wisdom today—and its claims still threaten the Cain in every one of us. The concern with life as a "good" is implicit in the first line of the psalm and waits the further statement of the last line.

V. Text and Deuteronomic Context in Psalm 133

The old wisdom saying and its perception are woven into a poem that has a larger and different social group in view. It is not necessary to insist that the saying had an independent existence in Israel's common stock of proverbs, though I suspect that was the case. It is enough to recognize the kind and substance of knowledge that the saying brings into the psalm at its beginning. The saying has been extended in a sequence of lines by the aesthetic device of repetition of themes and sentence patterns. The two added similes, which reinforce the first with new images of what is good, appear to be drawn from the cultic tradition of Jerusalem: Aaron, the name of the classic priest, and Zion, the name of Jerusalem as the elect city of God. The religious location of the chosen city of God where the priest presides over the institutions of the people of God is set alongside the social location of brothers' dwelling together as its appositional definition. The reference "there" in the concluding declaration refers to Zion envisioned as the sphere in which brothers dwell in unity. And the term "brothers" in this larger context assumes a connotation characteristic of Deuteronomy. Especially in Deuteronomic rhetoric, "brothers" is a way of speaking of the people Israel as an extended family in which the traditional obligations of one sibling to another are regarded as binding between members of "the people of the LORD."[5]

Deuteronomy is in fact, the best interpretive context for the entire final line of the psalm with its talk about enduring life as the blessing that the LORD has commanded. Of course, in the entire Old Testament life is regarded as dependent on God and a gift of God. Some of the psalms, for example, speak of the life-bestowing Presence in Zion's sanctuary.[6] But it is in Deuteronomy that the phrase, "The LORD will command the blessing . . ." is found.[7] And it is in Deuteronomic address that command and

---

5. E. Jenni, "אָח *'āḥ* brother," *TLOT* 1:73–77, esp. 76–77.
6. E.g., Pss 16:11; 21:4; 36:9.
7. Deut 28:8; cf. Lev 25:21.

blessing and life are brought together as interdependent motifs.[8] It is characteristic of Deuteronomy that life is related to obedience to the commandments of God.[9]

These congruencies with Deuteronomic theological tradition suggest the answers to a crucial question: How was this good and pleasant unity that is the manifestation and experience of enduring life to be accomplished by this larger and diverse family? The answer lies in the exhortation: "See, I set before you this day life and good, death and evil . . . therefore choose life, that you and your descendants may live, loving the LORD your God, obeying his voice, and cleaving to him; for that means life to you" (Deut 30:15–20; RSV). The torah was the LORD's provision of a center and a conduct, a basis of life and a way of living for a conflicted family of "brothers." Hear the torah and one heard the blessing of abiding life commanded. Psalm 133 thinks of Israel, not just as a nation, but as a social unit with a transcendent source. The relational ethos of blood kinship is transcended. The fabric of interdependence that involves identity with the other and responsibility for the other is spread across old boundaries that define and limit living.

The psalm's content, title, and the collection of "songs of ascent" in which it stands all point to the use for which it was composed. The occasion was probably the pilgrimage to the holy city to celebrate Tabernacles, the festival in which the pilgrims built booths and dwelt together during its course to enact their identity as a community created by the salvation of God. It is an anthem whose proper context is that place where movement toward God's promise of the unity required for life becomes visible.

In imagination one can hear the measures of Psalm 133 echoing across the ridges around Jerusalem at festival time—Israelites on pilgrimage because they had long since learned it was not enough to be kindred or neighbors or fellow citizens of one Kingdom. The centrifugal forces always at work in their mortality tore them apart, set tribe against tribe, rich against poor, resident against stranger, strong over weak. But in the covenant place they heard the message: "Hear O Israel, the LORD is our God, the LORD alone" (Deut 6:4), and faced the power who, against all that fragmented, drew them together. And in the covenant exhortation they were taught "the path that the LORD your God has commanded you, so that you may live" (Deut 5:33), and learned the guidelines for living together. When the Covenant claimed them, life won and the history of God in their living became a little stronger.

---

8. Deut 30:15–20.
9. G. Gerleman, "חיה *ḥyh* to live," *TLOT* 1:417.

VI. Text and Ongoing Contexts in Psalm 133

There is, as far as I can find, no specific allusion to Psalm 133 in the New Testament, as is the case with so many other psalms. But its theme and concern appear in many places. In a letter of one of the early Christian communities the writer observed: "We know that we have passed from death to life because we love one another [literally: the brethren (τοὺς ἀδελφούς)]" (1 John 3:14). If we ask how this new religious community learned that, and how they came to be calling one another brothers and sisters, the best place to go for an answer is a story about Jesus of Nazareth (Mark 3:31–35). During the controversy and confusion provoked by his activity, his family feared he had lost his mind and came to the house where he was. They stood outside and called to him. A crowd was sitting around him and they said to him, "Your mother and your brothers and sisters are outside, asking for you." He replied, "Who are my mother and my brothers?" He looked around on those who sat about him and said, "Here are my mother and my brothers! Whoever does the will of God is my brother and sister and mother." This abrupt rupture of the kinship relation and its interests, and its replacement by another kinship group created by his person and the enactment of God's will in his mission, is astonishing. It signals the subordination of every natural, ethnic, and national dependence for identity and ethos to a new overarching community centered solely in him. It was a move that impelled the reach of the Christian community across every boundary in the societies and nations of the Roman Empire. Now it was possible to sing "How good and pleasant it is when brothers and sisters live in unity" within new horizons of expectation that stretched toward the whole family of humanity.

With its passage through that context, Psalm 133 entered the history of Christian praise and thought. And, of course, it lived on in the worship and piety of Judaism. It was incorporated into the cycle of lectionary readings in synagogue and church to be heard again and again in a repetition that colored the consciousness of many generations. The poem was translated, first into Greek and Latin, then into other languages, cast in the form of hymns and paraphrases. Of the countless contexts in which it was used, some are still visible. I mention several of these, only as illustrations.

Augustine noted in the fifth century C.E. that "The sound of the first verse is so sweet that it is chanted by persons who know nothing of the rest of the Psalter."[10] In what was certainly a bit of an overstatement he also said that the psalm gave birth to the monasteries; it was like a trumpet-call

---

10. Quoted in J. J. Stewart Perowne, *The Book of Psalms* (2 vols.; Andover: Warren F. Draper, 1898) 2:395.

to those who wished to dwell together as brethren. So in those days Psalm 133 had become a lovely slogan to articulate the joy believers experienced in a community that had more purchase on the future than the dying Roman culture around them. And it had become one of the texts by which the emerging monastic communities understood their character and purpose.

John Calvin's passion for biblical praise gave the psalms new vitality in congregational worship. Many in the early Reformation committed metrical versions of the entire Psalter to memory. In one of the orders for the celebration of the Lord's Supper, the first verse of Psalm 133 was said, just after the words of institution, as "The Peace." Its use interpreted the sacramental communion as the constitution of a family through whose unity God bestowed the blessing of life.

In the *Book of Common Prayer*, Psalm 133 is designated as a psalm for use in services of Christian Unity. In such a context it is a two-edged sword. It speaks judgment on the Church's vulnerability to the power of race, nation, and particular history to define the catholic fellowship by division. But it remains a gracious encouraging invitation to pilgrimage toward the center that unites.

And, finally, one illustration from a contemporary setting: Some years ago in Little Rock, Arkansas, the synagogue which belonged to the congregation of Beth Ahabah burned down. An arrangement was worked out for the Jewish congregation to share the building of the Second Presbyterian Church. On Saturday, the Jews worshiped in the building and called it a synagogue—on Sunday, the Presbyterians worshiped there and called it a church. The alternation lasted several years. As time passed the alternation changed to a conversation and the conversation to discovery of each other that had remarkable effect on both communities. When the new synagogue was dedicated, the Presbyterians were honored guests and in the service were given a banner which now hangs in their church. On it, Ps 133:1 is inscribed in Hebrew:

מה־טוב ומה־נעים שבת אחים גם־יחד

In all these contexts, a micro-fraction of the whole history, Psalm 133 brings two contributions. *First*, it elicits and forms into language the original insight of the old saying with which it begins. Where that occurs, consciousness is focused on the need and the innate longing for a unity of persons equal to the demands of life. *Second*, it sets that predicament and possibility of human existence in the perspective of faith in the covenant-making God of Israel and the community-forming event of Jesus Christ. The psalm reveals that God is the power who withholds life from the rejection of interdependence, and is the source who provides life as a blessing when people let the divine purpose bring them together.

The two contributions generate an eschatological tension. In every occasion where the truth of the psalm's wisdom is acknowledged and the power of the promise believed, a sense of pilgrimage is created, a movement toward a place where the family of humankind shall appear. Such occasions become a foretaste, an earnest, a proleptic and symbolic enactment of an environment defined alone by the human need for life and the divine will to bless.

Edmond Fleg, a Jewish poet who lived through the Holocaust, wrote a poem about Passover. It raises a vision that defies the worst experience of violence against the human family that our recent history can provide. I use it as a conclusion, to discern, as only poetry can, the place toward which the pilgrimage moves.[11]

Awake, Awake! Behold and see!
On all the peaks, on all the plains,
In closed valleys, open gulfs,
On all the seas and archipelagos
The table for mankind is laid!
And on the table made of wood, from every wood,
A napkin that is spread for all,
Woven with all the fires that flow down from all the skies.
The cover is laid, the cups are blessed,
Creation all around communicates.

And here—among the beasts
That far outnumber
All mankind, the Wolf walks with the Lamb,
Making the Peace of the World!

Behold, they are come, their naked bodies tinted,
The men whose lips are black . . .
And see here, squatting quite close to them
The men whose skulls are red . . .

And here, from out their distant world
The men whose skulls are yellow . . .

And here—now come the men with white foreheads . . .

---

11. My copy of this poem is a translation of a version of Edmond Fleg, *Nous de l'espérance* (Miroir 3; Angers: Masque d'or, 1949) 105–6, as printed in a book by Edmund Jacob that, unfortunately, I no longer own and cannot locate.

Arise, arise! Your place is empty in their midst,
Their faces shine with happiness
All round that immense table!
Behold, they have broken the Bread!
Behold, they have raised the Wine!
Listen, they have prayed in the silence.

The Holy Supper of Mankind begins!

Certainty, Ambiguity, and Trust: Knowledge of God in Psalm 139

CAROLYN PRESSLER

———◆———

I. Introduction

It is both fitting and humbling to dedicate this essay to Patrick D. Miller, a brilliant and beloved teacher, mentor, and friend. Miller's chapter on the poetry of the psalms is among the most helpful discussions of Hebrew poetics available and his interpretation of Psalm 139 wonderfully illustrates how consideration of their poetic nature can deepen one's interpretation of the psalms.[1] Moreover, the following essay has its roots in a paper written some fifteen years ago for his seminar on the Psalms.[2] I offer it to him with deep gratitude and affection.

Psalm 139 has a rich and diverse history of interpretation. For John Calvin, the psalm was evidence of God's inescapable judgment;[3] it has also been the last words with which martyrs protested their innocence.[4] Most often lauded as a hymn praising God's all-encompassing knowledge, presence, and power, it has also been interpreted as the cry of one for whom God is an ambiguous and even oppressive presence.[5] Scholars have

---

1. Patrick D. Miller, "Poetry and Interpretation" and "Psalm 139" in his *Interpreting the Psalms* (Philadelphia: Fortress, 1986) 29–47, 144–53.

2. The interpretation set forth in that essay was further developed in my installation address: "Ambiguity and Certainty in the Knowledge of God: A Close Reading of Psalm 139 and Exodus 3:14," *Voices of United* (January 2000) 14–18.

3. John Calvin, *Commentary on the Book of Psalms* (trans. J. Anderson; Grand Rapids: Eerdmans, 1949) 207–8.

4. According to Rowland E. Prothero (*The Psalms in Human Life* [London: John Murray, 1909] 209), Blaise Pascal described his sister going to her death along with other victims of persecution with the words of Psalm 139 on her lips.

5. Walter Harrelson captures well the ambiguity of the psalm: "In this remarkable poem . . . we have a portrayal of a person for whom God is at once a glorious and an oppressive presence" ("On God's Knowledge of the Self, Psalm 139," *CurTM* 2 [1975] 261–65; citation from 262).

variously described the genre of the psalm as hymn, lament, didactic or wisdom poetry, protestation of innocence, and "mixed." Especially given the high artistry of the psalm, such multiple, disparate interpretations raise the possibility that its author deliberately incorporated divergent or equivocal elements into the poem. At the same time, the widely diverse interpretations of the psalm serve as a powerful reminder that any interpretation of it is, at best, one of many plausible readings. In this essay, I examine the poet's use of carefully contrasting language and ambiguous terms or phrases as an expression of ambivalence towards a God whose presence is experienced as potential threat as well as potential salvation. According to this reading, recollection of God's intimate involvement with the psalmist since conception reframes the psalmist's ambivalence, resolving ambiguity into trust.

II. Certainty

At first reading, Psalm 139 seems to be a witness to certainty rather than ambiguity. Indeed, the poem expresses no doubt whatsoever that God exists and that the psalmist is known by God. The poet uses a careful choice of pronouns, repetition, and merismus to establish the psalmist's overwhelming experience of God's piercing knowledge.

The opening words of the psalm, "O Yahweh,"[6] center the prayer solidly within the context of an "I-Thou," or, rather, a "Thou-I" relationship. The next words establish that the psalmist's awareness of God is first of all a primal experience of being examined and known.[7] "*You* know," the psalmist exclaims; the "you" (אתה) of v. 2 is emphatic. Moreover, "You know *me*." The cry has to do with personal relationship, rather than with divine omniscience in any abstract sense.

The poet's repeated use of the verb "to know" hammers home the intensity of God's knowledge of the psalmist. Four times in the first four verses, the poem asserts God *knows* (ידע) the petitioner. Related verbs pile up: God examines (חקר), discerns (בין), sifts through (זרית), is familiar with (סכן) this one!

God knows *all* of the psalmist's life. The poet employs merismus (citing two poles like "alpha and omega" to indicate a whole) and implicit contrasts in order to impress upon the listener the totality of God's knowledge. God knows "when I lie down and when I rise" (v. 2) and sifts "my walking and my

---

6. Translations of Psalm 139 are my own and come from work I did for Miller's Psalms seminar at Princeton Theological Seminary in Spring 1987.

7. I use the term "psalmist" to refer to the implied singer of the psalm, as distinct from its composer, to whom I refer as the "poet" or "author."

reclining" (v. 3). The phrases, reminiscent of Deut 6:7, refer to all of the psalmist's behaviors. Yahweh recognizes all angles of this one's life: pressing "behind and before" (v. 5). Indeed, God knows the psalmist inside and out: acts, thoughts (v. 2), and words (v. 4). Whether near (v. 5) or far off (v. 2), the psalmist is never outside of the sphere of divine consciousness.

The knowing God is everywhere present. The poet answers the rhetorical question of v. 7, "where could I flee?" emphatically: "nowhere." "Heaven" and "Sheol" constitute another merismus: neither the highest nor the lowest points in the cosmos, nor any place in between provide a corner where the psalmist may escape God (v. 8). With references to "wings of dawn" and "outermost sea" (v. 9), the poet's attention shifts from cosmos to earth, and from vertical to horizontal. The image seems to trace the course of the sun traveling through the heavens until it sets in the West. Neither the farthest East nor the uttermost West, nor any point in between is free of God's presence.

Other ancient Near Eastern texts connect the outermost reaches of the sea to Sheol. There, it was believed, the sun went down to complete its circuit through the underworld.[8] The poem begins to build an implicit contrast between the places of light and life, where one would expect God to be present, and the places of death and sun's setting where divine presence is not expected. And yet, in Sheol also, God is there. The image of the sun moving through the sky is temporal as well as spatial. From earliest dawn to day's end, God is inescapably there. God's ineluctable presence extends through all time as well as all space.

One cannot escape; neither can one hide. While the vocabulary and syntax of vv. 11–12 present several problems, it is clear that the poet first imagines, then rejects an attempt to evade God. In v. 11b the psalmist seems to desire darkness to be as light now is, that is, all around him or her, but recognizes that the effort to hide would still be vain. Light and darkness, day and night, all are alike to God.

III. Ambiguity

The psalm expresses no ambiguity at all about God's knowledgeable presence—and that is precisely the problem. The psalmist experiences the inescapable presence of God as possibly salvific, but also as potentially threatening. Is God a damning judge or a sustaining guide, an enemy or a friend? The poet has chosen words carefully to convey ambivalent human response to the overwhelming experience of divine power. Repeatedly, a

---

8. While maintaining the fullness of the earth/cosmos, vertical/horizontal imagery, Othmar Keel rightly suggests that the West is connected with Sheol in Psalm 139 (*The Symbolism of the Biblical World* [trans. T. Hallett; New York: Seabury, 1978] 23–24).

word with negative connotations is set against a more positive term that expresses the same phenomena. Such ambivalence is already hinted at in the first verse. The verb "to examine" (חקר) has potentially threatening overtones. Used metaphorically, it tends to involve taking action to establish the truth in a case of law. At one time it may have involved an ordeal.[9] While God's "knowing" (ידע) can also refer to judgment (Ps 73:11), most often for God to know a person or nation leads to restoration and healing. In the laments, divine knowledge of the one praying is evoked to motivate God to act on the petitioner's behalf (see Pss 31:7; 69:5, 19; 142:3).

The psalmist's ambivalence about the experience of divine scrutiny is clearly captured in v. 3, which the NRSV renders "You search out my path and my lying down." "Search out" is a very benign translation of the Hebrew verb זרית, which literally means "winnow, scatter, disperse."[10] The word is frequently found in biblical poetry, almost always with reference to judgment. "You . . . *have scattered* us among the nations" (Ps 44:11); because of the Israelites' grumbling, God "swore to . . . disperse their descendants among the nations, *scattering* them over the lands" (Ps 106:26–27). A just king "*winnows* all evil with his eyes" (Prov 20:8). In contrast, the verb in the second half of v. 3, "to be familiar with" (סכן), carries the positive meaning "to be of use, profit, or service."

The ambivalent language continues in vv. 7–12, as the psalmist considers the possibility of escape. Under the pressure of God's ambiguous scrutiny, the beleaguered psalmist longs to flee, as Jacob flees from his murderously angry brother, as Hagar flees from her abusive mistress, or as Jonah flees from God—but flight is impossible. Even at the farthest edges of the sea, the outermost West, the end of the day, God's hand would lead (נחה), as a shepherd leads sheep—or perhaps seize (אחז) as one seizes a prisoner (v. 10).[11] For good or ill, God's hand guides and grasps.

In addition to close, yet contrasting terms, the poet conveys the double-edged experience of divine knowing through deliberately ambiguous terms

---

9. M. Tsevat, "חָקַר *ḥāqar*," *TDOT* 5:148–50.

10. I take זרית as the *hipʿil* of זרה. Some have understood זרית as a denominative of the noun, זרת, meaning "encompass." Such a denominative is not otherwise attested in Biblical Hebrew, however. Moreover, even if that was the primary meaning of the word, the negative meaning of זרית would not be lost on the hearers.

11. The first verb in v. 10 has the positive meaning "to guide or lead." The second verb, אחז, can be used positively. Psalm 73:23–24a resembles 139:10: ואני תמיד עמך אחזת ביד־ימיני בעצתך תנחני, "I am continually with you. You hold my right hand. By your counsel you guide me." In this instance, the verb אחז is used in an avowal of confidence. Usually, however, אחז means "to seize" in the negative sense. One is seized by traps (Job 18:9) or by anguish or fear (Exod 15:14; Ps 48:6). God's hand seizes in judgment (Deut 32:41) and even with violence (Job 16:12). Would those listening not have heard reverberations of being caught and rendered powerless?

and phrasing, that is, single words or phrases that carry multiple meanings.[12] The ambiguous language expresses an exquisitely ambiguous experience of the Holy One. Such ambiguity is found in v. 5: "You hedge me in
behind and before; you lay your hand on/against me." "Hedge," צור, is used
once in Biblical Hebrew to refer to closing one's hand around something
valuable, but its basic meaning is warlike, that is, "to besiege." The word is
saved from sounding unambiguously hostile by the similarity in sound between it and the noun צור, "rock," a common image of divine protection. It
also calls to mind the verb יצר, "to form or create" (cf. v. 16). God is besieging the psalmist—or could it be that God is protecting and/or creating him
or her? To "lay hands on someone" has the same double meaning in Hebrew
that it does in English. It may be an act of blessing or protection (Gen
48:14; Exod 33:22), but may also be hostile (Job 13:21). God's "hand," God's
power, can punish or protect.

The ambiguity of the psalmist's experience of God is most fully expressed in the hymnic line of v. 6: פלאיה דעת ממני נשגבה לא־אוכל לה. This
pivotal verse declares something about God's knowledge, but what? The
adjective פלאיה (*Kethib*) is found elsewhere only in Judg 13:18 (in masculine
form), where God's name is described as too פלאי for a human being to
know and survive. The verbal root of the word means to be wonderful or
difficult; in both Judges 13 and Ps 139:6, the adjective seems to refer to aw-
ful, awe-inspiring numinous power. The last half of the verse is also ambiguous. The NRSV's translation of לא־אוכל לה, "I cannot attain it," is typical.
However, elsewhere in the Bible, the verb יכל plus the preposition ל followed by a noun or pronoun is found only in adversarial contexts and has to
do with one's ability, or lack of ability, to overcome or prevail against the
adversary.[13] The verse is genuinely ambiguous. It carries two meanings. The
translation offered by the NRSV provides the most common understanding
of the verse: "Such knowledge is too wonderful for me; it is so high that I

---

12. Paul R. Raabe convincingly documents a number of examples of ambiguity used
as a poetic device ("Deliberate Ambiguity in the Psalter," *JBL* 110 [1991] 213–27). The
multivalence inherent in poetry and the potential for confusing translation uncertainty
with deliberate ambiguity raise the issue of controls. Raabe sets out three criteria for determining whether a perceived textual ambiguity is a deliberate literary device. First, the
multiple meanings of the word or phrase must be established for the term in Hebrew,
not deduced from cognate languages. Second, there must be support for each meaning
of the term or phrase within the passage. Third, the ambiguity must carry theological or
semantic significance. I would add to Raabe's criteria that identifying a repeated pattern
of ambiguous terms strengthens the probability that any given instance is intentional.
Moreover, the artistry of the poem is also a factor; presumably good poets do not use
language that denotes more than one meaning unintentionally.

13. See Gen 32:25; Num 13:30; Judg 16:5; 1 Sam 17:9; Esth 6:13; Ps 129:2; Jer 1:19; 15:20;
20:10; 38:22; Obad 7.

cannot attain it." But the verse may also be rendered "Such knowledge is too *difficult* for me; it is high; I cannot prevail against it."[14]

The first half of the psalm conveys God's knowledge of and presence to the psalmist as certain and intensely personal, but also as double-edged. As Walter Harrelson writes, the poem "presents to us that familiar ambivalence that the faithful feel toward the God who is at once their very life and breath and also their scourge and nemesis."[15] To borrow Judith Plaskow's fine phrase, it "names the power in the world that makes us know our vulnerability."[16]

IV. From Ambiguity to Mystery, From Ambivalence to Trust

The twin themes of God's knowledge of and God's inescapably close relationship to the psalmist continue in the third section of the psalm, vv. 13–18. But in my judgment the mood of the psalm shifts in v. 13 from ambivalence, bordering on dread, to trust. Perhaps God's ineluctable presence, God's discernment of the psalmist in darkness as in light, calls to mind the hidden place where life begins. The psalmist recollects that God was creatively present even in the womb. Elsewhere in the Bible, the motif of God's intrauterine involvement functions as a word of assurance. In Ps 71:6, remembering God's support from the womb serves as a basis for renewed trust and hope. Psalm 22:9–10 depicts Yahweh as midwife, both to encourage the lamenter and to motivate God to act by lifting up the Creator's responsibility for the creature. In Isa 44:2, 46:3–4, and 66:8–9 God reminds Judah that the ground of hope is the One who forms, carries, and delivers the people from the womb.[17] In our passage, also, the recognition that God has created and known the psalmist from the womb transforms the experience of God's knowledgeable, unavoidable presence.

Moving through vv. 13–18, we encounter words and motifs that were ambiguous in the first half of the psalm but that are now uttered in unalloyed praise. "I praise you, for I am awesomely, wonderfully made; your works are wonderful!" (v. 14). The phrase echoes v. 6 in its hymnic form and repetition

---

14. The translation of the verse in the NJPSV (Tanakh) maintains the ambiguity: "It is beyond my knowledge; it is a mystery; I cannot fathom it."

15. Walter Harrelson, "On God's Knowledge of the Self," 263.

16. Judith Plaskow, "Facing the Ambiguity of God," *Tikkun* 6 (1991) 70, 96.

17. The author of Job distorts this motif of divine compassion, using birthing language to underscore God's betrayal of expected responsibility and compassion (Job 10:8–14). God's agency in conception and gestation can also serve as the basis of divine authorization (see Isa 49:1, 5; Jer 1:5).

of the root פלא. But, as the glad cry "I praise you" makes clear, what had earlier been experienced as both "wonderful" and "difficult/powerful" is now seen as unambiguously wonderful. In the first section of the poem, the psalmist complains that God lays a siege (צור) behind and before. Now, memory of God's gracious creation of the psalmist leads to praise for all the days that God has formed (יצר; v. 16).

Similarly, the poet takes up words and motifs that carried negative connotations in the first half of the psalm and reuses them as images of life and protection. The work that makes the psalmist pause in wonder is that God knit together the poet in the mother's womb (v. 13), and intricately wove them in the depths of the earth (v. 15). In v. 15, "depths of the earth" may refer to the mythic creation of humankind within Mother Earth. It may also simply be a metaphor for the womb. Elsewhere in the Bible, "depths of the earth" refers to Sheol,[18] the place of death, the place where, in v. 8, the psalmist would flee from God's spirit, but could not. Here the dark, hidden place is the domain of life, a secret recess where God intricately shaped the psalmist's frame. Moreover, in the life-giving womb, divine vision is providence, not scrutiny. Far from longing for the possibility of hiding from God in darkness (vv. 11–12), by v. 16 the psalmist recognizes that God's "eyes beheld" the psalmist's unformed substance in order to bring life. Similarly, the psalmist has learned to view God's inescapable presence as unambiguously positive. In the first half of the poem there is no place (vv. 7–10) and no time (vv. 11–12) within which the psalmist can escape Yahweh's scrutinizing presence. Now, the poet rejoices that there are no days outside of God's providential care (v. 16). Both birth and death are held by God. Verses 13–16 look back to the psalmist's birth; v. 18 looks ahead to death: "I come to an end; I am still with you."

Ambivalence, then, is resolved not into certainty but into trust. Like v. 6, v. 18 speaks directly to the psalmist's knowledge of God, and to the limits of that knowledge. In v. 6, the poet recognized that divine knowledge is too powerful for a human to attain to or to prevail against. Now, in v. 18, the psalmist declares that God's thoughts are vast beyond count—greater than the human mind can comprehend. But while earlier the psalmist was pitted powerlessly against divine knowledge, in v. 18, God's weighty uncountable thoughts are "dear." Here, too, the poet uses an ambiguous term,

---

18. "Depths" (תחתיות) and "earth" (ארץ) are found together five other times in Biblical Hebrew. In four of these, the phrase is in contexts where it clearly means the underworld (Ps 63:10; Ezek 26:20; 32:18, 24). The fifth instance is in a hymn that exhorts the heavens and the depths of the earth to shout for joy (Isa 44:23). The author of the Isaiah passage appears to have chosen a name for Sheol in order to emphasize the totality of the cosmos that is called upon to praise Yahweh.

יְקָר. The word seems to have two different meanings. Commentators point
to an Aramaic meaning of the term as the basis for the translation "weighty"
(so NRSV). The primary meaning of the term in Hebrew, however, is "precious, dear."[19] Unlike v. 6, however, the ambiguity of God's thoughts in v. 18
points not to God's two-edged relationship to the psalmist, but to Yahweh's
unfathomable mystery, a mystery that is both profound and cherished. As
Miller rightly notes, the section ends with an ambiguous phrase: "I come to
an end" could refer to attempts by the psalmist to count God's thoughts or
to the end of the psalmist's life.[20] In either case, God is present: "I am still
with you." Ambivalence finds resolution in confident relationship. Double-
edged experience of the Deity is transformed into trust by the remembered intimacy of the womb.

V. Certitude and Full Circle

The mood shifts yet again in vv. 19–24. As occurs so often in the Psalter,
trust opens up the possibility of entreaty. The psalmist's initial plea is jarring: "slay the wicked!" The cry is so abrupt and (to twenty-first century
ears) so abrasive that a number of commentators suggest that the verses
were not originally part of the psalm and excise them from their interpretations. While talk about hating enemies might indeed be disturbing,
it nevertheless belongs to the thought-world of the psalms. Hatred of
wickedness and wicked persons occurs and recurs in the Psalter as a sign of
righteousness. But in Psalm 139, the imprecation does more. It signals a
movement in the psalmist's relationship to God. In vv. 1–12, God is perceived as "other," possibly as a rock or refuge, but certainly as a besieging,
scrutinizing presence. Now, at the end of the psalm, the enemy is no longer
the deity, but the wicked.[21] Now, the psalmist seeks to be aligned with

---

19. BDB 429 gives "be precious, prized, valued" as the primary definition of יְקָר. Cf.
HALOT 2:431–32.

20. Miller, *Interpreting the Psalms*, 148–49. Miller's cogent argument for translating
הֲקִיצֹתִי as "I come to the end," rather than "I awake," influenced my translation of this
verse and was later adopted by the NRSV.

21. As noted above, biblical scholars have classified Psalm 139 in widely (even wildly)
divergent ways. Many recent commentators follow Sigmund Mowinckel in classifying it
as a protestation of innocence (*The Psalms in Israel's Worship* [trans. D. R. Ap-Thomas; Oxford: Basil, 1962] 131). The artist who created the poem seems to have incorporated into
it elements from a range of poetic genres. Motifs associated with protestations of innocence in other psalms seem to be particularly prominent, however. Such motifs include
the use of verbs related to the image of God as judge (בחן, חקר), and the hatred of the
wicked. If the psalm is, indeed, a protestation of innocence in the face of false accusations, then the imprecation can also be understood as a cry of rage and pain, the
protest of injured innocence unable to defend itself. The emotion behind the prayer,

Yahweh, hating those who reject God. Nonetheless, in the context of a discussion of ambiguity and certainty, the verses may function best as a warning. In vv. 19–22, ambiguity is resolved not into trust, but into certitude; the distance between God and the self collapses. Such certitude is hazardous, easily able to become an excuse to absolutize one's own perspectives and interests and/or a justification for violence against others who think differently. For those who, unlike the psalmist, have the power to act upon it, certitude is especially dangerous.[22]

The last two verses of the psalm blur the sharp line that vv. 19–22 have drawn between the psalmist and the wicked. The psalmist turns back from self-righteousness to acknowledge the possibility of walking in a "hurtful" or idolatrous way. The plea turns back from thoughts of enemies to the central concern: relationship with God. "Examine me, O God, and know my mind; try me and know my anxious thoughts. See if there is any vexatious [or idolatrous] way in me, and lead me in the way of everlasting life" (vv. 23–24).

The language of these concluding verses echoes the words with which the psalm opens: "examine," "know." The tone of the words is very different, however. In the opening verses, the verbs are declarative and, according to my reading, at least partly complaint. "You have searched me and known me . . . winnowed, scattered me, you besiege me front and back!" The psalmist begins by viewing him or herself as an unwilling object of divine scrutiny. The psalmist ends with the verbs in the imperative: "Search me! Oh, yes, do know me!" The psalmist is now a willing participant in the divine examination.

The author of Psalm 139 has used a multitude of poetic devices to interweave certainty and ambiguity, mystery, and trust. From the space created by the recollection of God's involvement in the womb, the psalmist finds grounds, finally, not for certitude, but for trust. Looking back from that point of intimate memory, what had seemed to be divine scrutiny is recognized as divine solicitude. Mystery is not eliminated; God's being may still not be grasped or defined. God's thoughts are unfathomably weighty, as countless as the sand. But what the psalmist *can* know is God's trustworthy presence: "I come to the end—I am still with you" (v. 18b).

---

dangerous for those with the power to act upon it, is more readily understood when voiced by one powerless against intolerable persecution.

22. Walter Brueggemann has explored this dimension of the psalm in his essay "The Cunning Little Secret of Certitude," *Church and Society* 87 (1997) 63–80.

Quoth the Raven:
Psalm 147 and the Environment

JAMES LIMBURG

I. Introduction

In an important editorial in *Theology Today*, Patrick D. Miller writes the following: "Reticent to speak about the state of theology or its future, I will boldly suggest that an even more important enterprise at this chronological turning point is assessing *the state of the world*."[1] Miller goes on to commend the work of the Worldwatch Institute (www.worldwatch.org) and calls attention to the "Millennial Edition" of its annual report, *State of the World 1999*. He quotes a statement from Lester Brown, leader of the Institute, summarizing the world's situation at the edge of a new millennium:

> The Earth's forests are shrinking, fisheries are collapsing, water tables are falling, soils are eroding, coral reefs are dying, atmospheric CO_2 concentrates are increasing, temperatures are rising, floods are becoming more destructive, and the rate of extinction of plant and animal species may be the greatest since the dinosaurs disappeared 65 million years ago.[2]

The editorial goes on to speak of the "prophetic" stance of the work of the Worldwatch Institute and their indications of "things we can do to build a sustainable society." Miller continues, "[t]he producers of *State of the World* do not provide theological grounds for their critique, but they do expect communities of faith to contribute to and support the vision of a different future."[3]

Miller's editorial concludes with a number of suggestions for the work of the church at this time of the turn of the millennium. Among these is a call for "rethinking creation with the help of Scripture." The present essay

---

Author's note: This essay is dedicated to Patrick D. Miller, whom I have known as helpful thesis reader, insightful teacher and author, patient editor, and good friend.
1. Patrick D. Miller, "The State of the World," *TT* 56 (1999) 147.
2. Ibid., 148.
3. Ibid., 148–49.

is intended as a response to Miller's call by offering an ecological reading of Psalm 147. By this I mean a consideration of the psalm that asks not only what it says about God, or about God and human beings, but about God, humans, and the earth and its creatures.[4]

II. Reflections on Psalm 147

¹Praise the LORD!
How good it is to sing praises to our God;
      for he is gracious, and a song of praise is fitting.
²The LORD builds up Jerusalem;
      he gathers the outcasts of Israel.
³He heals the brokenhearted,
      and binds up their wounds.
⁴He determines the number of the stars;
      he gives to all of them their names.
⁵Great is our Lord, and abundant in power;
      his understanding is beyond measure.
⁶The LORD lifts up the downtrodden;
      he casts the wicked to the ground.

⁷Sing to the LORD with thanksgiving;
      make melody to our God on the lyre.
⁸He covers the heavens with clouds,
      prepares rain for the earth,
      makes grass grow on the hills.
⁹He gives to the animals their food,
      and to the young ravens when they cry.
¹⁰His delight is not in the strength of the horse,
      nor his pleasure in the speed of a runner;
¹¹but the LORD takes pleasure in those who fear him,
      in those who hope in his steadfast love.

¹²Praise the LORD, O Jerusalem!
      Praise your God, O Zion!

---

4. Claus Westermann has been especially sensitive to what the Bible says about nature and to the importance of that material for Christian faith. For example, Westermann notes that Psalm 148 is seldom used in Christian worship because such worship deals almost exclusively with relationships between God and humans, and other creatures hardly ever appear. See his "Mensch, Tier und Pflanze in der Bibel," in *Gefährten und Feinde des Menschen: Das Tier in der Lebenswelt des alten Israel* (ed. Bernd Janowski, Ute Neumann-Gorsolke, and Uwe Gleßmer; Neukirchen-Vluyn: Neukirchener, 1993) 90–106.

¹³For he strengthens the bars of your gates;
    he blesses your children within you.
¹⁴He grants peace within your borders;
    he fills you with the finest of wheat.
¹⁵He sends out his command to the earth;
    his word runs swiftly.
¹⁶He gives snow like wool;
    he scatters frost like ashes.
¹⁷He hurls down hail like crumbs—
    who can stand before his cold?
¹⁸He sends out his word, and melts them;
    he makes his wind blow, and the waters flow.
¹⁹He declares his word to Jacob,
    his statutes and ordinances to Israel.
²⁰He has not dealt thus with any other nation;
    they do not know his ordinances.
Praise the LORD!

As the NRSV divisions indicate, the psalm divides into three parts. Each part is made up of the elements of a hymn, with a *call to praise* in the imperative mood, followed by *reasons for praise*. Each part also contains some *observations* about God.

Praise the Lord! (vv. 1–6)

Part 1 (vv. 1–6) begins with a *call to praise* in v. 1 ("Praise the LORD!"). The verse continues by offering an *observation* in praise of praise. My literal translation follows:

It is good to make melody [*zammĕrâ*] to our God
It is pleasant (to sing) fitting praise [*tĕhillâ*].

Verses 2 and 3 provide *reasons* for praising the Lord. The reasons have to do with the delivering act of the Lord who is rebuilding the capital city, bringing in those who had been exiled, and healing broken bodies and broken hearts. The references to gathering the outcasts (v. 2) and strengthening the city's defenses (v. 13a) point toward the period of rebuilding Jerusalem after the Babylonian exile.[5] The imagery here is that of a new exodus, bringing the exiles home to a land where children will grow up in safety and where there will be *šālōm,* that is, good crops, peace, and prosperity (v. 14).

---

5. Note that the same expression "outcasts of Israel" is used in reference to the gathering of exiles in Isa 11:12 and 56:8. The same word for "gathering" the exiles also occurs in Ezek 39:28.

There is no doubt about who is responsible for this new beginning. The subject of the verbs in vv. 2 and 3 is the Lord, the one who builds, gathers, heals, and binds up.

After this description of the Lord's actions in history, the psalm speaks of the Lord's work in nature as another *reason* for praise (v. 4). The Lord counts out (*mnh*; see Ps 90:12 for the same verb) a determined number of stars and names each one of them. Numbering and naming are indications that the Lord has power over these created entities (Gen 2:18–20).

In Hebrew, the statement in v. 5 stands out from its context as a nominal sentence. It offers a theological *observation*—a statement about God—that is of foundational importance for the entire psalm:

> Great is our Lord, and abundant in power;
>   his understanding is beyond measure.

The expression "our Lord" (cf. "our God" in v. 1) calls to mind the statement which frames another psalm that reflects on the heavens:

> O LORD, our Lord, how majestic is your name in all the earth.
>   (Ps 8:1, 9)

These comments about the power of the Lord in the realm of nature are followed by yet another *reason* for praise drawn from the Lord's work in the everyday arena of history: the Lord lifts up the beaten down and punishes the wicked (v. 6).

Sing to the Lord! (vv. 7–11)

This second segment of the psalm is made up of the same formal elements as the first. A pair of imperatives (*'ĕnû*, "sing"; *zammĕrû*, "make melody") constitute a *call to praise*, followed by *reasons for praise* (vv. 8–9), and the section concludes with an *observation* about God and people (vv. 10–11).

Of particular interest for the environmental theme are the *reasons* for singing praises given in vv. 8–9. This time, the reasons for praise have to do with the Lord and nature or the nurturing care of God.

The psalm speaks first about rain.[6] The Lord must prepare the rain carefully. The Lord sends a cloud cover, then the rain, with the result that the grass grows (v. 8; cf. the growth of choice wheat in v. 14b).

Second, the focus is on the animals. The Hebrew word *bĕhēmâ* ("animals") refers to both domestic and wild creatures.[7] But then the psalm focuses in on the most helpless of creatures, the young ravens:

---

6. Cf. the importance of water in Ps 104:5–16.
7. See *HALOT* 1:111–112; BDB 96–97.

> He gives to the animals their food,
>   and to the young ravens [*libnê ʿōrēb*] when they cry. (v. 9)

Young ravens are also mentioned in Job 38:41:

> Who provides for the raven [*lāʿōrēb*] its prey,
>   when its young ones [*yĕlādāw*] cry to God,
>   and wander about for lack of food?

The idea behind these verses is reflected in the widespread notion that raven parents abandon their young.[8] Since no one pays attention to the hungry cries of these tiny creatures, God hears them and feeds them. And thus we should praise God for this divine care for the least of God's creatures. The 12th–13th-century Jewish exegete David Kimchi, for example, supposed that this text referred to the fact that adult ravens left their young ones in trouble

> since these are white at birth and their mothers desert them and do not bring them their prey, for they imagine that they are not their offspring because they are white . . . and the Holy One, blessed be he, provides for them mosquitoes which they devour.[9]

Jesus, too, spoke of God's care for ravens:

> Consider the ravens: they neither sow nor reap, they have neither storehouse nor barn, and yet God feeds them. Of how much more value are you than birds! (Luke 12:24)

After this focus on God and the earth and its creatures, the psalm offers an *observation* on the Lord's relationship to people. God is not impressed by the strength of the sturdiest draft horse, nor the speed of the fastest runner. The Lord takes pleasure in those who place their confidence in the Lord's reliable love (*ḥesed*; vv. 10–11).

---

8. The notion of neglectful raven parents persists today. Note the contemporary German expressions *Rabenmutter, Rabenvater, Rabeneltern*, for parents who abandon their children. However, this charge of parental neglect against ravens appears to be untrue, at least for the modern raven. In a fascinating study, biologist and raven expert Bernd Heinrich identifies the biblical raven with the modern common raven, *Corvus corax* (*Ravens in Winter* [New York: Random House, 1989] 23). In an equally intriguing subsequent work, Heinrich observes that "Ravens are unjustly accused of being poor or uncaring parents because their young beg for food so noisily. Although hunger increases the volume of their begging yells, that volume is itself a product of natural selection" (idem, *Mind of the Raven* [New York: HarperCollins, 2000] 7).

9. Cited in Siegfried Risse's valuable treatment of this psalm, *"Gut ist es, unserem Gott zu singen": Untersuchungen zu Psalm 147, seiner Einbindung in das Schluss-Hallel und seinem Verständnis in der jüdischen und christlichen Tradition* (Münster: Oros Verlag, 1995) 255.

Praise the Lord, Jerusalem! (vv. 12–20)

The final section of the psalm is made up of a double *call to praise*, this time identifying those who should praise:

Praise [*šabbĕḥî*] the LORD, O Jerusalem!
Praise [*halĕlî*] your God, O Zion! (v. 12)

As in the other two sections, this call to praise is followed by *reasons* for praising (vv. 12–19) and an *observation* about the Lord and Israel in the context of all the nations (v. 20).

The psalm began by speaking about the delivering work of the Lord (vv. 2–3). Now it speaks of the Lord's activity of blessing (v. 13b) as a reason for praising.[10] First of all, the Lord provides a situation of security in Jerusalem so that children can grow up in safety and peace (vv. 13–14a). But it should be noted given our environmental theme that the focus then shifts to the Lord's blessings in the sphere of nature. The Lord provides fertility so that farmers can grow crops and produce food (v. 14b).

The theme of vv. 15–19 is the word of the Lord ("his word" in vv. 15, 18, 19). While the word of God can bring about events in history (Isa 9:8; 55:10–11; Jer 23:18–20), the emphasis here is on God's word and nature (cf. Genesis 1). That word causes snow and hail, frost and cold (vv. 16–17), but also times of warmth and thawing (v. 18). These weather phenomena affect all people (cf. Matt 5:45) or no people whatsoever (cf. Job 38:26). But God has also sent a special word to the people of Israel, namely the directives found in Israel's Scripture (v. 19).

This psalmist is given to generalizing theological *observations* (vv. 1b, 5, 10–11). After reflecting on the Lord's special relationship to Israel, the psalm concludes as it began with a call to "Praise the Lord!" (v. 20).

III. Psalm 147 and Psalms 146–150

The immediate literary context for Psalm 147 is the set of five psalms of praise that conclude the Psalter.

The Shape of Psalms 146–150

After a two-psalm introduction and five psalms of Lament (Psalms 3–7), the Book of Psalms concludes with five psalms of praise, each framed with "Praise the Lord" (*halĕlû yāh*). This concluding quintet is introduced by the closing lines of the alphabetical acrostic Psalm 145:

---

10. For the distinction between God's delivering and blessing work, see Claus Westermann, *Blessing in the Bible and the Life of the Church* (OBT; Philadelphia: Fortress, 1978).

My mouth will speak the praise of the LORD,
and all flesh will bless his holy name forever and ever. (Ps 145:21)

Psalm 145 promises that all flesh will praise the Lord; the next five psalms articulate the progressive fulfillment of that promise. Psalm 146 expresses the resolve of an individual, "I will praise" (v. 2). Psalm 147 calls upon the people of Jerusalem/Zion to praise (v. 12). Psalm 148 expands the call to praise to encompass all heavenly beings that the Lord has created (vv. 1–6) and then to all created entities in the heavens and on earth, including fire and frost, mountains, plant and animal life, as well as humans (vv. 7–12). With Psalm 149 the focus narrows, now calling upon the faithful (vv. 1, 5, 9) in Israel/Zion (v. 2) to praise. Finally, the invitation to praise expands to include "everything that breathes" (Ps 150:6). The shape of the Psalter, then, suggests that Psalm 147 is to be understood as a part of this "Concluding Hallel" that comprehensively includes all of creation in its summons to praise.

God in Psalms 146–150

What do Psalms 146–150 say about God? Psalms 146–148 speak much about God the *Creator*. The Lord has made heaven, earth, and the sea and its creatures (Ps 146:5–6) and has created the sun, moon, stars, and heavenly beings (Ps 148:5–6). The Lord has actually numbered and named the stars (Ps 147:4).

Some of these psalms also speak of the Lord as the *Caregiver* for all of creation. The Lord provides clouds and rain to make grass and wheat grow (Ps 147:8–9, 14b) and gives food to hungry people (Ps 146:7b) as well as to animals and young ravens (Ps 147:9). The Lord grants times of security, peace, and prosperity so that children can grow up well-nourished and in safety (Ps 147:13–14).

All five psalms also portray God as *Deliverer*, working God's purposes in the historical arena. The Lord executes justice, setting prisoners free (Ps 146:7) and rescuing those who have been in exile (Ps 147:2–3). The Lord gives special attention to the oppressed and hungry, the blind and the burdened, the stranger, the orphan and the widow (Ps 146:7–9), and the humble (Ps 149:4). The Lord punishes the wicked (Pss 146:9; 147:6), gives the Lord's people victory over their enemies (Pss 149:4–9; 148:14), and performs "mighty deeds" (Ps 150:2).

These references to the creating, caregiving, and delivering acts of God in history all function within the structure of these hymns, providing *reasons for praising* (Pss 147:2–3; 149:4–9; 148:14) or for being happy since their God is the God of Jacob (Ps 146:5–7).

Psalm 150 as a Concluding Summary

Finally, Psalm 150 offers a summary on the theme of praise. Who should be praised? God in God's sanctuary (v. 1). Why should God be praised? Because of God's mighty deeds and greatness (v. 2). How should God be praised? With all types of orchestral instruments, including brass, strings, and percussion (v. 3–5). And who should do the praising? Everything that breathes (v. 6).[11]

In sum, the five psalms concluding the Psalter are hymns expressing praise. The fundamental form of each of these hymns is a *call to praise* in the imperative mood coupled with *reasons for praising*. The call to praise is not directed only to human beings. All forms of plant and animal life, as well as other natural entities, including planetary and astral life in the entire universe, are considered together as created by God, and as such are exhorted to praise. Psalm 147, with its call to praise because of the Lord's creating, caregiving, and delivering work, fits well into the context of the Psalter's concluding quintet.

IV. Psalm 147 and the Environment[12]

The significance of Psalm 147 in the context of Miller's call for "rethinking creation with the help of Scripture" must now be addressed.

Two Biblical Models

Elsewhere I have suggested an ecological reading of Scripture that asks not only what the Bible says about God and humans, but about God, humans, and the earth and its creatures.[13] One may observe that the Bible ex-

---

11. See James Luther Mays, *Psalms* (Interpretation; Louisville: John Knox, 1994) 449–51.

12. From the vast sea of literature on religious dimensions of environmental issues, note especially the following: Thomas Berry, *The Dream of the Earth* (San Francisco: Sierra Club, 1988); Dieter T. Hessel, ed., *Theology for Earth Community: A Field Guide* (Maryknoll: Orbis, 1996); and Larry Rasmussen, *Earth Community and Earth Ethics* (Maryknoll: Orbis, 1996). On the Bible and environmental issues, see: Gene Tucker, "Rain on a Land Where No One Lives: The Hebrew Bible and the Environment," *JBL* 116 (1997) 3–17 (note the extensive bibliography there); Janowski, Neumann-Gorsolke, and Gleßmer, ed., *Gefährten und Feinde des Menschen*, passim; Bernd Janowski, "Auch die Tiere gehören zum Gottesbund: Gott, Mensch und Tier im alten Israel," and "Herrschaft über die Tiere: Gen 1,26–28 und die Semantik von *RDH*," in idem, *Die rettende Gerechtigkeit* (Neukirchen-Vluyn: Neukirchener, 1999) 3–32 and 33–48 (note the extensive bibliography on 27–32).

13. See, for example, James Limburg, "What Does It Mean to 'have dominion over the earth?'" *Dialog* 10 (1971) 221–23; idem, "The Responsibility of Royalty: Genesis 1–11 and the Care of the Earth," *WW* 11 (1991) 124–30; idem, "Who Cares for the Earth?:

hibits two basic models of the relationship between humans and the earth and its creatures. According to the "dominion over" model, human beings are charged with *responsibility for* the earth and its creatures. The "dominion over" language appears in Gen 1:26–28, Ps 8:6–8, and Wis 9:1–2. Genesis 2 expresses the notion of humans ruling over the rest of creation in terms of tilling and keeping the garden (2:15) and in the account of naming the animals (2:19–20). Yet another expression of humans ruling over the animals is found in the flood narrative where human beings organize, rescue, and set free the animals in the ark (Genesis 6–9).

Alongside this "dominion over" model, the Bible also articulates the notion of the commonality that humans have with the rest of creation — what might be designated the "solidarity with" model. This is especially true for the relationship between humans and animals: both are creatures of the sixth day of creation and both are referred to the same table for food (Gen 1:26–30). Human beings have in common with the animals the fact that both were made of the same raw material (*'ădāmâ*, "the ground," Gen 2:7–9, 19) and that both are animated by the same "breath of life" (Gen 1:30; 2:7). In fact, the Hebrew name for the individual man or for humankind as a whole, *'ādām*, links human beings to the earth or ground, *'ădāmâ*.[14] There are further hints at commonality between humans and animals: both went together into Noah's ark and came out of the ark together (Genesis 6–9). In Psalm 104, humans do not rule over the other creatures, but simply appear among them. In fact, human beings appear quite late in Psalm 104, first mentioned only with v. 14.[15]

Humans and the Environment in Psalms 146–150

In Psalms 146–150, the *solidarity* that humans have with the earth and its creatures is stressed. In the framework of each psalm, humans are exhorted to praise. But this summons to praise is not directed exclusively to humans. Other created things are also called to praise: sea monsters, lions and tigers, cows and sheep, snakes and eagles, even hills and mountains, apple

---

Psalm Eight and the Environment," *Word and World Supplement 1* (1992) 43–52; and idem, "Down to Earth Theology: Psalm 104 and the Environment," *CurTM* 21 (1994) 340–46.

14. The same link is reflected in the words "human/humus" and "earthling/earth." See Patrick D. Miller, Jr., *Genesis 1–11: Studies in Structure and Theme* (JSOTSup 8; Sheffield: JSOT Press, 1978) 37–42; and Phyllis Trible, *God and the Rhetoric of Sexuality* (OBT; Philadelphia: Fotress, 1978) 75–82.

15. Rüdiger Bartelmus ("Die Tierwelt in der Bibel I," in Janowski, Neumann-Gorsolke, and Gleßmer, ed., *Gerfährten und Fiende des Menschen*, 269) writes, "When the poet finally speaks of humans beings in v. 14, this is not as the 'crown of creation,' but as an equal among equals as the synonymous parallelism clearly indicates: 'You cause grass to grow for the cattle, and plants for people to use'" (my translation).

trees and cedars (Ps 148:7–10)! When it comes to praising God, humans, apparently, are nothing special!

This sense of *solidarity* in praise extends even beyond the earth: angels, sun and moon, and shining stars are all part of the chorus of those praising God. "All God's children got a place in the choir" declares the old song. These psalms are even more inclusive. The choir of praisers includes all God's human children, but also God's other creatures and all things that exist on the earth and even in the universe. These, too, are God's children! All of us, the whole family on our "blue planet," (and elsewhere as well) are in this together![16]

Psalm 147 and the Environment

And now what of Psalm 147? What does it say about God, humans, and the earth and its creatures?

The theme of human "solidarity with" the rest of creation is sounded clearly. Just as the Lord is shown to be a Caregiver by providing food for humans ("he fills you," v. 14), the Lord is also a Caregiver for the animals, even the helpless young ravens (vv. 8–9), by providing food for them as well. The divine word is sent to Israel in the form of written directives (v. 19) and to the earth in the form of the nurturing cycle of the seasons (vv. 15–18). God's people and God's earth are both addressed by the same word from God (vv. 15–19).

One hears little of the "dominion over" theme in Psalm 147. Perhaps one could imagine that the "statutes and ordinances" express this theme (v. 19). But like the other psalms in the grouping 146–150, the emphasis is on the fact that humans, along with the earth and its creatures, are all together in the great scheme of life unfolding on this planet. These psalms are a reminder that all of us sharing this earth are interdependent.

This is an important reminder in the context of conditions on our planet at the beginning of the third millennium as reported in *State of the World 1999*. When our planet loses its forests (the lungs of the planet) or topsoil (the food provider) or clean water or air or varieties of species, then the whole earth is impoverished. We are family. All of us who call spaceship earth our home are in this together!

---

16. Terence Fretheim ("Nature's Praise of God in the Psalms," *Ex Auditu* 3 [1987] 17, 23, 27) comments on praise of God from the non-human world: "one has to be converted into a mode of perceiving reality that, at the least, is less anthropocentric and more inclusive of the value of the nonhuman for the world and for God. . . . Each entity has its own distinctiveness and complementarity in praising according to its intrinsic capacity and fitness. . . . But each is also part of the one world of God contributing to the whole. The model of the symphony orchestra comes to mind. . . . Inarticulateness does not disqualify one from praise. At the human level one thinks of praise offered by those who dance or play musical instruments."

At the center of this psalm, amid the sounds of musical productions in the temple (vv. 1, 7) and wind and rain and hail in the countryside (vv. 8; 17–18), is the sound of the desperate crying of a nestful of hungry young ravens (v. 9). Even though the parents of these creatures may be neglectful (or *seem* that way), says the psalmist, our God is not. The Lord who brought the exiles home, who set the stars in the sky and moves the clouds across the heavens, who sends hail and snow and cold, who communicates by his word, this is the God who hears the cry of the hungry young ravens and responds by providing them with food. The voice of the young raven is, therefore, somehow at the center of this psalm.

And should a Bible reader at some midnight dreary, pondering "weak and weary, over many a quaint and curious volume of forgotten lore . . ."— should some such Bible reader ask whether the Lord might forget to feed those tiny birds, or whether the steadfast love of this God (v. 11) could ever fail, that faithful Bible reader might be surprised to hear, in the quiet of that midnight hour, a mysterious, rasping, haunting, voice declaring but one word:

"Nevermore."[17]

---

17. See Edgar Allen Poe, "The Raven," in idem, *The Tell-tale Heart and Other Writings* (New York: Bantam, 1982) 396.

Prayer and/as Self-Address:
The Case of Hannah

J. Gerald Janzen

———◆———

I. Introduction

Among biblical women, Hannah is most often celebrated for the song she sings after the birth of Samuel (1 Sam 2:1–10). But her earlier prayers in distress (1 Sam 1:3–18), though indicated only indirectly, are the human foundation of her subsequent song. Her movement from prayer in distress to song of praise parallels the movement in psalms of individuals (e.g., Psalms 22; 116), and the movement of her ancestors from the cries and groanings of the Israelites in Egypt (Exod 2:23–25) to the hymn of praise after the deliverance at the sea (Exod 15:1–21). This same movement marks the book of Psalms as a whole. Although in this last example the movement oscillates between complaint and praise, nevertheless, after the opening two psalms, the psalter continues with the next dozen or so psalms voicing various kinds of individual or communal cries for help, and it closes with a virtually unbroken series of psalms of thanksgiving and praise.

Hannah's life, then, as it comes to expression in her prayers, exhibits in miniature the pattern that marks the life of Israel as a whole. In this paper, I wish to examine one aspect of her prayer, namely, her speaking to herself in 1 Sam 1:13, and to bring that into sharper focus through close attention to the Hebrew idiom, *dibbēr ʿal lēb* (RSV: "speaking in her heart"; NRSV: "silently"). As I will show, this idiom, though distinctive in its application to Hannah, fittingly connects this aspect of her prayer to the frequent appearance of "self-address" in the Psalms and in other biblical prayers.

Author's note: Since our first semester together, in the 1959 Fall Seminar of G. E. Wright and F. M. Cross, Patrick D. Miller and I have discovered again and again the truth of Prov 27:17: "Iron sharpens iron, and one person sharpens the wits of another." I offer this essay in celebration of Miller's own scholarship and of his gifts as a wit-sharpening editor of the work of so many others.

II. Comfort: God's and the Self's

The notion of self-address in prayer appears within the context of one of the recurrent images for the divine-human relation, God's parental care for people. In Ps 27:10, the psalmist cries out, "If my father and mother forsake me, / the LORD will take me up."[1] In exile, Zion cries out, "The LORD has forsaken me, my Lord has forgotten me," and God answers,

> Can a woman forget her nursing child,
>   or show no compassion for the child of her womb?
> Even these may forget,
>   yet I will not forget you. (Isa 49:14–15)

The image of parental divine compassion and care, implicit in Psalm 27 and clear in Isaiah 49, is elaborated in Isa 66:10–13:

> Rejoice with Jerusalem, and be glad for her,
>   all you who love her;
> rejoice with her in joy,
>   all you who mourn over her—
> that you may nurse and be satisfied
>   from her consoling breast;
> that you may drink deeply with delight
>   from her glorious bosom.
> For thus says the LORD:
> I will extend prosperity to her like a river,
>   and the wealth of the nations like an overflowing stream;
> and you shall nurse and be carried on her arm,
>   and dandled on her knees.
> As a mother comforts her child,
>   so I will comfort you;
> you shall be comforted in Jerusalem.

This parental image of the relation between God and Israel accords with the relation between God as *'Ēl Šadday* and Israel's ancestors in Genesis. There, *'Ēl Šadday* is the giver of the blessings of heaven above and the earth beneath, blessings of breast and womb (Gen 49:25), and is invoked (Gen 43:14; answered in 43:29–30) as the divine source of compassion.[2] These themes of nurture and compassion converge in Isa 66:10–13. The act of nursing in response to the infant's cry of hunger is itself an act of com-

---

1. Modifications of the NRSV are identified by an asterisk.
2. See the contribution by Sakenfeld in this volume.

passion. So the divine compassion extended to Israel in exile is movingly imaged as a mother soothing a distraught child at the breast and playing with it on her knees.

Psalm 131 presents this image of divine parental care, as well as the issue of "self-address" in prayer, that lies at the center of my argument. The psalmist finds herself in a state of perplexity that threatens to overwhelm her. Frequently in the psalms, such perplexity arises because the psalmist, though protesting innocence, is accused by others of suffering affliction on account of some wrongdoing. If that is the case with this woman, she may be compared with Job.[3]

For his part, Job counters the accusations of his friends with protestations of innocence and accusations against God—against *'Ēl Šadday*, the name by which God is so frequently designated in this book.[4] When God finally answers him out of the whirlwind (in part as *'Ēl Šadday*; see 40:1), Job realizes that the issues he has been wrestling with cannot be humanly fathomed. So he confesses—in words like those in Psalm 131—"I have uttered what I did not understand, / things too wonderful for me, which I did not know" (42:3). In saying this, he may be said to rediscover the wisdom hidden in the proverb, "Trust in the LORD with all your heart, / and do not rely on your own insight" (Prov 3:5). The wisdom tradition repeatedly calls on people to forsake naiveté and vigorously to seek wisdom. But, as this proverb warns, the danger is that humans may come to rely on the wisdom they have acquired, and forget that human understanding must sooner or later give way to unreserved trust in God's wisdom and goodness.

How long has it taken the woman of Psalm 131 to arrive at the resolve, "I do not occupy myself with things too great and too marvelous for me" (v. 1)? And how does she arrive there? Perhaps by hearing God's direct spoken response to her repeated cries, the way Job finally did? I think not. Psalm 131 traces a different path than the straightforward one of human distress,

---

3. Patrick D. Miller discusses connections between Psalm 131 and Job 42:1–6 in his *They Cried to the Lord: The Form and Theology of Biblical Prayer* (Fortress Press: Minneapolis, 1994) 239–43. This follows immediately on his discussion of Hannah's prayer and hymn in 1 Samuel 1–2 (pp. 237–39). I am indebted to Miller especially for his translation of Psalm 131, which is adopted in this paper. For further recent scholarly work on this psalm, see his references (pp. 414–15).

4. Of its forty-eight occurrences in the Old Testament, *Šadday* (or *'Ēl Šadday*) occurs seven times in Priestly contexts relating to Israel's ancestors, and thirty-one times in the book of Job. The other ten occurrences are scattered in other contexts. The two occurrences in Ruth 1:20–21 relate to existential issues similar to those in the ancestral narratives, 1 Samuel 1, and the book of Job. For a brief exploration of Job and Naomi as existential counterparts, and for further discussion of the significance of *Šadday* themes and their bearing on Job's dilemma, see my essay, "Lust for Life and the Bitterness of Job," *TT* 55 (1998) 152–62. Cf. also Sakenfeld's contribution in this volume.

direct divine response, and human consolation derived from that response. That path is laid out in v. 2: "I have calmed and quieted my soul, / like a weaned child with ['al] its mother; / my soul is like the weaned child that is with ['al] me." The psalmist does not speak of God calming and quieting her soul. She speaks of calming and quieting *her own soul*.

She accomplishes this calming through the activity of self-address. The image of the *weaned* child is critically important to understanding how such self-address can provide comfort for a soul in a situation of distress. In Isaiah 66, the comfort that comes to Zion is likened to the comfort extended to a nursling (a *yônēq*). A weaned child (*gāmûl*) does not cease to seek comfort from its mother, but it receives that comfort in a different way. It may come to its mother and still be taken up into her bosom, but something has begun to replace the consolation of the nursing breast. At one stage, a "pacifier" or "soother" serves as a transitional means of comfort. The mother (or father or older sibling) may extend the soother to the child, but eventually the child will place the soother in its own mouth. Later still, the child may resort to some personally selected equivalent, such as a blanket.

What is happening here? Psychologists speak of the process by which the child internalizes the inter-personal dynamic of soothing, so that what originally was the mother's soothing of the child becomes the child's *self*-soothing. As the mother had soothed the child, so now the child sooths itself; yet the self-soothing remains in some sense a drawing upon the soothing extended to it by the mother.[5] A dramatic example of this occurred in the midst of a near-tragedy in Midland, Texas in 1987 when 18-month-old Jessica McClure fell down an old abandoned well. Because of the danger of a cave-in, the rescue dragged on for hours. In the meantime, rescuers lowered a two-way microphone into the well to offer reassurance to the presumably terrified child. To their amazement, instead of a terrified child, they found a reasonably calm little girl who they heard singing to herself songs that her mother had often sung to her.

So it is, I suggest, in Psalm 131. The woman says to God that she cannot fathom the issues that trouble her; but she has calmed and quieted her soul "like a weaned child with its mother; my soul is like the weaned child that is with me." As Miller notes, the preposition (*'al*) repeated in these two lines has the basic meaning, "upon," so that the child here may not be sim-

---

5. In *Playing and Reality* (Routledge: London and New York, 1989), D. W. Winnicott discusses weaning as a psycho-social process involving, among other things, the child's movement from being soothed in breast-feeding to its ability to soothe itself by means of what he calls "transitional objects." As the following story shows, the "transitional object" may take the form of songs or words learned from the mother and now recited to oneself.

ply "with" its mother, but *on* her lap or bosom.[6] That, indeed, is precisely how this preposition works in Isa 66:12: "you shall nurse and be carried *on* [*ʿal*] her arm, and dandled *on* [*ʿal*] her knees." The weaned child of Psalm 131 no longer nurses, but it can still be held; and as the mother holds it, she observes it becoming quiet.

Deeply troubled by something she cannot understand, the psalmist notices what any observant parent notices in such a situation: while, on the one hand, the calming and quieting is an interpersonal process, on the other it is also a process internal to the child. As the mother reflects on how the child calms and quiets itself within her embrace, she calms and quiets herself, as it were, on God's bosom, trusting in God with all her heart, and relying not on her own insight. Then she turns to her community, calling on it to "hope in the LORD / from this time on and forevermore" (Ps 131:13). If she thus extends her comfort to others, it is by calling on them to calm and quiet their own soul in times of distress. This is not simply an exhortation to "boot-strap" self-help; nor is it simply passive acquiescence in God's sustaining help. It is a mode of that fathomless mystery where the human spirit and the divine spirit commune together, at a depth that lies beyond human understanding.[7]

III. Self-Encouragement in the Worship of God

This way of viewing Psalm 131 may illuminate a similar dynamic of self-address in prayer found in Psalm 42–43 (understood here as a single prayer-text). The psalmist begins by voicing a soul-thirst for God and a longing to see God's face. But in place of God's satisfaction of that thirst (as in Isa 66:11), the psalmist can only drink his own tears. Yet even as he does so, he assuages his thirst also with the memory of his participation in processions to God's house, processions filled with so many people's glad shouts and songs of thanksgiving that he was buoyed along joyfully by them. Encouraged by this memory of communal buoyant song, he may be said to calm and quiet his soul like the woman in Psalm 131:

> Why are you cast down, O my soul,
> and why are you disquieted within me?

---

6. Miller, *They Cried to the Lord*, 239.

7. The best discussion of this mystery known to me occurs in S. T. Coleridge, *Aids to Reflection* (ed. John Beer; Princeton: Princeton University Press, 1993) 78–79. In this passage, Coleridge explores the implications of Rom 8:26, and arrives at his famous description of the "unknown distance" between the deepest reach of human consciousness and the depth of the human spirit where the "first acts and movements of our own will" interact with the Spirit of God.

Hope in God; for I shall again praise him,
    my help and my God. (Ps 42:5)

The exhortation to "hope in God" which the woman in Ps 131:3 directs
toward Israel, the speaker in Psalm 42–43 directs to himself. He is both the
encourager and the one being encouraged; and the source of the encouragement is the sustaining recollection of previously being borne along and
participating in the worship that ended in God's house where his soul in
the past had slaked its thirst and he had beheld the face of God. Having internalized that earlier communal dynamic, he is able to reenact it within
himself when he is cut off from his community and feels cut off from God.
What is especially noteworthy is the oscillation between distress and self-
comfort, as the refrain of 42:5 recurs in 42:11 and 43:5.

The repeated self-address is not simply a soliloquy, but occurs within a
psalm that begins as address to God (42:1) and approaches its end in the
same way (43:4). The self-address and the third person references to God
are embraced within, and thereby are an integral part of, the address to
God. Just as the weaned child's self-calming in Psalm 131 draws on the internalized calming of the nursing mother, and occurs on her bosom, so the
very ability of this psalmist to call on himself to hope in God is derived
from earlier hope-filled communal songs of assurance, and takes place
within the bosom of his address to God. These two Psalms, then, 131 and
42–43, should alert us not to interpret third-person awareness of God in
the midst of prayer, or self-address in that context, as lapses from the spirit
of prayer, but as integral aspects of it. Such prayer dynamics are one aspect
of the "weaning" that is part of the spiritual growth that biblical religion
calls its adherents to, a weaning in the course of which, as the mother's
comfort is internalized, distress is transmuted into trust.[8]

What we may call the self-relation in prayer is present graphically in
Psalms 131 and 42–43. This aspect of prayer is present much more perva-
sively, if less obviously, in the psalms than often meets the eye of readers of
modern English translations. We have already seen that Psalm 131 ends with
a call to Israel, in the imperative voice, to hope in the LORD; and we have
seen that in Psalm 42–43 this call is self-directed. It is typical in the Psalms
that parallel to this self-directed call, the speaker may, by the use of the plural imperative, call likewise upon others. So, for example, the exhortations
in Psalm 100 are all in the plural imperative. But in another standard form,
the speakers include themselves among the persons being exhorted. This
form uses verbs in the cohortative mood, or first-person indirect impera-

───────────────

8. Viewed in this context, the book of Job testifies to the stringent conditions under
which such weaning is sometimes undergone.

tive. The plural form of the cohortative mood (e.g., "Let us sing unto the LORD") is used to exhort one's cohorts *and oneself* to engage in some action. Psalm 95 provides a good example. A second-person imperative, "O come" (vv. 1, 6) is followed by reiterated first-person plural cohortatives, "let us" (vv. 2–3, 6). But the cohortative can also occur in the singular, "let me . . . ." In such a usage, "the *cohortative* expresses the direction of the will to an action and thus denotes especially self-encouragement (in the 1st plural an exhortation to others at the same time), a resolution or a wish, as an *optative*."9 The singular form of the cohortative occurs frequently in psalms of individual complaint or praise. From over fifty instances, we may note the following examples.

Psalm 146 opens with the plural imperative call to "Praise the LORD" (in earlier parlance, "Praise ye the LORD"). But whereas in Psalms 148, 149, and 150 this opening call is followed by repeated verbs in the plural imperative, in Psalm 146 the call is re-directed inward to the speaker, with the singular imperative, "Praise the LORD, O my soul," followed immediately by the singular cohortative, "Let me praise the LORD as long as I live; let me sing praises to my God while I have any being."* Psalm 103 opens with the re-iterated singular imperative, "Bless the LORD, O my soul; / and all that is within me, bless his holy name." At the end, after a series of plural imperatives calling various creatures to "bless the LORD," the psalm ends as it began, "Bless the LORD, O my soul." Psalm 104 opens like 103, but unlike Psalm 103, at the end it shifts to a series of singular cohortative verbs:

> Let me sing to the LORD as long as I live;
>> Let me sing praise to my God while I have being.
> May my meditation [*śîaḥ*] be pleasing to him,
>> for I rejoice in the LORD.* (Ps 104:33–34)

One common call to praise involves the imperative plural use of the verb "sing" (*šîr*). It first appears on the lips of Miriam, who calls to Moses and all Israel, in Exod 15:21, "Sing [pl.] to the LORD, for he has triumphed gloriously." As I have argued elsewhere, it is this call which evokes the song in 15:1–18, a song which begins, "Let me sing unto the LORD, for he has triumphed gloriously."*10 In this instance, the imperative call of Miriam and her sister song-leaders evokes an individualized response in Moses and the

---

9. GKC §48e (emphasis theirs).

10. Exod 15:19–21 is introduced in Hebrew (and in earlier English translations) by the conjunction "for," and functions as an *analepsis* which belatedly gives the reason for the singing in 15:1–18. This *analepsis* (working like "for" in Gen 20:18) is obscured in the NRSV which omits the "for." For fuller discussion, see my paper, "Song of Moses, Song of Miriam: Who is Seconding Whom?" *CBQ* 54 (1992) 211–20.

people of Israel. We have already seen how, in Psalm 146, this call-and-response can occur within the individual psalmist. When we see this verb, "let me sing," sprinkled some ten times throughout the Psalms, and this same cohortative form, "let me," of other verbs likewise so sprinkled, we may conclude that the act of self-encouragement in worship of God, as an internalization of the call from others to such worship, is characteristic of biblical prayer.

Whether directed to others or to oneself, the call to praise most naturally arises in response to some helping action of God. But it can also occur in the midst of trouble or distress, prior to the appearance or the assurance of such help. Psalm 57 opens with a plea for God's help when surrounded by enemies, a plea punctuated by an assertion of confidence in that help (v. 3) and ending, even before help arrives, in a self-directed call to praise (vv. 7–9). The imagery in this call is striking:

> My heart is steadfast, O God,
>   my heart is steadfast.
> Let me sing and make melody.
>   Awake, my soul!
> Awake, O harp and lyre!
>   Let me awake the dawn.
> Let me give thanks to you, O Lord, among the peoples;
>   Let me sing praises to you among the nations.*

The imagery shows the psalmist engaging in an act of praise while still in an embattled situation. The soul will not be wakened to praise by the dawning of God's help. Rather, while the psalmist still lies in existential darkness, he will rouse his soul from its sleep; and his soul, moved to praise, will waken his instrument; and by this means he will awake the dawning of the Lord's favor.

As this psalm shows, the self-directed call to praise is not simply a response to divine action, it can become a prayer initiative in the midst of trouble. We see this again in Psalm 13, which begins with the desperate cry, "How long, O Lord? Will you forget me for ever?" Acknowledging that God alone can intervene lest he sleep the sleep of death (v. 3), the psalmist somehow finds the ability to rouse himself to praise (vv. 5–6):

> But I have trusted in your steadfast love;
>   my heart shall rejoice in your salvation.
> Let me sing to the Lord,
>   because he has dealt bountifully with me.*

Sometimes the self-directed call in the midst of distress is not a call to praise but a call not to lose heart or lose confidence in God. Psalm 25 begins,

To you, O Lord, I lift up my soul.
O my God, in you I trust,
>   let me not be put to shame;
>   let not my enemies exult over me.
Let none who wait for you be put to shame;
>   let them be ashamed who are wantonly treacherous.*
>   (Ps 25:1–3)[11]

The cry to God for help is accompanied by an assertion of trust in God. And this assertion is followed by a self-directed cry of encouragement not to become ashamed, not to allow the enemy's treacherous and hateful exultations against the psalmist (vv. 2–3, 19) to become overwhelming. It is they, instead, who should be ashamed. It is easy to allow the hateful tauntings of one's enemies to prevail over one's own sense of acceptance before God. So the continuing appeal to God for help is punctuated again by the call to oneself not to become ashamed by them, but rather to take refuge from them in God (v. 20).[12]

The same pattern is seen in Jeremiah. Beleaguered by those who resist his prophetic message, Jeremiah calls on God for help, and affirms God as his refuge (Jer 17:14–17). Then he cries out:

Let my persecutors be put to shame,
>   but let me not be put to shame;
let them be dismayed,
>   but let me not be dismayed.* (Jer 17:18)[13]

This is his faithful response to God's exhortation to him in the context of his call to the prophetic task:

But you, gird up your loins; stand up and tell them everything that I command you. Do not be dismayed by them, or I will dismay you before them. And I for my part have made you today a fortified city, an iron pillar, and a bronze wall, against the whole land—against the kings of Judah, its princes, its priests, and the people of the land. They will fight against you; but they shall not prevail against you, for I am with you, says the Lord, to deliver you.* (Jer 1:17–19)

---

11. The third-person Hebrew verbs translated "Let none/Let them" are grammatically jussive and function as third-person indirect imperatives. The nrsv's "Do not let me" obscures the self-directed address here.

12. Other examples of this pattern include Pss 31:1–2, 11–18; 71:1.

13. The nrsv's "Do not let me be ashamed/dismayed" obscures the self-directed address.

On the one hand, Jeremiah is given God's assurance of protection against his enemies. On the other hand, he must appropriate that assurance; and one way in which he is able to do that is to refuse to allow his enemies' opposition and plots against him to throw him into such dismay that he abandons his calling. When, then, in chapter 17 he affirms God as his refuge, he also calls on himself not to be dismayed and not to be put to shame.

IV. *sîaḥ: The Means of Self-Encouragement*

I have been exploring ways in which the act of prayer can include aspects of self-address that have the aim of encouraging one's self in a stance of faithful trust in God despite circumstances. One Hebrew word that includes this connotation (a term which appears on Hannah's lips) is the verb *sîaḥ* and its cognate nouns. We have already encountered this word in Ps 104:33–34:

> Let me sing to the LORD as long as I live;
>   Let me sing praise to my God while I have being.
> May my meditation [*sîaḥ*] be pleasing to him,
>   for I rejoice in the LORD.*

BDB offers the following meanings for the verb: "1. Complain; 2. Muse, meditate upon, study; 3. Talk about, sing."[14] As these summary definitions indicate, the word can be used to indicate a variety of moods and activities in various situations. Most often, what one muses or meditates on, or sings and talks about, is either God's *tôrâ* (so, repeatedly, in Psalm 119) or something God has made or done in the past that evokes thanks and praise (Judg 5:10; Pss 105:2; 143:5; 145:5; Prov 6:22). But frequently the speaker is in distress, and here the word is typically translated "complaint" or "mediation" (in which case I take the psalmist's troubles to be the *focus* or the *basis* of the meditation) (see Pss 55:2, 17; 64:1; 77:3, 6, 12; 142:2; Job 7:11, 13; 9:27; 10:1; 21:4; 23:2; Prov 23:29). In these passages, I would suggest that *sîaḥ* does not refer simply to the psalmist's complaint or trouble as such, but also to the psalmist's appeal to the character and the prior actions of God as a basis for God's hoped-for action in the present. The occurrences in Psalm 77 are particularly noteworthy. The psalmist, deeply distressed over some personal situation, has been crying out to God for a long time, and refuses either to give up or to accept false comfort. Three times he uses the verb *sîaḥ*; and the contexts suggest its rich range of meaning (cohortative singular verbs are marked with a †):

---

14. BDB 966–67. The definitions and discussions in *HALOT* 3:1319–21 and *TWAT* 8:757–61 are similar, but fuller, with bibliography of more recent analyses of the root.

I †think of [literally: *remember*] God, and I †moan;
    I †meditate [*sîaḥ*], and my spirit faints. (77:3)
I consider the days of old,
    and †*remember* the years of long ago.
I commune with my heart in the night;
    I †meditate [*sîaḥ*] and search my spirit. (77:5–6)
I will call to mind [literally: *remember*] the deeds of the LORD;
    I will †*remember* your wonders of old.
I will meditate on all your work,
    and †muse [*sîaḥ*] on your mighty deeds. (77:11–12)

Here, the verb *sîaḥ* describes a deep inner wrestling that moves the psalmist at times to cry aloud (v. 1), at times to moan inarticulately (v. 3), and at times to descend into soundless agony (v. 4). At the heart of the agony is the tension between the psalmist's experience and conviction of God's steadfast love and compassion and the absence of any sign of that love and compassion in the present situation. What is it that sustains the psalmist, that moves him to cry out unwearyingly and to refuse any false comfort (cf. Jer 6:14)? It is the recollection of what God has done in the past (Ps 77:13–20). This recollection is not a passive recall—it is an intentional act, carried out in a spirit of self-exhortation and self-encouragement. This is indicated in part by the repeated use of the singular cohortative form of the marked verbs. It is indicated also by the psalmist's self-dialogue, as he communes with his heart, mediates, and searches his spirit. When his heart or spirit questions whether God has spurned and forgotten him forever (vv. 7–9), he comforts and encourages himself with recollections of God's wonders of old (vv. 11–20).

That such activity, however plaintive, is an act of loyalty and trust in God is underscored in the book of Job. This sufferer repeatedly uses terms that we will hear on Hannah's lips, as he says, "I will not restrain my mouth; I will speak in the anguish of my spirit; I will complain [*sîaḥ*] in the bitterness of my soul" (Job 7:11; similarly 10:1; 23:2; cf. 7:13; 21:4). From the connotations of *sîaḥ* in Psalm 77, we may suppose that Job's *sîaḥ* included both references to God's past benevolent actions (e.g., Job 29), and the absence of any sign of God's benevolence in the present (e.g., Job 30). And the pervasive presence of such complaints in the psalms and elsewhere would suggest that they, no less than praise, are a sign of one's loyalty and trust in God.[15] But Job's friends think he has gone too far. As Bildad asserts in 15:4,

---

15. On the psalms of complaint as expressions of loyalty and trust, see James Luther Mays, *The Lord Reigns: A Theological Handbook to the Psalms* (Louisville: Westminster/John Knox, 1994) esp. 23–39.

"You are doing away with the fear of God, / and hindering meditation [*śîaḥ*] before God." Job is not the only one to have his *śîaḥ* misinterpreted. As the psalms attest, and as we shall see in the case of Hannah, the struggles of the soul with God and with itself before God can be badly misread by the very persons one might have hoped would read them aright.

V. Hannah's Meditation and Self-Address

Like Sarah, Rebekah, Rachel, and Tamar before her, Hannah is childless. Her plight is economic, religious, and social. Without children, she is vulnerable to economic hardship if her husband dies, she lacks the most palpable evidence of the favor of the God who is giver of the "blessings of breast and womb," and she is vulnerable to the condescending pity and belittling contempt of other women—especially her co-wife, Peninnah—who have themselves received such blessing in abundance.

The occurrence of several terms in the standard vocabulary of complaint, both in the narrative and on Hannah's lips, identifies her prayer as typical of anyone in distress. She weeps and she fasts (1 Sam 1:7–8); she is sad in heart (v. 8), bitter in soul (v. 10; RSV and NRSV: "deeply distressed"), hard pressed in spirit (v. 15; RSV and NRSV: "sorely troubled"), and afflicted (v. 11). She persists in prayer (v. 12) with great intensity, weeping copiously (v. 10) and pouring out her soul before God (v. 15), until, finally, she makes a vow, promising that if God will give her a child she will dedicate it in life-long Nazirite service (v. 11). As she says in response to Eli's obtuse challenge, "I have been speaking out of my great anxiety [*śîaḥ*] and vexation all this time" (v. 16). This vexation (*ka'as*) may arise over her economic vulnerability and her sense of neglect at God's hands; but the sharpness of its bite comes from Peninnah, her rival (*ṣārâ*, v. 6). In its masculine form (*ṣār*) this latter word occurs over two dozen times in psalms of complaint or psalms of thanksgiving for deliverance, where it is a term for the psalmist's adversary (e.g., Pss 3:1; 13:4; 27:2; 78:42). We may suspect that, like many adversaries in the psalms, and like Job's friends, Peninnah falsely accuses Hannah of some personal failing as the reason for her plight.

In all this, Hannah is presented as typical of the faithful Israelite at prayer amid prolonged distress. But two items of description are distinctive to her. First, her adversary's severe provocation[16] causes her, not simply to become irritated (v. 6 RSV, NRSV), but literally, "to thunder."[17] A bold

---

16. Or "vexing," v. 6. Note verbal *kā'as*, like nominal *ka'as*, "vexation," in v. 16.

17. I see no reason to take *har'îm* (*hip'il* of *r'm*) as textually problematic. It is a vivid figure for Hannah's cry of complaint. As such, it resembles the usage of the verb *šā'ag*. The latter verb and its cognate noun refer literally to the roaring of a lion; but figuratively it can refer to the activity of rapacious rulers, foreign invaders, and Israel's God in

image! In the Bible, the figurative use of the verb, "to thunder" aptly images God's self-revelation to creation or against God's foes (e.g., 1 Sam 2:10; 11:10). But it can also characterize creation's address to God in praise (Pss 96:11; 98:7; RSV and NRSV, "Let the sea roar"). Hannah's thundering is not in praise but in complaint.[18] By this bold image she appears as a soul mate of Job who is portrayed as a roaring lion (Job 3:24, where NRSV "groanings" translates *šĕʾāgâ*, a word usually indicating the roaring of a lion), a braying ass, and a bellowing ox (Job 6:5).

Before we examine the second peculiar phrase, we may note that Hannah applies to herself the word *śîaḥ*. RSV and NRSV render this noun, "anxiety" (v. 16). I take the term to refer not simply to her anxiety but to the whole range of her prayer activity, an activity whose range has been canvassed above and is exemplified in Psalm 77. In this activity, the person in distress appeals to God for help, questions God's faithfulness, asserts continuing trust in God, calls to mind God's goodness as manifest in previous acts of blessing or deliverance, and, addressing to oneself communally-learned words of reassurance and comfort, rouses oneself to continue in prayer and even praise in the midst of affliction.[19] That her use of the word *śîaḥ* carries so rich a connotation—including self-soothing—is supported by the second phrase applied to her in a novel way, *dibbēr ʿal lēb*.

The narrator tells us that Eli observes Hannah's mouth. The NRSV translates, "She was praying silently," while RSV, closer to the Hebrew idiom, translates, "She was speaking in her heart" (v. 13). Neither is precise. The Hebrew idiom, *dibbēr ʿal lēb*, in all its other occurrences conveys a quite specific connotation. A speaker, seeking to assuage the grief, allay the anxiety, reassure the guilty fearfulness or mollify the outraged indignation of another party, literally "speaks upon [ʿal] the heart" of that party. At times (as in Gen 50:21; Isa 40:1–2) the accompanying verb *niḥam* describes the speaker as seeking to convey "comfort." In its other ten occurrences in the Old Testament, this idiom indicates the reassuring address of one party to another.[20] Only here, in 1 Sam 1:13, are speaker and addressee *one and the same* person. Conventional translations such as "speaking in her heart," or "praying silently," obscure what Hannah is doing here.[21] In using this idiom

judgment or redemption. The storm theophany in Job 37:4 portrays God as both roaring (*šāʾag*) and thundering (*harʿîm*). If intense, perhaps even aggressive human cries to God in distress can be portrayed with the verb *šāʾag* (Ps 38:9) and its cognate noun (Pss 22:2; 32:3; Job 3:24), they can surely be portrayed also as "thundering."

18. When George Herbert, in his sonnet on "Prayer," characterizes prayer as "reversed thunder," one may wonder whether he has Hannah in mind.

19. Cf. the contribution by Sauter in this volume.

20. Gen 34:3; 50:21; Judg 19:3; Ruth 2:13; 2 Sam 19:8; 2 Chr 30:22; 32:6; Isa 40:2; Hos 2:16.

21. In its full listing of the idiom, *dibbēr ʿal lēb*, BDB 181 follows its citation of 1 Sam 1:13 with the comment, "seemingly from context *ʿal* for *ʾel, to her heart, to herself*," and

to characterize her interior speaking or praying, the narrator identifies its specific point. Like the woman in Psalm 131, and like the speaker in Psalm 77 and repeatedly in Psalm 42–43, *Hannah is comforting and encouraging her complaining self.*

But this is not simply a bootstrap type of "self-help" for it is grounded in and appropriates the community's experience of and testimony to the goodness and active (if sometimes hidden) presence of God in the midst of trouble. In Psalm 77, the psalmist draws on the tradition of God's saving acts through the leadership of Moses and Aaron in the exodus from Egypt. In Psalm 42, the psalmist draws on past personal experiences of participation in acts of worship that ended on a note of glad shouts and thanksgivings in the house of God. In Psalm 74, in the face of the desecration and destruction of the sanctuary, the psalmist draws on traditional imagery for God's activity in creating and ordering the world as a habitable place (vv. 12–17). And the exilic prophet, in obeying the heavenly summons to "comfort, comfort my people" and to "speak tenderly to Jerusalem" (*dibbēr ʿal lēb*, Isa 40:1–2), recalls to the exilic community's mind the richly diverse traditions of God's activity in creation, promises to and blessings upon the ancestors, deliverance in the exodus, leading and provision in the wilderness, entry into the land, and covenanting promises concerning David and Zion.

What traditions and stories would Hannah meditate on in her complaint over her barrenness in the face of Peninnah's prolific brood of children? Stories like those told about Naomi and Ruth? About the midwives in the midst of oppression in Egypt (Exodus 1)? About the female ancestors in Genesis—Sarah, Rebekah, Leah and Rachel, and Tamar? Especially, perhaps, the story of Rachel *vis-à-vis* her sister and co-wife, Leah?[22]

---

references S. R. Driver, *Notes on the Hebrew Text of the Books of Samuel* (2d ed.; Oxford: Clarendon Press, 1960), where Driver writes, "not, of course, as Is. 40, 2 al. in the sense of *consoling*" (14). Driver takes the usage to be "another instance of *ʿal* = *ʾel*" and cites Gen 24:45 (*dibbēr ʾel lēb*); and Gen 8:21 and 27:41 (*ʾāmar ʾel lēb*) in support of the meaning, "to herself." But even this construal provides no ground for the translation, "speaking *in* her heart," which would presuppose the standard idiomatic preposition *bĕ-*. Whether the preposition be *ʿal* or *ʾel*, it identifies not *the locus* of the speaking but *the one spoken to.* Driver's "not, of course . . . in the sense of *consoling*" begs the question. In view of the self-consoling aspects of prayer canvassed above, there is no reason to rule out such a meaning here; and, in view of Eli's obtuse misconstrual of Hannah's prayer as inebriated self-address (on which see below), such a meaning is actually quite appropriate here.

22. In this paragraph, I am taking the biblical corpus as a total narrative world as presented by the final redactors, inviting us to reflect on the thematic interplay between its various parts. Historically speaking, during the last years of the Tribal Period a woman in Hannah's plight would have been familiar with the stories of earlier women in the community whose similar plight, brought to God in prayer, had been happily resolved.

But Eli mistook her for a drunken woman. He may have seen others whose festive drinking during communal celebration brought them to such a state. But how could he mistake her *śîaḥ*, in particular her self-comforting, for inebriation? Perhaps because the two behaviors have a common aim. The Bible celebrates the capacity of wine to "gladden the human heart" (Ps 104:14). More somberly, the mother of King Lemuel in Prov 31:2–9 depicts the way in which those "afflicted" and in "bitter distress" (literally, "the bitter in soul," like Hannah in 1 Sam 1:10), attempt to drown their troubles in strong drink. Who has not witnessed a person "in his cups" speaking to himself in sympathetic aggrievedness over his lot, both lamenting his situation and consoling himself in it? In terms of both motivation and behavior, the actions of self-comfort in prayer, and self-comfort in wine or strong drink, may be confused in the eyes of the imperceptive bystander.[23]

But the eventual outcomes are profoundly different. And one may ponder the question as to the spiritual legacy which Hannah bequeaths to Samuel, through her refusal to join the others in their eating and drinking until God answers her prayer, and through her vow that the son granted to her will become a Nazirite, forswearing wine and strong drink as well as the razor. Both her own song in 1 Sam 2:1–10, and Samuel's epoch-making vocation in Israel, are humanly grounded in her faithful, prayerful travail in 1 Samuel 1. In a retrospect opened up by Paul's words in Romans 8, one may hear her *śîaḥ* as her plaintive yet hopeful participation in the groaning and travail of the whole creation. In its internal thundering, inaudible to the ears of Eli, one may also hear her *śîaḥ* as the echo within her own heart of the Spirit of God who, with unutterable groanings, makes intercession for her and her people. The outcome, of course, in Hannah's case, is the song of thanksgiving in 1 Sam 2:1–10.

---

23. Interestingly, drunkenness and Spirit-filled singing are contrasted in Eph 5:15–20 as ways of coping with "evil days." Given the equivalency, in Mark 2:6–8, of the expressions "in their/your hearts" and "within [or to] themselves" (RSV; cf. NRSV), and especially in view of 1 Cor 14:28, "if there is no one to interpret, let them be silent in church and speak to themselves and to God," perhaps Eph 5:19 may be translated, "singing psalms and hymns and spiritual songs *to* (or *within*) *yourselves,* singing and making melody to the Lord *in your hearts*." Shades of Hannah!

Naomi's Cry:
Reflections on Ruth 1:20–21

KATHARINE DOOB SAKENFELD

———◆———

I. Introduction

In a region of northeastern India, the Christian wedding sermon typically emphasizes that just as Eve was made from the rib of Adam, so now the
source of life for the new bride should be her husband. She is no longer considered connected to her birth family. Village elders reinforce the theme.
Women informants report that when a woman from this context is wid-
owed, she becomes "a shadow"—physically, socially, emotionally.

Elsewhere in India, women friends bring a colorful new *sari* and fresh
flowers to a newly bereaved woman and dress her elaborately to sit one last
time in the presence of her husband's body. It is her "last time to be dressed
as a married woman." Once the funeral ceremonies are complete, she will
never again wear flowers and bright colors.

An Indian shopkeeper claims he does not have the item a young widow
wants to purchase. When she points it out in plain sight behind the counter,
he states the reality already known to both of them. It is early morning, and
he cannot risk making his first sale of the day to an "unlucky person."

Stories like these, so different from the experiences typical of my own
cultural context, could no doubt be multiplied from many different settings
in our contemporary world. Might they be similar to those of biblical Israel? What customs surrounded a widow's life there, and what was the emotional experience of widowhood like for women then? Although the Old
Testament insists on God's special concern for the widow (e.g., Ps 68:5
[Heb 6]; 146:9)[1]—with a corresponding legal tradition requiring a measure

Author's note: The essay is dedicated to Patrick D. Miller with deep gratitude for his
contributions to biblical scholarship and especially for his many acts of friendship and
support as a faculty colleague.

1. Most often coupled formulaically with the orphan (fatherless) and the stranger
(resident alien). For an analysis of the place of the Hebrew widow as sociologically on the
fringes of society, see Paula S. Hiebert, "The Biblical Widow," in *Gender and Difference in*

of protection and support for the widow (e.g., Exod 22:22 [Heb 21]; Deut 24:17, 19–21) and with evaluation of the community and its leaders by their concern for these especially marginalized women (e.g., Isa 1:17, 23)—it offers little insight into the longer term grieving process or social effects of widowhood for women in that culture. We have brief notices about individuals or communities grieving for someone who has died, but in these narratives the individual mourners are usually men, and the reports generally focus only on the immediate time (sometimes specified as seven or thirty days) after the death. Recognizing these limitations, the present essay turns to Naomi's words to the women of Bethlehem as an entry point into the reality of her grief. The approach will be literary and intertextual, giving attention to clues from the vocabulary of Naomi's cry and its placement within the larger narrative. It is hoped that a closer look at Naomi's cry may offer points of contact with women's (and men's) grieving in our own time.

II. Naomi's Cry: A Prayer of Lament?

The book of Ruth is permeated by the theme of care and blessing. In a book noted for the high proportion of direct speech by comparison to third person narration, characters repeatedly invoke divine blessing upon one another or bless God for an experience of providential care. Naomi says to her daughters-in-law, "May the LORD deal kindly with you" (1:8); Boaz and the reapers exchange greetings, "The LORD be with you," and "The LORD bless you" (2:4); in the field, Boaz says to Ruth, "May the LORD reward you . . . may you have full reward from the LORD, the God of Israel" (2:12); Naomi says to Ruth, "Blessed be the man who took notice of you" (2:19) and then, after learning the man's identity, continues, "Blessed be he by the LORD whose kindness has not forsaken the living or the dead" (2:20). In the encounter at the threshing floor, Boaz says to Ruth, "May you be blessed by the LORD" (3:10); at the village gate, the people say to Boaz, "May the LORD make the woman who is coming into your house like Rachel and Leah" (4:11); and, after Ruth gives birth, the village women say to Naomi, "Blessed be the LORD, who has not left you this day without next of kin" (4:14). All of this God-talk by the principal and supporting characters evokes in the reader the picture of a God presumed to offer providential care.

Ancient Israel (ed. Peggy L. Day; Minneapolis: Fortress, 1989) 125–41. On the relative invisibility of poor women in the Old Testament, see Phyllis Bird, "Poor Man or Poor Woman?: Gendering the Poor in Prophetic Texts," in idem, *Missing Persons and Mistaken Identities: Women and Gender in Ancient Israel* (OBT; Minneapolis: Fortress, 1997) 67–78.

In the midst of this deep-rooted theme, Naomi's words to the village women who are astir over her return to Bethlehem strike a sharply discordant note:

> Call me no longer Naomi,
>> Call me Mara,
>> for the Almighty has dealt bitterly with me.
> I went away full,
>> but the Lord has brought me back empty;
> why call me Naomi
>> when the Lord has dealt harshly with me,
>> and the Almighty has brought calamity upon me? (Ruth 1:20–21)

Although anticipated by Naomi's words to Ruth and Orpah in 1:13, Naomi's cry here is conspicuous for its length, its poetic structure, and the sheer force of its "anti-caring" picture of God.

The title of this essay is intended to evoke the title of Patrick D. Miller's volume, *They Cried to the Lord: The Form and Theology of Biblical Prayer.*[2] Exploring the implicit content of Naomi's cry and how her cry functions within the overall context of blessing that dominates the book, the essay suggests possibilities for understanding Naomi's words in the general context of lament before God. This perspective on Naomi's cry was raised for me in part by Miller's treatment of Baruch's lament recorded in Jeremiah 45. In his "Structural Outline of Prayers for Help and Intercession in Prose Texts," Miller notes that "Jeremiah's scribe, Baruch, receives a word of divine assurance (a salvation oracle) after having cried out in complaint to God."[3] Baruch said (as reported in God's words in the oracle of salvation), "Woe is me! The Lord has added sorrow to my pain; I am weary with my groaning and find no rest" (Jer 45:3). In these brief recorded words, it should be observed that Baruch does not in fact address God, but speaks of the deity in the third person. Why, then, has Miller categorized Baruch's words as prayer? The unstated rationale is not difficult to discern. In the first place, oracles of salvation as a genre often appear in response to prayer and frequently include quotations from the petitioner within the oracle.[4] Furthermore, the phrasing attributed to Baruch has resonances with various texts from the Psalter (e.g., Pss 13:2 [Heb 3]; 22:2 [3]; 31:10 [11]; 38:17 [18]; 107:39; 116:3).

---

2. Patrick D. Miller, *They Cried to the Lord: The Form and Theology of Biblical Prayer* (Minneapolis: Fortress, 1994).

3. Ibid., 356.

4. Miller offers numerous examples (ibid., 141–62). See also the contribution by Janzen in this volume.

Naomi's cry also speaks of the deity in the third person. But the text contains no oracle of salvation, and the narrative context makes clear that Naomi is addressing not God but the women of Bethlehem. Thus it is not discussed in Miller's volume. A survey of a representative sample of contemporary literature about lament and grief reveals that reference to Naomi's cry is conspicuous by its absence, whether in literature about Old Testament prayer or psalms of lament or in literature about biblical resources for counseling persons in the midst of grieving the loss of a family member or close friend. Again, this absence is not surprising, for Naomi's words are not cast in the form we usually recognize as prayer. Yet certain clues in her words and in the overall literary features of the book suggest that her cry might appropriately be considered in these contexts. This essay will first examine critical words in the cry itself from an intertextual perspective, then turn to comment on the place of these verses in the literary structure of the story.

III. Naomi's Cry in Intertextual Perspective

Several key words of Naomi's cry evoke themes from other parts of the Old Testament. Although a number of the connections have been mentioned briefly by various commentators, the overall effect of the choice of vocabulary in Ruth 1:20–21 deserves additional attention. Perhaps most conspicuous, and therefore an appropriate starting point, is Naomi's use of "Shaddai" (usually translated "the Almighty") along with the more usual Yhwh ("Lord") when she speaks of God. As is often pointed out, her references to the deity are laid out chiastically, with Shaddai encompassing Yhwh.[5] Campbell comments that the term Shaddai appears often in "contexts of lament/complaint . . . judging . . . [and] blessing or curse."[6] Reflection on the use of Shaddai in the Old Testament canon offers intertextual clues to the significance it carries in the context of Naomi's cry. As is well known, the term appears principally in the books of Genesis and Job, while it is non-existent or rare in other books, including the Psalms.

The distribution of Shaddai in Genesis is indeed concentrated in contexts of blessing. The connection with the context of Ruth may be developed more specifically in several respects, however, as a review of the six

---

5. For treatments of the literary structure of Naomi's words, see especially Tod Linafelt, *Ruth* (Berit Olam: Studies in Hebrew Narrative and Poetry; ed. David W. Cotter; Collegeville: Liturgical, 1999) 19; and Frederic W. Bush, *Ruth, Esther* (WBC 9; Dallas: Word, 1996) 90.

6. Edward F. Campbell, Jr., *Ruth* (AB 7; Garden City: Doubleday, 1975) 77. Campbell's primary focus is upon the etymology and historical use of the term.

occurrences in Genesis will indicate.[7] In Gen 17:1, God appears to the patriarch Abram under the name El Shaddai, announcing a covenant and numerous descendants. In this context, Abram's name is changed to Abraham (v. 5), and the promise is given that he will be ancestor of many nations and that kings will come from his line (v. 6). An everlasting covenant with his offspring and the gift of the land are assured (v. 7). Genesis 28:3–4 recounts the words of Isaac's blessing of Jacob. Invoking the name El Shaddai, Isaac recalls God's blessing of Abraham, emphasizing numerous descendants, a "company of peoples," and possession of the land. In Gen 35:9–12, we read of God's appearance to Jacob. Again using the name El Shaddai, the command to "be fruitful and multiply" (implying numerous offspring) is given, together with reiteration of the promise of nations, kings, and land (vv. 11–12). In this same context, Jacob's name is changed to Israel (v. 10). This theme is underscored yet again in Gen 48:3–4, as Jacob/Israel on his deathbed recounts to his son Joseph the story of this appearance of El Shaddai. Recalling the promise of numerous people and the land, the dying ancestor pronounces a blessing that incorporates his grandsons Ephraim and Manasseh into full participation alongside his own sons as heirs to the promise.

In these four closely related texts from Genesis, three themes lend intertextual depth to Naomi's use of the name Shaddai. *First*, the name appears in Genesis in the context of *promise of numerous offspring*; by contrast, Naomi's cry is called forth by *the loss of her offspring*, as well as of her husband and the possibility of bearing more children. As she puts it, she went away "full" (despite having fled a famine) but has been brought back "empty" (bereft of husband and sons). She has expressed this emptiness earlier in her words to Ruth and Orpah about her inability to bear more children, even if she had another husband (1:11–12). Shaddai, the One who promises many offspring, has taken away those whom she had.[8]

Second, in Genesis both Abraham and Israel *receive their new names* in the context of promise from El Shaddai. Naomi in her pain *asks that her name be changed* because of what Shaddai has done: "call me no longer Naomi, call me Mara. . . . Why call me Naomi?" As the deity offers a play on words in

---

7. Five occurrences use the expression "El Shaddai"; four of these are generally assigned by scholars to the Priestly source or tradition of the Pentateuch (Gen 17:1; 28:3; 35:11; 48:13). The sixth occurrence, part of a presumably far older tradition in the poem of Genesis 49, reads simply "Shaddai." Discussions of source analysis and of the relative dating of the various texts continue in the scholarly literature, but their outcome is not essential to the intertextual thematic reflection undertaken here.

8. Bush (*Ruth, Esther*, 97) rightly points out that Naomi's concern is centered primarily on the security of family life, not on matters of levirate marriage. See also my assessment in Katharine Doob Sakenfeld, *Ruth* (Interpretation; Louisville: John Knox, 1999) 6–7.

proposing a reason for Abraham's new name ("ancestor of a multitude"; Gen 17:5), so Naomi's self-renaming plays on the word "bitter," which is her characterization of the action of God and of the state of her own life as a result of that action.

Third, the Genesis promise of kings from the line of Abraham evokes the larger context of the story of Ruth as the story of the ancestry of King David. The narrator of Ruth has set this theme in motion by the identification of Naomi's husband and sons as "Ephrathites from Bethlehem in Judah,"[9] a theme that will be brought to resolution with the identification of Ruth's son as ancestor of David (4:17, 18–21). For the intertextual reader, Naomi's use of the name Shaddai evokes not only the inversion of the motifs of offspring and the renaming of a protagonist, but also calls attention to the near failure of the emergence of David from the seed of Abraham. In this sense, Naomi's use of Shaddai might even be said to evoke the motif of threat to the divine promise that permeates the ancestral narratives of Genesis.[10]

The two remaining uses of Shaddai in Genesis contribute further to the picture thus far developed. Genesis 43:14 records Jacob/Israel's hope that the man in Egypt (Joseph) will release Jacob's hostage son Simeon if Jacob allows his youngest son Benjamin to go to Egypt. In this context Jacob says to his sons, "May El Shaddai grant you mercy before the man. . . . As for me, if I am bereaved of my children, I am bereaved."[11] As in Ruth, the context is one of concern for offspring, and here the possibility of losing them. Finally, the name Shaddai appears in the long poem of Genesis 49, Jacob's last words to his sons, in the section concerning Joseph (vv. 22–26). The textual and translation difficulties of this poem are well known, but it nevertheless appears probable, if not completely clear, in this section that the full range of the blessing of Shaddai pronounced upon Joseph includes "blessings of the breasts and of the womb" (v. 25). Once again, the term is associated with

---

9. Cf. Mic 5:2 and Sakenfeld, *Ruth*, 20.

10. A fourth intertextual resonance evoked by the term Shaddai might be suggested in the symmetry between Jacob's incorporating his grandsons as offspring at the level of his sons and the words of the village women, "A son has been born to Naomi" (4:17), as they name Ruth's baby at the end of the story. The genealogy of 4:18–22, however, proceeds strictly through Boaz (not Elimelech) and the generations of males; thus, finding the theme of an adoptive grandson through the presence of the term Shaddai is at best tenuous. Nonetheless, Jacob's speech incorporating Ephraim and Manasseh refers to the death of Rachel and her burial "on the way to Ephrath (that is, Bethlehem)" (Gen 48:7), opening up a potential intertextual connection to the reference to Rachel, Ephrathah, and Bethlehem in Ruth 4:11.

11. Compare Gen 42:36, where Jacob specifies his loss of children with the words "Joseph is no more, and Simeon is no more, and now you would take Benjamin."

blessing of family and offspring, even as in Ruth it is associated with the loss of this blessing in life.

The second major Old Testament context for the term Shaddai is in the book of Job. Here the term appears some thirty times scattered throughout the poetry, with particular concentrations in chapters 22 and 27. Although it is far beyond the scope of this essay to explore the function of this name in its Joban context, the usage in Job 27:2 is of particular intertextual significance for Ruth. In an oath formulation, Job speaks of God as Shaddai "who has made my soul bitter." As commentators have often noted, this association of Shaddai with Job's bitterness uses the same terminology (*mrr*) found in Naomi's cry. Campbell makes a step in the direction of the present essay as he suggests a possible comparison between Job's frustrated attempt to understand his situation and the mood expressed in Naomi's cry.[12] The thematic connection of the two works may be pressed further,[13] for in each case loss of children and the loss of material well-being shape the situation of the complainant. To be sure, the cases are not fully symmetrical. Job has lost his health, while Naomi has not; Naomi has lost her spouse, while Job has not. And because the name Shaddai appears also in the speeches of Job's friends, not solely on the lips of Job, one cannot associate it specifically with the circumstances of his complaint. Nonetheless, the association of Shaddai, bitterness, and a speech of complaint addressed to others links Naomi and Job as characters, even as the broad pattern of loss, complaint, and restoration links the two books thematically.[14]

The context of Job 27:2 may also shed light, albeit indirectly, on an interpretive crux in Ruth 1:21. Scholars have long debated the significance of the phrase "the LORD has testified against me" (MT: *ʿānâ bî*). The Greek and Old Latin read "has afflicted me," as if from the *piʿel* of a different *ʿnh* root.[15] The idiom of *ʿnh* in the *qal* plus the preposition *bĕ-* (of person), as in the MT, is generally recognized to refer to giving unfavorable testimony in a legal case. Possibly the ancient translators found this meaning awkward or inappropriate for Naomi's words and therefore translated from the root "to afflict" (*piʿel*), even though a prepositional object of person with *bĕ-* in this meaning is not otherwise attested. Naomi says God has "dealt bitterly," "brought back empty," "brought calamity." The choice of a meaning

---

12. Campbell, *Ruth*, 77.

13. See J. Gerald Janzen, "Lust for Life and the Bitterness of Job," *TT* 55 (1998) 152–62, esp. 155–56.

14. See Kirsten Nielsen, *Ruth* (OTL; Louisville: Westminster John Knox, 1997) 51.

15. The NRSV's "dealt harshly with me" may reflect an effort by the translators to carry forward both meanings, although it appears to lean toward the Septuagint.

"to afflict" appears to fit this context nicely. And yet the undercurrent or overtones of law court language in Job 27:1–6 may suggest that a juridical note of protest is sounded by Naomi as well.[16] Although Shaddai had made Job's life bitter, Job swears by Shaddai that he will not speak "falsehood" or "deceit"; he will maintain his "integrity." He will not concede that he has sinned either to placate his friends or to make easy sense of the God whose actions have so hurt and mystified him (see also Job 23:2–7). In evaluating this possibility, certain uses of the juridical idiom ʿnh + b- take on particular significance. Although the idiom refers to testifying against the accused, it does not follow in every case that the accused party is in fact guilty. This is seen first of all in an example from Job, in which Eliphaz addresses Job: "your own lips testify against you [yaʿănû-bāk]" (15:6).[17] Yet the reader knows of Job's innocence. Similarly, Samuel calls upon all Israel to testify against him (ʿănû bî; 1 Sam 12:3), but the rhetorical intent is clearly one of declaring his innocence. And in classic lawsuit imagery (Mic 6:3), God calls the people to testify (ʿănēh bî; NRSV: "Answer me!") about what God has done to/for them, in a setting that obviously presumes divine innocence.

In light of these examples, and with consideration of Job's insistence on his innocence and integrity despite Shaddai's bitter dealing with him, Naomi's statement that God has "testified against" her does not lead necessarily to the conclusion that she herself believed she was guilty of some wrongdoing or offense against God (or that the narrator assumed such guilt on her part). Naomi gives no indication that she considers herself deserving of the bitter dealing, emptiness, and calamity that has befallen her. It can equally well be argued that rather than implicitly accepting blame, she makes here a defiant, if frustrated and deeply hurt, expression of her innocence. Like the action of God in the life of Job, divine action in the life of Naomi is bitter and yields bitterness precisely because it is so utterly inexplicable.[18]

---

16. The oddity of the juridical idiom in Ruth is that God is placed in the role of witness rather than judge. Possibly this uncharacteristic construction accounts for the Versions' move toward the verb "to afflict." Campbell (*Ruth*, 77) suggests that God is portrayed as judge in the second verb of the couplet, translating "pronounced evil sentence upon me." See below, n. 25.

17. Elsewhere Job himself apparently speaks of false or misleading testimony against him (16:8), but the text of 16:7–8 appears defective and cannot be translated with certainty. If the NRSV's reading of these verses is plausible, then Job's physical condition caused by God is the testimony (clearly misleading and false, from Job's point of view) against him. Such a reading brings Job 16:8 close to the judicial sense suggested here for Ruth 1:21.

18. One ought still to ask whether the reader of the text must attribute a single clear intent to Naomi's words. Unlike Job, Naomi does not explicitly claim that she was innocent of wrongdoing. Were the village women whom Naomi addressed certain of her

Thus far we have seen that Naomi's use of Shaddai resonates intertextually in two ways. With respect to Genesis, it elucidates the content of her cry as a reversal of blessing in the face of bereavement—the loss of offspring and her self-renaming, as well as the story's larger motif of kingship. With respect to Job, it suggests that her bitterness is fueled not just by the fact of her loss, but also by her own sense of integrity and innocence in the face of God's inexplicable action. She has lost not only her husband and sons, but also her way of making sense of her life. As with Job, we may imagine a range of emotions covered under the theme of bitterness: anger, resentment, despair, grief, resignation, frustration. We may imagine that Naomi, although she does not ask, would wish like Job for her chance to confront the deity who has brought her into the depths.

Psalm 91 offers a third locus for intertextual reading of Naomi's use of Shaddai. The connection is highlighted by the rarity of the term Shaddai in the Psalter, where it occurs elsewhere only in Ps 68:14 [Heb 15].[19] As with the Genesis passages, the focus is on the contrast between Naomi's situation and the theme of Psalm 91. "You . . . who abide in the shadow of Shaddai will say to the LORD, 'my refuge'" (vv. 1–2). "He will cover you with his pinions, and under his wings you will find refuge" (v. 4). The psalm assures the faithful of divine protection from all manner of trouble; no "calamity" (*rāʿâ*) shall befall those who have made the LORD their "refuge" (vv. 9–10). How starkly opposite is Naomi's experience: Shaddai has "brought calamity" (*hēraʿ*) upon her! It is as if Naomi's very choice of words sets out to proclaim that the psalmist's assurance does not resonate with the truth of her life. In this respect, she expresses herself in a form that is known from a number of psalms of lament, the complaint against God in the form of an assertion,[20] except that her words are not addressed directly to God. As Miller puts it with regard both to prose and psalm prayers, "The present circumstances of distress seem to indicate to the ones praying a terrible

---

intent? Indeed, was Naomi herself certain? The book of Ruth is characterized throughout by ambiguity of expression, as shown by Campbell (*Ruth*, 131) for the narrator's art in chapter 3, and as suggested by Danna Nolan Fewell and David Miller Gunn (*Compromising Redemption: Relating Characters in the Book of Ruth* [Louisville: Westminster/John Knox, 1990]) for many of the speech quotations throughout the story. Today's grief counselors know that many bereaved persons move back and forth between believing that God has punished them, raging against the unfairness of God, and simply being frustrated by the mystery of their loss and pain. Perhaps Naomi's words portray some of the same ambivalence.

19. Mitchell Dahood has argued for a third instance in Ps 32:4. See his *Psalms I: 1–50* (AB 16; Garden City: Doubleday, 1966) 194. The reading is provocative but remains disputed.

20. Miller (*They Cried to the Lord*, 76) cites as examples Pss 44:9 [Heb 10]; 60:1; 88:5 [6], 15–18 [16–19].

inconsistency on the part of God. The Lord seems to have caused or allowed things to happen in a way inappropriate to the faithfulness and compassion that are characteristic of the Lord of Israel."[21] If we accept the supposition of Naomi's implicit claim of innocence (via the intertextual connection with Job), then we have space to hear her implicit protest that God is not providing the care and protection promised to and expected by the faithful. A refuge from calamity seems far from her present experience of God. She has not been spared terror and destruction (Ps 91:3–4); to the contrary, "Shaddai has brought calamity" upon her.

The possibility of this intertextual reading is underscored by the imagery of finding refuge under God's wings. This imagery of divine wings is not common in the Old Testament. Beyond Psalm 91, it appears five times in the Psalter (Pss 36:7 [Heb 8], 57:1, and 61:4 [5] with the same verb of "finding refuge"; also 17:8 and 63:7 [8]), each time in a prayer for help. Outside the Psalter the metaphor appears only in Ruth 2:12, as Boaz speaks to Ruth of her finding refuge under the wings of the God of Israel. Further on in the story, the term "wing" (NRSV: "cloak") is used with reference to Boaz's garment, in a phrase that appears to have connotations of marriage (3:9). Through Ruth's commitment to Naomi (concretized in Ruth's commitment to place, to people, to Yhwh, and eventually to Boaz), the refuge of God's wings, so absent from Naomi's experience as she returns, may again become apparent in Naomi's life.

Beyond the use of Shaddai in Psalm 91, the appearance of the noun "calamity" (v. 10), as noted above, provides a second point of contact between the psalm and Naomi's words. A number of commentators have pointed also to similarities between Naomi's use of the verb r^{cc} (*hip'il*) and its occurrence in prayers of complaint on the lips of Moses and Elijah.[22] It is to these passages and their intertextual enrichment of our hearing of Naomi's cry that I now turn.

Two narratives record Moses' complaints about calamity brought by the God who has commissioned him as leader. The first instance follows Moses' initial approach to Pharaoh, which led to the command to make "bricks without straw" and the subsequent anger of the Israelite supervisors. Moses complains to the Lord that God has brought calamity upon (NRSV: "mistreated") the people by sending him. The only effect has been that Pharaoh has brought calamity upon them, while God has taken no action for their deliverance (Exod 5:22–23). In response (6:1), God promises Moses anew that the Pharaoh will indeed let the people go. Despite this

---

21. Ibid., 71.

22. For example, Campbell, *Ruth*, 77; Linafelt, *Ruth*, 20; E. John Hamlin, *Surely There Is a Future: A Commentary on the Book of Ruth* (ITC; Grand Rapids: Eerdmans, 1996) 23.

reply focused on the deliverance of the people, the concern of Moses' cry is not necessarily solely for the fate of the people. The setting of his complaint immediately after the supervisors express their wrath against him suggests that Moses is at least as much complaining to God about his personal plight, and his question "Why did you ever send me?" certainly has a tone of personal frustration.

That Moses' personal experience is at stake in the first story is further suggested by the clear prominence of his own concerns in the second of his complaints using the verb *r*ʿʿ. During the wilderness sojourn the people become dissatisfied with manna and begin weeping and wishing for meat and other foods they had known in Egypt (Numbers 11). At this, Moses complains to God, "Why have you brought calamity [*hărēʿōtā*] on your servant?" (11:11; my translation). With passionate rhetoric Moses insists that the problem is of God's making; he says he has no place to get meat and that the burden of leadership is too great for him; he insists that if God cannot treat him better, then God should kill him to put him out of his misery (*r*ʿʿ). In response, God provides a system of shared leadership and announces a plan to provide meat for the people.[23]

The story of the prophet Elijah's encounter with the widow of Zarephath (1 Kgs 17:8–24) offers a third narrative instance of complaint about God's bringing calamity upon a person. Through the power of God at the word of Elijah the woman and her son are rescued from starvation by a never-empty jar of meal and jug of oil. Yet subsequently the boy becomes so ill that "there was no breath left in him." Confronted angrily by the woman, who somehow holds Elijah accountable for this turn of events, Elijah complains to God, "have you brought calamity [*hărēʿôtā*] even upon the widow with whom I am staying, by killing her son?" (17:20). He then prays that the child's life be restored, and the child revives. In response, the widow acknowledges Elijah as truly a "man of God." In this third example, the prayer of complaint is clearly on behalf of someone else (as in Moses' prayer in Exodus 5). Like both previous examples, the prayer presumes that God had started an action of deliverance through the speaker but had not brought it to appropriate fruition; thus God is called to account by the complainant. In this third story, as in the first, one may see an implicit personal complaint on the part of Elijah. Although the calamity befalls the widow, her wrath is expressed against Elijah (just as the Israelite supervisors express wrath against Moses) and his credibility is on the line. The widow's response at the end of the narrative reinforces this supposition.

---

23. Since God had been angered by the people's desire for other food and dissatisfaction with the manna (v. 10), the meat is to be provided in excess as a form of judgment for their complaining rejection of God (vv. 19–20).

Out of a large number of occurrences of the verb r^{cc} (*hipʿil*), these three narratives have appropriately been singled out for connection with Naomi's cry because in common with her cry they express the pain of the complainant about the action of God in someone's life.[24] Yet their interpretive potential deserves further elaboration.[25] Whether personal petition or intercessory prayer or an implicit combination of both, each complaint assumes the innocence of the speaker and of the parties interceded for.[26] This assumption of innocence furthers the intertextual proposal above that Naomi's use of Shaddai be read in light of Job's point of view. Yet there is of course a major difference between Naomi's cry and this set of texts: these three are addressed to God while Naomi's is not; Moses and Elijah apparently expect God to respond, while one would most easily infer that Naomi does not. Even in the case of Job, complaints about God addressed to his friends do incorporate hope for some response from God.[27] In the face of this difference, what connections are possible? This question brings the essay at last to its opening concern: how Naomi's cry can be read in relation to prayers of lament or complaint.

IV. Naomi's Cry and/as Lament

Linafelt suggests a possible direction as he points out that "Naomi—unlike the paradigmatic prophets Moses and Elijah—has never been addressed by God or called to some great task. Rather, like Ruth . . . Naomi must endure hardship and uncertainty without the benefit of an active God underwriting and endorsing her affairs."[28] It is certainly true that Naomi has not been addressed or called by God. But this absence of God's

---

24. Human beings rather than God are the subject of the verb in many other instances. In the remaining instances in which God is the subject, the texts generally deal with punishment for clearly identifiable individual or communal disobedience.

25. Campbell (*Ruth*, 77), followed by Bush (*Ruth, Esther*, 93) introduces these Moses and Elijah narratives primarily to argue for a juridical meaning of "pronouncing evil sentence," thus finding a closer poetic parallel meaning to the juridical idiom "testify against" of the previous line. Bush repeats Campbell's mistaken citation (a typographical error?) of the idiom under consideration as r^{cc} *hipʿil* plus preposition *bĕ-*, whereas Ruth and the two pentateuchal passages in fact use the preposition *lĕ-* (*ʿal* in 1 Kgs 17:20). This proposal of a juridical connotation is tenuous in my view, as it seems strained to find the notion of "God's presumed verdict and the onset of punishment" (so Campbell) in each story. The Moses narratives in particular seem focused more on delay of fulfillment of promise rather than onset of judgment.

26. Note that in Numbers 11 Moses petitions only for himself; he does not intercede for the people, although God must deal with their behavior in order to address Moses' complaint.

27. For a treatment of Job in relation to the psalms of lament, see Claus Westermann, *The Structure of the Book of Job* (Philadelphia: Fortress, 1981).

28. Linafelt, *Ruth*, 20.

voice has to do not just with the contrast between her status and that of paradigmatic prophets, for other less central biblical characters pray to God and receive answers,[29] and the psalms of lament could be prayed by ordinary individuals. I suggest rather that Naomi's words fit a literary pattern that is consistently carried through in the entire book of Ruth: No one in these four chapters addresses any second person prayer to God, nor does God speak to any of the characters. In this respect, the narrative of Ruth finds its place at a point between the narratives of the Pentateuch and historical books on the one hand, where prayers to God and speeches by God (directly or through intermediaries) are a regular feature, and on the other hand the book of Esther (in the MT), where God is not mentioned overtly at all. As reviewed in the introduction to this essay, the Ruth narrative includes invocations of God's blessing, but their second person address is to other human characters in the story. There are exclamatory words of thanksgiving, blessing God for events that have transpired, but again these are in third-person form, as if intended for the ears of the human conversation partner in the narrative. Surely God, whose actions of providing food for the people of Bethlehem (1:6) and giving conception to Ruth (4:13) form a framework for the human actions of the story, is supposed to have heard these invocations and exclamations, despite their form of address. In the overall structure of the narrative, each invocation of blessing upon another person is eventually fulfilled not by divine intervention, but by faithful human action.[30] Yet such fulfillment does not mean that God is absent. Rather, God is at work through the intricate web of human interaction portrayed in the story.

In this literary environment, it seems to me reasonable to imagine Naomi's cry in the same way. Her words are addressed to the village women, but at some level they are meant for God to hear. Within Naomi's own sequence of longer speeches in the narrative, an ABCB′A′ pattern can be discerned: two moments of cry against God (B, B′) are separated by silence (C) and bracketed by words of blessing (A, A′). Initially Naomi commits her daughters-in-law to God's care: "May the LORD deal kindly with you. . . . May the LORD grant that you may find security . . ." (1:8–9; A). The next phase of her conversation with Ruth and Orpah introduces the theme of her subsequent cry to the women in Bethlehem: "It has been far more bitter for me than for you, because the hand of the LORD has turned

---

29. For example, Manoah, Samson's father, in Judg 13:8; and Abraham's servant (seeking a bride for Isaac) in Gen 24:12–14. Of course, the relative importance of these characters by comparison to Naomi is debatable, but the point is that they are not of the stature of Moses or Elijah in the tradition.

30. Sakenfeld, *Ruth*, 14–16, 47–48. Cf. David M. Gunn and Danna Nolan Fewell, *Narrative in the Hebrew Bible* (New York: Oxford University Press, 1993) 157.

against me" (1:12–13; B). There is silence as Ruth and Naomi proceed to Bethlehem (1:18; C). Following the silence comes Naomi's cry (1:20–21; B'). Then, after Ruth returns from gleaning, Naomi first blesses the unknown man who aided Ruth, then blesses the LORD when that man turns out to be a near kinsman of hers (2:19, 20; A'). If Naomi supposes God will hear her words of concern and blessing; why should she not hope that God will hear (or at least overhear) her cry as well?

Kathleen Billman and Daniel Migliore have drawn attention to Jeremiah's report of the cry of Jacob's wife Rachel, her refusal to be consoled over the loss of her children (Jer 31:15). They point out that although Rachel's weeping is not addressed to God, a direct response of God is immediately proclaimed.[31] "There is a reward for your work . . . there is a hope for your future" (31:16–17). Rachel's children will return from exile. Like Miller's work on Old Testament prayer, this important study of prayers of pain and protest in relation to theology and pastoral care makes no reference to Naomi's cry. Yet this work too contains themes that point toward Naomi's words. Rachel, for instance, is coupled with Job as "a resister, a protester who refuses the consolations of orthodox theology and conventional pastoral care."[32] The importance of full expression of the depth of grief, with all its fear and anger, is lifted up. Following the work of Donald Capps, Billman and Migliore recognize that the words of the grieving person addressed to a grief counselor are implicitly addressed to God.[33] The point here is not to place the women of Bethlehem in the role of grief counselors, but rather to suggest yet again that Naomi's words addressed to others may be seen as implicitly addressed to God. Although the depth of complaint found in Jeremiah's laments and in some psalms suggests that there is nothing we cannot say to God, it is still true that many people find it easier to express their most vehement protests to other people rather than directly to God. In the words of Billman and Migliore, "Whether or not the cries of pain and protest are identified as prayer by the afflicted, when suffering is experienced in the presence of God, the prayer of lament is in the process of formation.[34] Capps further suggests that it may be the catharsis of full expression of grief that opens the door for the mourner to begin to trust others and God again.[35] Naomi's ability to pronounce blessing first upon an

---

31. Kathleen Billman and Daniel Migliore, *Rachel's Cry: Prayer of Lament and Rebirth of Hope* (Cleveland: United Church Press, 1999) 2. The title of the present essay plays on their book title, as well as Miller's *They Cried to the Lord.*

32. Billman and Migliore, *Rachel's Cry,* 3.

33. Ibid., 84. Cf. Donald Capps, *Biblical Approaches to Pastoral Counseling* (Philadelphia: Westminster, 1981) 88.

34. Billman and Migliore, *Rachel's Cry,* 139.

35. Capps, *Biblical Approaches,* 88.

unnamed kind person and then specifically upon the deity whom she had earlier declared to have brought calamity reflects this kind of movement. In a similar way, Naomi's giving of practical advice to Ruth about how to behave in Boaz's fields (2:22) and her later resumption of planning for longer term security (3:1) suggest that she has moved from the depths of despair to some sense of herself and her ability to deal with her world.

Is there then an implicit "answer" to Naomi's cry, to her implicit "prayer" or prayer "in the process of formation"?[36] Just as no one prays directly to God in the literary form of the book of Ruth, so also God's response to Naomi's cry is not direct intervention of speech or word, but is implicit, taking shape in the actions of Boaz, Ruth, and the men and women of the village.[37] Life cannot go backward, the deaths of Naomi's husband and sons cannot be reversed, but parts of her emptiness can be filled: with food (twice Boaz has Ruth bring a generous supply of grain to Naomi: 2:14–18 and 3:17), with the loyalty of a daughter-in-law (who is counted by the village women as more to Naomi than seven sons; 4:15), with an adoptive grandson in apparent defiance of traditional genealogical practice (as she lays Ruth's baby in her bosom and the women say, "a son is born to Naomi"; 4:17).

Because Naomi does not speak in the final scenes of the book, we do not know what she thought as she took the child in her arms.[38] We must not imagine that Boaz, Ruth, and Obed could just replace Elimelech, Chilion, and Mahlon. Those who grieve do not "just get over it." Yet the narrative suggests that through the actions of faithful people around her who embody divine faithfulness Naomi is not left in a condition of unrelieved calamity and bitterness. She is offered anew the affection of others, the security of economic survival and of family relationships, and the assurance of care for her time of old age, and she is able to experience these basics of human existence as real and meaningful. What better response could there be to her cry? Would that the widows of India with whom this essay began, and indeed the widows of every culture, could receive such a response.

---

36. It should be noted that only Naomi of the three main characters receives no explicit invocation of blessing on her behalf. Thus her cry is all the more poignant. Yet blessing does in the end come to Naomi also.

37. The contrast between the books of Ruth and Job in this regard is dramatic, despite the similarity of theme suggested above. In the end of the book of Job, God speaks at length, and Job speaks to God. Then God "restores" Job's fortunes; the expression is one of direct intervention. In the book of Ruth, we hear no "where were you when I laid the foundations of the earth" (Job 38:4), nor do we hear Naomi recant her accusations against God. God does intervene in providing Ruth conception (4:13), but this divine action is only possible in the context of the many human actions that have resulted in Ruth's marriage to Boaz.

38. See Fewell and Gunn, *Compromising Redemption*, 65, 105.

Jonah 2: A Prayer Out of the Deep

GERHARD SAUTER

———◆———

Sometimes a child dreams unutterably horrible things: "I am being dragged into the depths by a waterfall. Through all the water I can still make out a rocky shore in front of me, and I hope that with my last bit of strength I can climb onto it. But then yet another whirlpool grabs me; the water opens up like a throat, and I fall another story deeper. When I look up, I can see a little bit of sky through an opening above. Perhaps I can manage to overcome this chasm, to climb back up one story—but no. The water drags me to a new depth, and this goes on and on. Soon I cannot see the slightest patch of sky, and I feel only endless rivers of dark power that entangle me in an abyss. I am hopelessly at its mercy."

This is not just a nightmare. It is a metaphysical dream, and because of this, more than just a dream. The abyss out of which we can never climb is precisely the depth from which the psalmist prays, "Out of the depths I cry to you, O LORD. Lord, hear my voice" (Ps 130:1–2a). It is an immeasurable depth that reaches much further than the feeling of being down below and not above. Even when we feel ourselves oppressed, burdened, and feeble, we can still see, for a while, what is above, or at least others that are above. However, with this ceaseless falling, there is no longer any "above" of which to speak: the very distinction of "above" and "down below" loses its meaning. All is swallowed up by the "down below."

Jonah is thrown into exactly such a place. He is supposed to go to the metropolis of Nineveh to deliver a message from God. Nineveh is the capital of a power-hungry kingdom, a very dark place. What light would a word of God be able to bring about there? Therefore Jonah cleared out, and with that sought to free himself from his task—but how he deceived himself! Through his flight, he drove himself into an inconceivable catastrophe.

Author's note: As a systematic theologian, I greatly admire the ability of Patrick D. Miller to integrate historical-critical research into biblical theology. He understands theology as a service of and to the Church. I am very thankful for his friendship and for our many "Transatlantic" discussions.

The ship on which Jonah hid himself traveled into a great storm. When the storm did not calm down, Jonah was thrown into the turbulent sea. He was helplessly at the mercy of the floods. He could still thrash about there for a while, and there was at least the tiniest prospect that the storm could calm down, making it possible for a ship to come by and rescue him. And then something actually does appear on the horizon. Yet what comes nearer is a monstrosity the likes of which had never been seen or encountered before. It is much worse than waves as tall as houses. A sea monster bears down on him and then devours him. As the sea monster dives beneath the waves, it takes Jonah down, down below. Jonah can do absolutely nothing.

One might compare here the somewhat similar account of Baron von Münchhausen. The Baron, however, renowned for his lies and tall tales, does not allow a fish to swallow *him*! No, on the contrary, he takes it—the powerful but willing whale—by the reins and rides it through the sea, all the way to the bottom of the ocean where he plays all sorts of mischievous games. After resurfacing, he is attacked by a pirate ship. A fight flares up, Münchhausen strikes the ship in two, and his whale-horse swallows the front half of the ship with all its passengers. This mouthful, however, does not agree with the whale. As Münchhausen comments,

> The ship that my traveling companion swallowed laid all too heavily in his stomach; also, a dulled murmuring, which I heard now and then, convinced me that the swallowed pirates were probably still alive; at least not all of them were dead. Since we have the story of Jonah, this circumstance should no longer astonish a good Christian.[1]

Unfortunately, the Baron's story turns out very badly, at least for the poor whale, who dies of digestive problems.

How completely different it is for Jonah, the helpless prophet! Instead of mastering the whale he is mastered *by it*. For three whole days and three long nights he can manage no more than a single prayer. But the fish, at least, has covered a great distance in this time period. It serves as Jonah's transportation. Jonah is thrown onto the land, precisely at the spot that he wanted to avoid at all costs: on the shore where the road to Nineveh began. Of course, Jonah is also saved by this action. If God had heard him earlier, then the fish would have given Jonah up before they reached the shore,

---

1. Erwin Wackermann, ed., *Wunderbare Reisen zu Wasser und Lande, Feldzüge und lustige Abenteuer des Freiherrn von Münchhausen, wie er dieselben bei der Flasche im Zirkel seiner Freunde selbst zu erzählen pflegt* (2d ed. reprinted; Hamburg: Hoffmann & Campe, 1966 [London, 1788]) 332.

and it would have turned out very badly for the prophet who would have drowned miserably.

During this rescue Jonah is a laughable figure. One can perhaps recall an old painting of this scene that arouses more sympathy for the poor fish, chased through the sea, than for Jonah.[2] When the fish spits out Jonah, it seems as if it had been sick, so that our compassion turns toward the fish, leaving Jonah lying on the beach. So, relieved by a mighty belch, the fish rids itself of Jonah, as if to say, "Thank God, I am finally done with him. He lay long enough in my stomach, that indigestible man of God!"

The laughing fades away, however, when we return to Jonah in the unfathomable depth of the belly of the fish. Three days and nights, and only a single prayer! That prayer is a lament and a song of thanks—a psalm like many others. Such a psalm really belongs in the temple, when those who have been rescued bring their sacrifices after a danger has been withstood. The belly of a fish is a highly peculiar place for such a prayer—much too dark, and ominous, with no way out. Isn't it much too early, in the belly of a fish, to be voicing such thanks?[3]

This is a very artistically composed psalm, as if the person praying had considered—in peace and with time to concentrate—how a beautiful song of God's praise should look and sound, a song that thanks God for the experience of not being abandoned by God, not even in the whirlpool of floodwaters or in the abyss of the sea.[4]

I called to the LORD out of my distress,
    and he answered me;
out of the belly of Sheol I cried,
    and you heard my voice.
You cast me into the deep,
    into the heart of the seas,
    and the flood surrounded me;
all your waves and your billows

---

2. E.g., there is an old tapestry in the Löwenburg in Kassel, Germany, that depicts the scene in such fashion.

3. Hans Walter Wolff, *Obadiah and Jonah* (Minneapolis: Augsburg, 1986) 128–31, notes that Jonah's psalm does not fit with the surrounding narrative context. He also notes that the usual solution to this problem is to posit that the psalm was a separate composition that was added to the story of Jonah at a later date. I will suggest below an alternative to this usual redaction-critical reading of the hymn, namely, that rather than praying the "wrong" kind of psalm (or seeing the psalm as a later interpolation), Jonah prays *a piece of memorized liturgy*. Cf. also the contribution by Williamson in this volume.

4. The artfulness of the psalm leads some to conclude that the psalm is a composition of stereotypical elements from other psalms or that it is a later addition (see previous note).

passed over me.
Then I said, "I am driven away
    from your sight;
how shall I look again
    upon your holy temple?"
The waters closed in over me,
    the deep surrounded me;
weeds were wrapped around my head
    at the roots of the mountains.
I went down to the land
    whose bars closed upon me for ever;
yet you brought up my life from the Pit,
    O LORD my God.
As my life was ebbing away,
    I remembered the LORD;
and my prayer came to you,
    into your holy temple.
Those who worship vain idols
    forsake their true loyalty.
But I with the voice of thanksgiving
    will sacrifice to you;
what I have vowed I will pay.
Deliverance belongs to the LORD! (Jonah 2:2–9)

Buried alive, should Jonah have prayed like this?[5] Is this prayer fitting for a stiff-necked prophet who wanted to flee from God? The sailors first threw him in the water to be rid of him, and then he fell more deeply and more hopelessly into the abyss of the fish. How is it that he noticed precisely there that precisely by means of this catastrophe he had fallen into God's hands? God had protected him, when God sent the fish to take Jonah to where he should have been—if, that is, he had obeyed God's bidding from the start.

---

5. Phyllis Trible, *Rhetorical Criticism: Context, Method, and the Book of Jonah* (GBS; Minneapolis: Fortress, 1994) 160–73 argues that the psalm functions satirically since it seems to contradict Jonah's earlier and later attitudes in such a strong way. Understood this way, the psalm sets up the ironic contrast to Jonah's later response to the repentance of Nineveh and God's mercy. But the psalm functions on more than just a literary level. I would like to emphasize the *biblical-theological* character of this prayer that questions the distance of space and the sequence of present and future time and, above all, that questions the self-recognition of the praying person. In this I am arguing along the lines of Patrick D. Miller's exemplary research on the correlation of prayer and theology: *They Cried to the Lord: The Form and Theology of Biblical Prayer* (Minneapolis: Fortress, 1994).

It is Jonah's awareness of God in the belly of the fish that makes his prayer completely unexpected. From his cell on death row, he sees himself again in the temple, in the company of those who are bringing their thank-offerings to God for having been rescued. Those people are doing just what he wants to do, too.

It is also very important to note that Jonah, in his distress, thinks no more about the reason for his flight, about his discontentment, nor about the God who accepts others, others who have no entitlement to that acceptance whatsoever. Now, when Jonah himself sits in a mess, he is not brave enough to bear the consequences of his rebellion against God. Instead of crying out for God's forgiveness, he cries out without inhibition for God to save him. All of a sudden, he only knows to speak of God as Savior. And now he is also ready to swear loyalty to God and to believe that God is Lord of heaven and earth. He is ready to believe that God's arms reach to the depths of the seas, yes, even to the innards of a monster. One would think that if Jonah has recognized that this is God's purpose—to save even him—then he might also recognize that saving might also be God's purpose for even godless Nineveh. Surely now Jonah would have nothing against God's purposes and would no longer resist God's plan. (Of course, readers of chapters 3 and 4 know this is not the case!)

So, yes, in this light, Jonah's prayer is out of line and goes too far. But does not every sincere prayer go too far? Is not every prayer out of line? Prayer goes beyond all that we can know of ourselves and what we can request of ourselves, beyond our judgment about ourselves and about others! Prayer may even go beyond what is expected of us and what we expect of ourselves! Do not our own prayers also live from a confidence, from an unfathomable hope? Our hope is that what we pray, what we more wrongly than rightly want to bring before God (and, with completely unsuitable words, no less!)—that all these really ascend to God and reach God in God's holiness. We hope this despite the fact that, like Jonah, we pray from a peculiar, gloomy, and threatening place in which we can sense very little of God. And if it seems peculiar to us that Jonah suddenly speaks at odds with what we have learned about him (and will learn about him), this really shouldn't surprise us. In Jonah's prayer, he—not unlike we ourselves—places himself in the company of many, many others who are bringing thank-offerings to God.

We place ourselves in the same way when we pray. Are we not suddenly transported by each of our prayers into the company of all those who call upon God with their complaints, their pleas, their praise and thanks? Do we actually stand alone in our place when we stand before God? No, we always pray *with others*, even if we do not really know it at that moment, and perhaps never foresee it or even dream it. Each prayer puts us in an

inestimable throng of men and women who pray.[6] There, not one more
word could be counted. There, we can give our consent, without being certain beforehand, to what we thought ourselves incapable of saying. And
therefore it does not matter at all if our prayer is original or something we
have memorized. And if it does not matter for us if the prayer we pray is
something original or something memorized, then perhaps the same is true
of Jonah.

Jonah's prayer consumes the entire time he is in the belly of the fish, as
if no extra time remained for another thought. Perhaps—who knows?—
Jonah prayed this prayer often earlier in his life. Perhaps it is because of
that that this prayer rises to his lips even as the water rises right up to his
neck and then reaches over his lips. He keeps praying—up to the point
when he cannot utter one more word. But even then the thought of this
prayer comes to him. So it is for us when we are reduced to no more than
thoughts, to barely more than instinctive reaction. At such times, we grasp
desperately after what remains in our memory, what we have learned by
heart, so much so that it becomes a part of our hearts.[7] It is when we are in
the innards of the fish with the water rising over our lips that what we really
have in our heart rises up out of it. During our moment of greatest danger,
this is something other than what we are able to recite with fitting words or
in wholly well-formed sentences. We grasp for a prayer that has sunk into
us. In that kind of prayer we speak differently. We blurt it out uncontrolla-
bly in the blink of an eye. And, before we can get a hold on ourselves, we become something different through that prayer.

In his prayer, Jonah lets himself become involved in it. Moreover, in his
prayer, Jonah lets himself into it. He falls into it so completely that *he
changes. He speaks completely differently* about God and about himself than he
was capable of earlier. Earlier, he had grumbled about God's judgment and
God's goodness. He had concerned himself with the outcome of God's
word of judgment and concluded that he did not want to be a part of God's
plan. Jonah had intended to interrupt God's plan with his flight. Yet now, in
the moment of prayer, he finds himself praying a completely different
prayer than even he might have anticipated.

Nothing else occurs to Jonah than to call on God as the one who could
save him from his danger. He turns himself to this God and his prayer pen-
etrates into God's holy temple. In speaking this prayer, Jonah already *looks*

---

6. Cf. Miller, *They Cried to the Lord*, 185: "The explicit reporting or telling of God's
deliverance to a wide audience, therefore, is one of the most noticeable features of this
song of thanksgiving [Psalm 22]. Indeed there is an unending echo of reporting and proclamation to others."

7. See the contribution by Janzen in this volume.

back on his distress. This is the *second change*, no less miraculous than the first. He thanks God in the unlit confines of his cell on death row. He does not suddenly, heroically outgrow his childishness. But he says far more in this moment than he is able to articulate. He speaks differently about God and completely differently about himself than what can be expected of him in this situation, slung here and there without an above or below and with no view out. But isn't every prayer like this to some extent—an unreasonable expectation that surpasses what is expected of us?

Now what remains is the power of one more prayer from the heart. Jonah speaks here like many others, whom waters of every type have swallowed up, who have been dragged into the deep. This prayer might be a song that he had sung frequently in the house of God or that he had learned in his religious training. Perhaps, in such lethal danger, he squeezed out only a very few words, "Lord, help!" or "O Lord, my God!" Yet with this shred of a prayer the whole meaning of the prayer is nevertheless present. Perhaps not for Jonah himself, since he can say absolutely no more, let alone think as far as God's temple, but the entire prayer unfolds itself before God. And we can listen to it.

We *must* listen to it. We have a part in Jonah's prayer, just like we have a part in the prayers of so many others who have been in dark places before us. Perhaps that is also the reason why something still occurs in us when we find ourselves yet again in the belly of a fish; when we find ourselves lying in bed with a high fever capable of no thought, let alone a well-constructed sentence, or when we pray with someone who is terminally ill, who perhaps can form only a single word. Yet, with that one word they can remember an entire prayer that they can no longer put together. A friend once wrote to me about a very serious illness, in which he was no longer able to pray. In retrospect, this reminded him of his dying mother, who repeated only one word, "Forever," from the psalm in which is it written, "And I will dwell in the house of the Lord for ever" (Ps 23:6; KJV).

Or, we could think of the Russian pilgrim who spent all his energy and attention on the short prayer, "Lord Jesus Christ, have mercy on us!"[8] Finally the pilgrim could pray nothing else, nothing more, and yet with this prayer, somehow, all that a person could say before God had been said. Such prayers belong to us like our heartbeat. It is not so much that we are bringing something to God, but that in the heartbeat of this remembered prayer, God carries our life for us.

In the weak sound of Jonah's heartbeat in the belly of the fish is a trace of what Paul writes, "We do not know how to pray as we ought"

8. Emmanuel Jungclausen, ed., *Aufrichtige Erzählungen eines russischen Pilgers* (7th ed.; Freiburg/Basel/Wien: Herder, 1999).

(Rom 8:26).[9] But do we ever really know what to pray or how to pray rightly? The unpronounceable sigh comes before God; in our words of prayer, we are brought before God. There we find ourselves again, completely different than we found ourselves before. And, again, we are not alone in sighing such a sigh.

"Salvation comes from the Lord": Has such a prayer taken root in our hearts? Perhaps other, similar words of prayer have taken root, for example, the call to worship, which one can hear in German Reformed worship: "Our help comes from the Lord who made heaven and earth, whose Word and faithfulness remain eternally, who does not let fall the work of his hands." This prayer echoes in Jonah's prayer, "Deliverance belongs to the Lord" (Jonah 2:9b). Has this prayer buried itself so deeply in our memory that it can burst out of the deepest recesses, when we need it most, when we can say no more?

God, the Lord over life and death, is the one who hears a voice out of the deep, even when that voice should really be silent before that Hearer and before all other ears. This is the God whose hand reaches to the metaphysical depths, and not just *to* the depths, but rather *into* the depths—even into the depths where this hand cannot be felt. This is demonstrated ironically in that the monster, which swallowed up and traveled to the saving shore, comes to be at the very place where we would wish, at all costs, not to be. The belly of the fish became the saving hand of God that enfolded Jonah, even though Jonah did not have the slightest notion of this. Jonah prayed in his deep despair to God, who saved him, who far surpassed his perception of the situation, just as every prayer that comes out of the depths of the heart greatly surpasses all our possibilities and expectations.

Jesus speaks about these three days and three nights in the belly of the fish when he denotes the time between Good Friday and Easter, between his death and his resurrection (see Matt 12:40). He, too, was swallowed up by death, dragged down into the depth of the world of the dead. But he was not disobedient like Jonah was; rather, he was obedient unto death, even death on a cross. He gave himself into God's hands and this landed him in the grave. But there—even there!—he was not abandoned by God.

Prayer leaves room for God, then, whether in the belly of the fish or in the world of the dead, because each hearing of prayer is a sign of salvation out of death. All our prayers are lifted up by God, because they speak of God in ways other than we ourselves are able to say, think, or even dream.

---

9. Miller, *They Cried to the Lord*, 321: "Here, therefore, Paul takes us into that crucial dimension of prayer that is to the forefront in the Old Testament, the prayer according to God's will."

Songs in a New Key:
The Psalmic Structure of the
Chronicler's Hymn (1 Chr 16:8–36)

MARK A. THRONTVEIT

———◆———

I. Introduction

The primary objective of chapters 13–15 in the Chronicler's[1] narrative entails a description of the tortuous journey of the ark of the covenant, the visible symbol of God's presence, to its permanent site in Jerusalem.[2] In chapter 16, the Chronicler celebrates the meeting of that objective with a great hymn of thanksgiving constructed from portions of three existing psalms (Ps 105:1–15 = vv. 8–22; Ps 96:1b, 2b–10b, 11a–13a = vv. 23–33; Ps 106:1, 47–48 = vv. 34–36).

Scholarship has long been aware of the Chronicler's hymn, yet matters of unity and authorship have dominated scholarly interest until fairly recently.[3] Readers interested in matters of theology or exegesis are often

---

Author's note: It is a pleasure to offer this essay on the intersection of Psalms and Chronicles in honor of Patrick D. Miller, tireless advocate for biblical readings of theology and theological readings of the Bible; passionate preacher of God's word; editor, author, and *Doktorvater* who, twenty-two years ago, managed to find these marvelous psalms in the bowels of Chronicles and surprise me with them as part of my Hebrew exam.

1. In this study, "the Chronicler" will be used to designate the anonymous author of 1–2 Chronicles, a work composed in Jerusalem sometime during the Persian Period. The books of Ezra–Nehemiah, while sharing some of the concerns of the Chronicler and coming from roughly the same time, are from a different hand. For a concise treatment of these issues, see Ralph W. Klein, "Chronicles, Book of 1–2," *ABD* 1:992–1002.

2. For recent, rhetorically informed presentations, see Leslie C. Allen, "The First and Second Books of Chronicles," in *NIB* 3:382–83; and Tamara Eskenazi, "A Literary Approach to Chronicles' Ark Narrative in 1 Chronicles 13–16," in *Fortunate the Eyes That See: Essays in Honor of David Noel Freedman in Celebration of His Seventieth Birthday* (ed. Astrid Beck et al.; Grand Rapids: Eerdmans, 1995) 258–74.

3. Recent scholarship affirms the text's unity. Those who question it essentially follow Martin Noth, who regards vv. 5–38 and 41–42 as secondary (*The Chronicler's History* [trans.

directed to consult the relevant sections of a good Psalms commentary! This, however, neglects the importance of context and falsely suggests that these psalms mean the same thing in both canonical settings. Just as a Sousa march sounds brighter when transposed and played in a higher key, so the Chronicler's transposition of these songs to David's time results in a shift in the character of their message for the post-exilic community and, I would argue, for us.

Fortunately, the growing interest in synchronic approaches to biblical texts has emphasized matters of structure and context over such diachronic matters as unity and authorship. This has resulted in a small but important body of literature devoted to the analysis of these songs in a new key as a psalmic hymn in its own right, with a particular setting, function, message, and audience.

Trent C. Butler was the first to seriously challenge investigations limited to descriptions of textual differences and the question of authorship by demonstrating that the hymn conforms well with the Chronicler's familiar theological perspective.[4] Soon thereafter, J. A. Loader offered a detailed structural outline of the hymn based upon rhetorical and stylistic observations.[5] Andrew E. Hill furthered Loader's rhetorical analysis by pointing to the chiastic ordering of the imperatives that introduce the underlying psalms ("Give thanks," v. 8; "Sing," vv. 9, 23; "Give thanks," v. 34).[6] Building upon another of Hill's observations, R. Mark Shipp suggested that the levitical activities prescribed in v. 4b ("give thanks," "praise," and "remember") structure the Chronicler's hymn and provide a "connective echo"[7] that anchors the hymn in its narrative context.[8] Most recently, John W. Kleinig, in a study of the basis, function, and significance of choral music in Chronicles, has offered a thorough literary analysis of the hymn.[9]

H. G. M. Williamson; JSOTSup 50; Sheffield: JSOT Press, 1987] 35). Regarding authorship, only C. F. Keil thinks David is the author (*The Books of the Chronicles* [Edinburgh: T. & T. Clark, 1872] 211–18). Peter R. Ackroyd doubts that the Chronicler composed or arranged the psalm (*I & II Chronicles, Ezra, Nehemiah* [London: SCM, 1973] 64–65).

4. Trent C. Butler, "A Forgotten Passage From a Forgotten Era (1 Chr. XVI 8–36)," *VT* 28 (1978) 142–50.

5. J. A. Loader, "Redaction and Function of the Chronistic 'Psalm of David,'" in *Studies in the Chronicler* (Ou-Testamentiese Werkgemeenskap in Suider-Afrika 19; ed. W. C. van Wyk; Johannesburg: Ou-Testamentiese Werkgemeenskap in Suider-Afrika, 1976) 69–75.

6. Andrew E. Hill, "Patchwork Poetry or Reasoned Verse? Connective Structure in 1 Chronicles XVI," *VT* 33 (1983) 97–101.

7. Ibid., 99.

8. R. Mark Shipp, "'Remember His Covenant Forever': A Study of the Chronicler's Use of the Psalms," *ResQ* 35 (1993) 31–39.

9. John W. Kleinig, *The Lord's Song: The Basis, Function and Significance of Choral Music in Chronicles* (JSOTSup 156; Sheffield: JSOT Press, 1993) 133–48.

Tamara Eskenazi captures the state of this emerging scholarly recognition of the hymn's poetic character and reminds us of its unusual nature when she states, "The thanksgiving psalm extols God's wondrous deeds in hyperbole that is common in poetry. The use of poetry, however, is uncommon in Chronicles."[10] Nevertheless, despite general scholarly recognition of the hymn's poetic character, there is little scholarly consensus regarding the relationship between its poetic character and its contextual function and message. Is its purpose to attribute the contemporary practice of psalm singing to David? Is its purpose primarily liturgical, or is there an element of proclamation present in the Chronicler's reworking?[11] Solutions to such questions are further hindered by the lack of consensus regarding the hymn's structure. Most scholars find four divisions,[12] but divisions of two,[13] three,[14] five,[15] six,[16] and even eight[17] regularly appear in the literature. Unfortunately, rationales for these proposed structures are rarely provided.

---

10. Eskenazi, "Ark Narrative," 269.

11. For a brief overview of the questions see Frederick J. Gaiser, "Songs in the Story: A Study of the Place of the Songs of Lament and Praise in the Historical and Narrative Literature of the Old Testament and the Apocrypha" (D. theol. diss., University of Heidelberg, 1984) 286–91.

12. H. G. M. Williamson, *1 and 2 Chronicles* (NCB; Grand Rapids: Eerdmans, 1982) 128–29: vv. 8–13; 14–22; 23–33; 34–36a; followed by W. Johnstone, *1 and 2 Chronicles* (JSOTSup 253; Sheffield: Sheffield Academic Press, 1997) 192–94. John Sailhamer, *First and Second Chronicles* (Chicago: Moody, 1983) 45: vv. 8–13; 14–22; 23–30; 31–36. Hill, "Patchwork Poetry," 100: vv. 8; 9–22; 23–33; 34–36; followed by Martin J. Selman, *1 Chronicles* (TOTC; Leicester: IVP, 1994) 168–72. Shipp, "Remember," 34–37: vv. 8–14; 15–22; 23–33; 34–36; followed by Samuel E. Balentine, "'You Can't Pray a Lie': Truth *and* Fiction in the Prayers of Chronicles," in *The Chronicler as Historian* (ed. M. Patrick Graham et al.; Sheffield: Sheffield Academic Press, 1997) 255. Leslie C. Allen, "First and Second Chronicles," 3:401: vv. 8–22; 23–30; 31–33; 34–36.

13. Johnstone, *1 and 2 Chronicles*, 175: vv. 8–22; 23–36. Sara Japhet, *I & II Chronicles: A Commentary* (OTL; Louisville: Westminster/John Knox, 1993) 316: vv. 8–33; 34–36 (but see n. 14 below). In addition to his structural analysis (see n. 15 below) Kleinig also sees two main sections, a psalm of thanksgiving in vv. 8–34 and a summary petition in vv. 35–36a (*The Lord's Song*, 142–44).

14. Loader, "Psalm of David," 71–72: vv. 8–22; 23–33; 34–36a; followed by Simon J. De Vries, *I and II Chronicles* (FOTL 11; Grand Rapids: Eerdmans, 1989) 151; Leslie C. Allen, *1, 2 Chronicles* (The Communicator's Commentary 10; Waco: Word, 1987) 116–18; and Japhet, *I & II Chronicles*, 312.

15. Kleinig, *The Lord's Song*, 143–44: vv. 8; 9–22; 23–30; 31–33; 34.

16. John W. Watts, *Psalm and Story: Inset Hymns in Hebrew Narrative* (JSOTSup 139; Sheffield: JSOT Press, 1992) 156; and J. A. Thompson, *1, 2 Chronicles* (NAC 9; Nashville: Broadman, 1994) 140–42: vv. 8–13; 14–22; 23–29; 30–33; 34; 35–36a.

17. Keil, *Chronicles*, 211: vv. 8–11; 12–14; 15–18; 19–22; 23–27; 28–30; 31–33; 34–36.

In his discussion of poetry and interpretation, Patrick D. Miller addresses the importance of both exegetical and stylistic evidence in the analysis of texts:

> This means that poetry and interpretation are not matters that should be dealt with separately; rather, a deeper sensitivity to the poetic character of the text can enhance our understanding, and attention to poetic features may aid the interpretive process and its results. Even more, they may do much of the task of enabling us to appropriate the word of the psalm or the biblical poem as our own.[18]

Far too often, the perceived development of themes determines the structural analysis of texts, without reference to corroborating stylistic evidence. This has certainly been true for treatments of 1 Chr 16:8–36.

Miller's plea for the integration of the stylistic aspects of texts is also found in another article:

> The full hearing of the Psalms will be greatly enhanced when the familiar tendency to abstract content from form or to empty form of its content is overcome. To know the Psalms are poetic is not to forget that they are Scripture. To read and hear them as Scripture requires that one receive them also as poetry. From either direction, *understanding* is all.[19]

The present study echoes this claim that identification of structure leads to clearer perception of function and message. This will be illustrated by offering an examination of 1 Chr 16:8–36 that is sensitive to both thematic and stylistic evidence. The investigation begins with an annotated translation displaying what I believe to be the major divisions of the hymn, followed by an examination of three structural analyses seeking acceptance today. An argument for my own proposal and a brief discussion of its ramifications conclude the study.

II. Translation and Division of 1 Chr 16:8–36

In the following translation I have intended to be quite literal. The translation essentially follows that of the RSV (except in word order), sacrificing eloquence in order to display the structure of the individual divisions and their arrangement. Justification of the divisions themselves appears in section IV.

---

18. Patrick D. Miller, *Interpreting the Psalms* (Philadelphia: Fortress, 1986) 30. See the similar remarks of Leslie C. Allen regarding the central section of Psalm 103 (*Psalms 101–150* [WBC; Waco: Word, 1983] 21).

19. Patrick D. Miller, "Current Issues in Psalms Studies," *WW* 5 (1985) 143.

1 Chr 16:8–36

I. Thanksgiving Hymn: vv. 8–34

A. Introductory Calls to Praise

[8]O give thanks to the LORD, call on his name; make known among the
peoples his deeds!

[9]Sing about him, sing hymns concerning him;[20] tell of all his wonderful
works!

[10]Glory in his holy name; let the heart of them rejoice who seek the LORD!

[11]Seek out the LORD and "his strength;"[21] seek his face regularly![22]

[12]Remember the (his) wonderful works that he has done; his signs, and the
judgments of his mouth,

[13]O seed of Israel[23] his servant, O children of Jacob his chosen ones!

B. Thanks for Past "Judgments"

[14]He, the LORD, is our God; his judgments are in all the earth.

[15]He remembers[24] forever his covenant, the word he commanded to a
thousand generation(s),

[16]that he cut with Abraham, even his oath to Isaac,

[17]that he established as a statute to Jacob, to Israel (as) an everlasting
covenant,

[18]by saying, "To you I will give the land of Canaan, (as) the portion of your
inheritance."

[19]When they[25] were an insignificant people, few in number and merely
aliens there,

---

20. For this use of the preposition see P. A. H. de Boer, "Cantate Domino: An Erroneous Dative?" in *Remembering All the Way* (OTS 21; ed. A. S. van der Woude; Leiden:
Brill, 1981) 55–67; cited in Kleinig, *The Lord's Song*, 139.

21. I.e., "the ark"; cf. Pss 78:61; 132:8; see NJPSV (Tanakh).

22. תמיד has the sense of "regularly" here as opposed to its usual sense of "continually"; see Japhet, *I & II Chronicles*, 311.

23. Ps 105:6 reads אברהם, "Abraham," followed by RSV. Most commentators now recognize that the Chronicler traces the origin of the people to the patriarch, Israel, rather
than Abraham. See, e.g., H. G. M. Williamson, *Israel in the Books of Chronicles* (Cambridge:
Cambridge University Press, 1977) 62; and Sarah Japhet, "Conquest and Settlement in
Chronicles," *JBL* 98 (1979) 217.

24. Reading 3ms perfect זכר with Ps 105:8, LXX[B] (LXX[AL] participle), RSV, NEB, NIV,
and REB. The MT reads 2mp imperative זכרו, "Remember." Recent scholarship prefers
the MT and sees it as one of several chronistic alterations that make the psalm contemporary. While the concept of God's remembering the covenant is well established (see
Gen 9:15, 16; Exod 2:24; 6:5; Lev 26:42, 45; Pss 106:45; 111:5) there are no other instances
of the people remembering, or being called to remember, *the covenant*. Furthermore, the
uncontested presence of זכרו in v. 12 has already called the community to remembrance.

25. Reading the 3mp suffix בהיותם with Ps 105:12, the LXX, the Vulgate, RSV, NAB,
NASB, NIV, and NRSV. The MT, the Peshitta, the Targum, NJB, and NJPSV (Tanakh) read

[20]they wandered from nation to nation, from one kingdom to another people,

[21]he allowed no one[26] to oppress them, and warned kings on their account:

[22]"Touch not my anointed ones; and to my prophets do no harm!"

C. Thanks for Present Sovereignty

[23]Sing about the LORD, all the earth; proclaim from day to day his deliverance![27]

[24]Declare among the nations his glory; among all the peoples his wonderful works!

[25]For great is the LORD, and greatly to be praised; indeed, revered is he above all gods.

[26]For all the gods of the peoples are nothing, but the LORD the heavens has made.

[27]Splendor and majesty are before him; strength and joy are in his place.[28]

[28]Ascribe to the LORD, O families of the peoples,
   ascribe to the LORD glory and strength,

[29]ascribe to the LORD the glory due his name,
   bring an offering and come before him,[29]
   worship the LORD in holy majesty!

B'. Thanks for Future "Rule"

[30]Tremble at his presence, all the earth![30] Then will the world be established, never will it totter![31]

[31]Let the heavens rejoice and the earth be glad, that they may say[32] among the nations, "The LORD is king!"

[32]Let the sea and all that fills it roar; let the field and all within it exult!

---

a 2mp suffix בהיותכם ("when you were"). A 3mp reading connects v. 19 with what follows, a 2mp reading ties v. 19 to what precedes. Both translations are equally possible. The Chronicler's interests and audience argue for the latter, hence the recent shift in scholarly acceptance. Structural considerations may favor the former, however, as will be argued in the third section of this study. On the ambiguity, see Japhet, *I & II Chronicles*, 319.

26. Ps 105:14 reads אדם for לאיש.

27. Ps 96:1a, 2a are omitted, creating a new parallel between vv. 1b and 2b.

28. Ps 96:6: במקדשו, "in his sanctuary," for במקמו. The Chronicler alters the source to make the psalm fit David's time before the building of the temple.

29. Ps 96:8: לחצרותיו, "into his courts," for לפניו. See previous note.

30. Ps 96:10a appears at 1 Chr 16:31b where the imperative has become a jussive.

31. Ps 96:10b is omitted. The verbs are clearly Niphal imperfects suggesting, along with the אז, the future aspect.

32. The Chronicler has changed an imperative to a jussive. Jussives (precatives) with simple *waw* usually imply purpose; see Ronald J. Williams, *Hebrew Syntax: An Outline* (2d ed.; Toronto: University of Toronto Press, 1976) § 181.

³³Then will the trees of the forest rejoice before the LORD, when³³ he comes to rule (judge)³⁴ the earth!

A′. Concluding Call to Praise

³⁴O give thanks to the LORD! For he is good, for his covenant loyalty is forever!

II. Concluding Liturgy: vv. 35–36

Liturgical Summons

³⁵ᵃSay:

Petition

³⁵ᵇ"Save us, O God our savior,³⁵ [gather us] and deliver us³⁶ from the nations,
to give thanks to your holy name, and to glory in your praise."

Benediction

³⁶ᵃ"Blessed be the LORD, the God of Israel, for ever and ever."

Congregational Response

³⁶ᵇThen all the people said,³⁷ "Amen!" and "Praise the LORD!"

III. Three Structural Analyses

Contemporary scholarship has essentially offered three options regarding the structure of the Chronicler's hymn. Virtually every proposal presented above appears as a variant of one of these three. To these we now turn. The three representative treatments are by R. Mark Shipp, John W. Kleinig, and James W. Watts.³⁸

---

33. Despite Miller's vigorous defense of causal כי at this juncture in Psalm 96 in response to Crüsemann's argument for a deictic or emphatic reading in the hymns of praise in general, a temporal reading expressing "when" as well as "why" seems best (Patrick D. Miller, *They Cried to the Lord: The Form and Theology of Biblical Prayer* [Minneapolis: Augsburg Fortress, 1994] 358–62; Frank Crüsemann, *Studien zur Formgeschichte von Hymnus und Danklied in Israel* [WMANT 32, Neukirchen-Vluyn: Neukirchener Verlag, 1969] 32–35).

34. The point of the three middle divisions, as well as Psalm 96, is the coming rule of the LORD (v. 31b = Ps 96:10). "Rule" is often a better translation of שפט than "judge" because of the latter's legal connotations in English. See NJPSV (Tanakh), NAB, and James Luther Mays, *Psalms* (Interpretation; Louisville: John Knox, 1994) 309.

35. Ps 106:47: יהוה אלהינו, "O LORD our God," instead of אלהי ישענו.

36. Ps 106:47 lacks והצילנו, "and deliver us," but the LXX lacks וקבצנו, "and gather us." L. C. Allen suggests a conflated text (*The Greek Chronicles: The Relation of the Septuagint of I and II Chronicles to the Massoretic Text* [2 vols.; VTSup 25, 27; Leiden: Brill, 1974] 1:217). Japhet recommends omitting "gather us" (*I & II Chronicles*, 319).

37. Ps 106:48: ואמר, "and let (all the people) say," for ויאמרו.

38. Shipp, "Remember," 34–37; Kleinig, *The Lord's Song*, 141–44; Watts, *Psalm and Story*, 155.

R. Mark Shipp: "Remember, Praise (Sing), and Give Thanks!"

The most common structural analysis sees a correspondence between the main divisions of the Chronicler's hymn and the three psalm fragments of the underlying sources (Pss 105:1–15; 96:1b, 2b–13a; 106:1, 47–48). Of the many scholars making use of this schema, Loader, Hill, and especially Shipp have provided stylistic rationales for their proposals.[39]

Shipp begins with Hill's suggestion that 1 Chr 16:4b provides the structural key to the thanksgiving hymn: "And he set before the ark of Yahweh some of the ministering Levites, for the purpose of *causing remembrance, giving thanks*, and *praising* Yahweh, the God of Israel" (my emphasis). Shipp proposes that the three infinitive constructs of v. 4b correspond to both the major divisions in the hymn as well as the psalmic sources appropriated by the Chronicler, as follows:

1. An "Introductory Section" (vv. 8–14) in which the three verbal roots of v. 4b appear in reverse order (ידה, "give thanks," v. 8; הלל, "praise," v. 10; and זכר, "remember," v. 12) and that corresponds to Ps 105:1–7.

2. A "Remember Section" (vv. 15–22), introduced by the imperative זכרו ("remember"; v. 15), that corresponds to Ps 105:8–15, a recital of God's covenant loyalty that Israel is urged to recall.

3. A "Praise Section" (vv. 23–33), introduced by the imperative שירו ("sing"; v. 23), that corresponds to Psalm 96, a hymn celebrating God's rule.[40]

4. A "Giving-Thanks Section" (vv. 34–36), introduced by the imperative הודו ("give thanks"; v. 34), that corresponds to Ps 106:1, 47–48.

Shipp is to be commended for his attempt to blend rhetorical and thematic evidence. Nevertheless, a number of points require discussion. The observation that the repetition of the three infinitive constructs of v. 4b in vv. 8, 10, and 12 serves as a "connective echo" linking the hymn to its immediate narrative context seems well founded. Why the division should continue through v. 14, however, is more problematic. All of the interpretive benefits derived from this observation would still apply in a division ending

---

39. Other scholars who see the three underlying psalms as structurally constitutive include Loader, who claims the correct sequence of vv. 30–33 is 30a, 31b–30b, 31a–32a, 32b–33a, 33b ("Remember," 71–72), followed by De Vries, *I and II Chronicles*, 151; Hill, "Patchwork Poetry," 100, followed by Selman, *1 Chronicles*, 168–72; Balentine, "You Can't Pray a Lie," 255; Allen, *1, 2 Chronicles*, 116–18; and Japhet, *I & II Chronicles*, 312.

40. Shipp, "Remember," 34 n. 15 is not accurate. Based upon the rest of his essay I have reconstructed what I take his meaning to be. Surely his "(2)" requires a reference to vv. 15–22, and the psalmic reference must be Ps 105:1–15, not "105:15." His "(3)" would then refer to vv. 23–33 (presently unmarked), and vv. 34–36 would become (4) not "(3)" as in the note.

at either v. 12 or v. 13. In fact, the three verbs, highlighted by the repetition, suggest an ABA′ pattern in which vv. 8 and 9 (introduced by הודו) and v. 12 (introduced by זכרו) frame vv. 10 and 11 (introduced by התהללו). The repetition of נפלאתיו ("his wonderful works") in the A and A′ segments (vv. 9b, 12a) and two forms of בקש ("seek") in the B segment (מבקשי, "seekers of," v. 10b; and בקשו, "seek!" v. 11b) that frame yet another synonym of "seek," דרשו (v. 11a), further supports this arrangement. Verse 13 would then close the division by naming the, as yet, unnamed addressees of the preceding calls to praise God.

One assumes Shipp continues the division through v. 14 because of his decision to use the imperatives gleaned from the infinitive constructs in v. 4b as divisional markers. The second division (vv. 15–22) provides the strongest evidence for this approach in that this "Remember Section" does indeed begin with זכרו and contains material that Israel might reasonably be urged to recall. It should be noted, however, that Shipp here follows a recent shift in scholarship. Contemporary interpreters maintain that the 2mp imperative form of "remember" found in the MT is original, and is therefore a tendentious change from the 3ms perfect form ("he [God] remembers") found in Ps 105:15. But this is by no means certain. The textual evidence is mixed (see n. 24 above), displaying confusion in the transmission of the LXX as well as the MT. Yet, even Butler, whose seminal article in 1978 still makes the strongest case for reading the hymn as a meticulously crafted chronistic appropriation of these psalms aimed at a particular audience, makes no mention of the supposed alteration.[41] Furthermore, זכר is not a key term for the Chronicler. It appears only five times in 1–2 Chronicles, three of them in the hymn (i.e., from earlier psalmic source material; vv. 4, 12, 15); the other two in 2 Chr 6:42 and 24:22. Finally, if the Chronicler has introduced this change it would be the only imperative found in a division which, as will be argued later, is comprised of narrative and speech.

Concerning the third division, Shipp candidly admits that "The Praise Section" begins with the imperative שירו ("Sing!") and that "this presents an obstacle to (his) analysis."[42] He then argues that "praise" is the theme of the whole section, maintains that "sing" and "praise" are synonymous terms for the Chronicler, and points to the *puʿal* participle of "praise" in v. 25a.[43] While this is true, it is somewhat beside the point and calls into

---

41. Butler, "A Forgotten Passage." Cf. Williamson's cautious remarks (*1 and 2 Chronicles*, 129).

42. Shipp, "Remember," 36.

43. On this last point, see Balentine who otherwise strictly follows Shipp's proposal but here refrains from citing שירו and only mentions the appearance of מהלל, "praised" ("You Can't Pray a Lie," 255).

question a structural proposal that features introductory imperatives repeated from the narrative context as division markers.

Shipp's fourth division, "The Give-Thanks Section" (vv. 34–36), while
meeting the criterion of an introductory imperative repeated from v. 4b,
raises questions of a form-critical nature. Kleinig's observation that the
"liturgical rubric in v. 35a . . . separates the song of thanksgiving from the
petition with its doxology" is pertinent here.[44] Two-thirds of this section
devoted to the giving of thanks consists of petition (v. 35, though הודה does
appear in a purpose clause connected with the petition), benediction
(v. 36a), and congregational response (v. 36b). Similar difficulties arise in the
other proposals that assume the underlying psalms form the structural
framework for the Chronicler's hymn.

John W. Kleinig: "Give Thanks to the Lord, *Sing, and Remember!"*

A second approach to the structure of the Chronicler's hymn is exemplified in John W. Kleinig's detailed examination of the theological significance of choral music in the books of Chronicles.[45] Kleinig begins by
noting a number of devices that unify the psalm and distinguish its chief
parts.[46]

1. The liturgical rubric ואמרו, "Say," separates the song of thanksgiving
   (vv. 8–34) from the petition and following doxology (vv. 35–36a).
2. The song of thanksgiving, itself, is marked by the use of an inclusio
   with הודו ליהוה, "Give thanks to the Lord" (vv. 8, 34).
3. An inclusio formed by כל־הארץ, "all the earth" (vv. 23, 30), marks the
   intervening verses as a separate unit.
4. The repetition of two other imperatives (besides הודו) introduces
   two parallel poetic units: שירו, "sing" (vv. 9, 23), separates vv. 9–22
   from 23–30, and זכרו, "remember," (vv. 12, 15) identifies two segments
   within vv. 9–22.
5. Six common terms act as "catch words" that unify the material: עם,
   "people," vv. 8, 20, 24, 26, 28; גוי, "nation," vv. 20, 24, 31, 35; שם, "name,"
   vv. 8, 10, 29, 35; קדש, "holy," vv. 10, 29, 35; הודה, "give thanks," vv. 8, 34,
   35; and תהללה/הלל, "praise," vv. 10, 25, 35.

---

44. Kleinig, *The Lord's Song,* 142.
45. Ibid., 133–48. Leslie C. Allen's approach in his recent commentary mirrors
Kleinig's. While he collapses v. 8 into the following division and the congregational petition and response into the previous division, his designations "a call to Israel to praise
God (vv. 8–22), a call for praise throughout the earth (vv. 23–30), a call for cosmic praise
(vv. 31–33), and a call for Israel not only to praise but also to pray that fresh potential for
praise may be theirs (v. 34–36)" are virtually identical, ("First and Second Chronicles,"
3:401).
46. Kleinig, *The Lord's Song,* 142.

In addition, each new section and subsection is introduced by calls to praise expressed in imperative and jussive forms, frequently in clusters (vv. 8, 9, 12, 15, 23, 28, 31, 34).[47] Building upon the work of Keil, Becker, and Hausmann, Kleinig emphasizes that the originally unspecified audience of all these calls to praise moves from "Israel" (v. 13), through "the earth with all its ethnic groups" (vv. 23, 30), to "the whole cosmos" (vv. 31–32).[48] Kleinig then offers the following structural outline based upon his observations:[49]

A. *The Psalm of Thanksgiving: 1 Chr 16:8–34*
   1. *General Call to Thanksgiving:* 16:8   הודו ליהוה
   2. *Israel's Praise:* 16:9–22   שירו
      a. Call to musical praise (9–11)
      b. Double call to remembrance (12–22)
         (1) remembrance of the LORD's works (12–14)   זכרו
            (a) call to remember the LORD (12)
            (b) identity and status of audience (13)
            (c) content of remembrance (14)
         (2) remembrance of the LORD's covenant (15–22)   זכרו
            (a) call to remember the covenant with the ancestors (15–18)
            (b) Israel protected as result of this covenant (19–22)
   3. *International Praise:* 16:23–33   שירו
      a. The praise of the whole earth (23–27)
         (1) call to singing (23–24)   כל־הארץ
         (2) reasons for song (25–27)
      b. The praise of its peoples (28–30)
         (1) call to prostration in sacrificial worship (28–30a)   כל־הארץ
         (2) reason for prostration (30b)
   4. *Cosmic Praise:* 16:31–33
      a. Command for universal proclamation of the LORD's kingship (31–32)
      b. Result of proclamation (33)
   5. *Final Call to Thanksgiving:* 16:34   הודו ליהוה
B. *Summary Petition: 1 Chr 16:35–36a*
   1. Petition for Israel's Deliverance (35)
   2. Doxology (36a)

---

47. Ibid., 143.
48. See Keil, *Chronicles*, 214; J. Becker, *1 Chronik* (NEchtB; Würzburg: Echter Verlag, 1986) 72–74; J. Hausmann, "Gottesdienst als Gotteslob: Erwägungen zu 1 Chr 16, 8–36," in *Spiritualität: Theologische Beiträge* (ed. H. Wagner; Stuttgart: Calwer, 1987) 86–87.
49. Kleinig, *The Lord's Song*, 143–44. I have added the key structuring words in Hebrew.

Kleinig's sensitive reading of 1 Chr 16:8–36 takes careful notice of the thematic development of the hymn without overlooking its stylistic elements. Each of the stylistic devices Kleinig isolates is worthy of comment. To begin with, the separation of the song of thanksgiving from the petition and its doxology by means of the liturgical rubric, "and say" (v. 35a), is surely correct. This, along with the consequent recognition of הודו ליהוה as an inclusio marking vv. 8 and 34 as an introduction and conclusion, constitutes his most important contribution to the structural analysis of this text.

The supposed inclusio formed by the occurrence of כל־הארץ, "all the earth," in vv. 23 and 30, however, is less certain. The structural significance of this device, for Kleinig, is to isolate a section of "international praise" in which "all the earth" (vv. 23–27) and "its peoples" (vv. 28–30) engage in praise and sacrificial worship of the LORD. This section is preceded by a section of "Israel's praise" (vv. 9–22) and followed by a section of "cosmic praise" (vv. 31–33). As virtually all analyses take v. 23 as the start of a new section and v. 33 as the end of a section, these seem secure as boundaries. At issue is whether one or two sections lie between these boundaries, and if two, what their extent is. Shipp, and those who see the three psalms as the hymn's structural matrix, consider vv. 23–33 (= Psalm 96) as one section and assign no structural function to the repetition of כל־הארץ. Those who see two sections either begin the second at v. 30 (e.g., Watts, see next section) or, with Kleinig, begin the second section with v. 31. Clearly, both analyses are possible. The כל־הארץ in v. 30 either indicates the beginning of a new section or forms an inclusio with v. 23. For now, it should be noticed that כל־הארץ has already appeared (albeit with the preposition ב) in v. 14 where, as will be shown later, it initiates the primary structuring device of the hymn.

Kleinig also finds great significance in the repetition of the imperatives "sing" (vv. 9, 23) and "remember" (vv. 12, 15) that introduce new parallel units. Kleinig's elegant approach to the structure of the hymn based upon the placement of these imperatives invites acceptance. Three questions remain, however. First, one could agree with the major inclusio in vv. 8 and 34 without limiting the introduction to v. 8. This decision leaves vv. 9–11 somewhat isolated between the initial "give thanks" and the "remember" of v. 12. Kleinig's suggestion that these verses form a segment of "musical praise," while conducive to his overall thesis and consistent with the structuring role of "sing," is not compelling. Of the six imperatives only the first two ("sing" and "sing praises," v. 9a) and the jussive ("rejoice," v. 10b) are consistently seen in musical contexts. The remaining four imperatives ("tell," v. 9b; "glory," v. 10a; and "seek," whether דרש, v. 11a or בקש, v. 11b) are not. Japhet suggests that they are most commonly associated with the ark.[50] This seems to be a better explanation for their appearance at this juncture.

50. Japhet, *I & II Chronicles*, 318.

Second, this decision leaves the identity of the addressees of all those imperatives unknown until the middle of the second subsection of the second division (v. 13). As demonstrated in the discussion of Shipp's approach, vv. 8–13 display an overall ABA' structure that binds them together while still incorporating the three infinitive constructs of v. 4b and maintaining the identification of the addressees in the same unit.

Third, again, as in Shipp's approach, much structural weight is attached to the Chronicler's supposed tendentious change from "He (God) remembers" (Ps 105:8) to the plural imperative "You (Israel) remember" in v. 15. The tenuous nature of this approach was discussed there. Rejection of the MT reading, here, would eliminate Kleinig's double call to remembrance in vv. 12–22.

Finally, the list of catch words that unify the material should be expanded to include (ל)יהוה, "(to) the Lord" (vv. 8, 10–11, 14, 23, 25–26, 28a, 29b, 29a, 29b, 31, 33–34, 36a, 36b); and אלהים, "God, gods" (vv. 14, 25–26, 35). In addition, the following repetitions tie two of the three psalm-fragments together: משפטי/שפט, "judge, judgments" (vv. 12, 14, 33); נפלאתיו, "his wonderful works" (vv. 9, 12, 24); מלך/מלכים, "kings, be king" (vv. 21, 31); עז, "strength [ark]" (vv. 11, 27, 28); ישע/ישועה, "salvation, save" (vv. 23, 35); and עולם, "eternal, forever" (vv. 15, 17, 34, 36a [twice]).

James W. Watts: "A Levitical Medley"

In his investigation of hymns set within Hebrew narrative, James W. Watts provides the clearest articulation to date of the third structural proposal for 1 Chr 16:8–36, the outline of which follows:

1. Invocations to worship (vv. 8–13)
2. Exhortations regarding the covenant and reminders of God's faithfulness to the ancestors (vv. 14–22)
3. Call to recognize Yahweh among the nations and a declaration of Yahweh's superiority over foreign gods (vv. 23–29)
4. Nature's reverence for Yahweh (vv. 30–33)
5. Climactic exhortation to thanksgiving (v. 34)
6. Communal plea for salvation that Yahweh may be worshiped (v. 35)
7. Blessing and congregational response (v. 36).[51]

Watts's proposal resembles the previous two in some respects while being quite different in others. Like Kleinig, but unlike Shipp, Watts and other proponents of this proposal do not feel constrained to maintain the individual structures of the underlying psalms, as indicated by the definite

---

51. Watts, *Psalm and Story*, 156. Other scholars who share this proposal include Williamson, *1 and 2 Chronicles*, 128–29; Johnstone, *1 and 2 Chronicles*, 175; and Thompson, *1, 2 Chronicles*, 140–42.

break at v. 29. Again, like Kleinig, but unlike Shipp, proponents of this proposal tend to separate the petition, doxology, and community response of vv. 35–36 from the thanksgiving hymn proper of vv. 8–34. Like Shipp, but unlike Kleinig, these proponents tend to see vv. 14–22 as a single unit. But, in contrast to both Kleinig and Shipp, none of the proponents represented here has offered a rationale for their structural analysis beyond showing the development of theme.

Watts has suggested an outline that presents a thematic development of the Chronicler's hymn. This accounts for the general scholarly acceptance it enjoys. Nevertheless, a literary justification of this proposed structure has not appeared. While I do not necessarily concur with the exegetical results or the interpretation this thematic approach has uncovered, I do agree with the structural divisions proposed. The following proposal seeks to justify that structure while remaining open to other hermeneutical possibilities.

IV. A New Proposal

In some respects, my proposal is not "new" at all. The three proposals examined above all provide valuable insights into the structure of the Chronicler's hymn that I gladly incorporate. The most important structuring devices are as follows:

1. With Shipp and Hill, I agree that the imperatives "give thanks," "praise," and "remember" in vv. 8, 10, and 12 of the hymn are best seen as a "connective echo" to the infinitive construct forms of these verbs in v. 4b. I also agree with Shipp that the reverse order of their appearance is significant. I would maintain, however, that this significance is limited to the identification of the hymn's initial division in vv. 8–13.

2. With Kleinig, I agree that the liturgical rubric ואמרו (imperative: "Say!") divides the text into two major parts. These are the hymn proper (vv. 8–34) and a liturgical section comprising a summons to pray (v. 35a), a petition (v. 35b), a doxology/benediction (v. 36a), and a congregational response (v. 36b).

3. Each of these major parts is defined by an inclusio: the hymn by הודו ליהוה (vv. 8, 34) and the liturgical section by ואמרו (v. 35a) and ויאמרו (v. 36b).

4. Within the hymn proper, the repetition of the phrase (ב)כל־הארץ, "(among) all the earth," in vv. 14, 23, and 30 defines three central divisions: vv. 14–22; 23–29; and 30–33. The addition of vv. 8–13 as an introductory call to praise/thanksgiving and v. 34 as a conclusion, results in five divisions for the hymn itself. These divisions generally correspond to those proposed by Williamson, Watts, and Thompson on exegetical or thematic grounds.

In addition, each of the five divisions displays its own structural integrity in terms of both form and content. The first division (vv. 8–13) has been discussed to some extent in the reviews of Shipp and Kleinig. There it was maintained that the introductory הודו ליהוה (v. 8) forms an inclusio with v. 34, framing the entire hymn of thanksgiving. In addition, the three infinitive constructs of the programmatic v. 4b appear in reverse order in vv. 8, 10, and 12 establishing an ABA′ or ring structure with vv. 8–9, 12–13 framing vv. 10–11. The repetition of נפלאתיו in vv. 9 and 12 strengthens this structure as does the matching ABA′ alternation of synonyms for "seek" in the B portion (בקש, vv. 10b, 11b; דרש, v. 11a). The division closes in v. 13 with the delayed announcement of the addressees of the imperative calls to praise.

The second division (vv. 14–22) opens with the statement, "He is the LORD our God; his judgments are in all the earth." This first appearance of כל־הארץ signals the beginning of the second division. The next two appearances will mark the beginnings of the third and fourth divisions. Following this programmatic confession, the remaining eight verses form a repeated pattern that has more to do with narrative than poetry. This pattern consists of three verses of continuous narrative (vv. 15–17; 19–21), followed by God's direct speech (vv. 18, 22). Note the presence of *waw*-consecutive in the narrative sections (vv. 17, 20, 21) and the addition of "saying," immediately before the speech in v. 22 by KJV, NKJV, RSV, and NRSV. Both of these parallel, four verse segments provide theological warrant for the creedal statement of v. 14 by illustrating God's remembrance of the covenant (vv. 15–18) and God's protection during the wilderness wanderings (vv. 19–22).

The middle division (vv. 23–29) is marked in two ways. First, as in the second and fourth divisions, כל־הארץ in v. 23 signals a new beginning. Second, with the exception of הודו (vv. 8, 34), that functions as an inclusio for the hymn proper, שירו ("sing"; vv. 9a, 23) is the only imperative repeated in the hymn.[52] As such, it draws attention to this central division.

Unfortunately, the end is not so clearly marked. Shipp's proposal, that Psalm 96 forms the third division, continues through v. 33. As we have seen, however, there are problems with dividing the hymn this way in its new setting in Chronicles. Kleinig wants to close his division devoted to "international praise" after v. 30 in order to incorporate the inclusio formed by כל־הארץ, leaving vv. 31–33 as a fourth division, devoted to "cosmic praise." While Kleinig's analysis of vv. 31–33 works well on the level of theme or content, he is unable to produce any stylistic or literary devices to isolate this fourth major division. Textual matters also contribute to the complexity of the problem. The Chronicler has altered the parallelism of vv. 28–30 by moving Ps 96:10a, "Say among the nations, 'the LORD is king!'" to a

---

52. For the rejection of זכרו in v. 15 see n. 24 above.

position following Ps 96:11a (1 Chr 16:31a) and by changing the imperative to a jussive. He has also omitted Ps 96:10c, "He will judge the peoples with equity." This means the triple appearance of "Ascribe to the LORD" (vv. 28–29a, followed by "bring an offering and come before him," in v. 29b) is mirrored and extended in an extra, final colon in v. 29c, "Worship the LORD."[53] The poetic device of the extra colon in v. 29, coupled with the inclusio formed by the fourfold repetition of ליהוה in vv. 28–29 and v. 23 suggests that this central division extends from vv. 23 to 29.

The fourth division (vv. 30–33) is also marked with כל־הארץ. The inclusio formed between מלפניו, "before him" (v. 30),[54] and מלפני יהוה, "before the LORD" (v. 33) serves to frame this division characterized by a number of jussives summoning nature's praise.

The terse fifth division (v. 34) is defined by its introductory imperative הודו ליהוה that, together with v. 8, forms an inclusio for the entire hymn.

The following outline summarizes my proposal. As with Kleinig's proposal, I have indicated the relevant Hebrew structural elements in the margins:

I.   *Thanksgiving Hymn (vv. 8–34)*
   A   Introductory Calls to Thanksgiving (vv. 8–13)   הודו ליהוה
      B   For Past "Judgments" [שפט] (vv. 14–22)   (ב)כל־הארץ
         C   For Present Sovereignty (23–29)   שירו, כל־הארץ
      B'   For Future "Rule" [שפט] (vv. 30–33)   כל־הארץ
   A'   Concluding Call to Thanksgiving (v. 34)   הודו ליהוה
II.   *Concluding Liturgy (vv. 35–36a)*
   A   Liturgical Summons (v. 35a)   ואמרו
      B   Petition (v. 35b)
      B'   Benediction (v. 36a)
   A'   Congregational Response (v. 36b)   ויאמרו

It is easily seen in this outline that the five divisions of the hymn, and (possibly) the concluding liturgy, have been concentrically arranged. The introductory and concluding calls to thanksgiving (A, A') share the thematic phrase of the hymn, הודו ליהוה. As we have seen, the three central

---

53. Ps 29:1–2 displays the same three plus one, staircase trope but without the enclosed colon.

54. A concern to provide boundaries for the division may account for the Chronicler's otherwise inexplicable alteration of his source from מפניו, "before him" (literally, "from his face"; Ps 96:9b) to מלפניו.

divisions (B, C, B′) share the phrase (ב)כל־הארץ) and are identified by its presence. Framing the central section, C, sections B and B′ are thematically linked by מלך (vv. 21, 31); גוי (vv. 20, 31); and שפט (vv. 14, 33). The central division begins with the hymn's only repeated imperative, שירו. That the Chronicler's hymn falls into a concentric arrangement should come as no surprise. Japhet, Selman, and Kleinig have all recognized the concentric structure of the entire chapter:[55]

A David blesses the people (vv. 1–3; cf. 2 Sam 6:17–19a)
   B David appoints Levites for worship in Jerusalem (vv. 4–7)
      C The Chronicler's Hymn (vv. 8–36)
   B′ David appoints Levites and priests for worship at Gibeon (vv. 37–42)
A′ David blesses his house (v. 43; cf. 2 Sam 6:19b–20a)

This analysis suggests that the Chronicler's hymn is a rhetorically sophisticated example of the classic hymn of praise: a call to praise the Lord followed by a motive clause giving the reasons for praise.[56] Structurally speaking, A and A′, as pure calls to praise/thanksgiving, surround three motivations for that praise that progress temporally from the past through the present to the future, in BCB′, as follows:

- Verses 8–13 provide introductory calls to praise concluding with the addressees.
- Verses 14–22 supply the initial motivation for praise, namely, the recitation of God's mighty acts of judgment/salvation (v. 14b) in the past, as indicated by the perfect form of זכר and the *waw*-consecutive imperfect (i.e., preterite) verbs. The motivations include God's remembrance of covenantal promises to their ancestors (vv. 15–18) and protection from hostile neighbors (vv. 19–22).
- Verses 23–29 combine the formal elements of praise in a new way. Here, additional calls to praise (vv. 23–24, 28–29) frame two motive sections. The first chiastically asserts at the very heart of the hymn (vv. 25–26) the present sovereignty of Yahweh over "all the gods of the nations":

---

55. Japhet, *I & II Chronicles*, 312; Selman, *1 Chronicles*, 166; and especially Kleinig, who confirms the structure by listing several thematic links between paired divisions (*The Lord's Song*, 144–45).

56. For this understanding of the hymn of praise see Miller, *They Cried to the Lord*, 204–28, 358–62; and the recent treatment of J. Kenneth Kuntz, "Grounds for Praise: The Nature and Function of the Motive Clause in the Hymns of the Hebrew Psalter," in *Worship and the Hebrew Bible: Essays in Honor of John T. Willis* (ed. M. Patrick Graham et al.; Sheffield: Sheffield Academic Press, 1999) 148–83.

A For great is *Yahweh*, and greatly to be praised;
    B   indeed, revered is he above *all gods*.
    B′ For *all the gods* of the peoples are nothing;
A′ But *Yahweh* the heavens has made.

This first motivation for praise signaled its presence with a double use of causal כי, "for," so characteristic of the hymn of praise, at the start of both vv. 25 and 26. The second motivation for praise reverts to recitation, as in vv. 15–22. Here, however, God's present characteristics are recited in nominal sentences that imply and emphasize the present tense, "Splendor and majesty *are* before him; strength and joy *are* in his place" (v. 27).

If the previous two divisions provide reasons for praising the LORD based upon what God has done in the past and God's present sovereignty, vv. 30–33 boldly proclaim that the Chronicler's post-exilic community "ain't seen nothin' yet!" Imperfect verbal forms and a participle are used to make the point that "all the earth" should "tremble," now, before this faithful yet sovereign God because the world is about to be divinely "established, never to totter" (v. 30). The results will be so great that all of nature: heaven and earth, sea, field, forest and all they contain will confess to the nations that "Yahweh rules!" when he comes.

But not yet. The Chronicler's community, insignificant, few in number and regarded as aliens in their own land (v. 19), yet also encouraged by the testimony of the Chronicler's hymn to their God's past, present, and future devotion, are invited to "take it to the Lord in prayer" in the concluding liturgy that follows the hymn (vv. 35–36). In the petition, the community asks for salvation and deliverance, that their praise may continue, and, following a benediction, they respond as have countless congregations since with "Amen" and "Hallelujah."

Thus, at the heart of the Chronicler's sixteenth chapter, as David completes the important task of centralizing the ark, the symbol of the LORD's presence, in Jerusalem, the narrator pauses to remind his readers of the centrality of worship. The Chronicler's hymn, these songs in a new key, provide a model of worship in which proclamation leads to prayer and culminates in praise. It is one for which we can all "Give thanks to the LORD!"

Wild, Raging Creativity:
The Scene in the Whirlwind (*Job 38–41*)

KATHLEEN M. O'CONNOR

I. The Divine Speeches: Bully or Beauty?

The divine speeches in the book of Job are creation texts. Among the most exquisite poetry in the Old Testament, they should be numbered among other biblical creation accounts: Genesis 1–3, Proverbs 8, Psalm 104, Wisdom of Solomon 7–9, and sections of Second Isaiah. Within a feminist/liberationist hermeneutics, however, the divine speeches have hardly seemed helpful. Women do not figure in them, and they appear to inscribe violence and combat in the description of the deity. Much contemporary interpretation has thoroughly desentimentalized the God of Job to reveal *him* to be a patriarchal, overbearing, and dominating deity.[1]

In these approaches, God challenges Job in order to silence, overpower, and shame him. God shows the Divine Self to be the more Macho One who

---

Author's note: Patrick D. Miller is a scholar of extraordinary range and depth in the field of Biblical Studies. His mastery extends from ancient Near Eastern studies to literary and theological interpretation. Through his publications, as a distinguished professor, and as an editor who encourages and guides the work of other scholars, he continues to have a massive, positive influence on the field. I am delighted to contribute to this volume in his honor.

1. See Edwin Good, *In Turns of Tempest: A Reading of Job with a Translation* (Stanford: Stanford University Press, 1990); David Penchansky, *The Betrayal of God: Ideological Conflict in Job* (LCBI; Louisville: Westminster/John Knox, 1990); Susan E. Schreiner, *Where Shall Wisdom Be Found?: Calvin's Exegesis of Job from Medieval and Modern Perspectives* (Chicago: University of Chicago Press, 1994); David J. A. Clines, "Deconstructing the Book of Job," in idem, *What Does Eve Do to Help? And Other Readerly Questions to the Old Testament* (JSOTSup 94; Sheffield: JSOT, 1990) 118; and Jon D. Levenson, *Creation and the Persistence of Evil: The Jewish Drama of Divine Omnipotence* (San Francisco: Harper and Row, 1988). This listing, of course, overlooks other readings, such as Gustavo Gutiérrez, *On Job: God-Talk and the Suffering of the Innocent* (Maryknoll: Orbis, 1987) and J. Gerald Janzen, *Job* (Interpretation; Atlanta: John Knox, 1985), but the former views seem to be dominant.

out-talks Job the talker. The issues are predominantly ones of power and knowledge in a kind of intergalactic, pyrotechnical, and zoological rhetoric that falls upon Job like an asteroid from outer space. He is squashed. Splat!

I have some ideas about this. Maybe the point of view I just overstated represents in some cases a not-so-hidden supersessionism. Job needs the kind of revelation found in the New Testament. James G. Williams says, for example, "What Job calls for the Gospels focus on."[2] Or perhaps these interpretations reflect the turn to ethics in theology and the academy wherein power relations of justice and mutuality have become the touchstone of theological adequacy. As a Roman Catholic woman, for whom power relations of justice are of surpassing concern, how can I challenge such a starting point?

But these readings do not foreclose other possible readings. One of the few things about which commentators agree in Joban interpretation is that the divine speeches are beautiful in their literary structures and their imagery. Only rarely, however, does the beauty of the speeches receive critical attention.[3] In this paper, I propose that the divine speeches are not primarily about the bullying power of God; instead, they are about the potent beauty of creation, of God, and even of Job himself. To make these claims, I will draw upon form, setting, and the content of the divine speeches, and with the help of Elaine Scarry's theory of aesthetics, I will reflect on the significance of beauty in the speeches.[4] Then I will invent feminist meanings.

II. The Form and Setting of the Divine Speeches

Form. The speeches of God in the storm function as other texts typical to the wisdom genre: they give instruction through suggestion, juxtaposition, and indirection. They use the non-human world to provide knowledge about the human world. The rhetorical questions of the speeches function as a vehicle of divine instruction that invites Job and the reader to come to their own conclusions about events in the storm. The questions are not a mode of intimidation but a "Socratic" pedagogical device.

---

2. James G. Williams, "Job and the God of Victims," in *The Voice from the Whirlwind: Interpreting the Book of Job* (ed. Leo G. Perdue and W. Clark Gilpin; Nashville: Abingdon, 1992) 226. See also p. 220 on the "rivalry of God and Job," which leads me to the conclusion that Williams sees the speeches as God's power play.

3. The few works that do attend to beauty include Carol Newsom's "The Book of Job," *NIB* 4:317–634, and an essay by Corrine L. Patton, "The Beauty of the Beast: Leviathan and Behemoth in Light of Catholic Theology" (paper presented to the Old Testament Biblical Colloquium, Conception Abbey, Conception, Missouri, February 1999).

4. Elaine Scarry, *On Beauty and Being Just* (Princeton: Princeton University Press, 1999).

William P. Brown suggests that the larger genre underlying the divine speeches is the covenant lawsuit (*rîb*) in which the stars, the mountains, even creation itself are called forth as witnesses against humans.[5] God brings elements of creation forward as witnesses against Job, but neither accusations nor guilty verdict follow. Instead, the morning stars sing together and the heavenly beings shout for joy (Job 38:7). The earth changes like clay under sealing wax (38:14) and the dawn takes its post (38:12). Light disperses, wind scatters (38:24), and the water skins of the heavens tilt to water the earth (38:37). These aspects of creation are exquisitely beautiful, and they exist independently of Job.

Setting. The divine-human encounter takes place in a storm, a whirlwind (*hassĕ'ārâ*). This setting is a place of wild energy. Layers of meaning are associated with this storm. First, there are the obvious references to biblical theophanies (Exod 19:16; Pss 18:8–14; 104:3; Hab 3:14; cf. 1 Kgs 19:11–13). Second, and more subtly, the storm evokes Job's own stormy life, whipped about within and without by chaotic forces. And, third, if the storm is not only the divine venue for appearance but also an aspect of revelation, the storm itself implies a deity who is wild, beautiful, free, and deeply unsettling.

III. The Content of the Divine Speeches

The speeches themselves are about creation, its beauty and freedom — what ecologists might call the "the household of life." The subject of creation is first introduced by the addressee of the speeches, Job himself. In the curse of his birth (Job 3:1–7), Job tries to "uncreate" the world, to turn day into night, light into darkness, life into death.[6] In the divine speeches, God replies to Job's *rhetorical destruction* of creation with *rhetorical construction* and *recreation.* The divine questions restore the world from the bottom up, from pillars to stars to animals.

Divine questions about creation reveal that God's power and knowledge is superior to Job's. "Surely you know for you were born then" (38:21). But Job does not know. I would not challenge traditional interpretations here. Such interpretations frequently understand Job's lack of knowledge in the face of divine knowledge as part of God's silencing of Job. While I do not question Job's lack of knowledge, I want to consider the *interpretation* of this lack of knowledge. What if we shift the hermeneutical emphasis of the

---

5. William P. Brown, *The Ethos of the Cosmos: The Genesis of Moral Imagination* (Grand Rapids: Eerdmans, 1999) 340.

6. Leo Perdue, "Job's Assault on Creation," *HAR* 10 (1986) 295–315; Kathleen M. O'Connor, "Job Uncreates the World," *TBT* 34 (1996) 4–8.

questions from their interrogative aspects—"who?," "where?," "do you
know?," "have you?," so often recognized as intimidating—to the *content* of
the questions, the *subjects* about which Job is ignorant? Such a shift results
in a picture of what Dianne Bergant calls "the mind-boggling creativity" of
God and the overflowing beauty of the cosmos and its inhabitants.[7]

God's first speech concerns the habitat and its non-human inhabitants,
the second the specific inhabitants Behemoth and Leviathan. Here is but a
brief sample of the speeches' contents and the sense of "mind-boggling creativity" that they create.

The First Speech: Inanimate Creation (38:1–38)

God's questions convey divine pride and delight in the beauty and energy of creation.

> Who shut in the sea when it burst out of the womb? (38:8)

The sea, a traditional symbol of chaos, is here a newborn baby bursting
from the womb, yet penned in and swaddled in clothes of clouds, an infant
bursting into life, nurtured and protected.

> Have you commanded the morning since your days began,
>   and caused the dawn to know its place,
>   so it might take hold of the skirts of the earth,
>   and the wicked be shaken out? (38:12–13)
> Have you entered into the springs of the sea? (38:16)
> Have you comprehended the expanse of the earth? (38:18)
> Where is the way to the dwelling of light? (38:19)
> Who has cut a channel for the torrents of rain,
>   and a way for the thunderbolt? (38:25)
> Can you bind the chains of the Pleiades,
>   or loose the cords of Orion? (38:31)

To all these questions, Job's answer is "No." Job does not know, cannot understand, cannot bind and loose the constellations because they are un-
bindable, unloosable. But neither does God explicitly claim to do so. The
lightning flashes, the rain pours, the constellations are unbounded. Creation pulses with beauty and energy. God praises it all by means of these
questions. Rather than shaming Job, God glories in the world. The speech
conveys divine pride in the cosmos like that of a new home-owner showing
off her habitat.

---

7. See Dianne Bergant, *Israel's Wisdom Literature: A Liberation-Critical Reading* (Minneapolis: Fortress, 1997) 44.

The Second Speech: Animate Creation (38:39–40:30)

From the creation of the habitat, the Creator moves to its animal inhabitants. Why these animals? What do they have in common? Why animals at all? Carol Newsom has pointed to Othmar Keel's proposal that these animals derive from royal lists of hunted animals and the iconography of kings.[8] Keel's work may indeed provide the original source for this listing, but regardless of where they come from, each of the animals is also beautiful as well as wildly and exuberantly alive. Job, who shares the cosmic habitat with these wild creatures, has nothing to do with their care and feeding. And it can be argued that neither does God, especially if one considers that control is not the primary issue behind God's questioning.

1. Can Job hunt prey for lions? No, and although the question clearly implies that God can do so, that is not God's explicit claim here.[9] They hunt for themselves, these kings of beasts, these symbols of monarchs, and they flourish.

2. Does Job know when mountain goats give birth? No, but in spite of Job's ignorance, they do give birth, and their young ones grow up and go forth. Does God know this moment? Presumably, but neither is there indication that God is actively involved. Job does nothing. God does nothing.

3. Who let the wild ass go free? In its wild freedom it scorns the tumult of the city and ranges the mountain. Can Job tie the wild ox in the furrow with ropes and hinder its freedom? Clearly not, but—again—neither does God explicitly claim to do so.

4. And who makes the horse leap, paw, and laugh?

In each case, although the question may imply that God does these things, it does not require God to do so. What makes it even less clear that we are to see God as saying "I can do this, but you cannot," is that each of these animals is unbounded, fearless, and beautiful. Each follows its own way that Job (and God) can neither know nor control. And the only mention of divine control concerns the ostrich whom God created without giving it wisdom, yet even it is wild, fearless, and laughing (39:13–18). When God does claim to act using "I" language ("when I laid the foundations of the earth, I made the clouds for a garment, hail I have reserved for time of trouble"; 38:4, 9, 23), the speech accentuates divine creativity more than control. The text celebrates abundant, fecund life that needs no control.[10]

---

8. Newsom, "The Book of Job," 617. Othmar Keel's work is *Jahwes Entgegnung an Ijob: Eine Deutung von Ijob 38–41 vor dem Hintergrund der zeitgenössischen Bildkunst* (FRLANT 121; Göttingen: Vandenhoeck and Ruprecht, 1978).

9. But cf. Ps 104:21.

10. Brown, *Ethos*, 366.

The Monsters: Behemoth and Leviathan (40:6[15]–41:34)

Behemoth and Leviathan are central to interpretations that see Job shamed and God as controller. Richard Clifford, for example, argues that Behemoth and Leviathan are mere playthings in the powerful divine hands.[11] Others find more explicit violence in the texts. Tryggve Mettinger sees an "antagonistic theology" in Job;[12] and Jon D. Levenson writes, "While Behemoth is declared to be a creature of God, Leviathan is not so described in the longer section devoted to him. . . . We hear only of God's heroic capture and conquest of the great sea beast."[13] But do we really?

No. Instead, God brags about, celebrates, and praises these beautiful creatures, as if proud, even in awe, of them. God's questions neither assert nor imply divine conquest; rather, they show God rejoicing in these beasts' power, beauty, and independent fearlessness. If the ancient combat myth of creation lurks here, it has been seriously defanged. The text does acknowledge that only God can approach Behemoth with a sword (40:19), but there is no indication that God does, has done, or intends to do so. Instead, both animals become exemplars of divine pride, and as John G. Gammie proposed, both are mirrors of Job's self, his own beauty and fearlessness.[14]

Behemoth (40:15–24). "Look at Behemoth which I made just as I made you" (40:15), declares God. This command invites Job to compare himself to Behemoth.[15] The strong Behemoth—stiff-tailed, iron-boned—"is the first of the great acts of God, only its maker can approach it with the sword" (40:19). But the Creator does not do so. Instead of engaging in combat with God, Behemoth eats where all the wild animals play, rests under the lotus, finds a place in the shade among the willows, thus yielding a picture of harmonious contentment. Even if the river is turbulent, Behemoth "is not frightened; it is confident though the Jordan rushes against its mouth" (40:23). And, according to God's question, Job has fierce kinship with this beast. Job, too, is fearless and confident before his friends and before God. Even when a river of ridiculing words from his friends rushes against him, he continues to speak, and from the all-powerful Creator (12:13–25) he demands a hearing face-to-face (13:3). It is this fierce indepen-

---

11. Richard Clifford, *Creation Accounts in the Ancient Near East and in the Bible* (CBQMS 26; Washington, D.C.: Catholic Biblical Association, 1994) 196.

12. Tryggve Mettinger, "The God of Job: Avenger, Tyrant, or Victor?" in Perdue and Gilpin, ed., *The Voice from the Whirlwind*, 39–49, esp. 48.

13. Levenson, *Creation and the Persistence of Evil*, 49; see also Rene Girard, "Job as Failed Scapegoat," in Perdue and Gilpin, ed., *The Voice from the Whirlwind*, 192.

14. John G. Gammie, "Behemoth and Leviathan: On the Didactic and Theological Significance of Job 40:15–41:26," in *Israelite Wisdom: Theological and Literary Essays in Honor of Samuel Terrien* (ed. John G. Gammie et al.; Missoula: Scholars Press, 1978) 217–31.

15. Gammie, "Behemoth," 221.

dence that God recognizes and that God further invites in the introductions to the speeches. "Who is this that darkens counsel by words without knowledge? Gird up your loins like a man [*geber*]" (38:2–3; cf. 40:7). "Have you an arm like God and can you thunder with a voice like his?" (40:9). "Deck yourself with majesty and dignity. . . . [T]hen I will acknowledge that your own right hand can save you" (40:10–14). The same kind of questions that God asks Job about the animals, God must consider about Job.

Leviathan (41:1–34). The sea monster Leviathan is even more fearsome and resistant to capture. God also brags about him, this time at length, and asks over and over if Job can capture, tame, conquer, or injure this creature. How could he? No one can. Any hope of capturing it will be disappointed for even the gods are overwhelmed at the sight of it (41:9)! No one is so fierce as to dare to stir it up. Who can stand before, who can confront it and be safe, who under the whole heaven, who? The answer is no one, only God, but God does not. God is not in conflict with the symbol of chaos and terror. God is simply and eloquently proud:[16]

> I will not keep silence concerning its limbs,
>   or its mighty strength, or its splendid frame. (41:12)

Nor does God keep silent about its back (41:15), its teeth (41:14), or its breath of fire (41:21):

> It makes the deep boil like a pot;
>   it makes the sea like a pot of ointment. (41:31)
> On earth it has no equal,
>   a creature without fear.
> It surveys everything that is lofty;
>   it is king over all that are proud. (41:33–34)

Although both creatures are capable of ferocious battle, this text is not about battle, nor conflict, nor hostility with God, nor primarily about Job's inability to conquer these creatures. It is about God's pleasure in their beautiful wildness. In these speeches, God is superior to Job in strength, knowledge, and power, but God is not a bully. God may humble Job, put him in his place, and show him his creatureliness, but is Job's experience a humiliation or an invitation to grasp reality? God invites Job to step beyond his constricted view of himself, of God, and of the world. God challenges Job to recognize his participation in the beauty and wild freedom of creation and its Creator.

---

16. As Newsom observes ("The Book of Job," 617), there is no hostility between God and these beings.

IV. A Feminist Hermeneutics of the Divine Speeches

What significance can such an experience of beauty have for Job? Is emphasis on beauty in the speeches not simply another abstraction that ignores Job and his immense suffering? Elaine Scarry's book, *On Beauty and Being Just*, offers suggestive possibilities to the contrary. Beauty, she asserts, is sacred, unprecedented, life-affirming, life-saving, and life-giving.[17] It brings about a transformation at the very roots of the beholder's sensibility. It affirms one's being and becomes an occasion for "unselfing," freeing one to be in the service of something (or someone) else.

In this light, rather than ignoring Job, the divine speeches greet him, affirm him, bless him. Newsom proposes that Job gains an expanded moral vision of his place in the world during the storm.[18] But if Scarry's theory is correct, something more is taking place. The divine speeches not only expand Job's ethical frame "beyond family and village" to include the cosmos; the heart-stopping beauty revealed in the storm *transforms him*. According to Scarry, the experience of beauty with its intense and involuntary pleasure can have three effects:

- Beauty focuses one outward, requiring the relinquishment of one's imaginary position at the center of the world;[19]
- beauty creates a sharpened attentiveness, a "heightened state of alert," necessary also for recognizing injustice and for opening oneself to extend care toward the world;[20]
- beauty "incites, even requires" creativity in the replication of that which is beautiful.[21]

The experience of beauty is, therefore, the source of creativity.

Seen in this light, the beauty of the divine speeches in Job is not an accidental literary feature nor merely a pleasant harmonious aesthetic but revelation itself. The beauty in the storm is fearsome, wild, free. It is attracting power, akin to Rudolph Otto's notions of the *mysterium tremendum*, *mysterium fascinans*, what he calls "the sheer absolute wondrousness that transcends thought."[22] Job's experience of this beauty certainly does not

---

17. Scarry, *On Beauty and Being Just*, 23–28.
18. Newsom, "The Book of Job," esp. 625–27; and idem, "The Moral Sense of Nature: Ethics in the Light of God's Speech to Job," *PSB* 15 (1994) 9–27.
19. Scarry, *On Beauty and Being Just*, 50–58 and *passim*.
20. Ibid., 58.
21. Ibid., 5.
22. Rudolph Otto, *The Idea of the Holy* (Oxford: Oxford University Press, 1924) 81. I am grateful to Walter Brueggemann for this reference and, in what follows, to Christine Roy Yoder for suggestions regarding sight in the text of Job. Thanks also to poet and professor Alicia Ostriker for comments on an earlier draft of this paper.

explain his suffering but it does transform him nevertheless. I am not able here to analyze Job's responses in the storm and in the epilogue, but both texts point toward a Job *changed by beauty*. There is language of sight: "But now my eyes see you" (42:5); there is Job's unselfing: "I put my hand over my mouth, I am of small account," "I repent in/of/concerning dust and ashes" (42:6).[23] There is evidence that his focus turns outward as he repairs injuries, interceding for his friends (42:7–9) and extending extraordinary care to his daughters (42:13–15). Job has received a life-affirming greeting from another world and however we deal with the many lingering puzzles of this book, its beauty calls to readers if only we, in our flattened, technological, consumerist world, were but open to it.

Within a feminist/liberationist hermeneutics, then, the divine speeches invite us to open ourselves to the amazing beauty divinely loosed in the cosmos, to look for it, to let it whoosh through us, to heed it, and to obey. The speeches invite us to participate in God's wild, raging creativity, to replicate beauty, to create new beauty, to generate harmony and wild freedom in our work and relationships, to extend our realm of care from our families to the whole cosmos and its denizens, to make a world where creative flourishing is available to all beings. The speeches urge us to be like the animals and like the monsters, Behemoth and Leviathan—wild, fearlessly ourselves, exuberantly alive. They call us to pulse with life, to be strong, to yell and shout like Job, to find our place in the world and to take no one else's. They require us to throw off colonized spirits, self-silencing, great fears, endless self-critiques. They demand radical resistance to all forms of silencing, bullying, and denial of and destruction of the beauty and creativity of women, children, men. They call for the disciplined avoidance of such tactics ourselves with students, family, friends, women's groups, colleagues, communities. They invite endless, joyous labor for justice for the earth and for all its wondrous, wild, and creative creatures.[24]

---

23. For a brief discussion of many possible translations of this verse, see Newsom, "The Book of Job," 629.

24. Earlier versions of this paper were presented at the annual meeting of the Catholic Biblical Association, Feminist Hermeneutics Task Force, August, 1999; and in the Feminist Hermeneutics of the Bible Section at the annual meeting of the Society of Biblical Literature, November, 2000.

Part II

"As Just as This Entire Law"

*God's Nearness in the Torah
(Deuteronomy and Beyond)*

Law in the Service of Life:
A Dynamic Understanding of
Law in Deuteronomy

TERENCE E. FRETHEIM

I. Introduction

Christians commonly do not know what to do with the law texts in the Pentateuch. One practical effect of this uncertainty is that these texts are virtually ignored in the common lectionary. Besides the Decalogue, the exceptions are Deut 6:4–9 and Lev 19:11–18—probably because Jesus quotes from these texts and claims that no laws are "greater" than these and commends the scribe for saying that they are "more important" (Mark 12:28–34). There are many reasons Christians tend to ignore the law texts: their ancient cultural context; their claimed obsolescence; their hard-nosed, albeit selective, use by some believers; confusion over the polysemic word "law"; and their remarkable capacity to make readers feel uncomfortable (e.g., Exod 22:21–28; Deut 15:7–11). A less visible, but perhaps more basic reason for this neglect is the sense that Old Testament laws are to be understood in static terms, given by God and never to be changed; hence, readers will either agree or disagree and treat them accordingly. In this essay I will argue that *the legal texts themselves* understand the law in dynamic terms. I focus on the book of Deuteronomy, but draw other law texts into the conversation.

At stake in these reflections is not simply an understanding regarding whether and how individual laws pertain to Christian faith and life, but a

Author's note: It is a pleasure to be able to contribute this article in honor of Patrick D. Miller. I have learned much from Miller's sophisticated analysis of biblical texts and from his theological discernment. His encouraging of my own work has been greatly appreciated. This essay is much informed by his work on Pentateuchal law, especially his commentary, *Deuteronomy* (Interpretation; Louisville: John Knox Press, 1990), and his article, "The Place of the Decalogue in the Old Testament and Its Law," *Int* 43 (1989) 229–42.

continuing positive view of the basic concerns that undergird and inform these laws. Specifically, many laws articulate Israel's deep concern for justice for the less advantaged; by neglecting these law texts we lose so much grist for our consideration of these issues. More generally, these laws, both individually and in their entirety, are a gracious gift of God for the sake of the life, health, and well-being of individuals in community. This is made especially clear in the book of Deuteronomy. As Deut 5:33 puts it: these laws are given to God's people "that you may live, and that it may go well with you, and that you may live long on the land that you are to possess." God gives the law in the service of life. If for no other reason than that, they deserve our close attention.

Scholars have long been at work tracking the development of Israel's legal tradition. While the canonical presentation of the emergence of Israelite law covers a span of some forty years (from Mt. Sinai to the plains of Moab), interpreters usually understand that these laws developed over many centuries, from pre-monarchical times to the postexilic period. Various repetitions and inconsistencies in the laws have been especially important in drawing this conclusion. Broadly speaking, it is now commonplace to distinguish the Book of the Covenant (Exod 20:22–23:33), Deuteronomy 12–26, and the Priestly tradition (Leviticus); and that is the usual chronological ordering. At the same time, these complexes of law are themselves composite and it is usually thought that they underwent a complex development over many centuries in view of ongoing changes in community life before being drawn into their present canonical orbit.[1]

Yet, while there has been a long-standing awareness that Israel's laws developed over time and were not understood in a static sense, this has been more an historical judgment than a canonical one.[2] Does the *canonical* presentation of law, set as it is in the wilderness period, reveal a comparable perspective regarding law? In my judgment the answer is affirmative: despite the ascription of all law to the Mosaic era, there are several different signs that the law as canonically presented is not understood to be timeless and immutable.

I make several claims as a way of beginning. The laws that God gives Israel are understood basically in terms of creation and vocation. For example, for Deuteronomy to speak so basically and persistently of the law as

1. For a helpful analysis of the development of the Book of the Covenant, showing that it is not "an immutable, timeless law," see Paul D. Hanson, "The Theological Significance of Contradiction within the Book of the Covenant," in *Canon and Authority* (ed. George W. Coats and Burke O. Long; Philadelphia: Fortress, 1977) 110–31.

2. A recent, important book, focusing on this issue relative to the book of Deuteronomy that informs my discussion is Bernard M. Levinson's *Deuteronomy and the Hermeneutics of Legal Innovation* (New York: Oxford University Press, 1997).

being in the service of life and well-being means that its understanding of law is dynamic and is fundamentally creational in its orientation. To speak so of Deuteronomy also carries the claim that its understanding of law is seen basically in vocational terms. God gives the law not only for the sake of the life of those who receive it but also for the sake of the life of the neighbor, indeed all of creation, whom they are called to serve.

II. Creation and Law

Links between Deuteronomy and the creation story in Genesis have often been noted,[3] but here I speak of the relationship between law and creation in the Pentateuch more generally, a perspective in which Deuteronomy participates. The sequence of redemption followed by law in the book of Exodus can be misleading; it may prompt a view that God's act of salvation obligates obedience to the law.[4] But such an understanding cannot be maintained. Rather, Israel's laws are grounded in God's work in creation. As B. D. Napier stated long ago, "Hebrew Law, in its present total impression, has its clearest roots in [Israel's] creation-faith."[5] Generally speaking, that many Pentateuchal laws have their predecessors and parallels in other ancient Near Eastern cultures demonstrates their roots in creation rather than redemption (which Israel itself recognized, see below on Deut 4:8). More specifically, in his study of creation in Israel and the ancient Near East, H. H. Schmid claims unambiguously, "Legal order belongs to the order of creation." In his view, there is a symbiotic relationship between cosmic and social orders. Negatively, "an offense in the legal realm obviously has effects in the realm of nature (drought, famine) or in the political sphere (threat of the enemy)." Positively, the law is a means by which the divine ordering of chaos at the cosmic level is actualized in the social

---

3. For a brief summary, see Terence E. Fretheim, *The Pentateuch* (IBT; Nashville: Abingdon, 1996) 56–58.

4. An example of the difficulties such an understanding can generate may be seen in a statement by James W. Watts, *Reading Law: The Rhetorical Shaping of the Pentateuch* (Biblical Seminar 59; Sheffield: Sheffield Academic Press, 1999) 95: "Because YHWH has done and will do these things for Israel, Israel *owes* YHWH obedience" (emphasis mine; cf. similarly, 125: "the exodus has obligated Israel to YHWH"). The word "owes" draws on imagery from the world of finance and suggests that Israel is in debt to God and hence is obligated to repay God for what God has done. But if God is truly gracious, as Israel's central confession states (Exod 34:6–7), the language that Israel has an obligation to pay God back for services rendered compromises the claim regarding grace.

5. B. D. Napier, "Community Under Law: On Hebrew Law and Its Theological Presuppositions," *Int* 7 (1953) 413. Cf. Jon Levenson, "The Theologies of Commandment in Biblical Israel," *HTR* 73 (1980) 28–33. Important for these considerations generally is the work of Gustaf Wingren, especially his *Creation and Law* (Philadelphia: Muhlenberg, 1961).

sphere, which is thereby brought into closer conformity with the creation that God intended.[6] The law is given because God is concerned about *the best possible life* for *all* of God's creatures.

The book of Genesis supports this understanding of creational law. Law is integral to God's creative work and is formulated both as prohibition (Gen 2:16–17) and as positive command (Gen 1:26–28). Law is thereby recognized as a pre-sin reality, part and parcel of God's good creation, given for the sake of a good life for all its creatures. This creational law is reiterated and extended after sin enters the life of the world (Gen 9:1–7) and these early narratives reveal something of this creational law (e.g., the story of Cain and Abel assumes that Cain should have known that murder is wrong, Gen 4:10–13).

The ancestral narratives also witness to pre-Sinai law; especially to be noted is Gen 26:5 (cf. 18:19, 25): "Abraham obeyed my voice and kept my charge, my commandments, my statutes, and my laws." This text is no simple anachronistic reference to the law given at Sinai; it witnesses to the narrator's understanding of the place of law in the pre-Sinai period.[7] This text stands in basic continuity with earlier articulations of God's will in the creation. Abraham's conformation to the will of God shows that his life is in tune with God's creational purposes and models for later Israel the right response to law. These ancestral texts also demonstrate that law cannot be collapsed into the law given at Sinai. At the same time, they show that Sinai law basically conforms to already existing law; that is, the law given at Sinai stands in fundamental continuity with the law obeyed by Abraham.

The place of law in Exodus 15–18 makes the same point (e.g., 15:25b–26; 16:4, 26; 18:13–27). Exodus 18:13–27 may carry a special force, situated as it is just before the revelation at Sinai (and somewhat disjunctively so). Jethro identifies his wisdom regarding the right ordering of the community with what God has *commanded* (18:23), even though he had not received a revelation from God. This understanding is important for at least two reasons.

---

6. See H. H. Schmid, "Creation, Righteousness and Salvation: 'Creation Theology' as the Broad Horizon of Biblical Theology," in *Creation in the Old Testament* (ed. Bernhard W. Anderson; IRT 6; Philadelphia: Fortress, 1984) 104–5. He notes, for example, that Hammurabi's giving of the law occurs in a creation context, and "so does every Near Eastern legal code with the same structure" (105). See also Klaus Koch, "Is There a Doctrine of Retribution in the Old Testament?" in *Theodicy in the Old Testament* (ed. J. Crenshaw; IRT 3; Philadephia: Fortress, 1983) 57–87.

7. See James Bruckner, "The Creational Context of Law Before Sinai: Law and Liberty in Pre-Sinai Narratives and Romans 7," *Ex Auditu* 11 (1995) 91–110. See also his Luther Seminary dissertation, "A Literary and Theological Analysis of Implied Law in the Abrahamic Narrative: Implied Oughts as a Case Study," forthcoming from Sheffield Academic Press.

First, it makes possible a more open understanding of the ascription of the Sinai laws to God's specific revelation. If Jethro can attach a "God commands you" to his own discernment, then readers are put on the alert that the phrase "the LORD spoke to Moses" (or the like) does not necessarily exclude human insight and reflection in the development of these laws (though no explicit credit is so given). This understanding may be parallel to the description of mediated divine *action* in Exod 3:7–10 where both God and Moses are agents of the exodus, though God is often the only subject of the verbs (e.g., Exod 14:13, 31). This point may be supported by the textual recognition of the distinction between God speaking the Decalogue directly (see Deut 5:22–27) but mediating other laws through Moses. Even more, the additional distinction between law spoken by God to Moses (Sinai) and law spoken by Moses (Deuteronomy) makes the latter one step further removed from the mouth of God. In the latter, God's laws pass through a human mind (narratively) and that inevitably involves interpretation and reflection (see Acts 15:28, also in a law-giving context). God's revelation is therefore the decisive, but not the only factor in the giving of the law.

Second, "The *specific revelation of God at Sinai*, now to be presented, is thus seen to stand in *fundamental continuity* with the discernment of the will of God in and through *common human experience*."[8] To cast this point in general terms, human constructs for the ordering of community may be revealing of the divine intention quite apart from the reception of a specific divine directive to that effect. This observation, in turn, links back to the development of law in ancient Near Eastern societies and, I might add, in every society since that time.

This understanding may be supported further by Deut 4:6–8. As noted above, we know that many of Israel's laws find their parallel in ancient Near Eastern law codes. That Israel also knew this to be the case is clear from this text. Other peoples do have "statutes and ordinances," but they are not as "just" as Israel's (4:8); theologically, this recognizes the work of God the Creator among such peoples in the development of law. Note also that the difference in the "just" character of the laws involved pertains to the "entire law"; this may recognize that the *individual ordinances* of other peoples could not always be so described. Even more, the knowledge of the law by other peoples entails a quality of discernment on their part; they recognize the wisdom of Israel's laws (4:6; cf. their discernment in Deut 29:24–28; Jer 22:8–9). This text understands that ultimately there were human agents, both within and without Israel, involved in the ongoing evaluation and development of Israel's laws.

---

8. Terence E. Fretheim, *Exodus* (Interpetation; Louisville: John Knox, 1991) 200.

The law is given in creation for two fundamental reasons, both of which are basically concerned about life:

1. to preserve God's creative work in the face of threats that may arise to creation's well-being. For example, creation will not remain "good" and engendering of life regardless of what human beings do with the gifts they have been given. The created order is not so fixed that it is immune to significant damage; human sin can negatively affect the created order so that it ceases to serve life in the way that God intended (see Deut 11:13–17; Hos 4:1–3). The law is given in creation so as to keep cosmic order and social order integrated in a harmonious way. This creational context for law also means human beings are not free of creational demands just because they do not belong to the chosen people. It is just such an understanding that informs many biblical texts relating to non-Israelites (e.g., Deut 4:6–8; or the oracles against the nations, e.g., Amos 1–2).[9] Nations are held accountable to creational law quite apart from their knowledge of the God who gave it.

2. to serve the proper development of God's good but not perfect creation. The command to "subdue the earth" (1:28) indicates that the creation was not fully developed at the beginning. God does not establish the created order as a fixed, polished entity; it was not intended to remain forever just as it existed at the end of the first week of its life (as the history of nature well demonstrates). This openness to the future exists not only because God did not exhaust the divine creativity in the first week of the world (see Ps 104:30), but also because of the creative capacities built into the order of things and the charges given its creatures (see Gen 1:11–12, 20, 24, 28; 2:18–23).[10] To be sure, there are the great rhythmic givens of creation that perdure: seedtime and harvest, cold and heat, summer and winter, day and night (Gen 8:22; Jer 31:35–36), but God's creation is also understood to be a work in progress. God creates a paradise, but the effect is not a static state of affairs; the creation is a highly dynamic reality in which the future is open to a number of possible developments.

---

9. See John Barton, "Natural Law and Poetic Justice in the Old Testament," *JTS* 30 (1979) 1–14. Note that one perspective within later Judaism was that the law of Moses was preexistent, serving as the pattern God used in making the world.

10. On the interpretation of these texts as witnessing to a creation in process, see Terence E. Fretheim, "The Book of Genesis," *NIB* 1:343–46, 352, 357. For an important statement of this perspective, see Michael Welker, "What is Creation?: Rereading Genesis 1 and 2," *TT* 45 (1991) 56–71.

If the law was given in creation in the service of developing God's creation toward its fullest possible life-giving potential, then for the creation to stay just as God originally created it would be a failure of the divine design. Development and change are what God intends for the creation and human beings are charged with responsibilities for intra-creational development. A fundamental implication of this kind of reflection is that "natural law" is not understood to be a fixed reality; it, too, is open to development in view of a changing world. In other words, a proper creational understanding of law entails something other than the maintenance of the status quo; existing understandings of "natural law" are in need of ongoing scrutiny in view of what creation is becoming (and this is borne out by experience). For example, the command to "fill the earth" (Gen 1:28), understandable in view of its ancient setting, may need to be reexamined in view of changing population patterns. New situations will teach new duties in view of the developing created order, including natural law.

III. Law and Vocation

The covenant at Sinai with its accompanying laws is concerned most fundamentally with Israel's vocation in the world in the service of life. The Sinai covenant does not establish God's relationship with Israel; the Israelites are "my people" early in the book of Exodus (e.g., Exod 3:7–10). These people are the inheritors of the promises given to their ancestors (Exod 3:15–17; 6:4, 8), a covenant that God remembers (Exod 2:24; 6:4–5) as given to the ancestors and to their "descendants" (Gen 17:7). It is this ancestral covenant that grounds Moses' appeal to God when the people break the Sinaitic covenant (Exod 32:13), indicating that the Abrahamic covenant is more foundational for the God-Israel relationship. The Sinai covenant is a matter of Israel's vocation not its status. It is a formalization of Israel's role in the world—to be a holy nation and a kingdom of priests (Exod 19:5–6). The giving of the law to an already redeemed people is in the service of this vocation, to which the people agree to be obedient (Exod 19:8; 24:3, 7).

In being given the law at Sinai, Israel, like the first human beings, is caught up by God in a vocation that involves the becoming of the creation. Sinai law is not a new reality but a fuller particularization of how the community can take on its God-given *creational* responsibilities for the sake of life in view of new times and places. Sinai draws together previously known law and develops new law for this redeemed and called community. In most respects, Sinai is simply a regiving of the law implicitly or explicitly commanded in creation or made evident in common life experience (within Israel and without). The exodus gives Israel some new motivations for keeping the law, indeed empowers Israel to that end, but, as I have already noted above, the law is grounded in Israel's creation-faith, not God's re-demptive activity.[11] To obey the law is to live in harmony with God's inten-tions for the creation. As Deuteronomy never tires of telling readers, the law is given for the sake of the best life possible; the law stands in the ser-vice of a stable, flourishing, and life-enhancing *community* (the community language is important). Sinai law sketches a vocation to which Israel is called for the sake of the neighbor and the creation. Because of the way in which Deuteronomy often identifies the neighbor in relationship to spe-cific life situations (e.g., 24:10–22), it reveals a dynamic sense of law.

I return to the salvation wrought by God at Passover and sea crossing. When the Israelites sing the song of Exodus 15, "the LORD has become my salvation," it is important to note what salvation means in this context. Sal-vation means that the Israelites are delivered from the effects, not of their own sin, but of the sins of other people (the Egyptians). When God deliv-ers Israel from this abusive situation, the people are reclaimed for the life and well-being that God intended for the creation. As such, God's salva-tion stands, finally, in the service of creation, freeing people to be what they were created to be and having a re-creative effect on the nonhuman world as well, as life in the desert begins to flourish once again.[12] And the central concern of the law for the poor and other disadvantaged people is, for Deuteronomy, for the sake of life, or, in other terms, to make sure that God's *salvation* extends deeply into the life of the community.

God's work of salvation has the effect of reclaiming and enabling not only true human life and freedom, but also *responsibility* for the sake of life for all. As a newly redeemed community, Israel stands before God and is in effect addressed as human beings were on the sixth day of creation, called to take up this vocation.

IV. A Dynamic Understanding of Law

I now consider various matters that more fully indicate that the law is understood to be a dynamic rather than a static or fixed reality.

Law and Context

It is of no little import that the wilderness is the context for all Pen-tateuchal law. This is true of the major blocks of law given at Sinai and

---

11. For an earlier formulation of these understandings of law, see Terence E. Fret-heim, "The Reclamation of Creation: Redemption and Law in Exodus," *Int* 45 (1991) 354–65.

12. For details, see Terence E. Fretheim, "The Plagues as Ecological Signs of Histor-ical Disaster," *JBL* 110 (1991) 385–96.

Moab, but especially to be noted are the wilderness narratives (Exod 15:22–18:27; Num 10:11–36:13), where laws emerge periodically as new situations develop for the journeying community (e.g., Exod 15:25b–26; Numbers 15; 18–19; 27–36). The book of Deuteronomy, whether viewed canonically (forty years after Sinai) or historically (most basically, the seventh century B.C.E.), is a major exemplar of law emerging in view of changing circumstances (see further below). The forty years between Sinai and Deuteronomy should not be downplayed, especially in view of its recollection of Israel's most recent history and its anticipation of a new context in the promised land. This span of time is sufficient to demonstrate that the text recognizes that Israel's life situation has now changed and new formulations of law are needed. Deuteronomy would have to be interpreted quite differently if its laws had been given at Sinai.

In tracking the way in which the law is literarily presented in Exodus through Deuteronomy it is immediately apparent that law and narrative are interwoven.[13] In other words, the law is not presented as a code but is integrated with the ongoing story of the people of God, unlike the law codes of the ancient Near East (or of contemporary societies). Law for Israel is always intersecting with life as it is lived—filled with contingency and change, complexity and ambiguity.

That Israel's laws emerge in connection with the wilderness experience is significant; it indicates that the wilderness is an image for the basic character of law. On the one hand, the law provides something of a compass for wandering in the wilderness. On the other hand, the contingencies of wilderness wandering keep the law from becoming absolutized in a once-for-all form and content. Law in and of itself tends to promote a myth of certainty regarding the shape of life; actual life, however, especially when seen from the perspective of the wilderness narratives, is filled with contingencies, in which nothing on the ship of life seems to be tied down. This means that new laws will be needed and older laws will need to be revised or perhaps put on a back burner. So, for example, in Deuteronomy there are laws regarding kingship and prophecy in anticipation of the coming settlement in the land.

The image of wilderness lifts up that which is basic to the development of law (and all relationships for that matter): constancy and change. Law takes ongoing experience into account while remaining constant in its objective: the life, health, and stability of the community. Both constancy and change are basic to law because they are basic to life, indeed the life that God intends for all creatures. They are also basic for God, a matter to which I now turn.

---

13. For the theological significance of this literary reality, see Fretheim, *Exodus*, 201–7.

Law and God

That all Pentateuchal law is ultimately attributed to God has created something of a problem in thinking about the God of these texts, especially in view of their inconsistencies. Is God inconsistent or represented as inconsistent or is some other explanation possible? Various harmonistic efforts, both Rabbinic and Christian, have been attempted to make sure that a consistent God emerges, but at the expense of a straightforward reading of the text. At the same time, critical scholars sometimes make claims about God that may intensify the God issue unnecessarily. But some implications of the interweaving of law and narrative noted above deserve further consideration.

1. The law is a gracious gift of God. The law is more clearly seen to be a gracious gift because it is episodically integrated with the story of God's other gracious activities. God's actions in the narrative show that the law is not arbitrarily laid upon the people, but is given "for our good always, that God might preserve us alive" (Deut 6:24). The gracious purposes of God for Israel evident in the narrative demonstrate that the law is fundamentally gift, not burden.

2. The law given by God has a fundamentally personal and interrelational character. God introduces the law with highly personal statements regarding what God has done on behalf of the people (Exod 19:4; 20:2). Obedience to law is thus seen to be a response within a relationship, not a response to the law as law. Moreover, in the narrative, readers are confronted with a God who personally interacts with Israel through every stage of their journey. God's giving of the law does not stand at odds with this kind of interactive God-people relationship. And so God does not give the law in a once-for-all form but takes the ongoing relationship into account in giving shape to the law.

3. God's gracious gift of law meets a creational *need*. God's ongoing work of providence and salvation in Pentateuchal narrative is always related to the needs of the people, for example, delivering them from Egyptian abuse and providing food and drink in the wilderness. That God's narrative actions are so correlated with the people's needs argues for a comparable understanding of law. God's law takes into account what the people need for the best possible life. This means that the laws are not arbitrary; they are given in view of specific human needs, and this at several levels. For example, God gives the sacrificial laws in Leviticus 5 because of the people's need for atonement. At the same time, it is made clear that the wealth of the worshiper is taken into account in determining the type of offering. Individual situations of need affect how the law is to be applied.

4. The basic shape for a life lived in obedience to law is drawn most basically from Israel's narrative experience with God, rather than from

abstract ethical argument or even divine imperative. God "loves the strangers, providing them food and clothing. You shall also love the stranger, for you were strangers in the land of Egypt" (Deut 10:18–19). "Be merciful, just as your Father is merciful" (Luke 6:36). God's will for Israel does not remain at the level of general principle; it moves into life in all of its particulars, for that is where the law often makes the most difference for people's well-being (e.g., Deut 24:19–22).

That the law is developed as an exegesis of divine action means that believers are always being called to go beyond the law. The range of God's actions is not *legally* circumscribed (e.g., Jer 3:1–5, 11–12). God is always doing new things, and so this will mean imagining ever-new ways in which the law and the consequent shape of people's lives can reflect God's actions in the world. Such an understanding also prevents the believer from equating obedience to the law with doing what is right. Law may not have caught up with the community's confession regarding God or its understanding of life and well-being (and so it may be that the legal act is not necessarily a moral act).[14]

5. God does not simply give the law to the people by divine fiat; God accompanies the law with motivations to obey the law.[15] These motivations are revealing of the kind of God that stands behind the law; God does not just lay down the law, but gives Israel good reasons to obey. For Deuteronomy (e.g., 5:33; 22:6–7!), it is in Israel's self-interest and in the best interests of the human and nonhuman community, especially the vulnerable and marginalized, to obey—"that it may go well with you and that you may live long." This, of course, is not the language of reward; rather, such benefits are intrinsically related to the deed; they grow out of the deed itself. To obey is a reasonable thing to do (Deut 4:6); right obedience is always an intelligent obedience.[16] The concern of the law is not to bind Israel to some arbitrary set of laws but to enable them to experience the fullness of life in relationship.

The most basic motivation given Israel for obeying the law is drawn from its narrative experience with God as deliverer: "Remember that you were a slave in the land of Egypt" (e.g., Deut 24:18, 22). Because of God's stance towards the disadvantaged Israel must also shape its life toward the disadvantaged in ways both compassionate and just. God's saving deeds call forth this grateful response from Israel. For what is Israel to be grateful? Most basically, it is the gift of life, and obedience to law extends that gift out into all the highways and byways of the community.

---

14. Hanson, "Theological Significance," is particularly forceful on this point.
15. For a brief, helpful survey of these motive clauses, see Watts, *Reading Law*, 65–67.
16. See Miller, *Deuteronomy*, 55.

6. God's giving of the law, understood in vocational terms, means that God has chosen to use human agents in carrying out the divine purposes in the world. God moves over, as it were, and gives to the human an important role to play in taking initiative and assuming responsibility for the world of which it is a part, including furthering the cause of justice and good order in Israel and the larger creation. God is the kind of God who has chosen not to do everything "all by himself."

7. Given these comments about the law, let me interact briefly with statements about God made by two scholars who have been very helpful in developing our thinking about the law.

James W. Watts, in his excellent book, *Reading Law: The Rhetorical Shaping of the Pentateuch*, makes certain claims regarding the God of the law that are sometimes problematic.[17] He states: "Because YHWH rules in Israel, fidelity and obedience is demanded and enforced."[18] But this kind of formulation implies an unacceptable purpose for God's giving laws to Israel. It is as if God reasoned, "I'm king and you're my subjects, and hence you are obligated to obey me." God's purpose in giving the law looks quite different if understood in more creational and relational terms. That is, God gives the law and commands obedience for the sake of the life and well-being of the creatures, not out of a self-serving notion that the people *must* obey because God is, after all, their ruler.[19]

Bernard Levinson, in his article, "The Human Voice in Divine Revelation: The Problem of Authority in Biblical Law," asks some rhetorical questions about the God of the law that are also problematic: "Once a law is attributed to God, how can it be superseded, which is to say, annulled, without the prestige or authority of the divine law being thereby impaired? . . . Could one imagine, for that matter, that the divine himself should suddenly deem inadequate one of his own rules?"[20] These questions assume that the will of God (and God?) is immutable, at least as revealed in the law.

---

17. Watts, *Reading Law,* 91–109, claims that the primary metaphor for the God who gives the law is "just king." He draws this conclusion primarily on the basis of certain parallels with ancient Near Eastern law texts. He recognizes that kingship language for God in the Pentateuch is rare, but that recognition should have proved decisive in rejecting such a primary metaphor. If Israel did borrow legal ideas, conventions, genres, etc., it is remarkable that they did *not* bring the royal language along with it. The most likely reason is that Israel did not find royal images particularly helpful in thinking about their relationship with God. This is borne out by the uncommon use of this imagery in the rest of the Old Testament, where it is used primarily in contexts relating to other nations.

18. Ibid., 108.

19. See also the comments in n. 4 above.

20. Bernard Levinson, "The Human Voice in Divine Revelation: The Problem of Authority in Biblical Law," in *Innovation in Religious Traditions* (ed. M. Williams et al.; Berlin: Walter de Gruyter, 1992) 45.

But on what grounds is such a claim made? Why would a divine change in God's own law be considered problematic for either the law or God?[21] Would it not be much more problematic for both God and the law if God were not able to revise God's own law or to choose to set one or more laws aside in view of new needs in the people's lives? God's (and the law's) "prestige" and "authority" are more tied up with the divine ability to know what is best for people's lives, not the ability to put laws in place that never need changing. It might be noted that the *historical* recognition on the part of most scholars that the canon reveals an ongoing revision of God's own law has probably enhanced the divine reputation, not damaged it.

Law and Spirit

One of the more striking characteristics of the book of Deuteronomy is the passion and energy with which the law is set forth. The parenetic form of presentation ("preached law") addresses the reader directly. This spirit in which the law is presented reveals a dynamic understanding of law that often entails a degree of open-endedness. For example, Deut 15:7–11 speaks of the treatment of the poor in the language of spirit rather than letter: "do not be hard-hearted and tight-fisted toward your needy neighbor; you should rather open your hand, willingly lending enough to meet the need"; "give liberally and be ungrudging when you do so"; "open your hand to the poor and needy neighbor in your land."

This hortatory language is not related in a literal way to the actual law regarding remission of debts (15:1–3). Rather, the language urges readers to *interpret* the law and even go *beyond the law* (e.g., "give liberally"; "enough to meet the need"). Once this rhetoric is introduced into the text, then what it takes for individuals (or the community) to obey the law becomes a somewhat open-ended matter, subject to interpretation (for example, "liberally" is not defined and discerning what is "enough" to meet the need is left open). The laws regarding the less advantaged are often generally stated (e.g., Exod 22:21–24); what it means to care for them entails the use of the imagination (Exod 22:25–28 may provide an illustration of the general principle articulated in the prior verses).

Revision of Law within the Pentateuch

The literary history of Pentateuchal law is ostensibly denied by the attribution of all law to God in the wilderness setting. Levinson in his penetrating study of Deuteronomy seeks to uncover the human voice that lies

---

21. It might be noted that there are many texts in the Old Testament where the divine will changes in view of changing human circumstances, especially regarding announcements of judgment (e.g., Exod 32:14; 2 Kgs 20:1–7; Jer 26:18–19).

beneath the surface of the text. While some aspects of Levinson's proposal are problematic, his work opens up new avenues for conversation.[22] He speaks of a "rhetoric of concealment" in Deuteronomy whereby, through various literary devices, changes in the law are deliberately camouflaged through a variety of literary means, not least casting the whole in terms of its ancient Mosaic setting. They employed "the garb of dependence [on the Covenant Code] to purchase profound hermeneutical independence."[23] While the text of Deuteronomy presents the law in terms of the divine voice, Levinson's proposal reveals the concealed human voice in the material. His proposal joins other analyses of the text that give evidence for ongoing human involvement in the development of law.

I would like to pick up on a somewhat isolated statement by Levinson regarding the juncture between his historical work and the canonical shape of the law; he calls the inclusion of both the Covenant Code and Deuteronomy within the Pentateuch "a major irony of literary history."[24] In other words, the canonical process has given a status to the Book of the Covenant that the Deuteronomic authors would not have shared. Whatever one may think of Levinson's historical proposal, that Deuteronomy has been placed on a canonical continuum that includes older law, that very fact indicates that Deuteronomic law is considered a revision of prior law and has in turn been opened up for further revision.

Notably, the inconsistencies in the laws are not ironed out in the canonical form. What if one worked with the assumption that these inconsistencies are a plus and are revealing of a complex understanding of the development of law *within* the canonical shape of things? This dynamic understanding of the law may be demonstrated by a comparison of law texts

---

22. See Levinson, *Deuteronomy*. For Levinson, the Deuteronomic authors assert their freedom to revise the canonical law, but sense that they must do so "under the table," so to speak. They assume that their program would not be acceptable in Israel if presented in a straightforward way. Is it clear that they could not have done this more openly? Or, from another angle, who is fooling whom? In addition, if the Deuteronomists sensed that they could do this only in a subversive way, as Levinson claims, where from within Israel came the understanding that this would be an appropriate thing to do? If God had spoken in a prior generation, and this was generally recognized in Israel, whence their theological moxie that they felt that they could *completely* abrogate that earlier divine word? Levinson skirts the danger of making the Deuteronomists into religious charlatans; they camouflage their innovations "by feigning a cunning piety with respect to the very authoritative texts that they had subverted" (48). The Deuteronomists are "subversives," religiously intolerant and "tendentious" folk, who sought to "silence," indeed "eliminate" the opposition, defining their new vision as normative while regarding the existing legal traditions as "odious" and "deviant" (144–50). Such judgments on the prior tradition seem unlikely and, in any case, the final form of the canon declares otherwise.

23. Ibid., 149.

24. Ibid., 153 (cf. 94).

to one another. A long-recognized example are the changes that Deuteronomy makes with respect to the laws in the Book of the Covenant in view of new times and places (changes in Leviticus and Numbers could also be noted).[25] These changes are not explicitly acknowledged in Deuteronomy (hence Levinson's proposal), but readers of the final form of the Pentateuch would recognize them as such.

To illustrate this situation, two texts may be cited. The Ten Commandments, redactionally placed at a crucial position in both Exodus and Deuteronomy, introduce the two major bodies of law in the Pentateuch. Given their standing, it is striking that the Deuteronomic version varies from that in Exodus; the changes are minor, but that they exist at all is important. The coveting commandment(s) is notable, with the interchange of "house" and "wife" (Exod 20:17; Deut 5:21); this change may reflect a change in the status of women in Israelite society (and any contemporary revision would make sure that the "neighbor" is no longer only the male!). This change may be related to a more significant revision in the slavery laws where, for example, Deuteronomy does not distinguish between treatment of male and female slaves in their manumission whereas Exodus does (cf. Deut 15:1–18, esp. v. 17, with Exod 21:2–11, esp. vv. 2, 9).

This recognition of inner-biblical development in the law is of considerable import, not only for understanding biblical law but also for post-biblical developments. The tensions and inconsistencies in the law texts are testimony to the ongoing, unresting divine effort to link the law to life in ever new times and places. Watts says it well, "Contradiction in Pentateuchal law . . . authorizes legal change as a natural part of Torah."[26] Because God is the author of all these laws, Israel's legal traditions "cast God as the principal instigator of change within law."[27] If these law texts were (are) all smoothed over, then they would be testimony to an immutable law for which new times and places were irrelevant. The very roughness of the material is an ongoing witness to the changing character of life and the changing character of the will of God as it relates to that life. And so *development in the law* is just as canonical as individual laws or the various collections of law. God's will for Israel is understood to be a living will. God moves with this people on their life's journey and God's will for them changes because they are changing. For God's will to be linked to life in such a central way makes the law an even more gracious gift than it would be if understood as immutable.

---

25. Dale Patrick, *Old Testament Law* (Atlanta: John Knox, 1985) 97, lists twenty-two instances.
26. Watts, *Reading Law*, 119.
27. Ibid., 104.

Even more, the Pentateuch's *preservation of older law alongside newer law* is an important matter to consider. Leaving the Book of the Covenant stand in the canon in its given form along with Deuteronomy is not considered a threat to the law's integrity; rather, old law and new law remain side by side as a canonical witness to the process of unfolding law. At the same time, all laws remain God's laws—older laws from God and newer laws from God—and hence cannot be declared devoid of value. As such, the Book of the Covenant maintains its value for ongoing legal reflection and innovation. This means that in moving toward any new formulation of law, every word from God was thought to need careful consideration. In revising the law it was deemed necessary to go back over all the laws from God; it was precisely in the imaginative interaction of older laws and current laws that new laws were generated for changing times and places. As such, Pentateuchal law unfolds in a way comparable to the ways in which new law is developed in our own time, where older laws that are no longer "on the books" continue to be a resource for legal reflection.

And so, instead of an immutable, timeless law in the Pentateuch, we have preserved for us a developing process in which experience in every sphere of life over time is drawn into the orbit of the law and preserved for the consideration of successive generations. For the sake of the best life possible!

The New Testament Witness to This Pattern

The New Testament texts pick up on this Old Testament witness to a dynamic, unfolding law. The New Testament community doesn't simply accept every Old Testament law as binding law; it works through the laws in a variety of ways in view of the new situations in which it finds itself (e.g., Acts 15:1–35; note especially vv. 28–29). As such, it follows a trajectory already set by the Old Testament community.[28] The New Testament thereby provides a broad pattern for interpretation and sets an agenda for both church and society in its ongoing consideration of Old Testament laws.

For example, the laws regarding clean and unclean food are rethought (e.g., Mark 7:1–23; Acts 10:1–16) and the result is that older laws regarding these matters now have a different standing in the canon for Christians. At the same time, the food laws have not been cut out of the canon or declared of no value. They remain the laws of God for an ancient time and place, but they have an ongoing import precisely because of that. They served life at

---

28. Patrick Miller's reflections on this "trajectory" in both of the works cited in the note on p. 183 have been important for my thinking about relationships between Old Testament and New on matters of law.

one time and it remains to be asked: how might the most basic concerns that inform the food laws continue to be of value for contemporary life? One may well look to contemporary food laws designed to preserve life and health as descendants of that ancient biblical concern (e.g., the Food and Drug Administration). I would argue that every law of God continues to have value for contemporary communities *at some level*.

V. A Point of Contemporary Significance

Over the course of the last two centuries much blood has been spilled over the question of the continuing applicability of particular Old Testament laws. In the nineteenth century, disagreement over texts regarding slavery spawned conflict and split communities, churches, and families. In more recent times, disagreement over law texts regarding homosexual behavior threatens to do the same. In my estimation, these conflicts have not been accompanied by much sophistication in understanding how to work with these and other laws. However well-intentioned, such argumentation is all too often a cut-and-paste enterprise.

The post-biblical formulation of new laws by human beings should be seen as being in tune with the divine intention regarding creational life and well-being evident in biblical law. Because these ever-emerging laws, however, are usually associated with legislatures, courts, and church assemblies, and developed by human beings, we tend not to think of them as God's laws; but of course they are (see, e.g., Rom 13:1–7). It may well be that some of these newer laws will stand over against their biblical predecessors, but this would be not unlike their biblical predecessors in, say, Deuteronomy.

The above discussion of inner-biblical development in the law—as much a canonical reality as the laws themselves—may provide a canonical warrant for thinking through post-biblical developments in the law in a new way. Interpreters should not make a blanket statement about all biblical laws, as if they were all equally applicable or obsolete; we are called to study each and every law seeking to discern whether it continues to serve the life and health of the community and see what might come of that conversation. While the New Testament has done some of that work for us regarding Old Testament laws, we are called to do a careful and thorough consideration of *all* biblical law, to think through God's purpose in giving it and to read back through it for insights it may continue to provide in moving toward new formulations. It is precisely in the interaction of older words from God and newer words from God, words that may stand in tension with one another, that revisions or abrogations of law are determined and new laws are developed.

If it is granted that the biblical law texts witness to a dynamic process of revising law in view of new times and places, then that testimony provides an important canonical basis for considering every biblical law as open to revision, but without treating any one of them with disdain. This way of thinking about biblical law may change attitudes toward the law and, I might add, toward the God who has so graciously given us such a dynamic law for the sake of life.

How Does Deuteronomy Do Theology?
Literary Juxtaposition and Paradox in the
New Moab Covenant in Deuteronomy 29–32

DENNIS T. OLSON

———◆———

I. Introduction

In his *Introduction to the Pentateuch*, R. Norman Whybray notes the importance within Deuteronomy of the Sinai or Horeb covenant between God and Israel with its reiteration of the Ten Commandments in Deuteronomy 5 (first given in Exodus 20) and their expansions in the statutes and ordinances that follow in Deuteronomy 6–28. Then he notes,

> In ch. 29, however, there is reference to a *second* covenant now made, after the proclamation of the laws, in the land of Moab, a covenant made "*in addition to* the covenant that he had made with them at Horeb" (v. 1). The significance of, and the necessity for, this second covenant has never been satisfactorily explained. . . . This second covenant is found nowhere else in the Old Testament. Various attempts at explaining it have been made. . . . Whatever may be the solution of the problem, this second covenant detracts from the "once-and-for-all" character of the Horeb-Sinai covenant as presented in the rest of the book, and must be regarded as an unexplained anomaly.[1]

A number of studies have analyzed in helpful ways many elements of the history, content, structure, and theology of the Moab covenant section in Deuteronomy 29–32. The purpose of this essay is to review some of this scholarship in order to examine these chapters and their theological method of reflection. My thesis is that the mode of theologizing in the

Author's note: It is with great pleasure, gratitude, and admiration that I dedicate this article to my dear colleague, mentor, and friend, Patrick D. Miller. Miller's warm personality, gracious spirit, wise counsel, theological sensitivity, and learned scholarship have touched and shaped my own life and work in many important ways over our past fifteen years together as faculty colleagues at Princeton Theological Seminary.

1. R. Norman Whybray, *Introduction to the Pentateuch* (Grand Rapids: Eerdmans, 1995) 97–98.

Moab covenant of chapters 29–32 is an integral part of a literary strategy of juxtaposition and paradox employed by the later editors of the final form of Deuteronomy. This strategy of paradox and juxtaposition evident in 29–32 serves to reframe the older Deuteronomic material (chapters 5–28) in light of the theological crisis brought on by the Babylonian exile of 587 B.C.E.[2] This reframing was achieved by adapting a tradition that was widely known and available in the ancient Near East at the time, namely, the tradition of Neo-Assyrian vassal treaties. The exilic or postexilic editors then combined this treaty or covenant tradition with a number of other Israelite traditions to create a mosaic of paradoxes and juxtapositions that work theologically with some of the most basic and ultimate issues of theology and faith.

II. The Problem of the Moab Covenant and Deut 29:1

Deut 29:1 reads, "These are the words of the covenant that the LORD commanded Moses to make with the Israelites in the land of Moab, in addition to the covenant that he had made with them at Horeb." The first critical issue that arises with the Moab covenant is to determine whether this verse functions as a superscription to the chapters that follow it or as a subscript that concludes the section of chapters that precede it (chapters 5–28). The two options are reflected already in the differences in verse numbering between the English version (29:1) and the Hebrew version (28:69). The latter number reflects the Masoretic *pārāšâ*, or paragraph division, which places the verse at the end of the section, referring backward to the chapters that precede it. Understood in this way, the "Horeb covenant" in the verse may refer to an earlier covenant text like Exodus 20 or Deuteronomy 5 (the giving of the Ten Commandments at Mount Sinai/Horeb). The "Moab covenant" would then consist of the whole of Deuteronomy 5–28 which presents a second and expanded version of the same Sinai/Horeb covenant. This would imply a thematic and theological continuity with the older covenant, not an essentially new covenant. On the other hand, the English versification reflects the tradition of the Septuagint and the Vulgate, both of which number the verse as the first of a new section. If Deut

---

2. Israel's exile from the land of Canaan and the possibility of a return to the land are explicitly mentioned at two key points in Deuteronomy: 4:25–31 and 29:19–30:10. These explicit allusions to the exile have led many scholars to understand the present form of chapters 4 and 29–30 as products of an exilic or early postexilic redaction or addition (post-587 B.C.E.). See, e.g., Jon Levenson, "Who Inserted the Book of the Torah?," *HTR* 68 (1975) 203–33. The Song of Moses in Deuteronomy 32 is probably a much earlier, pre-exilic text, but it has now been incorporated with the later exilic or postexilic materials of chapters 29–30, along with chapter 31, under the umbrella of the larger Moab covenant complex of chapters 29–32.

29:1 begins an entirely new unit described as the Moab covenant, then we are likely to see two different covenants existing simultaneously within the single book of Deuteronomy: a Horeb covenant (Deuteronomy 5–28) and a Moab covenant (Deuteronomy 29–32).

The most thorough debate on this question has been carried on by H. F. Van Rooy and Norbert Lohfink. Van Rooy's principal argument is semantic in nature. The phrase in 29:1, "the words of the covenant," occurs a total of ten times in the Old Testament. Among those ten occurrences, "the words of the covenant" typically refer to covenantal obligations *and* the covenantal curses that will come upon those who disobey the obligations. For example, Jer 11:8 reports these divine words concerning the ancestors of Israel, "Yet they did not obey. . . . So I brought upon them all *the words of this covenant*, which I commanded them to do, but they did not" (emphasis mine). Here the phrase appears to signify both the commandments to be obeyed as well as the punishments for their disobedience. Thus, Van Rooy argued that the clearest referent for the phrase in Deut 29:1 was what preceded, namely, all the statutes and ordinances in Deuteronomy 1–27 as well as the extensive list of curses in chapter 28 which immediately come before 29:1. Van Rooy maintained that one does not find any comparable list of covenantal laws and punishments in the chapters that follow (chapters 29–30). They are simply an "exhortation" to follow the Deuteronomic covenant and do not in themselves constitute a new covenant document. Deuteronomy 1–28 is the Moab covenant to which 29:1 refers, and this large block is bracketed by a superscription in 1:1 ("These are the words that Moses spoke . . .") and a concluding subscript in 29:1 ("These are the words of the covenant that the Lord commanded Moses to make . . ."). Van Rooy saw the repetition of "these" and "words" in both 1:1 and 29:1 as a sign of intentional editorial bracketing of the entire section of chapters 1–28 as under the umbrella of the "Moab covenant."[3]

Norbert Lohfink concedes that the phrase, "These are the words of the covenant . . . ," in 29:1 may at some *earlier* stage of the book's history have functioned as a subscript pointing back to the statutes and curses of at least chapters 5–28. However, what may have once been a concluding subscript in 29:1 has been altered by later editors to fit into a governing series of superscriptions which provide the overall structure for the book of Deuteronomy in its final form.[4] Each of these key superscriptions contains the

---

3. H. F. Van Rooy, "Deuteronomy 28:69 — Superscript or Subscript?" *JNSL* 14 (1988) 215–22.

4. Norbert Lohfink, "Dtn 28,69 — Überschrift oder Kolophon?" *BN* 64 (1992) 44. See also Georg Braulik, *Deuteronomium II: 16,18–34,12* (NEchtB; Würzburg: Echter, 1992) 210. Interestingly, one of the earliest known commentators to explicitly propose 29:1 as a superscription to the following chapters — one that introduced an altogether new and

demonstrative article (*'ēlleh* or *zō't*) and a designation of the material that
follows according to the following scheme:

1:1 — "These are the words that Moses spoke . . ." (followed by largely
narrative material in chapters 1–4).

4:44 — "This is the law [*ḥattôrâ*] that Moses set before the Israelites
. . . " (followed by the Decalogue given at Mount Horeb in chapter 5
and the expansive "statutes and ordinances" [6:1] of chapters 6–28).

29:1 — "These are the words of the covenant that the LORD commanded Moses to make with the Israelites in the land of Moab in addition to the covenant that he made with them at Horeb" (followed
by the covenant material in chapters 29–32).

33:1 — "This is the blessing with which Moses, the man of God,
blessed the Israelites before his death" (followed by Moses' blessing
of the twelve tribes [chapter 33] and the account of Moses' death on
Mount Nebo [chapter 34]).[5]

In the present form of Deuteronomy, *none of these formulas functions as a concluding subscript but only as a superscription*, introducing the section that follows it.

Moreover, Lohfink argues that the phrase in Deut 29:1 actually finds
more resonance forward in chapters 29–32 than backward to chapters 5–28.
"Words" can refer not only to obligations and curses for disobedience but
also cultic and ritual texts.[6] Chapters 29–32 consists of a ritual of covenant-

---

different Moab covenant in addition to the Horeb covenant—is a Jewish interpreter
who argued against the *pārāšâ* division of the Hebrew tradition, Rabbi Abravanel (1437–
1508 C.E.). Concerning the Moab covenant which he saw as consisting of Deuteronomy
29–30, he wrote: "This passage is still due to happen, because its promises were not yet
fulfilled, neither in the first nor in the second Temple; this one is our consolation and
hope, this is the overall healing to all our miseries" (cited in Alexander Rofé, "The Covenant in the Land of Moab [Deuteronomy 28:69–30:20]: Historico-Literary, Comparative, and Form-critical Considerations," in *Das Deuteronomium: Enstehung, Gestalt und
Botschaft* [ed. Norbert Lohfink; Louvain: Louvain University Press, 1985] 311).

5. Lohfink, "Dtn 28,69," 44. One of the earliest scholars to note this editorial framework of four superscriptions was Paul Kleinert, *Das Deuteronomium und der Deuterono-
miker: Untersuchungen zur alttestamentliche Rechts- und Literargeschichte* (Leipzig: Velhagen
& Klasing, 1872) 167. Examples of theological interpretations of Deuteronomy that incorporate this overarching structure of superscriptions in Deuteronomy include Patrick
D. Miller, *Deuteronomy* (Interpretation; Louisville: John Knox, 1990); and Dennis T.
Olson, *Deuteronomy and the Death of Moses: A Theological Reading* (OBT; Minneapolis: Fortress, 1994).

6. See Deut 29:19: "words of this oath"; and 1 Kgs 8:59: the "words" King Solomon
spoke in the context of offering sacrifices and prayer at the Temple.

making which may properly be described as "these . . . words of the covenant." Finally, Lohfink notes that the word "covenant" itself is very rare in the preceding chapters. It occurs only once in the statutes of Deuteronomy 12–26 and not once in the blessings and curses in chapters 27–28. In contrast, the word "covenant" appears repeatedly in chapter 29 following the superscription in 29:1 — 29:9, 12, 14, 21, 25.[7] Thus, the formula, "These are the words of the covenant . . . ," *clearly points forward* to the covenant-making ceremony in chapters 29–30, the accompanying succession of covenant leadership from Moses to Joshua as well as the writing down of the book of the Torah in chapter 31, and the rehearsal of God's covenant relationship with Israel in the Song of Moses in chapter 32.[8]

III. The Horeb Covenant, the Moab Covenant, and Neo-Assyrian Treaty Forms

As we will see, the Moab covenant in Deuteronomy 29–32 offers something qualitatively new and different from the structure and themes of the old Horeb covenant presented in Deuteronomy 5–28. This qualitative difference was necessitated by a decisive historical experience in Israel's life as a people, the exile of Judah to Babylon in 587 B.C.E. (see 2 Kings 24–25). Although we will see that important differences exist, it is also important to note that the Horeb and Moab covenants share a crucial common literary ancestor, namely, the Neo-Assyrian treaty form dating from the eighth and seventh centuries. This treaty form was apparently well known and widespread among the nations and cultures of the ancient Near East.

Consider first the Horeb covenant and its use of the treaty form. The old "if . . . then . . ." form of the Horeb covenant and its blessings and curses were modeled after the Neo-Assyrian suzerainty treaties of the time. These

---

7. Lohfink, "Dtn 28,69," 50.

8. Scholars differ on the extent of the section introduced by the superscription in 29:1, whether chapter 29 alone, chapters 29–30, or the whole of chapters 29–32. For example, J. Gary Millar argues that the Moab covenant encompasses only chapter 29. He suggests that chapter 30 represents yet a third "new covenant" in addition to the Horeb covenant (Deuteronomy 5–28) and the Moab covenant (chapter 29). He believes the theologies of chapters 29 and 30 are incompatible with one another as one covenant. See J. Gary Millar, *Now Choose Life: Theology and Ethics in Deuteronomy* (Leicester, England: Apollos, 1998) 93. Others see the Moab covenant as including chapters 29–30 but not 31 and 32. See Gerhard von Rad, *Deuteronomy: A Commentary* (OTL; Philadelphia: Westminster, 1966) 178. A thorough and convincing defense for all of chapters 29–32 being subsumed under the Moab covenant is Norbert Lohfink, "Der Bundesschluss im Land Moab: Redaktionsgeschichtliches zu Dtn 28,69–32–47," *BZ* 6 (1962) 32–56. Lohfink demonstrates the redactional connections and artful shaping of this entire complex, bracketed by Moses climactic speech in chapters 29–30 and Moses' climactic song in chapter 32.

treaties or covenants were political documents between one powerful king
(the suzerain) and another less powerful king or ruler (the vassal). The treaties contained the following well-known elements: (1) preamble, (2) historical prologue (containing the beneficial actions that the suzerain had done
for the vassal), (3) stipulations (obligations of the vassal in light of the suzerain's activity), (4) an invoking of witnesses (often deities), and (5) a list of
blessings and curses (consequences of obedience and disobedience).[9] The
old Horeb covenant of Deuteronomy transposed and adapted this political
treaty form into a covenant between God (the suzerain) and Israel (the vassal). Partial elements of the treaty form may be seen in Deut 5:6a (preamble:
"I am the LORD your God"), 5:6b (historical prologue: "who brought you out
of the land of Egypt"), 5:8–26:19 (stipulations: the Decalogue and all the
statutes and ordinances which are vastly greater in number in Deuteronomy
than in the typical suzerainty treaty), and 27–28 (the blessings and curses in
an "if . . . then" form until 28:45–48 when the form is broken and the future
is depicted as predetermined toward an unavoidable exile and judgment).

The tragedy of the Babylonian exile led to this "fracturing" of the very
end of the old Horeb covenant itself, namely, the form of blessings and
curses that conclude the Horeb material in chapter 28. Later exilic editors
introduced a key grammatical shift in the enumeration of the Horeb covenant curses in Deut 28:45–48. In the preceding list in 28:1–44, the curses
and blessings remain open possibilities and are entirely dependent on Israel's apparently free decision to obey or to disobey God. This conditional
syntax is the typical form of the Near Eastern treaty. The conditional
clause that begins 28:15 rules over the entire section of curses in 28:15–44:
"*If* you will not obey the LORD your God." But in Deut 28:45–48, the text
shifts abruptly from this conditional mode into a declarative and narrative
mode. The syntactical structure changes dramatically from 28:15, which is
an open-ended conditional clause, to a declared state of fact that will assur-
edly happen in the narrated future in 28:45. The conditional clause ("*if* you
will not obey . . . then . . .") now becomes a causal or explanatory clause—
"All these curses *shall* come upon you . . . *because* you did not obey." This is to
say that the curse shifts here at the very end of the Horeb covenant from a
conditional possibility to a *narrated future reality*. A focus on human freedom
and ability to choose wisely to obey and act righteously ("if . . . then") is
here juxtaposed with a focus on a determined future which no human
choice can avert: "all these curses shall come upon you." This subtle change
in syntax introduced here at the end of the Horeb covenant in chapter 28
provides already a glimpse into one of the key paradoxes or juxtapositions

---

9. Dennis J. McCarthy, *Treaty and Covenant* (2d ed.; AnBib 21A; Rome: Pontifical Biblical Institute, 1981) 199–205.

that will be featured in the Moab covenant of chapters 29–32: the paradox and interplay of divine determination with human freedom and power.

Elements of the Neo-Assyrian treaty form are also taken up and significantly reshaped in the new Moab covenant of Deuteronomy 29–32. Thus, one may see some evidence of a preamble (29:1), historical prologue (29:2–9), stipulations (29:16–19), witnesses (30:19: "heaven and earth"), and curses (29:20–28). Although the treaty form is one traditional element which was used and adapted by the writers of chapters 29–32, there is much more going on in these chapters that responds to the issues and dilemmas posed by Judah's exile to Babylon and its loss of temple, king, and land. Indeed, Deuteronomy 29–32 brings together and reinterprets through juxtaposition a whole host of traditional materials.

IV. Deuteronomy 29–32 as an Adaptation and Juxtaposition of Traditional Elements

The Moab covenant is constructed through an artful juxtaposition of many earlier traditions and motifs. They may be listed as follows:

1. 29:2–3—"you have seen all that the LORD did before your eyes in the land of Egypt . . . signs and . . . wonders"—an echo of the old Horeb covenant; Deut 5:6 (Decalogue), 6:22; 7:19; 26:8.
2. 29:4—"the LORD has not given you a mind to understand, or eyes to see, or ears to hear"—an echo of Isa 6:9–10 where the prophet is instructed by God to prophesy "so that they may not look with their eyes, and listen with their ears, and comprehend with their minds" (see also Isa 42:18–20; 43:8; and Jer 5:21).
3. 29:7–8—a reference to the defeat of King Sihon and Og previously recounted in Deut 2:26–3:22 (see also Num 21:21–35).
4. 29:13—an appeal to the covenant promise made to the ancestors, grounded in Genesis 15 and 17.
5. 29:14–15—an adaptation of Deut 5:3 which drew the covenant from the past into the present ("Not with our ancestors did the LORD make this covenant, but with us, who are all of us here alive today"). Deut 29:14–15 uses similar language to open up the covenant from the present into the future ("I am making this covenant. . . . Not only with you who stand here with us today . . . but also with those who are not here with us today").
6. 29:23—a reference to the destruction of Sodom and Gomorrah in Genesis 19, which reflects an interest in what happens to the other nations and in what the other nations believe about Israel and Israel's God.

7. 30:6 — a clear allusion to Deut 10:16 where God commands Israel, "Circumcise, then, the foreskin of your heart; and do not be stubborn any longer." However, here in a bold reinterpretation, God promises to achieve what Israel alone has been unable to achieve: "The LORD your God will circumcise your heart and the heart of your descendants, so that you will love the LORD your God with all your heart and all your soul" (a strong echo of the central confession of the Horeb covenant in the "Shema" of Deut 6:4–5).[10]

Along with these significant traditions that are taken up in the Moab covenant, we must also count the poetic Song of Moses (Deuteronomy 32) which most scholars see as an ancient and traditional song. Similar ancient poems like the Song of the Sea in Exodus 15 or the Song of Deborah in Judges 5 were supplemented with later prose reinterpretations that now precede them in the present form of the text (Exodus 14 and Judges 4, respectively). In a similar way, the Song of Moses has been supplemented and restated in two prose additions that precede it: chapters 29–30 (the covenant liturgy of Moab) and chapter 31 (the covenant leadership and text of Moab).

These three parallel versions of the Moab covenant — the covenant liturgy of chapters 29–30, the covenant leadership and text of chapter 31, and the covenant song of chapter 32 — share a threefold movement from (1) the affirmation of God's past faithfulness to (2) the present reality of human limits and death, and, finally, to (3) the future activity of God, who alone has the power to overcome human limits and disobedience through an inscrutable but assured divine justice and compassion.[11] Along the way, the exilic constructors of the new Moab covenant will do their theological thinking by means of a process of literary juxtaposition of paradoxes, affirming simultaneous truths that seem contradictory. This paradoxical method should not be surprising in that the writers present the Moab covenant "*in addition to* the covenant" which God made at Horeb (29:1). Juxtaposition, retaining conflicting perspectives, seems to be characteristic of these exilic or postexilic Moab covenanters.

V. Time and Juxtaposition in Deuteronomy 29–30

This threefold movement is first illustrated in chapters 29–30, which begin by affirming God's past faithfulness (29:2–8). The chapters then proclaim the limits of human knowledge (29:4, 29), the limits of human obedi-

---

10. See the contributions of Lemke and Brueggemann in this volume.
11. See further Olson, *Deuteronomy and the Death of Moses*, 129–52.

ence (29:18–19), and the ultimate limits of human life and power as curse and exile crowd in upon God's people (29:18–28). But mysteriously (29:29: "secret things"), God will "restore your fortunes and have compassion on you" even "if you are exiled to the ends of the world" (30:3, 4). God's unbounded compassion breaks the barriers of finite time and space so that God is present in every place we call "this place" (29:7; 30:11–14) and in every day we call "this day" (29:4, 10, 12, 13, 14, 15; 30:11, 15, 16, 18, 19).

One of the central juxtapositions or paradoxes in Deuteronomy 29–30 is the affirmation of both *divine determination* and *human freedom*. One encounters here the unprecedented (for a Deuteronomist) notion of God circumcising the heart of Israel. God promises to set the human intellect and will ("the heart") toward God in obedience and devotion. The Horeb covenant had emphasized the appeal to the human will to be obedient through command and persuasion: "Circumcise, then, the foreskin of your heart (10:16)." In light of the exile, the Moab covenant provides a dramatic alternative: only God can create obedience. And yet the paradox is that the new Moab covenant also is emphatic in calling Israel to exercise its own will and freedom to "choose life" as God presents two paths: "if you obey" or "if your heart turns away" (30:16–17). One is reminded here of the juxtaposition in Exodus 8–11 of God's hardening of Pharaoh's heart alongside texts that speak of Pharaoh hardening his own heart and confessing his sin and responsibility in willfully resisting God's commands (compare Exod 8:15 and 9:27 with 10:1). We sense that the Deuteronomists are bumping up against "secret things" (see Deut 29:29), truths that transcend human knowing and thus require paradox and the affirmation of seemingly contradictory positions to articulate them.

A related paradox is the affirmation both that obedience and loyalty to God seem *very difficult* for Israel to maintain (29:22–28) and yet the statement that the commandments are *not difficult* and very near to the heart so that they are easily obeyed (30:11–14).

Another juxtaposition puzzling to those who desire more linear truths is the *collective* responsibility and *communal* consequences of Israel's rebellion on one hand and the sudden interruption with a concern for singling out *individuals* for their sin on the other. Deut 29:18–21, with its focus on individual sinners, is often seen by commentators as a clumsy insertion into what is otherwise an "all-Israel" perspective. However, I would argue that this is another example of theology by uneasy juxtaposition, affirming both collective responsibility as well as individual obligation apart from what happens to the larger community. Neither perspective alone captures the truth about the relationship of individuals and communities: at times it is proper to emphasize one or the other, but neither dimension can be ignored.

A final juxtaposition is the one posed by Deut 29:29: "The secret things belong to the LORD our God, but the revealed things belong to us and to our children forever, to observe all the words of this law." This is not so much a paradox as a claim about the *limits of human knowledge* in the face of the *constant human yearning* to observe and make conclusions about the ways of God and humans. Immediately before this verse, people from other nations are observing the devastation of the land and searching for an answer, "Why has the LORD done thus to this land?" They will conclude, "It is because they abandoned the covenant of the LORD." But the acknowledgement that the cosmos holds "secret things" also suggests that sometimes there will be no answers to questions like "Why?" or "How long?"

VI. Time and Juxtaposition in Deuteronomy 31

Chapter 31 likewise displays this threefold movement from past to present to future. We move from God's past blessings (31:1–6) to the present limitations and impending death of the individual Moses (31:14–15), whose death prefigures the rebellion and death of the whole community in exile (31:16–21, 27–29). In response to human limits and death, God provides concrete and intimate means by which the faith and traditions of Moses can be carried forward to future generations: transfer of leadership from Moses to Joshua (31:7–8, 14–15, 23), Moses writing down the book of the Torah to be read orally to future generations (31:9–13, 24–29), and a song that will serve as a witness against the people (31:19, 22, 30).

An intriguing juxtaposition in this section is a physical one in 31:26 when Moses instructs the Levites who carry the ark of the covenant to take the book of the Torah that he has written and "put it beside the ark of the covenant." According to the Horeb covenant in Deut 10:2, 4–5, the ark is a box that contains the two tablets of stone on which God had written the Ten Commandments. The tablets represent the only direct and unmediated text of God's word. The ark and its tablets come to rest eventually in Solomon's temple in Jerusalem (1 Kgs 8:9). The Babylonian exile presumably resulted in the destruction of the temple and its contents, including the ark and the tablets. They do not reappear again in the building of the second temple after the exile. Thus, this exilic Moab covenant juxtaposes the unmediated divine words on stone tablets that eventually disappear and are not recoverable with the humanly mediated and secondary words of Moses' book of the Torah. There is a further complication in that Deuteronomy's narrator juxtaposes the book that Moses writes, which is placed alongside the ark, and the book of Deuteronomy itself, which recounts the writing of Moses' book. They are two different books, although tradition eventually identifies this Mosaic book of the Torah with not only Deuteronomy but

the whole Pentateuch of Genesis–Deuteronomy. We have access to Moses'
book only secondarily through the book of Deuteronomy, however, since
we do not have a copy of Moses' book itself. We have only Deuteronomy
which reports its writing.[12] Thus, Deuteronomy itself recognizes that it is,
in a sense, thrice-removed from the direct word of God—the Ten Commandments in the ark as the first step, Moses' book of the Torah beside the
ark as the second step, and the book of Deuteronomy itself as the third
step away from the unmediated word of God.

Another juxtaposition in this section emerges when we compare the visible theophany of God's appearance at the tent of meeting where "the
LORD appeared at the tent in a pillar of cloud" (31:14–15) with the focus on
God's presence being mediated through a book and its oral reading in generations to come. The Horeb covenant is predominantly a covenant of the
ear. The people hear the voice of God out of the fire, a fire that streams
from heaven down to the mountain like a pipeline carrying the divine word
(Deut 5:24–26). In contrast to other biblical theologies, Deuteronomy affirms that only God's name (not God's full presence) dwells in the earthly
temple (12:5). God is transcendent, and the petitioner can only ask God to
"look down from your holy habitation, from heaven, and bless your people
Israel" (Deut 26:15). But alongside this verbal, aural, and distant God who is
mediated secondarily through a book and a teacher/preacher, is placed a
full-fledged theophany of God. Horeb is not the once-and-for-all revelation. God can appear again and does so at this crucial transition between
the death of Moses and the rise of Joshua as the people's new leader. The
appearance of God here also affirms that somehow God is near in and
through the written book and its oral reading through leaders of the community. God will be as present through the book, the leader, and the song
as much as God was present with Moses at Mount Horeb, the only other
theophany Deuteronomy records.

VII. Time and Juxtaposition in Deuteronomy 32

The Song of Moses itself also moves from the confession of God's past
gracious acts (32:3–14) to the people's past and present rebellions by which
they will experience the limits and curses of human life (32:15–35). The future will also involve judgment, but when the LORD "sees that their power
is gone," when they have come up against their ultimate limits, then God
will have compassion on them and win victory on their behalf (32:36–43).

---

12. See the insightful study of Jan-Pierre Sonnet, *The Book within the Book: Writing in
Deuteronomy* (Leiden: Brill, 1997) 235–61.

The song is full of juxtapositions and contrasts, but the strongest is God's proclamation after recounting the jagged history of Israel's rebellions and God's punishments: "See now that I, even I, am he; there is no god beside me. I kill and I make alive; I wound and I heal; and no one can deliver from my hand" (Deut 32:39). The affirmation of God as one who both kills and makes alive, wounds and heals, will be experienced by Israel over and over as unfathomable, unjust, or capricious (see Ecclesiastes, Job, the psalms of lament). Yet there is also solace and hope in this affirmation for "indeed the Lord will vindicate his people, have compassion on his servants, when he sees that their power is gone" (32:36).

Another intriguing paradox is the affirmation that there are no other gods besides the Lord (32:39) and the contrasting acknowledgement of the existence of other gods for other nations in Deut 32:8–9, at least in the pre-Masoretic tradition. The Septuagint and Qumran readings of this verse agree in reading "[the Most High] fixed the boundaries of the peoples according to the number of the gods [literally, "the sons of the gods], the Lord's own portion was his people, Jacob his allotted share."[13]

VIII. Conclusion

I have moved from a focus on one particular verse, Deut 29:1, to a larger examination of the entire Moab covenant section in Deuteronomy 29–32. In doing so, I have noted the method of the exilic writers of this section in posing contrasts and paradoxes as the only adequate means of wrestling with the difficult theological issues that faced them, particularly in light of the exile and the theological crisis it created in Israel's understanding of its relationship to God. There is more work here yet to be done. It would be important to test the results of this study against an examination of the other clearly exilic text in Deuteronomy, namely, chapter 4.[14] The results

13. The MT apparently sought to avoid the notion of Israel's God as one among other gods and thus reads v. 8 as "he fixed the boundaries of the peoples according to the number of the sons of *Israel*" (emphasis added). The Song of Moses is likely an ancient poem and may well reflect an earlier time in Israel's history when it acknowledged the existence of other gods along with Israel's own God (see also Psalm 82). For a treatment of this text which also interacts with other texts from Deuteronomy, see Patrick D. Miller, "God's Other Stories: On the Margins of Deuteronomic Theology," in *Realia Dei: Essays in Archaeology and Biblical Interpretation in Honor of Edward F. Campbell, Jr. at His Retirement* (ed. Prescott H. Williams, Jr. and Theodore Hiebert; Atlanta: Scholars Press, 1999) 185–94.

14. An insightful reading of Deuteronomy 4 by Stephen Geller, *Sacred Enigmas: Literary Religion in the Hebrew Bible* (London: Routledge, 1996) 30–61, provided a helpful stimulus for thinking about the theological method of juxtaposition and paradox in the exilic or postexilic writers of Deuteronomy 4 and Deuteronomy 29–32.

of this study may also be valuable in rethinking the relationship of the wisdom tradition and the theological perspectives of the exilic writers of Deuteronomy 29–32. Deuteronomy is often posed as antithetical to books like Job or Ecclesiastes, but at least these chapters of Deuteronomy may offer some ways by which wisdom may be pulled more closely into the mainstream of biblical theology.

Keep/Observe/Do—Carefully—Today!
The Rhetoric of Repetition in Deuteronomy

BRENT A. STRAWN

———◆———

"In art, too, repetition is a sign of maturity, of assurance and strength."[1]
"'Repetition' is and remains a religious category."[2]

I. Introduction

In the scholarly literature on Deuteronomy, statements about the book's style are among those most frequently encountered. That style, or what might better be called Deuteronomy's rhetoric, is typically said to be hortatory, proclamatory, even "preachy."[3] It is also said to be prolix, redundant, even monotonous—especially in its repetition of certain key words and formulae.[4]

Unfortunately, beyond identifying exhortation and repetition as two main components of Deuteronomy's rhetoric, scholars usually have little more to say. Instead, these elements, whether they are spoken of approvingly or disparagingly, have been used most often by scholars to track the

Author's note: It is a true and distinct honor and privilege to dedicate this essay to Patrick D. Miller, who first led me into the (Hebrew) rhetoric of Deuteronomy and who, I am happy to say, never restrained himself from participating in and seconding its proclamatory rhetoric! There is no doubt in my mind that these two aspects, Miller's teaching and preaching (perhaps it would be better to speak of his teaching/preaching or preaching/teaching), have had a decisive impact on my own occupational and vocational pursuits.

1. Bruce F. Kawin, *Telling It Again and Again: Repetition in Literature and Film* (Boulder: University Press of Colorado, 1989) 181.

2. Søren Kierkegaard, *Fear and Trembling; Repetition* (trans. and ed. Howard V. Hong and Edna H. Hong; Kierkegaard's Writings 6; Princeton: Princeton University Press, 1983) 326.

3. See, e.g., Moshe Weinfeld, *Deuteronomy and the Deuteronomic School* (reprinted; Winona Lake, Ind.: Eisenbrauns, 1992) 1.

4. See, e.g., Ernst Sellin and Georg Fohrer, *Introduction to the Old Testament* (Nashville: Abingdon, 1968) 167. John William Wevers has tracked the same tendency in LXX Deuteronomy (*Text History of the Greek Deuteronomy* [MSU 13; Göttingen: Vandenhoeck & Ruprecht, 1978] 86).

influence of Deuteronomy in other portions of the canon, most notably in the Deuteronomistic History.[5] With regard to repetition specifically, previous scholarship has typically employed it in source-critical and/or tradition-historical pursuits, finding in it proof of development, the existence of literary seams, redaction, and the like.[6]

But much more can be said about repetition and exhortation—especially when they are found together, as they are in Deuteronomy—especially with regard to their *rhetorical effect* and *theological function*. The present essay draws upon various treatments of repetition in literature, film, and discourse analysis[7] to argue that repetition in Deuteronomy functions to leave the reader—or, perhaps better, the hearer—of the book with

---

5. See, e.g., Martin Noth, *The Deuteronomistic History* (2d ed.; JSOTSup 15; Sheffield: JSOT Press, 1991) 18. For listings of terms and phrases that occur in Deuteronomy and other books, especially those in DtrH, see Weinfeld, *Deuteronomy and the Deuteronomic School*, 320–65; S. R. Driver, *A Critical and Exegetical Commentary on Deuteronomy* (3d ed.; ICC; Edinburgh: T & T Clark, 1902) lxxviii–lxxxiv, xci–xciv; and idem, *An Introduction to the Literature of the Old Testament* (New York: Meridian Books, 1960) 99–102.

6. See, e.g., A. D. H. Mayes, *Deuteronomy* (NCB; Grand Rapids: Eerdmans, 1981) 34–35; Rolf Rendtorff, *The Old Testament: An Introduction* (Philadelphia: Fortress, 1986) 150; and Thomas B. Dozeman, *God on the Mountain: A Study of Redaction, Theology and Canon in Exodus 19–24* (SBLMS 37; Atlanta: Scholars Press, 1989) 148 and n. 11—both of the latter on Wellhausen's assessment and historical (diachronic) use of repetition. To some extent, Dozeman follows in this diachronic tradition, though with significant nuance. The same holds true of Bernard Levinson's important work, *Deuteronomy and the Hermeneutics of Legal Innovation* (New York: Oxford University Press, 1997), though it should be noted that he takes issue with both classical diachronic approaches to the problem of repetition as well as synchronic approaches that treat the phenomenon "as deliberate rhetorical emphasis" (p. 27).

7. Especially Kawin's work, *Telling It Again and Again*; but also J. Hillis Miller's work, *Fiction and Repetition: Seven English Novels* (Cambridge: Harvard University Press, 1982); and other theoretical works on repetition from a discourse perspective. For the latter, see especially Barbara Johnstone, ed., *Repetition in Discourse: Interdisciplinary Perspectives* (2 vols.; Advances in Discourse Processes 47–48; Norwood: Ablex, 1994); idem, "An Introduction," *Text* 7 (1987) 205–14; Neal R. Norrick, "Functions of Repetition in Conversation," *Text* 7 (1987) 245–64; Deborah Tannen, "Repetition in Conversation as Spontaneous Formulaicity," *Text* 7 (1987) 215–43; and idem, "Repetition in Conversation: Toward a Poetics of Talk," *Language* 63 (1987) 574–605. To my knowledge, the extensive theoretical work on repetition has not been applied to Deuteronomy, though one should note Dozeman, *God on the Mountain*, 145–75, who discusses Kawin's and Miller's work with reference to the problem of repetition in Exodus 19–24 (and beyond). Even so, Dozeman interacts primarily with Miller, citing Kawin only in passing. Levinson, *Deuteronomy*, 156–57 has discussed Kierkegaard's *Repetition* with reference to Deuteronomy but, again, only briefly and in a less direct fashion than that undertaken here. Finally, Timothy A. Lenchak, *"Choose Life!": A Rhetorical-Critical Investigation of Deuteronomy 28,69–30,20* (AnBib 129; Rome: Pontifical Biblical Institute, 1993) 130–35, treats some discourse works on repetition, but cites neither Kawin nor Miller.

a few key items in mind. These include, above all, characteristic Deuteronomic *verbs*, "keep/observe" (שמר), "do" (עשה), and "listen/hear/obey" (שמע); and the typical *objects of those verbs*: "law" (תורה), "commandment(s)" (מצות/מצוה), and the ubiquitous "statutes and ordinances" (חקים ומשפטים). When the reader/hearer is done with Deuteronomy these are what remain—in ear, mind, and heart. This *rhetorical effect* produces, in turn, an *ethical and theological result*: one who *really does do* the law, does it quite carefully at that, and does it, furthermore, within the primary timeframes of the book: "now, today, always" (כל הימים; היום הזה; היום).

II. Repetition in Deuteronomy and Beyond: A Functional Typology

Statements about repetition in Deuteronomy abound, but are not uniform. Although positive assessments are made occasionally,[8] more frequently the statement appears to be negative. Consider the following:

> The language and style . . . of all the sermons in Deuteronomy, appear at first sight to be framed in a somewhat conventional way, and the continual repetition of phrases seems almost monotonous.[9]

> [The speeches'] characteristic features are not only the style, which is broad, often overloaded and seemingly prolix (and the easy Hebrew!), but also [the] paraenesis, i.e., constantly repeated admonitions to observe the commandments, often bound up with the promise of blessings on life in the promised land.[10]

Whatever the exact intent of these citations, it is the negative assessment that seems to dominate scholarly treatments of Deuteronomic repetition. Perhaps this is because, as J. P. Fokkelman has recently reiterated, repetition is in bad company today.[11] We learn from an early age to avoid it: it is an indication of poor style, bad writing, and so forth. Negative assessments of repetition also enjoy a long history in Classical rhetoric[12] and in

---

8. See, e.g., Driver, *Deuteronomy*, lxxxvii–lxxxviii, who writes that the discourse is "never (in the bad sense of the term [!]) rhetorical, always maintains its freshness, and is never monotonous or prolix." Cf. ibid., lxxxiv; idem, *Introduction*, 102; and James Muilenburg, "A Study in Hebrew Rhetoric: Repetition and Style," in *Congress Volume: Copenhagen, 1953* (ed. George W. Anderson; VTSup 1; Leiden: Brill, 1953) 100.

9. Gerhard von Rad, *Deuteronomy: A Commentary* (OTL; Philadelphia: Westminster, 1966) 20.

10. Rendtorff, *The Old Testament*, 151–52.

11. See J. P. Fokkelman, *Reading Biblical Narrative: An Introductory Guide* (Louisville: Westminster John Knox, 1999) 112.

12. Too much repetition, in particular, was a bad thing. Note, e.g., *homiologia* (tedious or redundant style) and *pleonasmus* (needless repetition)—not to mention *tautologia*. These

still earlier work.[13] Fokkelman rightly observes, however, that this situation is in marked contrast to the practices of the biblical text. That contrast, furthermore, poses a problem insofar as "we run the risk of misunderstanding and misjudging forms of [biblical] repetition."[14] It is noteworthy in this regard, for example, to observe that even recent treatments of repetition in biblical texts typically place special emphasis, not on repetition proper, but on variation-within-repetition.[15] Hermeneutical significance is found especially there—on *variation* and *difference*—even though the subject at issue, repetition, is dominated by *similarity*.[16] It is also significant that most treatments of repetition in the field of biblical studies deal only with the phenomenon in *narrative*. Treatments of repetition within the legal mate-

---

terms belong to repetition at the clause/phrase/idea level (see Richard A. Lanham, *A Handlist of Rhetorical Terms: A Guide for Students of English Literature* [Berkeley: University of California Press, 1969] 125). Note further that one of the categories of good style, *dignitas*, is marked by "embellishment by a *variety* of figures tastefully used" (ibid., 116; emphasis mine).

13. Note, e.g., the following lines from the Middle Kingdom Egyptian work, *The Complaints of Khakheperre-sonb*: "Had I unknown phrases, / Sayings that are strange, / Novel, untried words, / Free of repetition; / Not transmitted sayings, / Spoken by the ancestors!" (*AEL* 1:146).

14. Fokkelman, *Reading Biblical Narrative*, 112–13; citation from 113. So also Robert Alter, *The Art of Biblical Narrative* (New York: Basic Books, 1981) 88 who states that the "extraordinary prominence of verbatim repetition" in the Bible is a barrier to modern readers to whom it appears "primitive" (cf. p. 96).

15. This is true, I believe, of both Alter, *The Art of Biblical Narrative*, 88–113 ("The Techniques of Repetition"), see especially 91, 96–97 (where he contrasts prose repetition with poetic parallelism), 104, 112; and Meir Sternberg, *The Poetics of Biblical Narrative: Ideological Literature and the Drama of Reading* (Bloomington: Indiana University Press, 1987) 364–440. See also Dozeman, *God on the Mountain*, 148; and David M. Gunn and Danna Nolan Fewell, *Narrative in the Hebrew Bible* (Oxford Bible Series; Oxford: Oxford University Press, 1993) 148, 155. An exception to this judgment is Muilenburg, "A Study in Hebrew Rhetoric," who emphasizes *both* (the "intimate relation between old and new" in repetition; p. 98), but who also devotes his primary attention to "actual repetition" (p. 99).

16. At the very least, one must grant that similarity is *as important as* difference to the concept of repetition. Interestingly, the recent emphasis on difference within repetition corresponds, in part, to the two types of repetition that Miller lays out: that of repetition based on *similarity* (mimesis, which implies the existence of an archetype of sorts) and that of repetition based on *difference* (ungrounded doubling, which implies no archetype). See Miller, *Fiction and Repetition*, 1–21, esp. 5–6. If this is accurate, most theorists seem to have tended to favor the latter type. One wonders if this emphasis on difference is theoretically related to the importance of difference in structuralism. Whatever the case, *both* sameness *and* difference are important. "A cultural account that looks at difference needs to acknowledge sameness; one that understands discourse as linearity needs to accede to cyclicity and repetitiveness" (Greg Urban, "Repetition and Cultural Replication: Three Examples from Shokleng," in Johnstone, ed., *Repetition in Discourse*, 2:160).

rial are rare and, when present, typically concerned with other, more dia-chronic issues.[17]

But it must be said in response to negative assessments of repetition that it has not always been so. Despite their generally negative view of repetition, some of the Classical rhetoricians considered it a highly useful device, especially in suasive speech. And, regardless of the canons of Classical rhetoric, Hebrew literature abounds in repetition in both prose and poetry.[18] Indeed, some scholars have argued that repetition is built into the very structure of the Hebrew language itself—not only in its syntax, but even its morphology (consider the limitations of the tri-consonantal root).[19] One might well wonder, then, if contemporary distastes for repetition are not only anachronistic with reference to the Old Testament, but also if they have little to do with rhetoric *qua* rhetoric and more with favoring modern, predominantly literate culture (and literacy) over pre-modern, predominantly oral culture (and orality).[20] In any event, whatever the origins of scholarly estimations of Deuteronomy's repetition and whatever its possible oral traditions or origins may be, there can be no doubt that Deuteronomy is a *literary* text,[21] and is, simultaneously, shot full of repetition. But this begs the question for, as Sternberg has pointed out, the use of repetition in literary texts is not required nor expected.[22] Why, then, is

---

17. See the work of Guy Lasserre, *Synopse des lois du Pentateuque* (VTSup 59; Leiden: E. J. Brill, 1994), esp. 116–50, which lists a number of parallels to the Deuteronomic law code, but which is not concerned with the kind of close (micro-level) and intra-Deuteronomic repetition that is my primary concern here. A good treatment of repetition in legal material with an eye toward persuasion can be found in the work of James W. Watts, *Reading Law: The Rhetorical Shaping of the Pentateuch* (Biblical Seminar 59; Sheffield: Sheffield Academic Press, 1999), esp. 61–88.

18. If one includes repetition not only of key words, but also of motifs, themes, sequences of action, and so forth, the amount of repetition in the Old Testament multiplies exponentially. For these and other types of repetition see Alter, *The Art of Biblical Narrative*, 95–96; Miller, *Fiction and Repetition*, 1–2.

19. See Israel Eitan, "La repetition de la racine en Hébreu," *JPOS* 1 (1921) 171–86; cf. Alter, *The Art of Biblical Narrative*, 92; Muilenburg, "A Study in Hebrew Rhetoric," 101. Such a phenomenon is, of course, not restricted to Hebrew. See Barbara Johnstone et al., "Repetition in Discourse: A Dialogue," in Johnstone, ed., *Repetition in Discourse*, 1:11.

20. According to Sternberg, a literate culture can forego repetition more easily than an oral one given the former's various media possibilities (*Poetics of Biblical Narrative*, 368–69; also 374, 387–88, 406). Still, as the works cited in this essay amply attest, even highly literate cultures (and media) abound in repetition.

21. See, e.g., the work of Jean-Pierre Sonnet, *The Book within the Book: Writing in Deuteronomy* (Biblical Interpretation 14; Leiden: Brill, 1997); and idem, "Le Deutéronome et la modernité du livre," *NRTh* 118 (1996) 481–96.

22. See n. 20 and note, additionally, that there are other legal *corpora* that do not evidence the same type of repetition.

there so much repetition—verbatim and near-verbatim—in Deuteronomy, a literary text that could easily avoid such? Perhaps a better question, and a more answerable one, is *what is the function(s)* of this repetitive rhetoric?

There can be no singular response to the latter question. The functions of repetition are legion and polyvalent.[23] Context is everything: each instance of repetition must be evaluated on its own.[24] To complicate matters, there has been no shortage of treatments of repetition. According to J. Hillis Miller,

> The history of Western ideas of repetition begins, like our culture generally, with the Bible on the one hand and with Homer, the Pre-Socratics, and Plato on the other. The long centuries of Biblical hermeneutics whereby the New Testament was seen in one way or another as repeating the Old are still supposed in the use of Biblical types in *Henry Esmond* or *Adam Bede*. The modern history of ideas about repetition goes by way of Vico to Hegel and the German Romantics, to Kierkegaard's *Repetition*, to Marx (in *The Eighteenth Brumaire*), to Nietzsche's concept of the eternal return, to Freud's notion of the compulsion to repeat, to the Joyce of *Finnegans Wake*, on down to such diverse present-day theorists of repetition as Jacques Lacan or Gilles Deleuze, Mircea Eliade or Jacques Derrida.[25]

There is not space here to fully engage this history of scholarship. Still, among the theorists that Miller includes in his own study of repetition is Bruce F. Kawin, whose typology of repetition is both insightful and generative when applied to Deuteronomy.

Kawin's Typology of Repetition

"Life takes its tone and character from repetition," begins Kawin, but immediately notes the contemporary tendency to neglect and devalue repetition. Things that are capable of being repeated are thought of as "lower" or "more boring." In contrast, "the ultimate romantic experience of our culture is First Love" and we try to do everything at least "once."[26] But even extraordinary events are often deemed such because "they approximately repeat earlier experiences, or because they fulfill earlier expectations long rehearsed in fantasy; so that in both instances an event may have an air of familiarity about it even as it is occurring."[27] Kawin argues

---

23. See, e.g., Sternberg, *Poetics of Biblical Narrative*, 375–87, 438–39; Muilenburg, "A Study in Hebrew Rhetoric," 99; and Johnstone, "Repetition in Discourse," 6–19, esp. 10–11 on the function of repetition always remaining open. See further the works in the annotated bibliography (275 items) in *Repetition in Discourse*, 2:176–98.

24. Sternberg, *Poetics of Biblical Narrative*, 387–88, 437.

25. Miller, *Fiction and Repetition*, 5; see also 233–34 n. 3.

26. Kawin, *Telling It Again and Again*, 1.

27. Ibid., 2.

that novelty is, in fact, exhaustible; the search for it leads ultimately to boredom. Repetition, on the contrary, has the ability to move us "as time moves, in the present—the only existing tense."[28]

Kawin is careful to draw a distinction between repetition and repetitiousness. Repetition is "when a word, percept, or experience is repeated *with equal or greater force* at each occurrence." Repetitiousness is "when a word, percept, or experience is repeated *with less impact* at each recurrence; repeated *to no particular end*, out of a *failure of invention* or *sloppiness of thought*."[29] It is the unfortunate inability to distinguish between these two that has led to misconceptions of repetition. Even so, there is a shadow-side of repetition, one that is not unrelated to repetitiousness, that is frequently encountered, especially in the first type of repetition Kawin discusses: destructive repetition.

1. *Destructive Repetition.* To this first category in Kawin's typology belongs repetition that has either "gone flat or has actually had a destructive effect on its material."[30] For Kawin, Sigmund Freud's conception of "repetition compulsion" provides an excellent example of this phenomenon. Freud uses this concept to speak of the repetition of certain, usually negative, patterns of behavior and the unavoidable nature of that repetition.[31] This compulsion to repeat pathologies is, in fact, what facilitates the therapeutic process of transference between patient and therapist.[32] This repetitive process is largely *un*conscious, but not necessarily neurotic. Even so, Freud calls the compulsion to repeat "the manifestation of the power of the repressed."[33]

Why do people repeat in this way? At least one answer is that people attempt to *master* various situations through repetition. As an example, Freud cites children at play.[34] It is a small step to apply this insight to adults who are often prone to choose familiar over unfamiliar modes of action, even if those produce suffering and hardship.

---

28. Ibid., 3.

29. Ibid., 4 (emphases mine).

30. Ibid., 10.

31. See Sigmund Freud, *Beyond the Pleasure Principle* (trans. and ed. James Strachey; New York: W. W. Norton and Company, 1961); and idem, "Further Recommendations in the Technique of Psycho-Analysis: Recollection, Repetition and Working Through," in idem, *Collected Papers* (trans. Joan Riviere; 5 vols.; New York: Basic Books, 1959) 2:366–76. Note also Gregory Zilboorg's introduction to Freud, *Beyond the Pleasure Principle*, xxxiii.

32. Freud, *Beyond the Pleasure Principle*, 19, 22, 42. Cf. Kawin, *Telling It Again and Again*, 16.

33. Freud, *Beyond the Pleasure Principle*, 21.

34. Ibid., 16, 42; Kawin, *Telling It Again and Again*, 16.

From Freud's work and other examples, Kawin concludes that a type of destructive repetition exists. Perhaps the most innocuous form of destructive repetition is *habit*: "Repetition without insight or excitement creates routine, takes the life out of living, and *cannot cause us pain*."[35] But at what price is this peace—if it is that? Happily, in contrast to destructive repetition, Kawin has delineated two *positive* or *constructive* types that differ mainly in how they employ memory.

2. *Emphasizing, Echoing, Building.* The first type of positive repetition is "involved with the concepts of past and future, and believing in the integrity of memory, builds repetitions one on the other toward some total effect; this 'repetition with remembering' takes place in cumulative or 'building time.'"[36] This emphatic, "outright" repetition "aims to make us remember something."[37] Repetition is used in this way in poetry, for instance, where it lends a source of lyrical strength to the work. Kawin claims that the Old Testament itself offers "some of the finest and most familiar examples of the beauty and strength of repetition."[38] This kind of repetition is not repetitious, according to Kawin, "because each rediscovery is preceded by a conclusion that, closing the matter for us, frees us to experience each repetition as something new."[39] It is thus critical to the function and apprehension of this type of repetition that it takes place *in time*. It is "a sequence that begins the viewer in it again as it begins again."[40] It can thus function in expressive and didactic ways, especially because it *"makes intense and solid through persistence.* Repeated enough, a word or idea or phrase or image or name will come to dominate us to such an extent that our only defenses are to concede its importance or turn off the stimulus completely."[41]

3. *The Continuous Present (Transcendence).* The second type of positive repetition considers

> the present the only artistically approachable tense, [and] deals with each instant and subject as a new thing, to such an extent that the sympathetic reader is aware less of repetition than of continuity; this "repetition without remembering" takes place in "continuing time."[42]

---

35. Kawin, *Telling It Again and Again*, 20 (emphasis his).

36. Ibid., 33; cf. p. 34 and Frank McConnell's remarks in the foreword to *Telling It Again and Again*, xiv.

37. Kawin, *Telling It Again and Again*, 35.

38. Ibid., 38; see 38–43 for a treatment of Old Testament texts, esp. and interestingly, Ecclesiastes.

39. Ibid., 41. Cf. Johnstone, "Repetition in Discourse," 10.

40. Kawin, *Telling It Again and Again*, 47.

41. Ibid., 49–50 (emphasis his). George Orwell's *Nineteen Eighty-Four: A Novel* (New York: Harcourt, Brace and World, 1949) comes to mind.

42. Kawin, *Telling It Again and Again*, 33; cf. McConnell's remarks in the foreword (p. xiv).

Kawin treats the notion of continuing time, or repetition that takes one out of time, under the rubric of transcendence. Drawing most notably on Gertrude Stein and Søren Kierkegaard (among others), Kawin argues that repetition can be understood as transcendent because it transports one to a moment that is fully *present*, fully *now*, and by definition, therefore, outside of time-consciousness and time itself. Beginning over and over again feels *atemporal*. Of course, it only *feels* that way and is not *really* that way unless one can forget—forget that one has already been here before. This is what Kawin means by stating that this type of repetition can only take place *without* voluntary memory. One cannot voluntarily remember that one has done this or that before, been here or there before. That would be to place one's self in *building* time (see above), not *continuing* time. But *in*voluntary memory is another matter: "When the impression literally repeats, we are in its time. Involuntary memory is a time-warp that not only returns the past to us, but returns us to the past, makes us who we were when we lived in that time."[43] So, as "long as we do not falsify our past with possession and fear and remembering, we can in the instants of its *repetition* live both in the ordinary 'now' and in the 'then made now'—transcending our life in space by discovering our freedom in time."[44] In this space, then, there is only "now" and variations of "now," or what Kawin and others have called "the continuous present." And, as should be obvious from the above, in contrast to the first type of positive repetition, this second type of positive repetition deals largely with exact repetition or the nearest the artist can get to that: near-repetition.[45]

The power that repetition has to negate time is due in part to the fact that repetition is "minimum syntax: a word relating to and acting on itself. ... The word, and then the word." In this sense, repetition "takes the word further, into its inherent preverbal timelessness."[46] Repetition's quality of being the exact same thing all over again "makes us doubt that this thing was ever not here, or that there was any time in which it could have not been here, any time other than this time."[47] But, again, this effect is contingent on the person(s) involved being *truly involved*; the repetition must be *felt*, must be *real*:

> It is further true that nothing actually felt, nothing real in its moment is boring. Sexual intercourse, for example, loses neither its attractiveness nor its

---

43. Kawin, *Telling It Again and Again*, 84.
44. Ibid., 85.
45. Many theorists argue that exact repetition is impossible or nearly so. On near-repetition see ibid., 7; Sternberg, *Poetics of Biblical Narrative*, 390; Fokkelman, *Reading Biblical Narrative*, 112–22, esp. 121–22.
46. Kawin, *Telling It Again and Again*, 176.
47. Ibid., 104; cf. also p. 3.

reality through being repeated; its felt intensity is entirely independent of previous experience. Why, since it is the same every time, does it not become boring? The answer is, because it is interesting to us: it proceeds from our basic needs, it is urgent and pleasant and present. It is outside time, and therefore outside futility.[48]

Repetition in Deuteronomy

Before proceeding to an analysis of Deuteronomic repetition in light of Kawin's typology, it is necessary to step back and repeat (!) that Deuteronomy is replete with repetition. The notion of repetition is already present in the *title* of the book—at least as that has been brought into English via the Septuagint, even if, as some argue, that is a misinterpretation of the Hebrew of Deut 17:18.[49] Further, the *structure* of the book itself is repetitive; the book employs repetition on the *macro-structural level(s)*. There are, for example, two introductions (1:1–4:40; 4:44–11:32), two sections of blessings and curses (27:11–13; 28:3–6, 16–19 and the remaining curses in chapter 28), and two poems of Moses (32:1–33; chapter 33).[50] Missing from this listing is the repetition of covenant/covenant-making in Moab (29:1 [Heb 28:69]); the repetitions of speeches by Moses; the repeated superscriptions that mark those speeches; and the material that follows the Decalogue, whether it be in chapters 5–11 or in the central law code (12–28), which is a working out, or repetition of sorts, of the Decalogue or the great/first commandment.[51] Of course, the Decalogue itself is a repetition—within the final form of the Pentateuch—of the version found earlier in Exod 20:1–17.

The last item is yet another example that Deuteronomy's repetition extends beyond itself, crossing over and beyond the book's literary boundaries. This is especially true in the legal material where Deuteronomy picks up on and reiterates legislation from elsewhere in the Pentateuch, particu-

---

48. Ibid., 2; see also x, 151.

49. LXX: τὸ δευτερονόμιον τοῦτο, "this second law"; MT: את־משנה התורה הזאת, "a copy of this Torah."

50. See Moshe Weinfeld, "Deuteronomy, Book of," *ABD* 2:171; idem, *Deuteronomy 1–11* (AB 5; New York: Doubleday, 1991) 9.

51. See Georg Braulik, "The Sequence of the Laws in Deuteronomy 12–26 and in the Decalogue," in *A Song of Power and the Power of Song: Essays on the Book of Deuteronomy* (SBTS 3; ed. Duane L. Christensen; Winona Lake: Eisenbrauns, 1993) 313–35; idem, "Zur Abfolge der Gesetze in Deuteronomium 16,18–21,23: Weitere Beobachtungen," *Bib* 69 (1988) 63–92; Stephen A. Kaufman, "The Structure of the Deuteronomic Law," *Maarav* 1/2 (1978–1979) 105–58; Norbert Lohfink, *Das Hauptgebot: Eine Untersuchung literarischer Einleitungsfragen zu Dtn 5–11* (AnBib 20; Rome: Pontifical Biblical Institute, 1963); and Dennis T. Olson, *Deuteronomy and the Death of Moses: A Theological Reading* (OBT; Minneapolis: Fortress, 1994) 49–125. Olson also argues that Deuteronomy 5 is a type of "blueprint" for the rest of the book (see ibid., 40–48), which, accordingly, would be a repetition and elaboration of that blueprint.

larly the Book of the Covenant (Exod 20:22–23:19). In this sense, the book's Greek title, whatever the demerits of its origin may be, is well chosen. But Deuteronomy's repetition works forward, as well as backward, as the book not only repeats earlier legislation but also makes its rhetoric known and felt in subsequent portions of the Old Testament.

These considerations demonstrate that Deuteronomy also knows of repetition on the *micro-structural level(s)*. Smaller units—laws, sentences, clauses, words—are also repeated. And repeated. And repeated. Extensively. The primary concern of this essay, however, is not with the exact details of all this repetition,[52] but the method and meaning of it. In addressing these, it is instructive to ask to which one (or more), if any, of Kawin's types does Deuteronomy's repetition belong.

III. The Emphasis of / on Emphasis: The Rhetoric of Deuteronomy's Repetition

In my judgment, Deuteronomy's repetition falls, not under Kawin's first category of negative, destructive, or compulsive repetition, but among his two positive types: those of emphasis and transcendence. This decision against compulsion and in favor of emphasis and transcendence is not arbitrary; it is *textual*. As Kawin points out, "[o]ne of the principal characteristics of useless repetition is that it locks a work or a life into an unfulfillable compulsive cycle."[53] But Moses is at pains in Deuteronomy to indicate that this material *is* fulfillable (see, e.g., 30:11–14, 19b–20). The specific content of Deuteronomic repetition; its connection to persuasion, didacticism, and memory; and textual enactments of that repetition are all additional factors that support a positive—emphatic and transcendent—understanding of Deuteronomy's repetitive rhetoric. Each of these items are treated below with special attention to the *ethics* of the rhetoric—*what it does* and *how it does* it.

The Content of Repetition in Deuteronomy

The *content* of Deuteronomy's repetition is arguably the most important item to consider in evaluating its overall effect. That content, in brief, seeks

---

52. The raw data has been collected in the works of Moshe Weinfeld, John W. Wevers, and Norbert Lohfink. For the MT, see Weinfeld, *Deuteronomy and the Deuteronomic School*, 320–65; and Lohfink, *Das Hauptgebot*, 295–312. For the LXX, see Wevers, *Text History of the Greek Deuteronomy*, 86–99 (I thank Julie A. Duncan for drawing my attention to the listing in Wevers). Virtually every commentary on Deuteronomy or introduction to the Old Testament also provides at least a few examples of this type of micro-structural repetition.

53. Kawin, *Telling It Again and Again*, 12.

to inculcate life. The famous "choose life!" passage (30:19b) comes to mind, as do the many other texts dealing with life[54] and long life, especially in the land.[55] Still other texts promise prosperity (רבה), blessing (ברכה/ברך), or general goodness (יטב).[56] Equally important are the *numerous motivation clauses* that serve to underscore and motivate Israel's keeping of the law.[57] Rifat Sonsino has estimated that the percentage of motivated regulations in Deuteronomy is as high as fifty percent.[58] Patrick D. Miller puts it well, then, when he writes:

> That the exercise of power was by persuasion and rhetoric is seen in the covenant document par excellence, Deuteronomy. It set up a structure for existence—social, political, economic, and religious—that depended upon the willingness of the people to accede to the demands of the covenant, a willingness that was elicited in large part by preaching, testimony, self-understanding, and self-indictment through song and instruction taught and learned by the people.[59]

The content of Deuteronomy's repetition, therefore, is not only explicitly concerned with life, prosperity, and blessing, but the very repetitive rhetorical strategy of the book motivates one to enact these laws, statutes, and ordinances by means of valid and persuasive reasoning. Indeed, these two things are often interconnected: many of the life-in-the-land passages, for example, belong to the motivational clauses.

Still further, it is often the case that other repetitions, beyond those dealing explicitly with life or blessing, are equally positive. So it is that one encounters repeated references to the God who "brought out" (יצא)[60] or "ransomed" (פדה)[61] Israel from Egypt/the house of bondage, which is certainly among the great deeds "that Yahweh did" for Israel.[62] And God is not

---

54. E.g., חיה + למען (in order to/so that + live): 4:1; 5:33; 8:1; 16:20; 30:6, 19; cf. 6:24; 30:16.

55. E.g., ימים + ארך (to prolong + days), frequently with למען (in order to/so that): 4:40; 5:16, 33; 6:2; 11:9, 21; 22:7; 25:15; 30:20; 32:47; cf. 4:26; 17:20; 30:18.

56. For an extensive listing, see Weinfeld, *Deuteronomy and the Deuteronomic School*, 345–50.

57. E.g., אשר/ל/למען + טוב/יטב (so that/to/in order to + good/to be good): 4:40; 5:16, 29, 33; 6:3, 18; 12:25, 28; 19:13; 22:7.

58. Rifat Sonsino, *Motive Clauses in Hebrew Law: Biblical Forms and Near Eastern Parallels* (SBLDS 45; Chico: Scholars Press, 1980) 221.

59. Patrick D. Miller, *The Religion of Ancient Israel* (Library of Ancient Israel; Louisville: Westminster John Knox, 2000) 5; cf. idem, *Deuteronomy* (Interpretation; Louisville: John Knox, 1990) 12.

60. See 4:20, 37; 5:6, 15; 6:12, 21, 23; 7:8, 19; 8:14; 9:26, 28–29; 13:5 [Heb 6], 10 [Heb 11]; 16:1; 20:1; 26:8; 29:25 [Heb 24].

61. See 7:8; 9:26; 13:5 [Heb 6]; 15:15; 21:8; 24:18.

62. עשה + יהוה: 1:30; 3:21; 4:3, 34; 7:18; 11:4, 7; 29:2 [Heb 1], 24 [Heb 23]; 31:4.

finished. Repeatedly it is asserted that God "swore" (שבע)[63] or "promised" (דבר)[64] to give (נתן)[65] the land and, now, "is giving" (נֹתֵן)[66] the land to Israel. More generally, the LORD is repeatedly said to be an agent of blessing.[67]

The extent of this repetition is impressive and is but the beginning of a partial listing. In the face of such rhetoric, it is not surprising to find the injunction for Israel to "do what is right (and good) in the sight of the LORD (your God)" repeated five times.[68] Indeed, nowhere is repetition more pronounced in Deuteronomy than with reference to *obedience*. Note the following collocations:[69]

- שמר + לעשות or שמר + עשה (keep + do): 4:6; 5:1, 32; 6:3, 25; 7:11, 12; 8:1; 11:22, 32; 12:1, 32 [Heb 13:1]; 13:18 [Heb 19]; 15:5; 16:12; 17:10, 19; 19:9; 23:23 [Heb 24]; 24:8; 26:16; 28:1, 13, 15, 58; 29:9 [Heb 8]; 31:12; 32:46.
- שמר + מצוה(מצות)/חקים/עדות/משפטים (keep + commandment[s], statutes, decrees, or ordinances): 4:2, 6, 40; 5:1, 10, 12; 6:2, 17; 7:9, 11, 12; 8:1, 2, 6, 11; 10:13; 11:1, 32; 12:1; 13:4 [Heb 5]; 16:12; 26:16, 17; 28:9, 13, 15, 45; 30:10, 16.
- שמר + כל המצוה/כל מצותי/מצותיו (keep [often with עשה (do)] + the entire commandment or all my/his commandments): 5:29; 6:25; 11:8, 22; 13:18 [Heb 19]; 15:5; 19:9; 26:18; 27:1; 28:1, 15; cf. 30:8 (עשה without שמר).
- שמר/עשה + כל דברי התורה הזאת (הכתובים בספר הזה) (keep or do + all the words of this Torah [that are written in this book]): 17:19; 28:58; 29:29 [Heb 28]; 31:12; 32:46.
- שמע + אל מצות יהוה (listen + to the commandments of the LORD): 11:27, 28; 28:13; cf. 11:13.
- שמע + בקולו/בקול יהוה (listen + his voice or the voice of the LORD): 13:4 [Heb 5], 18 [Heb 19]; 15:5; 26:14, 17; 27:10; 28:1, 2; 30:8, 10.

---

63. See 1:8, 35; 6:10, 18, 23; 7:8, 12, 13; 8:1; 10:11; 11:9, 21; 19:8; 26:3, 15; 28:11; 30:20; 31:7, 20, 21, 23; 34:4.

64. See 1:21; 19:8; 27:3.

65. In addition to the texts cited in the two previous notes, see 1:36; 2:12, 19, 36; 3:18; 4:38; 8:10; 9:23; 12:1, 15; 26:9; 28:52.

66. See 1:20, 25; 2:29; 4:1, 21, 40; 5:16, 31; 9:6; 11:17, 31; 12:9; 15:4, 7; 16:20; 17:14; 18:9; 19:1, 2, 10, 14; 21:1, 23; 24:4; 25:15, 19; 26:1, 2; 27:2, 3; 28:8; 32:49, 52.

67. See 1:11; 2:7; 7:13; 12:7; 14:24, 29; 15:4, 6, 10, 14, 18; 16:10, 15; 23:20 [Heb 21]; 24:19; 28:8, 12; 30:16.

68. 6:18; 12:25, 28; 13:18 [Heb 19]; 21:9; contrast 17:2; 31:29.

69. These follow Weinfeld, *Deuteronomy and the Deuteronomic School*, 336–37 (see further 332–39) though at times my presentation of the total number and location of the occurrences differs. If the present listing reflects an improvement, it is due to the advantages of computer software, in this case BibleWorks for Windows (Version 4.0; Big Fork, Montana: Hermeneutika Bible Research Software, 1999).

To be sure, these formulations are not identical—each is distinct and should not be simplistically identified with the others—but they are sufficiently similar to muddle their precise differences in a listener's/reader's mind. That is, can a listener/reader—whether novice or experienced—describe in detail the subtle nuances between

- כי־תשמר את־כל־המצוה הזאת לעשתה אשר אנכי מצוך היום, "if you carefully keep the entirety of this commandment, which I am commanding you today" (19:9); and
- כי־תשמע אל־מצות יהוה אלהיך אשר אנכי מצוך היום, "if you listen to the commandments of the LORD your God, which I am commanding you today" (28:13)?

This *muddling effect* is made even worse (or better, as the case may be) by other, closely similar, collocations not presented here. But the corollary of this muddling effect is, paradoxically, a *sharpening* one: it is a heaping up, a getting-at-by-all-possible-means. This effect, in short, actually functions to underscore a singular point: "keep/observe/do!" In fact, keep/observe/do *carefully,*[70] *exactly* as God commanded![71]

The verbal emphasis is thus quite clear. But the identification of *what*, exactly and carefully, one is to keep/observe/do is equally as repetitive and similarly confusing. Consider the following collocations:[72]

- חקים + משפטים (statutes + ordinances): 4:1, 5, 8, 14, 45 (with עדות [decrees]); 5:1; 6:20 (with עדות); 11:32; 12:1; 26:16.
- מצות + חקים/חקות or חקים/חקות + מצות (commandments + statutes or statutes + commandments): 4:40; 6:2, 17 (with עדות intervening); 10:13; 27:10; 28:15, 45; 30:10.
- מצות משפטים or חקות משפטים וחקות or חקים מצות ומשפטים or חקות ומצות ומשפטים (statutes, commandments, and ordinances; or statutes, ordinances, and commandments; or commandments, ordinances, and statutes): 8:11; 11:1; 26:17; 30:16.
- המצוה/המצות + חקים ומשפטים (the commandment[s] + statutes and ordinances): 5:31; 6:1; 7:11.

As if these were not enough, there are still more formulations—those that take Yahweh or Yahweh's way(s) as the verbal object, for instance—that are not included in this listing.[73] Keeping all of these items straight is no less difficult or confusing than was the case with the verbs themselves.

---

70. נשמר/השמר + בנפש/לנפש/לך/לכם (watch + you/yourself): 4:9, 15, 23; 6:12; 8:11; 11:16; 12:13, 19, 30; 15:9; cf. 23:9 [Heb 10]; 24:8 (both of the latter without pronoun or נפש).

71. E.g., כאשר/כ־ + צוה יהוה (just as/as + the LORD commanded): 1:3, 19; 2:37; 5:32; 34:9; cf. 5:33.

72. See Weinfeld, *Deuteronomy and the Deuteronomic School*, 339–40.

73. See ibid., 332–33.

And yet, the point is the same. The rhetorical issue is not precise colloca-
tion or whether each specific formulation means something in contrast to
its near-identical siblings. Instead, it is a case of *heaping up* in the textual environment (whether oral or written), which leaves the reader/hearer without escape from these terms. One *must* obey/observe/enact — and must
do that *carefully*.[74] This much is clear from the repetition. And now it is
equally clear *what* one must obey: it has to do with the statutes and ordinances, the commandments and the laws, the Torah and the testimonies,
Yahweh and Yahweh's ways. And, of course, Deuteronomy's repetitive rhetoric is also quite clear on what one is *not* to do/obey,[75] as well as the precise
manner in which one is to perform this mandated obedience and disobedience. Finally, it is highly pertinent in light of Kawin's emphasis on the continuing present to note that Deuteronomy also repeats itself on the *when* of
this obedience. There is a constant emphasis on "today" (היום הזה/היום) or
"always" (כל הימים).[76]

Also important are the specific *subjects* of the majority of these verbal
formulations. The subjects are invariably *the second person* — sometimes imperative[77] — whether singular or plural: "you." Second-person address lends
to the commandments "a sense of immediacy and urgency lacking in the
hypothetical formulation of (usually) third-person casuistic laws. . . . Hearers and readers are likely to feel directly addressed and therefore obliged
to respond."[78] Without engaging the vexed question of the switch in

---

74. Or, *à la* Kawin, turn the stimulus off completely (see n. 41 above). Deuteronomy's
motivation clauses, however, would obviate this move even while its possiblity is granted.

75. See, e.g., ibid., 320, 339–41.

76. See ibid., 356–57. יום occurs 167 times in Deuteronomy. Though not all of these
are directly connected to parenesis, and instead describe specific periods of time, duration, or the like, the vast majority of instances are in service to the hortatory statements
of Moses. For the background and function of the "today" passages in Deuteronomy, see
Weinfeld, *Deuteronomy and the Deuteronomic School*, 174; Robert Polzin, "Deuteronomy,"
in *The Literary Guide to the Bible* (ed. Robert Alter and Frank Kermode; Cambridge:
Belknap, 1987) 92–93; and E. Theodore Mullen, Jr., *Narrative History and Ethnic Boundaries: The Deuteronomistic Historian and the Creation of Israelite National Identity* (Semeia
Studies; Atlanta: Scholars, 1993) 75.

77. Somewhat surprisingly, the frequency of imperatives in Deuteronomy is low. According to my search, there are only 112 imperatives in the book. Of course, if one
counted negative commands, the number would increase. L. J. de Regt, *A Parametric
Model for Syntactic Studies of a Textual Corpus, Demonstrated on the Hebrew of Deuteronomy 1–
30* (Studia Semitica Neerlandica 24; Assen: Van Gorcum, 1988) 95, 114–15, argues that
clauses in which legislative rules are formulated and in which imperatives occur, do not
appear together, and "seem to be mutually exclusive" (95). This is further evidence that
the vision of Deuteronomy is "persuasively taught rather than forcefully dictated" (Olson, *Deuteronomy and the Death of Moses*, 4).

78. Watts, *Reading Law*, 64. Sonsino identified direct address as one of the legal
forms found only in biblical law (*Motive Clauses*, 36–38).

grammatical number (*Numeruswechsel*) in Deuteronomy, it can be stated simply that this effect is felt whether the addressee is designated in the singular or plural.

In sum, the content of Deuteronomic repetition—in verbal emphasis, object, and addressee—is clearly of the emphatic variety. Repeated formulations with attention to the present and "always" may also relate this repetition to Kawin's transcendent type. But before a final decision can be made on this point, there are other aspects of Deuteronomy's repetition that must be considered.

Repetition, Persuasion, and Didacticism

Repetition is highly effective in *suasive* discourse, be it oral or literary.[79] As already noted, despite some distaste for repetition, the Classical rhetoricians also realized its importance and effectiveness. Quintilian, for instance, wrote: "Our aim must be not to put him [the judge] in a position to understand our argument, but to force him to understand it. Consequently we shall frequently repeat anything which we think the judge has failed to take in as he should."[80] To this end, repetition was frequently utilized by Classical rhetoricians, especially in the conclusion (*epilogos* or *peroratio*) of their arguments.[81] It also figures into discussions of arrangement (*taxis, dispositio*) and style (*lexis, elocutio*).[82] More recent studies of rhetoric, both oral and written, continue to note the effectiveness of repetition within persuasive intent.[83]

---

79. It is not necessary to decide between oral or written environments at this point. Note Watts, *Reading Law*, 61 n. 1: "The distinction between hearers and readers, which has been so fruitful for studies of orality and literacy, is blurred by the practice of reading aloud for aural reception" (see also p. 65). Regardless of environment, then, Deuteronomy's repetition is suasive. For more on Deuteronomy and oratory, see Weinfeld, *Deuteronomy and the Deuteronomic School*, 3, 8, 171–73, 176–77; Alter, *The Art of Biblical Narrative*, 89–90; and von Rad, *Deuteronomy*, 29.

80. Quintilian, *Institutio Oratoria*, 8.2.22–24 (cited in Watts, *Reading Law*, 70 and n. 38).

81. See, e.g., Aristotle, *On Rhetoric*, 3.19 (1419b); however, he criticizes earlier rhetorical handbooks for too much repetition in the *proemium* (entrance or *exordium*). In conclusions, repetition functions as a type of recapitulation, a refreshing of the memory. In this light, Deuteronomy's repetition functions as a constant refreshing of the memory (see further below).

82. Note, e.g., the repetition of letters, syllables, or sounds (e.g., alliteration, assonance, *parechesis, parimion*) that was frequently lauded by ancient rhetoricians. On these terms, as well as others, see Lanham, *A Handlist of Rhetorical Terms*, 124–25.

83. See, e.g., James W. Cox, *Preaching: A Comprehensive Approach to the Design and Delivery of Sermons* (San Francisco: Harper and Row, 1985) 231; and Raymond S. Ross, *Understanding Persuasion* (3d ed.; Englewood Cliffs; Prentice Hall, 1990) 161–63. Kenneth Burke, *The Philosophy of Literary Form: Studies in Symbolic Action* (3d ed.; Berkeley: University of California Press, 1973) 217 has noted "the power of endless repetition" in more ominous ways ("to a disturbing degree") in Hitler's *Mein Kampf.*

The motivated nature of Deuteronomic law is again pertinent here since at least one function of the motive clauses is to strengthen the persuasive appeal of the legal material. Moreover, "[t]he motivations attached to laws point out *the didactic intent* in their formulation, wishing to instruct hearers/readers not only in specific regulations but also in the law's foundations in Israel's communal experiences and religious ideas."[84] It is not only the motive clauses that do this, however; the exhortations found throughout the material also make didactic purposes explicit. Moreover, many theorists have pointed to didacticism as a primary function of repetition.[85]

In short, Deuteronomy seeks to *teach* and *persuade*.[86] This is widely known and frequently said about Deuteronomy's rhetoric, but it is equally true of the book's *repetition* for the purpose of repetition is "to point, to direct a hearer back to something and say, 'Pay attention to this again. This is still salient; this still has potential meaning; let's make use of it in some way.'"[87] Repetition is thus hermeneutically helpful and instructive.[88]

Here too, then, Deuteronomy's repetition largely falls under Kawin's second, emphatic type. After all, Deuteronomy repeats the Sinai-Horeb

---

84. Watts, *Reading Law*, 67 (emphasis mine).

85. See, e.g., Martha S. Bean and G. Genevieve Patthey-Chavez, "Repetition in Instructional Discourse: A Means for Joint Cognition," in Johnstone, ed., *Repetition in Discourse*, 1:207–20; Russell S. Tomlin, "Repetition in Second Language Acquisition," in Johnstone, ed., *Repetition in Discourse*, 1:172–94; and Tannen, "Repetition in Coversation as Spontaneous Formulaicity," 215–17.

86. One need not take these insights and the obvious similarities to wisdom traditions and put them to work in hypotheses about the origin of Deuteronomy though obviously Weinfeld has attempted to do that in systematic fashion (*Deuteronomy and the Deuteronomic School*; for particular phraseological links, see 362–63). It is interesting, however, to consider connections between didacticism and the presentation of the learner as a *child* in Wisdom Literature. Deuteronomy also knows of repetition to children (see, e.g., 6:7, 20–25) but, more generally, one wonders if the repetitive didacticism of Moses in Deuteronomy makes Israel/the reader out to be child-like, if only because "[i]n the instruction of the young . . . iteration proved an effective device for stamping the mind with the things that must be remembered" (Muilenburg, "A Study in Hebrew Rhetoric," 100). For further studies on the use of repetition in speech with children, especially in language acquisition, see Johnstone, "An Introduction," 205–14. Cf. also Freud on repetition and children.

87. Johnstone, "Repetition in Discourse," 13. Cf. James E. Porter and Patricia A. Sullivan, "Repetition and the Rhetoric of Visual Design," in Johnstone, ed., *Repetition in Discourse*, 1:27–28; and Watts, *Reading Law*, 61, 70–71, 88, esp. 71.

88. See J. Miller, *Fiction and Repetition*, 1–2; Sternberg, *Poetics of Biblical Narrative*, 368; Gunn and Fewell, *Narrative in the Hebrew Bible*, 148; Wolfgang Iser, *The Act of Reading: A Theory of Aesthetic Response* (Baltimore: The Johns Hopkins University Press, 1978) 94 (cf. also p. 209); and Norrick, "Functions of Repetition in Conversation," 257. It must be admitted that repetition is not full-proof in controlling meaning control. See Steven Cushin, "'Air Cal Three Thirty Six, Go Around Three Thirty Six, Go Around': Linguistic Repetition in Air-Ground Communication," in Johnstone, ed., *Repetition in Discourse*, 2:62.

event and its legislation throughout chapters 5–28 (especially) and undertakes yet another, different type of repetition in the Moab covenant (chapters 29–30; see especially 29:1 [Heb 28:69]).[89] Still more to the point, Moses makes clear that the Sinai-Horeb event is not just "back then" but is present; the cutting of the covenant is "with us, those of us here today, all of us who are alive" (5:3). In this nexus, elements of emphatic repetition (beginning the viewer in it again as it starts again) and transcendent repetition (the continuous present and the ubiquitous "today") combine.

Repetition and Memory

While repetition, by today's standards, might make for *boring* literature, it is equally true that repetition makes for *highly effective* literature. At least part of that is due to repetition's connection to memory. At this point the oral vs. written question might be more significant as there have been a number of studies that demonstrate that repetition works especially well when it is originally (or) primarily *oral* in presentation. Simply put, people remember what they have heard and heard often.[90]

Even so, the function of repetition as mnemonic device is not restricted to its use in oral contexts. The issue is also related to the nature of repetition and/as suasive rhetoric. Whatever the case, it is clear that Deuter-

---

89. The Moab covenant may be related to repetitions that repeat archetypal actions performed "in the beginning of time." See Kawin, *Telling It Again and Again*, 91, 94 and Mircea Eliade, *The Myth of the Eternal Return* (trans. Willard R. Trask; Princeton: Princeton University Press, 1965). Note also Olson's contribution to the present volume.

90. E.g., Aristotle, *On Rhetoric*, 3.12.2 (1413b): "*asyndeta* and constant repetition are rightly criticized in writing but not in speaking, and the orators use them; for they lend themselves to oral delivery" (the translation is from Aristotle, *On Rhetoric: A Theory of Civic Discourse* [trans. George A. Kennedy; New York: Oxford University Press, 1991] 255). Cf., more recently, Alter, *The Art of Biblical Narrative*, 90. Many more works could be summoned in support of these sentiments. See, e.g., Walter J. Ong, *Orality and Literacy: The Technologizing of the Word* (London: Routledge, 1982), esp. 33–36, 39–41; Birger Gerhardsson, *Memory and Manuscript: Oral Tradition and Written Transmission in Rabbinic Judaism and Early Christianity* with *Tradition and Transmission in Early Christianity* (Grand Rapids: Eerdmans and Livonia: Dove, 1998) 122–70, esp. 148–56, 163–70; Susan Niditch, *Oral World and Written Word: Ancient Israelite Literature* (Library of Ancient Israel; Louisville: Westminster John Knox, 1996) 10–11, 13–14; Johnstone, "Repetition in Discourse," 8; and, more generally, William M. Schniedewind, "Orality and Literacy in Ancient Israel," *RSR* 26 (2000) 327–32. Note also Watts, *Reading Law*, 70 (see also pp. 61, 71, 88) who thinks that in a public recitation, repetition would largely provide "thematic unity, emphasis and mnemonic effect." Variation, on the other hand, would have served to maintain audience interest. This may be correct, but it is the repetition that would primarily indicate *what* the people are to remember. One additional item that should be mentioned in connection with orality is the importance of intonation and performance in oral environments. See, e.g., JoEllen M. Simpson, "Regularized Intonation in Conversational Repetition," in Johnstone, ed., *Repetition in Discourse*, 2:48.

onomy places a special — and repeated! — emphasis on *memory*.[91] An interesting example of the effect of Deuteronomy's repetition on memory is found in some of the Dead Sea Scrolls. Julie A. Duncan has shown that the excerpted biblical manuscripts that include passages from Deuteronomy often have alternative, slightly expanded readings. Apparently, these are the result of a scribe copying by memory and being influenced by other, closely similar passages.[92] This example shows that the muddling effect of Deuteronomy's repetition is quite real and that, especially due to instances of near-repetition, it complicates memory while simultaneously producing a sharpened focus on concepts that are closely similar and frequently repeated.

Textual Enactments of Deuteronomy's Repetition

Repetitions of Deuteronomy's own repetitive rhetoric elsewhere in the Old Testament are extensive. These might be termed *textual enactments* of Deuteronomic rhetoric. A particularly fascinating example of this enactment and its positive outcome is found in 2 Kgs 23:25, a text describing Josiah, the ultimate Deuteronomic king:

> Before him, there was no one like him: a king who turned to the LORD with all his heart, and with all his soul, and with all his might [בכל-לבבו ובכל-נפשו ובכל-מאדו], according to all the law of Moses [ככל תורת משה]. And no one like him arose after him.

Not only does Josiah repeat and enact Deuteronomy's repeated phrase "with all the heart and with all the soul (and with all the might) [בכל לב ובכל נפש (ובכל מאד)]" (4:29; 6:5; 10:12; 11:13; 13:3 [Heb 4]; 26:16; 30:2, 6, 10), he does this *exactly* (cf. ככל תורת משה), in the full phrase as set forth in the Shema (6:5: בכל-לבבך ובכל-נפשך ובכל-מאדך). Textual enactments such as

---

91. Note זכר, "remember" (5:15; 7:18; 8:2, 18; 9:7, 27; 15:15; 16:3; 12; 24:9, 18, 22; 25:17, 32:7) and לא שכח, "do not forget" (4:9, 23; 6:12; 8:11, 14, 19; 9:7; 25:19; 26:13; 31:21; 32:18). For a study of the memory motif in Deuteronomy, see Edward P. Blair, "An Appeal to Remembrance: The Memory Motif in Deuteronomy," *Int* 15 (1961) 41–47, esp. 45 on the objects of remembrance in Deuteronomy. Notably, Blair highlights the ability of memory to actualize.

92. See Julie A. Duncan, "Considerations of 4QDt[j] in Light of the 'All Souls Deuteronomy' and Cave 4 Phylactery Texts," in *The Madrid Qumran Congress: Proceedings of the International Congress on the Dead Sea Scrolls, Madrid 18–21 March, 1991* (ed. Julio Trebolle Barrera and Luis Vegas Montaner; 2 vols.; STDJ 11; Leiden: E. J. Brill, 1992) 1:199–215; and idem, "Excerpted Texts of Deuteronomy at Qumran," *RevQ* 18 (1997) 43–62. It is noteworthy, in contrast, that 11QTemple removes many of the repetitions of Deuteronomy (see Emanuel Tov, "*Deut.* 12 and *11QTemple* LII–LIII: A Contrastive Analysis," *RevQ* 15 [1991] 169–73).

Josiah's show that Deuteronomy's repetitive rhetoric is effective, doable, and, in this case at least, beneficial.

These enactments are also another example of *the deep connection between the psyche—that is, human behavior—and the structures of repetition*. Repetition is deeply connected to what we do and even why we do it. This finds support in the work of Freud, more negatively, and in the work of Kierkegaard, more positively.[93] Although Kierkegaard knew of negative repetition, he also spoke of the positive variety, a kind that demonstrated that repetition was a religious category—an element of the eternal and timeless. Even Freud, despite repetition compulsion, knew of enjoyable and pleasurable repetition, especially in children.[94] But the connection between repetition and behavior should not be construed only in an individualistic or intrapsychic fashion. E. Theodore Mullen, Jr., among others, has argued that Deuteronomy is comprised of community-constitutive discourse.[95] This business of community creation, constitution, and maintenance is furthered, in the case of Deuteronomy, by its extensive and excessive repetition. And, *à la* Freud, Deuteronomy's rhetoric also knows of repetition that has to do with joy and enjoyment.[96]

IV. Dis/orientation and Surrender: The Aesthetics of Repetition in Deuteronomy

One final and important element remains to be treated: *the aesthetics of repetition* in Deuteronomy. Aesthetics are a main consideration in Kawin's typology because "[s]uccessful repetition depends both on the inherent interest of the recurring unit and on its context."[97] Much of what has already been said above applies to any discussion of the aesthetics of Deuteronomic repetition. Even so, two particular aesthetics should be lifted up.

---

93. See Kierkegaard, *Repetition*, 131–33, 149, esp. 131 and 132.

94. Freud, *Beyond the Pleasure Principle*, 42. See also Johnstone, "Repetition in Discourse," 6–7.

95. Mullen, *Narrative History and Ethnic Boundaries*, 55–85. Note esp. Mullen's important observation that the Israel that is created in Moses' speeches is one that does not yet exist. Part of Deuteronomy's function, then, is "to supply the defining characteristics to that people that will then be applied to the latter groups who accept this as a part of their ethnic history and authoritative account of their temporal and spatial origins" (p. 58). Cf. further pp. 75, 79, and, more recently, Walter Brueggemann, *Deuteronomy* (Abingdon Old Testament Commentaries; Nashville: Abingdon, 2001) 18.

96. See, e.g., שׂמח, "rejoice": 12:7, 12, 18; 14:26; 16:11, 14, 15; 26:11; 27:7.

97. Kawin, *Telling It Again and Again*, 4–5; see also Johnstone, "Repetition in Discourse," 9.

The *first aesthetic*, touched on above under the rubric of *muddling*, is this: the similar and repeated language, themes, passages, words, and the like in Deuteronomy have a *disorienting* effect, causing one to feel as if one is "Lost in Deuteronomy."[98] But, while it is probably true that it is repetition at the micro-structural level(s) in Deuteronomy that is most disorienting in its tendency toward near-verbatim repetition, even macro-structural repetition can bring the reader back and forth in Deuteronomy, not permitting a simplistic linear flow or "plot" progression. This disorienting effect would be greatest, no doubt, in an oral/aural environment for a first-time hearer, but the same holds true, in my judgment, for a first-time (and perhaps even a multiple-time) reader. How could either of these audiences differentiate or even recall significant differences between 6:6–9 and 11:18–20 after just one, initial reading/hearing? This disorientation diminishes as one moves through Deuteronomy, if only because the laws frequently become more specific and thus more distinguishable.[99] Yet, simultaneously and concurrently, the opposite effect (the *sharpening* element discussed earlier) is taking place: The disorientation caused by repetition at the macro-structural level(s) is countered by an orientation caused by the high instance of repetition (especially) at the micro-structural level(s).[100] Again, there is a massive amount of this latter type of repetition in Deuteronomy, but it is imperative to remember that not all of it occurs with equal frequency. The clear preponderance of repetition favors the verbs, words, and phrases mentioned above: hear, keep, do; Torah, statutes, ordinances; and so forth. Moreover, even some of the macro-structural repetition is in service to this type of orientation. This is especially true of the repetitions that bring the reader/hearer back to the Ten Commandments or to the most important word (the Shema).[101]

The *second aesthetic* has less to do with Deuteronomy itself; instead, as "aesthetic" implies, it has to do with *our own involvement and assessment* of

---

98. Cf. Weinfeld, *Deuteronomy and the Deuteronomic School*, 173: "The deuteronomic orator often employs rhetorical phrases . . . and he repeats these phrases again and again as if to hypnotize his audience." Note also Johnstone, "Repetition in Discourse," 17 on repetition functioning as *dis*intensification.

99. See von Rad, *Deuteronomy*, 19–20, though the connection of even the later laws and their structure to the earlier materials (especially the Decalogue), and thus that repetition of a sort, must not be forgotten.

100. Cf. the dynamic discussed in Watts, *Reading Law*, 71; and note Tannen, "Repetition in Conversation as Spontaneous Formulaicity," 223 who notes that altered forms of set expressions can actually be enhanced by connection to other set expressions.

101. For the first/great commandment, see S. Dean McBride, Jr., "The Yoke of the Kingdom: An Exposition of Deuteronomy 6:4–5," *Int* 27 (1973) 273–306; and Patrick D. Miller, Jr., "The Most Important Word: The Yoke of the Kingdom," *The Iliff Review* 41 (1984) 17–29, esp. 18–19 on repetition underscoring its importance.

this repetition. Kawin's work underscores the importance of this involvement at every turn: the positive effects of repetition are only experienced if they are *truly experienced*, if they are *really felt* and this, of course, means if *we* truly experience them, if *we* really feel them.[102]

On the one hand, this is, or should be, a most obvious point in the contemporary climate of hermeneutics and biblical studies. *We*, after all, are the ones interpreting these texts, interacting with them and affecting them in the process. But the obviousness of that enterprise does not make this insight any easier to swallow, for it would indicate, as Sandra Schneiders has rightly pointed out, that the process of "[e]ntering into the world projected by the text is not first and foremost an exercise of discursive rationality, but a process of aesthetic involvement"—even aesthetic surrender.[103] That is, we must surrender to the aesthetics of the text, at least for the duration of the experience, if we are ever to understand it aright. In the case of Deuteronomy, this would entail giving ourselves over to its repetitive rhetoric with the possibility, perhaps even the likelihood, that we would emerge on the other side transformed by that rhetoric—suddenly attuned to the suasive mood, the content of the actions enjoined, and the objects of the verbal commands, not to mention to the One who commands. Repetition's connection to this second aesthetic requires us to carry the point yet one step further: Could it be that our negative assessments of Deuteronomy's repetitive rhetoric have more to say about *us* than they do about the book and its rhetoric?

V. Conclusion:
The Theological Result(s) of Repetition in Deuteronomy

In closing, it must be granted that instances of repetition that are less connected to the overall rhetorical force of Deuteronomy do exist. But it is the *ethical* repetition that is most pronounced. This observation indicates that, in contrast to previous scholarly perspectives, it is the suasive nature of Deuteronomic repetition that is most important and that cannot be

---

102. See, e.g., Kawin, *Telling It Again and Again*, 33, x, 151, 172–73; as well as the two essays by Tannen ("Repetition in Conversation" and "Repetition in Conversation as Spontaneous Formulaicity") and the literature cited there.

103. Sandra M. Schneiders, *The Revelatory Text: Interpreting the New Testament as Sacred Scripture* (2d ed.; Collegeville: Liturgical, 1999) 172; see further 172–78. Schneiders rightly points out that this type of engagement is not uncritical. One may decide, after surrendering for the duration, that the text or some of its parts is/are to be rejected or, at the very least, that the dialogue between interpreter and text "not only permits but demands development of both" parties involved (p. 175). It is not, then, in the final analysis, "blind submission to what the text says" (p. 177). Cf. the contribution by Fretheim in this volume.

overlooked or neglected, whatever else one might think of it or do with it. Indeed, this suasive intent is the primary purpose of the repetition and its *raison d'être*.

Several points must be made in conclusion:

1. The rhetoric of repetition in Deuteronomy suggests that the importance and meaning of repetition is found not only in difference, but also in similarity, in emphasis, even in muddled redundancy.

2. In the main, Deuteronomic repetition seems to fit the Kawinian category of emphasis. But its tendency to begin again and again, and its enactment, especially in the present and continuous timeframe(s) of the book, indicate that it also belongs to Kawin's category of transcendence. There is, however, one notable difference: for Kawin, transcendent repetition must take place without memory. Deuteronomy, by contrast, is quite emphatic—and repetitive!—that one *must* remember and not forget. This does not necessarily mean that Deuteronomic repetition is not transcendent for Kawin speaks of yet another category that blurs the distinction between emphasis and transcendence. To this category belong those works that describe "eternity in an hour"—that is, "works that exist on the margins of both time-systems, whose characters move both in time and in eternity."[104] It may very well be that Deuteronomy belongs to this tertiary, hybrid category. This would certainly help to explain the book's ability to function at many different times and places, including within the canon of Scripture, both "today" and "always."

3. But the pragmatic question must still be addressed: does Deuteronomy's repetitive rhetoric really work? Greg Urban has written that

> for something to be replicable and hence capable of forming part of socially circulating discourse, and, therefore, also part of culture, it is helpful and perhaps essential that it be built around a structure of internal repetition. . . . The repetition picks out what it is about the discourse that is *replicable*.[105]

According to this, there *is* much in Deuteronomy that is (and was) replicable. Moreover, Scripture is quite clear that, despite possible doubts to the contrary, Deuteronomy's repetition was effective. The Old Testament knows of positive, textual enactments of Deuteronomy's rhetoric and these come from disparate time periods. The specifics of that effect, therefore—especially its *first* instance—are not the primary issue. Scholars have discussed at least three audiences for the book of Deuteronomy (the literary, the Josianic/monarchic, and the exilic) and it is more significant to ask

---

104. Kawin, *Telling It Again and Again*, 72.

105. Greg Urban, "Repetition and Cultural Replication," in Johnstone, ed., *Repetition in Discourse*, 2:160.

whether and how these various audiences would have experienced this effect. There can be little doubt from texts like Deut 17:18–20; 31:9–13; 2 Kgs 22:11–23:25; and Ezra 7:73–8:12 that Deuteronomy (or something like it) was to be read/heard (and was read/heard) periodically and was to make (and did make) a significant impact in vastly different contexts and periods.[106] At this point, the importance of the septennial reading of Deuteronomy prescribed in 31:9–13 cannot be overstated.[107]

The rhetorical impact of Deuteronomic repetition is felt whether the book is read or heard. It is that rhetorical force, not its specific or original delivery that is of primary import. Indeed, the repetition itself fosters the impetus and motivation to return to the words and study them again. After all, the fact that one must keep/observe/do—carefully—all this Torah/these words/commandments/statutes and ordinances, and so forth, means that one must go back and learn these latter in great detail.[108] To come full circle, the intimate familiarity with Deuteronomy that comes from such repetitive (!) study actually works against the rhetorical effect produced in an initial hearing or reading. It diminishes, that is, the "Lost in Deuteronomy" feeling. When one knows Deuteronomy well, one is not lost at all. But this only serves to underscore that the rhetoric of Deuteronomy accomplishes its task remarkably well. It wants us to keep its words—to do them and do them carefully—and by the time we have *superseded* that rhetoric we have, in all actuality, *succumbed* to it. In so doing, we have been transformed into the people of God that Deuteronomy so desperately seeks.[109] So, again,

---

106. See, recently, Daniel J. Harrington, *Invitation to the Apocrypha* (Grand Rapids: Eerdmans, 1999) 11–13, 23, 25, who has highlighted the impact of Deuteronomy on the book (and character) of Tobit. Note also Agrippa's (I or II?) reading of Deuteronomy at Tabernacles in *m. Soṭah* 7:8. I thank James VanderKam for bringing this text to my attention.

107. Note William L. Holladay's application of the septennial reading in his treatment of Jeremiah (*Jeremiah 1: A Commentary on the Book of the Prophet Jeremiah Chapters 1–25* [ed. Paul D. Hanson; Hermeneia; Philadelphia: Fortress, 1986] 1–2). For more recent times and contexts, appeal might be made to the eleven *parashot* and thirty-one *sedarim* in Deuteronomy, which, though they divide the text into smaller parts, nevertheless expose the reader/listener to large sections of the book at a time. For two commentaries that take these divisions very seriously, see Jeffrey H. Tigay, *Deuteronomy* (Philadelphia: Jewish Publication Society, 1996); and Duane L. Christensen, *Deuteronomy* (2 vols.; WBC 6A–B; Nashville: Thomas Nelson, 2001–2002).

108. On going back to the beginning and starting over again, see Watts, *Reading Law*, 83; Johnstone, "Repetition in Discourse," 7, 18; and Rebecca S. Gault, "Education by the Use of Ghosts: Strategies of Repetition in *Effi Briest*," in Johnstone, ed., *Repetition in Discourse*, 1:139–51.

109. See Watts, *Reading Law*, 57: "Deuteronomy obliges Israel not only to legal obedience but also repetition of the book's own rhetoric of persuasion through reenactment, both by individuals (6.2–25; 17.18–20) and by the nation as a whole (11.29; 27.12; cf.

any inability we may have with respect to Deuteronomy's repetition may very well go beyond our inability to appreciate that repetition and include our inability to enact it as well.

4. Of course, it must be admitted that not everything is so easy, not even in the face of an overwhelming, pervasive, and persuasive repetitive rhetoric like that of Deuteronomy. This, too, is signaled in repetition; there is something about repetition that evidences a difficulty in the subject matter. So Kawin, quoting Ecclesiastes: "'Man cannot utter it,' but he can utter around it. He can, through repetition, 'make it manifest.'"[110] Repetition helps the speaker/writer talk around an issue that is unclear and uncertain, that is hard to say and hard to say right. Perhaps the repetition around obedience in Deuteronomy is similar: it is hard to get obedience said right and even harder to get it done right. Perhaps the rhetoric of repetition in Deuteronomy, then, despite urging this obedience upon all of us who take up the book, nevertheless understands and acknowledges the difficulties involved in this, *even within the very rhetoric that urges it upon us.*

Perhaps related to the difficulty repetition attempts to counter is the observation that repetition sometimes functions as a means to gain or regain control.[111] Was the Israelite audience who heard Deuteronomy out of control? *Which* Israelite audience? An out-of-control scenario certainly makes sense with the presentation of the Josianic reform in Kings,[112] but it may also make sense of the narrative audience, insofar as Moses is about to die and lose control of Israel. Deuteronomy is his last opportunity to get some words in edgewise. And this, again—always again!—reminds us of why repetition is there in the first place: to remind us, over and over and

---

31.10–13)"; and P. Miller, *Deuteronomy*, 10: "Thus the Book of Deuteronomy is to be understood backwards; its significance is its summarizing and closing of the foundational period. Deuteronomy signals that the period is over. That very fact, however, means that the book is also to be understood from the future. Its impact is not fully comprehended apart from reading the books that follow and sensing sharply that the word of the Lord in Deuteronomy *is always set for future generations.* The intentionality of the book prohibits its ever being viewed as over and done, an enterprise belonging only to the past. No other book of the Old Testament is so straightforward and self-conscious about *its character as a guide for the future*" (emphases mine).

110. Kawin, *Telling It Again and Again*, 7–8, citing Qoh 1:8. See also Dozeman, *God on the Mountain*, 173–75; and, further, Kawin, *Telling It Again and Again*, 50–51, 61–62.

111. See above on Freud and note Johnstone, "Repetition in Discourse," 19.

112. Cf. Kawin, *Telling It Again and Again*, 122 (a quotation from Stein): "The excitingness of pure being had withdrawn from them [the words]; they were just rather stale literary words. Now the poet has to work in the excitingness of pure being; he has to get back that intensity into the language." If repetition is a part of getting that intensity back into the language, one wonders what had become stale in the Josianic or exilic periods that Deuteronomy's rhetoric sought to address.

over again, to keep/observe/do, carefully, today! I close with the words of
Patrick D. Miller: "From the beginning, its [Deuteronomy's] words have
claimed that its readers' lives depend upon careful attention to them. So
read on, carefully."[113] The present essay would add only that the book's
words—*repeated* words—urge one additional item: to not only read on, but
also to *live* on, carefully.[114]

---

113. P. Miller, *Deuteronomy*, 17.

114. An early version of this essay was drafted at the Mount Calvary Monastery and
Retreat House in Santa Barbara, California. I am deeply thankful to Carlos Estrada for
making that trip possible. I am also grateful to Bill T. Arnold, Nancy R. Bowen, Henry
W. Rietz, Brad D. Strawn, and Christine Roy Yoder for reading and commenting on an
earlier draft of this paper.

Divine Warrior Theology in Deuteronomy

Richard D. Nelson

I. Introduction

The book of Deuteronomy represents an extended period of creative, constructive theologizing. A likely scenario suggests that this book began as a covert undertaking by dissident Jerusalem scribal circles during the reign of Manasseh, with collaboration from conservative rural landowners, elements of the priesthood, and those schooled in wisdom. Traditional legal materials formed the basis for a document fashioned on the model of Assyrian loyalty treaties. In order to encourage acceptance, this developing textual package incorporated motivational rhetoric attached to the laws themselves and layered into introductory and concluding frameworks. In Josiah's reign, this underground reform theology emerged as an accessible "published" document and temporarily became public policy. Subsequent additions fit Deuteronomy to new ideological situations and literary contexts. Chapters 1–3 and 31 connected it to the Deuteronomistic History. The Song of Moses (chapter 32) offered a prophetic theology of history, and the Blessing of Moses (chapter 33) emphasized Deuteronomy as Moses' final testament.[1]

Author's note: This essay is offered with grateful appreciation to Patrick D. Miller, my teacher and friend, who has contributed richly to our understanding of both Deuteronomy and the Divine Warrior.

1. For the general viewpoint adopted here, see Frank Crüsemann, *The Torah: Theology and Social History of Old Testament Law* (Minneapolis: Fortress, 1996) 207–15; and Rainer Albertz, *A History of Israelite Religion in the Old Testament Period* (2 vols.; OTL; Louisville: Westminster/John Knox, 1994) 1:197–206. On Assyrian influence, see Eckart Otto, *Das Deuteronomium: Politische Theologie und Rechtsreform in Juda und Assyrien* (BZAW 284; Berlin: Walter de Gruyter, 1999); and Hans Ulrich Steymans, *Deuteronomium 28 und die adê zur Thronfolgeregelung Asarhaddons: Segen und Fluch im Alten Orient und in Israel* (OBO 145; Freiburg: Universitätsverlag Freiburg Schweiz, 1995). For an overview of compositional matters, consult Thomas Römer, "The Book of Deuteronomy," in *The History of Israel's Traditions: The Heritage of Martin Noth* (ed. Steven L. McKenzie and M. Patrick Graham; JSOTSup 182; Sheffield: Sheffield Academic Press, 1994) 178–212.

Characteristic of this enterprise was a potent theological creativity that reused traditional concepts in innovative ways. For example, the tradition of the covenant relationship with Yahweh was elevated into a principal theme and enriched through the format of the Assyrian loyalty treaty. Deuteronomy transformed old laws into new social programs (e.g., Deut 14:22–29 and 15:1–11; cf. Exod 21:2–11; Lev 25:39–46; 27:30–33; Num 18:21–32) and dethroned kingship from its ruling position (Deut 17:14–20). The principle of Yahweh's unity and incomparability (6:4) validated a radical call for cult centralization (Deuteronomy 12).

In the same way, successive redactions of Deuteronomy transformed Israel's tradition of Yahweh as the Divine Warrior and the institution of sacral war into potent theological tools to serve new theological purposes.[2] Some special features of Deuteronomy's presentation of sacral war are immediately apparent. The ark does not represent the presence of the Divine Warrior, but rather serves simply as a law depository (contrast Num 10:35–36 with Deut 10:1–5; 31:9). Priests have no sacral or oracular duties in warfare; they merely deliver a reassuring oration before battle (contrast Num 10:1–9 or 1 Sam 23:9–12 with Deut 20:2–4).

This study examines the ways in which Deuteronomy took up the complex of traditions and ideologies that scholarship has categorized under the concept of "the Divine Warrior." In the culture of Israel, this Divine Warrior came to life in poetry, song, liturgy, and myth, as well as in the actual (or nostalgically-imagined) practice of sacral war. The developing book of Deuteronomy transformed these Divine Warrior traditions by using them as rhetorical instruments to advance its own theological agenda. This transformation can be briefly outlined as follows:

In the central (and older) portions of Deuteronomy—the exhortations of chapters 6–11 and the law code of chapters 12–26—the Divine Warrior tradition is used primarily to advocate: (1) the strictest avoidance of internal apostasy and (2) a precautionary destruction of all nonorthodox cult objects and apostate persons (see section II below). At the same time, this central section of Deuteronomy also uses Divine Warrior and sacral war motifs to warn readers about the dangers of false self-assurance (section III), to inculcate appreciation for Yahweh's good gifts (section IV), to encourage humane behavior towards nature and marginalized human beings (section V), and to advocate a general concern for propriety (section VI).

---

2. In this article, "Divine Warrior" refers to the mythic presentation of Yahweh as a warrior god. "Sacral war" designates the practice of warfare as a religious activity. For general background, see Patrick D. Miller, Jr., *The Divine Warrior in Early Israel* (HSM 5; Cambridge: Harvard University Press, 1973); Manfred Weippert, "Heiliger Krieg in Israel und Assyrien," *ZAW* 84 (1972) 460–95; and Sa-Moon Kang, *Divine War in the Old Testament and in the Ancient Near East* (BZAW 177; Berlin: Walter de Gruyter, 1989).

Chapters 1–3, added at a later stage in the book's development, utilize the ideology of the Divine Warrior to teach a lesson about the perils of disobedience and the rewards of faithful obedience (section VII). The Song of Moses in Deuteronomy 32 takes up the prophetic notion of the Divine Warrior as one who fights against Israel's enemies but who may also choose to turn against Israel. This is done in order to set forth a theocentric explanation for the vicissitudes of Israel's recent history (section VIII). Finally, the Blessing of Moses in Deuteronomy 33 uses the Divine Warrior image to emphasize Israel's fortunate status as a people gifted with the law, blessed by riches, and protected from enemies (section IX).

II. Sacral War against Apostasy (Deuteronomy 7, 13, 20)

Eliminate Those Who Worship Other Gods and Their Cult Objects
(Deut 7:1–5, 16–26)

These verses link sacral war with a call to eradicate alien cults. Consequently, there is an emphasis on Israel's role as a partner of the Divine Warrior in eliminating the nations (7:2, 16, 24). Verse 1 reminds the reader that the setting of Moses' discourse is the threshold of conquest and turns the topic to the threats posed to faith and obedience that Israel will face in the land. It must remain aloof from alien peoples and destroy them and their religion. This call for nonassociation (vv. 1–5, 16–26) frames Israel's elective and blessed relationship with Yahweh (vv. 6–15). Verse 17 is one of three citations in Deuteronomy of Israel's dangerous, erroneous thoughts that focus the theological hazards of their new situation, in this case, fear of the enemy (7:17).[3]

At first sight there seems to be an irreducible logical tension between the command to obliterate the nations and the simultaneous prohibition of social contacts with them. However, this apparent contradiction makes it clear that the text is not really about a long-past conquest but the situation of its contemporary (7th century B.C.E.) readers. The conquest is a distant memory. The real issue is a contemporary alien presence and ideology that threatens Israel's orthodoxy. The text demands total destruction and a policy of social separation simultaneously because both tactics work together to protect national identity and pure worship. By the time of Manasseh or Josiah, the six nations catalogued in v. 1 are no more, so, by default, sacral war annihilation must be applied to disloyal cult objects. This radical demand is thus a wake-up call directed at antireform factions and at the inertia and conservatism of the general populace. *Ḥērem* ("devoted" for

---

3. The other two are false self-sufficiency (8:17) and the idea that the conquest is proof of righteousness (9:4).

destruction) is a powerful rhetorical alarm intended to energize supporters and silence critics of Deuteronomy's policies.[4]

The text begins with a call for a complete disassociation from the nations in vv. 1–5. A series of prohibitions in vv. 2–3 promotes a watertight separation that makes any common life impossible. The standardized list of enemy nations communicates the overwhelming odds that the power of the Divine Warrior can overcome. Because these are victories of the Divine Warrior, these populations naturally fall into the state of *ḥērem* (v. 2) and must be eradicated along with the images and cult apparatus of their gods (vv. 5, 26). In this way, *ḥērem*, a traditional aspect of sacral war against *external* enemies, has been converted into an expression and a guarantee of *internal* religious loyalty. The call to show no mercy suggests that readers might be likely to do so, that is, to be apathetic in the face of apostasy. Those subject to *ḥērem* are no longer alien peoples, but nonorthodox and apostate neighbors and their religious paraphernalia.

A wooden Asherah pole, along with the altar and stone pillar, was a standard fixture for a local, open-air shrine (Judg 6:25–30), and was associated with the cult of Yahweh, perhaps as a mediator of fertility.[5] This campaign against indigenous Asherah poles, as well as the call to destroy the stone pillars (Deut 7:5; 12:3) that Israel's *own ancestors* had once erected (Gen 28:18, 22), shows that Deuteronomy is reacting to contemporary dangers under the guise of foreign survivals.

Verses 17–24 return to the topic of vv. 1–5. Moses gives the classic admonition of the sacral war tradition: "do not fear."[6] Such fear might seem logical since the enemy's power is so overwhelming (vv. 1, 7, 17), but the evidence of the even greater power of the Divine Warrior counters this. Verse 21 utilizes hymnic language about the Divine Warrior "in the midst" (Deut 1:42; 23:14; Ps 46:5) who is "great and dreadful" in Zion (Pss 47:2; 99:2–3). A rationalized answer is given to the question of why such alien influences should still exist in the readers' own day (v. 22). Moses describes the glorious progress of the coming conquest with its divinely induced panic (vv. 20, 23), but the surviving influences of these nations represent an unfinished task. In this contemporary sacral war struggle, Yahweh does not act alone. Of course, Yahweh is the subject of most of the conquest verbs,

4. Yoshihide Suzuki, "A New Aspect of ḤRM in Deuteronomy in View of an Assimilation Policy of King Josiah," *AJBI* 21 (1995) 3–27. Christa Schäfer-Lichtenberger, "JHWH, Israel und die Völker aus der Perspektive von Dtn 7," *BZ* 40 (1996) 194–218, believes the annihilation commands counter the dangers of exile.

5. See John Day, "Asherah in the Hebrew Bible and Northwest Semitic Literature," *JBL* 105 (1986) 385–408; and Othmar Keel and Christoph Uehlinger, *Gods, Goddesses, and Images of God in Ancient Israel* (Minneapolis: Fortress, 1998) 327–36.

6. See H. F. Fuhs, "יָרֵא *yārē*'," *TDOT* 6:290–315, esp. 304–5.

but Israel too must "make an end of them," "blot out their name," and "destroy them" (vv. 22, 24).

In vv. 25–26, echoes of past sacral war victories lead into a challenge to eliminate alien religious objects. From a practical standpoint, to renounce alien gods means to deny them their liturgical service and suppress temptation by destroying their shrines and associated paraphernalia. Once again, this is really an attack on Israel's own altars, pillars, Asherah-poles, and images, under the analogy of alien cults. Verses 25–26 make the demands of v. 5 more explicit and precise by using three of the repellent categories by which Israel categorized elements of its world. Even precious metals associated (as foil overlays or jewelry) with these images fall into the categories of *tôʿēbâ* ("repugnant") and *ḥērem*, and are catalogued as *šeqeṣ* ("detestable," using the derived verb). Total eradication is mandated, lest Israel itself be contaminated by the contagious category of *ḥērem*.[7] Verse 26 ends with a climactic and decisive use of the genre of priestly declaration (Lev 13:8, 15, 17; cf. Ezek 18:9; Hag 2:14): "it is *ḥērem*."

Destroy All Who Promote False Worship (Deut 13:12–18)

Chapter 13 urges fidelity and drastic action in the face of apostasy by offering three potential cases, each focusing on a refrain advocating worship of "other gods" (vv. 2, 6, 13).[8] These illustrate extreme boundary situations demanding total loyalty. Religious treason does not threaten from outside, but from deeds done "in the midst" (*qereb*) of the people (see vv. 5, 11 ["in your midst" is omitted by NRSV], 14). These are not just theoretical dangers, but part of the readers' actual experience. Yahweh's apparent inability to protect Judah from external threats must have led to calls for less exclusive religious behavior (2 Kgs 16:18; 18:22; Jer 44:16–18). Formerly Canaanite cities assimilated into the royal state would naturally continue aspects of their local religion. More generally, the traditional practices and loyalties of the people as a whole fell short of the orthodoxy expected by Deuteronomy. Over against these very real temptations, the text is uncompromising: Engage in ruthless internal sacral war and *ḥērem* against renegade cities!

---

7. On these categories, see Richard D. Nelson, *Raising Up a Faithful Priest: Community and Priesthood in Biblical Theology* (Louisville: Westminster/John Knox, 1993) 17–38. On *ḥērem* specifically, see idem, "*Ḥērem* and the Deuteronomic Social Conscience," in *Deuteronomy and Deuteronomic Literature* (ed. Marc Vervenne and Johan Lust; BETL 133; Leuven: University Press, 1997) 39–54, esp. 41–49. Note that *ḥērem* was evidently contagious (see Josh 6:18; 7:12)!

8. See Paul E. Dion, "Deuteronomy 13: The Suppression of Alien Religious Practices in Israel during the Late Monarchical Era," in *Law and Ideology in Monarchic Israel* (ed. Baruch Halpern and Deborah Hobson; JSOTSup 124; Sheffield: Sheffield Academic Press, 1991) 147–216.

The third case advocating worship of "other gods" (vv. 12–18) is climactic, a mass defection followed by a mass action of punishment and decontamination. Casting the case as a little hypothetical drama creates personal involvement on the part of the reader. The repetition of "among you" (vv. 13, 14) also aims at reader interest. The attractiveness of the temptation is underscored by use of the potent verb *ndḥ* (*hipʿil*; v. 13, cf. vv. 5, 10). This denotes "thrust someone away" from Yahweh or Yahweh's way, but also implies "seduce, entice" (see Prov 7:21). A rhetoric of emotional language seeks to carry the day with the reader, as though much resistance to these harsh demands is expected. Gods not known (v. 13) are opposed to Yahweh's past gracious acts (vv. 12, 17). Such behaviors are "repugnant" (*tôʿēbâ*; v. 14). Yahweh's "compassion" is assured for those who obey, in contrast to "fierce anger" (v. 17).

The case begins with the mechanism of its discovery as news or rumor (v. 12; cf. 17:4). Passing mention of Yahweh's gift (v. 12) underscores the depravity of the crime. The "you" addressed is the whole nation, but as the rebellion is described, what was "your town" in v. 12 becomes "their town"[9] in v. 13. The triple repetition of verbs in v. 14a underscores that careful investigation is conducted, and in v. 14b the roots *ʾmn* ("true") and *kwn* ("certain") point to an assured verdict. Verse 15 replaces the capital punishment language of the first two cases in vv. 5 and 9–10 with sacral war terminology. This is because individual malefactors have been replaced by a community capable of resistance. The apostate town becomes the object of sacral war, dealt with as though it were part of the pagan nations of the land. The motivation of population increase (v. 17) intends to counteract any hesitation caused by the potential loss of a whole city.

Kill All Who Do Abhorrent Things for Their Gods (Deut 20:1–4, 10–18)

Deuteronomy describes war as it thinks it ought to be waged, depicting the proper role of the "citizen soldier" in a restored and reformed practice of sacral war. These laws go beyond the traditions of conquest to comment on the policies and difficulties of the late monarchy. They reflect the technology of siege warfare, the politically motivated use of forced labor, and the problems of a nonprofessional army facing a technologically superior foe. These citizen soldiers who attack distant cities are settled, with houses and vineyards. The strong topical connection between vv. 10–14 and 19–20 suggests that vv. 15–18 form a secondary insertion. It is widely accepted that vv. 15–18 represent a later and harsher rethinking of the more moderate vv. 10–14. Verse 15 creates a bridge between the two viewpoints by introducing the geographic distinction of "far" and "near."

---

9. MT: עירם. The suffix is not reflected in the NRSV.

Verses 1–14 deal with war in a realistic and practical light. Aggressive attacks on cities are in view, perhaps a reflection of the revival of national aspirations under Josiah. However, Israel's wars are to be wars consonant with their nature as Yahweh's people. The standard themes of sacral war are present. A reduced army is no problem. The exodus is the basis for faithful confidence (v. 1), which is the unconditional requirement for any sacral war (v. 8). The text simply assumes that wars fought to subjugate others and enjoy plunder are a fact of life. The fruits of such victories, including the slave labor of conquered peoples, are gifts of Yahweh (v. 14). For this reason, the dangers of war are not to undermine the enjoyment of life's sweetest blessings (vv. 5–7). If Israel can enjoy the spoils of war without bloodshed, that is preferable (v. 10); if not, the onus lies squarely upon the enemy (v. 12). Respect for noncombatants (vv. 11, 14) excludes wanton atrocities. These are not wars of any king, but wars of the people ("you go out," "you draw near") under team leadership (v. 9).

In contrast, vv. 15–18 turn from general rules for warfare to the topic of the conquest of the land. Apprehension over the temptations of foreign worship replaces the issues of a political covenant and the economic value of a conquered population. In place of an offer of life or the grant of survival to noncombatants, the total extermination of *ḥērem* comes into play. This harsher attitude towards the enemy represents the same thinking that is found in 7:1–5, 17–26 and 13:12–18, namely, that the extermination of apostasy labeled as "abomination" (*tôʿēbâ*; 7:25–26; 13:14) should be accomplished through the application of *ḥērem* (7:2, 26; 13:15, 17). Once again, the ruthless atmosphere of sacral war is utilized in the service of Deuteronomy's call to eliminate apostasy. For Deuteronomy, the danger threatened in v. 18 is already a present reality and must be cancelled out.

III. False Assurance (Deut 9:1–6)

Deuteronomy's emphasis on Yahweh's decisive role as Divine Warrior serves to counter Israel's self-important claims. Deuteronomy seeks to counteract any narcissistic, boastful theology that would collapse the tension between divine grace and human obedience. Such boasting is prevented by a reminder of Yahweh's actual motivations in the conquest and of Israel's constant opposition to Yahweh. Verses 1–3 describe sacral war victory, and vv. 4–6 warn about false conclusions that might be drawn from it.

Two overlapping rhetorical forms are present in vv. 4–7a. On the one hand, these verses present a "schema of evidence from history."[10] Verses

---

10. See Norbert Lohfink, *Das Hauptgebot: Eine Untersuchung literarischer Einleitungsfragen zu Dtn 5–11* (AnBib 20; Rome: Pontifical Institute, 1963) 125–36. Other examples are Deut 4:37–40; 7:7–11; and 8:2–6.

4–5 present the evidence, v. 6 sets forth the conclusion in the form of what is to be known, and v. 7 the consequences of this lesson from history in the form of remembering. At the same time, the argument uses a rhetorical form described as an "internal monologue."[11] Israel's erroneous monologue (v. 4a) is set up by the situation of Divine Warrior victory (vv. 1–3) and then is followed by a listing of realities that counter this incorrect thinking.

Divine Warrior and sacral war notions dominate the counter-argument. Yahweh's effectiveness as warrior is evidenced by a capacity to overcome fortifications and the proverbial Anakim (vv. 1–2) and to do so "quickly" (v. 3). The Divine Warrior will be Israel's vanguard (v. 3; note the emphatic grammar). "Devouring fire" is a weapon of the Divine Warrior (Isa 29:6; 30:27, 30).[12] Moses begins by imitating the style of a sacral war sermon (cf. 20:2–4), but turns this genre to a different rhetorical purpose, not encouragement but warning. Israel dare not take Yahweh's good gifts as evidence of their own righteousness. On the contrary, the conquest represents punishment on the indigenous inhabitants and a fulfillment of Yahweh's oath. Ancient thought patterns would have taken it for granted that victory should go to the just as a matter of course. Thus, Israel is tempted to engage in a binary juridical logic: our victory means our righteousness. Moses insists on a counter logic: "our victory means enemy wickedness, yes, but also Yahweh's promise to our ancestors. Do not think your victory means that Yahweh has judged you innocent as though in a judicial battle. Yes, your foes are guilty and will get what they deserve, but you are guilty too." The reader must understand the fate of these wicked nations in light of 8:19–20. The reader is just as vulnerable as they are to the judgment of the God of history!

IV. Appreciation of God's Gifts (Deut 20:5–8)

The practice of granting deferments from battle was common in the ancient world, as evidenced by the Gilgamesh epic and the Legend of Keret.[13] Originally, these were based on notions of the danger of persons in certain liminal or threshold states taking part in a sacral enterprise. Each of the first three scenarios for deferment requires two things of the warrior: that he has entered into a brand new liminal situation and that the dynamics of that situation have not yet been completed. A new act of construction or

---

11. See F. García López, "Analyse littéraire de Deutéronome, V–XI," *RB* 84 (1977) 481–522, esp. 484, 495–96; and *RB* 85 (1978) 5–49, esp. 17–19, 21.

12. See Patrick D. Miller, Jr. "Fire in the Mythology of Canaan and Israel," *CBQ* 27 (1965) 256–61; reprinted in idem, *Israelite Religion and Biblical Theology: Collected Essays* (JSOTSup 267; Sheffield: Sheffield Academic Press, 2000) 18–23.

13. *ANET*, 48 (lines 50–53), 143–44 (lines 96–103, 184–91).

planting or betrothal has not yet been transformed into the corresponding normal situation by dedication, profanation, or marriage.[14]

Deuteronomy sets its own stamp on these traditional exclusions. Although scholars have sometimes spoken of a humane ethic at this point or of the protection of family life, it is really an appreciation of the genre of "futility curses" that opens the door for a proper interpretation. These are rhythmic antithetical parallels in which potential projects and benefits are initiated, but then success or reward is thwarted (cf. Deut 28:30–33a, 38–41). In the operation of such a curse, death in battle would break the natural relationship of act and expected consequence, the relationship between an initial step and the natural next step in continuity with it. This was viewed as undermining a natural and expected order of the world. Engaging in war must not endanger this cosmic order, nor undercut someone's rights to enjoy the completion of what has been started. Israel is not to come under the power of such a curse, but rather to enjoy the good things given by Yahweh.[15]

Deut 20:8 is of a different character and returns to the problem of fear addressed in v. 1. Here the issue for deferment is not the private rights of an individual, nor a liminal condition, but the psychological effect of panic on one's "brothers." Such an exemption flies in the face of all state compulsion in warfare.

V. Humane Behavior (Deut 20:19–20; 21:10–14)

Protect Trees That Give Food (Deut 20:19–20)

This law seeks to limit the practice of complete devastation in war, as described, for example, in 2 Kgs 3:19, 25. Until the reader reaches Deut 20:20, what is being prohibited in warfare seems to refer to any trees. Verse 20 sounds like a narrowing redefinition of v. 19 (suggesting that a comprehensive ban on cutting trees has been restricted to food trees), but even here cutting down trees is only for the purpose of building a counter-wall, not an act of vandalism or psychological warfare. "Many days" (NRSV: "a long time") adds to the pressure to take drastic action as the need for wood would increase as the siege dragged on. There is a double motivation for this law: the importance of food to the besieging army and what sounds like sympathy for the trees themselves. The first motivation is much the same

---

14. "Enjoy its fruit" is literally "to make profane use of" after a sacral period (Lev 19:23–25).

15. W. M. de Bruin, "Die Freistellung vom Militärdienst in Deut. xx 5–7: Die Gattung der Wirkungslosigkeitssprüche als Schlüssel zum Verstehen eines alten Brauches," *VT* 49 (1999) 21–33.

as 20:14 ("you may eat"), and in fact v. 19 sounds like a limitation or control on the permission to plunder given by v. 14. The second anthropomorphizing, "environmental" argument may relate to the impropriety of breaking the natural connection between act and consequence, intention and result. Just as one should be concerned with breaking the connection between planting a vineyard and eating its fruit (20:6) or a female bird's ability to produce young (22:6–7), so Israel should not destroy a tree's ability to produce food.

Treat Responsibly a Wife Captured in War (Deut 21:10–14)

This law consists of a case (21:11–13) and a subcase (v. 14). A proper understanding depends on how one divides the protasis and apodosis. Most likely, the legal demands start at the point of the change in subject in v. 12b ("she shall shave," cf. NRSV, NJB, NAB). The main case of this law validates marriage to a captive woman who would have no legally recognized relative to act for her, making normal contractual marriage arrangements impossible. Before consummation of the marriage can take place, she must be appropriately integrated into her new family via a right of passage. The subcase protects her from a reduction to slave status in case of a later divorce.

The law envisions a situation in which a man takes a woman captive and brings her to his house in order to marry her, but it does not overtly prohibit battlefield rape. Nor does it explicitly exclude the practice of enslaving her and then having sexual relations with her outside of marriage. In this particular case, marriage is in the picture because of the man's choice and loving desire. She has full status as a wife and is given time to adjust to her new situation. In choosing to marry her, however, he must be willing to lose his claim to her potential value as a slave, because marital sex creates a relationship of marital responsibility.

The acts required of her are symbolic of her change in status. Her month-long isolation ("remain in your house") is a classic example of the liminal state characteristic of rites of passage that separate persons from an old status and incorporate them into a new one.[16] It is also likely that this month gives her time to menstruate to demonstrate she is not pregnant. She puts aside her former life and captive status, represented by her clothes, hair, and nails. Changing clothes (Gen 35:2) and shaving (Lev 14:8–9; Num 6:9) were part of the transition rituals of purification (cf. Joseph's transition from prison to freedom, Gen 41:14). The wife-to-be is shedding bits of her former self.

---

16. On the liminal state, see Victor W. Turner, *The Ritual Process: Structure and Anti-Structure* (Ithaca: Cornell University Press, 1977) 94–130, esp. 102–6.

The double marriage formula of v. 13 emphasizes that a standard full marriage is in view. Therefore, he is to treat her like any Israelite wife, giving her a proper divorce and releasing her as a free woman. He is not to sell her for money (v. 14). The verb often translated "sell" should be understood as "exercise one's power of commercial disposal."[17] The important point is that she is to be treated like the Israelite brother in 24:7. If he cannot be sold, neither can she. The justification for her status as free woman is that her husband has "dishonored her" (*'nh*). Although this is usually used for forced or adulterous sex, here the connotation must be more neutral, "had sex with her" (cf. Exod 21:10 where the root denotes a wife's sexual rights).[18]

This law is notable for what it envisions, not just for what it requires. In terms of women and war, the only case offered is one in which a captive woman is desired for marriage and brought home — as though saying implicitly that this is what should be the norm. Of course, to read this law as representing a positive gain for the woman requires the reader to adopt its androcentric perspective. It is hardly the breakthrough in gender relations that some interpreters have made of it! The law assumes the victorious male's right to capture a woman for the purpose of marriage. Her consent to this arrangement is beside the point. Moreover, what real protection is provided by discharging her as a "free" woman into a patriarchal society without any protective family structure? Nevertheless, here, as in the case of fruit trees endangered by the practice of total war, Deuteronomy utilizes the context of sacral warfare to promulgate laws promoting humanitarian behavior.

VI. Propriety (Deut 23:9–14)

Sacral war involved abstinence from sexual relations on the part of the participants (1 Sam 21:4–5; 2 Sam 11:11). The Divine Warrior is present in the sacral war camp, so the ritual impurity imparted by sexual relations (Lev 15:18, 24) has to be prohibited. Unless driven away, Yahweh is present (Deut 7:21; 20:1, 4) and can be expected to perform a liberating, saving act of sacral war victory (Deut 23:14). Yahweh's departure would turn victory into defeat.

The introduction to these commands against ritual impurity marks this as a "when-you-go-out" sacral-war law like Deut 20:1 and 21:10. Deuteronomy 23:11–12 represent a third person casuistic law, and vv. 13–14 are a positive command in the second person. These two laws are surrounded by

---

17. *HALOT* 2:849.

18. For further discussion, see Carolyn Pressler, *The View of Women Found in the Deuteronomic Family Laws* (BZAW 216; Berlin: Walter de Gruyter, 1993) 14–15.

the inclusive topic of what must be avoided: "any impropriety" (v. 10), "anything indecent" (v. 15). Two possible violations illustrate the general concept of war camp sacrality, one involving the purity of the body, the other the purity of sacral space.

The purity of the body is associated with "what happens at night" (v. 10)—this is usually understood as a seminal emission by analogy with Lev 15:16. The purity of space reflects the attitude of Ezekiel's refusal to bake with human excrement (Ezek 4:12–15). The 'erwat dābār (v. 15; literally "nakedness of a thing"; NRSV: "anything indecent") refers broadly to a shameful matter or behavior. "Nakedness" is something better left unseen (e.g., Gen 9:22; Lev 20:17), something to be countered by "covering" (Deut 23:13). In fact, "cover" and "nakedness" form a standard word association (Gen 9:23; Exod 28:42; Ezek 18:7; Hos 2:9). A generalized and unexplained 'erwat dābār on a wife's part can lead to divorce (Deut 24:1); here it would lead to Yahweh "turning away."

This law immediately follows 23:1–8, a section that regulates those who may be admitted to the assembly (qāhāl) of Israel, especially when it is gathered for worship. This redactional ordering suggests an associative identification of the war camp with the whole community and its purity. Although Deuteronomy is hardly a priestly document in the sense of Leviticus, it is still not entirely uninterested in matters of purity and sacrality, something demonstrated by the inclusion of laws such as 14:3–21, 15:21, and 17:1. So also, in this chapter, a law about the practice of sacral war and the aversion of the Divine Warrior to unseemly behavior has been taken up to promote general wholesomeness and propriety in community life.

VII. A Lesson From History (Deuteronomy 1–3)

The first three chapters of Deuteronomy focus on a lesson from history. Unbelief and disobedience have meant defeat (1:19–46); faith and obedience produce sacral war victory (2:1–3:17). These are "case studies" of disobedience and obedience. The first case motivates faithful obedience by portraying a disobedient, perverted sacral war. In chapters 2 and 3, other "case studies" of successful obedience provide positive counter examples.[19]

---

19. Norbert Lohfink, "Darstellungskunst und Theologie in Dtn 1:6–3:29," *Bib* 41 (1960) 105–34; reprinted in idem, *Studien zum Deuteronomium und zur deuteronomistischen Literatur I* (SBAB 8; Stuttgart: Katholisches Bibelwerk, 1990) 15–44; William L. Moran, "The End of the Unholy War and the Anti-Exodus," *Bib* 44 (1963) 333–42; and Patrick D. Miller, "The Wilderness Journey in Deuteronomy: Style, Structure, and Theology in Deuteronomy 1–3," in *To Hear and Obey: Essays in Honor of Fredrick Carlson Holmgren* (ed. Paul Koptak and Bradley J. Bergfalk; Chicago: Covenant Publications, 1997) 50–68; reprinted in idem, *Israelite Religion and Biblical Theology: Collected Essays* (JSOTSup 267; Sheffield: Sheffield Academic Press, 2000) 572–92.

By means of these stories, the law proclaimed by Deuteronomy is set into the context of an annulled relationship that can nevertheless be revitalized after a journey by the next generation. Readers are to identify themselves with this new generation that has a new chance to choose obedience. From now on, things must be done Yahweh's way and be based on trust in Yahweh's ability to act.

Unbelief and Disobedience Lead to Disaster (Deut 1:19–46)

Israel's disobedience is cast in the worst possible light so that it may function as an effective contrast to the victories of the next generation. Sending spies is the unanimous (cf. "all of you," v. 22) suggestion of the people. The spies fulfill only part of the task assigned in v. 22, reporting just on the first item, the land. Their "word" is really a confession of Deuteronomistic faith rather than useful military data. This adds to the shock when Israel proves unwilling to attack. Rebellion follows immediately, almost inexplicably, after the spies' positive report. The text has "set up" the reader to expect a positive response; however, the people have only really heard what the narrator has not yet recounted, the negative, delayed message they repeat in v. 28.

That this is not a tactical decision but an abandonment of faith is made clear in vv. 27–28. The people furtively grumble in their tents, impugning Yahweh's motives and commitment. They proclaim an "anti-credo," a perversion of proper faith, setting forth a reversed interpretation of the exodus (contrast 5:6). Yahweh "hates," rather than loves (contrast 4:37; 7:8). They annul the faith required in sacral war with the accusation that Yahweh wishes "to destroy us" (contrast 7:23–24; 12:30) and express a self-fulfilling reversal of proper sacral war formulas ("hand us over to the Amorites"). It is enemy hearts that are supposed to melt (Josh 2:11; 5:1), not those of Israel! In a proper sacral war, Israel's weakness in contrast to the strength of the foe is supposed to point positively to Yahweh's power. Here the people have it backwards, so that the enemy's strength is used to support disbelief instead of wonder at the work of God.

Moses seeks to counter this with an encouraging sacral-war sermon (vv. 29–33), offering three reasons why Israel should not fear: the Lord has already fought for them (v. 30), carried them like a child (v. 31), and guided them on their journey (v. 33). This speech responds directly to Israel's grievances. Verse 27 is countered by v. 31, a response to the objection about divine motives and attitude. Verse 33 answers the question of v. 28, "Where are we headed?" From a literary standpoint, this speech introduces tension-building delay before the expected negative reaction of Yahweh. From a theological perspective, this is a sort of "short historical credo" that counters the "anti-credo" professed by the people. The bottom line is the rebuke of v. 32: the people's reaction stems from an incomprehensible absence of trust.

Verse 34 shifts the scene from Moses to Yahweh, connecting directly to v. 28 as though Moses has never spoken. Yahweh swears a "counter oath" to that sworn to the ancestors (1:8). Successful progress must be put "on hold" until this oath has run its course and a new generation can replace the old (cf. 2:14). The point is that exclusion is universal for the truly guilty, while promise must await those who have not been faithless.

In vv. 41–45, Israel moves from the disobedience of inaction to the disobedience of self-chosen action. The proposal to "go up" stands in sharp contrast to their unwillingness to "go up" in v. 26a. Yahweh's warning in v. 42 is unambiguous: "I am not in your midst." The result of Israel's "go it alone" anti-sacral war is the precise reversal of the panic and pursuit of genuine sacral war (v. 44). The story of defeat ends where it began, at Kadesh-barnea (vv. 19, 46). This conveys the futility that Israel's rebellion has brought about.

Faith and Obedience Lead to Success (Deut 2:1–3:17)

This section is organized by encounters with five peoples on a journey from south to north. The first three encounters are peaceful; the last two are sacral war victories. Two great changes in Israel's situation have taken place. The former generation has died off (at the Zered, 2:14–16), and Yahweh has again begun to function as Divine Warrior (at the Arnon, 2:25). Because the plot has moved beyond anti-sacral war in the direction of genuine sacral war, the peoples that Israel confronts are now appropriately fearful (2:4).

There is a sharp line between old failures and new opportunities. Verse 15 emphasizes that the extinction of the rebellious generation was not due to natural causes only, but to the actions of Yahweh the Divine Warrior. This is accentuated by the verb *hmm/hwm*, "roust out, throw into confusion," with reference to the "divinely-induced panic" of sacral war (cf., e.g., Exod 14:24; Deut 7:23; Josh 10:10; Judg 4:15; 1 Sam 7:10). Yahweh's destructive "hand" is also part of Divine Warrior ideology.[20] The shocking message is that Yahweh the Divine Warrior prosecuted sacral war against the faithless generation.

Israel shares the Transjordan with other nations to whom Yahweh the Divine Warrior has given land (2:5, 9, 19). The sovereignty of these other nations is under Yahweh's protection. Israel's own conquest is thus justified and assured by being only one element in Yahweh's extensive realignment

---

20. Patrick D. Miller, Jr. and J. J. M. Roberts, *The Hand of the Lord: A Reassessment of the "Ark Narrative" of 1 Samuel* (JHNES; Baltimore: The Johns Hopkins University Press, 1977).

of ethnic geography. The theology of the "ethnographic notices" (2:10–12, 20–23) builds on this concept and makes it more explicit. Israel's "salvation history" of destroying, dispossessing, and settling in place of the previous inhabitants follows an earlier pattern set by Yahweh's actions in behalf of the Edomites and Ammonites.

Verses 24–36 are a doxological description of how Yahweh gave Israel a wonderful victory. The decisive command and promise of vv. 24–25 mean that the Arnon marks the change from peace to war. The piling up of Divine Warrior language indicates assured victory: "handed over," "dread and fear," "tremble and be in anguish." The text uses the Divine Warrior language of Exod 15:14–16 to express the enemy's terror. Israel exhibits obedience, faith, and courage (2:33b, 34, 37; 3:3b) but Yahweh is the one who does everything really significant (2:30, 33a, 36b; 3:3a). Total victory is pledged by Yahweh (2:24–25, 31; 3:2) and underscored by *ḥērem* (2:34–35; 3:6–7), the extent of land acquisition (2:36; 3:4), and the defensive strength of the captured cities (2:36a; 3:5). The report about Sihon carries the main narrative and ideological load. The victory over Og is largely a parallel replay that seconds and underlines the primary Sihon story.

Glorious triumphs given to a new generation reverse in every way the previous generation's failure of nerve and obedience. The spies that triggered Israel's fear (1:23) are replaced by messengers who provoke Sihon's overconfidence (2:26). The land that Yahweh is giving (1:25; 2:29) is approached once more, but this time Israel's unwilling rebellion (1:26) is replaced by Sihon's unwilling defiance (2:30). Now Israel believes Yahweh's promise of victory and obeys the comforting call "do not fear" (1:21; 3:2). The attacks launched by Sihon and Og parallel that of the Amorites (1:44; 2:32; 3:1), but at this point the outcome exemplifies true sacral war. Conquest of high and fortified cities (2:36; 3:5) cancels out earlier discouragement about such obstacles (1:28). *Ḥērem* emphasizes this as a sacral war victory won by Yahweh (2:34–35), to whom the captives belong by right of conquest. The "*ḥērem* inventory" of 2:34 (and 3:6) emphasizes the obedient totality of this slaughter.[21]

VIII. The Divine Warrior as Both Enemy and Defender (Deuteronomy 32)

The Song of Moses uses Divine Warrior imagery to present a theory of history in accord with prophetic theology. The punishing wrath of the

---

21. The "*ḥērem* inventory" is a formulaic list of what was treated as *ḥērem* (see Josh 11:14 and the Mesha Inscription [*ANET*, 320 (lines 16–17)]).

Divine Warrior that would normally be expected to destroy Israel's enemies is startlingly turned against the people (vv. 22–25). However, in the end, when Yahweh considers Yahweh's own reputation and self-interest (vv. 26–27) and the character of Israel's foes (vv. 28–33), the Divine Warrior turns against those who have harassed and maltreated Israel (vv. 39–43).

Yahweh's plan for the destruction of Israel is described in mythic Divine Warrior terms (v. 22). Yahweh uses the weapon of fire. This fire moves downward from its heavenly starting point to Sheol (v. 22a) and to the earth (v. 22b). The language is that of total reach and immense destructive power—a disturbance at the deepest level of the cosmos, even to the world of the dead.

In vv. 23–24 Yahweh's anger turns from the cosmic horizon to focus on Israel. The Divine Warrior will use up a quiverful of arrows (cf. v. 42; Ezek 5:16; Pss 7:13; 38:2; Job 6:4). One thinks immediately of lightning, but perhaps the list that follows enumerates these arrows as a larger arsenal of weapons (thus the colon at the end of v. 23 in NRSV). If so, it would be appropriate to translate the verb *šlḥ* in v. 24 as "shoot" (NRSV: "send"; cf. Ps 18:14). The arrows of the Divine Warrior are wasting hunger, consuming pestilence, bitter epidemic, the teeth of beasts, and poison of things that crawl in dust. The translation "pestilence" is based on the parallelism here and in Hab 3:5. Behind this usage is the figure of the (often sinister) god *Rešep*, who appears as an attendant of the marching Divine Warrior in Hab 3:5. Perhaps *Rešep* is portrayed here as a demon in Yahweh's service. *Qeteb*, "epidemic," may also be a demon and "beasts" may refer to Behemoth, supposed by many to have been a mythic creature (Job 40:15–24).[22] In v. 25, the acts of the Divine Warrior against Israel merge with what one might expect of God towards the "enemy" in v. 27. The destruction by the Divine Warrior is total, expressed in the language of the polar opposites of location, sex, and age.

At the end of the poem, the Divine Warrior returns in a saving, positive role. The "see now" of v. 39 refers to the realities expressed in previous verses. In contrast to vv. 37–38, one must not imagine these catastrophes mean that Yahweh has lost power! The divine attributes of traditional poetry deny such a conclusion (1 Sam 2:6–8; Isa 43:10–11, 13; Hos 6:1–2). Yahweh is the only god with the true powers of the Divine Warrior: "I kill and I make alive; I wounded,[23] but I heal, and no one can deliver from my hand."

The Divine Warrior lifts a hand in v. 40, marking a transition to warlike action and dividing vv. 37–39 from 41–42. In context, this seems to be an act of oath taking (Gen 14:22; Ezek 36:7), although it could conceivably indicate

---

22. Paolo Xella, "Resheph," *DDD*, 700–703; Nicholas Wyatt, "Qeteb," *DDD*, 673–74.
23. Note the perfect tense, referring to Israel's experience earlier in the poem.

the martial gesture of the Divine Warrior's upraised fighting arm, familiar in iconography (cf. Ps 10:12).[24] Verse 41 gives the content of Yahweh's oath. The nations Yahweh utilized to punish Israel are now seen as Yahweh's enemies because of their brutal actions. The Divine Warrior's sword (v. 25a) is now turned against them and the retribution language of v. 35 is picked up again. Yahweh's sword flashes because it is lightning itself (Hab 3:11; cf. Nah 3:3). "Takes hold on judgment [or justice]" is a striking phrase, as though justice is itself used by Yahweh as a metaphorical weapon.

Untangling the intermixed predicates of v. 42 expands the verse into: "I will make my arrows drunk with blood, with the blood of the slain and the captive; and my sword shall devour flesh from the head of the wild-haired enemy." The arrows directed against Israel in v. 23 are now reversed. The powerful images of the ravenous sword (2 Sam 2:26; 11:25; Isa 1:20) and thirsty arrows evoke bloody, physical violence. The "blood of the captive" may refer to wounded captives or those who are put to death because *ḥērem* is being applied.

Picking up the theme of repaying the enemy, the poem returns in v. 43 to the initial apostrophe of vv. 1–3, addressing heaven and heavenly beings and calling on them to praise the Divine Warrior.[25] The poem ends significantly with Yahweh's concern once again focused on Israel. The need to "atone" may refer to the polluting effects of blood violently shed on the land.

The Song of Moses uses the image of the Divine Warrior to explain not only Israel's victories, but also its defeats. Defeat and destruction have resulted from apostasy (vv. 15–18). Any potential for restoration and victory, however, rests entirely on Yahweh's own character and self-concern (vv. 26–27).

IX. The Divine Warrior Gives Law and Blessing (Deut 33:2–5, 26–29)

The Blessing of Moses points forward to the conquest and to the land of promise, advancing the themes of abundance, security, and valor by describing how Israel's future life will take shape. Verses 2–5 and 26–29 frame

---

24. Johan Lust, "For I Lift Up My Hand to Heaven and Swear: Deut 32:40," in *Studies in Deuteronomy* (ed. F. García Martínez et al.; VTSup 53; Leiden: Brill, 1994) 155–64. For the iconography of the Divine Warrior's outstretched arm, see Othmar Keel, *Wirkmächtige Siegeszeichen im alten Testament: Ikonographische Studien zu Jos 8,18–26, Ex 17,8–13, 2 Kön 13,14–19 und 1 Kön 22,11* (OBO 5; Freiburg: Universitätsverlag Freiburg Schweiz, 1974) 158–60.

25. See NRSV. The text of this verse has generated considerable discussion (see Eugene Ulrich et al., ed., *Qumran Cave 4 IX: Deuteronomy, Joshua, Judges, Kings* [DJD 14; Oxford: Clarendon, 1995] 139–42). The earliest recoverable text consists of six lines as preserved by 4QDeut^q.

the tribal blessings. Perhaps these framing verses were an independent hymn into which the blessings were inserted at the catchphrase "tribes of Israel" (v. 5), or perhaps they were composed in order to fuse the earlier individual blessings into the story of "all Israel." Verse 4 ties the theophany of the Divine Warrior into the book of Deuteronomy by connecting it to Moses, the giving of law, and the gathered nation. Both introduction and conclusion describe the Divine Warrior approaching to help the people (vv. 2 and 26–27).

The introductory verses describe the Divine Warrior coming from the southern mountains, perhaps Yahweh's ancient pre-Israelite home. A mythic pantheon of divine beings is fully subordinated to Yahweh. The kingship of the Divine Warrior is linked to Moses as lawgiver by connecting the Sinai of theophany (v. 2) with the place of lawgiving and human assembly (vv. 3–5).

Verse 2 has not been transmitted correctly and is hard to interpret, especially the last line (v. 2b), which seems to be irretrievably corrupted.[26] "Shone" evidences the solar aspects of Yahweh's theophany (cf. Mal 4:2; Hab 3:3–4). The "myriads of holy ones" are the Divine Warrior's army of numinous beings. Verse 3 is also a problem, in part because of confusion about pronoun references. I will limit myself to the observation that "his holy ones" refers to the makeup of the Divine Warrior's army, although these may be humans (taking "his" as Israel) or nonhuman powers ("his" as a divine reference). These "holy ones" are in "your" hand (in your charge or by your side) and march (or fall) at "your" feet, emphasizing the subordinate relationship of these warriors to Yahweh.[27]

The focus of the concluding frame is security and divine protection. Verses 26 and 29 form an envelope with "none like" Yahweh and "who is like?" Israel. The uniqueness of Yahweh (v. 26) entails the uniqueness of elected Israel (v. 29). Verses 26–27 are about Yahweh the Divine Warrior and vv. 28–29 are about Israel protected by the Divine Warrior.

The Divine Warrior rides through the skies (cf. Isa 19:1; Pss 18:10; 68:4, 33; 104:3), returning to image of vv. 2–3. A poetic parallelism equating Israel's help and Yahweh's majesty (v. 26b) offers powerful theological comfort. Verse 27 is obscure. I translate conservatively as "A dwelling place is the ancient God, and underneath are the eternal arms; he drove out the enemy before you and said, 'Destroy!'" "Underneath" means underneath those

---

26. In the observations that follow, I follow the reconstruction of the NRSV.

27. "By your side" is supported by Zech 4:12. "March" takes *whm tkw* as the *puʿal* of *tkh*: "and they crowded together" (?; see *HALOT* 4:1730). "Fall" begins from the Old Greek ("they are under you") and postulates an erroneous division of *himtakkû* (from *mkk* with infixed *t*), "they sink, bow down."

whom God supports; the divine arms are Israel's underpinning (cf. Hos 11:3).[28] Verses 27b–28 describe three connected actions in *waw*-consecutive imperfect: Yahweh "drove out" and "said"; as a result, "Israel lives." "Alone" (NRSV: "untroubled") implies either left alone after the enemy has been expelled or unafraid to be alone (see Num 23:9). Verse 28b connects the triumphs of the Divine Warrior to the rich blessings of the land. Verse 29 portrays Israel's special fortunate state as a people whose uniqueness consists in being saved by Yahweh. The Divine Warrior embodies a complete armament: the shield of defense and the sword of offense.

Chapter 33 employs the Divine Warrior image in a way that in some respects is more traditional and conservative than anywhere else in Deuteronomy. The warrior God is viewed in an uncomplicated way as the source of Israel's prosperity and security. The advent of this One from Sinai means that Israel is a special people gifted with law (vv. 5, 21), blessed by riches (vv. 13–16, 19, 23, 28), and victorious in battle (vv. 7, 11, 17, 22, 25, 29).

---

28. NRSV: "He subdues the ancient gods, shatters the forces of old." This treats *mˁnh* as a *piˁel* participle of *ˁnh* ("humble"), transposes *wmtḥt* into *wmḥtt* ("who shatters"; *piˁel* participle of *ḥtt*), and understands "arm" as a metaphor for "powers."

Reading Deuteronomy 5 as Narrative

Norbert Lohfink

I. Introduction

Deuteronomy 5 is probably best known as the chapter in the book of Deuteronomy that contains the *Decalogue*. Given the Decalogue's significance, one's attention is almost automatically directed to it, with the result that the narrative within which it is embedded easily escapes the scholar's attention. Exceptions to this judgment consist mostly of those discussions treating textual strata, the dating of such strata, and parallel texts.[1] All of these are significant concerns, to be sure, but the chapter itself is rarely envisioned as a *narrative*.[2] This is the task I would like to undertake here. My analysis is based on the final form of the text,[3] and some of my observations

Author's note: Among the many works by Patrick D. Miller's works is an excellent commentary on the book of Deuteronomy (Patrick D. Miller, *Deuteronomy* [Interpretation; Louisville: John Knox, 1990]). So, there seemed nothing more fitting with which to honor Miller (with whom I have long maintained a lively exchange of ideas and offprints) than a small study preliminary to the commentary on Deuteronomy that Georg Braulik and I have been working on for many years. The essay is offered as a small token of my appreciation.

1. Recent studies tend to be more cautious with regard to the number of textual strata that can be identified. See, e.g., R. Achenbach, *Israel zwischen Verheißung und Gebot: Literarkritische Untersuchungen zu Deuteronomium 5–11* (Europäische Hochschulschriften Theologie 422; Frankfurt: Lang, 1991) 31–64; and, before him, C. Brekelmans, "Deuteronomy 5: Its Place and Function," in *Das Deuteronomium: Entstehung, Gestalt und Botschaft* (ed. N. Lohfink; BETL 68; Leuven: University Press, 1985) 164–73. Studies that treat the chapter as a unity frequently prefer a late dating.

2. The most useful study in this regard is J.-P. Sonnet, *The Book within the Book: Writing in Deuteronomy* (Biblical Interpretation Series 14; Leiden: Brill, 1997) 42–51; however, Sonnet only deals with certain narrative aspects.

3. I consider the "final form" to be, not simply the MT, but rather the oldest text that can be reconstructed with the help of external textual witnesses. Outside of the Decalogue, the text-critical differences are minimal. There is no indication in the MT of a new redactional intention, by which someone had once again managed to alter the narrative. Nor does the thesis of A. Rofé, "Deuteronomy 5:28–6:1: Composition and Text in the Light of Deuteronomic Style and Three Tefillin from Qumran (4Q 128, 129, 137),"

261

regarding the text's structure, its legislative character, and its stylistic details that I have discussed in an earlier publication are only briefly summarized here.[4] Furthermore, I shall refrain from addressing questions about textual strata or about intertextual connections to texts outside of the book of Deuteronomy proper.[5]

II. *Chapter 5 as Part of the Overall Narrative of Deuteronomy: The Tension between Fabula and Narrative Structure*

Deuteronomy is a narrative book. That narrative begins in Deuteronomy 1 at the point when Israel is preparing to cross the Jordan. Indeed, for the reader, this event is a fixed point in the familiar history of the people. This starting point is appropriate for a story that contains the constitutive elements of Deuteronomy and Joshua, if one ascribes the basic text of Deuteronomy 1–3 to a Josianic "Deuteronomistic conquest narrative." It is equally appropriate for a story that continues on until the exile, if one should read Deuteronomy 1–3 as the beginning of a unified composition called the "Deuteronomistic History." Finally, it is also a plausible opening for the book of Deuteronomy itself for contemporary readers of the Bible.

Even so, the narrator immediately abandons this starting point. He lets Moses speak and Moses looks back and narrates the history of the past thirty-eight years, which explains how the current situation came about. In other words, the original starting point of the narrative is immediately erased. The narrated story—in the form of a narrative within the narrative—begins still further in the past with the departure from Horeb, which is a rather unusual opening for the historical story line. It is unusual because, for instance, it must be *presupposed* that the reader knows what the word "Horeb" signifies.[6] For the original addressees, this presupposition may not have been self-evident,[7] but for readers of the Pentateuch in its

---

Hen 6 (1984) 1–14, appear viable to me when he argues that what follows 5:29–30 is secondary. The tefillin are not sufficient as textual witnesses to warrant such a postulation.

4. N. Lohfink, *Das Hauptgebot: Eine Untersuchung literarischer Einleitungsfragen zu Dtn 5–11* (AnBib 20; Rome: Pontifical Biblical Institute, 1963) 140–52. In that study, I avoided the term "narrative," as I applied this word primarily to the type of "narrative" that we find in the Tetrateuch and in the historical books. In a broader sense, however, Deuteronomy 5 should also be considered a "narrative."

5. I am thereby following up on my analysis of Moses' first address published in my article "Narrative Analyse von Dtn 1,6–3,29," in *Mincha: Festgabe für Rolf Rendtorff zum 75. Geburtstag* (ed. Erhard Blum; Neukirchen: Neukirchener, 2000) 121–76.

6. The narrator introduces this term already in 1:2.

7. This is true if the name "Horeb" (for Sinai) was a Deuteronomic invention. So L. Perlitt, e.g., "Sinai und Horeb," in *Beiträge zur Alttestamentlichen Theologie: Festschrift*

final form it does not pose too large of a problem, since the holy mountain, Sinai, was known to have been called "Horeb" in preceding books. So nothing is narrated here—not even by Moses—about Horeb or about the events that took place there. Moreover, even the exodus is referred to only *in obliquo*, in the context of the murmuring of the people (1:27), in Moses' denunciation of the people's murmuring (1:30), and in an allusion to the destruction of the Egyptians in the Sea of Reeds (2:14–15).[8] The narration proper concerns only the *departure* from Mount Horeb.

One might argue that this shows that, for Moses, what is *past* is no longer important, only what is *future*—the final destination, the land. This would explain why only the movement toward the land is narrated. But, regardless of that possibility, a story that begins in this way appears to be left hanging in mid-air. Or, alternatively, it seems based on external elements, which can only be known from other texts. As a result, the story lacks its own, comprehensive interpretation of and vision for the very foundation on which it is constructed. Such a situation raises narratological challenges, if not outright intellectual tensions.

This state of affairs is further intensified when, after 4:1, the law becomes the topic of discourse and when the Horeb events are necessarily brought into the discussion (4:10–14)[9]—as is inevitable with the topic of "law." Everything that appears later in Deuteronomy 5 is already mentioned here: the fire on the mountain, Israel at the foot of the mountain, the proclamation of the Decalogue, the tablets of the law, and God's commission of Moses to teach the חקים ומשפטים ("statutes and ordinances"). The more Moses engages the topics of law and covenant, the stranger it appears to the reader that the Horeb events were not represented in the narrative at the beginning of the book, and that the actual narrative commences *only after* these events. In accordance with these questions, which are almost systematically elicited by the book-narrator, Moses, after a short intervening report that serves an emphasizing function (4:41–43) as well as another introduction (4:44–5:1a), returns in 5:1 to the beginning of the book and shifts the beginning of the narrative back yet again. In Deuteronomy 5, Moses finally provides an extensive description of the Horeb events, which are further supplemented later in Deuteronomy 9.

---

für Walther Zimmerli zum 70. Geburtstag (ed. Herbert Donner, Robert Hanhart, and Rudolf Smend; Göttingen: Vandenhoeck, 1977) 302–22.
    8. See W. L. Moran, "The End of the Unholy War and the Anti-Exodus," *Bib* 44 (1963) 333–42.
    9. For a rhetorical-stylistic analysis of this text see, esp., G. Braulik, *Die Mittel deuteronomischer Rhetorik erhoben aus Dtn 4,1–40* (AnBib 68; Rome: Biblical Institute Press, 1978) 28–34.

Leaving aside 4:10–14 for the time being, it can be said that, stylistically-
speaking, we are dealing here with two, or better, three flashbacks. In the
narrated world (the *fabula*), the starting point of the story is moved back
twice. The narrator *begins* at the river Jordan and *then* has Moses refer back
to the departure from Horeb. Only after the gradually unfolding discourse
about law and covenant virtually requires it, does Moses make reference to
an *even more remote past*. Then, finally, Horeb becomes the point of departure for the story. The narrative in Deuteronomy will never reach farther
back than Horeb, thus making it something of a primeval or primordial
event. It is at Horeb that Israel's existence in the land finds its justification,
and it is therefore an appropriate beginning for the Deuteronomistic
History, which tells the story of a "Horeb-Israel."[10] In this sense, Deuteronomy 5 is much more than a minor narrative framework for the Decalogue. It is *the* foundational narrative of Deuteronomy—even of the entire
Deuteronomistic History.

Only in Deuteronomy 31 does it become fully clear why the appearance
of Horeb in the narrative is necessary. The reason is that leadership must
be transferred from Moses to Joshua. This transfer necessitates a covenant
renewal, and a new, objective ratification of the law. Moses' first speech
must extend all the way back to the departure from Horeb in order to explain why he must now be replaced by Joshua when Israel crosses the Jordan. The transfer of authority cannot take place without a new ratification
of covenant and law. But that, in turn, is not intelligible unless the Horeb
events are narrated. The very logic that necessitates the inclusion of Horeb
into the *fabula* is itself worked out by the narrative. This is the purpose behind the layering of voices (the narrator's and Moses') and of the various
narrative retrogressions that it renders possible.

Moses narrates the Horeb events in two stages: He *begins* (Deuteronomy 5) by showing that the Decalogue (the "Horeb-covenant" insofar as
it is a text) gives rise to the Torah (the law to be confirmed by oath in the
"Moab-covenant"). *Later* (Deuteronomy 9–10), he shows that even in the
very hour of its ratification, the Horeb covenant must be upheld by God
vis-à-vis Israel's apostasy. In Exodus 32–34, a new covenant is made by God

---

10. This idea is generally ignored in the currently-fashionable theory that knows of
only two (initially competing) origin myths for Israel: the ancestral myth and the exodus
myth. This theory generally includes Deuteronomy with the latter myth and therefore
has to view occurrences of the names of the patriarchs in Deuteronomy as later additions in the redaction of the Pentateuch. But, in reality, what Deuteronomy presents is
a third origin myth—the "Horeb-Israel" myth—and this already at an early point in the
development of the book. See N. Lohfink, *Die Väter Israels im Deuteronomium* (OBO 111;
Freiburg: Universitätsverlag / Göttingen: Vandenhoeck & Ruprecht, 1991).

while the people are still at Sinai, immediately after Israel's breaking of the covenant. It is thus no coincidence that there are implicit parallels in language between Exodus 34 and the "new covenant text" in Jeremiah 31.[11] The situation is quite different in Deuteronomy 9–10, however. The tablets are shattered, but there is no new text, only *new tablets* with *the old text*—the Decalogue. Even the Deuteronomic Torah is no "new" covenant text with respect to the Decalogue, but serves only as its explication. God is faithful to the Horeb covenant despite Israel's apostasy at the very moment of the primordial act itself. In a very real sense, then, the Torah in Deuteronomy is set from the start on top of the chasm of Israel's sin, with only God supporting it above this chasm.[12]

In 10:11, Yhwh issues a command to Moses, which parallels the command for departure in 1:6–8. The former is the commission of the leader, complementary to the latter, which was addressed to the entire people. Both commissions overlap also in their use of language:

Deut 10:11	*Deut 1:7–8*
. . . למסע . . .	פנו וסעו כלם . . .
ויבאו וירשו את־הארץ	באו ורשו את־הארץ
אשר־נשבעתי לאבתם	אשר נשבע יהוה לאבתיכם . . .
לתת להם	לתת לזרעם[13] אחריהם

This comparison shows that, in 10:11, Moses' narrative arrives at the point within the *fabula* where his narrative started in 1:6. Thus, although the two Horeb narratives in Deuteronomy 5 and 9–10 appear toward the end of the Deuteronomic narrative plot, within the *fabula* they immediately *precede* the material narrated by Moses at the beginning in Deuteronomy 1–3. This material connects seamlessly to what preceded in the *fabula*. The connection is intended to be noticed by the reader. Moses does not make any further references to past history after 10:11, which thereby closes the narrative circle. In short, Deuteronomy 5 recounts the *beginning of the book's story*. This fact underscores the importance of its content.

---

11. See C. Dohmen, "Der Sinaibund als Neuer Bund nach Ex 19–34," in *Der Neue Bund im Alten: Studien zur Bundestheologie der beiden Testamente* (ed. E. Zenger; QD 146; Freiburg: Herder, 1993) 51–83.

12. See N. Lohfink, "Der Neue Bund im Buch Deuteronomium?," *ZABR* 4 (1998) 100–125.

13. The MT's להם ו is secondary, a later adaptation to the Priestly expression. Cf. SamP. For a more extensive treatment, see Lohfink, *Die Väter Israels*, 28–30.

III. A Deed about Legal Acts:
The Genre Theory of the Book-Narrator

In Deuteronomy 5, as already in Deuteronomy 1–3, Moses recounts the past events that his audience has experienced. He explicitly negates the distinction present after Deuteronomy 1–3 between the exodus-generation, which has since died in the wilderness, and the generation of his present audience. According to Moses' account, those listening to him themselves stood at the foot of Horeb (5:3).[14] Once again, readers are expected—on the basis of the Tetrateuch (specifically, the book of Exodus)—to be familiar with the events discussed here. Here too, Moses' primary goal is clearly much more than the simple conveyance of information; it is quite clear—even more so than in Deuteronomy 1–3—that he has other, very specific plans. The book-narrator deals with this issue reflexively, primarily through a gradual change in his superscriptions:

- 1:1: "These are the words that Moses spoke to all Israel."[15] "All Israel" simply refers to the present audience. There is, at the very least, no mention of a formal or official assembly.
- 1:5: "Moses began [הואיל] to render effective [באר] this Torah [which can only refer to Deuteronomy 5–28] as follows." In other words, he did not recite it immediately nor did he write it down, but began with remote actions necessary to bestow it with legal force,[16] that is, to actually make a covenant (cf. Deut 28:69).
- 4:44: "This is the Torah that Moses set before the Israelites." Here a new element is introduced. "Set before" (שים + לפני) refers to a legal covenant offer. The object of this offer is the same Torah which was identified in 1:5, and for which the text will now be provided.
- 4:45: "These are the decrees [העדת], (that is to say) the statutes and ordinances [החקים והמשפטים]17 that Moses stated to the Israelites." The

---

14. One should not think that the present generation were infants at Horeb, since Moses identifies them as *covenant partners*, which can only refer to *adults*. We are dealing with a cultic identification of the generations.

15. Translations are my own.

16. I shall give the reasons for this interpretation of באר in another publication. For the best discussion up to this point, see L. Perlitt, *Deuteronomium* (BKAT V/1; Neukirchen-Vluyn: Neukirchener, 1990) 22–23. But I disagree with his conclusions.

17. Though the MT reads והחקים, the *waw* should be deleted. This is based upon SamP, which should be considered in comparison with the parallels in 5:31; 6:1, 20; 7:11. The reading is crucial as it concerns the question of whether the word introduces an apposition, or whether it continues a series of terms. I have discussed this question in greater detail elsewhere: see N. Lohfink, "Die *ḥuqqîm ûmišpāṭîm* im Buch Deuteronomium und ihre Neubegrenzung durch Dtn 12,1," in idem, *Studien zum Deuteronomium und zur deuteronomistischen Literatur II* (SBAB 12; Stuttgart: Katholisches Bibelwerk, 1991) 229–56, esp. 230.

Torah (i.e., instruction) is now circumscribed in the language of legislation.

* 5:1: "Moses convened all Israel." Aside from this passage, such a convocation is mentioned only in 29:2.[18] The terminology describes a formal assembly. If it should imply—on the *fabula* level—a continuation of the assembly in Deuteronomy 1–4, which is quite possible, the terminology explicitly designates the formal character of the convocation, which was not the case in 1:1.

By now, Moses has also provided a short recapitulation of the Horeb events (4:10–14) strategically embedded in the parenetic portion of his first speech, which—as suggested earlier—anticipates all the central elements of Deuteronomy 5, though without the direct address of Deuteronomy 5.[19] The two divine speeches of Deuteronomy 5 are referred to, but are not quoted; their content is only summarized (4:13, 14). On the other hand, Moses cites a divine speech that does not appear in Deuteronomy 5: the command to Moses to convoke an assembly, which was to set the Horeb events in motion (4:10). This quotation is followed by a narrative element—also lacking in Deuteronomy 5—a remark about Israel assembling together (4:11).

Moses pursues very clear rhetorical goals with his proleptic summaries of the Horeb theophany. At a later stage of his parenesis (in 4:15, 36), he will revisit those elements which differ from the later narrative—the fire from which God spoke was blazing up into the heavens (4:11) and no form was to be seen (4:12). However, even though he considers such distinctions to be significant, Moses nevertheless also provides an outline of the subsequent full narrative and identifies its constitutive elements: the Decalogue, which represents a covenant founded by God (4:13), and the commission to Moses to teach Israel חקים ומשפטים (4:14). Both of these items fall in the sphere of legal discourse.

Unlike 1:6, Deuteronomy 5 specifically identifies Moses' rhetorical aim in the very first sentence. In 1:6, Moses launched immediately into his narration:

---

18. For the significance of this overlap in formulation for the *fabula* of Deuteronomy, see N. Lohfink, "Zur Fabel des Deuteronomiums," in *Bundesdokument und Gesetz: Studien zum Deuteronomium* (ed. G. Braulik; Herders biblische Studien 4; Freiburg: Herder, 1995) 65–78, esp. 67–71; and idem, "Bund als Vertrag im Deuteronomium," *ZAW* 107 (1995) 215–39, esp. 229–31.

19. For a comparison of the two accounts of the Horeb events, see D. Knapp, *Deuteronomium 4: Literarische Analyse und theologische Interpretation* (Göttinger theologische Arbeiten 35; Göttingen: Vandenhoeck, 1987) 57–62. Knapp's reading is diachronically oriented and primarily discusses similarities and dissimilarities between Deuteronomy 4 and 5. He also presupposes a reconstructed, early version of Deuteronomy 5, which comprises only a portion of the present text.

The LORD our God spoke to us at Horeb, saying . . .

In 5:1, Moses begins with a call to listen, an apostrophe, a topical summary, and a description of the legislative situation, before parenetically expanding his call to listen:

> Hear, O Israel,
>> the statutes and ordinances [את־החקים ואת־המשפטים]
>> that I am formally presenting you today in view of your
>>> acceptance;[20]
> you shall learn them by heart
> and pay heed to observe them. (5:1)

Moses thus carries out the command that he mentioned in passing in 4:14. In Deuteronomy 5, he is already beginning to teach the חקים ומשפטים, although it quickly becomes clear that the חקים ומשפטים in their actual wording will commence only in 12:1.[21] After this detailed outline of what he is about to do in the next 22 chapters, Moses can begin a narration, although after such an introduction it is somewhat surprising that there is narration (and not legislation proper) at all.

Given this state of affairs, one almost wishes that Moses would have made a statement to this effect: "I shall quickly review the historical context from which the חקים ומשפטים are derived." Instead, he proceeds in a stylistically more elegant fashion. He presupposes that the reader has read the preceding chapters, and therefore begins his narrative in a manner parallel to his first narration:

לאמר   בחרב   יהוה אלהינו דבר אלינו   1:6

יהוה אלהינו כרת עמנו ברית בחרב (5:5) לאמר   5:2

This parallelism is reinforced, as the reader will later discover, by the fact that these passages are the only two divine words among all the lengthy speeches in the book of Deuteronomy, which God, according to Moses, addresses to *all of Israel*. Elsewhere God only speaks to him alone, which demonstrates clearly that 5:2, as 1:6 in the beginning of the book, introduces a narrative.

Furthermore, the parallelism with 1:6 via the keyword "Horeb" also indicates the exact point in time to which the reader has to return. Since God's work at Horeb is identified (the making of a covenant), we are no longer simply dealing with a physical departure from a geographic locale. A short preview of what is to follow next was already given by Moses in 4:10–14.

---

20. On the significance of the terminology used here (literally: "that I am speaking in your ears today"), see Lohfink, *Das Hauptgebot*, 274–75.

21. See Lohfink, "ḥuqqîm ûmišpāṭîm," 244–48.

One can therefore expect that the subsequent narrative will be oriented toward legal matters. This is reinforced by the introductory sentence (5:1) that announces חקים ומשפטים. But, in legal discourse, narrative is specially suited for a particular genre: that of legal deed. Should one expect something of this kind to follow?

If one anticipates this type of genre, one should expect a thematically-organized narrative structure, as was the case in the sequence of proleptic references in 4:10–14. One might also expect a certain ancient Near Eastern style of legal record that summarizes positions and statements in "quotations" (*Sprechurkunden*). Such short speech summaries in the form of quotations were already seen to be characteristic of the narrative style of Deuteronomy 1–3.

IV. Two Scenes:
The Narrative Structure of Deuteronomy 5

The narrative that is Deuteronomy 5 is framed, as mentioned earlier, by two direct addresses to the assembly (see 5:1 and 5:32–6:3). A shared key-term in both of these addresses is the double expression חקים ומשפטים (5:1 and 6:1), which is preceded by the call to listen שמע ישראל (5:1)—alluded to in 6:3 and serving as a new introduction in 6:4. The following analysis focuses only on the framed narrative, which consists of two distinct parts:

1. 5:2–22   Proclamation of the Decalogue in a Theophany at Horeb
2. 5:23–31   Installation of Moses as mediator of the law

A closer analysis yields the following outline.[22]

1	Frame: Introductory Parenesis
	Scene I: Proclamation of the Decalogue
2–5	*Introduction to* Speech
6–21	Cited Words of God: The Decalogue
22	Concluding Notes
	Scene II: Installation of Moses as Mediator of the Law
23	*Introduction to* Speech
24–27	Cited Speech: Request of the People's Representatives
28a	*Introduction to* Speech
28b–31	Cited Response by God: Installation of Moses
5:32–6:3	Frame and Parenetic Continuation

---

22. For an outline in rather juridical terms, see Lohfink, *Das Hauptgebot*, 143–44.

Part I is introduced by a proleptic summary, a virtual title or heading.

> The LORD our God made a covenant with us at Horeb. (5:2)

Strictly speaking, this is *an introduction to direct speech*, since the sentence ends in 5:5 with לאמר. Inserted are parenthetical remarks that explicate the meaning of "with us" (5:3) and that suggest the contextual setting of the events (5:4–5), even describing the role of Moses (5:5a). In doing so, 5:4–5 splits the "us" of 5:3 into a "you" (5:4) and an "I" (5:5). In 5:5b the explanation then returns to the "you."[23] This split is deliberate, although it represents a rather unusual narrative style: On the one hand, the narrator hurries with full force towards the Decalogue, but, on the other, allows some details to emerge in passing and thus manages to outline the entire scenario.[24] Be that as it may, everything hinges on the Decalogue, which is cited in 5:6–21. We may note a certain tension between the narrative's tendency to represent events and the tendency of legal discourse to cite texts.

For the reader of the book of Deuteronomy in its present form, the introduction in Deuteronomy 5 is all the more conspicuous, since even the brief summary of the Horeb-events in 4:10–14 followed a more normal narrative structure: God issued a call for the people to assemble at the mountain, God provided an explanation for the call, and the people followed God's call (4:10–11). Furthermore, the description of the theophany in 4:11 was more complete than in 5:4–5:

> the mountain was blazing up, with fire into the heart of the heaven, darkness, cloud and gloominess. (4:11b)

But it is precisely the comparison of these two texts that demonstrates how differently Deuteronomy 5 introduces the Horeb-events. The recounting of the event in Deuteronomy 5 proceeds hurriedly towards the citation of the Decalogue. The end of Scene I (5:22) marks a formal completion of the scene. It is set apart from the Decalogue by the reflexive expression "these words," after which the entire scene is summarized—with even more detail

---

23. In the explanation of the Mosaic role of mediation, the place of YHWH's speech (בהר מתוך האש; "at the mountain, out of the fire") is also split into two short sentences in a chiasm which frames the statement regarding Moses: "you were afraid מפני האש" ("because of the fire") and "you did not go up בהר" ("the mountain").

24. This narrative style has the further effect that key terms appear repeatedly at the beginning of a sentence. What results is that the verb appears, according to syntactical rules, in the *qāṭal*, not the *wayyiqṭōl*, form. At the end of Scene I, we then find two verbs in the *wayyiqṭōl* form (5:22b). Brekelmans, "Deuteronomy 5," 169, does not recognize the true reason for these different verb forms.

than at the beginning of the scene—and one last piece of information is added: the production and distribution of the stone tablets.[25]

Scene II begins with a temporal clause (-ויהי כ), which picks up key elements from the preceding scene and connects them to the new scene (5:23a). There are two speeches: the pleading of the people with Moses (5:24–27) and a positive response to their plea, which is given, not by Moses, but by God (5:28b–31). The replacement of the expected response by Moses with a word from God dissolves the scenic compactness. Only Moses hears the words of God. Moses insinuates that God does not even leave him enough time to respond himself, since God intervenes while the people are still speaking to him:

> The LORD heard how you were loudly speaking to me, and the LORD said to me. . . . (5:28)[26]

How and where God spoke to Moses remains open. Only the content of the divine speech is important (5:28b–31).

God's answer at the end suggests the closing of the scene but also the inclusion of another, subsequent scene—one that is *not* subsequently narrated. Moses is to send the people back to their tents (5:30) and to meet God alone in order to receive the חקים ומשפטים, which, according to 5:1, he is about to set before Israel. There is no explicit indication that Moses executed the divine commands; it goes without saying that he has done so. The quotation of the divine speech leads, not to narrative enactment, then, but directly into a parenetic address[27] that, in itself, has a very solemn

---

25. Considering the legal character of the text, it remains an open question if, as far as the *fabula* is concerned, the written production and the handing over of the tablets was carried out immediately at the end of the proclamation of the Decalogue. Deuteronomy 9:9–11, at least, clarify that the delivery took place after Moses' forty-day stay on the mountain. Deuteronomy 5:22 therefore anticipates the narrative. Sonnet, *Book within the Book*, 45, maintains that this does not refer to the inscription of the tablets and cites 4:13 and 5:22 in support. I am unconvinced by this argument, since 5:22 also speaks of the delivery of the tablets. The *fabula* remains ambiguous with regard to the inscription; the possibility of a proleptic remark cannot be excluded.

26. Readers will take note of this, especially if they keep the corresponding scene in Exod 20:18–21 in mind. In that text, Moses himself responds to the people, while comments about the people's absence and Moses' approaching the cloud constitute the closing of the scene.

27. It remains open to debate whether Moses has already reported what he is about to recite here during the stay at mount Horeb, or whether he has kept it in his heart for the past forty years. The latter is perhaps the more immediate understanding, but the text is ambiguous on this matter. It is equally possible that a reader of the Pentateuch, remembering the Book of the Covenant in Exodus 20–23, would assume the former reading. If this is the case, one is required to see the Book of the Covenant as a variation

palindromic structure (5:32–6:3).[28] Moses begins by admonishing the people to observe the Decalogue (5:32–33).[29] Then, at the center of the structure (6:1) we find the anticipated title for what follows. Moses can now, finally, begin the recitation of the חקים ומשפטים that God has conveyed to him (6:1).

Both scenes in Deuteronomy 5 are intrinsically "showing" rather than "telling," but in both parts there are elements that prevent Moses from providing a full scenic deployment. At the beginning, he is driven by haste to get to the divine word, the Decalogue. Haste also drives him to the second scene, which he subsequently neglects to continue narrating as soon as the divine word has legitimized his subsequent proclamation of the law. Thus, from a narratological perspective, we get here a characterization of Moses. It shows indirectly, but also quite clearly, that he no longer wishes to narrate. He is pressed to proclaim the law and narrates only because and only as long as it is necessary to legitimate his actions. The genre of the chapter is thus clear: It deals with the conveyance of legally-oriented divine words, almost as if proceedings edited at Horeb were read and reviewed. The style of Moses' narration thus confirms what the introductions by the book-narrator have already suggested.

V. The "Assembly":
The Conjunction of the Two Scenes

Both scenes are artfully joined together by Israel's experience of the theophany. As already mentioned earlier, the theophany scene was at first portrayed with fairly broad brush-strokes (5:4, 5b). At the conclusion of the scene, it is enriched by new elements—the cloud and the darkness, and then by the divine voice/thunder (5:22):

			בהר מתוך האש	5:4
			מפני האש / בהר	5:5
קול גדול	הענן והערפל	בהר מתוך האש		5:22

---

in form and content from the Deuteronomic law. Such a reading is not simple, but it is also not so farfetched for a genetic consideration (see most recently Sonnet, *Book within the Book*, 46–48). Perhaps it is precisely this idea that is suggested here and possibly also insinuated in 1:18.

28. For a more detailed analysis, see Lohfink, *Das Hauptgebot*, 66–68.

29. It is often erroneously supposed that the reference is immediately to the Deuteronomic laws. S. R. Driver, *A Critical and Exegetical Commentary on Deuteronomy* (3d ed.; ICC; Edinburgh: T. & T. Clark, 1902) 88, concludes on the basis of the perfect form of צוה, that these laws had already been proclaimed to the people at Horeb. For a comprehensive discussion of the reference to the Decalogue, see G. Braulik, "Die Ausdrücke für 'Gesetz' im Buch Deuteronomium," in idem, *Studien zur Theologie des Deuteronomiums* (SBAB 2; Stuttgart: Katholisches Bibelwerk, 1988) 11–38.

The closing frame resumes the imagery of the introductory frame, without, however, preserving its brevity. This later expansion is deliberate, and the supplemented elements are instantly utilized. The beginning of the second scene connects itself to the end of the first scene, as the more complete description of the theophany in 5:22 is immediately picked up in chiastic fashion by 5:23, which constitutes the basis for the development of Scene II. The parallels are almost identical in vocabulary with only two exceptions. In 5:23, מתוך ("out of") refers, not to fire (האש), but to the darkness (החשך); and הענן והערפל ("the cloud, and the thick darkness") is replaced by החשך ("the darkness") probably in accordance with the first change. Darkness is in the depth of the fire. This results in the following structure:

5:22	בהר מתוך האש הענן והערפל קול גדול
5:23	כשמעכם את־הקול מתוך החשך וההר בער באש

Thus, it is not the content of the Decalogue, but rather the theophany experience (cf. 5:5b) that precipitates the second scene, although there is certainly reference to God's words. From the terror of the theophany emerges a strong desire—namely, that further speeches by God should come from a greater distance.[30]

This chiastic structure, which provides both cohesion and emphasis, encompasses yet another element by means of Moses' address to "Israel," which is characterized anew at this transitional point. The name "Israel" occurred in the introduction: "Hear, O Israel" (5:1); from v. 4 on, Moses uses

30. In the plea to Moses, after כבודו ("his glory"), which occurs only once in Deuteronomy, two elements of this description of the theophany are picked up. These elements carry the plea through three sequential verses by means of a three-fold repetition, each chiastically structured:

5:24	קול מתוך האש
5:25	האש הגדולה קול
5:26	קול מתוך האש

A comprehensive analysis of the motif of speaking from the midst of the fire is found in J. Wilson, *Out of the Midst of the Fire: Divine Presence in Deuteronomy* (SBLDS 151; Atlanta: Scholars, 1995) 54–81.

the second person address "you." In the conclusion to this scene, however, he speaks about the words that YHWH has spoken to "your [plural] entire assembly" (5:22: אל־כל־קהלכם)—not, that is, simply to "us" or to "you" (plural). It is perhaps precisely by God's addressing the people directly and so creating a covenant that Israel *becomes* a קהל, an assembly.[31] The term "assembly" (קהל) is certainly used deliberately,[32] since it is hereafter used throughout Deuteronomy to describe the Decalogue-theophany, which is referred to as having taken place at the יום־הקהל ("the day of the assembly").

In 5:22, the exact reference is to כל־קהלכם ("your whole assembly"). I have argued elsewhere that the expression כל־קהל ישראל in Deuteronomistic literature (and in the Chronicler's History) does not refer to a plenary assembly of all Israel, but rather designates a specific institution, which one could describe as a council of the elders of all Israel.[33] Whether such an institution actually existed at any point in Israel's history is an open question, but the Deuteronomistic History refers to such an institution and gives it this name. If this is correct, the same institution could be referred to in 5:22 by its grammatically-contextualized form כל־קהלכם. If so, it was not the entire people who heard the words of the Decalogue, but only Israel's *council of elders*. This is, perhaps, rather unlikely if only because instead of כל־קהלכם—a phrase that occurs nowhere else in the Old Testament—a more precise identification by the exact name would have been possible.

It is thus more probable that Israel as such was perfectly constituted only through the Horeb covenant. Only by this event did it *become* a קהל *in the exact sense of the word.* This קהל then had its own official representation, namely a *council of elders*. If so, the word קהל is used in 5:22 in order to evoke an association with the elders of Israel in 5:23. At the end of 5:23, in the passage that corresponds to 5:22 within the symmetrical structure of the text, it is not the entire assembly that approaches Moses, but rather "all the authorities of your tribes and your elders" (כל־ראשי שבטיכם וזקניכם; 5:23).[34] Thus, Horeb marks not only the origin of Israel as a קהל, but also of Israel's

---

31. The LXX translates קהל here with συναγωγή, as it does generally in Genesis–Numbers, though that term is found only once more in Deuteronomy (33:4: συναγωγαῖς Ιακωβ for קלהת יעקב). Elsewhere in Deuteronomy and in the later books, the usual term is ἐκκλησία.

32. The verb of 4:10 already points to this.

33. N. Lohfink, "Zur Fabel in Dtn 31–32," in *Konsequente Traditionsgeschichte: Festschrift für Klaus Baltzer zum 65. Geburtstag* (ed. Rüdiger Bartelmus, Thomas Krüger, and Helmut Utzschneider; OBO 126; Freiburg Schweiz: Universitätsverlag / Göttingen: Vandenhoeck, 1993) 255–79, esp. 275–78.

34. Note the following attestations of both expressions in Deuteronomy:

• ראשי שבטיכם—1:15; 5:23; 29:10. There are text-critical problems in 1:15 and 29:10,

representative body—the כל־קהל ישראל—which, although it does not yet bear this name, is already recognizable through its functioning members. The relation of Moses to the כל־קהל ישראל, then, is just the same as Moses' relation to the entire people earlier in 5:5.

Perhaps the double expression "all the authorities of your tribes and your elders" in 5:23 is pleonastic. The tribal authorities *are* perhaps the "elders of Israel." If this is correct, it could even be only a twelve-member council. More likely, the "elders" are a larger group of important figures. Important for the purposes of the narrative is the fact that the plea to Moses was not voiced by a vast assembly, *but by an authorized body of representatives*. It is this group that is responsible for Moses' commission by God as transmitter of the Torah, and this group will reenter the picture at the closing of the covenant in 27:9–10.

The experience of the theophany is again the subject of the representatives' speech in 5:24. The contrast between the two parts of this chapter as well as their connection point is therefore quite clear.

This connection to 5:22 is also maintained throughout the book, since the phrase יום הקהל is used in all its occurrences within Deuteronomy to refer to the Horeb theophany and the installation of Moses as mediator.[35] So much for the obvious terminological cross-references; more allusive intertextual relations are identified differently and are discussed below. Suffice it to say here that all events narrated in Deuteronomy 5, of both scenes, are later identified on the basis of the transition from the first scene to the second.

VI. Request and Acceptance:
Inner-Deuteronomic Intertextuality I

As I've already indicated, the reader who reads the opening of the Horeb narrative in 5:2 is reminded of the opening of Moses' first speech in 1:6. Furthermore, the Decalogue now introduced is a divine word that is addressed to all of Israel; again, such a situation is only found once earlier, in 1:6–8. In this light, one suspects that Deuteronomy 5 may contain other

---

but 1:13–15 does deal with the installation of tribal authorities, even if the *terminus technicus* is secondary.

• זקנים—5:23; 27:1; 29:10; 31:9; 31:28 (the last has כל־זקני שבטיכם). The "city-elders" are not considered in this list. In the Deuteronomic portrayal of the covenant in Moab, the "elders" of 5:23; 27:1 and 31:9 are one and the same group. See Lohfink, "Bund als Vertrag," 233–37.

35. See 9:10 and 10:4 (at the beginning and end of the second Horeb narrative); and 18:16 (legitimation of future prophecy in Israel). All three passages also make use of other vocabulary characteristic of Deuteronomy 5.

intertextual connections with Moses' first speech, and that suspicion is confirmed.

The beginning of the second scene of Deuteronomy 5 corresponds almost word-for-word to the event that prompted the spy-story.[36] After Israel's arrival at Kadesh-Barnea, Moses resumes the divine words of 1:6–8, after which the Israelites make a proposal of how to proceed next. The same pattern follows immediately after the proclamation of the Decalogue by Yhwh. The two texts correspond closely to each other:

ותאמרו	כלכם	ותקרבון אלי	1:22
ותאמרו כל־ראשי שבטיכם וזקניכם		ותקרבון אלי	5:23–24

The two proposals differ in content, but the response is the same. In each case, the suggestion is met with approval and with the same response. In the former, the response is approval by Moses, which he himself reports; in the second, it is approval by Yhwh, who is directly quoted by Moses.

הדבר	וייטב בעיני	1:23
כל־אשר דברו	היטיבו	5:28

Of course it makes a rather large difference whether it is Moses or God who gives the approval. God also responds in the story of the spies sent to scout out the land, albeit at a later time (1:34). We can thus compare God's responses to the two situations in chapters 1 and 5. In both passages, God's reaction is introduced with the same wording: Yhwh has heard what the people demand:

לאמר	ויקצף וישבע	וישמע יהוה את־קול דבריכם	1:34
ויאמר יהוה אלי...		וישמע יהוה את־קול דבריכם	5:28

The instances of approval by Moses and by God occur at different points within the sequence of events, with the divine word constituting the closing of the event in each case. The following table demonstrates the succession of events:

Yhwh's word to Israel	*Yhwh's word to Israel*
Proposal by Israel of how to proceed	*Proposal by Israel of how to proceed*
Approval by Moses	
Spies: Departure and Return	

---

36. This parallel has a precedent in 1:9–18, where the first Yhwh-speech (1:6–8) is followed by a proposition by Moses to the people (1:9–13) that is favorably received (1:14: טוב הדבר). Moses then carries out the proposition, in effect rehearsing the pattern.

Israel's sin	
Moses' intervention: futile	
Y̨ʜᴡʜ *hears*	Y̨ʜᴡʜ *hears*
Yʜᴡʜ's wrath	**Approval by Yʜᴡʜ**
Yʜᴡʜ rescinds everything	**Yʜᴡʜ approves everything**
Moses must die	(Moses is successful)

The astute reader of Deuteronomy 5 is bound to notice the parallels between the two chains of events and may very well deduce that things went badly in Deuteronomy 1 because Moses responded on his own accord without waiting for God's reaction. Perhaps it is even significant that the people themselves (1:22: "all of you"), rather than their legitimate representatives (5:23: "tribal authorities and elders"), approach Moses.[37] In Deuteronomy 1, it is the convergence of a general popular opinion and the consent too easily given by the leader that leads to sin, which Moses is then unable to contain. But, in Deuteronomy 5, the plea of qualified representatives, on the one hand, and the restraint of the people's leader with regard to God's own reaction, on the other, leads to a positive outcome. Did Israel and Moses learn from the past? It is precisely at this point that the reader must also recognize an element of irony. For if one were to pose such a question, one would have fallen victim to the temporal shift in the narrative structure, since the events of Horeb (that is, Deuteronomy 5) occur *prior* to the events of the spies (that is, Deuteronomy 1) on the level of the *fabula*. Thus, Israel and Moses behaved correctly at Horeb, and it is thus all the more poignant that they make the wrong choice in a structurally-identical situation, when the conquest of the land is at hand. How is this possible? This question persists, but is answered in Deuteronomy 9–10, where it becomes clear that Israel had, in fact, already fallen into sin while Moses was with God on the mountain.

Hence, the suggestion that Moses should function as the people's mediator is by no means only or simply the result of a commendable "fear of God" on the people's part, but is shown later in the book to be an example of the people's tendency towards apostasy. In the spy story, Israel reinterpreted God's command to depart from Horeb, and turned it into a command that led to failure. And this is not the first time. Already once before Israel had turned a command—the first commandment of the Decalogue—into its opposite, and worshiped a golden calf instead of God.[38] We

---

37. This idea is, however, quite uncertain. See Lohfink, "Narrative Analyse," 169.

38. Another minute difference in Deuteronomy 5 also indicates that the people's reaction is not as it should be. Israel requests that Moses alone should hear and then "tell"

must therefore once again invert the sequence of events in the *fabula*. Since Israel had already broken the covenant at Horeb, they continue to mistrust God in the wilderness. This idea, which is specifically expressed in 9:22–24,[39] is the reason why the Horeb story in Deuteronomy 9–10 was included in the central parenetic section. This is explained by 9:7–8, which is to be read in light of 9:22–24, and it once again supports the idea that Deuteronomy 9–10 brings the Mosaic narrative circle to a close.

VII. "Fear": Inner-Deuteronomic Intertextuality II

There are several other intertextual connections between Deuteronomy 5 and the rest of the book. There is a broad narrative continuation in Deuteronomy 9–10 of the subjects of sin, intercession, and forgiveness. Later, within the laws themselves, the law about prophecy suddenly refers back to Deuteronomy 5, repeating its narrative in a way that Israel's prophets are also legitimated by the Horeb events (18:16–20). The discovery by commentators that the Deuteronomic laws not only implement statutes related to the Decalogue (5:31, cf. 4:5, 10, 14; 6:1; 12:1),[40] but also are arranged according to the sequence of the Decalogue, reaffirms the close connection between the two scenes in Deuteronomy 5. Of course this is not explicitly said in Deuteronomy 5,[41] unless the double expression חקים ומשפטים points to this idea, as I have suggested elsewhere.[42]

Rather than exploring that idea further here, I would like to point to a more subtle and yet important intertextual trajectory of Deuteronomy 5 based on the verb ירא, "to fear." This word occurs only twice in Deuteronomy 5, at the beginning and again at the conclusion of the two scenes taken together (5:5, 29). So it belongs to the framework that links the two

---

(דבר) Israel the words of God (5:27). God grants this request, but with the charge that Moses "teach" (למד) his laws to the people of Israel (5:31). See Sonnet, *Book within the Book*, 47.

39. For a closer analysis of the "theology of justification" in the wilderness passages around Deuteronomy 8, see R. Gomes de Araújo, *Theologie der Wüste im Deuteronomium* (ÖBS 17; Frankfurt: Lang, 1999) 115–271.

40. On the importance of the "land" as purview of the laws see Lohfink, "*ḥuqqîm ûmišpāṭîm*."

41. See, above all, G. Braulik, *Die deuteronomischen Gesetze und der Dekalog: Studien zum Aufbau von Deuteronomium 12–26* (SBS 145; Stuttgart: Katholisches Bibelwerk, 1991); and, further, N. Lohfink, "Kennt das Alte Testament einen Unterschied von 'Gebot' und 'Gesetz'?: Zur bibeltheologischen Einstufung des Dekalogs," in idem, *Studien zur biblischen Theologie* (SBAB 16; Stuttgart: Katholisches Bibelwerk, 1993) 206–38.

42. Lohfink, "*ḥuqqîm ûmišpāṭîm*," 231–40; idem, *Höre, Israel! Auslegung von Texten aus dem Buch Deuteronomium* (Welt der Bibel 18; Düsseldorf: Patmos, 1965) 70–71.

scenes. According to 5:5 (in the introduction to the first scene), the Israelites did not ascend the mountain, for they "*were afraid* because of the fire." That same fear—though the word is not specifically mentioned—leads to the request for Moses to serve as mediator. Fear is the justification for this request in a very concrete way. It is fear for one's own life or fear of death, which lurks in the divine fire, as the following texts indicate:

> 5:24: "that a God may speak to someone and the person may still *live*."
> 5:25: "why should we *die*? . . . we shall *die*."
> 5:26: "the voice of the *living* God speaking out of fire . . . and remained *alive*?"

Everything revolves around the motifs of "life" and "death." In responding, God interprets this fear *positively*, as a genuine and commendable "fear" of God.

> 5:29: "If only they had such a mind as this, to fear me and to keep all my commandments [i.e., the Decalogue] always. . . ."

We may initially see this explanation of deep fear being equated with obedience to the commandments as a reinterpretation, but perhaps that is mistaken. Perhaps the point, instead, is to infuse the blunt and dull expression of that period, "fear of God," with a new and terrifying experience.

Deuteronomy 4 has already identified the infusion of "fear" as the purpose of the Horeb events (4:10). With a view toward the future, the fear that was awakened in Israel at Horeb was to persist throughout the generations. The parenesis that follows the Horeb story incorporates the motif of "fear" into its framework (see 6:2, 13, 24).[43] After chapter 7, it moves to the background, but after the second Horeb narrative, it reemerges in chapter 10 (10:12, 20; see also 10:17, 21). The word "fear" is thus an evocative term associated with the Horeb experience and the resulting relationship of Israel to God. The expression "fear of God," known throughout the ancient Near East—which is in itself no more "loaded" than our own concepts of "religion" or "faith"—took on, therefore, a very specific meaning for Israel, which is directly based on the Horeb theophany. This association has two distinct implications.

1. References to the fear of God establish a connection between *cultic gatherings* and the original events at Horeb. Most important in this regard is the commandment to recite the Torah every Sabbath year before all of

---

43. On this element, which joins Deuteronomy 5 and 6, see Lohfink, *Das Hauptgebot*, 76 and 158.

Israel at the feast of tabernacles (31:9–13). In a solemn assembly of all Israel, the people's experience of Horeb is to be regained through the reading of the Torah. A central element here is again the fear of God (31:13).[44] The same formulations also appear, albeit in more concise form, in the important centralization law of annual tithing (14:22–27). The tithe is to be brought to the sanctuary, where it is consumed by all Israel in a great feast. Here too the experience of fear at Horeb is to be revived (14:23). This feast probably took place during the celebration of tabernacles,[45] which was combined with a public recitation of the Torah every seven years (31:9–13). A ritual banquet, which is not mentioned in Deuteronomy 5, thus reestablishes the basic atmosphere of Deuteronomy 5. The same atmosphere must also be reestablished on a daily basis for Israel's king (17:14–20), who is to live under the shadow of Horeb at all times. For this reason he is required to read the Torah every day, so that the fear of God may be awakened in him (17:19). Of interest is the difference of the king's law to the law about prophecy in Deuteronomy 18, in which there is a narrative reference back to the "day of assembly" but without a mention of the word "fear" (18:16). The prophet is thereby included, so to speak, within the succession of Moses, whereas the king belongs to the people to which Moses mediates the Torah.

2. But the term ירא does not only describe the high-points and the center of Israel's existence; it also points to its low points and to its margins. The so-called בערת-laws (literally, "purgation laws") are characterized by the בערת-formula: "So you shall purge the evil from your midst" (or the like, frequently with elaborations). These laws always deal with crimes deserving death and always correspond to a Decalogue commandment, which has given rise to the theory that the Decalogue represents a list of crimes punishable by death in Israel.[46] Below is a table of these laws, in which the last

---

44. N. Lohfink, "Glauben lernen in Israel," *KatBl* 108 (1983) 84–99; now revised in idem, *Das Jüdische am Christentum* (Freiburg: Herder, 1987) 144–66 ("Der Glaube und die nächste Generation"). The motif of "learning," which is associated with "fear" in all of these passages, is examined by G. Braulik in "Deuteronomy and the Commemorative Culture of Israel: Redactio-Historical Observations on the Use of למד," in idem, *The Theology of Deuteronomy: Collected Essays of Georg Braulik, O.S.B.* (trans. Ulrika Lindblad; North Richland Hills, Tex.: BIBAL, 1994) 183–98.

45. G. Braulik, "Von der Lust Israels vor seinem Gott: Warum Kirche aus dem Fest lebt," in *Den Himmel offen halten: Ein Plädoyer für Kirchenentwicklung in Europa: Festschrift für Paul M. Zulehner* (ed. Isidor Baumgartner, Christian Fiesl, and Andras Mate-Toth; Innsbruck: Tyrolia, 2000) 92–112, esp. 100.

46. N. Lohfink, "Die Zehn Gebote ohne den Berg Sinai," in idem, *Bibelauslegung im Wandel: Ein Exeget ortet seine Wissenschaft* (Frankfurt: Knecht, 1967) 129–57. Of fundamental importance is the study by J. L'Hour, "Une legislation criminelle dans le Deutéronome," *Bib* 44 (1963) 1–28. According to L'Hour (pp. 9–14), the second and third law in Deuteronomy 13 also belong to this group of laws, although the verb בער is missing in

column lists the corresponding commandment in the Decalogue.[47] The cases to be considered here are in bold type.

13:1–5	A prophet preaches apostasy from Yhwh	I
13:6–11	**Family members or friends secretly entice people to apostasy**	**I**
13:12–18	A city in Israel commits apostasy from Yhwh	I
17:2–7	Someone worships the host of heaven	I
17:8–13	**Rejection of a decision by the central court**	**V and VII**
19:11–13	Murder	V
19:16–21	**False Witness**	**VIII**
21:1–9	Murder of and by an unknown person	V
21:18–21	**An obstinate and defiant son**	**IV**
22:13–21	A woman who entered marriage without being a virgin	VI
22:22	Adultery	VI
22:23–24	Intercourse with one engaged to another	VI
24:7	Kidnapping	VII

In each of the four בערת-laws emphasized here,[48] we find an expansion of the בערת-formula that involves the motif of "fear." The news of the execution of a Decalogue-transgressor functions to install new fear in Israel. There can be no doubt that the connection to Israel's fear of death, experienced during the Horeb theophany, is deliberate. In two of these passages "all Israel" is referred to; in a third, "the entire people."

The laws regulating capital punishment represent the boundary of Israel's social order. It is here, where social cohesion is endangered, that the memory of the Horeb events, narrated in Deuteronomy 5, returns.

In this way, the narrative of Deuteronomy 5 weaves its way through the entire book. The society envisioned here finds here the positive center of its experience in the feast, as well as the place where its very existence is threatened in crimes punishable by death.[49]

---

them. I would not go so far as to suggest that it should be reconstructed hypothetically. All three laws constitute a unified group, and thus do not always need to contain every element of the formula.

47. Numeration of the Decalogue follows Roman Catholic practice.

48. Each of these laws belongs to a different group of laws. The elements relevant for our purposes are therefore found once in each group of laws up to chapter 21. This pattern does not continue after chapter 22.

49. The essay was translated by Armin Siedlecki. My thanks go to him and to the editors for their help bringing the essay into English. I would also like to thank Georg Braulik and Dieter Böhler for their critical review of the manuscript.

The Travail of Pardon:
Reflections on slḥ

Walter Brueggemann

———————◆———————

I. Introduction

The book of Deuteronomy offers the normative statement of covenantal theology in ancient Israel. In that covenantal theology, deriving from Moses but situated a long time later, Israel is set in a Torah-relation of command and obedience. That relationship of command and obedience, moreover, carries with it non-negotiable sanctions, so that the rhetoric of "if . . . then" is definitional for this presentation of faith.

The rigorous requirements of Torah obedience are indeed doable (Deut 30:11–14). However, in the life of Israel, the doable is in actuality not done, at least according to the Deuteronomistic History. Here, the not-done Torah evokes the negative sanctions of curse, causing the destruction of Jerusalem, the dislocation of many of the faithful, and the eventual exilic situation of the sixth century. This sequence of negativities, in the purview of Deuteronomy, is fully explained and justified in terms of covenant requirements, failures, and sanctions. Such a construal of lived experience is clear enough and fully understandable.

And yet, given the air-tight logic of covenant, the most important question remains—namely, what next? The future of Israel with its God depends upon reentry into the covenant. That reentry is to be premised on "repentance" whereby Israel, now failed, re-engages the commandments of covenant. That notion of repentance is clear enough and fits the uncompromising expectation of the Torah. But in this paper I want to push beyond the return of repentance, to see if initiative from God's side—forgiveness—is a working theme in the covenant theology of exilic Israel. I

Author's note: I am glad to offer this paper to Patrick D. Miller in thanks for his scholarship that lives precisely at the interface of academy and church, and for his unfailing and generous kindness to me.

will consider specifically the term *slḥ* ("pardon") as a clue to the developing pastoral possibility for restoration in an alienated community that seems only partially able to undertake repentance. While the theme of "pardon" seems to move beyond the primary assumptions of the covenantal theology of Deuteronomy, I shall consider whether such a motif actually emerges from that covenant theology.

II. *Yhwh: A God Who Pardons*

It is notoriously difficult now to suggest an early dating for any text; we may begin, nonetheless, with the claim that Israel's oldest theological understanding of Yhwh includes a glad affirmation of a readiness and capacity to pardon. We may consider the creedal response to the violation of covenant in Exod 34:6–7 as a source for Israelite theology.[1] In that stylized assertion, Yhwh's capacity for pardon is explicit, even as it is crucial in context:

> The LORD, the LORD,
> a God merciful and gracious,
> slow to anger,
> and abounding in steadfast love and faithfulness,
> keeping steadfast love for the thousandth generation,
> forgiving iniquity and transgression and sin.

That readiness to pardon is deeply qualified by the provision of v. 7b, suggesting that pardon is not a facile matter for this God who takes covenant requirements seriously:

> Yet by no means clearing the guilty,
> but visiting the iniquity of the parents
> upon the children and the children's children,
> to the third and the fourth generations.

In the reuse and quotation of the text in Num 14:18, the same two-sided characterization of Yhwh is given.[2] In both cases, the confessional formulation of forgiveness is with the verb *nś'*. In both cases, Moses petitions Yhwh to "pardon" (*slḥ*) the iniquity of the people (Exod 34:9; Num 14:19). In Exod 34:10, Yhwh's response to the petition to pardon is to provide a new covenant; in Num 14:20–23, Yhwh's response is a readiness to pardon, but with deep and brutal qualification. "Pardon" is thus one of Yhwh's

---

1. On this text, see Walter Brueggemann, *Theology of the Old Testament: Testimony, Dispute, Advocacy* (Minneapolis: Fortress, 1997) 215–28.
2. See also Jonah 4:2; Pss 86:15; 103:8; 145:8; Neh 9:17.

available responses, but it is not lightly or readily granted. Still, in these early texts, the capacity for pardon with the verb *slḥ* is nevertheless available in the character of YHWH. It remains to see what is made of that available dimension of YHWH in the trajectory of Deuteronomy.

III. The Problem of Pardon in Deuteronomy

In the book of Deuteronomy, the issue of forgiveness and pardon is not a primary agendum. We may suppose that it is only in the late, emerging parts of the book of Deuteronomy—late and emerging in the sixth century—that the crisis of pardon even surfaces. Prior to that, in the primary tradition of Deuteronomy, perhaps linked to the hopeful act of reform, obedience to Torah is seen as fully possible and therefore there is no need to ponder pardon. However, in the later part of Deuteronomy, specifically in 29:20–30:20, Patrick D. Miller detects three themes in sequence:[3]

1. Curse (29:20–28);
2. Preaching of Repentance and Restoration (29:29–30:14); and
3. Covenantal Decision (30:15–20).

Three comments seem appropriate regarding the text and Miller's rendering. First, of the second element on "Preaching of Repentance and Restoration," Miller writes:

> The marvelous thing about this text is that it arises out of the harsh realities of disobedience, judgment, and exile and yet dares to assert the new possibilities not only of God's mercy and pardon but of the people's full obedience to the Lord's way. The church has called this justification of the unrighteous and sanctification. In the covenant at Moab, it is blessing for those who have been judged and obedience. Either set of categories confronts us with the powerful grace of God and the transformation of life that it can effect.[4]

While Miller rightly sees grace offered here, the trajectory from these texts moves well beyond this way of affirming God's grace. That is, the "powerful grace of God" offered in 29:29–30:14 turned out not to be an adequate formulation for the circumstance of exile and needed to be developed in the tradition beyond this formulation.

Second, the urgency of a covenantal decision in 30:15–20 is yet again a return to a tight, symmetrical "if . . . then" conditional statement in which the offer of grace is simply a permit to reenter into the demand of the "as . . . if" relationship. This is a characteristic Deuteronomic affirmation, but

---

3. Patrick D. Miller, *Deuteronomy* (Interpretation; Louisville: Westminster/John Knox, 1990) 211–15.

4. Ibid., 213.

one that is deeply circumscribed in comparison with more belated interpretations of grace.

Third, the "curse" of 29:20–28 is handled by Miller as "language typical
of the treaty curses . . . a stereotyped question and answer schema."[5] This is
surely correct, and yet this "typical/stereotyped" curse seems to not take
account of the remarkable negation stated concerning YHWH in the only
passage that employs *slḥ* in the book of Deuteronomy:

> the LORD will be unwilling to *pardon* them, for the LORD's anger and
> passion will smoke against them. (29:20)

The negative verdict is upon the Israel that turns away from YHWH to serve
other gods and that went in "our own stubborn ways" (29:18–19). This is
presumably the generation that disobeyed Torah and evoked the distortion
that produced exile. The accent for that generation is on "unwilling to
pardon."

My point is to notice that: (a) the force of the negation in 29:20 is as
strong as the positive in 29:29–30:14; and (b) the connection between the
negation and the affirmation is made by the "after all these things" (30:1),
presumably referring to the destruction and exile, when Israel is to turn
and repent. It is clear that the "powerful grace of God" consists in receptiv-
ity to repentance for the coming generation, but not in any forgiveness or
pardon for the disaster-evoking generation that precedes. It is clear that re-
ceptivity to repentance is indeed powerful grace. The severe negative of
29:20, however, even if stereotypical, set me to wondering about "pardon"
in Deuteronomy, and how rigorous and uncompromising the "if . . . then"
of the covenant is, even in the restored covenant of 30:15–20.

IV. Solomon's slḥ: Kings vs. Chronicles

Out of that strong denial of pardon in Deut 29:20, I want to consider
uses of *slḥ* in other materials that I consider closely linked to and perhaps
derivative of the problem posed by that denial. There are only two programmatic uses of the term *slḥ* in the Deuteronomistic History.[6] The first
of these is the prayer of Solomon in 1 Kings 8 that is strategically important
to the larger narrative of the history.[7] Whereas the earlier material in this
chapter, especially vv. 12–13, offers the temple as a place of presence, the

---

5. Ibid., 211–12.
6. I exclude 2 Kgs 5:18, which I take to be incidental and not programmatic for the
larger narrative.
7. See Dennis J. McCarthy, "II Samuel 7 and the Structure of the Deuteronomic History," *JBL* 84 (1965) 131–38. Even though McCarthy focuses on 2 Samuel 7, his analysis ap-
preciates the decisive placement and function of 1 Kings 8 in the larger narrative.

later Deuteronomistic material resists the claim of presence (see v. 27) and instead offers the temple as the access point to Yhwh's forgiveness. In 1 Kgs 8:30, 34, 36, 39, and 50 (see parallels in 2 Chr 6:21, 25, 27, 30, 39), the term *slḥ* is used to designate the temple as the proper place of petition and pardon even, we should note, for those "carried away captive to the land of the enemy" (v. 46). In vv. 34, 36, and most elaborately v. 50, the petition to pardon is preceded by an anticipation of repentance, "if they turn [*šûb*]" (vv. 33, 35, 47–48). Such anticipation of repentance does not precede vv. 30 and 39, but the implication is apparently the same.[8] The prayer in the mouth of Solomon is a bold and confident one, counting on Yhwh's readiness to accept repentance and to grant pardon to those who turn. The assumption is the same as that made in Deut 30:1–10, with the same term *šûb*.[9] Two observations are in order. First, the premise of forgiveness is the repentance of Israel. Yhwh's grace consists in a readiness to accept Israel's return to obedience. Second, the use of the term "pardon" is on the lips of Solomon as a petitionary imperative. It is not an assurance given by God. Thus it makes a claim that contradicts the negation of Deut 29:20, but does so in an act of Israelite hope, apparently in the conviction that the efficaciousness of the temple as access point to Yhwh more than overrides the rejection based on Torah. I suggest that the positive possibility affirmed by Solomon reflects temple theology, wherein the conditionality of Yhwh is less stringent than in the Torah traditions. Temple is here offered as a more receptive vehicle for forgiveness.[10]

Immediately upon the conclusion of the temple dedication in 1 Kings 8, the text of 1 Kgs 9:1–9 reiterates the rigorous "if . . . then" of the Torah, as though to counter the offer of temple forgiveness. The relation of 8:31–54 to 9:1–9 is not unlike Deut 30:1–10 and 30:15–20, an invitation to turn, followed by an "if . . . then" assertion of life. The positive "if . . . then" of 1 Kgs 9:4–5 and its negative counterpart in vv. 6–9 —culminating in the explanation of "why has the Lord done such a thing to this land and to this house" (vv. 8–9)—is preceded by an oracle of assurance in v. 3. The divine oracle

---

8. Hans Walter Wolff, "The Kerygma of the Deuteronomic Historical Work," in Walter Brueggemann and Hans Walter Wolff, *The Vitality of Old Testament Traditions* (2d ed.; Atlanta: John Knox, 1982) 83–100, has fully appreciated the theme of "turn" (*šûb*) for the shape and theology of the larger narrative. It is worth noting, in passing, that Wolff regards Deut 4:29–31 along with Deut 30:1–10 and 1 Kgs 8:46ff. as later elements in the narrative. Such a critical distinction is not especially pertinent to the point made here.

9. See also Jer 36:3, also a Deuteronomistic formulation.

10. On the ways in which 1 Kings 8 both voices and moves beyond temple theology, see Jon D. Levenson, "From Temple to Synagogue: 1 Kings 8," in *Traditions in Transformation: Turning Points in Biblical Faith* (ed. Baruch Halpern and Jon D. Levenson; Winona Lake: Eisenbrauns, 1981) 143–66.

would seem to be a direct response to the "prayer and plea" of Solomon in 1 Kings 8; we might thereby expect an assurance of the pardon for which Solomon prays. What is odd is that there is no offer of pardon here, but only a stringent "if . . . then" that culminates in a heavy threat. That is, the temple offer of pardon is recontextualized in Torah theology so that there is no offer of pardon, but only yet another insistence upon obedience.

The absence of an assurance of pardon that might be commensurate with the petition is made more obvious by the contrast in the parallel statement of 2 Chr 7:12–14. The response of YHWH to Solomon's prayer is formally the same in 2 Chronicles 7, and concludes in vv. 17–22 with a formula of "if . . . then." But between the assurance of hearing in v. 12 and the "if . . . then" of vv. 17–22, the Chronicler has the following:

> If my people who are called by my name humble themselves, pray, and seek my face, and turn from their wicked ways, then I will hear from heaven, and will forgive [*slḥ*] their sin and heal their land. (2 Chr 7:14)

The condition of turning is the same, but the assurance of pardon is explicit with the use of *slḥ* that the Deuteronomistic presentation seems unwilling or unable to utter. Whereas 1 Kings 8 has *slḥ* as a petition on the lips of Solomon, the Chronicler is able to have the same term as an assurance on the lips of YHWH. This later theological development in the Chronicler flies in the face of the negation of Deut 29:20. The conditional "turn" persists, but now there is an explicit readiness on the part of YHWH, albeit qualified, to pardon. That readiness, however, comes outside of and after the Deuteronomic and the Deuteronomistic. Thus the temple prayer, a petition and a hope, is the only time in the Deuteronomistic History that "pardon" (*slḥ*) is continued as a sustained, positive theme.[11]

V. The Failure (and Transformation) of Repentance

It turns out that the hope of Solomon, who staked everything on the temple, was only an interim possibility in the royal narrative. The only other use of *slḥ* in the books of Kings is the verdict rendered on Manasseh.[12] It is clear that Manasseh and Josiah are paradigmatic figures in the royal narrative.[13] Josiah is the "turner" par excellence:

---

11. See the vexed usage of the term "pardon" in Jer 5:1, 7, in the same broad tradition.
12. Again excepting 2 Kgs 5:18.
13. The paradigmatic quality of the contrast between the two kings is not unlike that of Ahaz and Hezekiah in the book of Isaiah, on which see Christopher R. Seitz, *Zion's Final Destiny: The Development of the Book of Isaiah: A Reassessment of Isaiah 36–39* (Minneapolis: Fortress, 1991) 195–202 and *passim*.

... because your heart was penitent, and you humbled yourself before the LORD ... and because you have torn your clothes and wept before me, I also have heard you, says the LORD. (2 Kgs 22:19)

Before him there was no king like him, who turned to the LORD with all his heart, with all his soul, and with all his might, according to all the law of Moses; nor did any like him arise after him. (2 Kgs 23:25)

Josiah is the perfect Torah-keeper who enacts the "if" of Torah and is entitled to the "then" of covenant blessing. Josiah is the one who fully enacts the repentance of Deut 30:1–10, who should therefore make possible a way of life in Jerusalem.

But whereas Josiah enacts Deut 30:1–10 and is a "turner" to life, his positive generativity is countered, according to this presentation, by Manasseh who embodies the fickleness of Deut 29:18–20. In the end-game of royal narrative, the negation of Deut 29:20 is reiterated concerning Manasseh as a warrant for the final destruction of the city:

Surely this came upon Judah at the command of the LORD, to remove them out of his sight, for the sins of Manasseh, for all that he had committed, and also for the innocent blood that he had shed; for he filled Jerusalem with innocent blood, and the LORD was not willing to *pardon*. (2 Kgs 24:3–4)

Indeed, 2 Kgs 24:4 directly matches Deut 29:20, both passages use *slḥ* governed by *l˒ ˒bh*—YHWH unwilling to pardon.

The story of king and temple thus winds down in a failure to pardon. There had been repentance ... on the part of Josiah. The repentance of Josiah, however, coming after the disobedience of Manasseh, was not enough. Indeed, in this telling of the royal tale, there is *not enough repentance* to evoke *pardon*. Repentance, even that of Josiah, is an inadequate antidote to the systemic, long-term disobedience of royal Israel epitomized by Manasseh. The question that arises is anticipated by Moses:

they and indeed all the nations will wonder, "Why has the LORD done this to this land? What caused this great display of anger?" (Deut 29:24)

The question is reiterated in 1 Kgs 9:8, after the interim offer of the temple. The question haunts the narrative, as it haunted the generation of Israel that lived in the wake of the events of 587 B.C.E. Why? Because repentance did not avail. Because repentance, even of the deepest kind—from Josiah—could not counter the evil that had evoked the curse.

Given that deep negative, we may notice one more use of *slḥ* that is akin to 2 Kgs 24:4. In Lam 3:40–45 the themes of "return" and "pardon" are taken up:

> Let us test and examine our ways,
>   and return [*šûb*] to the LORD.
> Let us lift our hearts as well as our hands
>   to God of heaven.
> We have transgressed and rebelled,
>   and you have not forgiven [*slḥ*].
> You have wrapped yourself with anger and pursued us,
>   killing without pity;
> you have wrapped yourself with a cloud
>   so that no prayer can pass through.
> You have made us filth and rubbish
>   among the peoples.

This generation must still live in an unpardoned state. One can, however, see the beginning of movement in the poem beyond that forlorn state in which devastated Israel has no recourse. For as the poem moves beyond YHWH's anger in vv. 43–45, the "enemy" begins to appear as the perpetrator of the trouble. In response to Israel's "I am lost" (v. 54), there is now from YHWH "Do not fear" (v. 57). There is not yet rescue; but it is already clear here that YHWH is now repositioned *vis-à-vis* Israel after v. 45. The ground for the repositioning would seem to be Israel's humiliation at the hands of the enemy, and Israel's daring capacity to speak the trouble to YHWH in ways that move YHWH to response. In the movement of the poetry from v. 40 to v. 60, the divine subject has been changed by the Israel that speaks. What had evoked YHWH's *rage* now makes Israel subject to YHWH's *pity*. Now it is Israel's *need* and not Israel's *failure* that matters to YHWH. This is not at all what Deut 30:1–10 means by "turning." This is a turn *on the part of YHWH* rather than on the part of Israel; this makes newness possible.[14] Israel turns not in order to admit failure but to plead for help (v. 40). The news of v. 57 is that help is on the way, the help an unpardoning God had not until now been willing to give.

VI. A New Thing: Unmotivated Forgiveness

No more is heard elsewhere in Scripture of the "not pardoning" expressed in Deut 29:20 and 2 Kgs 24:4. Now, finally, I will consider the an-

---

14. Reference might usefully be made to the same turn in Ps 90:13, where the verb is parallel to *nḥm*, a term also important for the offer of grace in Second Isaiah.

nouncement of pardon that takes repentance into account but that does
not wait for repentance on the part of Israel. It is not clear that the texts I
cite are directly linked to the tradition of Deuteronomy; but I take it as
plausible that they are derived from and represent movement that can be
understood as part of the same trajectory. It turns out that the absolute negation of Deut 29:20, voiced in 2 Kgs 24:4 with particular reference to Manasseh but with the entire Jerusalem enterprise in purview, was not the last
word. Miller has already seen that it is not the last word in Deuteronomy,
since Deut 29:20 is followed by 29:29–30:20. Here I will explore other evidence that the absolute negative of Deut 29:20 is actually penultimate and
therefore not as absolute as it was intended to be heard in its utterance.

It is commonly noticed that Second Isaiah begins (Isa 40:8) and ends
(55:10–11) with reference to Yhwh's decisive word that fulfills its own purpose. It is not so often noticed that the framing of Second Isaiah is not only
by "the word" but by an announcement of *pardon*. In 40:1–2, there is a declaration of pardon, or at least an assertion that enough has been suffered
for sin by those displaced from Jerusalem. This is clearly not the same as repentance, but rather a sense that the punishment has run it course. In 55:6–
9, where *slḥ* occurs in parallel to *rḥm* ("mercy"), there is an offer of pardon
to which exilic Israel is summoned. The ground of the offer is that Yhwh's
"thoughts" and "ways" are beyond the thoughts and ways of Israel. Presumably the thoughts and ways of Israel in exile are that the exile is to perpetu-
ity (as voiced in Deut 29:20 and 2 Kgs 24:4), but Yhwh's "otherwise" is for
homecoming (Isa 55:12–13). The appropriation of "pardon and mercy," however, is indicated by the imperatives, "seek" (Isa 55:6a), "call" (v. 6b), and
"turn" (v. 7b). The first two imperative verbs simply reinforce "turn," which
brings this text into complete alignment with Deut 30:1–10 where repentance is the condition of restoration. This Deuteronomy-like invitation is a
move beyond the harsh judgment of First Isaiah in the same way that Deut
30:1–10 follows after the harshness of 29:20.[15] In both cases, the harshness
is overcome by a willingness to offer pardon.

Beyond the affirmation of pardon-cum-repentance in Isa 55:6–9, there
are three texts in the tradition of Jeremiah that seem to be a later development in the same trajectory, given the close connection between Deuteronomy and the tradition of Jeremiah. The best known of these is Jer 31:31–
34. The offer of a new (renewed?) covenant is cast as a remarkable prophetic

15. On the connections between Second Isaiah and the Deuteronomic traditions,
see Walter Brueggemann, "Isaiah 55 and Deuteronomic Theology," *ZAW* 80 (1968) 191–
203, and more recently, Marvin A. Sweeney, "The Book of Isaiah as a Prophetic Torah,"
in *New Visions of Isaiah* (ed. Roy F. Melugin and Marvin A. Sweeney; JSOTSup 214; Sheffield: Sheffield Academic Press, 1996) 50–67.

oracle of promise. The single matter that is of interest here is that in v. 34, the conclusion and ground of the newness is precisely pardon:

For I will *forgive* [*slḥ*] their iniquity, and remember their sin no more.

The assurance of pardon and the forgetting of sin are voiced as a unilateral act by YHWH, without any seeking, calling, or turning—that is, without any repentance on the part of Israel. Pardon is a genuine *novum* on the part of YHWH, the breaking of all vicious cycles of alienation that permits a new start with YHWH.[16] The connection to Deuteronomy is well articulated by Robert Carroll:

> I would regard the relation between 31.31–34 and the Deuteronomistic strand in the tradition to be one of critical dialogue. . . . The Deuteronomists believed that the covenant had been broken and therefore had become inoperable. Late additions to their work allow for the possibility of Yahweh's restoration of the nation and the divine circumcision of its mind after it has turned back to him (Deut. 30.1–10). But of a new covenant the Deuteronomists know nothing. . . . The author of 31.31–34 transcends that limitation by asserting the divine initiative beyond human turning and the making of a new *bᵉrît*. It is a post-Deuteronomistic hope but one which has learned its theology from Deuteronomism and made the leap of hope into the utopian future.[17]

I shall return to this "leap of hope" in a moment. Here I only note that it is a leap beyond the repentance that is the ground of pardon even in the most generous parts of Deuteronomy.

In what is likely an even later oracle in the Jeremian tradition, Jer 33:4–9 makes an abrupt and heretofore unknown turn. Jer 33:4–5 announces YHWH's word concerning Jerusalem, which is about to be filled with the dead due to YHWH's hidden face. After this announcement of destruction, the fresh assertion of vv. 6–9 is staggering in its form. The series of first person verbs, grounded in nothing from Israel's side, amounts to a total offer of pardon:

I will heal,
I will reveal,
I will restore,
I will build,
I will cleanse,
I will pardon.

16. See Thomas M. Raitt, *A Theology of Exile: Judgment/Deliverance in Jeremiah and Ezekiel* (Philadelphia: Fortress, 1977) for an extended treatment.

17. Robert P. Carroll, *Jeremiah: A Commentary* (OTL; Philadelphia: Westminster, 1986) 613–14.

The outcome is "prosperity and security." By v. 6, nothing is recalled or operative from vv. 4–5.

Finally, in Jer 50:17–20, in a prose promise in the midst of the oracle against Babylon, another promise from YHWH is offered that begins in punishment for Babylon and ends in pardon for Israel (v. 20). Nothing is made of it, but the report in v. 17 may suggest that YHWH's new initiative toward Israel is a response to and compensation for the victimization of Israel by the enemies. Here the work of Assyria and Babylon is not regarded as an outcome of YHWH's authorization but is simply brutalizing imperial activity, in the face of which pardon by YHWH is a welcome, transformative alternative. It should be noted that here the promise of pardon is to "the remnant," that is, the community of survivors after the deportation. This use of "remnant" does not, however, refer to the religiously privileged, but simply to those fortunate enough to survive the ordeal of imperial aggression.

VII. Adjudicating Pardon

Our survey of the material concerning pardon (*slḥ*) traverses a broad sweep from *absolute rejection* (Deut 29:20; 2 Kgs 24:4; Lam 3:42) to a *bid for repentance* (1 Kgs 8:30–51; Jer 33:6; Isa 55:7), through an *insistence on the cruciality of obedience without pardon* (1 Kgs 9:4–9; made clear by the variation in 2 Chr 7:14), to *a full, unilateral pardon without reference to repentance* (Jer 31:31–34; 33:8; 50:20). From this sequencing of material, we may consider three questions:

1. Is this trajectory of pardon a legitimate extrapolation from Deuteronomy? Obviously I think so. Miller's judgment about Deut 29:20–30:20 is that this material is an assertion of "the powerful grace of God." In the confines of Deuteronomy, however, the offer of YHWH's pardon does not move outside the limits of covenantal symmetry within a condition of obedience.[18] That is, pardon depends on becoming fully obedient, probably fully obedient *before pardon*. It is an act of grace on the part of YHWH to leave open a return to full obedience, but it is a limited offer, an offer also sounded in Deut 4:29–31 and 1 Kings 8.

But because the tradition of Deuteronomy is covenantal and genuinely interactionist, it is clear that the absolute negation of Deut 29:20 (and 2 Kgs 24:4) or the limited offer via repentance is not sufficient (Deut 30:1–10; Isa 55:6–9). I suggest that because, already in Deuteronomy, this is a God whose "heart is set" (*ḥšq*) on Israel (Deut 7:7; 10:15), this deep emotional, passionate yearning on the part of YHWH for Israel is operative in

---

18. Miller, *Deuteronomy*, 213, shows himself to be a discerning Calvinist theologian by seeing the interface in the text of "justification of the unrighteous and sanctification."

Deuteronomy in a way that will not let absolute negation be the last word. Thus the "not pardon" and the negative use of the term *slḥ* in Deut 29:20 already inchoately introduce questions, constraints, and challenges beyond "not pardon," and raise questions about other options from the God "whose heart is set."

The trajectory beyond "not pardon" to "pardon" is accomplished in two theological maneuvers. The first, on which Miller eloquently comments, is that Yhwh will permit recalcitrant Israel back into a covenant of obedience. This is no small matter after what appears to be termination. But the second move, surely also propelled by *ḥšq*, is a *free pardon* in which past affronts are not mentioned and no summons to repentance is even issued. Whether this second move, perhaps hinted at in Isaiah 55 but made explicit in the traditions of Jeremiah, is genuinely rooted in Deuteronomy is open to question. But there can be no doubt that the tradition of Jeremiah is deeply situated in the world of the Deuteronomistic History.

Beyond that, however, it may be suggested that the crisis of pardon, seeded in Deuteronomy, is not one among many such traditions, but it is the *central* tradition that poses the entire problem of the future in an exilic context of covenant canon-making. Thus these several traditions, I propose, all converge around this emergency question. The lived experience of destruction and dislocation required a rhetoric of severity. The severity of absolute negation could hardly be avoided. Deeply rooted in Yhwh's own covenant embracing character, however, is the theological force that causes the theme of *slḥ* to admit of no single assertion; the term, reflective of a theological emergency, becomes an arena for dangerous interpretive play in which the strictures of Torah, the vagaries of lived experience, an Israelite capacity for candor and hope, plus Yhwh's own *ḥšq* all converge in a suggestive spectrum of interpretive conviction.

2. Does this spectrum of interpretive opinion have a theological coherence to it? By identifying two theological maneuvers, (a) conditional pardon via repentance and (b) unilateral pardon without a call to repentance, I may seem to suggest a kind of developmental sequence to these texts. While such a development is not impossible, given the lived crisis of the sixth century, it is not definitional to my argument. I mean rather to insist that the covenantal symmetry of obedience is the defining rubric in all of these traditions. That symmetry of obedience can produce either an absolute negative or it can result in a summons to repentance.

What is odd and curious is the "leap" to a third posture of pardon—unconditional forgiveness—that seems provisionally to violate the symmetry of obedience. Along with Carroll, however, I suggest that the "leap" that goes beyond the symmetry of obedience is inchoately already given in the texts of symmetry. This relationship of Yhwh and Israel is not strictly contractual, but it is grounded in passion and commitment, the very factors that require genuine interpersonal interaction that goes beyond technical or juridical guidelines. Thus whatever may be said about the historical-critical relation of these several texts to each other, their theological coherence evidences Israel's daring traditionists struggling, once the notion of *slḥ* has been uttered, to discern what the tension, the severity of punishment, and the asymmetry of pardon may preclude or permit.

3. We may move into a more speculative realm to ask about the reasons why the "leap" in pardon eventuated in these traditions. A "suspicious" response might be that such an assertion of pardon met a pastoral need of a community in crisis, so that the oracles are made to say what needs to be said. A more "transcendent" view might say simply that in the mystery of God's way with God's people, the oracles of God disclose great depth to God's grace.[19]

I suggest we need not choose between the pastorally pragmatic and the theologically inscrutable justifications. Within that matrix, however, we may suggest two other matters that are to some extent obvious in the text. First, the judgment of "not pardon" has run its course and expired it claim. In the older assertion of Exod 34:6–7, the resolve to "visit iniquity" upon the parents is qualified by "the third and fourth generations." That is, the punishment may last a long time, but eventually it reaches its statute of limitation. We may also suggest that the remarkable assertions of Jer 31:34, 33:8, and 50:20 are made possible at the limit of the fourth generation, a recognition perhaps also evident in Isa 40:2.

Second, there is an inclination to identify Israel first as *perpetrator*, but then as *victim*.[20] As long as Israel is the guilty perpetrator, as with Manasseh, pardon is not easily forthcoming. It is, however, hinted in Jer 50:17–28 that Israel is victim, with no hint of any role as perpetrator. This sort of statement, surely with reference to 587 B.C.E., is astonishing, for it completely disregards the earlier prophetic notion that Nebuchadnezzar (and before him the Assyrians) had moved against Israel only at the behest of YHWH as punishment from YHWH (see Isa 10:5–11; 47:6; Jer 25:9; 27:6).

---

19. On a later exposition of this aspect of the issue see William Stacy Johnson, *The Mystery of God: Karl Barth and the Postmodern Foundations of Theology* (Columbia Series in Reformed Theology; Louisville: Westminster John Knox, 1997). There is no doubt that Karl Barth locates the possibility of forgiveness deep in the mystery of God.

20. I have learned of the interface of the categories of "perpetrator" and "victim" from Paul Ricoeur, *The Symbolism of Evil* (Boston: Beacon, 1967) 232–78, even though Ricoeur focuses upon matters other than those that concern me here. His mention of Jer 31:31–34 (ibid., 241) indicates that Ricoeur is not only reading Genesis 2–3, but is concerned with the "dialectic of judgment and mercy" as it permeates Israel's articulation of its faith.

The point is perhaps even more clear in Lam 3:40–66. I began my treatment of that poem above with the stanza of vv. 40–42, because that is where the term *slḥ* occurs. In v. 42, Israel's guilt is acknowledged and is taken as the proper ground for God's anger. But then in v. 52, the poem turns. Israel's enemies are "without cause." The prayer of petition (vv. 55–56) evokes Yhwh's "Do not fear" (v. 57). From that point on in the poem, Israel's role of abused victim is explicated. To be sure, the term "pardon" does not recur in the poem, but the salvation oracle of v. 57 indicates a glad, attentive response on the part of Yhwh. The guilt of v. 42 is completely overridden by the sense of victimization. Clearly, Yhwh will come in fresh ways to this people that is now not perpetrator but victim. How this poetic maneuver is accomplished in the ongoing reflection of exile is not obvious. Still, it is apparent that the deep sense of guilt has run its course, a fact that makes the idea of free pardon by Yhwh more credible.

These possible responses to the questions of legitimacy, extrapolation, coherence, and theological rationale (all considered above) suggest that the tradition of pardon, rooted in Deuteronomy, is a major theological agenda that receives a great deal of Israel's continued and belated interpretive energy.

VII. Present-Day Crises of Pardon

Finally, given that Patrick Miller is a deeply committed churchman, let me reflect briefly on the ways in which this convergence of *absolute negation*, summons to *the symmetry of obedience*, and *unconditional pardon* continues to be pertinent to the church. I identify three "crises of pardon" that continue to haunt in deep ways the church in the United States and its society:

1. The barbarism of slavery and the ensuing racism evident in every facet and dimension of our common life;
2. The unparalleled act of barbarism in Hiroshima and Nagasaki that bespeaks Western savagery toward Asia in a most particular way, but more largely epitomizes U.S. hegemony as the "last superpower";
3. The durable shame of Vietnam, the untold costs of which continue in visible and in hidden ways among us.

Other such "crises of pardon" could readily be added to this list. These are representative and typical of the deep theological crises that mark our society where raw power has become utterly separated from God's will in the world. I suggest that the taxonomy of pardon that I have traced from the trajectory of Deuteronomy is a way in which such "crises of pardon" bear upon long-term interpretive tasks. In each of these cases, as with many others we could add, it is too easy, as is our wont, to imagine easy, free pardon. It is excessively bourgeois, I suspect, to imagine a credible repentance that promptly "puts all this behind us." It is thinkable, but hardly bearable, to imagine that any of these acts might place us permanently beyond pardon from God. Yet the interpretive task is not to select one of these options. It is rather to recognize that such a lived, visible fissure as 587 B.C.E. along with its desolation-like moral fissure, requires long term interpretive staying power. By noting the use of the term *slḥ* and its several uses in the trajectory, we are able to see how Israel, in its desolation, understood and stayed at such an interpretive task that was unavoidable, but that admitted of no easy or obvious resolution.

To conclude: It is clear that the theological notion of "pardon" entailed an immense field of interpretive imagination for Israel. That field of imagination included: (a) harsh judgment, (b) *quid pro quo* reconciliation on the basis of repentance, and (c) a free offer of a new start by YHWH, the offended party. In contemporary social transactions, in both the church and larger society, it is clear that this "immense field of interpretive imagination" is still at work, or at least potentially available. The maintenance of community requires ordered, accountable relationships with firm sanctions. Israel, however, discovered that in the end the future is only possible by a large gesture of compassion on the part of the offended party. In contemporary imagination, that same discernment surfaces here and there yet again, as theological models sometimes inform social relationships.

Circumcision of the Heart:
The Journey of a Biblical Metaphor

WERNER E. LEMKE

I. Introduction

In this essay, I propose to examine the meaning and development of the
biblical metaphor of the "(un)circumcised heart." In the Old Testament,
this metaphor appears for the first time in certain legal and prophetic texts
of the 7th and 6th centuries B.C.E., specifically in Lev 26:41; Deut 10:16;
30:6; Jer 4:4; 9:25–26; and Ezek 44:7, 9. I hope to show that this metaphor
was part of a larger biblical-theological trajectory in the development of
Israelite religion during that period, which found its most concentrated
expression in such biblical books as Deuteronomy, the Psalms, Ezekiel,
and especially, Jeremiah. Occasioned most likely by Israel's experience of
national destruction and exile, it placed pronounced emphasis on the human heart and the interior or spiritual nature of the relationship between
God and the people.

II. The Metaphor in Its Immediate Biblical Context

I turn first to a brief analysis of the texts in which the metaphor of the
(un)circumcised heart is used explicitly, at the same time attempting, in so
far as possible, to place these texts in some kind of chronological sequence.
But before examining these texts in which the rite of circumcision is alluded to metaphorically, a brief word regarding the origin and meaning of
the ritual practice of circumcision in the biblical period is in order. Circumcision was not unique to ancient Israel, but is attested among other ancient

---

Author's note: It is my hope that this essay will be a fitting tribute to Patrick D. Miller,
whom I consider to be one of the outstanding Old Testament theologians of our generation, as well as a dear colleague and personal friend ever since we started together in the
graduate program in Old Testament and Ancient Near Eastern Studies at Harvard University more than four decades ago. May God bless you, my friend.

Near Eastern nations, though by no means all. Thus, for instance, circumcision was practiced by the Egyptians and Northwest Semitic peoples related to the Hebrews, though not by East Semitic peoples, like the Assyrians and Babylonians, nor by Sea Peoples like the Philistines.

While the practice of circumcision is attested since the early third millennium in the ancient Near East, its precise origin and meaning is not recoverable, though in all likelihood it may have had to do with initiation and/or marriage rites. That this may have been true for ancient Israel as well is suggested by such texts as Exod 4:25 and the story of Genesis 34. More common in Israel, however, was the circumcision of the newly born, which may have been associated with notions of a sacrifice of redemption, though the most prevalent notion came to be that of inclusion in the covenant community. This is clearly the case in the Priestly writer's version of God's covenant with Abraham found in Genesis 17, where circumcision has become a covenantal sign and obligation. While the practice of circumcision is attested as early as the pre-monarchic period, it is also clear that the rite did not gain special theological significance until the period of the exile, when Israel was cut off from its official temple cult and lived as captives among uncircumcised people. At that time, circumcision and sabbath observance become major means for Israel's religious differentiation from pagan nations.[1]

With this much by way of background on the literal meaning of the rite of circumcision, let us now turn to an examination of those passages in which "circumcision of the heart" functions as a theological metaphor, beginning with a text in Deuteronomy.

Deut 10:16

> Circumcise then the foreskin of your heart and do not stiffen your neck any more.[2]

This verse is embedded in a larger hortatory section (Deut 10:12–22) in which the author reminds Israel of its basic obligations before God and which is introduced by a rhetorical question, the answer to which is immediately provided:

> And now, O Israel, what does Yahweh your God ask of you? But this: To fear Yahweh your God, to walk in all his ways, to love him, and to

---

1. For further information on the subject, see Robert G. Hall, "Circumcision," in *ABD* 1:1025–31 and the literature cited there. See also Rainer Albertz, *A History of Israelite Religion in the Old Testament Period* (2 vols.; OTL; Louisville: Westminster / John Knox, 1994) 2:407–8.
2. Translations, unless otherwise indicated, are my own.

serve Yahweh your God with all your heart and all your soul, by keeping the commandments and statutes of Yahweh which I am commanding you this day, for your own good. (10:12–13)[3]

The answer to the question is couched in characteristically Deuteronomic
formulations, found repeatedly throughout the hortatory prologue of Deuteronomy 5–11, and presents itself as a concise summary of God's requirements of Israel in response to God's gracious initiatives on behalf of Israel.
It is followed by a reference to God's greatness manifested in creation and
to God's election of Israel out of all nations (10:14–15). Then follows the
verse under consideration with its twofold injunction to circumcise the
heart and to be stiff-necked no longer (10:16). Its appearance at this juncture seems a bit abrupt and unexpected, raising the question of whether it
might be a secondary insertion, rather than integral to the original narrative. In support of such a suggestion, the following observations can be
made. First, the omission of v. 16 would cause no disruption in the flow of
the narrative, either in terms of syntax or content. While the Hebrew *kî*
clause in v. 17 could be read as providing a motivation or rationale for the actions enjoined in v. 16, it fits even better as a motivation for God's election
of Israel out of all the nations (v. 15), which God was free to do as creator of
heaven and earth and all that is in it (v. 14) and as "God of gods and Lord of
lords" (v. 17a). And, just as the description of God's essential character in vv.
14–15 moves from creation to the realm of history, so also does vv. 17–18.
Thus the omission of v. 16 would create a uniform and balanced description
of God's nature and character (vv. 14–18), before launching into a series of
injunctions directed at Israel and rooted in God's character and Israel's exodus experience of God (vv. 19–22).

A second reason for questioning the originality of v. 16 has to do with
the appropriateness or fit of the two metaphors used in a Deuteronomic
context. Neither of them is a characteristically Deuteronomic idiom, although the second—regarding the stiffening or hardening of the neck—
occurs more frequently in the book than the first. Reference to Israel as a
"stiff-necked people" is found also in Deut 9:6, 13; and 31:27, where, however, the Hebrew adjective *qāšeh* is employed rather than the *hipʿil* of the
verb *qāšāh* as in 10:16. That usage is dependent on the older narrative of Israel's idolatry in the golden calf episode at Sinai, where the idiom occurs
for the first time in the Old Testament (see Exod 32:9; 33:3, 5; 34:9) and from

---

3. As Miller observes in his commentary on Deuteronomy, this rhetorical question is
reminiscent of Micah 6:8 and the answers given in each case seek to summarize the
essentials of Israel's relationship with God. Patrick D. Miller, *Deuteronomy* (Interpretation; Louisville: John Knox, 1990) 125.

which the author of Deuteronomy derived it. The use of the *hipʿil* of the verb *qāšāh*, however, is not found in that older narrative, nor elsewhere in Deuteronomy, though it is found frequently elsewhere in the Old Testament, occurring mostly in later texts.[4]

As for the first metaphor relating to the circumcision of the heart, it occurs once more in Deut 30:6, though in a different context than 10:16, moreover, in 30:6 it belongs to one of the latest redactional layers of the book. This latter reference sheds no light on the origin of the metaphor in 10:16, unless, of course, one wishes to argue that 10:16 derives from the same late redactional layer as 30:6. A further difficulty with 10:16 is the seemingly unmotivated and isolated appearance of the circumcision metaphor in it. Moshe Weinfeld seeks to provide an answer to this problem with the following observation:

> The election of the fathers and especially the election of Abraham, which was sealed by the covenantal sign of circumcision (Gen 17), triggered the idea of circumcision here. The Deuteronomic author, however, interpreted circumcision in a figurative manner: not circumcision of flesh but circumcision of heart, in other words, of spirit and soul.[5]

While it is true that Deuteronomy knows of God's love for and election of Israel's ancestors, nowhere does it single out Abraham or mention the covenantal sign of circumcision. Circumcision plays no role in the book of Deuteronomy, and where the ancestors are mentioned at all, it is usually collectively and with reference to God's love for or oath and promise to them, rather than the covenant of circumcision.[6] Furthermore, it is generally agreed that the Genesis 17 version of God's covenant with Abraham, with its pronounced emphasis on the covenantal sign of circumcision, is a uniquely Priestly notion not found in the earlier epic version of God's covenant with Abraham in Genesis 15. Thus Weinfeld's suggestion regarding what triggered the introduction of the idea of circumcision in the text under consideration is plausible only if one assumes either: (a) that P antedates and was known to the author of Deuteronomy; or (b) that Deut 10:16 is a later, post-Priestly, editorial addition presupposing the Pentateuchal narrative in its final and essentially complete form. If, on the other hand,

---

4. See, e.g., 2 Kgs 17:14; Jer 7:26; 17:23; 19:15 (all in prose texts); 2 Chr 30:8; 36:13; Neh 9:16, 17, 29; and Prov 29:1.

5. Moshe Weinfeld, *Deuteronomy 1–11* (AB 5; New York: Doubleday, 1991) 437.

6. Cf. Deut 1:8; 4:37; 6:10; 7:8; 9:5, 27; 29:13; 30:20; and 34:4. Where names are mentioned, Abraham is never mentioned alone, but always as part of the triad Abraham, Isaac, and Jacob. In two instances, the ancestors are alluded to collectively without any names (Deut 4:37 and 7:8). Incidentally, it is not surprising that in a book originating in Northern Israelite circles, Abraham should not be singled out for specific attention.

one wishes to maintain both the priority of D over P as well as the originality of Deut 10:16, then the introduction of the metaphor of the uncircumcised heart is a rather isolated and unexpected invention by the author of
Deuteronomy, who used it essentially as a synonym for the more commonly known metaphor of the stiff neck. Both suggest a willful lack of re-
sponsiveness to the divine will and covenantal obligation. But there is yet
another possibility for explaining the origins of this metaphor, as will become apparent by examining the next text in which it also occurs.

Jer 4:3b–4

Till your fallow ground and do not sow among thorns!
Circumcise yourselves unto Yahweh and remove the foreskin of your
 heart!
O men of Judah and inhabitants of Jerusalem,
lest my wrath break forth like fire and burn, with none to quench it,
on account of the evil of your doings!

In contrast to the verse that we just considered, the date and authorship of
this text can be established with a high degree of confidence. There is wide
agreement among commentators that these words derive from the prophet
Jeremiah and that they were first uttered during the early phases of his prophetic ministry, sometime during 627–605 B.C.E.[7]

The passage forms the conclusion to part of a larger pericope in Jer 2:1–
4:4, in which the prophet accuses his people of apostasy and pleads with
them to repent of their evil ways and to return to God. Two metaphors are
used in our text to state the prophet's concluding appeal, one drawn from
agriculture and the other from social custom. If Israel is to fulfill its divine
mission to the world (see v. 2b and cf. Gen 12:3), then it must prepare the
soil of its heart through deeds of penitence and righteousness, rather than
sowing on soil hardened and choked by evil deeds. The expression "till your
fallow ground" (*nîrû lākem nîr*) is found only here and in Hos 10:12. In view
of the well-known fact that Jeremiah, particularly in his earlier utterances,
exhibits extensive affinities to Hosea, it is likely that he derived this imagery from that 8th-century prophet. The second metaphor reinforces the
idea that a true turning to Yahweh cannot be superficial, but involves genuine deeds of penitence that move beyond externals to matters of the heart

---

7. So, e.g., John Bright, *Jeremiah* (AB 21; New York: Doubleday, 1965) 26; William
Holladay, *Jeremiah 1* (Hermeneia; Philadelphia: Fortress, 1986) 63; William McKane,
Jeremiah 1–25 (ICC; Edinburgh: T & T Clark, 1986) 88–90; Wilhelm Rudolph, *Jeremia*
(2d ed; Tübingen: J. C. B. Mohr, 1958) 28–29; and J. A. Thompson, *The Book of Jeremiah*
(NICOT; Grand Rapids: Eerdmans, 1980) 217.

or will, or the innermost orientation and aspirations of the human soul. As
in the case of Deut 10:16, so in Jer 4:4 the people are expected, indeed commanded, to take an active part in this process. If Deut 10:16 antedates Jer
4:4, then it is possible that Jeremiah was dependent for the use of this imagery upon the author of Deuteronomy, but this should not be taken for
granted or assumed. As we have seen above, there is some evidence to suggest that the Deuteronomy text may belong to later redactional stages in
the composition of the book, and that it could be dependent on Jeremiah
for the use of this metaphor. It is also conceivable that neither is dependent on the other, but that each arrived at the expression independently or
from a common source not known to us.[8] Be that as it may, the rest of v. 4
specifies the addressees of this command and provides a motivation clause
with specified consequences in the event of disobedience, all in language
that is stereotypical of Jeremiah. Thus the combination of "men of Judah
and inhabitants of Jerusalem" occurs most frequently in Jeremiah.[9] The
"inhabitants of Jerusalem" referred originally to the pre-Israelite inhabitants of Jerusalem or Jebusites (cf. Josh 15:63). Then, after David captured
the city from them and made it into his capital for the United Kingdom of
Israel and Judah, the term designated all the inhabitants of the royal capital.
Belonging to neither Judah nor Israel, and consisting of a mixed population
made up of indigenous Canaanites, Israelites, Judeans, and foreigners in the
service of the royal establishment, the inhabitants of Jerusalem came to be
differentiated from the free landowners or citizens of the two sister kingdoms of Judah and Israel known respectively as "men of Judah" or "men of
Israel." Following the destruction of Northern Israel in 722 B.C.E., only Judeans and the inhabitants of Jerusalem remained as identifiable social and
political entities; this was the situation in the time of Jeremiah. In the postexilic period, even that distinction became increasingly meaningless and
eventually was lost altogether. In the Chronicler's History, "inhabitants of
Jerusalem" and "(people of) Judah" are used essentially as synonymous
terms.[10]

Another stereotypical expression in our text found most commonly in
Jeremiah is the combination "the evil of your (their) doings" (*rōaʿ maʿallêkem*). While the expression is not unique to Jeremiah and occurs a few

---

8. In this connection it is worth noting that the precise formulations are not identical. Whereas Deut 10:16 says *ûmaltem ʾet ʿārlat lĕbabkem* "circumcise the foreskin of
your heart," Jer 4:4 says *himmōlû layhwh wĕhāsîrû ʿārlat lĕbabkem* "circumcise yourselves
unto Yahweh and remove the foreskin [read the sg. for the MT's pl.] of your heart."

9. Cf. Jer 4:4; 11:2, 9; 17:25; 18:11; 32:32; 35:13; and 36:31 (in reverse order). Elsewhere
in the Old Testament, it occurs in only the four following texts: Isa 5:3; 2 Kgs 23:1; 2 Chr
34:30; and Dan 9:7.

10. Cf. 2 Chr 20:15, 18, 20; 21:11, 13; 31:4; 32:33; and 33:9.

times elsewhere in the Old Testament, only in Jeremiah has it become a common and standard indictment of the nation's wrongdoings.[11] Corresponding to this negative indictment of the people regarding "the evil of their doings," is the opposite positive admonition "amend (or: improve) your doings" (*têṭîbû maʿallêkem*), found uniquely in the Jeremiah tradition.[12] All of this suggests that we are dealing here with a text that is an authentic expression of both the prophet's diction and message. Could the same be said also of the particular idiom regarding the circumcision of the heart? Indeed there are a couple of other passages in Jeremiah that are relevant to this question and which suggest that the use of the circumcision language in a metaphorical sense is not unique to Jer 4:4.

Jer 6:10

> Against whom shall I speak or testify that they might listen?
> Behold their ear is uncircumcised, they are unable to listen.
> See the word of Yahweh has become for them an object of scorn;
> they take no delight in it.

While the precise terminology of Jer 4:4 (or Deut 10:16) is not present in this text, the metaphorical use of circumcision is very much in evidence. That this occurs in another text from Jeremiah which is also generally acknowledged to be authentic and as coming from the same early period of the prophet's ministry is surely significant and may have bearing on the question of the provenance of this metaphor. Whereas in Jer 4:4 the organ needing circumcision was the heart, here it is the ear that is said to be "uncircumcised" (*ʿărēlâ*)—that is, is incapable of listening to God's prophetic word. Both expressions belong to the same complex of ideas and form a consistent spiritual metaphor, the heart being the seat of human intention and volition and the ear that of intentional hearing and obeying.[13] Thus, in essence, the prophet is saying that his people are lacking in both ability and

---

11. Cf. Jer 4:4; 21:12; 23:2, 22; 25:5; 26:3; and 44:22. Elsewhere it is found only in Isa 1:16; Hos 9:15; Deut 28:20; and Ps 28:4.

12. Cf. Jer 7:3, 5; 18:11; 26:13; and 35:15.

13. The only other body part involved in a metaphorical use of circumcision in the Old Testament are the lips. Twice in the Mosaic call narrative of Exodus 6, Moses doubts that Pharaoh would listen to him and describes himself as *ʿaral śĕpātayim* "uncircumcised of lips" (vv. 12 and 30). Unlike the Jeremiah passages involving heart and ear, no moral or spiritual failure is implied by Moses' or the Priestly author's use of this idiom. It merely suggests Moses' lack of eloquence, already attested to in the earlier epic version of the story, though in different words (cf. Exod 4:10: *kî kĕbad-peh ûkĕbad lāśôn ʾānōkî*, literally, "for I am heavy of mouth and tongue"). Thus P's use of the circumcision metaphor implies a physical or emotional impediment, rather than a moral or spiritual one, and is thus of a different order than Jeremiah's.

willingness to heed God's word and to repent of their evil ways. The expression regarding God's word becoming an object of scorn is another idiom unique to Jeremiah, which is found only here and in Jer 20:8.

Jer 9:24–25

> Behold days are coming, utterance of Yahweh,
> when I will deal with all who are circumcised in foreskin,
> that is with Egypt, and with Judah, and with Edom, and with the
>   Ammonites, and with Moab, and with all those whose hair at the
>   temple is cut and who dwell in the desert.
> All the nations are uncircumcised, and all the house of Israel is
>   uncircumcised in heart.

This text is beset with some ambiguities, and scholars differ on the question of its meaning, date, and provenance. As regards meaning, Holladay observes that "one hardly knows whether it is badly framed and/or badly preserved, or whether it is making a subtle and ironic point, or both." But then he goes on to interpret it as "so ironic a judgment speech that it can only be genuine to [the prophet Jeremiah]."[14] Others consider it to be a later addendum to the prophet's authentic oracles in chapter 9. I see no compelling reason for denying this passage to the prophet, however. In both language and thought it fits in well with Jeremiah's other utterances involving the use of the circumcision metaphor. All the characteristic circumcision terminology is used (cf. "to circumcise," *mûl*; "foreskin," *ʿārĕlâ*; and "to count as uncircumcised," *ʿārēl*) and Israel is singled out as being "uncircumcised in heart." The characterization of certain desert nations as "those whose hair at the temple is cut" (*kol-qĕṣûṣê-pēʾâ*) is found only in two other Jeremiah texts.[15] As suggested by Rudolph, the nations cited in this text originally may have been part of an anti-Babylonian coalition, such as that mentioned in Jeremiah 27.[16] At any rate, the passage presently announces that at some time in the future this group of nations, all of whom in contrast to the Babylonians practiced physical circumcision, would soon be the objects of God's judgment. Hence, while they may have been circumcised in the flesh, they were really uncircumcised in the metaphorical sense of "sinful and deserving of God's judgment," like other nations. Judah is lumped together indiscriminately with these other pagan nations and singled out for special condemnation, for while it may have observed the

---

14. Holladay, *Jeremiah 1*, 319–20.
15. Cf. Jer 25:23 and 49:32. This custom may be related to a prohibition found in Lev 19:27.
16. See Rudolph, *Jeremia*, 65.

physical rite rigorously, it was really "uncircumcised of heart" (*'arlê-lēb*) — that is, spiritually disobedient to and out of harmony with God's will.

Thus, this text, along with the other two from Jeremiah that we have examined, exhibits a coherent and consistent spiritual use of the circumcision metaphor. In light of this, as well as the frequency and prominence of its occurrence in the book of Jeremiah, it is not implausible to suggest that this metaphor may have originated with that prophet rather than with some other author. But before we can pursue this suggestion further, we need to examine briefly the remaining three texts in which the circumcision of the heart metaphor occurs.

Lev 26:41–42

> When I also will have been hostile to them and will have brought them into the land of their enemies, then their uncircumcised heart will be humbled and they will pay for their iniquity. Then I shall remember my covenant with Jacob; I shall also remember my covenant with Isaac and also my covenant with Abraham; and I shall remember the land.

This prose passage is part of the epilogue to the Holiness Code (Lev 26:3–46). The epilogue consists of three sections: (1) a description of the blessings that would ensue if Israel remained faithful to its covenant obligations (vv. 3–14); (2) a lengthier section describing dire consequences that would ensue in the case of covenant breaking (vv. 14–45); and (3) a conclusion to the entire Holiness Code of Lev 17–26 (v. 46). In form and function, the epilogue is similar to the blessings and curses section of ancient Near Eastern vassal treaties, as well as those of Deuteronomy 28. However, in its present form, the curses of the second section are mitigated by promises of a more hopeful nature relating to the future restoration of some survivors to their ancestral land (vv. 40–45). These verses envisage a future when the surviving exiles will confess and repent of their sins and those of their ancestors (v. 40). Having suffered the consequences of their iniquity, "their uncircumcised heart will be humbled (or: humble itself)" (*yikkāna' lĕbābām he'ārēl*). The verb admits either a passive or reflexive translation, thus leaving somewhat in doubt whether this is something they will be capable of doing themselves or whether this will be brought about by some other agent, such as God.[17] The latter seems more likely in the light of God's

---

17. The association of the verb *kāna'* with "heart" as the subject is unique and puts this text at some distance from Deut 10:16 and Jer 4:4 where the verb *mûl* "to circumcise" is used. The avoidance of using the latter verb with anything but physical circumcision suggests Priestly influence on or authorship of this text.

unilateral and unconditional promises in vv. 42 and 44–45. In spite of all
their transgressions, God would not destroy them utterly nor ever break
his covenant with Israel, whereby all major covenant traditions, both ancestral (v. 42) and Mosaic (v. 45), are mentioned specifically in support of
that divine promise. The entire pericope (vv. 40–45) reflects the experience
of exile and stands under the influence of the thought not only of Jeremiah,
but even more so the thought and language of Ezekiel and other exilic
priestly authors. Thus it should be dated no earlier than the late exilic or
even early post-exilic period.[18] The next text to be considered comes from
a similar situation and general time frame.

Deut 30:6

> And Yahweh your God will circumcise your heart and the heart of
> your descendants,
> so that you will love Yahweh your God with all your heart and with all
> your soul, in order that you may live.

This text is part of a passage envisaging the future restoration of Israel following her destruction and exile (Deut 30:1–10). As in the case of Lev
26:40–45, so Deut 30:1–10 presupposes the reality of the exilic situation
and appears to be a later interpolation in its present literary context, as suggested by most commentators.[19] Both passages also occur in concluding
epilogues to the legal portions of their respective books and seek to miti-
gate or look beyond the consequences of covenant breaking (see Lev 26:3–
39 and Deut 28:1–68). Other than these formal or functional similarities,
however, these texts are quite different in linguistic vocabulary and mode
of expression. Whereas the Leviticus text exhibits a Priestly vocabulary,
Deut 30:1–10 is distinctly Deuteronomic in flavor.[20] In all probability it

---

18. In his commentary on Leviticus, Baruch A. Levine, in an extensive excursus on
Lev 26:3–46, has demonstrated that the epilogue to the Holiness Code has received several significant additions emerging "from the actual experience of exile, most poignantly,
the hope for God's forgiveness and the prospect of restoration" (Baruch A. Levine, *Leviticus* [Philadelphia: Jewish Publication Society, 1989] 275). Following a suggestion by
H. L. Ginsberg, Levine goes on to distinguish several layers of additions to the epilogue,
to the latest of which he assigns vv. 40b–43, which include the text under consideration.
As regards its date, the present author is in agreement with Levine's conclusion that "at
the earliest, the completed Epilogue takes us to the end of the exile, possibly to the first
period of return after the edict of Cyrus the Great, issued in 538 B.C.E." (p. 280).

19. So, e.g., Miller, *Deuteronomy*, 212; and Jeffrey H. Tigay, *Deuteronomy* (Philadelphia:
Jewish Publication Society, 1996) 432.

20. Note, for instance, the repeated use of the root *šûb* ("to repent, return, restore
the fortunes"), the emphasis on "loving and obeying Yahweh with all one's heart and with
all one's soul," "observing all his commandments and decrees written in this book of the
law," and the like.

derives from an exilic Deuteronomistic historian standing under the influence of the prophet Jeremiah. Whatever the case, Deut 30:1–10 envisages a time following Israel's destruction and dispersal among the nations (see v. 1: "When all these things have happened to you"), when the surviving exiles would remember Moses' Torah and admonitions, repent of their sins, and turn to the Lord their God with all their heart and soul, as a result of which God would then restore their fortunes and bring them back to their ancestral land and bestow blessings upon them again as in former times (vv. 1–5). So far the syntax of the passage is conditional in form, with vv. 1–2 forming the protasis spelling out the conditions and vv. 3–5 forming the apodosis envisaging consequences that would ensue if the conditions were met. That is, *if* the exiled survivors of Israel and their descendants turn to the Lord in penitence and obey him in wholehearted devotion, *then* God would restore their fortunes and bring them back to the land of their ancestors.

But in the second half of this passage (vv. 6–10), the conditional language appears to have been abandoned in favor of unconditional statements regarding God's future and unilateral action. While it is possible to read these verses also as conditional by extending the apodosis of vv. 3–5 through v. 9 and by rendering v. 10 as a restatement of the protasis of v. 2, a causal or even emphatic rendering, which continues the focus on God's unilateral future action with Israel, is to be preferred, not only on linguistic and syntactical grounds, but for reasons of context and meaning.[21]

While on first sight the use of the circumcision metaphor in v. 6 appears to be simply an echo of Deut 10:16, upon closer examination it reveals a rather significant difference in meaning, signaled by a change in the subject of the action. That is, whereas in Deut 10:16 the circumcision of the heart was an action enjoined upon human beings (as in Jer 4:4), in Deut 30:6 it has become an action which God will perform for human beings, thus enabling them to love God with all their heart and soul. In similar fashion there appears to be a significant theological shift in the passage of Deut

---

21. Cf. NIV: ". . . if [*kî*] you obey the LORD your God and keep his commands and decrees that are written in this Book of the Law and [*kî*] turn to the LORD your God with all your heart and with all your soul." While the conjunction *kî* may at times introduce a conditional sentence or "if" clause, this is usually only the case in series of casuistic laws and not in narrative prose such as this text, where the more usual choice for "if" would have been *'im*, as in v. 4. The latter is the preferred conjunction in conditional sentences, whereas *kî* occurs predominantly in causal or object clauses. See GKC 491–98. Thus, in the context of this passage, a causal or emphatic rendering of *kî*, beginning already at v. 9b and extending through v. 10, is to be preferred: "For [*kî*] Yahweh your God will again delight in your well-being, just as he delighted in your ancestors; for [*kî*] you will obey Yahweh your God by keeping his commandments and decrees which are written in this book of the law, because [*kî*] you will return to Yahweh your God with all your heart and with all your soul!" So, similarly, the NJPSV.

30:1–10 itself: What vv. 1–5 had envisaged as a conditional promise or future possibility, has become in vv. 6–10 an unconditional promise or certain future reality. This shift does not necessarily indicate a change in authors, but could have taken place in the mind of the same author in the light of changing realities during the exile and his own further reflections on the history and destiny of his people. Given Israel's history of unfaithfulness, covenant breaking, and seeming inability to love and obey the Lord wholeheartedly, this author, possibly under the influence of the thought and utterances of prophets like Jeremiah (e.g., 31:33) and Ezekiel (e.g., 36:26–27), came to the conclusion that if Israel was ever to resume life in the promised land as God's covenant people, then this would come about not so much by human effort, but only by a new divine initiative of grace. God's circumcision of the human heart would be this kind of divine act of grace, enabling Israel to do what it had been unable to do for itself—namely, to love God with all their heart and soul and to live in true faithfulness and obedience to God.[22]

Ezek 44:6–9

> Say to the rebellious house of Israel, thus says the Lord God:
> Enough already of all your abominations, O House of Israel, admitting foreigners, uncircumcised of heart and uncircumcised of flesh, to be in my sanctuary, to defile my house, when you offer up my food, the fat and the blood. You have broken my covenant with all your abominations, and have not discharged the duties pertaining to my holy things, but have appointed them to discharge the duties of my sanctuary in your stead.
> Thus says the Lord God:
> Let no foreigner, uncircumcised in heart and uncircumcised in flesh, enter my sanctuary, no foreigner whatsoever among the Israelites.

This text is part of a larger unit (Ezek 44:4–31) dealing with legislation pertaining to temple personnel and who may rightfully discharge the priestly duties relating to the service at the sanctuary. Three groups of people are mentioned: Priests, Levites, and foreigners. Only descendants of the Zadokite line may perform priestly duties at the central sanctuary (44:15–31); Levites shall serve as lesser clergy performing menial services for the priests (44:10–14); and foreigners residing among the people of Israel are to be barred altogether from service at the temple (44:6–9). The polemical nature of this chapter is quite evident and the issues raised in it were acutely debated during the early post-exilic period of the late sixth

---

22. See the contributions by Olson and Brueggemann in this volume.

and early fifth century B.C.E., in conjunction with the rebuilding of the temple and the resumption of the sacrificial cult there. This text clearly argues for a more restrictive policy than that reflected in the practices of the First Temple period.[23] A contrary view, advocating the inclusion of those foreigners who by their actions signal their desire to be part of God's covenant community, finds expression in Isa 56:1–8. It is clear that the more restrictive view eventually carried the day and became official policy in Jerusalem under Ezra and Nehemiah (see Ezra 10 and Neh 9:2). It is most likely, therefore, that the text under consideration dates to the period of the early restoration and derives from redactors in sympathy with the narrower Zadokite priestly ideal.[24]

A closer look at the peculiar use of the circumcision metaphor in our text further underscores this conclusion. Twice foreigners, whether in the singular (v. 9) or in the plural (v. 7), are described by the pejorative label "uncircumcised of heart" (*'erel* or *'arlê-lēb*) and "uncircumcised of flesh" (*'erel* or *'arlê-bāśār*). While the first expression is found only once elsewhere in the Old Testament (Jer 9:25, on which it may be dependent), the second expression is unique to this text, as is the combination of the two.[25] There is a sense in which the conjoining of the adjective "uncircumcised" with the noun "flesh" is unusual and redundant, for the adjective alone, unless otherwise specified, was sufficient to refer to "fleshly circumcision." The use of such a redundant expression makes sense only when another kind of circumcision, such as that of the heart, had entered the picture.

Certainly the combination of the two expressions into one stereotypical cliché was intentional and polemical in nature. Whereas in all the other passages where the metaphor occurred, it was used to differentiate one kind of Israelite from another, here it is used indiscriminately to refer to

---

23. The book of Deuteronomy contains provisions granting priestly privileges at the central sanctuary to Levites (cf. Deut 18:1–8). That even non-Israelites performed more menial services at the Temple is suggested by such passages as Deut 29:11 and Josh 9:21, as well as by the cultic practices of surrounding nations. Among the Phoenicians, for instance, foreigners living under the protection of the deity constituted a distinct class of cult personnel. Cf. Georg Fohrer, *Ezechiel* (HAT 13; Tübingen: J. C. B. Mohr, 1955) 248.

24. This conclusion is also supported by Walther Zimmerli's observation: "Thus Ezek 44:6ff. stands at an appreciable distance from the genuine oracles of Ezekiel" (*Ezekiel 2* [Hermeneia; Philadelphia: Fortress, 1983] 453).

25. Elsewhere in the book of Ezekiel where the Hebrew word *'ārēl* is used, it always occurs in the absolute and never in the construct state. See Ezek 28:10; 31:18; 32:19, 21, 24, 25, 26, 27, 28, 29, 30, and 32. All of these occurrences come from the oracles against foreign nations, specifically Tyre and especially Egypt, and involve the use of the root as a plural noun form in a strongly pejorative sense. That is, Israel's enemies are promised one of the worst fates imaginable, which is to descend to the netherworld and make their grave among the uncircumcised in the deepest regions of Sheol.

foreigners only. Furthermore, the combination of the two expressions into one cliché suggests that they are viewed by the author of this text as essentially one. In other words, all foreigners who are uncircumcised in flesh are, by definition, also uncircumcised in heart. The close correlation between the two in effect obliterates the distinction between them, which all the other texts we have examined were so careful to make. It constitutes essentially a dismissal of the metaphorical in favor of the literal meaning of circumcision, which is also born out by the subsequent disappearance of the metaphor from the rest of the Old Testament. What we are witnessing here in this text, then, is *the end or reversal of the spiritualization of circumcision* evidenced in all the other texts examined so far. It could also be described as the "deconstruction" or "re-institutionalization" of a metaphor. In the religious perspective of the author of Ezek 44:6–9, as in that of the Priestly stratum of the Pentateuch, the only circumcision that mattered for inclusion in the religious community was the physical or ritualized one.

III. The Metaphor in Its Wider Biblical Context

Having examined seven key texts in which the metaphor (or a close variant thereof) occurs, we shall now take a brief look at a wider field of semantic expression and theological affirmation found in the literature of the period in which our metaphor makes its appearance. That this metaphor was part of a larger theological trajectory or complex of ideas is suggested first and foremost by several texts that speak of the importance of the heart in Israel's relation to God. We already had occasion to note the prevalence of heart language in Deuteronomy. In addition to the two texts considered above (Deut 10:16 and 30:6), emphasis on serving or loving God with all one's heart if also found in Deut 6:5; 10:12; and 11:13, 18. A similar concern with the human heart is also evidenced in the writings of the prophets Jeremiah and Ezekiel.

Jeremiah, for instance, frequently accused his contemporaries of walking or acting "in the stubbornness of their heart."[26] Judah is accused of not returning to the Lord "with her whole heart," but only in pretense (Jer 3:10); and elsewhere Jeremiah wonders whether the "hearts" of his prophetic opponents will ever turn back or repent (Jer 23:26). So pervasive and ingrained is Judah's sinfulness that it is likened by the prophet to being inscribed with an iron pen or etched with a diamond tip "upon the tablet of their hearts" (Jer 17:1). Such hearts can therefore only be "devious above all

---

26. Hebrew *bišrîrût libbām* appears to be a characteristic expression of Jeremiah; cf. Jer 3:17; 7:24; 9:14; 11:8; 13:10; 16:12; 18:12; 23:17. Elsewhere in the Old Testament, it occurs only in Ps 81:13 and Deut 29:19.

else" (Jer 17:9). In view of the depth of the human predicament and the seeming inability of human beings to extricate themselves from their sinful proclivities by their own power, Jeremiah at some point came to the realization that God would have to bring about profound changes in the human heart in order to make a renewal of the broken covenant relationship with Israel possible.[27] And this brings us to the best known of all the texts in the book of Jeremiah involving the use of the metaphor of the heart, the "new covenant" passage in Jer 31:31–34. The text is so well known that there is no need to reproduce it or discuss it at length here.[28] It suffices simply to point out that the renewal of the covenant relationship between God and Israel would be entirely the result of God's unilateral redemptive and forgiving activity, rather than by human effort or deserving. Among the things that God would do for Israel in that day would be to put God's Torah or instruction within them and to "write it upon their hearts" (31:33). Not only does this text envisage an internalization of the relationship between God and people, it also clearly shifts the initiative for this from the human to the divine partner.

Similar promises regarding Israel's future restoration are found elsewhere in Jeremiah, though with slightly different wording. In Jer 24:7, God makes the following promise to the exiles of Judah: "I will give them a heart to know that I am the LORD; and they shall be my people and I will be their God, for [*kî*] they shall return to me with all their heart." The final clause in this verse introduces a certain amount of ambiguity into the statement, for it could also be read as conditional (i.e., ". . . *if* they return to me with all their heart"), in which case God's redemption would be dependent on Israel's prior repentance. In the present context of 24:4–7, however, the emphasis is clearly on God's future redeeming action, rather than on human

---

27. This point is made persuasively and with extensive documentation in Jeremiah Unterman's work, *From Repentance to Redemption: Jeremiah's Thought in Transition* (JSOTSup 54; Sheffield: JSOT Press, 1987). Unterman distinguishes three stages in the development of Jeremiah's thought. During the first stage, the prophet preached repentance, believed in its possibility, and saw it as a prerequisite for redemption. During the second stage (597–587 B.C.E.) after his calls for repentance went largely unheeded by the people and punishment had overtaken them in the form of the first deportation, the element of divine mercy now becomes more prominent than that of human repentance in his thinking and utterances. During the third and final stage of the destruction of Jerusalem and the ensuing exile of the people, talk about human repentance is abandoned in favor of emphasis on God's unilateral and unconditional work of redemption, rooted solely in Yahweh's eternal commitment to and love for Israel.

28. For a summary of my views regarding the meaning and implications of this text, see Werner E. Lemke, "Jeremiah 31:31–34," *Int* 37 (1983) 183–87. See also Unterman's detailed analysis of Jer 31:27–37 (*From Repentance to Redemption*, 89–110), with which I am in essential agreement.

obligations, which makes it preferable to read this clause as an affirmation, rather than as a condition. In other words, the author is not so much setting forth conditions for God's future restoration of Israel as he is announcing the certainty of it. Even the people's penitential turning to Yahweh is not so much an exhortation to human action, as it is a prediction of a future reality, assured precisely because God will have a hand in it: "I will give them a heart to know that I am Yahweh" (v. 7). A similar promise is made in another text coming from approximately the same period. In a letter to the exiles, after admonishing them to settle down and prepare for a lengthy stay in Babylon (29:1–9), Jeremiah goes on to speak of their eventual restoration by God (29:10–14), including the resumption of a right relationship with God involving the human heart: "You will seek me and you will find me, for [*kî*] you will search for me with all your heart" (29:13). As in the case of 24:7, the final clause is ambiguous, and some translators prefer to render it as a conditional, rather than a causal or affirmative clause. Given its historical and literary context, however, I prefer to read it as an indicative statement regarding God's future activity on behalf of Israel.[29]

There is no ambiguity about the unconditional nature of God's promise of redemption in a final Jeremiah text we need to look at briefly. In Jer 32:39–40, God is represented making the following promise to Israel: "I will give them one heart and one path, so as to revere me always, for their own good and that of their children. I will make an everlasting covenant with them, that I will never turn away from doing good to them; and I will put reverence for me into their heart, so as to never depart from me again." In this text, as in Jer 31:31–34, the unilateral and unconditional nature of God's future redemptive activity on behalf of Israel is quite evident. Repentance is not even mentioned, no human obligations are specified. God alone will perform the necessary operations on the human heart to make possible a reverent and abiding relationship between Israel and God.

While they use different words and images, all of these Jeremiah texts speak essentially about the same thing, namely, the restoration of the covenant relationship between God and people, initiated unilaterally by God, rooted in God's forgiveness and loving faithfulness, and involving the interiorizing of the divine-human relationship in the human heart.

A similar vision regarding Israel's future involving the metaphorical use of the heart, though with slightly different imagery, is also found in the utterances of Ezekiel. Like his older contemporary Jeremiah, Ezekiel also spoke of the corruption of the human heart, which could be stubborn (2:4;

---

29. See also Unterman's observation regarding both Jer 24:4–7 and 29:10–14: "in these prophecies repentance takes a secondary position and God's promise of redemption takes center-stage" (*From Repentance to Redemption*, 87).

3:7), full of pride (28:2, 5, 17; 31:10), and given to idol worship (14:3, 4, 7; 20:16). Israel deserved God's judgment and did not merit redemption or restoration. Nevertheless, Ezekiel also announced the future restoration of Israel, which God would bring about simply for the sake of his own name or honor among the nations. That God's work of restoration would also involve changes in the human heart and an interiorizing of the divine-human relationship is envisaged in three different passages of the book. Toward the end of his lengthy discourse on the problem of divine retribution and human responsibility, Ezekiel admonishes the exiles as follows: "Cast off from you all your rebellious acts and get yourselves a new heart and a new spirit! For why should you die, O house of Israel?" (Ezek 18:31). The conjoining of "spirit" with "heart" is unique to Ezekiel and not found in either Deuteronomy or Jeremiah. But, as in the case of Deut 10:16 and Jer 4:4, the renewal of the heart and spirit here is part of an appeal to repentance and hence something human beings can and are expected to do for themselves. Elsewhere in Ezekiel, just as in Deuteronomy and Jeremiah, this expectation is abandoned in favor of attributing the renewal of the heart solely to God. Thus in the context of a prophecy predicting the return of the exiles to their homeland, God makes the following promise: "And I will give them a new[30] heart and a new spirit I will place within them. I will remove the heart of stone from their flesh and give them a heart of flesh" (Ezek 11:19). Similarly in Ezek 36:25–27:

> And I will sprinkle upon you clean water and you shall be clean from all your defilements, and from all your idols I will cleanse you. And I will give you a new heart and a new spirit I will place within you. I will remove the heart of stone from your flesh and give you a heart of flesh. My spirit I shall place within you, and thus I will bring about that you will walk in my statutes and carefully observe my ordinances.

Two things are quite evident in this last text. First, as in the case of the Jeremiah passages examined above, this future redemption of Israel will be the result of God's sovereign initiative and not Israel's penitential action. The new spirit that God will place within them is God's very own spirit, which would thus ensure that Israel would be able to walk in God's statutes and ordinances (v. 27). In other words, Israel's obedience to God would be the

---

30. The MT reads *'eḥād*, "one." The LXX reflects Hebrew *'aḥēr*, "another," which in view of the second half of the verse makes more sense than the MT, the "other" heart being the "heart of flesh" rather than the "heart of stone." With a few MSS and versions, and in the light of the close parallel in Ezek 36:26 where the "new heart" is identified with the "heart of flesh," we prefer, however, the reading *ḥādāš*, "new," to either the MT's *'eḥād* or the LXX's *'aḥēr*.

result of, and not a precondition for, God's work of redemption and renewal. Second, and quite unlike Jeremiah, a distinctively Priestly perspective is evident in this text.[31] The renewal of the human heart and spirit is conceived and described in terms of lustration and purification, distinctions between clean and unclean, and the ritual observance of statutes and ordinances. The dangers inherent in such an understanding of the renewal of the heart are evident. Instead of signifying the interiorizing or deepening of the divine-human relationship, the metaphor may now be employed to signify a new externalization or ritualization of that relationship. That this danger was real and that the heart metaphor was in fact subverted in this fashion by a subsequent editor of the book of Ezekiel, was demonstrated above in the analysis of Ezek 44:6–9. While I am not prepared to argue that Ezek 36:25–27 has already taken the fateful step which the author of 44:6–9 has taken, its particular utilization of the new heart and spirit metaphor could easily encourage others to move in that direction.

Before concluding this section I want to look at one other text in which the metaphorical use of "heart" and "spirit" language figures prominently; this is the well-known fifty-first psalm. Psalm 51 is a penitential psalm dealing with the problem of human sin. The psalmist displays a profound sense of awareness of the human predicament of sin and guilt, as well as the need for divine forgiveness. The psalmist is also aware of the fact that there is nothing s/he or any other human agency, such as the cult, can do to deal with the problem. The poet arrives at the conclusion that only God is capable of dealing with the problem of human sin and that nothing short of a creative divine act relating to the human heart and spirit can resolve the human predicament of sin. And so, in the context of his prayer for divine forgiveness, the following petition is made by the psalmist: "Create for me a clean heart, O God, and a steadfast spirit make new within me!" (Ps 51:12). As in the case of Ezekiel, but unlike Jeremiah, heart and spirit are here conjoined. Proximity to the thought of Ezekiel is also suggested by the use of the verb *ḥiddēš* "to make new or renew" in association with "spirit," which brings to mind Ezekiel's predictions about the "new" heart and spirit which God would give to Israel.[32] Priestly perspectives can also be seen in the use of the adjective "clean," though its use here is clearly metaphorical or spiritualized. The renewal of heart and spirit, for which the psalmist prays, is

---

31. Differences in eschatological hope between Ezekiel and Jeremiah are also aptly delineated by Moshe Weinfeld in his article, "Jeremiah and the Spiritual Metamorphosis of Israel," *ZAW* 88 (1976) 17–56.

32. Cf. Ezek 11:19; 18:31; and 36:26. By contrast, Jeremiah does not speak of a "new" heart or spirit, but only of a "new covenant" (Jer 31:31).

likened to a new act of creation, as suggested by the use of the technical term *bārāʾ* "to create," thus emphasizing the sovereign and unilateral nature of this divine activity.[33] This text is a profound theological statement concerning the interiorizing and deepening of the divine-human relationship. It demonstrates that such insights were not confined to prophetic, or prophetically influenced, literature such as that of Jeremiah or Deuteronomy, but could also arise in the context of a more priestly or cultically-oriented piety, such as that reflected in the Psalms. Yet the author of this psalm managed to avoid some of the dangers and pitfalls of cultic piety, such as its tendency toward reductionist ritualization of the divine-human relationship, as is evidenced by the poet's concluding reflections in vv. 18–19 which emphasize the interior or spiritual nature of this relationship: "For you do not delight is sacrifice, were I to bring a burnt offering, you would not be pleased. My sacrifice, O God, is a broken spirit, a broken and crushed heart, O God, you will not despise."[34]

To summarize: I have attempted to place the texts utilizing circumcision of the heart language into a wider biblical context by examining other biblical texts utilizing metaphorical heart language, but without circumcision. It has been shown that the metaphor under consideration is not an isolated phenomenon, but rather part of a larger theological trajectory concerned with the renewal and spiritual nature of the divine-human relationship. By and large, this trajectory appears in roughly the same time frame and body of literature associated with the destruction of Jerusalem, the Babylonian captivity, and early restoration; in other words, from ca. 625–515 B.C.E., and is found chiefly in Deuteronomy, Jeremiah, Ezekiel, Second and Third Isaiah, and the Psalms. Among this literature, the metaphor is most prominently developed in the book of Jeremiah.[35] We also noticed a significant development in this theological trajectory involving a shift in emphasis from human to divine agency. Whereas initially human beings could be enjoined to participate in the circumcision or renewal of their heart, increasingly it came to be seen as the result of God's sovereign and gracious initiative. Lastly, we also witnessed the incipient deconstruction

---

33. The verb is used only of divine (never human) activity in the Old Testament and occurs predominantly in Second Isaiah and the Priestly stratum of the Pentateuch.

34. With many commentators, I consider vv. 18–19 to be the original ending of the psalm and vv. 20–21 to be a later addition, made probably during the early restoration period, which apparently has misunderstood the profound theological perspective and message of the psalm.

35. In support of this claim, see also the important article by Weinfeld ("Jeremiah and the Spiritual Metamorphosis") in which the author examines other important elements in this larger theological trajectory so prominently displayed in Jeremiah.

and eventual eclipse of the heart metaphor in texts influenced by certain Priestly perspectives, such as Ezek 36:27; 44:7–9; and of course P, in which the metaphor has been abandoned entirely in favor of single-minded emphasis on physical circumcision as a *status confessionis*. It appears that in spite of occasional opposition by certain prophetic circles, such as those associated with Third Isaiah, the priestly and theocratic ideal prevailed throughout the later biblical period. Only one kind of circumcision now mattered, and that was physical and literal. Talk about the metaphorical or spiritual variety of circumcision disappeared from the theological horizon of the Old Testament, until it was revived in later Jewish and early Christian literature. To trace the history of that revival would be a fascinating topic in itself, but one which limitations of space do not permit us to pursue further in this essay.[36] Suffice it to conclude this study with some theological reflections of a more general nature.

IV. Concluding Theological Reflections

First, in this investigation of a biblical metaphor for spiritual renewal, I have attempted, among other things, to do biblical theology of the type advocated by Patrick Miller in his recent presidential address to the Society of Biblical Literature.[37] Like Miller, I have tried to engage several biblical voices in conversation around a common, theme, namely that of the true nature of the divine-human relationship. To Miller's conversation partners of Deuteronomy and Psalms, I added other Torah and prophetic voices, especially that of Jeremiah who played a key role in this conversation. We heard chords that created not only harmony, but also dissonance of a sort. Yet it is precisely this that leads to greater theological insight and understanding, for the whole is always greater than the sum of the parts. Miller's suggestions regarding the doing of Old Testament Theology is, I believe, a fruitful and workable one which I have tried to emulate here.

Second, this investigation of the metaphor of the circumcision of the heart yielded insights not only into the essentially spiritual nature of the divine-human relationship, but also the tensions that exist between it and

---

36. For one such attempt, see the article by R. LeDeaut, "Le thème de la circoncision du coeur (Deut xxx 6; Jer iv 4) dans les versions anciennes (LXX et Targum) et à Qumran," in *Congress Volume: Vienna, 1980* (ed. J. A. Emerton; VTSup 32; Leiden: E. J. Brill, 1981) 178–205.

37. Patrick D. Miller, "Deuteronomy and Psalms: Evoking a Biblical Conversation," *JBL* 118 (1999) 3–18. Toward the end of this article, Miller raises the question of whether there is any coherence in the theology of the Old Testament, given the varied voices found in it. He goes on to suggest that one way of working on that issue "may be to acknowledge the different voices but to engage them in ways that draw them together in the kind of conversation I have sought to elicit here" (p. 17).

the more external or institutionalized manifestations of all religions. At some point all religions seem to arrive at the realization that just going through the motions of ritual, or giving lip service to belief, is simply not enough. True religion takes place in the human heart, that is, it involves the whole human self in a transformation of the mind, will, affections, desires, motivations, and actions. It does not really matter too much what we call it, whether we call it "circumcision of the heart," or "baptism of the spirit," or some similar kind of expression. Physical circumcision in the flesh is not enough; mere baptism with water is not enough! The particular metaphor employed is not as significant as the reality to which it points and from which it must be distinguished, if it is to avoid misappropriation for a new externalization or ritualization of the divine-human relationship. This, however, appears to be a perennial problem and never-ending struggle for human beings, which may be beyond their ability to resolve completely and for which, in the final analysis, they need the help of God.

Huldah, the Prophet:
Reading a (Deuteronomistic) Woman's Identity

RENITA J. WEEMS

I. Introduction

She has been called by some "the first biblical text critic."[1] Others have
dubbed her "the founder of biblical studies."[2] She is the first figure in Scripture, male or female, whose contribution to biblical history centered on
verifying a written document as sacred and holy writ. But talk about the
prophet Huldah in my seminar class some fifteen years ago when I was a
graduate student at Princeton Theological Seminary centered more on her
forgotten status than her lofty contribution. "Despite the role she played in
inspiring the canon she is one of the most overlooked figures in the Bible,"
is the way Patrick D. Miller, I believe, referred to the lady prophet in
2 Kings 22 in his lecture that day on the editorial activity of the Deuteronomistic scribes. Like most graduate students who don't dare let onto their
peers and instructor how little they actually know about the topic around
the seminar table, I kept my ignorance about Huldah the prophet to myself.
But I recall scribbling her name down in the margins of my notes that day
(which was my reminder later when I reviewed class notes that this was
something I needed to brush up on before the next class!). Miller's lecture
that afternoon was not on Huldah, nor was it about women in ancient Israel, nor even about Hebrew prophets. But in his lecture on the origins and
transmission of the book of Deuteronomy, his casual comment about Huldah's role in confirming, in 621 B.C.E. that the Torah scroll found during
some Temple repairs was indeed the word of God, proved to be a windfall
for me sitting, as I often did, in class wondering to myself what in the world
possessed me to seek a Ph.D. in Old Testament Studies. Huldah soon became my secret role model. Other female prophets were mentioned in class

---

1. Baruch Halpern, "Huldah, the First Biblical Text Critic," *Other Side* 35/2 (1999)
51–53.
2. Arlene Swidler, "In Search of Huldah," *TBT* 98 (1978) 1783.

that semester, and many other (male) prophets who acted as mouthpieces
for Yʜᴡʜ before and after 621 ʙ.ᴄ.ᴇ. would occupy my attention during my
studies at Princeton. But the image I conjured up in my mind of a woman
sitting at her desk in the middle of the day hunched over a dusty manuscript, peering intently down at its contents, consumed with deciphering
the meaning hidden in the script, captured my imagination.[3] I continued to
have my doubts about my future in the discipline, but now, having been introduced to Huldah, I could take comfort in the fact that at least I didn't
have to invent myself. There was precedent in Scripture that one could be a
professional interpreter of scripture *and also* a woman. So, among other
things, I want to thank Pat Miller, my professor and dissertation adviser,
for bringing Huldah the prophet to my attention.

Until 621 ʙ.ᴄ.ᴇ., no writing had been designated as Holy Scripture. The
scroll discovered in the temple, containing as it did warnings and legislation
thought to be from the prophet Moses, would become the impetus for a
flurry of scribal and theological editorial activity.[4] As a result of Huldah's
proclamation one of the most important revival movements to sweep the
tiny southern kingdom began. Instigated by King Josiah (ca. 640–609), the
movement launched both political and religious reforms throughout the
land and reached not only into Judah but Samaria also, inspired as it was by
the newly discovered Deuteronomic legislation that had come to the attention of the king. In addition to these reforms, Israel's ancient traditions
were reworked to compile a history of Israel from the wilderness period to
the climatic fall of the northern and southern kingdoms. With Mosaic legal
traditions providing the major framework for its history, this work sought
to demonstrate that Israelite and Judean history, which climaxed in the fall
of Samaria and Jerusalem and the exile, was the story of repeated periods of
human idolatry and apostasy followed by acts of divine retribution. The
"Deuteronomistic History" is the way the work would come to be designated by scholars, beginning with Martin Noth, with Joshua–2 Kings being
the constituent books of the history.[5] By proclaiming this first scroll as rep-

---

3. Admittedly, such an image was borne strictly out my literary imagination. The
text simply says the king's delegation went to consult her as the king had ordered. Did
they hand the scroll to her for her review? Exactly what took place during their consul-
tation, we are not told. The narrator's failure to specify left me free to let my imagination
go in its own direction.

4. Based on the kind of reforms undertaken, scholars have long maintained that the
scroll validated by Huldah as Yʜᴡʜ's words contained core chapters of what we know
now as the book of Deuteronomy.

5. Martin Noth was the first to explore extensively the literary and ideological unity
of Judges–2 Kings in his monograph *The Deuteronomistic History* (2d ed.; JSOTSup 15;
Sheffield: JSOT Press, 1991), first published in German in 1943.

resentative of holy writing, Huldah started a process that centuries later would result in dozens of scrolls being produced, collected, and shaped into what is now known as the Old and New Testaments.[6]

Despite all that, surprisingly little biographical detail is offered about the woman prophet who started it all. We are introduced to her through her duties as a prophet, as an exegete of a rediscovered Torah scroll, as a mouth-piece for Deuteronomi(sti)c ideology, as a spokesperson with a single mission. But as to whom Huldah was as a woman and an individual, nothing is offered; though that has never stopped readers from ascribing a personal identity and personality to Huldah. Nor has it stopped her from capturing the imagination of generations of scholars and ordinary readers alike. In fact, commentators never fail to marvel at the king choosing *a woman* to authenticate the most auspicious discovery of his reign. I will argue here that the narrator of 2 Kings relies precisely upon readerly surprise at Huldah's gender to reinforce his point about the gravity of the times. Of course, women being sought out for aid by desperate leaders during times of crises was not unknown. Saul, for instance, beside himself with worry over an impending battle with the Philistines, urged the medium at Endor to bring up Samuel from the dead in order that he might seek his advice (1 Sam 28:8–14). Barak and the citizens of Israel sought the prophet Deborah's help when time came to battle the Canaanites while Sisera relied upon the counsel of Jael the Kenite when Barak's army had him cornered (Judg 4:17–22). Similarly, in the 2 Kings narrative, Huldah embodies both in gender and in oration the gravity of Josiah's situation and the inevitable doom upon the nation. Huldah's gender is central to the narrator's message. But by limiting his description of her to her name, her status as wife of the king's valet, and her dwelling in a section of Jerusalem beyond the borders of the royal guild of scribal activity, the narrator contrasts her marginal status to that of the elite policy-makers who seek her out. Readers are not allowed the privilege of being mere spectators of the story. Instead, we are made to experience

---

6. The dating and compositional stages of the Deuteronomistic History (DtrH) is a much debated area of scholarship. Noth considered the work the product of one author/compiler working during the exile. Other proposals have spun off from there with some agreeing with Noth, others arguing for preexilic and exilic editions of the work, and still others opting for multiple exilic redactions of the composition. The view taken here is that while reforms similar to the ones Josiah undertook were also implemented by King Hezekiah (ca. 715–687 B.C.E.), suggesting the possibility that the Mosaic legal traditions were not completely unknown in Judah in the first half of the seventh century, DtrH as an active scribal school probably began compiling materials in earnest under Josiah (640–609 B.C.E.) so as to legitimate his anti-Assyrian inspired religious and political reforms. But the edition of the work of most interest in this paper is the one produced during exile where the emphasis would be upon narrating the events that led to the fall of the southern kingdom and signifying the irreversibility of Judah's fate.

what even the most elite company of the day was blind to: the inevitability of Judah's doom.

The less we are allowed to know about the woman prophet, the larger she looms in both the narrative and in the reader's imagination. The mystery surrounding the newly discovered Torah scroll and the mystery of the woman who interpreted it become one. While it is tempting to confuse her role identity with her personal identity, we are constantly forced to ask ourselves what we do and do not know about Huldah, from a historical and literary point of view. We are also forced to ask how that knowledge, or lack thereof, both constructs identity and complicates identity—in biblical texts as well as in our own reality. In fact, identity—the nation's, Huldah's, God's, even that of the real, flesh-and-blood readers—is constantly being written and rewritten, examined and reexamined, imagined and reimagined in this Deuteronomistic saga of ambition, repentance, and failure.

II. Huldah within the Deuteronomistic Tradition

The story recounting the rediscovery of the Torah scroll and Huldah's role in confirming it as the words of Yhwh is found in 2 Kings 22, with a slightly different version recounted in 2 Chronicles 34. Following the narrative details of the former, the story goes that while cleansing and restoring the temple as ordered by the young, spirited king Josiah, the high priest Hilkiah discovered a scroll (2 Kgs 22:8). The high priest turned the scroll over to Shaphan, the king's secretary, who in turn read aloud the contents of the scroll to the unsuspecting king (vv. 9–10). Upon hearing the words of the scroll, the king tore his garments in an act of contrition. He perceived the words' implications for his people and for himself, but couldn't be certain until (in good Deuteronomistic fashion) the words proclaimed in the name of Yhwh on the scroll were confirmed by a prophet (vv. 11–13).[7] The king ordered Hilkiah, Shaphan, and the rest of the royal cabinet to "go, inquire of the Lord . . ." (v. 13). They set out for the Northwest section of Jerusalem, known as the Second Quarter, to meet with the prophet Huldah, wife of Shallum, the king's valet (v. 14). She confirmed the king's impressions that the document was indeed the book of the law spoken through Moses and that its contents spelled doom for Judah just as the king suspected. Yhwh was indeed about to bring disaster upon the inhabitants of the land because they had abandoned the covenant with Yhwh and had

---

7. The notion that Yhwh always makes the divine will known to the king and people through prophets is a patent tenet of the Deuteronomistic tradition. Most scholars recognize that 2 Kgs 17:7–23 is a key passage for shedding light on Deuteronomistic ideology. The editor makes clear that the reasons for Samaria's doom was the nation's repeated failure both to heed Yhwh's commandments and to heed the warnings of the prophets Yhwh repeatedly sent to the nation (vv. 13–14).

provoked Yhwh's anger with their acts of idolatry and apostasy (vv. 15–17). Judah was doomed: "Thus says the Lord, I will indeed bring disaster on this place and on its inhabitants" (v. 16). As for the king, because his heart grew contrite upon hearing Shaphan read the contents of the scroll, Yhwh was granting him a reprieve. He could take assurance in the promise that "you will be gathered to your grave in peace" (*běšālôm*; v. 20).

According to the story, Hilkiah, Shaphan, and the rest of the delegation took Huldah's words back to the king. The king, to his credit, tried to obviate the inevitable by calling the inhabitants together for a covenant renewal ceremony. Measures were also taken to purge the land of any and all vestiges of foreign worship practices left over from previous generations (2 Kgs 23:1–25). Indeed, the king suggests in 22:13 that part of his own worry about the scroll's meaning for the present had to do with his knowledge of how previous generations have utterly failed to abide by its contents ("our ancestors did not obey the words of this book"). But his reforms were all in vain.[8] The wheels of justice were already beginning to grind against Judah. From as far back as the days when the northern kingdom fell, Judah stood under condemnation (17:19). And, after the abominable idolatrous practices (re)introduced in Judah during the reign of Manasseh, it was just a matter of time when the axe would fall (21:1–15).

While her most obvious task in the narrative is to authenticate the scroll that King Josiah's delegation brings to her, Huldah's office as a prophet required her to go beyond the king's assignment and take her prophetic duties one step further by interpreting the scroll's meaning for Judah. This task establishes Huldah as a true prophet—one who fits the criterion for becoming a part of the Deuteronomistic canon. In the end, history confirmed Huldah's oracle concerning Judah: "I will indeed bring disaster on this place and on its inhabitants—all the words of the book that the king of Judah has read."[9] Approximately three decades later, Judah was besieged by and fell to Babylonian forces (2 Kings 24–25).

This prophet does not only divine what lay ahead for the southern kingdom. The king's personal fate also becomes a part of her prophetic purview. Unlike the prophets Samuel, Ahijah, Nathan, Elijah, Elishah, and Micaiah

---

8. A sampling of the places where the reforms outlined in 2 Kings 23 resonate with what we find in Deuteronomy include: centralizing worship in Jerusalem and abolishing surrounding cult sites (Deuteronomy 12); ridding the land of diviners (Deuteronomy 18); and celebrating Passover (Deuteronomy 16).

9. How were kings and kingdoms to distinguish true from false prophets? Only time and history will be able to distinguish one from the other, according to Deut 18:22. Huldah was a true prophet because history proved her correct. While her oracle is in direct response to the king's desire to confirm that the Torah scroll is authentic, one can only believe that Huldah, as unequivocal as her words appear at first glance, held out hope as a prophet that Judah might change its ways and avert disaster.

who condemned the kings to whom they were sent, Huldah tried to secure Josiah's place in history by announcing that he personally would be spared the judgment that awaited Judah. Of course, Josiah didn't exactly live out his old days quietly, as one who would expect from the phrase "gathered to your grave in peace." In fact, less than a dozen years later, Josiah would die at Megiddo in a battle against Pharaoh Neco (609 B.C.E.), as the latter was on his way to assist Assyria in curbing Babylon's growing hegemony in the area (23:28–30). Huldah's seeming blunder about Josiah's fate is "the one fly in the ointment" in an otherwise commendable execution of duties.[10] That the Deuteronomistic editors chose not to excise Huldah's prophecy from the accounts attests to what appears to be the oracle's overall importance to the momentous events that took place during the final decades of the seventh century.

As for her specific prediction about Josiah, the passage is the subject of much debate. Some commentators have argued that Huldah's oracle, which focuses on both Judah's fate and the king's personal fate, is a composite work deriving from separate sources.[11] Medieval commentators who insisted upon the integrity of Huldah's oracle explained away her seeming blunder by arguing that the prophecy never meant to say that the king would die nonviolently. Rather, what Huldah meant was that the king would die before Judah's calamity and thus be spared the grief of witnessing Judah's disastrous ruin.[12] But others like Baruch Halpern have shown that, theological rationalizations aside, the narratological evidence suggests that the prophet's words to the king (and to Judah) were not meant to be a precise prediction of Judah's calamity. Nor were her words to Josiah hinting at the precise circumstances surrounding the king's death.

Placing Huldah's oracle side-by-side with other prophetic sayings in the Old Testament indicates that her words were meant to inspire the people to repentance rather than to condemn them eternally. Assuring the king that he would be "gathered to his ancestors in peace" meant only that he would be buried in peace with his ancestors, not that he would necessarily live a long life and afterwards die of natural causes. Written as it was during

10. Baruch Halpern, "Why Manasseh Is Blamed for the Babylonian Exile: The Evolution of a Biblical Tradition," *VT* 48 (1998) 497.

11. See Antony F. Campbell and Mark A. O'Brien (*Unfolding the Deuteronomistic History: Origins, Upgrades, Present Text* [Minneapolis: Fortress, 2000] 458) who argue that Huldah's original oracle was concerned only with confirming the Torah scroll as legitimate. Accretions were later added by editors working during or after the exile to explain the causes for the exile, laying the blame on the institution of kingship in Israel and/or on the abominations committed by the inhabitants.

12. See Halpern's summary of the medieval and modern proposals for interpreting Huldah's oracle ("Why Manasseh Is Blamed," 493–501).

Josiah's time (and before his death), Huldah stood in the tradition of prophets before and after her saying: "Doom is coming unless you change your ways."[13] Josiah's contrition was symbolically the first step in forestalling disaster. But, in the end, neither his piety nor the acts of cult purification he initiated would be enough, says the Deuteronomist.

What is clear in all this is that the writer of 2 Kings had a special interest in the final decades of the seventh century—special enough, in fact, to retain Huldah's enigmatic interpretation of Judah and the king's fate. Indeed, upon closer examination, one discovers that Huldah's prophecy and the whole complex of material about the king functions as a fitting end, or *inclusio*, to the entire complex of historiographic material extending from Deuteronomy to 2 Kings. The religious and political reforms that Josiah initiated through the discovery of the Torah scroll[14] function as a fitting climax to the compilation which begins with Moses' recitation of the law and the warnings found in the book of Deuteronomy. Huldah's interpretation of Judah's disaster only confirms the curses and calamities that centuries earlier the prophet Moses had warned his audience would await them if they failed to live up to the stipulations of the covenant. Though one hesitates to argue that the Deuteronomistic scribes saw Huldah as a clear successor to Moses' prophetic ministry, one is struck by the ways in which her oracle stands in the tradition of Deuteronomistic spokespeople who came on the scene at critical junctures in Israel's history to harken back to the touchstones of Deuteronomistic teaching: covenant loyalty, right worship, and the opportunity to repent and mend their ways before it was too late.

A common literary feature of the Deuteronomistic tradition is to insert editorial expositions or valedictory speeches on the mouths of eminent spokespersons (e.g., Moses, Joshua, Samuel, David) as a way of summarizing some of the decisive junctures in Israel's history. If a prophetic figure couldn't be found, the narrator/editor then offered his own editorial on the period. For example, in Joshua 23, Joshua summarized the story of Israel's conquest of Canaan, again reminding them of their disobedience, but ultimately emphasizing YHWH's fidelity and challenging them to observe "all

---

13. Ibid., 498. See also Christopher R. Seitz, *Zion's Final Destiny: The Development of the Book of Isaiah: A Reassessment of Isaiah 36–39* (Minneapolis: Fortress, 1991).

14. The matter of the divergent chronology given to Huldah's prophecy by 2 Kgs 22:15–20 and by 2 Chr 34:23–28 *vis-à-vis* Josiah's reforms continues to be a lively and fascinating topic of scholarly debate. For two helpful discussions of issues involved, see Halpern, "Why Manasseh Is Blamed"; and David A. Glatt-Gilad, "The Role of Huldah's Prophecy in the Chronicler's Portrayal of Josiah's Reforms," *Bib* 77 (1996) 16–31. That the reforms were already underway by the time Huldah was approached, however subtle and modest they may have been in the beginning, is evident from the fact that temple improvements had already begun.

that is written in the book of the law of Moses" (Josh 23:6). But to do justice to Israel's failure to dispossess the remaining inhabitants of the land, the editor later steps in and summarizes where Israel had gone wrong (Judg 2:11–15). Similarly, the editor's voice comes through loud and clear when the time comes to describe and explain the downfall of the northern kingdom (2 Kgs 17:7–23). Later, in 2 Kings 21, the inference is that things had deteriorated so much during Manasseh's reign that no prophet was on hand to denounce the abominations Manasseh wrought upon the kingdom and their consequences upon Judah. So the narrator provided his own editorial judgment (2 Kgs 21:1–18).

At other times, however, prophets arose who offered the people the opportunity to repent and avert disaster. The amount of material devoted to the ministries of the ninth-century prophets Elijah and Elisha by the Deuteronomistic school suggests that both were seen as faithfully following in the footsteps of Moses the exemplar prophet of the tradition. Their preaching hearkened back to core Deuteronomistic teachings on covenant loyalty, repentance, and monotheistic worship. But YHWH did not allow prophetic activity to end with Elijah and Elisha. Later, in the eighth century, prophets such as Isaiah, whom Hezekiah consulted in times of crisis (2 Kings 19), and Huldah, who stepped out of the shadows to consult with Josiah and his delegation (2 Kings 22), rose up. And then there was Jeremiah, who tried—in vain—to persuade two Judean kings, Jehoiakim and Zedekiah, to trust YHWH, and whose preaching resounds with Deuteronomistic ideology and phraseology. Despite each prophet's ministry, the people ultimately failed to yield their whole heart to YHWH, obeying YHWH's stipulations; therefore, the monarchy's final collapse was justified.

What specific role does Huldah's oracle play in this doomed saga? By the time of the exile, Huldah's oracle hammers at the reader the effects of the southern kingdom's cumulative sin. Her interpretation of the scroll as a warning for Judah concerning its downfall confirmed prophetically, without mentioning it, exactly what the editor had already proclaimed earlier in 2 Kgs 21:10–16. Like Samaria, Jerusalem, too, would fall. As noteworthy as his efforts were to lead the people to repent and expurgate from Jerusalem all traces of the idolatrous worship practices which had climaxed during the reign of his grandfather Manasseh (2 Kgs 23:1–27), Josiah could not in the end reverse time.[15] His own "untimely" death signaled that and served as the beginning of the end.

---

15. For the Deuteronomist, it was during the reign of Manasseh, Josiah's grandfather, that the kingdom reached the pinnacle of its evil ways (2 Kgs 17:1–18). While the Deuteronomist paints a harsh picture of Manasseh and attributes Judah's fall uncategorically to Manasseh's abominations, the Chronicler insists that, while he was a wicked king, he

Unlike the major prophets Isaiah and Jeremiah, whose names are appended to books purporting to offer insight into the prophet's professional and personal life, and unlike minor prophets living roughly around the same time as Huldah—prophets like Zephaniah, Nahum, and Habakkuk, whose oracles were collected and canonized—there is no book named in Huldah's honor. No body of writing remains to distinguish her work from that of other prophets living and working about the same time. This, even though she herself was obviously literate. This, even though her oracle set in motion widespread reforms throughout Judah and parts of Samaria. It is her reputation as a prophet with expertise in legislation that brings her to the attention of Josiah and her readers. She filled a very real void in the cataclysmic events of the seventh century. Here was a prophet, a spokesperson in the Deuteronomistic tradition, who could see what no one else could see at the time: Time was running out for Judah.

III. *A Commentary on Gender*

Commentators have had a lot to say about the fact that Huldah was female, and not male. The chauvinism of some of their logic is a commentary itself. For example, the medieval Jewish exegete Rashi, famous for his exegetical goal of recovering the "plain sense" (*pĕšaṭ*) of the text, opined that Josiah solicited Huldah instead of the other prophets living in Jerusalem because he expected a woman to reply more gently than would, say, someone like Jeremiah.[16] A Protestant scholar, John Gray, writing on 2 Kings centuries after Rashi, defended Josiah's choice of Huldah with the following statement: "it was probably felt that such independent spirits [as those of Jeremiah and Zephaniah] would have given an answer which the priests considered *ultra vires*, whereas Huldah, the wife of a minor Temple official, would have given the divine authority to what they sought without embarrassing them."[17] Both statements show how deeply ingrained stereotypes affect readers' readings and how they affect readings for centuries on end. To their credit, however, both Jewish and Protestant interpreters have seen Huldah in a more positive light. Early Jewish interpreters saw in Huldah's expertise inspiration for their own tradition of biblical study and midrashic

---

nevertheless repented toward the end of his reign and became a religious reformer before the Assyrians carted him off in fetters to Babylon (2 Chr 33:1–20).

16. Rashi's commentary on the Torah is the most widely studied of all the medieval Jewish commentaries. See the translation by Morris Rosenbaum and Abraham M. Silbermann, *Pentateuch with Targum Onkelos, Haphtaroth and Prayers for Sabbath and Rashi's Commentary* (London: Shapiro, Vallentine & Co., 1946).

17. John Gray, *I & II Kings: A Commentary* (2d. ed.; OTL; Philadelphia: Westminster Press, 1970) 726.

commentary, and so in general judged her positively—despite some pretty chauvinistic reasoning given to the king's choice to consult her. One Jewish tradition held that Huldah was in fact the head of a school of learning during her day and that the southern gates to the temple, which were supposedly named in her honor, actually opened onto her academy.[18] One Protestant interpreter has argued that, despite being a woman, Huldah was chosen over Jeremiah because she was literate. Arguing that Jeremiah was illiterate and had to rely upon the services of his scribe Baruch ben Neriah (see Jeremiah 36) to write down his oracles suggests that he lacked the literacy skills to decipher the scroll's contents.[19]

As well meaning as some mean (or meant) to be, few commentators have ascribed much literary or theological significance to Huldah's presence in 2 Kings. Despite her expertise, she was in the end a woman outgunned by the ambitions of the men around her, a lackey for Josiah, a spokesperson for Deuteronomi(sti)c ideology, chosen because she was female more than because she was competent. She was not an authoritative figure. And such a perspective is right, at least in part. Historically speaking, Josiah probably did have ulterior reasons for consulting Huldah. He may indeed have expected a woman to respond differently from a man. What else he expected from her and whether she spoke as he expected, we do not know. We can only guess. Contemporary readers are left to guess based upon their own biases and notions about women, about women prophets, and about women serving in public offices.

In fact, that Huldah was a woman is not incidental to the story told by the Deuteronomistic narrator who is selective about what he says about her. Neither is her gender incidental to the signs and the times in which she lived. That Huldah was female only reinforced the narrator's message. A woman knew what the king only suspected, what the inhabitants in Jerusalem were deafly ignorant about, and what was patently evident to the narrator/editor centuries later: Judah was doomed. The narrator relies upon the audience's curiosity about Huldah being female to dramatize his point about the inescapability of Judah's fate. All other details about her paled in significance when compared with the fact that a woman was able to perceive the signs of the times. But female prophets were not unheard of. Despite the many speculations about her gender, Huldah stood in a long

18. Cf. *b. Meg.* 14b. To understand the genesis of the tradition that saw Huldah as head of her own academy, see the Targumic rendering of 2 Kgs 22:14 where *mišneh* is translated as "study" instead of "second." Rashi in particular argued that the gates named in Huldah's honor led to her academy (see his comment on *b. Meg.* 14b).

19. William E. Phipps, "A Woman Was the First to Declare Scripture Holy," *BRev* 6/9 (April 1990) 15.

tradition of women who throughout the Former Prophets showed themselves to be quick-witted and wise, discerning and able to invoke YHWH's words for circumstances when the time called for them to do so. We know that speechmaking was not a male activity alone. The Queen of Sheba, the wise women of Tekoa and Abel-Beth-Maacah, and Abigail, among others, also spoke at critical junctures in the history of Israel to confirm YHWH's will to a divinely chosen leader and to call Israel to renewed obedience. By restricting details about Huldah other than her gender, her husband's name, and the section of city she lived in, the narrator both tantalizes his audience and makes them strain forward to peer closer at the few clues he did see fit to leave. The fact that beyond the parallel story of Josiah's reforms in 2 Chronicles 34 this sketchily delineated female prophet is mentioned nowhere else in Scripture only adds to her mystique and forces us to peer closer at the ways the imaginative worlds of readers and texts intersect and bump heads with each other.

IV. Women's Stories and Women's Identities

We see already from the examples above how eager readers are to assign motive and meaning to characters they encounter in texts. Indeed, the less detail given about a character, the more readers impute significance to the few details that are offered, the more inclined they are to draw on their own experiences to help make the character come alive and gain significance in the narrative.[20] Many women graduate students in Bible of my generation had favorite female biblical characters whose stories we read and reread when we were still students. The contributions of these women to biblical history served as touchstones for our own ambitions and achievements in the public realm. But once we took our place in the guild of scholars such naive ways of reading and such pre-critical praise of biblical women had to be abandoned. We learned to accept detachment from our female subjects as part of the discipline of becoming educated. If we continued to care about or identify with women in the Bible, we learned as scholars to camouflage our interests by framing whatever we wrote or said about them in terms of their function in Scripture as stereotypes, literary representations, or social constructions of the ancient world that shaped them. Mainstream patriarchal biblical criticism taught us to talk about the ancient women of Israel, no matter how valiant or victimized they appeared, as products of

---

20. For a helpful discussion of how ambiguity ("gapping") functions in narratives, how authors manipulate gaps (poetic uncertainty), and how readers navigate gapping in the reading process, see "Gaps, Ambiguity and the Reading Process," in Meir Sternberg's *The Poetics of Biblical Narrative: Ideological Literature and the Drama of Reading* (Bloomington: Indiana University Press, 1987) 186–229.

their social world. Feminist biblical criticism taught us to view them as "male-authored characters [who] reveal more about the wishful thinking, fears, aspirations, and prejudices of their male creators than about real women's lives/experience/perceptions."[21] Of course, some women in some biblical texts fared better than others, depending upon the literary genre that bore us their story. In the mythopoeic world of Genesis and in the discursively symbolic world of Proverbs, women like Eve, Sarah, Hagar, Rebekah, Rachel, and the ideal woman in Proverbs 31 come off more as literary representations of the archetypal wife and mother concocted by ancient male narrators for the purposes of narrative plot-making than they do as real flesh-and-blood ancient women with complex needs and interests.[22]

In the historiographic texts of Deuteronomy–2 Kings, which recount the saga of Israel's ambivalent struggle for national identity—a saga interlaced throughout with ambition, bloodshed, and sexual violence—the story is not much different. Women like Deborah, Jael, the wise woman of Tekoa, Tamar, Bathsheba, Rizpeh, and Huldah come across as subordinate characters, supporting actresses, bit players in a larger plot that revolves around the unpredictable passions of men.[23] As Phyllis Bird says succinctly: "The[y] [women in the Bible] are necessary to the drama and may even steal the spotlight occasionally; but the story is rarely about them."[24] Even the prophet Huldah, who seems to stand on her own feet in the Deuteronomistic Historian's story as one whose expertise in verifying ancient legislation was sought after, proves in the end to be a shadowy figure in his-

---

21. Esther Fuchs, "The Literary Characterizations of Mothers and Sexual Politics in the Hebrew Bible," *Semeia* 46 (1989) 152.

22. Ibid., 138. Neither multi-faceted nor well-developed in their roles, biblical mother figures, argues Fuchs, succumb to "literary flatness" when compared to the portrait of biblical father figures. The gender constraints inscribed in the biblical literary world in which they live result in women in the Bible lacking both the human and the literary complexity of their male counterparts. Christine Roy Yoder has recently argued, however, that what others have viewed as skewed (Fuch's "flat") characterizations of women in Proverbs may nevertheless be based in part on the lives of real women in the Persian Period. See her *Wisdom as a Woman of Substance: A Socioeconomic Reading of Proverbs 1–9 and 31:10–31* (BZAW 304; Berlin: Walter de Gruyter, 2001).

23. So subordinate a role does Huldah play in the Deuteronomistic tale about Josiah and the reforms of the seventh century that some scholars have devoted pages to thrashing out the relationship between Josiah, the Torah scroll, and the book of Deuteronomy without so much as mentioning once Huldah's relationship to any of the items in question. For a recent example of a modern text that completely ignores Huldah while purporting to describe the Bible's origins and the role the law scroll of 621 B.C.E. played in inspiring Holy Writ, see Richard Elliott Friedman, *Who Wrote the Bible?* (San Francisco: HarperCollins, 1987).

24. Phyllis Bird, *Missing Persons and Mistaken Identities: Women and Gender in Ancient Israel* (OBT; Minneapolis: Fortress, 1997) 34.

tory. Not enough detail is provided to allow us to fully assess her actual position in Israelite society or even her representativeness as a female prophet in the southern kingdom during that period.

We do know that Huldah is one of four named women in the Old Testament who are remembered as prophets. The others are Miriam (Exod 15:20–21) and Deborah (Judg 4:4–16), both pre-exilic prophets; and Noadiah (Neh 6:14), who was active during the postexilic period. While Huldah's professional identity in Scripture is that of prophet, she *functions* in 2 Kings 22 more in the tradition of her Deuteronomistic female predecessors, the wise women of 2 Samuel 14 and 20 who also spoke authoritatively and persuasively to royal male figures who crossed their paths. Like these wise women, Huldah does not enjoy an official position within the established inner circle of prophets and scribes, but it does appear that her special talents in certain areas of law and prophecy caused her to be called upon from time to time to perform special duties for the royal court. It is likely that being female, in part, accounts for these figures' more marginal status. Because of this social status, the wise women use proverbs, taunts, rhetorical questions, and psychological pressure in their dealings with men of power. But unlike her predecessors, Huldah the prophet did not have to resort to such tactics to carry out her duties. Her speech in 2 Kings 22 is direct and unequivocal.

The wise women of Tekoa and Abel are further marginalized by their anonymity in the Old Testament. Huldah, however, has the honor of being identified with a proper name. The only other personal detail allowed is her husband's name ("Shallum [son of Tikvah, son of Harhas]"), and where she lived ("in Jerusalem, in the Second Quarter"). It was not uncommon for married women to be introduced in these texts as the "wife of so-and-so." But it is uncommon for a narrator to comment on the section of city where a person dwelt. This is a gratuitous detail, uncharacteristically given, and surely significant when provided. An informed audience can be expected to have appreciated the hint. Situated on the western hill of Jerusalem, the Second Quarter section was a part of the city that had been enclosed by a city wall in the late eighth century during the time of King Hezekiah. That it had been opened and expanded to include residents by the time of King Josiah has led some to speculate that Huldah was a descendant of the northern kingdom, as she was living in an area that was designed to accommodate those who had sought refuge in Judah and Jerusalem as a result of Assyria's invasion into the northern kingdom.[25] This could be still further

---

25. See the commentary on 2 Kings by Robert R. Wilson in *The HarperCollins Study Bible: NRSV* (ed. Wayne Meeks et al.; New York: HarperCollins, 1993) 598. Unfortunately, little is known about this section of the city during the reign of Josiah.

indication of Huldah's marginal social status within Jerusalemite circles. Is it possible that the Second Quarter was a section of the city looked down upon by inhabitants of Jerusalem, housing as it perhaps did, descendants from the North whose traditions differed from, and were sometimes at odds with, those of the South? If so, there is the possibility that the narrator is also playing on stereotypical attitudes towards northerners, not only those towards women. But despite her marginality, Huldah may very well have been a legal expert with northern ties, a descendant of northern prophetic circles in particular, head of a circle of scribes living in the Second Quarter who had devoted themselves to preserving their northern Mosaic heritage. All of this may just explain why Huldah (and not, say, Jeremiah or Zephaniah) was consulted when the scroll containing Mosaic legislation was happened upon during temple repairs.

As striking a figure as she is, however, Huldah has no function in the Deuteronomistic narratives beyond her speech legitimating the Torah scroll. Her character lacks any depth of characterization, leaving her to bloom more in the mind of her readers than on the pages of Scripture. We know what she said but we do not know her reactions to what she was asked to do. That kind of character information is supplied for women elsewhere in the Old Testament. For example, in the story about Solomon and his foreign visitor, the Queen of Sheba, the admiring queen admitted that she was at first skeptical about the report of King's Solomon's wisdom and wealth, but decided to come see for herself (1 Kgs 10:6–10). We get some notion of the queen as a bold, curious sort who could not rest until she knew if this was true. This female character comes across as a woman with personality, identity, and initiative. It is not a lot, but it is enough to make her an individual in her own right and not simply a mouthpiece for the narrator.[26] In comparison, Huldah is one-dimensional, especially in light of her contribution.

Despite a somewhat flat, lackluster portrait, and despite a lack of concrete historical data to help us grasp the real life circumstances of professional women like Huldah and the lives of other ordinary ancient women in Israel, there are nevertheless some interesting things one can glean from the choices the narrator made in weaving this national saga together to (re-)present the world of kings, high priests, domination, reform, revolt, doom, and God. While Huldah herself lacks depth, the story about her and its insertion into this otherwise androcentric saga lend considerable depth, dimension, and pathos to this account of the last decades of Judah. We have

---

26. For an excellent discussion of the ways in which anonymity and personal identity are constructed in biblical narratives, see Adele Reinhartz, *"Why Ask My Name?": Anonymity and Identity in Biblical Narrative* (Oxford: Oxford University Press, 1998).

seen that gender is not insignificant for the narrator of 2 Kings 22, though Huldah is still more of a male-authored character than a real flesh-and-blood ancient woman. The narrator makes no apology about the fact that the king sought out the counsel of a female prophet. He leaves the audience to react on their own. In fact, he relies upon the audience's reaction to reinforce his point. *Even a woman* (granted, one renowned and skilled) could see toward the end of the seventh century that the kingdom was doomed to disaster.[27] Why couldn't the leading men see the same thing? Despite whatever commendable reforms King Josiah had already set in motion, Judah's fate was sealed. Like Samaria before it, the tiny kingdom of Judah was fated to fail (2 Kgs 21:10–15). Even a woman could perceive that. And not only was she a woman. She was an *outsider*. As the wife of the king's valet, she was not part of the inner royal circle. As a northerner, she held different beliefs and traditions. But she knew what those on the inside did not. How blind could the nation at large be to the ways and will of YHWH?

Finally, what better way to expose the deluded hopes, the narrow thinking, and nervous ambitions of men than to juxtapose them against the insight and talent of a weaker character who fades in and out of the shadows? Stories are hardly built around minor characters. But minor characters like Huldah do have a way of sneaking up on the narrative sometimes and stealing the spotlight from those accustomed to having it. Huldah the prophet, wife of Shallum the king's valet, enters the narrative unannounced and unexpectedly, and she departs from the narrative unobtrusively and without a trace of her true identity. For the brief moment she is on stage, she piques the audience's curiosity and captures their imaginations. Her story, extraneous thought it may be, becomes *the* point of the larger story.

V. *Reading a Woman's Life*

With little biographical detail to go on, readers are left to their own imagination when trying to reconstruct a life for Huldah. That her professional role as a prophet completely overshadowed her husband's role as the king's valet has made some wonder about her marriage.[28] Some have seen

---

27. There is always the possibility, of course, that Huldah is (one of) the narrator(s)/ Deuteronomistic scribe(s) who is recounting this story of the Torah scroll's discovery and the role she played in interpreting it and warning the inhabitants. But the point remains the same. Storytellers, even those weaving quasi-biographical tales, know that in order to tell a good tale they must be willing to exploit their audiences' fears, stereotypes, and prejudices about the world, about certain kinds of characters, and even about themselves as one of the characters, if they must, in order to lend irony, suspense, excitement, and charm to their tales.

28. Elizabeth Cady Stanton referred to Huldah as a "statesman" who was in a position to teach even kings: "While Huldah was pondering great questions of State and

her status as outsider to the royal court of Jerusalem as justification for positing her as a prophet of Yʜwʜ's consort, Asherah.[29] The point here is that with little to fix her solidly in the narrative, Huldah emerges for some as a fascinating silhouette lurking in the shadows of the 2 Kings narrative. Not uncommonly in the destabilizing world of postmodernist readings, principal players find themselves eclipsed by bit players, major characters are supplanted by minor characters, speakers in the text get drowned out by those silenced in the text, and the lesser-known become more fascinating than the well known. Whereas in previous decades readers were expected to submit themselves to the reality of the text and were warned against prying into the ulterior aims of the text ("pay no attention to that man behind the curtain"), in recent years readers have insisted upon peering behind the veil that divides them from authors, narrators, editors, spinmasters, and scribes, wanting to know how characters are manipulated and the way reality gets constructed.

Sometimes the boundary between reader and character blurs, however. While scholars are trained to maintain some distance between themselves and the texts/characters they study, there are plenty of examples where scholars have had to admit that that isn't always possible. We have had to admit that we have cared about characters, we have identified with characters, we have found ourselves drawn into the lives of the characters we've encountered in these texts.[30] It is a rare reader indeed who is able to preserve forever the boundary between reader and character. Even characters we loathe are those whose point of view we tried to inhabit, but discovered that we could not. Conversely, those characters we admire and identify with are not just ones with whose point of view we sympathize. They are the ones we identify with our own point of view. We do not enter their world so much as they enter ours.

Ecclesiastical Law, her husband was probably arranging the royal buttons and buckles. . . . Marriage, in her case, does not appear to have been any obstacle in the way of individual freedom and dignity" (_The Woman's Bible_ [2 vols.; New York: Arno, 1972 (original: 1898)] 2:82).

29. See Diana Edelman, "Huldah the Prophet—of Yahweh or Asherah?" in _A Feminist Companion to Samuel and Kings_ (ed. Athalyah Brenner; Sheffield: Sheffield Academic Press, 1994) 230–50.

30. For essays by contemporary feminists on women in the Bible, see _Out of the Garden: Women Writers on the Bible_ (ed. Christiana Büchmann and Celina Spielgel; New York: Fawcett Colombine, 1994) and _Reading Ruth: Contemporary Women Reclaim a Sacred Story_ (ed. Judith A. Kates and Gail Twersky Reiner; New York: Ballantine Books, 1994). For more explicit discussions by biblical scholars on the intersection of their personal history with their biblical scholarship, see _The Personal Voice in Biblical Interpretation_ (ed. Ingrid Rosa Kitzberger; London: Routledge, 1999). There are also my own essays/Bible lessons written as nonacademic womanist commentary on select women in the Bible: _Just A Sister Away_ (Philadelphia: InnisFree Press, 1987).

For example, as a young graduate student in biblical studies, there was just so much I wanted to know about Huldah and her world but could never find out. How long had she been working as a prophet before she finally had a chance to strut her talents? Was she able to divine the scroll's authenticity after one swift reading, or did she ask the delegates for a few days with the recently-found document, promising to give the king an answer after she had had time to read it, compare it with other traditions, and to consult with YHWH about the matter? What role, if any, did she play in the subsequent reform movement that Josiah launched throughout Judah and Samaria? What role, if any, did she play in subsequent measures taken to preserve the Torah scroll, to develop it, edit it, and assemble other similar traditions to go along with it?

With nothing to prevent my imagination from wandering I imagined Huldah coming to the door of her home that day looking harried and peeved at Hilkiah and Shaphan's unannounced visit—feeling much like the poet May Sarton who often howled about the inconsiderateness of fans and devotees who intrude upon their favorite writers for advice and encouragement, insisting that they read their unsolicited (and often ill-written) manuscripts.[31] I imagine Huldah annoyed that the knock at the door came at the time that it did. She throws open the door and greets her guests with an annoyed expression on her face. As she stands in the door wondering what would bring such well-dressed strangers to her door in the middle of the day, in the background one child is crying at the top of her lungs, while two others are underfoot, peering up at the strangers from beneath her robe. The family goat dashes past Huldah, past the startled strangers, into the yard, no doubt to relieve herself in the garden Huldah kept just beyond the front entrance. Huldah avoids looking straight into the men's faces, and they are careful not to look straight at her. They fumble and stutter, obviously nervous and awkward about approaching a woman who is no relation to them. All Huldah can make out above the din of the crying baby and the children's laughter is something about her being a prophet, her ties to the North, the law, the king, Judah and Samaria, and YHWH, as one of them stands pointing to a musty, dusty scroll under his arm. She fixes her eyes on the tattered scroll and recognizes the faint script written on it.

Another image comes to mind. Huldah is sequestered in a room of her own when the knock at the door comes. She leaves it to one of the servant girls to answer. Past the age of lust and lactation, free from the sexual demands of a husband and the nurturing demands of children, she is old

---

31. For Sarton's deeply moving tales of relocating to homes in New Hampshire and Maine in the hopes of finding a balance between her desire for solitude and her need for companions and affirmation, see her two popular journals, *Plant Dreaming Deep* (New York: Norton, 1968) and *Journal of a Solitude* (New York: Norton, 1973).

enough to be left alone, to read alone, study, or simply *be* with her own private thoughts—free to listen for God, free to listen to God, or perhaps just
free to think a thought all the way through. And then comes the sound of
strange feet shuffling in the front room. She hears her name. One of the
servants peers into her private quarters and announces the guests in the
other room. She comes out of her room to find what appears to be several
elite ruffians standing before her with sheepish looks on their faces, and a
weathered scroll under the arm of one of them. The dusty, tattered look of
the scroll reeks of something mysterious. Nothing was more fascinating to
her than the secret world of the printed word. Scrolls and books reminded
her of the precious spices Hebrew women kept sealed in the hem of their
garments to perfume their bodies and to keep safe from the reach of
thieves. She listens impatiently to the men's speech, anxious to unroll the
scroll and to see what divine secrets it might reveal.

Part of readers' fascination with the stories of women in the Bible—despite all that they may come to know about the hopelessly patriarchal character of the world, literary and historical, that these women inhabited—
has to do with the insatiable appetite readers have for stories in general.
Reflecting on readers' unquenchable appetite for narratives that purportedly give them access into the deeply personal experiences of protagonists
and the private musings of authors, Jill Kerr Conway writes:

> Theory can help us read religious stories about women with more critical
> awareness. Gender studies can help us pay attention to when and where
> women autobiographers seem to have trouble with their narrative. But the
> answer to the question of why readers like to read stories, why individuals sit
> down at desk or table and tell stories, lies not in theory but in cultural history.
> It has to do with where we look when we try to understand our own lives,
> how we read texts and what largely unexamined cultural assumptions we
> bring to interpreting them.[32]

It is the chance to see how people, fictional or real, biblical and modern,
men and women, negotiate the world, make sense of their lives, live out
their deepest callings, do what they have to do, and how they stay (or not
stay) sane that makes readers—in their never-ending quest for scripts they
can live by—latch onto particular texts, characters, and stories and that
makes them return to those texts, characters, and stories again and again.
In short, there is something deeply satisfying about being allowed into the
experiences of another person, fictional or real. Despite all my training I
never fully gave up on Huldah as my secret role model. Despite (or perhaps

---

32. Jill Kerr Conway, *When Memory Speaks: Reflections on Autobiography* (New York: Alfred A. Knopf, 1998) 4.

because of) her cameo appearance in 2 Kings, despite (or perhaps because of) her role as a mouthpiece for Deuteronomi(sti)c ideology, despite (or perhaps because of) the role she plays in the otherwise male-dominated world of kings and kingdoms, despite (or perhaps because of) all that we don't know about her—her script reminds us of the impermeability of identity. It forces us to fill in the blank and does not allow us the comfort of being impartial spectators. With serious imaginative effort we try to pry open the door to texts and stories that we believe can satisfy our curiosity, and that will make us think about and see the world and ourselves in new ways. We marvel to find on the other side of the door blurry figures like Huldah who steal our attention away from the main characters, who confirm and ridicule our prejudices, who make us see something about the world and ourselves we otherwise couldn't have seen without them, and who leave us with more questions than they answer—forcing us to go deeper within ourselves for the answers we seek.

Prophets and Kings:
A New Look at the Royal Persecution of Prophets against Its Near Eastern Background

J. J. M. ROBERTS

The conflict between prophet and king is a well-known phenomenon in biblical literature. The Bible is replete with stories about the persecution of prophets by kings. In addition to a number of generalized statements about the state-sponsored murder of prophets (1 Kgs 18:4; 19:10, 14) or of attempts to silence them (Amos 2:12; Micah 2:6; Isa 30:9–11), there are a number of accounts of the execution, imprisonment, or intimidation of particular prophets. Zechariah the son of Jehoiada was executed at the command of Joash (2 Chr 24:20–22). Jehoiakim extradited Uriah the son of Shemaiah from Egypt where he had fled and had him put to death (Jer 26:20–23), and he would have done the same to Jeremiah if it had not been for Jeremiah's powerful patron, Ahikam the son of Shaphan (Jer 26:24). Jezebel threatened to kill Elijah (1 Kgs 19:2), an unnamed king of Israel threatened to kill Elisha (2 Kgs 6:31–33), and the Judean king Amaziah threatened an unnamed prophet with death (2 Chr 25:15–16). Another Amaziah, the priest of Jeroboam II's royal sanctuary at Bethel, warned Amos to flee from Israel (Amos 7:12–13), and Jeremiah (Jer 20:1–3; 32:2–3; 37:11–16), Micaiah (1 Kgs 22:26–27), and Hanani (2 Chron 16:7–10) were all imprisoned for their prophetic activity. The narrative presentation in these accounts and the usual reading of these texts in the modern religious communities for whom these texts are authoritative tend to portray such prophets as heroic victims of powerful, evil, corrupt, and ultimately foolish

Author's note: Patrick D. Miller has been an esteemed and stimulating colleague for many years and a dear friend for even longer. His critical interest in and encouragement of my work on Israelite and Near Eastern prophecy was the driving force behind the recent publication of my collected essays by Eisenbrauns, which includes a new transliteration and English translation of all the Mari prophetic texts (see J. J. M. Roberts, *The Bible and the Ancient Near East: Collected Essays* [hereafter *BANE*; Winona Lake, Ind.: Eisenbrauns, 2002]). So it is only appropriate that I honor him with a new study of an aspect of Israelite prophecy that draws on this Near Eastern background.

rulers. But the ethical slant reflected in these stories is dependent on the acceptance of a particular religious point of view—that the prophets in question had indeed been given a true message from Israel's God, Yahweh.

The same writers who portray the persecution of the true prophets of Yahweh as a despicable act have no ethical problem with the slaughter of the prophets of Baal or even with the execution of Yahwistic prophets that they consider false. Elijah's slaughter of the prophets of Baal (1 Kgs 18:40) is portrayed in a positive light, though this was the reason Jezebel sought to kill him (1 Kgs 19:1–2). The Deuteronomistic Historian (Dtr) also gives high marks to Jehu for annihilating all the worshipers of Baal in Israel; neither Jehu's deception nor his bloodletting, which troubled Hosea (Hos 1:4), bothered Dtr. Dtr's only problem with Jehu was his failure to do away with the Yahwistic high places (2 Kgs 10:9–31). Moreover, Dtr praises Josiah for removing the pagan priests and for slaying the priests of the high places of Samaria (2 Kgs 23:5–9, 20). In the same way, the Chronicler praises king Asa of Judah for entering into a covenant with his people to kill all those who did not seek Yahweh the God of Israel (2 Chr 15:13), and Jehoida's murder of Mattan, priest of Baal, is portrayed as a positive action (2 Chr 23:17). Even Jeremiah, who suffered so much at the hand of Judean kings, seems undisturbed by his prophecy that Yahweh would hand over Ahab, son of Koliah, and Zedekiah, son of Maaseiah—two Judean prophets working among the Babylonian exiles—to Nebuchadnezzar, the Babylonian king, and that he, in turn, would burn them alive (Jer 29:21–23). It is clear from the context that Jeremiah is not censuring Nebuchadnezzar's action; the false prophets were simply getting what they deserved. Although Jeremiah accuses the two prophets of adultery (29:23), his real complaint against them—as against their fellow prophet, Shemaiah of Nehelam (29:24–32)—was that their prophecies kept the Judean community in exile stirred up with false expectations that Babylon would be overthrown and that the exiles would soon return to Judah.[1]

This harsh attitude toward both foreign prophets and false prophets of Yahweh was in fact encoded in the Deuteronomic law. It demanded that the death penalty be imposed on any prophet who advocated worshiping other gods, no matter how impressive the prophet's powers might appear to be (Deut 13:1–5). Moreover, the law lumped the prophet who presumed to speak his or her own ideas in the name of Yahweh in the same category with the prophet who spoke in the name of another god: both were to be put to death (Deut 18:18–20). On the other hand, one was obligated to obey

---

1. It was the political unrest and turmoil created by their prophecies, rather than adultery, which would have led Nebuchadnezzar to execute Ahab and Zedekiah. So also Wilhelm Rudolph, *Jeremia* (HAT 12; Tübingen: Mohr, 1958) 169.

the real words of Yahweh that would be spoken by the true prophet. The problem, however, lay in determining which prophet was actually speaking the true word of Yahweh, and which was proclaiming falsehood in the name of Yahweh (Deut 18:21–22), and this problem was never satisfactorily solved in the Old Testament.

Once the serious difficulty of distinguishing between true and false prophecy is fully recognized, the sometimes harsh royal response to prophetic activity seems far less irrational. The prophets seldom spoke with one voice, and it was not self-evident to their contemporaries which prophet was telling the truth and which was lying. Any ruler, even a devout servant of Yahweh, when confronted by a prophet claiming to have a message from Yahweh, had to decide whether the prophet had indeed received a message from God and whether that message was reliable. These were actually two separate questions. *First*, it was important to decide whether the *prophet had actually received* a message from the deity. Prophets sometimes simply gave their own opinions or the opinions they had been paid to speak. Jeremiah accused his prophetic opponents of speaking their own opinions (Jer 14:14), and Nehemiah discovered that the prophet Shemaiah had not been sent to him by Yahweh, but by Nehemiah's enemies, Tobiah and Sanballat (Neh 6:10–13). Nehemiah even suggests that a number of other prophets who gave him messages calculated to terrify him were not in the service of Yahweh (Neh 6:14). Interestingly enough, Jeremiah is accused of the same kind of treachery after the murder of Gedaliah, when the people ask him to inquire of Yahweh for them as to whether they should stay in Judah or flee to Egypt. He gives them an oracular response that they should stay in Judah, but his message is rejected with the following telling words:

> You are telling a lie. The LORD our God did not send you to say, "Do not go to Egypt to settle there"; but Baruch son of Neriah is inciting you against us, to hand us over to the Chaldeans, in order that they may kill us or take us into exile in Babylon. (Jer 43:2–3)

But even if one were convinced that the prophet had indeed been sent by the deity and was speaking the message given by the deity, that did not answer the *second* question: *whether or not the message were true*. Deities were known to lie.[2] According to the Micaiah ben Imlah story, even Yahweh

---

2. See my treatment of the false oracles given by deities in J. J. M. Roberts, "Does God Lie? Divine Deceit as a Theological Problem in Israelite Prophetic Literature," in *Congress Volume: Jerusalem, 1986* (ed. J. A. Emerton; VTSup 40; Leiden: E. J. Brill, 1988) 211–20, now reprinted in my *BANE*, 123–31.

might resort to sending a lying spirit into the mouth of his prophets if it suited his purposes (1 Kgs 22:19–23).

There was ultimately no way to guarantee the truthfulness of the deity. A deity was more apt to lie to a person who had angered the deity by disobedience or neglect, so one could attempt to keep the deity happy by humble and obedient attention to the deity's will, and, at least in Mesopotamia, when one consulted the oracle, one always implored the deity to tell the truth. Nevertheless, there was no way to control or test the veracity of the divine word before the fact. One simply had to trust the deity.

The reliability of the prophet, however, was subject to more control. In Mesopotamia, a prophet's message was checked by testing it against the more standard divination by liver omens. If the liver omen confirmed that the prophet had received his or her message from the deity, then the prophet's word would be considered more seriously. The liver omens themselves were confirmed by taking multiple omens to see if they consistently agreed. To prevent collusion between the prophets or omen experts, kings were known to separate them into as many as four isolated groups so that one would receive four independent responses. If they all agreed, so the logic went, then the deity had indeed given the message. Unfortunately, there is very little evidence indicating how Israelite kings determined the veracity of prophetic oracles, but Jehosphaphat's request for a second prophetic opinion in the Micaiah ben Imlah story suggests that kings in Israel and Judah made analogous attempts to confirm the authenticity of prophetic oracles (1 Kgs 22:5–7).

Whatever royal controls the Israelite and Judean kings may have employed to sort out genuine prophetic messages from human imitations, the biblical material suggests that Judean and Israelite prophets often gave a sign that the message they were proclaiming was a true message from God. In semi-legendary narratives about famous prophets, these signs sometimes have miraculous qualities. Thus, in the narrative about Hezekiah's recovery from his illness, Isaiah's prophecy is confirmed by having the shadow from the sundial move in the opposite direction from what was normal (2 Kgs 20:8–11). Prophets may occasionally have claimed the power to give such signs. Isaiah offered Ahaz his choice of signs, whether it was as deep as Sheol or high as heaven (Isa 7:11). But the normal signs one finds in the prophetic corpus are more mundane. They often revolve around time limits.[3] When Ahaz refused to ask for a sign, the sign Isaiah gave him was a time limit: by the time the expected child of a pregnant woman known to

---

3. See my extended discussion of prophetic time-limit signs in J. J. M. Roberts, "Of Signs, Prophets, and Time Limits: A Note on Psalm 74:9," *CBQ* 39 (1977) 474–81, now reprinted in idem, *BANE*, 274–81.

both Ahaz and Isaiah had reached the age of weaning, the threat to Jerusalem from Aram and Israel would be a thing of the past (Isa 7:16). Isaiah gave a similar time-limit sign to his Judean audience in connection with the birth of his son Maher-shalal-hash-baz (Isa 8:4), and later, during Sennacherib's siege of Jerusalem, Isaiah is reported to have offered a similar time-limit sign to confirm his oracle that Sennacherib would not capture the city:

> And this shall be the sign for you: This year eat what grows of itself, and in the second year what springs from that; then in the third year sow, reap, plant vineyards, and eat their fruit. The surviving remnant of the house of Judah shall again take root downward, and bear fruit upward; for from Jerusalem a remnant shall go out, and from Mount Zion a band of survivors. The zeal of the LORD of hosts will do this. (Isa 37:30–32)

In fact, even the story of Hezekiah's healing contains such a time-limit sign. In the version of the story found in 2 Kings, Isaiah is sent back to Hezekiah with this message:

> Thus says the LORD, the God of your ancestor David: I have heard your prayer, I have seen your tears; indeed, I will heal you; on the third day you shall go up to the house of the LORD. I will add fifteen years to your life. I will deliver you and this city out of the hand of the king of Assyria; I will defend this city for my own sake and for my servant David's sake. (2 Kgs 20:5–6)

Note that the recovery from the illness within three days functions to confirm the reliability of the other promises—the extra fifteen years of life and the deliverance from Assyria. In the Kings narrative, Hezekiah then asks for a sign that he will recover within three days, and it is only then that the miraculous sign of the retreating shadow is given (2 Kgs 20:8–11), but in the parallel in Isaiah, the miraculous sign has totally displaced the sign of the recovery in three days (Isa 38:4–8).

The so-called false prophets also gave such signs. Jeremiah's opponent, Hananiah son of Azzur, prophesied:

> Thus says the LORD of hosts, the God of Israel: I have broken the yoke of the king of Babylon. Within two years I will bring back to this place all the vessels of the LORD's house, which King Nebuchadnezzar of Babylon took away from this place and carried to Babylon. I will also bring back to this place King Jeconiah son of Jehoiakim of Judah, and all the exiles from Judah who went to Babylon, says the LORD, for I will break the yoke of the king of Babylon. (Jer 28:2–4)

In this case, the passage of two years proved Hananiah wrong and Jeremiah right, but one could not always count on the failure of the signs given by false prophets. Deuteronomy reckons with the possibility that the signs given by such a prophet may come to pass. But even if the signs given by a prophet come to pass, Deuteronomy states that if the prophet urges one to turn to other gods than Yahweh, that prophet's message is to be rejected, and the prophet is to be put to death (Deut 13:1–5).

This whole discussion of the ambiguity surrounding the reliability of the prophetic word simply underscores the fact that a king in antiquity could never rely solely on the prophetic word in planning his social, political, military, and diplomatic policies. Kings surrounded themselves with royal counselors and military advisors, and they tried to stay informed of developments throughout their regions of interest by a system of informants, spies, and well-placed diplomats. The prophetic word was only one element in the mix that resulted in particular royal decisions. When the prophetic word confirmed or complemented the other sources of information, it was appreciated. But the prophetic word often conflicted inconveniently with the other determining factors in royal policy; in such cases, it led to serious internal conflict within government circles.

This is clear from the Mari archives, deriving from Mesopotamia in the first half of the second millennium B.C.E., where the prophetic word could be a seriously disruptive impediment to government plans. A provincial governor fully engaged in bringing in the wheat harvest certainly did not welcome the appearance of a prophet who announced the demand of the god that the governor drop whatever he was doing, and immediately construct a new gate.[4] One may suspect that Zimri-Lim, the king of Mari, was

---

4. This is text no. 9 in my treatment of the Mari prophetic texts in my *Bible and the Ancient Near East*, 182–85. It corresponds to A.4934. = *ARM* III 78 = *AEM* I/I, 221. The text reads as follows:

[1][*a-na be-l*]*í-ya* [2][*qí*]-*bí-ma* [3][*um-ma*] *Ki-ib-ri-*ᵈ*Da-gan* [4][ìʀ]-*ka-a-ma* [5][ᵈD]*a-gan ù* ᵈ*Ik-ru-ub-Il ša-al-mu* [6][*a-l*]*um Ter-qa*ᵏⁱ *ù ḫa-al-ṣú-um ša-lim* [7][*a-n*]*a* [*š*]*e-i-im ša ḫa-al-ṣí-ya e-ṣé-di-im* [8][*ù*] *a-na* ᴷᴵ.ᵁᴰʰⁱ·ᵃ *na-sa-ki-im* [9][*a-ḫa-a*]*m ú-ul na-de-e-ku* [10][*ša-ni-ta*]*m aš-šum a-bu-ul-lim* ɢɪʙɪʟ [11][*e-pé-ši*]-*im i-na pa-ni-tum* [12][x x x] ˡᵘ*mu-uḫ-ḫu-ú-um* [13][*il-li-ka*]*m-ma* (or: [*iq-bé-e-e*]*m-ma*) [14][*i-ta-aš-ša*]-*aš* [15][*um-ma šu*]-*ma* [16][*a-na ši-pí-ir a-bu*]-*ul-lim* [*š*]*a-a-ti* [17][*qa-at-ka šu-k*]*u-un* [18][*i-na-an-na u₄-u*]*m ṭup-pí an-né-e-em* [19][*a-na ṣe-e*]*r be-lí-ya ú-ša-*[*b*]*i-lam* [20][ˡᵘ*mu-u*]*ḫ-ḫu-ú-um šu-ú i-tu-ra-am-ma* [21][*ki-a-am*] *iq-bé-e-em* [22][*ù da*]*n-na-tim iš-ku-na-am um-ma-a-mi* [23][*šum-ma*] *a-bu-ul-lam ša-a-ti* [24][*ú*]-*ul te-ep-pé-ša* [25][*ku-r*]*u-ul-lum iš-ša-ak-ka-an* [26][*ú-u*]*l ka-aš-da-tu-nu* [27][*an-n*]*i-tam* ˡᵘ*mu-uḫ-ḫu-*[*u*]*m šu-ú* [28][*iq-b*]*é-e-em ù a-na e-b*[*u-ri-im*] [29][*pu-u*]*l-lu-sa-ku sú-ḫu-u*[*r*] [30][*ki-ša*]-*di-ya ú-ul e-l*[*e-e*] [31][*šum-ma*] *be-lí i-qa-ab-bi* [32][*né-eḫ-ra-rum li-il-l*]*i-kam-ma* [continues on left side, but broken]

[1][To] my [lor]d [2][sp]eak: [3][Thus says] Kibri-Dagan, [4]your [servant]: [5][D]agan and Ikrub-Il are well. [6]The [c]ity Terqa and the district is well. [7]I am not negligent

irritated by the repeated prophetic warnings that he should restrict his movements outside the citadel;[5] from the warnings themselves it is clear that the king was reluctant to submit to these restrictions. One may also wonder how pleased Zimri-Lim was with the violent prophetic opposition to the treaty with Eshnunna that he was in the process of negotiating.[6]

---

[8][t]o harvest the [g]rain of my district [9][and] to pour it out on the threshing floors. [10][Another m]atter: Concerning [the mak]ing of the new gate [11]earlier [12][PN], the ecstatic, [13][cam]e to me (or: [spok]e to me), and [14][being troubl]ed, [15][he] spoke [as follows]: [16]["To the work on] that [ga]te [17][pu]t [your hand."] [18][Now on the da]y that I sent this my tablet [19][to] my lord, [20]that [ecs]tatic returned to me, and [21]spoke [as follows] to me, [22][and] he put it to me strongly, saying: [23]["If] that gate [24]you do [no]t make, [25][a cal]amity will take place. [26]You have accomplished no[thing at all."] [27][Th]is is what that ecstatic [28][to]ld me, but with the har[vest] [29]I am [preo]ccupied. I am not able [30]to turn my neck. [31][If] my lord commands, [32][let some help co]me to me, and. . . .

5. E.g., no. 41 (*BANE*, 232–33 = A.2209 = *AEM* I/I, 216). The text is as follows:

[1]*a-na be-lí-ya* [2]*qí-bí-ma* [3]*um-ma Tè-bi-ge-ri-su* [4]*ìr-ka-a-ma* [5]*u₄-um a-na ṣe-er Aš-ma-a[d]* [6]*ak-šu-du i-na ša-ni-i-im u₄-m[i-im]* [7]*lúna-bi-i*meš *ša ḪA.NA*meš *ú-pa-ḫ[i-ir]* [8]*te-er-tam a-na ša-la-am be-lí-y[a]* [9]*ú-še-pí-iš um-ma a-na-ku-ma* [10]*šum-ma be-lí i-nu-ma ra-ma-[ak-šu]* [11]*i-pé-šu* U₄-7-KAM *i-na ka-[wa-tim]* [12][*iš]-[š]a-ab-ma i-na šu-ul-mi-[im]* [13][*a-na a-l]im*ki [*i-tu-ur-ra-am]* (Break of about 8 lines) [1'][*um-ma-mi u₄]-um [a-na An-nu-ni-tim]* [2']*ša ka-wa-tim [be-lí il-la-ku]* [3']*be-lí pa-ga-a[r-šu]* [4']*li-iṣ-ṣú-ur [ṣa-bu-um]* [5']*i-na re-eš be-lí-[ya li-zi-iz]* [6']*ù ma-ṣa-ra-at [a-lim*ki] [7']*lu-ú dan-[na]* [8']*a-na na-ṣa-ar pa-ga-ri-[šu]* [9']*be-lí a-aḫ-šu la i-na-ad-di*

[1]To my lord [2]speak: [3]Thus says Tèbi-gerišu, [4]your servant: [5]On the next day after I arrived [6]before Ašmad, [7]I assemb[led] the prophets of the Haneans. [8]I had them take an oracle for the wellbeing of [9]my lord. I said, [10] "If my lord, when he makes [his] ablutions, [11]stays outsi[de the walls] for seven days, [12][will he return to the c]ity in safet[y]?" (Break of about 8 lines) [1'][saying, "On the d]ay [my lord goes] [2'][to Annunitum] outside the walls, [3']let my lord guard himself. [4']Let [the army] [5'][stand] at the disposal of [my] lord, [6']and let the guard over [the city] [7']be reinfor[ced]. [8']In guarding himself [9']my lord should not be negligent.

6. See texts no. 20 (*BANE*, 202–3 = A.1047 = *ARM* X 80 = *AEM* I/I, 197), 34 (*BANE*, 220–25 = A.925 + A.2050 = *AEM* I/I, 199), 36 (*BANE*, 226–27 = M.11046 = *AEM* I/I, 202). Text 20 reads as follows:

[1]*a-na Ka-ak-ka-bi* [2]*qí-bí-ma* [3]*um-ma* míI-ni-ib-ši-na-ma [4]*i-na p[a]-ni-tim Še-le-bu-um as-sí-in-nu* [5]*te-er-tam id-di-[na]m-ma aš-pu-ra-kum* [6]*i-na-an-na* I míqa-ma-[t]um [7]*ša* dD[a-gan] ša Ter-qa*ki* [8][*i]l-li-ka-am-ma* [9][*k]i-a-am iq-bé-e-em* [10][*u]m-ma ši-i-[m]a* [11]*ša-li-ma-tum ša* LÚ ÈS.N[UN.NA]*ki* [12]*da-aṣ-tum-ma* [13]*ša-pal* IN.NU.DA *mu-ú* [14]*i-il-la-ku ù a-na še-tim* [15]*ša ú-kà-aṣ-ṣa-ru a-ka-am-mi-is-sú* [16]*a-al-šu ú-ḫa-al-la-aq* [17]*ù ma-ak-ku-ur-šu* [18]*ša iš-tu aq-da-mi* [19]{šu} *šu-ul-pu-tam ú-ša-al-p[a-a]t* [20]*an-ni-tam iq-bé-e-em* [21]*i-na-an-[n]a pa-ga-ar-ka* [22]*ú-ṣú-ur ba-lum te-er-tim* [23]*a-na li-ib-bi a-lim* [24]*la te-er-ru-u[b]* [25]*ki-a-am eš-me um-ma-a-mi* [26]*a-na ra-ma-ni-šu iš-ta-na-ar-[ra]-a[r]* [27]*a-na ra-ma-ni-ka la ta-áš-t[a]-na-ar-ra-a[r]*

[1]To my Star [2]speak: [3]Thus says Inibšina: [4]Earlier Šelebum, the cult homosexual, [5]gave me an oracle, and I sent it to you. [6]Now a *qammatum* [7]of D[agan] of Terqa

One should also note the striking breach of diplomatic protocol by the prophet of Marduk in Babylon. Hammurabi of Babylon had allowed Ishme-Dagan of Ekallatum, the long-time enemy of Zimri-Lim of Mari, to take up temporary residence in Babylon while he was recovering from an illness. Yet despite Ishme-Dagan's status as an official diplomatic guest of the state, the prophet of Marduk repeatedly stood outside in the street in front of Ishme-Dagan's Babylonian residence and publicly proclaimed Marduk's imminent judgment on the former king of Ekallatum.[7] Unless

[8][c]ame to me, and [9]spoke as follows, [10]saying: [11]"The peaceful words of the man of Ešnunna [12]are only treachery. [13]Below the straw water [14]runs. But into the net [15]which he ties I will gather him. [16]His city I will destroy, [17]and his treasure [18]which is from ancient times [19]I will surely plunder." [20]This is what she said to me. [21]Now guard [22]yourself. Without an oracle [23]do not enter [24]into the center of the city. [25]Thus I have heard them say, [26]"By himself he keeps moving around." [27]Do not keep moving around by yourself.

7. Text no. 55 (*BANE*, 246–49 = A.428 = *AEM* I/2, 371). It reads as follows:

[1][*a-na be-lí-ya qí-bí-ma*] [2][*um-ma*] *Ya-ri-im-*[d][IM ÌR-*ka-a-ma*] [3]*aš-šum ṭe₄-em e-le-e Iš-* [*me-*d*Da-gan*] [4]*a-na É-kál-la-tim*[ki] [5][*š*]*a be-lí iš-te-né-mu-ú mi-im-*[*ma*] [6]*a-na É-kál-la-tim*ki *ú-ul i-*[*le-e*] [7]*a-wa-tu-šu it-ta-ab-še-e-m*[*a*] [8]*i-ta-ti-šu ir-ṭú-pu ša-ḫa-ra-am* [9]lú*a-pí-lum ša* d AMAR.UTU *i-na ba-ab é-kál-lim* [10]*iz-zi-iz-ma ki-a-*[*a*]*m iš₇-ta-na-as₆-si* [11]*um-ma šu-ma Iš-me-*d D[*a-g*]*an i-na qa-at* d AMAR.UTU [12]*ú-ul uṣ-ṣí ša-ḫar-ra-am* [13]*i-ka-aṣ-ṣa-ar* [14]*ù iḫ-ḫa-ab-ba-as-sí-im* [15]*an-né-e-tim i-na ba-ab é-kál-lim* [16]*iš₇-ta-ás-si-ma* [17][*ma-am-ma-a*]*n mi-im-ma ú-ul iq-bi-šum* [18]*ki-ma pa-ni-šu-un-ma i-na ba-ab Iš-me-*d*Da-gan* [19]*iz-zi-iz-ma i-na pu-ḫu-ur ma-a-tim ka-li-ša* [20]*ki-a-am iš₇-ta-na-ás-si um-ma-a-mi* [21]*a-na sa-li-mi-im ù dam-qa-tim ša-ka-nim* [22]*a-na ṣe-er* SUKKAL ELAM.MA-*tim ta-al-li-ik-ma* [23]*ki-ma dam-qa-tim ša-ka-nim* [24]*ni-ṣi-ir-ti* d AMAR.UTU *ù a-lim* KÁ.DINGIR.RA ki [25][*a*]-*na* SUKKAL ELAM.MA-*tim tu-še-ṣí* [26][*ka*]-*re-e ù na-ak-ka-ma-ti-ya ta-ag-mu-ur-ma* [27][*g*]*i-mi-il-li ú-ul tu-te-e-er* [28][*ù*] *a-na É-kál-la-tim*ki *ta-at-ta-al-la-ak* [29][*ša*] *ki-ma ni-ṣi-ir-ti ú-še-ṣú-ú* [30][*ta-a*]*r-di-is-sà la i-ša-al-la-an-*[*ni*] [31][*an-né*]-*e-tim i-na pu-ḫu-ur m*[*a-a-tim*] [32][*ka-li-ša iš₇-t*]*a-na-ás-su-ú* [33][*ma-am-ma-an ú*]-*ul iq-bi-*[*um*] [34][. . . . .] [35][. . . . .] [36][. . . . . *m*]*u-ur-ma* [37][. . . . . *u*]*ḫ-šu-nu-ma* [38][. . . . . *É-k*]*ál-la-tim*ki [39]*iṭ-ṭà-ra-ad ù* LÚ *šu-ú* [40]*mu-ur-ṣa-am ra-bé-e-em* [41]*ma-ru-uṣ ba-la-as-sú* [42]*ú-ul ki-in*

[1][To my lord speak]: [2][Thus says] Yarim-[Adad, your servant], [3]Concerning the report about Iš[me-Dagan] going up [4]to Ekallatum, [5]which my lord keeps hearing, he [6]did not [go up] to Ekallatum at all. [7]Words about him have started, [8]and they constantly circulate around him. [9]The respondent of Marduk stood in the gate of the palace, [10]and keeps crying out as follows, [11]saying, "Išme-D[ag]an will not escape from [12]the hand of Marduk. As a sheath (of grain) [13]it (the hand of Marduk) will tie (him), [14]and he will be chopped up by it." [15]These things he kept crying out in [16]the gate of the palace, [17][and no on]e said anything to him. [18]In the same way he stood before them in the gate [19]of Išme-Dagan and in the assembly of the whole land [20]he keeps crying out as follows, saying, [21]"To make peace and friendship [22]you went to the ruler of Elam, [23]and in order to make friendship [24]you took out the treasure of Marduk and the city of Babylon [25]to the ruler of Elam. [26]The [si]los and my stores you used up, and

the Babylonian crown was actually behind this breach of protocol for its own reasons, this behavior certainly would not have helped Hammurabi's diplomatic relations with Ekallatum.

Such prophetic actions, and others like them, for which there are many biblical parallels, complicated royal policy on a number of levels. One of the headaches prophetic activity introduced into the process of royal deliberations was *a major security issue*. In Israel, as in the rest of the Near East, it was believed that God or the gods directed the outcome of human affairs, so it was important to have divine approval for a course of action before embarking upon it. Unfortunately, there was no way for the crown to address the relevant questions to the deity without revealing something of the king's sometimes sensitive contingency plans to the human medium of revelation, whether it was an oracle priest, prophet, dreamer, or some other type of diviner. If one wanted a clear answer from the deity, one had to present the deity with a clear question, but the clearer the question, the more transparent to the medium would be the king's proposed plan of action, and there was always a danger that the medium would intentionally or inadvertently reveal those secrets to an enemy agent. To counter such a threat, the mediums at Mari had to take an oath of loyalty to the king.[8] In

---

[27]you did not return my favor. [28][And] will you go away to Ekallatum? [29][The one who] removed my treasure [30]shall not ask me for its [int]erest." [31][Thes]e things [he kep]t crying out [32]in the assembly [of the whole] la[nd]. [33][No one] spoke [to him]. [34] . . . . [35] . . . . [36] . . . . [37] . . . . [38][. . . . . . to E]kallatum [39]he sent, and that man [40]is sick with a serious illness. [41]His life [42]is not firm.

8. Text no. 57 (*BANE*, 250–53 = M.13091 = *AEM* I/1, 1):

[1][i-na te-re-e-et Zi-im-ri-Li-im be-lí-ya] [2][i-na ne-pé-eš₁₅-tim ma-li i]š-ša-k[a-nu-ma a-am-ma-ru] [3][ú-lu-ma i-na te-re-et mu-ú]š-ke-nim [4][i-na ne-pé-eš₁₅-tim ma-li i]š-ša-ka-nu-ma a-am-ma-r[u] [5][UZU le-em-na-am ù la da]m-qa-am ma-li a-am-ma-ru [6][a-na ᵐZi-im-ri-Li-im be-lí-ya] lu-ú a-qa-ab-bi la a-ka-at-ta-mu [7]UZ[U l]e-[em-na-am ù la dam-qa-a]m ša i-na te-re-et [8]ᵐZi-im-ri-L[i-im be-lí-ya i-n]a ᵘᶻᵘiz-bi-im ù i-na ᵘᶻᵘIZ.MI-im [9]iš-ša-ak-ka-nu-ma a-am-ma-ru [10]a-na DUMU a-wi-lu-tim šum-šu la a-qa-ab-bu-ú [11]ù a-wa-tam na-ṣ[í-i]r-tam ša a-na te-re-e-tim e-pé-ši-im [12]ᵐZi-im-ri-Li-im b[e]-lí i-qa-ab-bé-e-em [13]ù a-na DUMU MÁŠ.ŠU.SU₁₃.SU₁₃ tap-pé-e-ya i-qa-ab-bí-ma e-še-em-mu-ú [14]ú-lu-ma i-na te-re-e-tim e-pé-ši-im i-na qa-at M[ÁŠ.ŠU.SU₁₃.SU₁₃ tap-p]é-e-ya [15]ši-ra-am ša-a-tu a-am-ma-ru [16]a-wa-tam ša-a-ti lu-ú a-na-aṣ-ṣa-a[r] [17][a-wa-a]t DUMU a-wi-lu-tim šum-šu ša pé-em na-ak-[ra-am i-da-bu-bu-ma] [18][l]a ú-še-eṣ-ṣú-ú-ši be-lí ša-[lu-um-ma i-ša-lu-ma] [19]a-na ba-ar-tim le-mu-un-tim ù [a-na la ba-la-ṭí-im] [20]ša Zi-im-ri-Li-im be-lí-ya te-re-[tim ú-še-pé-šu] [21]a-na DUMU a-wi-lu-tim šum-šu la e[-ep-pé-šu] (Three lines erased) [22]ú e-pí-iš ba-ar-tim [l]e-mu-un-tim [a-na na-pí-iš-tim] [23]ša Zim-ri-Li-im be-lí-[ya] [24]ša a-na te-re-e-tim e-pé-[š]i-im i-qa-ab-bé-e-em [25]ù [a-na] DUMU.M[ÁŠ.ŠU].SU₁₃.SU₁₃ tap-pé-e-ya i-qa-ab-bé [26][e-še-em]-m[u-ú] ú-lu-ma i-na te-re-e-tim [27][i-na qa]-at DUMU.MÁŠ.ŠU.SU₁₃.[SU₁₃] tap-pé-e-ya [a]-a[m-m]a-ru [28][la a-ka]-at-ta-mu-šu i-na u₄-mi-šu-ma [29][a-na Zi-im]-ri-Li-im be-lí-ya lu-ú a-qa-ab-[b]i [30][lu

it they swore to reveal to the king everything the deity revealed to them, whether good or bad, but at the same time they swore to keep the message of the oracle totally secret from other ears. Moreover, if they somehow became aware that someone was having oracles taken with any evil intent toward the king, they were to report that to the king immediately. Such precautions show that the authorities were afraid that the mediums would leak sensitive information. On at least one occasion a military commander from Mari refused to supply the Mari mediums with the animals necessary to take omens because they were reporting the omens to Hammurabi of Babylon, who was temporarily allied with Mari, though Hammurabi insisted on keeping several advisors in his inner circle who had been servants of Ishme-Dagan of Ekallatum, Mari's old enemy.[9] The commander from Mari clearly considered the security risk of leaked information greater than the risk of marching without the omens. The problem was heightened if the mediums or prophets were opposed to the course of action the king

---

a-ša-a]p-p[a-a]r la a-ka-ta-mu-š[u p]a-né-šu la ub-ba-lu ³¹[É]-*ti-ya ù ra-pa-aš* É-
ti-ya ³²[*a-na] na-pí-iš-ti Zi-im-ri-Li-im be-lí-ya* ³³[   ] *li-ib-bi-ya ga-*
am-ri-im ³⁴[   ] *ra-tim-ma* [. . . .
¹'[   ] *ki-ma ša ša-la-mi-ya ù ku-ši-ri-ya* ²'[*la] e-ep-pé-šu ša na-ṣa-ar na-pí-iš-ti*
³'[   ]-*ya Zi-im-ri-Li-im be-lí-ya ep-pé-*[o] ⁴'[*a-di] ba-al-ṭà-ku lu-*⟨ú⟩ *e-ep-pé-eš*

¹[In the taking of oracles for Zimri-Lim my lord], ²[in the extispicy, all that i]s pro[duced and that I see], ³[or in the taking of oracles for an ord]inary person, ⁴[in the extispicy, all that i]s produced and that I see, ⁵[the bad and unf]avorable omen, all that I see, ⁶I will surely tell [to Zimri-Lim, my lord]; I will not conceal it. ⁷The b[ad and unfavorab]le omen which is produced and I see ⁸in taking oracles ⁹for Zimri-L[im, my lord, i]n an abnormal birth or in an *izmum* ¹⁰I will not tell to anyone whomever. ¹¹The secret word which Zimri-Lim, my lord, ¹²will say to me for the purpose of making oracular inquiry, ¹³or which he will say to a diviner, my colleague, and which I hear, ¹⁴or in the making of an oracular inquiry by the hand of a diviner, my colleague, ¹⁵that ominous sign I see, ¹⁶that word I will certainly guard. ¹⁷The word of anyone whomever who [speaks] with hostile intent, ¹⁸and does not want it brought out, who wishes [to attack] my lord, ¹⁹and [who wants] ora[cles taken] in preparation for an evil rebellion ²⁰or [for an assassination] of Zimri-Lim, my lord, ²¹for any such person, whomever it is, I will not d[o it]. (Three lines erased) ²²And the one who makes an evil rebellion [against the life] ²³of Zimri-Lim, [my] lord, ²⁴who speaks to me about taking oracles, ²⁵or who speaks to a diviner, my colleague, ²⁶[and I he]a[r] or I see in the oracles ²⁷[performed by the h]and of a diviner, my colleague, ²⁸[I swear I will not] conceal it. In that very day ²⁹I will surely tell [Zim]ri-Lim, my lord, ³⁰[or I will wri]te him. I swear I will not conceal it. I will not show him favor. ³¹. . . . of my house and the enlargement of my house ³². . . . for] the life of Zimri-Lim, my lord, ³². . . . of my complete heart ³³. . . . break ¹'. . . . as my wellbeing and my success ²'. . . . I swear I will not] do. With regard to protecting the life ³'. . . . of Zimri-Lim, my lord, I will act. ⁴'. . . . as long] as I live, I will surely act.

9. See Jean-Marie Durand, *AEM* I/I, 104, and the further discussion on p. 21.

was contemplating. It is not clear how sensitive the treaty negotiations with Eshnunna were, but the prophetic opposition to this treaty and the prophets' insistence that Zimri-Lim should make no treaty without consulting the deity first, would have made it very difficult to keep these negotiations secret if that had been the king's desire.

By contrast, it is clear that Hezekiah tried to keep his negotiations with Babylon and Egypt very secret. Isaiah complained that Judah's leaders made a treaty without consulting Yahweh (Isa 30:1–2; 31:1). Isaiah even suggests that Judah's leaders thought they could keep their plans hidden from Yahweh (Isa 29:15–16). Hezekiah's desire for secrecy is quite understandable. Treaty negotiations with Egypt or Babylon was tantamount to rebellion against Assyria, and his Assyrian overlord had many agents in the area. If word of Hezekiah's disloyalty reached Assyria too soon, before Hezekiah's defensive alliances and other defensive preparations were in place, the revolt had little chance of success. Thus it was critical to his plans to keep these negotiations secret. Given such a need for secrecy, it was important to keep this information from Isaiah, who had to have been considered a serious security risk. The prophet was known to be violently opposed to any policy that relied on foreign alliances rather than on Yahweh, and his public display of opposition to earlier attempts at negotiating alliances made it obvious that he would not keep quiet on the issue. Early in Hezekiah's reign (713–711 B.C.E.), when Ashdod revolted against Assyria and tried to get Egypt, Judah, and other neighboring states to join in the revolt, Isaiah urged the royal court to answer these messengers from Ashdod negatively; Yahweh's people would find their refuge in Zion, which Yahweh had founded (Isa 14:32). Moreover, to underscore his message, Isaiah walked around Jerusalem during this extended period naked and barefoot to symbolize what would happen to Egypt and Ethiopia, the major powers thought to be supporting this revolt (Isa 20:1–6). If Assyria led the Egyptians and Ethiopians away naked and barefoot as prisoners of war, the rebels in Ashdod obviously had no hope, and it would clearly be folly for Judah to get involved.

Whatever alerted them, the Assyrians heard about Ashdod's revolt and their negotiations with the surrounding states, and the Assyians moved quickly, crushing the revolt and pacifying the whole area. Yamani, the hapless ruler of Ashdod, escaped to upper Egypt, where he found asylum for several years, but eventually the Ethiopian king Shebitqo, for his own reasons, extradited Yamani to Assyria in chains.[10] It is no wonder, then, that the Judean court, when plotting revolt less than a decade later against the new Assyrian king Sennacherib, did not want a repeat of that earlier fiasco,

---

10. See Grant Frame, "The Inscription of Sargon II at Tang-I Var," *Or* 68 (1999) 31–57, esp. 36 lines 19–21.

and thus they tried to cut Isaiah and apparently other prophetic figures out of the loop.[11] But the presence of foreign ambassadors in Jerusalem and the sending of Judean caravans with heavy tribute to Egypt could not be kept secret from Isaiah, and his opposition to the royal policy was public, bitter, and bitingly sarcastic. In blasting the folly of Judah's attempt to buy worthless Egyptian help, help from the same Egyptians who had abandoned its ally Ashdod to its fate a few years earlier, Isaiah dismissed Egypt as "the sea monster who sits still" (Isa 30:7).[12] When Isaiah learned that Hezekiah had shown his treasury to the ambassadors from Babylon, he warned the king that he would lose all those treasures to Babylon (Isa 39:6).

That brings up a *second concern* that royal officials had about prophetic opposition. There was not only the security issue; there was *the matter of public opinion*, which even in a monarchical system was far more important than we may be inclined to think. The ancients believed that God or the gods spoke through prophets, so if a respected prophet spoke against government policy, particularly against the government's policy in instigating an obviously dangerous revolt, the prophetic critique could undermine public support for the revolt and seriously undermine the morale of the military personnel. No one wants to risk sacrificing himself in a battle that the gods have already proclaimed a lost cause. This was why, during the Babylonian siege of Jerusalem, the royal officials went to king Zedekiah seeking the death penalty against Jeremiah. They had heard Jeremiah proclaiming that Jerusalem would surely fall to the Babylonians and that only those who surrendered would survive, while those who remained in the city would die one horrible death or another. They complained to the king:

> This man ought to be put to death, because he is discouraging the soldiers who are left in this city, and all the people, by speaking such words to them. For this man is not seeking the welfare of this people, but their harm. (Jer 38:4)

Even in antiquity it was hard to prosecute a war if public opinion were solidly against it. Rehoboam, Solomon's successor, discovered this when he tried to muster his troops to force the breakaway, northern tribes to accept

---

11. For an extended discussion of this point, see J. J. M. Roberts, "Blindfolding the Prophet: Political Resistance to First Isaiah's Oracles in the Light of Ancient Near Eastern Attitudes toward Oracles," in *Oracles et Prophéties dans L'antiquité: Actes du Colloque de Strasbourg 15–17 Juin 1995* (ed. Jean-Georges Heinz; Université des Sciences Humaines de Strasbourg, Travaux du Centre de Recherche sur le Proche-Orient et la Grèce Antiques 15; Strasbourg: De Boccard, 1997) 135–46, reprinted in idem, *BANE*, 282–91.

12. NRSV: "Rahab who sits still."

his rule. His attempt was blocked by the prophetic proclamation of Shemaiah in which Yahweh prohibited the war, announcing that the split was Yahweh's own doing (1 Kgs 12:22–24). Rehoboam was undoubtedly displeased by the oracle, but even a king cannot make a war if the troops will not follow, and both troops and commanders could be very reluctant to follow if the oracles were negative. Saul could not get his troops to follow him in a night attack when he could not get a positive oracle from Yahweh (1 Sam 14:36–46), and there are numerous examples from Mesopotamia where, despite orders from higher authorities, an army refused to march against the enemy until the oracles were favorable.

Moreover, from the king's point of view, the prophetic word could have a dangerous impact, not just on general public opinion, but on the opinion and actions of the movers and shakers of society. Negative oracles about the king or positive oracles addressed to a potential rival of the king could provoke an assassination attempt or an all-out revolt. That is why the loyalty oath was imposed on the Mari diviners, and that is why Saul was so upset when he learned that Ahimelech had taken oracles for the fugitive David at Nob.[13] According to the biblical text, Jeroboam's revolt against Solomon was provoked by an oracle of Ahijah the Shilonite (1 Kgs 11:26–40), and it was a negative oracle given by Elisha for the sick Aramean king Ben-hadad that emboldened Ben-hadad's servant Hazael to murder the king and seize the throne of Damascus for himself (2 Kgs 8:7–15). It was also a prophetic oracle that ignited the revolt of Jehu, a revolt that resulted in the death of the kings of both Israel and Judah, nearly obliterated both royal houses, and decimated the cultural elite of Israel (2 Kgs 9–10). Prophetic oracles were not the innocent things for which they are sometimes mistaken. From the royal point of view they could be the equivalent of *qešer*, "rebellion" (Isa 8:12; cf. Amos 7:10), and they had the potential to be quite deadly. Hosea's words, "Therefore I have hewn them by the prophets, I have killed them by the words of my mouth" (Hos 6:5a), were more than mere rhetoric.

It is no wonder then that kings sometimes responded violently to the threat they perceived from the prophetic word. The royal suppression, persecution, and execution of oracle-givers presented in the biblical tradition as opposed to Yahweh's will are favorably reported in the biblical text. But even the royal suppression, persecution, and execution of what the biblical tradition regards as the genuine prophets of Yahweh must be seen as a rational act. Within the ancient Near Eastern context, if one believed that a Jeremiah had truly been sent with a genuine and reliable oracle from

---

13. See J. J. M. Roberts, "The Legal Basis for Saul's Slaughter of the Priests of Nob (1 Samuel 21–22)," *JNSL* 25 (1999) 21–29.

Yahweh, it would, of course, be folly to oppose him, much less persecute him. If, on the other hand, one rejected his claims and believed him to be a paid agent of the Babylonian enemy, then the execution of Jeremiah that is demanded by the royal officials was a perfectly reasonable, legal, and moral course of action. Everything hinged on which belief about the particular prophet were true, but how one resolved that quandary was never self-evident to the contemporaries of the prophets.

From Mountain to Mountain: The Reign of God in Daniel 2

C. L. SEOW

―――◆―――

I. Introduction

Daniel 2, with its tantalizing account and interpretation of Nebuchadnezzar's dream of a magnificent multipartite statue, has had a vigorous and controversial hermeneutical "afterlife." The greatest controversy among interpreters has always revolved around the identity of the fourth regime, represented by the fourth part of the statue.[1] That regime is of particular interest, for the text claims that God will bring about yet another reign at that time—one that will render all the others nugatory but that will itself be enduring (v. 44). The dominant view among commentators through the ages is that the four parts of the statue represent four empires that will emerge successively in history, each one beginning only after its predecessor is finished. Yet, apart from the certainty that the first is the Babylonian kingdom of Nebuchadnezzar, there has been no consensus on the referents of the rest of the statue. For most exegetes in antiquity and still some today, the fourth power must mean the Roman Empire, and so the second must be Medo-Persian and the third Hellenistic.[2] For a majority

Author's note: I count it a great privilege to be able to make this contribution in honor of Patrick D. Miller, a dear friend and esteemed colleague. There is no scholar for whom I have higher respect, nor is there another from whom I have learned more about what scholarship in service to the academy and the church should be.

1. For a judicious and thorough review of the various positions, see the classic survey in H. H. Rowley, *Darius the Mede and the Four World Empires in the Book of Daniel: A Historical Study of Contemporary Theories* (Cardiff: University of Wales Press, 1959) 61–182.

2. This view is evident already in Josephus (*Ant.* X.276) and the Talmud (*b. Šebu.* 6b; *ʿAbod. Zar.* 2b). According to Cyril of Jerusalem (*NPFN*[2], VII, 108), this was also the dominant tradition among the earliest Christian exegetes. Thus, for instance, Hippolytus (*ANF*, V, 210), Origen (PG XII, 59), Eusebius of Caesarea (PG XXII, 793), John Chrysostom (PG LVI, 206–7), and Jerome (PL, XXV, 634) all held this view. Among modern scholars, this position is no longer the dominant one, although there are still some able adherents. See, for instance, J. C. Baldwin, *Daniel* (TOTC; Leicester: 1978) 161–62; S. R. Miller, *Daniel* (NAC 18; Nashville: Broadman and Holman, 1994) 95–99.

of historical-critics, however, the fourth must be the Hellenistic Empire, and so the second and third refer to Media and Persia, respectively.[3] These two views have been far and away the most prevalent, although various other proposals have been proffered from time to time.[4] Whatever these four great powers represent, they will, according to Daniel's explication of the dream, be crushed by "a stone hewn not by hands" from a mountain— a stone that will itself become a mountain filling all the earth (vv. 34, 45). There can be little doubt that divine intervention is meant in this imagery, but interpreters cannot agree if the stone symbolizing the reign of God would be an individual (the Jewish messiah or Christ in his first or second advent) or a corporate entity (the Jewish nation or the church).[5]

It is a curious oddity in the history of exegesis that the meaning of the dream has more often than not been sought entirely in the account of the dream (vv. 31–35) and its interpretation (vv. 36–45). It is as if the narrative framework in which they are set is but a vehicle to convey the dream oracle, which is supposed to be the primary focus of the chapter.[6] In consequence, there has been an inordinate preoccupation with questions of eschatology—determining what Daniel predicts will happen and when it will happen—and, hence, a disproportionate emphasis on chronology and especially on the identity of the fourth regime. Alternatively, for those who see the narrative as primary, the dream oracle merely serves the real purpose of the narrator: to show that true wisdom and knowledge come from God. The proclamation of a coming reign of God in the dream oracle is, therefore, entirely beside the point in this reading. As such, however, the chapter may be entertaining, but its message is largely platitudinous: the story underscores Daniel's extraordinary wisdom and insight and, indirectly through his example, calls for pious devotion to and dependence on God through prayer. In view of such tendencies, this essay offers a literary and theological rereading of the passage in its present form, arguing that the story from beginning to end portrays the nature of the reign of the God of Heaven, as it is manifested on earth. The chapter thus introduces a key

---

3. See the literature cited in G. Pfandl, "Interpretations of the Kingdom of God in Daniel 2:44," *AUSS* 34 (1996) 249–68; Rowley, *Darius the Mede*, 70–137.

4. At various points in history different powers have been named as the fourth regime, including the Saracens against whom the crusaders fought, the Ottoman Empire, or, as some Jewish interpreters see it, the Christian church. Others understand the dream to refer not to four kingdoms but to four kings—Nebuchadnezzar and his Neo-Babylonian successors, or four Assyrian, Persian, or Ptolemaic rulers. See the literature cited in J. E. Goldingay, *Daniel* (WBC 30; Waco: Word, 1989) 40–41, 51.

5. See J. A. Montgomery, *Daniel* (ICC; New York: Charles Scribner's Sons, 1927) 185–92.

6. So it is explicitly stated in A. Bentzen, *Daniel* (HAT 19; Tübingen: Mohr, 1937) 7.

theological theme that will be played out through the rest of the book, both in the example stories (chapters 1–6) and in the apocalyptic visions (chapters 7–12): the reign of God that is ever "now but not yet."[7] It also helps lay the foundation for the important notion of "the kingdom of God" and "the kingdom of heaven" in the New Testament.

II. Literary and Rhetorical Antecedents

In their consideration of the provenance of the passage, modern critics often point to parallels in other ancient Near Eastern royal dream accounts,[8] particularly the dreams of Nabonidus, which some have suggested may underlie the account in Daniel 2.[9] Accordingly, it is believed, the narrator adapted a traditional account about a dream of Nabonidus, substituting the name Nebuchadnezzar for Nabonidus.[10] Others critics, however, call attention to the presence of folkloristic motifs associated with certain genres of stories concerning the success of the wise courtier in a foreign court.[11] Inasmuch as the figure of Daniel appears to be a traditional one (see Ezek 14:14, 20; 28:3), with a possible antecedent in the legend of a certain figure by a similar name in Canaanite lore, one ought not to overlook the probable folkloristic background of the account.[12] Yet, the most compelling indications of the story's prehistory come in the way of literary and

---

7. Kingship is obviously a critical issue in the book. All told, the Hebrew and Aramaic words for it occur 69 times in the book, along with other terms for earthly or heavenly power.

8. See J. J. Collins, *The Apocalyptic Vision of the Book of Daniel* (HSM 16; Missoula: Scholars Press, 1977) 35; A. L. Oppenheim, *The Interpretation of Dreams in the Ancient Near East, with a Translation of an Assyrian Dream-Book* (TAPS; Philadelphia: American Philosophical Society, 1956) 245–54.

9. Thus, for example, W. von Soden, "Eine babylonische Volksüberlieferung von Nabunid in den Danielerzählungen," *ZAW* 53 (1935) 81–89; M. McNamara, "Nabonidus and the Book of Daniel," *ITQ* 37 (1970) 131–49; M. A. Beek, *Das Danielbuch: Sein historischer Hintergrund und seine literarische Entwicklung* (Leiden: Ginsberg, 1935) 39–47.

10. The hypothesis gained credibility with the discovery of fragments of the so-called "Prayer of Nabonidus" (4QPrNab = 4Q242) from Qumran, which refers tantalizingly to a Jewish diviner to whom Nabonidus appealed for help to overcome a disease. See J. T. Milik, "'Prière de Nabonide' et autres écrits d'un cycle de Daniel, fragments de Qumrân 4," *RB* 63 (1956) 407–15.

11. See S. Niditch and R. Doran, "The Success Story of the Wise Courtier: A Formal Approach," *JBL* 96 (1977) 179–99; cf. W. L. Humphreys, "A Life-Style for Diaspora: A Study of the Tales of Esther and Daniel," *JBL* 92 (1973) 211–23; J. J. Collins, "The Court-Tales in Daniel and the Development of Jewish Apocalyptic," *JBL* 94 (1975) 218–34.

12. See J. Day, "The Daniel of Ugarit and Ezekiel and the Hero of the Book of Daniel," *VT* 30 (1980) 174–84; H. H. P. Dressler, "The Identification of the Ugaritic Dnil with the Daniel of Ezekiel," *VT* 29 (1979) 152–61; M. Noth, "Noah, Daniel, und Hiob in Ezechiel xiv," *VT* 1 (1951) 251–60.

rhetorical echoes of other—almost certainly earlier—biblical traditions. Most widely recognized in this regard are the similarities that one finds with the story of Joseph in Egypt, especially in Genesis 41. In each case, we have a foreign ruler whose spirit is troubled by a dream, the failure of professional diviners to assuage the ruler's anxiety, a young Hebrew captive accomplishing what the experts could not, the faithful captive attributing his success to God, and the rewarding of the captive and his promotion to a position of enormous influence in the kingdom of his sojourning. Admittedly, these may be just the expected elements of the genre, as some have noted.[13] Still, a number of expressions in Daniel 2 are strongly reminiscent of the Joseph story in particular: Nebuchadnezzar had a dream and "his spirit was troubled" (*wattitpā'em rûḥô* in v. 1; *wattippā'em rûḥî* in v. 3; cf. *wattippā'em rûḥô* in Gen 41:8); the king summoned his "magicians" (*ḥarṭummîm*, v. 2) and "the sages of Babylon" (*ḥakkîmê bābel*, v. 12) to court, only to learn that none of them could explain his dreams (cf. Gen 41:8); the successful interpreter of the dream insists that it is God who has told the king what will happen in the future (vv. 28, 30; cf. Gen 41:16, 28). Poignantly, too, the setting of the story in the second year of Nebuchadnezzar's reign (v. 1), that is, the second year of Daniel's exile, echoes the fact that Joseph was called upon to interpret the Pharaoh's dreams after only two years of captivity in a foreign country (Gen 41:1).[14] The opening verse in the chapter, in fact, speaks to Nebuchadnezzar's *dreams* (*ḥălômôt*, 2:1; *ḥălōmōtâw*, 2:2), thus echoing the two dreams of Pharaoh, even though Nebuchadnezzar clearly had only one (cf. 2:3, 4, 5, 38). Indeed, the awkward and seemingly unnecessary reference to sleep coming to the king (*ûšěnātô nihyětâ 'ālâw*, v. 1)—after he had already dreamed—recalls the repetition of Pharaoh's dream after he awoke and fell asleep again (cf. Gen 41:4–5).[15]

Despite the apparent discrepancy with the preceding chapter (see 1:5, 18), the chronological notice in v. 1 is not out of place in its present canonical-literary context, for one gathers from it that Daniel's success is not on account of his education in the Chaldean academy. Even though the captive has not yet completed his three-year training, he is already able to best the fully-fledged Chaldean professionals and even able to save their lives

---

13. Niditch and Doran, "Success Story," 179–99.

14. This datum is a *crux interpretum.* Already in the OG (LXX⁹⁶⁷), "twelve" is read instead of "two," and some scholars emend accordingly. Others suggest reading (Aramaic) *št* ("six") rather than *štym* ("two"). Still others explain the apparent discrepancy in terms of different calendars, cultural differences in how one reckons time, different origin of the story, redactional oversight, and so on. See J. J. Collins, *Daniel* (Hermeneia; Minneapolis: Fortress, 1993) 154–55. None of these explanations is, in fact, convincing or necessary.

15. Attempts to emend the text or resort to an alternative root *hwh* ("to fall") are simply unconvincing. The MT is the *lectio difficior* and can only mean "sleep happened upon him (again)" (so Aquila and Syr).

(2:18, 24, 48). Salvation for these undeserving fools is mediated through this young captive, not on account of the skills that they have imparted to him nor even because of his own native ability, but only through the wisdom and power of God. Thus, like young Joseph in Egypt in his second year of his sojourn in Egypt, Daniel in the second year of his exile would enlighten his mighty captor and save others from certain death.

The account of Daniel 2 seems to be a development of the Joseph story, for Nebuchadnezzar here calls upon not only the "magicians" and the "sages," as the Egyptian ruler did,[16] he also consults with the Mesopotamian experts, the "exorcists, sorcerers, and Chaldeans" (v. 2).[17] Read in the light of the Joseph story, one may consider Daniel's success all the more remarkable; not only does he outperform a more diverse team of consultants than Joseph did, but the assignment at hand is far tougher than what Pharaoh had given Joseph. Whereas the Egyptian ruler had asked only for the interpretation of his dreams, the Babylonian king demands to know *both* the content of the dream *and* its interpretation, a point that is reiterated throughout the story (vv. 5, 6, 7, 9, 26, 30, 36). Yet, the purpose of all this is not merely to show that this captive novice has made fools of his captors so comically and also in such a marvelous fashion; more importantly, the message is *theological*: Daniel's success is due neither to his personal gifts nor to his Chaldean education, but to the wisdom and the power of God alone. Still, there is much more at stake in this narrative than the skillful interpretation of dreams by a wise and pious courtier. More so than the Joseph story, Daniel 2 calls attention to the triumph of divine wisdom and foreknowledge conveyed through a lowly exile, a faithful servant of God. The story illustrates the sovereignty of the God who humbles the mighty and exalts the lowly.

In this regard, the Daniel narrative is particularly reminiscent of the poems of Deutero-Isaiah, where one finds an unmistakable emphasis on the wisdom and foreknowledge of Israel's God over against the idols of the foreign nations (41:21–29; 43:9; 45:19; 46:1; 48:5–6, 16).[18] For this prophet,

---

16. On the Egyptian background of the word *ḥartummîm*, see T. O. Lambdin, "Egyptian Loan Words in the Old Testament," *JAOS* 73 (1953) 150–51; J. Vergote, *Joseph en Egypte* (Leuven: Leuven University Press, 1959) 66–73. The word does appear, though, in a few Neo-Assyrian inscriptions listing captive professionals from Egypt. See *CAD* Ḫ (Volume 6) 116.

17. The first two—Hebrew *ʾaššāpîm* and *měkaššěpîm*—are loanwords related to Akkadian *āšipu* ("exorcist") and *kišpū* ("sorcery"), respectively.

18. See, especially, P. von der Osten-Sacken, *Die Apokalyptik in ihrem Verhältnis zu Prophetie und Weisheit* (Theologische Existenz Heute 157; Munich: Kaiser, 1969) 18–27; J. Gammie, "On the Intention and Sources of Daniel I–VI," *VT* 31 (1981) 287–91; I. Fröhlich, "Daniel 2 and Deutero-Isaiah," in *The Book of Daniel in the Light of New Findings* (ed. A. S. van der Woude; BETL 106; Leuven: Leuven University Press, 1993) 266–70.

Israel's God is the one "who frustrates the omens of liars, and makes fools of diviners; who turns back the wise, and makes their knowledge foolish; who confirms the word of his servant, and fulfills the prediction of his messengers" (Isa 44:25–26a). The Chaldeans have too much confidence in their knowledge and wisdom, the poet observes, but their diviners will finally not be able even to save themselves (Isa 47:5–15, especially vv. 10, 13–14). The God of the Jewish exiles, by contrast, is able to reveal things concealed in darkness (Isa 45:3), secrets that are hidden and still unknown to humanity (48:6), for Yhwh is sovereign over light and darkness (Isa 45:7; cf. 42:16). Such, too, is the God to whom Daniel prays, for his God "reveals deep and hidden things; he knows what is in the darkness, and light dwells with him" (Dan 2:22). In the Deutero-Isaianic poems, the gods of the nations, unable to declare the things that will happen before they happen, are challenged to produce witnesses to vindicate themselves, so that those who hear the testimonies may say, "It is true!" (Isa 43:9). In Daniel 2, while the Chaldean experts are impotent in the face of Nebuchadnezzar's challenge and readily admit so, Daniel insists that his God is able to reveal mysteries and make known what will be in the future (v. 28). Eventually, after Daniel is able to bear witness to things that are to happen before they happen, it is the Chaldean king who confesses what is true: "Truly, your God is God of gods and lord of kings and the revealer of mysteries, for you are able to reveal this mystery" (v. 47). Thus, just as Deutero-Isaiah predicted the prostration of foreign rulers before the exiles (Isa 43:14; 49:7, 23), one finds Nebuchadnezzar prostrating before Daniel, the Jew in the service of a foreign ruler (Dan 2:46–47). Deutero-Isaiah envisioned that the exiles would eventually humble their adversaries and become to them like a new threshing sledge, "threshing mountains to dust and hills like chaff, so that the wind carry them off and scatter them" (Isa 41:15–16). Similar idioms are used in Daniel 2 of the stone that would crush the mighty powers of the world. Indeed, even though they are represented by metals, these foreign powers will become "like chaff of the threshing floor of summer," carried off by a wind until not a trace is left (v. 35). Daniel speaks of a stone hewn "not by hand" coming "from the mountain" (*miṭṭûrāʾ*, v. 45), a stone that will itself grow to be a great mountain (*ṭûr*) filling the whole earth (v. 35). Here the imagery of the stone hewn from the mountain may ultimately be derived from Deutero-Isaiah's exhortation to faithful Jews during the Babylonian exiles: "Look to the mountain [*ṣûr*] from which you were hewn, to the quarry from which you were dug" (Isa 51:1). Such literary and rhetorical allusions must surely be taken into consideration as one endeavors to understand Daniel's account and interpretation of the dream.

III. Literary Context and Hermeneutical Cues

The story begins with a chronological notice in reference to the reign (*malkût*) of Nebuchadnezzar (v. 1), and one is immediately given a sense in the narrative of both the power and limitations of such a reign. Despite his newfound power—it being but the second year of his reign—Nebuchadnezzar is frightened by a dream,[19] no doubt understood as a divinely initiated phenomenon. The king is terrified, despite all the impressions of his absolute power that the story portrays. He summons the presence of others at will, orders them to accomplish feats that no mortal can reasonably be expected to do, threatens the lives of any and all, and spares others by his whim. The salutation of the obsequious sages is formulaic and no doubt expected in royal protocol: "O king, live forever!" (v. 4). Yet, as the rest of the story unfolds, the emptiness of their courtesy will become all too obvious. Nebuchadnezzar's kingship can hardly be an eternal one! He has no control over time, much less eternity, even though he accuses his consultants of trying to buy time (*'iddānā'*, v. 8) and stalling until "time changes" (*'iddānā' yištannē'*, v. 9), and Daniel has to plead with him for time (*zĕmān*, v. 16).[20] At issue, it seems clear, is the nature of human kingship in history—both its power and its limitations.

The anxious despot summons his experts to "tell him his dreams" (v. 2), for he wants to "know the dream" (v. 3). Although the consultants are slow to catch on, the king is unequivocal that he means to know what the dream is and what it means. Throughout the first section of the account (vv. 1–12), there is a clash of expectations: the king demands the telling of the dream's content and its exegesis, but the Chaldean consultants want to uncouple the two tasks. They view the interpretation as a reasonable expectation of their trade,[21] but not the divining of its content, which requires nothing short of revelation. It is not entirely clear why the king does not provide the substance of his dream, as Pharaoh did for his would-be dream interpreters. Most commonly, commentators speculate that he has simply forgotten it. Others think it likely that he is deliberately withholding the

---

19. Those who seek to coordinate the chronological notice with historical data might point out that the second of Nebuchadnezzar's reign would be the year immediately following his decisive victory at the Battle of Carchemish. He has every reason to be confident, but he is terrified by a dream.

20. Time is obviously at issue in this story. Consider also the recurrence of *'lm* (vv. 20, 44), and references to the future in vv. 28, 29, 45.

21. Perhaps they are confident they can find the answers in the various dream manuals that give set solutions to mantic symbols. Indeed, a number of such reference works for professional interpreters have been discovered in the Levant. See Oppenheim, *The Interpretation of Dreams*, 222.

information as a test of the authenticity of the experts, a view that finds
some support in v. 9: "Tell me the dream, then, so that I may know that you
can give me its interpretation." Whatever the case, the primary concern of
the narrator seems to be the source and the agency of true wisdom and reliable knowledge that will allow the king to assuage his anxiety and allow
his subjects to survive his death threat.

After the king has asked three times for both the content and interpretation of the dream (vv. 3, 5–6, 8–9), the Chaldean charlatans finally get the
point and are forced to admit the limits of their ability (vv. 10–12). They do
not, however, deny the possibility of such knowledge, only that it is beyond
human capability. They admit that there is "no human on earth" (v. 10) who
can meet the king's unprecedented demand, only the gods can, but they
add immediately that the gods do not dwell with mortals (v. 11). They seem
to recognize where true knowledge ultimately lies, but their theology of
divine transcendence admits no consideration of divine immanence. They
do not entertain the possibility that the chasm between divine power and
mortal limitations may somehow be overcome.

Daniel, by contrast, does not have such theological reservations. Even
though he worships a transcendent deity, "the God of Heaven" (v. 18), he
does not hesitate to gather his Jewish companions to pray. Accordingly,
then, the mystery is revealed and Daniel on earth blesses "the God of
Heaven" (v. 19). His doxology (vv. 20–23) is similar in form and diction to
others found elsewhere in the Bible,[22] but it is not a mere pious interlude
or interpolation here in the narrative. Indeed, the hymn both summarizes
the theological issues raised so far in the narrative and anticipates the interpretation of the dream. It may even be argued that the doxology here is
theologically pivotal to the entire passage.[23]

Daniel begins blessing the God of Heaven (v. 19) by blessing "the name
of God" (v. 20). The "name of God" is, as most modern commentators recognize, God's hypostatic presence. So Israel's hymnic tradition contains
many references to the divine name as synonymous with the presence of
God (Pss 68:4; 113:1; 122:4; 135:1, 3). In Deuteronomy and the Deutero-
mistic History, in particular, it is God who has made the divine name "to
tabernacle" (lĕšakkēn) at the place where God has chosen (Deut 12:5, 11, 21;
14:23–24; 16:2, 6, 11; 26:2; cf. 2 Sam 7:13; 1 Kgs 8:16–20). And that "name theology" is nowhere more profoundly expressed than in Solomon's prayer at

---

22. See W. S. Towner, "The Poetic Passages of Daniel 1–6," *CBQ* 31 (1969) 319.

23. Whether or not one sees the doxology as part of a secondary addition, as L. F.
Hartman and A. A. Di Lella (*The Book of Daniel* [AB 23; New York: Doubleday, 1978] 139)
and others do, it not only is appropriate in its context but, indeed, provides an important theological lens through which to view the passage.

the dedication of the Jerusalem temple: "Will God, indeed, dwell on earth? Even the heavens and the heavens of heavens cannot contain You, how much less this House that I have built?" (1 Kgs 8:27). Even if God's abode is in heaven or beyond, according to this view, divine presence is still possible because the name of God is made to tabernacle among mortals in God's stead, and the God in heaven may still turn to hear human prayers (1 Kgs 8:27–53). The narrator of Daniel 2 invokes the name of God appropriately in response to the distinction that the Chaldeans make between the impotence of mortals on earth (v. 10) and the gods who do not dwell with humanity (v. 11). The name theology, however, affirms the simultaneity of divine transcendence and immanence, upholding the possibility that a God of Heaven could still hear the petitions of faithful people on earth.

The hymn returns to the issues that the narrative has implicitly raised so far. Wisdom, which the experts summoned by Nebuchadnezzar are supposed to have, and power, which is presumed to belong to the king, are, in fact, God's to give (v. 20). As already indicated, Nebuchadnezzar accuses the Chaldean sages of trying to "acquire time" (v. 8) and waiting for time to change (v. 9), and Daniel has to request the king to give him a period of time (v. 16). The hymn makes clear now, however, that it is *God* who changes times and periods (*měhašnē' 'iddānayyā' wězimnayyā'*, v. 21a). Whereas the Chaldeans bid the king to "live forever" (v. 4), Daniel's hymn blesses the name of God "forever and ever" (v. 20a). Indeed, the doxology asserts that the king himself is subject to the authority and power of God, for it is God who "removes kings and establishes kings" (v. 21b). It is God who is the true source of wisdom and knowledge, which the king's dream requires in order to be known; God is the one who reveals secrets and mysteries. And the wisdom and power of God are just what Daniel will mediate.

It has been observed that the doxology to the God of Heaven begins with Daniel blessing the name of God (v. 20), but by the time one gets to the end of it, the deity is addressed as "the God of my fathers" (v. 23).[24] The deity who is at once transcendent (the God of Heaven) and willing to be present (the name of God) is, for Daniel, none other than the God of his ancestors, a God who deigns to relate to a particular people. This divine designation is significant, inasmuch as its very first appearance in the Bible is in connection with God's self-revelation: God was revealed to Moses as YHWH, the distinctive name of Israel's God, the God of their ancestors (Exod 3:13–16; 4:5). That divine designation recurs, too, in the Deuteronomic tradition as a constant reminder of the ancient bond that Israel had with God. In the context of Daniel's doxology, then, one is to understand

---

24. D. N. Fewell, *Circle of Sovereignty: Plotting Politics in the Book of Daniel* (Nashville: Abingdon, 1991) 29.

that "the God of the fathers," whose self-revelation to Moses enabled Moses to confront Pharaoh's awesome power, is now revealing again, this time through his servant in exile, who is to confront another powerful and oppressive ruler in history. The God of Heaven is the God of Israel's ancestors, a transcendent God who nevertheless relates to a particular people and intervenes in history to deliver them. So the doxology begins with the affirmation that wisdom and power belong *to God* (v. 20), but it ends with wisdom and power given *to Daniel*, who is now enabled to address the king (v. 23). Calvin properly calls attention to the juxtaposition of wisdom with power here, even though Daniel is but a puny captive standing before his mighty captor.[25] The doxology implies that God's wisdom and power will be mediated through human agents, even those who are lowly and seemingly powerless.

IV. The Dream and Its Interpretation

The text is emphatic that the dream concerns events that have not yet come to pass as Daniel speaks: "what will happen in the latter days" (*mâ dî lehĕwē' bĕ'aḥărît yômayyā'*, v. 28), "what will be after this" (*mâ dî lehĕwē' 'aḥărê dĕnâ*, vv. 29, 45), "what will be" (*mâ-dî lehĕwē'*, v. 29). Of these various expressions, the first requires further consideration, for *'aḥărît yômayyā'* has often been taken literally to mean "the end of days," thus understood as an eschatological notion, whether broadly or narrowly conceived.[26] Yet, the word *'aḥărît* may refer indefinitely to the future, simply some time after the speaker's point of reference (e.g., Deut 8:16; Prov 23:18; 24:14; 25:8; Jer 29:11). In light of the many literary links between Daniel 2 and Deutero-Isaiah, it is also not amiss to note that the latter uses *'aḥărît* in reference to the telling of events before they happen, "the things to come" (see Isa 41:22; 46:10; 47:7). Moreover, the expression *bĕ'aḥărît yômayyā'* has a close parallel in the Akkadian idiom, *ina aḥrat ūmī* "at the end of days," which always means simply "in the future."[27] The Aramaic phrase (cf. also 10:14) is analogous to Hebrew *'aḥărît hayyāmîm*, an idiom that, in at least some if not all instances, refers to an unspecified time in the future (so especially in Gen 49:1; Num 24:14; Deut 4:30; 31:29).[28] So it is doubtful that the dream in the

---

25. Jean Calvin, *Daniel I* (Calvin's Old Testament Commentaries 20; trans. T. H. L. Parker; Grand Rapids: Eerdmans, 1993) 74.

26. So the LXX: *ep eschatōn hēmerōn*.

27. For this and the related idiom, *aḫrītiš ūmī*, see *CAD* A/1 (Volume 1) 194. The pertinence of the Akkadian expression, along with the sematically similar *ana arkāt ūmī* was pointed out long ago in B. D. Eerdmans, *The Religion of Israel* (Leiden: Brill, 1947) 322–23.

28. So G. W. Buchanan, "Eschatology and the End of Days," *JNES* 20 (1961) 188–93; J. T. Willis, "The Expression *be'acharith hayyamin* [sic] in the Old Testament," *ResQ* 22 (1979) 54–71. For a survey of the literature on this and related idioms, see G. Pfandl, *The*

first instance concerns an eschatological event in the sense of something in the distant future or at the end of history.[29]

The dream revolves around a statue, the Aramaic word here (*ṣalmāʾ*) being a cognate of the Akkadian term used for images erected to represent the presence of gods and kings. Since kingship is at issue, it is likely that a royal statue is meant, although in this case it is not the statue of an individual king but apparently a composite symbol of political power, represented by various regimes.[30] Royal statues were typically erected for propagandistic reasons. They were placed in the temple in various postures before divine images to represent the constant pious presence of the king before the deity, or they were placed in other public places, notably in vanquished territories, to remind the populace of the king's majesty and power.[31] Those placed in temples may, of course, be intended to impress the deity as well as the citizenry, and no one should be surprised to learn that those in the temples were frequently worshiped along with the divine images.[32] Needless to say, too, the size and splendor of the images enhanced their propagandistic effectiveness.[33] So in Mesopotamia, a king boasted of his well-wrought statue of gold, silver, and shining copper—a work of composite materials, not unlike the statue of Nebuchadnezzar's dream.[34] The latter is said to be huge and brilliant; constituted of gold, silver, bronze, and iron partly mixed with clay. Yet, despite its size, make, and obvious splendor, this statue is struck at its feet and utterly shattered by a stone hewn

---

Time of the End in the Book of Daniel (Adventist Theological Society Dissertation Series 1; Berrien Springs: Adventist Theological Society Publications, 1996).

29. See Collins, *Daniel*, 161; J. van der Ploeg, "Eschatology in the Old Testament," *OTS* 17 (1972) 90–91.

30. Cf. J. Steinmann, *Daniel* (Connaître la Bible; Bruges: Desclée de Brouwer, 1961) 49.

31. See J. Reade, "Ideology and Propaganda in Assyrian Art," in *Power and Propaganda* (ed. M. T. Larsen; Copenhagen: Akademisk Forlag, 1979) 329–43.

32. See the citations in *CAD* Ṣ (Volume 16) 81–82.

33. For various reasons, the epigraphic references to divine and royal statues far exceed the number of statues in the round that have been discovered so far. The latter, too, have tended to be of stone and either life-size or smaller. The inscriptions, though, abundantly attest to the existence of splendorous statues made of all kinds of materials, including gold, silver, bronze, and alabaster. The enormity of royal images is also well corroborated by many carvings—also called *ṣalmū* in Akkadian—on stelae and rock reliefs. In these latter, the kings are typically oversized, while other humans, when they are depicted, are diminutive. For some examples, see *ANEP*, 152–59.

34. R. C. Thompson, *The Prisms of Esarhaddon and Ashurbanipal found at Nineveh, 1927–28* (London: British Museum, 1931), Pl. 16, line 49. Statues made of different materials are known from the inscriptions from Mesopotamia. In the West, too, M. H. Pope and J. H. Tigay ("A Description of Baal," *UF* 3 [1971] 120) also call attention to an example from ancient Ugarit, made of five different metals, "similar to the image fashioned by Nebuchadnezzar."

"not by hands" (vv. 34, 45), an expression that occurs also in 8:25, meaning probably that it originates by divine will and power (cf. also Job 34:20).[35]

Daniel's interpretation begins with his address of Nebuchadnezzar as "king, king of kings" (v. 37). Yet, the superlative only highlights the irony that Nebuchadnezzar's kingship is, in fact, derived, for it is the God of Heaven who gives kingship, power, might, and glory (v. 38). There is another king above the earthly "king of kings" (see v. 47). Even if Nebuchadnezzar's kingship seems absolute and universal in human terms, it is ultimately derived from God, the creator of all (v. 38; cf. Jer 27:6; 28:14). Indeed, the language of the king's dominion over even the wild animals and the birds of heaven reflects creation theology (cf. also see Ps 8:6–9), particularly the notion of the creation of humanity in the divine *image* (*ṣelem*) and their God-given dominion over all other creatures of the universe (Gen 1:26).[36] The king is but a reflection, as it were, of divine kingship, power, might, and glory on earth—just as any human being might be a reflection of that presence, even if in less dramatic and obvious ways. Furthermore, Nebuchadnezzar is not the entire image, but only its head of gold. After him will come another reign, "inferior" to his in some undefined way, then a third that "will have dominion over all the earth," and then a fourth that would be as strong as iron, crushing and smashing "all these" (v. 40).

Exegetes through the centuries have, for the most part, assumed that four successive empires in history are at issue. Supporting that view, modern critics have added possible analogies, some even pointing to traditions that are supposedly antecedent to and influential upon Daniel 2. Most notable in this regard is Hesiod's *Works and Days* (1.109–201), which speaks of periods in human history in terms of four metals, and the *Bahman Yasht*, a ninth century (c.e.) Iranian prophetic text describing a vision of a tree with branches of various metals representing various periods in history.[37] Yet, it is debatable if the text has to do with successive kingdoms.[38] Even if the

---

35. Tantalizing in this connection is the repeated insistence of the prophets, notably Deutero-Isaiah, that the cultic images of the nations are powerless entities, the works of human hands (Isa 40:18–20; 41:6–7; 44:9–20). On these passages against their Mesopotamian backdrop, see M. B. Dick, "Prophetic Parodies of the Making of the Cult Image," in *Born in Heaven, Made on Earth: The Making of the Cult Image in the Ancient Near East* (ed. M. B. Dick; Winona Lake: Eisenbrauns, 1999) 1–53.

36. For the use of creation language and theology in Daniel, see J. B. Doukhan, "Allusions à la création dans le livre de Daniel," in *The Book of Daniel in Light of New Findings* (ed. A. S. van der Woude; BETL 106; Leuven: Leuven University Press, 1993) 285–92.

37. For a challenge to the view that the "four kingdom" schema is a result of external influence, see G. F. Hasel, "The Four World Empires of Daniel 2 against Its Near Eastern Environment," *JSOT* 12 (1979) 17–30.

38. Cf. C. Caragounis, "History and Supra-History," in van der Woude, ed., *The Book of Daniel in Light of New Findings*, 387–97.

statue does imply succession, the interpretation of it does not, for the stone shatters the entire statue all at once.[39]

Whatever the case, the identification of the first reign is indisputable, for Nebuchadnezzar is named: "You are the head of gold" (v. 38). One may take the cue from the opening verse in the chapter, which refers to the second year of Nebuchadnezzar's *malkût*, that the *malkûtā'* that God has given to him is simply that: Nebuchadnezzar's own reign, and not the duration of the Babylonian empire. Moreover, while it is clear that the second regime will come after the first (v. 39), nothing is said about how long each of the regimes will last. Indeed, the idea that the dream concerns successive empires spanning centuries is belied by the fact that the fourth regime is supposed to destroy "all these," implying that all others after Nebuchadnezzar's will still be in existence when the fourth reign comes to be.[40] The text may, therefore, be referring not to four different empires extending over several centuries, but to four *reigns*.[41] Indeed, the same word is used here as found elsewhere in the book for the reign of Nebuchadnezzar (4:26, 31, 36; 5:18), the reign of Belshazzar (5:26, 28; 8:1), the reign of Darius (6:26, 28), the reign of Cyrus (6:28), and the eternal reign of God (4:3, 34; 6:26; 7:27). Thus, the passing of Nebuchadnezzar's reign (*malkûtâ*) mentioned in 4:28 is not the end of the Babylonian empire *per se*, for Nebuchadnezzar, according to the book's own historiography, is succeeded by his "son" Belshazzar, whose own reign would end with the accession of "Darius the Mede" (5:31). Accordingly, then, the second regime is that of Belshazzar, who is portrayed as inferior to Nebuchadnezzar (see 5:22–29). The third regime would then be that of "Darius the Mede" (5:31; 6:28) and the fourth of "Cyrus the Persian" (6:28). Although the second regime is said to be inferior to Nebuchadnezzar's, no such thing is suggested of the others.[42] The third power will, indeed, be broad in scope: "it shall have dominion over all the earth" (*tišlaṭ bĕkol-'ar'ā'*, v. 39). And this is implicitly corroborated later in the book by the edict of Darius the Mede to "all peoples, nations, and languages that

---

39. See A. Momigliano, "The Origins of Universal History," in *The Poet and the Historian: Essays in Literary and Historical Biblical Criticism* (HSS 26; ed. R. E. Friedman; Chico: Scholars Press, 1983) 145.

40. Cf. H. L. Ginsberg, *Studies in Daniel* (New York: Jewish Theological Seminary, 1948) 6–7.

41. See the observation of B. D. Eerdmans in "Origin and Meaning of the Aramaic Part of Daniel," *Actes du XVIIIᵉ congrès international des orientalistes* (1932) 198–202. This position has been defended most recently by Goldingay, *Daniel*, 49–52.

42. One must be careful not to read into the text foreign valuations of the different metals. The four metals may not, in fact, indicate diminishing quality, the precise nature of which commentators have always had difficulty specifying. Rather, as Goldingay (*Daniel*, 49) suggests, "[g]old and silver are standard symbols for what is majestic and precious . . . bronze and iron for what is strong and hard."

inhabit the earth," invoking his own sovereignty over them (*bĕkol-šolṭān malkûtî*, see 6:25–26). Darius the Mede, the third ruler after Nebuchadnez-zar and the inferior Belshazzar, has dominion over all the earth. As for the fourth reign, it must be the fourth and last king explicitly mentioned in chapters 1–6, namely, "Cyrus the Persian" (6:28), who is portrayed in the book as the last king in whose reign Daniel served (1:21). As historians might point out, it was in the reign of Cyrus that the regimes of Belshazzar, the *de facto* ruler of Babylon when it fell at the hands of the Persian army, and the last Median kings were destroyed once and for all.[43] Thus, histori-cally, Cyrus, the fourth power, did destroy "all these." Herodotus, who notes the different ethnic background of the Persians and the Medes (1, 130), also tells of Cyrus himself being a product of mixed marriage (1, 107), an anath-ema to the Jews. The narrator may well be alluding to this background, for in Cyrus himself and in his political coalition, there was a "mixing of human seed" (*mitʿārĕbîn lehĕwōn bizraʿ ʾănāsāʾ*, 2:43).[44] In any case, it was he who brought about the unification of the mighty Persians and the Median king-dom that was breaking up; thus, an alliance of two unequal powers, a mixing of the strong (*taqqîpâ*) with the disintegrating (*tĕbîrâ*, v. 42).[45]

According to Daniel, it is "in the days of those kings" that the transcen-dent God will establish another regime that will never be destroyed and that will not be left to another people (v. 44). Indeed, that new power will crush and end all the others—the four—but it will stand forever.[46] This eternal regime is symbolized by a stone hewn not by hands that will annihi-

43. There is, as far as we know from historical records, no Median king by the name of Darius. Since it is the name of several Achaemenid rulers, it has been suggested that the Old Persian *Dārayarahu* ("He who holds firm the good") may have been a throne name for Gobryas. This is an old view, recently defended in K. Koch, "Dareios der Meder," in *The Word of the Lord Shall Go Forth: Essays in Honor of David Noel Freedman in Celebration of his Sixtieth Birthday* (ed. C. L. Meyers and M. O'Connor; Winona Lake: Eisenbrauns, 1983) 287–99. The suggestion that Darius may be a throne name is intrigu-ing, whether or not one accepts the equation of Darius the Mede with Gobryas, on which see Rowley, *Darius the Mede*, 19–29.

44. See M. Mallowan, "Cyrus the Great (558–529 B.C.)," in *The Cambridge History of Iran* (ed. I. Gershevitch; Cambridge: Cambridge University Press, 1985) 2:404. On the mixing of seed, see Ezra 9:2; Ps 106:35.

45. The passive participle *tĕbîrâ* does not, strictly, mean "brittle" (NRSV) or "fragile." It refers to something that is being broken or is disintegrating.

46. The notion of an everlasting regime that will have universal impact has an inter-esting parallel in the Akkadian *Prophecy of Uruk*, a *vaticinium ex eventu* predicting the reign of a king over the entire world and initiating a dynasty of kings that will exercise dominion like the gods forever. See H. Hunger, "Die Tontafeln der XXVII Kampagne," in *Vorläufiges Bericht über die von dem Deutschen Archäologischen Institut unternommenen Ausgrabungen in Uruk-Warka, 1968, 1969* (Berlin: Mann, 1972) 87, and the discussion in H. Hunger and S. A. Kaufman, "A New Akkadian Prophecy Text," *JAOS* 95 (1975) 371–75.

late the gold, silver, bronze, and iron and clay regimes (v. 45, cf. v. 35). Details in the account of the dream (vv. 34–35) and its interpretation (v. 45)
supplement one another. One learns in v. 45 that the stone is derived from
"the mountain" (*miṭṭûrāʾ*), the noun in the determinate state suggesting,
perhaps, that the reader is supposed to know which "mountain" is meant.[47]
The narrator is apparently drawing upon an idiom or a tradition that is familiar to those for whom the narrative was first intended. Moreover, the
text refers to gold, silver, bronze, and iron and clay being "crushed" (literally, "pulverized") so finely that they become "like chaff of the summer
threshing floor" and are carried away by wind until not a trace is left (v. 35).
Yet, it is patently strange to characterize the destruction of metals in this
way. The description may suggest, again, an imagery that is already familiar
to the original receptors of the message. Indeed, the imagery is much more
at home in Deutero-Isaiah's portrayal of the destruction of foreign nations.
The lowly exiles will be so empowered by God, the prophet maintains, that
they will pulverize (*dqq*) mountains and make hills "like chaff," so that these
mighty entities could be winnowed and carried away by wind (Isa 41:15–16).
It is pertinent to note, too, that in the same chapter, the poet envisions the
coming of a victor from the East (Isa 41:2), who most scholars properly
assume to be Cyrus (mentioned by name in Isa 44:28; 45:1). The presence of
such literary allusions in Daniel 2 prompted some scholars to conclude too
hastily that the stone hewn not by hands is, in fact, a reference to Cyrus.[48]
Yet, the addressee in Isa 41:15–16 can hardly be Cyrus. Rather, the feminine
markers point to the *tôlaʿat yaʿăqōb* ("Worm Jacob"; 41:14) as the antecedent.[49] The point of that passage is that even the despised and lowly (cf. Ps
22:6) may, contrary to expectation, be empowered to humble the lofty and
powerful. To Deutero-Isaiah, that is possible because Israel-Jacob is none
other than Yнwн's chosen servant, "the seed of Abraham," before whom
foreign potentates "will become as nothing and perish" (Isa 41:11; cf. 40:23–
24). Hope for the exiles lay in their divine election, the fact that they are
heirs to God's promise to Abraham. Hence, the poet encourages the exiles
to remember the divine promise to Abraham: "Look to the rock from

---

47. Theodotion, the OG, and the Vulgate also read *mṭwrʾ* in v. 35, but the MT and
other witnesses lack it.

48. Fröhlich, "Daniel 2 and Deutero-Isaiah," 270; Eerdmans, "Origin and Meaning,"
198–202.

49. Oddly, the MT has *mty yśrʾl* as parallel to *twlʿt yʿqb*. Most commentators recognize a textual corruption here and emend the text to read ⟨r⟩*mt yśrʾl* "louse Israel." See
K. Elliger, *Jesaja II* (BKAT 11; Neukirken-Vluyn: Neukircher, 1978) 146–47. G. R. Driver
("Linguistic and Textual Problems: Isaiah xl–lxvi," *JTS* 36 [1935] 399), argues for **mōt* on
the basis of a putative Akkadian noun, *mutu* ("a small louse," "cornworm"), but the existence of such a word in Akkadian is uncertain.

which you were hewn, and to the quarry from which you were dug. Look to Abraham your father and to Sarah who bore you; for he was but one when I called him, but I blessed him and made him many" (Isa 51:1–2). It is surely this "mountain" (*ṣûr*) to which Daniel now alludes, this mountain that is said to be "*the* mountain" (*ṭûrāʾ*) from which the stone hewn not by hands would be derived.[50] That stone is, therefore, the lowly and despised exiles, a remnant of "the mountain," as it were. The stone is the elect people of God, whatever their sociopolitical conditions may be, indeed, whatever their context. Thus, just as Deutero-Isaiah promised that the Jewish exiles in Babylon would in some sense render the powerful nations as nothing, so Daniel affirms that the exiles will annihilate all the foreign powers. Reflecting the pain of defeat and subjugation by foreign forces, the vision in Daniel points to a time when this entity would never again be destroyed or abandoned to "another people" (v. 44). It will be, on the contrary, an enduring sovereignty. Just as Deutero-Isaiah drew on the divine promise to Abraham to multiply (Gen 12:1–3), so the narrator of Daniel 2 envisions that the stone hewn "from the mountain" will grow again into a mountain so great that it will "fill all the earth" (v. 35). On the one hand, the imagery echoes the Isaianic vision of what will be "in the latter days" (*bĕʾaḥărît hayyāmîm*), when the nations of the world will come together to glorious Mount Zion, the abode of Yhwh's sovereignty (Isa 2:1–4; cf. Mic 4:1; Ps 22:27–28). On the other hand, it is reminiscent of Isaiah's vision of the glory or knowledge of God filling all the earth (Isa 6:3; 11:9; cf. 60:1–4).

V. Now but Not Yet

There is no question that the vision of the collapsing statue is about the decisive triumph of God and the universality of divine reign. Daniel's account of the dream, however, remains vague about how and when in the future that reign is to be manifested. The story, though, does not end with the interpretation of the dream. Indeed, it climaxes with the obeisance of Nebuchadnezzar and his acknowledgement of God on the one hand (vv. 46–47), and the exaltation of Daniel and his friends on the other (vv. 48–49). The similarities between the conclusion of Daniel 2 and the story of Joseph in Egypt have long been noted. Daniel is promoted after his successful interpretation of Nebuchadnezzar's dream, just as Joseph was promoted after successfully interpreting Pharaoh's dreams (Gen 41:37–45). Just as Joseph received authority over all the land of Egypt, so too Daniel is

---

50. Despite the common designation of the deity as "mountain" (*ṣûr*), it seems unlikely that "the mountain" in Daniel 2 is a direct reference to God, for the stone which comes from that mountain will grow into a mountain.

put in charge of the whole province of Babylon. Yet, there are important differences between the two stories. Pharaoh elevated Joseph so that the latter was revered everywhere he went, but Pharaoh also made it clear that he was superior to Joseph. In Nebuchadnezzar's case, however, he himself fell down on his face and prostrated himself before Daniel. He even instructs that a cereal offering (*minḥâ*) and oblations (*nîḥōḥîn*) be sacrificed to Daniel (*lĕnassākâ lēh*). The language of worship has proved to be an embarrassment to interpreters, since the text says nothing of Daniel's reaction to the gesture.[51] Some imagine that Daniel probably refused the honor, or that Nebuchadnezzar only tried to offer the sacrifices to Daniel but that the latter stopped him. Others frankly admit that Daniel's acquiescence is tantamount to acceptance; for all his faithfulness and wisdom, Daniel is finally a human being with his faults and foibles. Porphyry was, however, skeptical of the story's veracity, for it seemed to him highly improbable that the great king of Babylon would have so venerated a captive. In response to Porphyry, Jerome cites the desire of the Lycaonians to offer sacrifices to Paul and Barnabas on account of their performance of a miracle (Acts 14:8–18),[52] as well as the tradition that Alexander the Great venerated the high priest Joiada.[53] For Jerome, Dan 2:47 explains the true intention of Nebuchadnezzar's action: the king does not venerate Daniel so much as God.[54] The text is, in any case, silent about Daniel's response. It simply depicts Nebuchadnezzar, who is called "the king of kings" (v. 36), now fallen, with his face upon the ground, prostrate before the lowly Jewish captive. The prediction of the collapse of the mighty statue of kingship by a mere stone is foreshadowed, and even set in motion, in this event, for the "head of gold," is now on the ground.[55] The gestures of worship convey the point of the narrator that the reign of God is manifest in Daniel, who, as the rhetorical allusions to the Joseph story imply, is also the seed of Abraham. Whereas in Deutero-Isaiah, witnesses are unable to vindicate that the foreign gods are true (Isa 43:9), Nebuchadnezzar, having heard the telling of what will happen before they happen, now confesses theological truth.

---

51. On the probable cultic background of the terminology here, see B. A. Mastin, "Daniel 2:46 and the Hellenistic World," *ZAW* 85 (1973) 80–82.

52. While Daniel 2 says nothing of the sage's reaction, Paul and Barnabas are said to have rejected the veneration. Moreover, while the Acts parallel does caricature the bad theology of the unconverted, Porphyry's question of the historical likelihood of a great king bowing to a captive remains unanswered.

53. Josephus, *Ant.* XI.331–335.

54. PG XXV, 504–5. Translated by G. L. Archer, in *Jerome's Commentary on Daniel* (Grand Rapids: Baker, 1958) 33.

55. Cf. the collapse of Dagon's statue before the ark in Philistine captivity (1 Sam 5:1–5).

"Truly, your God is the God of gods and Lord of kings and the one who re-veals mysteries," he proclaims, "inasmuch as you are able to reveal this mys-tery" (v. 47). As Daniel's doxology has anticipated, the wisdom and power of God are evident in the wisdom and power of the exile Daniel, the ser-vant of God (vv. 20, 23). The reign of God is, in this way, already effected through this one who is "from the mountain." The promise that human power will be excelled by the enduring kingship of God is already coming to pass in this implausible way—through a human being, and a lowly one at that. The sacerdotal language of Nebuchadnezzar's obeisance before Dan-iel shocks the reader to this realization: the captive Daniel represents the reign of God!

The predicted growth of the stone is, likewise, also foreshadowed and its fulfillment set in motion in this event. Daniel predicted that the stone will grow to be "a great mount" (*tûr rab*, v. 35). Now Nebuchadnezzar liter-ally makes Daniel great (*lĕdānîyē'l* [*sic*; read: *lĕdānî'ēl*] *rabbî*), gives him very "great gifts" (*mattĕnān rabrĕbān*), and makes him chief (*rab*) of the governors of all the province of Babylon (v. 48). Three times in one verse the text im-plies that the Jewish exile is becoming *rab*, great. To be sure, that greatness is not yet to the extent predicted; the earth is not yet entirely filled. The greatness of the chosen servant of God is, for now, only over "all the prov-ince of Babylon" and over "all the sages of Babylon." Indeed, the exiles are still in the diaspora and required to function under foreign rule; Daniel himself is still "at the king's gate" (*bitra' malkā'*)—at the beck and call of earthly power (v. 49).[56] Still, the prediction of the dream oracle has been set in motion in this preliminary way. Not only did Daniel become great, at his behest, three other Jews—known by their humiliating, nonsensical exilic names (v. 49, contrast v. 17)—are promoted with him, again fulfilling the promised growth of the stone from the mountain. This is, indeed, how the reign of God is made manifest on earth: it is worked out incrementally through the quiet faith of individuals, often in ways that the world does not expect or recognize.

VI. *Postscript*

It seems clear that Daniel 2 has a prehistory. There are clues throughout of redaction: the king is intolerant of any attempt to buy time (v. 8), yet he grants Daniel reprieve (v. 16); Daniel appeared directly before the king in v. 16, but he has to be introduced by Arioch in v. 25; Daniel's three friends appear suddenly in v. 17, where they are referred to by their Hebrew names,

---

56. The "king's gate" is where the king's retainers wait to be summoned to duty. Cf. Esth 2:19, 21; 3:2–3. See H. P. Rüger, "Das Tor des Königs," *Bib* 50 (1968) 247–50.

have no part to play in the rest of the story, but are mentioned again in v. 49, this time by their foreign names. Some have posited plausibly that the oracle concerning the statue may have had an earlier (possibly Mesopotamian) origin and perhaps a different function than is now apparent; the dream oracle may have once served as political propaganda of some sort.[57] Accordingly, it may have been incorporated into the present narrative, which itself is modeled after the Joseph story and given a new meaning. The chapter's purpose now, so it has been suggested, is to demonstrate the superiority of wisdom properly conceived, namely, the superiority of wisdom that comes from God and the important place of piety.[58] That view presumes the subordination of the dream oracle to the narrative—to the extent that the dream oracle itself is nothing more than an illustration of the sage's God-given wisdom.

This essay argues, however, that the reign of God that culminates in the dream oracle is at the heart of the entire chapter. The preceding narrative, including the doxology, leads up to it, leaving interpretive cues along the way; the conclusion of the story illustrates the preliminary fulfillment of the oracle. Drawing on various sources and alluding to antecedent traditions, the narrator corroborates the message of comfort proffered to Babylonian exiles in the sixth century B.C.E. by the poet of Isaiah 40–55: God is the sovereign of history, even if that sovereignty is not readily evident in political realities. Indeed, the will of God will be effectuated through the ministrations of God's lowly servant. One may conjecture that the story in substantially its present form may have been formulated some time after Deutero-Isaiah, for Cyrus is no longer the benign conqueror ordained by the Sovereign of history. For the author of Daniel 2, hope resides not in Cyrus, who is just another oppressive power like the others before him. Rather, hope lies in the "stone hewn not by hands" from the mountain, namely, the heirs of the promise made to Israel's ancestors, the mountain to which Deutero-Isaiah bade the exiles to look. If the four regimes in the dream are, indeed, those explicitly named in the first half of the book (Nebuchadnezzar, Belshazzar, Darius the Mede, and Cyrus the Persian), then one may speculate that it was in the Persian period that the present form of the story was formulated. Certainly there is nothing in the passage that demands a date later than that. Still, the text does not name the

---

57. This is the position argued afresh recently in F. H. Polak, "The Daniel Tales in Their Aramaic Milieu," in van der Woude, ed., *The Book of Daniel in the Light of New Findings*, 249–65. Polak contends that the core of the story in Daniel 2 originated as anti-Nabonidus propaganda, but the piece was appropriated by Jewish exiles in the Persian period and then reworked in the Seleucid era.

58. See, for instance, J. J. Collins, *Daniel: With an Introduction to Apocalyptic Literature* (FOTL 20; Grand Rapids: Eerdmans, 1984) 52–53.

regimes beyond the first, leaving open the possibility of reading the story through different historical lenses. Indeed, it may be argued that the hermeneutical afterlife of the story begins within the book itself, with passages of later provenance, where the notion of the reign of God is given new life in new historical contexts. So one finds a reformulated four-regime schema also in Daniel's dream in chapter 7, a text that betrays the influence of chapter 2.[59] According to that version, where the fourth power is apparently identified with the reign of Antiochus IV Epiphanes, the divinely ordained reign will be given to someone who comes "with the clouds of heaven" and yet is "like a human being" (*kĕbar ʾĕnāš*, 7:13–14). At the same time, however, that enduring and indestructible reign ordained by God is supposed to be received by "the holy ones of the Most High" (vv. 13–28), an allusion to members of the divine council (cf. 4:17), but also a reference to their microcosmic counterparts on earth, namely, the faithful people of God (see, especially, 7:27). That enduring reign is, in all cases, still one that is at once of the God of Heaven and effectuated through the elect people of God on earth. That perspective of the reign of God is entirely in accordance with the intention of Daniel 2. Likewise, later interpretations of the stone hewn without hands as a reference to Christ (cf. Luke 20:18) or the Jewish Messiah,[60] or as denoting the new Jewish kingdom or the church, are all hermeneutically viable attempts to reappropriate the message of Daniel for their specific contexts. Indeed, the people of God at every time and in every place are to effectuate Daniel's prediction in their own context and, hence, become part of the stone from the mountain that will grow to be a mountain filling all the earth. They are part of that eternal and indestructible regime, at once brought about by divine initiative (hewn not by hands) and this-worldly (filling the earth), at once temporal (in history) and forever, at once now but not yet. That is a regime that belongs entirely to the transcendent God, who is "in heaven" but to whom one may nevertheless pray: "Your kingdom come, your will be done on earth as it is in heaven . . . for yours is the kingdom, and the power, and the glory forever. Amen" (Matt 6:9–13).

---

59. See Goldingay, *Daniel*, 148.

60. Cf. E. F. Siegman, "The Stone Hewn from the Mountain (Daniel 2)," *CBQ* 18 (1956) 364–79.

Sola Scriptura?
The Authority of the Bible
in Pluralistic Environments

MICHAEL WELKER

I. The Problem with Sola Scriptura

There is hardly a topic of theological dogmatics that has evoked such remarkable formulations and formulae as the topic "the Bible and the authority of Scripture." The notion of a "scriptural principle"; formulae such as *sola scriptura*, "Scripture's self-interpretation," the "infallibility of Scripture," the "external and internal clarity of Scripture"; as well as expressions such as "biblical theology" or "the Bible is true," belong to the defense arsenal that is supposed to ensure the authority of Scripture. To be sure, they are not equal in force or tone. Even so, these formulae and formulations, what I shall call "authority formulae," are remarkable because, on the one hand, they appear short and clear, but, on the other hand—unless they are accompanied by significant interpretation and qualification—they give rise to a wide variety of objections and false orientations. They rightly run repeatedly into opposition and protest.

When persons who possess a certain knowledge of the Bible encounter these authority formulae, they cannot help but be put off. In the Bible they meet a multiplicity of traditions, which not only exist in tension with each other, but which also stand in multiple tensions with our contemporary world of life and experience. In view of all this, to say that Scripture is infallible, or that Scripture interprets itself, comes across as highly questionable.

Author's note: Since 1988, I have had the joy of being in dialogue with Patrick D. Miller on many topics and questions regarding the interface between systematic and biblical theology. His insights have had major shaping effects on my theological thinking (see, e.g., my book *God the Spirit* [Minneapolis: Fortress, 1994] 125–26 n. 23) and on the work of several of my doctoral students. I have enjoyed our cooperation in various international and interdisciplinary research projects and have greatly appreciated his invitations to enter into interdisciplinary dialogue with young scholars in his doctoral seminars.

Suppose one responds by intensifying one's study of Scripture. One must then recognize—above and beyond the fact of tension-creating differences—that some of the biblical traditions present religious perspectives, moral viewpoints, and ways of regarding the world which are not only problematized by other biblical traditions but which many people today, even those with the best intentions, cannot share. In such a scenario, how can we speak of the "infallibility" of Scripture, or say that Scripture cannot err, or that Scripture "is true"?

Finally, suppose one points out that in reading the biblical traditions we must take note of the fact that they have developed over a period of more than a thousand years? In view of this fact, to speak of the external and internal clarity of Scripture, or to say that Scripture interprets itself, can appear to be mockery. Readers find themselves referred to an army of specialists—in theology, biblical exegesis, and historical and cultural disciplines—whose help they will need if they are to deal appropriately with sacred Scripture. It seems that the self-interpretation of Scripture and the principle "Scripture alone" are now out of the question.

When we confront the overwhelming complexity of the biblical traditions, another approach to Scripture presents itself with an attractiveness that is hard to resist. It starts with the assurance that the biblical details are not crucial. Persons interested in the Bible should concentrate on a personal encounter with God or on Jesus Christ or on salvation history or on the covenant or on atonement or on some other thread that runs throughout the whole of Scripture—whether in fact or only supposedly. But this imagined escape from the confusing complexity of the biblical traditions soon proves to be problematic. It merely introduces a religious, theological, or dogmatic *principle*—as an alternative to the authority of Scripture—that is now supposed to guide subsequent perspectives on Scripture. Some people, perhaps happy to have finally found a clear thread to guide them, will gladly exchange the unbearably complicated *authority of Scripture* for *this authority*. Others will undoubtedly note, however, that they have now been outfitted with a more or less powerful filter that substantially reduces the richness of the biblical traditions and requires continual foreshortenings and abstractions, as well as continual hermeneutic constructions that remain external to Scripture.

Once we have come this far, it is not hard to go still further in doubting and unmasking the authority of Scripture. Do we not uncover in the Bible many traces of positions that we would be only too glad to leave behind us: nationalism, patriarchy, and the glorification of violence? In view of the conflicts and contradictions between the various biblical texts, what are we to make of those texts' claim to truth? If we want to strive for honesty and truthfulness—including and especially in matters of faith—must we not at

least admit, alongside and in addition to Scripture, the validity of philoso-
phies; general theories; worldviews; moralities; historical, scientific, and
other rationalities; not to mention still other sources of knowledge? Isn't
the *sola scriptura* formula a wrong turn, or at least a one-sided idea in dire
need of correction?

When the aforementioned problems with the Bible and its authority
are clearly articulated, all authority formulae find themselves in a precari-
ous position. Indeed, they seem to be untrustworthy and untrue. If the
"scriptural principle" is the summary formula underlying the aforementioned authority formulae such as *sola scriptura*, the "self-interpretation of
Scripture," the "infallibility of Scripture," and the "external and internal
clarity of Scripture," must we not radically call into question the notion of
a "scriptural principle" in the first place? However we might specify and
give content to this principle, doesn't the notion of a "scriptural *principle*"
suggest a clarity and consistency that is simply not to be had when we consider more closely the internal constitution of the Bible?

The biblical tradition's complexity and abundant tensions have naturally not escaped the notice of the theologians who articulated the aforementioned authority formulae. Our first reading of the various authority
formulae has been consciously naive in its critique. We allowed ourselves to
be misled by talk of a "Scripture principle"—a formulation that is indeed
unfortunate and readily misunderstood. Our first reading thus needs to be
reexamined and corrected. If it is correct that Scripture cannot be brought
under one heading or reduced to one principle, what are the authority formulae saying? In what follows, I shall propose that we speak of the *fourfold
weight of Scripture*. First, I will clarify the Reformation's *sola scriptura* by
describing the authority of Scripture with regard to its fourfold weight.
Second, I will discuss the programmatic formula *biblical theology*, which
has—in its own way—also been understood as a type of authority formula.
Finally, I will show why the authority of Scripture verifies itself precisely in
pluralistic contexts that are critical of authority.

II. Sola Scriptura and the
Fourfold Weight of Scripture

"Scripture alone . . . *shall be queen*! Scripture shall be queen among the
oral and written testimonies to God and God's creative will!" That is the
unabridged version of Luther's *sola scriptura* formula.[1] Scripture is queen—

---

1. In a presentation at the Center of Theological Inquiry in Princeton, the North
American Reformation historian David Steinmetz has called attention to the fact that
the Reformers generally understood *sola scriptura* as *scriptura valde prima*.

but she is not God.[2] Scripture is not an authority that is automatically infallible in every word. Although Luther was a passionate defender of the *sola scriptura regnare*, he repeatedly warned against turning the Bible into a "paper pope." Scripture needs more than simply to be read with a raised voice. Scripture is testimony to God. It is God's word in human language and in human ways of seeing. More precisely, it is a multiperspectival testimony. Indeed it offers a "cloud of witnesses" (Heb 12:1), or better, an entire landscape of testimonies. It offers the best written collection of testimonies to God and God's will that Christianity possesses. Therefore Scripture should be queen among all other testimonies.

How could Luther and the Reformers maintain this with such great confidence? Although it does not occupy the highest place, we must *first* recognize the great *historical weight* of the biblical traditions. Over a period of at least one thousand years, and in the judgment of some biblical scholars over a period of nearly fifteen hundred years, the biblical traditions were prepared, gathered, compared with one another, related to one another, attuned to one another, and checked against one another. Thus we can also say that they "grew" over the course of centuries. These texts record a search for the knowledge of God that extended over more than a millenium. They also record the corresponding multiplicity of faith experiences of God. Scripture retains and documents a most impressive history of testimony.

By contrast, though, attention has repeatedly been focused on what Lessing called the "broad, ugly ditch" between our historical situation and the biblical traditions. The "long past world of the Bible" has repeatedly been written off along the lines of Hegel's aphorism: "In Swabia one says of that which happened long ago: It was so long ago that soon it will no longer be true. Thus Christ died for our sins so long ago that soon it will no longer be true."[3] However, such ironic statements fail to recognize that, in spite of all the undeniable distance and differences between the worldviews, rationalities, and moralities of the Bible and those of our time, in both cases it is human beings with their questions and their experiences of faith who are standing before God. Who are these human beings? They are deeply unsettled, afflicted, and despairing; they have experiences of good fortune, liberation, and hope; they have bodily needs similar to ours; they live with love and hate, hope and disappointment, sickness and death; they are ex-

---

2. See David H. Kelsey, *The Uses of Scripture in Recent Theology* (Philadelphia: Fortress Press, 1975); Hans Heinrich Schmid and Joachim Mehlhausen, eds., *Sola Scriptura: Das reformatorische Schriftprinzip in der säkularen Welt* (Gütersloh: Gütersloher Verlag, 1991); Richard Ziegert, ed., *Die Zukunft des Schriftprinzips* (Bibel im Gespräch 2; Stuttgart: Deutsche Bibelgesellschaft, 1994).

3. Johannes Hoffmeister, *Dokumente zu Hegels Entwicklung* (2d ed.; Stuttgart: Frommann, 1974) 358.

posed to the powers of nature and culture; they seek to direct and improve both their individual lives and shared human life, and in so doing repeatedly run up against their limits. To be sure, in many respects the color and contour of all these experiences in the biblical contexts differ from the color and contour of our experiences. Yet, again and again, in the midst of the distance and strangeness, an astonishing nearness emerges—not all the way down the line, but in relation to particular persons, situations, and constellations. Again and again the historical weight of Scripture will make itself felt in a great *existential richness*.

With its great historical weight and its richness encompassing both individual and societal human existence, the Bible has developed a two-thousand-year history of effects. Nothing argues for this history soon coming to an end, even though at the beginning of the third millenium the Western industrial nations are experiencing manifestations of religious decadence, a decline in religious educational formation, and even religious illiteracy. At the same time, we must see that even these religiously decadent societies are soaked through with the cultural substance of the Bible. This is true in these societies' educational formation, their customs, the ways they give rhythm to the year and to life, their art, and their ethos. Of course, by no means are this cultural substance and its influence an unqualified source of joy for everyone. For many they are a source of suffering. When we speak, then, of the *second* weight—the *cultural weight* of the Bible—we think of its open and implicit patriarchy, its ethnocentrism, its defense of worldviews that have been rendered scientifically problematic, and its functioning as a support both for ideologically authoritarian structures and for moralities that, at least from our perspective, are out of touch with the world.

Just as one cannot deny that these traits are found in the biblical traditions or that the biblical texts have repeatedly been used ideologically and for the oppression of human beings, one cannot truthfully embrace the clichés that highlight only those aspects. If we are to get a sense of the *cultural weight* of the biblical traditions as well as of their historical weight, we must emphasize their diversity, the diversity of their different "situations in life"—and thereby Scripture's diverse powers of influence and persuasion. Experiences of peace *and* of war, of liberation *and* of oppression, of joy *and* of distress accompany and mark the testimonies to God's presence *and* God's distance, to God's saving *and* God's judging actions. We find testimonies from Israel's existence prior to nationhood, from Israel's existence as a nation, and from Israel's existence after the collapse of the nation: testimonies of normative stability, of normative torpidity, and of normative crises. We find the unexamined assumptions of an ancient slaveholding society as well as important steps toward calling slavery into question and gradually doing away with it. We find many expressions of patriarchy and ethnocentrism and powers and voices that propagate new, liberating forms of shared human life. The biblical traditions critically engage a broad diversity of cultures, norms, and powers of their time. They call into question a great variety of political, social, and cultural contexts. They offer orientation and consolation in a great variety of situations of individual and communal development, formation, and crisis.

Yet the biblical traditions are not only a marvelously rich supply of faith testimonies that can and have mediated religious communications into a great variety of life situations. Over and above the historical and cultural weight of Scripture, we must give attention, *thirdly*, to its *canonical weight*. The biblical traditions do not simply offer a diffuse abundance and "plurality" of testimonies to God and God's activity, they offer numerous contrasting and interlaced testimonies to God and God's activity. As new situations arise, these testimonies refer to each other, learn from each other, criticize each other, and strengthen each other. Despite the fact that this internal dialogue strives towards consistency and coherence, it can and must not be reduced to only *one* principle. Rather, this internal dialogue itself is what constitutes the *canonical weight* of Scripture. This canonical dialogue greatly helps to fortify the certainty of faith precisely by repeatedly subjecting that certainty to healthy questioning. This dialogue of and within Scripture helps us to move from mere *certainties* to an increasingly comprehensive and profound *knowledge of truth.*[4]

The internal forces and dynamics that enter into constituting a canon are still relatively obscure to us. In a lecture on the occasion of receiving an honorary doctorate in theology in Münster, the Heidelberg Egyptologist Jan Assmann proposed a reconstruction of "five steps on the way to the canon."[5] Canonization is the preservation, in fixed collections of texts, of memories of broad and enduring scope and comprehensive, normative standards. According to Assmann, the need for canonization arises when human beings suffer radical collapse and disintegration. For Israel, the loss of their land, the deportation, and the Exile was such a collapse and disintegration, an experience of radical historical discontinuity. For the New Testament, the crucifixion of Jesus is also such a collapse and disintegration.[6]

4. See Michael Welker, "Theology in Public Discourse Outside Communities of Faith?," in *Religion, Pluralism, and Public Life: Abraham Kuyper's Legacy for the Twenty-First Century* (ed. Luis Lego; Grand Rapids: Eerdmans, 2000) 110–22.

5. Jan Assmann, *Fünf Stufen auf dem Wege zum Kanon: Tradition und Schriftkultur im frühen Judentum und in seiner Umwelt* (Münstersche Theologische Vorträge 1; Münster: Lit Verlag, 1999) 11–35.

6. For the literary development of the New Testament, the fall of Jerusalem and the burning of Rome should also not be underestimated.

These experiences of radical discontinuity, collapse, and threatening chaos find expression in potentially canonical texts. This radical discontinuity requires interpretation. It is important for the process of canonization that a certain *multiplicity* of interpretations, a limited multiplicity of exemplary possibilities be developed for explaining and bridging the catastrophe of discontinuity. Different views of the world, different views of history and of the future make possible these exemplary interpretations. Only when these interpretations are brought into mutual interconnection, only when a "pluralistic library"[7] of different perspectives on the crisis is present, only then does the substance of the canon come into being. This referential nexus can have several centers, but it also has limits. We still need to do more research on the theological reasons for the limits of the canon. With some texts on the margins of the canonical traditions, it is understandable why theologians and councils were sometimes uncertain whether they should include or exclude the texts in question. Karl Barth said that the canon "imposed" itself on the church.[8]

Andreas Schüle has suggested an alternative view to those of Assmann and Barth.[9] Schüle's position is that the postexilic experience of a discontinuity now overcome made possible a pluralism of interpretations, many of which, possessing complementary insight, could no longer be surrendered. As the church grew in multiple contexts, it, too, could not do without this pluralistic potential for theological knowledge. Thus Scripture acquired its canonical weight, which in turn set its historical weight and made possible its full cultural weight.

However, the historical, the cultural, and the canonical weight of Scripture is grounded in its fourth weight—the theological. The Bible is a highly complex testimony to God. More precisely, it is a complex nexus of testimonies, which together call attention to God's reality and God's activity in creation. Ultimately, the Bible's fourfold weight accrues to it on the basis of its object and its central content. On the basis of its content, Scripture guides our perception of God's activity among human beings[10] as well as our living memory and expectation of that activity. On the basis of its theological weight, Scripture guides historical, cultural, and ecclesial learning and growth in the knowledge of God. On the basis of its canonical composition and its theological weight, Scripture prevents premature (or final) closure

---

7. Heinz Schürmann, *Gottes Reich—Jesu Geschick* (Freiburg: Herder, 1983) 246.
8. See *KD* I/2, 473ff. and 597ff.
9. Andreas Schüle, *Israels Sohn—Jahwes Prophet: Zum Verhältnis von Religionsgeschichte und kanonischer Theologie anhand der Bileam-Perikope (Num 22–24)* (Münster: Lit, 2001).
10. R. Williams, "The Discipline of Scripture," in idem, *On Christian Theology* (Challenges in Contemporary Theology; Oxford: Blackwell, 2000) 44–59.

on these memories and anticipations, this learning and growth.[11] Precisely
because the Bible in its multiperspectival "testimony" refers to God and to
the divine action toward creation, the Bible itself becomes a living source.
It is on the basis of this internal constitution that people can ascribe to
Scripture the authority formulae that are so unpersuasive when regarded in
an isolated and superficial manner.[12] It is the biblical testimonies' reference
to the living God, to the God of Israel and to the revelation of God in Jesus
Christ, which gives those testimonies their coherence, their weight, and
their orienting power. The historical, the cultural, and the canonical weight
of Scripture are only a mirror and reflection of the theological weight bestowed upon Scripture by its content and object—the living God. Thus,
the great historical, cultural, and canonical weight that I have hinted at is
but a reflection of the glory of the living God, to which Scripture gives multiperspectival testimony.

For Christians, this glory of the living God is made manifest in the presence of the risen Christ.[13] The risen Christ is not simply the physically re-
vivified pre-Easter Jesus. Although a few resurrection testimonies seem to
suggest a confusion between resurrection and physical revivification, the
canonical material is compelling: What is at issue is a reality which, on the
one hand, shows traits of that which is available to normal sense perception, and yet which, on the other hand, has the character of a vision. The
texts tell of people falling on their knees in worship in light of a theophany,
a revelation of God. At the same time, the texts report doubt. The Emmaus
story is especially rich. The eyes of the disciples are kept shut so that they
do not recognize the risen Christ. In the ritual of the bread their eyes are
opened. But the very next verse says: "and he vanished from their sight"
(Luke 24:31). Instead of now complaining about a ghost, the disciples remember a second experience, also evidence but that at first had not been
revelatory for them: "Were not our hearts burning within us while he was
talking to us on the road, while he was opening the scriptures to us?" (Luke

---

11. See B. Oberdorfer, "Biblisch-realistische Theologie: Methodologische Überle-
gungen zu einem dogmatischen Programm," in *Resonanzen: Theologische Beiträge* (ed.
S. Brandt and B. Oberdorfer; Wuppertal: Foedus, 1997) 63–83; and Gerhard Sauter,
Grundlagen der Theologie (Göttingen: Vandenhoeck, 1998). See also James A. Sanders,
Canon and Community: A Guide to Canonical Criticism (GBS; Philadelphia: Fortress, 1984).

12. Only on the basis of this character of pluralistic testimony can we summarize, in
Luther's words, *scriptura "ipsa per sese certissima, facillima, apertissima, sui ipsius interpres, om-
nium omnia probans, iudicans et illuminans"* (*WA* 7, 97, 24–25).

13. For greater detail see Michael Welker, "Resurrection and Eternal Life: The
Canonic Memory of the Resurrected Christ, His Reality, and His Glory," in *The End of
the World and the Ends of God: Theology and Science on Eschatology* (ed. J. Polkinghorne and
M. Welker; Harrisburg: Trinity Press International, 2000) 279–90.

24:32). Witnesses recognize the risen Christ in personal address, in the breaking of bread, and in the opening of the Scriptures, as well as in luminous appearances, which *eo ipso* oppose the confusion of resurrection with physical revivification. It is important that a *multiplicity* of different experiences of the resurrected Christ give rise to the certainty that he is and remains present among us in a bodily way. By contrast, the stories of the empty tomb emphasize that a single revelation—even a spectacular one by means of heavenly messengers—does not yet evoke faith. Instead, the result is fear, terror, and silence (Mark 16:5–8). Or there is the rumor of a grave robbery or the subsequent propaganda (John 20:2, 13, 15; Matt 27:62–66; 28:11–15). Or the visions at the tomb are discounted as "an idle tale" (Luke 24:11).

The certainty that Christ is risen does not mean that he is present now in the same way that the pre-Easter Jesus was present in a particular location in space and time. Instead *the whole fullness of his person and his life* becomes present "in the Spirit and in faith." This presence in the Spirit and in faith is not something that makes sense to a naturalistic and scientific way of thinking. Therefore such thinking gets stuck over and over in the pros and cons of physical revivification. This reduces faith to a mere subjective opinion and the Spirit to a numinous entity. By contrast, the fullness of Christ's person and life comes to powerful expression in the canonical memory of the community of witnesses. By means of its canonical, cultural, and historical weight, Scripture can fulfill its task of serving to make the risen Christ richly present in canonical memory. In this process, the historical-critical reconstruction of past reality, as difficult and painstaking as it is, is just as important as the recognition that complex historical futures are co-present with the risen Christ—futures into which our existences and life stories are embedded. The risen Christ is not without his witnesses, not without his post-Easter body. Therefore, along with the indispensable historical-critical access to the biblical texts, newer "literary" approaches to biblical interpretation—now being imported into Europe from North America—and the socio-historical interpretation of Scripture are also critical. They are important in their attempt to correspond to Scripture's theological, cultural, and ethos-shaping weight in making the risen Christ present.

One cannot say, though, that we have even come anywhere near exhausting the creative interconnections between the various ways of approaching the biblical traditions. Under the programmatic formula of "biblical theology," some scholars—primarily in German- and English-speaking contexts—have been trying for a number of years now to draw attention to the significance of interdisciplinary theological work that can and must bring us forward on this path.

III. What Does the Expression
"Biblical Theology" Mean?

The expression "biblical theology" has been frequently employed in a manner not unlike the other authority formulae. According to Gerhard Ebeling's definition, which has been repeatedly cited in the secondary literature, "biblical theology" can be defined as theology in accordance with the Bible or the theology contained in the Bible.[14] For good reasons both exegetical and systematic theologians have treated these definitions with skepticism, indeed often with strong criticism. If "biblical theology" is to be understood as "theology" in the sense of (1) a comprehensively ramified nexus of thought and persuasion, or even a specific system, which (2) has been extracted from, or ultimately could be extracted from the Bible, then biblical theology is impossible. Biblical theology in that sense would contradict the multiplicity and vitality of the biblical testimonies and traditions emphasized earlier in this essay. It would also contradict the vitality of God's revelation, to which the various biblical traditions give testimony from their specific perspectives. The complex structure of the canon and the vitality of the canonical memory would be obscured by such a systematic conception of biblical theology, whether this theology were regarded as immanent in the Bible or as "accruing" to the Bible from outside, so to speak. Karl Barth was right to insist that it is misguided to "abstract from the Bible some concealed historical or conceptual system, an economy of salvation or a Christian view of things. There can be no biblical theology in this sense, either of the Old or New Testament, or of the Bible as a whole."[15]

However, we need not understand "theology" as talk of God in a comprehensively ramified nexus of thought. We can also, in all humility, understand "theology" as talk of God that is accompanied by certainty and directed toward truth, and that (1) has substantial content, (2) possesses public intelligibility and consistency, and (3) is capable of being substantively developed.[16] However unprepossessing and fragmentary this theology might be, it serves to strengthen the certainty of faith in the development of knowledge of God. This is the theology that is meant when it is said that every Christian is called to do theology. The Bible is undoubtedly full of such theology, indeed it is permeated by such theology. The most

---

14. G. Ebeling, "The Meaning of 'Biblical Theology'," in idem, *Word and Faith* (trans. James W. Leitch; Philadelphia: Fortress, 1963) 79–97. For more detail on the following discussion, see Michael Welker, "The Tasks of Biblical Theology and the Authority of Scripture," in *Theology in the Service of the Church: Festschrift for Thomas Gillespie* (ed. Wallace Alston; Grand Rapids: Eerdmans, 2000) 232–41.

15. *KD* I/2, §§19–21, 483.

16. See Welker, "Theology in Public Discourse," 110–22.

diverse theological efforts and enterprises could claim to be "biblical theology" in this basic sense, if they are merely somehow related to the Bible.

But upon closer examination, this use of the expression "biblical theology" proves to be counterproductive. There is not much help to be found in speaking of a theology that merely somehow refers to the Bible, or from making the trivial observation that the biblical texts are filled with and permeated by theology or theologies in this basic sense. To speak of "biblical theology" in this sense is pretentious since all Christian theology claims to relate to the Bible in some way and to correspond to Scripture in some sense. The expression "biblical theology" thus seems to place before us an unhappy alternative. Either "biblical theology"—in accordance with Ebeling's definition—propagates a notion of system and unity that is theologically and intellectually problematic,[17] or it lends inappropriate emphasis to the obvious points that the biblical texts speak of God in a qualified way and that Scripture, one way or another, is a source for Christian theology.

In spite of the problems I have named, and in spite of the risk of it being misunderstood as a pretentious assertion or as a theologically highly problematic authority formula, the expression "biblical theology" has emerged (and continues to do so) as an intradisciplinary and interdisciplinary concept of programmatic reform—especially in Germany and North America in the final third of the twentieth century. Journals, academic publishing series, conferences, and interdisciplinary research projects regularly employ the phrase "biblical theology" as a label. Note, for instance, the following series and journals: *Biblical Theology Bulletin* (1971–); Overtures to Biblical Theology (Philadelphia: Fortress, 1977–); Biblisch-Theologische Studien (Neukirchen: Neukirchener, 1977–); *Ex Auditu: An Annual of the Frederick Neumann Symposium on Theological Interpretation of Scripture* (Princeton: 1985–); *Jahrbuch für Biblische Theologie* (1986–). What might this development signify?

As early as the 1920s and 30s, processes of differentiation and specialization were taking place within the exegetical disciplines, especially in the English-speaking world. Although many scholars gave absolute priority to historical-critical exegesis, others argued that such an approach "divided the Bible into disjointed layers ... overemphasized the commonalities between the Bible and its cultural environment ... attached too much

---

17. For critical perspectives, see J. D. Levenson, "Why Jews Are Not Interested in Biblical Theology," in idem, *The Hebrew Bible, the Old Testament, and Historical Criticism: Jews and Christians in Biblical Studies* (Louisville: Westminster/John Knox Press, 1993) 33–61; D. Ritschl, "'Wahre,' 'reine' oder 'neue' Biblische Theologie?: Einige Anfragen zur neueren Diskussion um 'Biblische Theologie'," *Jahrbuch für Biblische Theologie* 1 (1986) 135–50; and Bernd Janowski, "The One God of the Two Testaments: Basic Questions of a Biblical Theology," *TT* 57 (2000) 297–324.

importance to the process of development, and . . . failed to meet the task of providing a truly theological interpretation of Holy Scripture."[18] This resistance to historical criticism and the effort to develop alternatives to it went under the heading (among other titles) "biblical theology." Beginning in the 1970s this programmatic concept (for reforming biblical studies) was picked up by systematic theology. A variety of motives have contributed to this recent development. Certainly one of the motives has been the exemplary systematic-theological creativity of many of the exegetical contributions to the discussion. The waning influence of philosophy and the increasing emergence of an orientation in systematic theology shaped by cultural history and other cultural disciplines have also suggested an increased need to take orientation from the biblical traditions. Both the diminution of the binding power of confessional writings and the interest in theological bases for orientation that enjoy ecumenical breadth are also part of the calculation in understanding this development. The same is true of the suspicion that those neo-Protestant and "postmodern" theologies that systematically neglect a substantive connection with the biblical traditions and distort them under reductionistic forms of thought provoke the self-secularization of churches in the Western industrial nations and contribute to the decline of religious educational formation.

Finally, the programmatic formula "biblical theology" is used to characterize nascent projects of interdisciplinary theological research and reflection. Here, however, one easily overlooks the fact that in the different theological disciplines this formula is connected with different governing conceptions and research intentions. At the same time, these different conceptions and intentions can certainly come to play complementary roles.

In the exegetical disciplines, "biblical theology" designates three enterprises in particular, namely:

1. to work against the disintegration of the discipline;
2. to reverse the tendencies toward self-secularization and transformation in research on the history of religions;
3. in the midst of the unmanageable abundance of detailed investigations of history generally and the history of religions specifically, to pose the question of "the unity" and "the *proprium*" of the biblical traditions, even if this question is regarded as a regulative one that only admits of provisional answers.

---

18. J. Barr, "Biblische Theologie," *Evangelisches Kirchenlexikon* (5 vols.; ed. Erwin Fahlbusch et al.; Göttingen: Vandenhoeck & Ruprecht, 1985–1997) 1:489.

In the disciplines of systematic and practical theology, the programmatic formula "biblical theology" is connected with the following three enterprises, among others:

1. to work toward theologically justifiable differentiations in critical engagement with forms of theological reflection that are reductionistic or with forms for thinking in a systematic-theological way that are inadequate;

2. to develop alternatives to specific systematic forms that primarily follow philosophical or other extra-theological rationalities and interests (this general category also includes attempts to develop alternatives to forms of religiosity that are marked by such extra-theological rationalities and interests);

3. to develop formulations for a diverse ecumenical culture that would enable us to understand the confessions as different ways of learning from Scripture and would offer new possibilities for mutual ecumenical appreciation and enrichment.

This complementarity of exegetical and systematic orientations gives rise to important tasks of mutual correction and supplementation between disciplines. Exegesis, with its historical-critical competence, must preserve systematics from moving too quickly to draw analogies or too quickly to move toward a "fusion of horizons." When exegetes propose and employ concepts of "unity," "the *proprium*," and the "center of Scripture," systematic theology and church history have the task of testing these concepts to see whether they can carry the load required of them in the contexts of contemporary thought and the history of dogma. In recent decades, a number of themes of unity and integration, or forms of thought designed to provide integration, have been proposed: the covenant, the mighty acts of God, atonement, Exodus and liberation—these are but some of the proposals, the validity of each of which has to be examined.

Modernistic thinking, which looks for the *one* continuum and the *one* principle that synthesizes *everything*, will see nothing but lost battles in the propagation of these diverse proposals. But it need not be so. Biblical theology can actually see in the limited capacity of various themes to integrate or unify something to be treasured. Instead of but one theme, the multiple themes of Scripture reveal connections in the pluralism of the canonical traditions. While it is certainly legitimate to strive for themes that offer the greatest scope and extent possible, what is of most importance is the finite *multiplicity* of *entrées* into the biblical traditions that are broadly supported in the canonical traditions. This multiplicity is of the utmost relevance in environments that are rightly termed "pluralistic."

IV. The Authority of Scripture
in Pluralistic Environments

One of the greatest cultural problems of our times consists in the fact that pluralistic cultures and societies have no clear conception of their internal constitution. Pluralistic cultures and societies notoriously confuse the constitution of pluralism with a diffuse plurality of individuals, lifestyles, groups, and institutional arrangements. In view of this diffuse plurality, some people rightly fear relativism, the threat of chaos, or the collapse of commonality and social connectivity. Others concoct conceptions, mostly illusory, of the infinite abundance of possibilities offered by this plurality. Still others call for authoritarian countermeasures against this chaos or put their hope in liberal forms of integration, as expressed in the statement: "We need this or that minimum commonality in order to get out of this mess." All these viewpoints have one thing in common: They haven't understood anything about pluralism. Pluralism does not simply bring with it disconnectedness, relativism, individualism, and the like, though these phenomena do occur in pluralistic environments. Rather, pluralism creates and cultivates *multi-systemic* forms, which, although they indeed develop great connective powers, do not develop *only one* socially and culturally unitive power. However, the various connective powers—those of the market, the media, education, politics, law, religion, and so forth—are relevant to the entire society and the culture as a whole. A specific multiplicity of systemic forms, which cannot be reduced to one single formula or one law, are necessary for the guidance and the welfare of "the whole."

In pluralistic contexts, a multiplicity of groups and associations attempt to influence this multi-systemic structure. We use the term "civil society" to denominate the numerous groups and associations that seek to influence, to stabilize or destabilize, to connect more strongly or separate more strongly the systemic forms of society such as law, education, and politics. Real pluralism brings a high degree of freedom and efficiency. But it also brings heavy burdens for persons who must live with increasing conflicts of interest, with tensions between their normative connections, and with fissures in their identity. These situations do not call for simplistic solutions brought about by an imposition of some supposedly global perspective. Instead, they call for differentiated aids to orientation that are able to speak in appropriate ways to diverse contexts. The family has expectations that differ from those of politicians, education has different expectations than the economy, law has different expectations than the media, and so on and so forth.

The multi-contextual and pluralistic constitution of the biblical canon enables it to respond in a differentiated way to such diverse contexts, rationalities, and thematic clusters. At the same time, the canonical webs of reference make it possible to establish subtle transitions and links between pluralistic contexts. Once a serious, specific, systematic connection is established—be it analogies in ways of posing questions or pursuing inquiries, or systematic contrasts or alternative visions between contemporary contexts and biblical ones—the results are typically fruitful and instructive interdisciplinary constellations. This method admittedly requires somewhat more loving care and effort than do attempts to find a religious formula which, by either authoritarian or liberal strategies of integration, is supposed to fit anything and everything. But to be precise, this method does not require more loving care and effort than we expect from the pastoral creativity which, whether in preaching, pastoral care, or teaching, interprets specific canonical texts for a specific situation or locates a specific situation in the analogous imaginative domain of a canonical context.

The great task for academic theology today is to elaborate specific models that allow the establishment of fruitful relations between the pluralistic canonical traditions on the one hand, and the orientation profiles and needs for orientation in societal and cultural pluralism on the other hand. In recent years, we have had encouraging experiences in various contexts.[19] Yet, we have also run up against devastating generalizing tendencies that refuse to engage in this work and which—for example, in the curricula of religious instruction in German schools—even contribute to the systematic

---

19. Here I name only four of the interdisciplinary projects in which I have had very encouraging experiences in the last several years:

- the dialogue between theology and natural science, including exegetes and specialists in cultural disciplines, especially at a series of consultations on eschatological themes at the Center of Theological Inquiry in Princeton: see Polkinghorne and Welker, eds., *The End of the World and the Ends of God*; and Michael Welker, "Springing Cultural Traps: The Science-and-Theology Discourse on Eschatology and the Common Good," *TT* 58 (2001) 165–76;
- the dialogue between theology and economics: a research project in Chicago and Heidelberg under the general theme of "Property and Possession," which focused on the symbols and rationalities of acquiring, having, and losing in economic and religious contexts (note that a volume entitled *Property and Possession*, edited by William Schweiker, is forthcoming);
- discussions involving theology, morality, and law: several events have occurred in connection with the Heidelberg graduate colloquium on "Religion and Normativity"; among the resulting publications is Jan Assmann, Bernd Janowski, and Michael Welker, eds., *Gerechtigkeit: Richten und Retten in der abendländischen Tradition und ihren altorientalischen Ursprüngen* (Munich: Fink, 1998);
- a number of interdisciplinary gatherings on the thematic complex of anthropology, personhood, and dignity: see, e.g., my introduction to *EvT* 60 (2000) 4–8; and N. H. Gregersen, W. B. Drees, and U. Görman, eds., *The Human Person in Science and Theology* (Edinburgh: T & T Clark, 2000) 95–114.

distortion of what the biblical traditions have to say.[20] But what, exactly, is a serious, specific, systematic relationship between the canonical traditions and the contexts of contemporary life?

To answer this question, we urgently need a cultural reorientation and a reorientation in educational politics. We need a new orientation that dispenses with fear of difference and of polycontextual and multi-systemic constellations. We need a new orientation that does not regard the search for the "master switch" or the "one size fits all" formula as the ideal solution to our quests for orientation. Instead we must learn to relate systemic differences to systemic differences. What does this mean?

The mere *observation* of thematic analogies, similar questions, and presumably similar figures of thought in canonical, historical, and contemporary contexts by no means suffices to meet theology's task in this pursuit. If we wish to go beyond a naive biblicism that tolerates a high degree of arbitrary associations, we must reconstruct analogous or contrary systemic differences in canonical, historical, and contemporary contexts. This means that a theme, a unit of content, a figure of thought, or a theoretical or practical problem is perceived in at least two different canonical contexts or historical contexts that stand in relation to the canon. Why is the item treated differently in context A than in context B? How do we evaluate this difference? What do we learn from it? We then relate this difference to an analogous difference in at least two contemporary contexts. In this way we can draw relations between presumed processes of development or decline that are instructive for each other. The challenge is to think not of a simple continuity, but of a threefold discontinuity. For example, it is senseless to want to "decide" a difference in the history of dogma or a contemporary theological question by appealing to only one portion of the biblical traditions. Different people center and select differently, and arrive at different results. The outcome is an indifferent juxtaposition of various results. By contrast, if we use at least two interfaces to mark differences and developments, the contexts begin to "talk" with each other and to set limits to the arbitrary drawing of relationships.

In concentrations of this kind—concentrations that are multi-systemic and sensitive to difference—the biblical traditions with their great historical, cultural, canonical, and theological weight can have an orienting effect. The finely-meshed interweaving of such concentrations prevents the process of making connections with the tremendous wealth of canonical traditions from becoming diffuse, disintegrated, and trivial. A theological

---

20. See Heinz Schmidt and Hartmut Rupp, eds., *Lebensorientierung oder Verharmlosung?: Die Lehrplanentwicklung des Religionsunterrichts in theologischer Kritik* (Stuttgart: Calwer, 2000).

endeavor that pays attention to themes, contexts, and rationalities must be focused by concentrations that are multi-systemic and sensitive to difference as that endeavor continually returns to the biblical traditions with new questions about the specific historical and cultural thematic possibilities for making connections between the biblical traditions and pluralistic contexts of both yesterday and today. The theological endeavor must learn to distinguish processes of convergence and divergence both historically and systematically. Rationally and thematically finely-meshed accounts, on the one hand, and challenges to counteract reductionistic developments, on the other hand, must be distinguished from each other, and must be justified with regard to their object and to the problem at issue.

In this development, we must rediscover the great significance of faith's knowledge and of spiritual and theological formation. We must also learn to attach new value to the power and dignity of *testimony* or *witness*. Witnesses' individual search for certainty and their communal search for truth are believable and trustworthy precisely because they can regard the perspectival and fragmentary nature of their knowledge and their contribution with untroubled respect.[21] They can live with the conscious thought: "This is *my* contribution, this is *our* contribution, to the search for knowledge of God and of truth." They can do so because they place themselves in canonical and ecumenical contexts that invite, encourage, and challenge them to respect the pluralistic constitution of these contexts, while remaining steadfast in opposition to relativism. The goal and the standard is not the search for final certainty, but the examination, growing completeness, development, justification, and—as need be—correction of certainty in the search for truth.[22]

---

21. For a recent attempt to do Old Testament Theology under the guiding rubric of "witness," see Walter Brueggemann, *Theology of the Old Testament: Testimony, Dispute, Advocacy* (Minneapolis: Fortress, 1997).

22. I thank John Hoffmeyer for translating this essay.

Bibliography of the Works of Patrick D. Miller
1964–2001

Brent A. Strawn

———◆———

The works are listed chronologically by year of publication with the following order prevailing within specific years: books (first authored, then edited),[1] articles, essays in books or dictionaries, and book reviews.[2] Multiple exemplars within these sub-categories are generally arranged alphabetically;[3] departures from this practice or from the other categorizations are present only when there were obvious reasons to do so. An attempt has been made to note reprints whenever possible.

Given Miller's prodigious work pace, this bibliography is now out-of-date (note the "In Press" section below). Furthermore, Miller's numerous contributions as an editor are, in the main, not listed on a per-volume basis in this bibliography. Nevertheless, the reader should note his editorship, whether alone or in concert with others, of the following publications:

- *Journals*:
  Theology Today (Book Review Editor: 1984–1990; Editor: 1990– ; note also nos. 178–179); and
  Interpretation: A Journal of Bible and Theology (Book Review Editor: 1966–72; Associate Editor: 1973–79; note also no. 55).
- *Commentary Series*:
  Interpretation: A Bible Commentary for Teaching and Preaching (Old Testament Editor; 20 Old Testament vols. to date; Atlanta and Louisville: John Knox, 1982–);

Author's note: I would like to thank Joan Blyth for both producing and providing an early version of this list and Linzie Treadway for help in double-checking many of the references.

1. Included here is a journal issue edited by Miller prior to his becoming Editor of that series (no. 178; cf. also nos. 179, 55).
2. Note that several of the book reviews in *Interpretation*, especially while Miller served as Book Review Editor, are unsigned.
3. Definite and indefinite articles are not treated as significant for alphabetization; book reviews are alphabetized by the author's last name.

Westminster Bible Companion (Series Editor with David Bartlett; 26 vols. to date; Louisville: Westminster John Knox, 1995–); and the currently underway

Abingdon Old Testament Commentaries series (General Editor; 2 vols. to date; Nashville: Abingdon, 2001–).

Additionally, Miller currently sits, or has sat, on a number of editorial boards for other journals and series.

Finally, a word on the book reviews: The bibliographical data for each volume reviewed varies in the respective publications. An effort has been made here to provide *title* information that is sufficient to facilitate any possible follow-up. At times this practice indicated abbreviating the published title information; at other times it involved adding information to the title. Similarly, in some instances, the title on the first page of an essay or journal article did not correspond to the title provided in that particular publication's Table of Contents. In such cases, I have followed the title that seemed most useful to the reader and that seemed more stylistically and/or grammatically correct. The interested reader will, in any event, have no problem locating the source in question using the bibliographical data provided herein.

1964

1. *Chart of Biblical History and Culture Manual* (Boston: United Church Press, 1964).
2. "Holy War and Cosmic War in Early Israel" (Ph.D. diss., Harvard University, 1964).
3. "Two Critical Notes on Psalm 68 and Deuteronomy 33," *Harvard Theological Review* 57 (1964) 240–43.

1965

4. "Fire in the Mythology of Canaan and Israel," *Catholic Biblical Quarterly* 27 (1965) 256–61. [Reprinted in no. 340]
5. "God the Warrior: A Problem in Biblical Interpretation and Apologetics," *Interpretation* 19 (1965) 39–46. [Reprinted in no. 340]
6. Review of R. Davidson, *The Old Testament* in *The Presbyterian Outlook* 147 (April 12, 1965) 15.
7. Review of D. Hillers, *Treaty-Curses and the Old Testament Prophets* in *Interpretation* 19 (1965) 372–74.
8. Review of G. E. Wright, ed., *The Bible and the Ancient Near East: Essays in Honor of William Foxwell Albright* in *The Presbyterian Outlook* 174 (September 6, 1965) 15.

1966

9. "*yeled* in the Song of Lamech," *Journal of Biblical Literature* 85 (1966) 477–78.

10. Review of M. Dahood, *Psalms I: 1–50* in *The Presbyterian Outlook* 148 (December 19, 1966) 19.

11. Review of A. Feuillet, *Johannine Studies* in *The Presbyterian Outlook* 148 (June 27, 1966) 19.

12. Review of V. Møller-Christensen and K. E. Jordt-Jørgensen, *Encyclopedia of Bible Creatures* in *The Presbyterian Outlook* 148 (February 21, 1966) 15.

13. Review of J. C. Trever, *The Untold Story of Qumran* in *The Presbyterian Outlook* 148 (March 7, 1966) 15.

1967

14. "El the Warrior," *Harvard Theological Review* 60 (1967) 411–31. [Reprinted in no. 340]

15. Review of G. W. Anderson, *The History and Religion of Israel* in *The Presbyterian Outlook* 149 (March 27, 1967) 15.

16. Review of H. H. Guthrie, *Israel's Sacred Songs: A Study of Dominant Themes* in *The Presbyterian Outlook* 149 (February 13, 1967) 15.

17. Review of H. F. Hahn, *The Old Testament in Modern Research* in *Interpretation* 21 (1967) 221.

18. Review of J. M. Myers, *Ezra, Nehemiah* in *The Presbyterian Outlook* 149 (January 23, 1967) 15.

19. Review of M. Noth, *Leviticus: A Commentary* in *The Presbyterian Outlook* 149 (March 6, 1967) 15.

20. Review of J. A. Sanders, *The Dead Sea Psalms Scroll* in *Interpretation* 21 (1967) 349.

1968

21. "The Divine Council and the Prophetic Call to War," *Vetus Testamentum* 18 (1968) 100–107. [Reprinted in no. 340]

22. "John L. McKenzie" in *The New Day: Catholic Theologians of the Renewal* (ed. Wm. Jerry Boney and Lawrence E. Molumby; Richmond: John Knox, 1968) 103–15.

23. Review of J. S. Ackerman, *On Teaching the Bible as Literature: A Guide to Selected Biblical Narratives for Secondary Schools* in *Interpretation* 22 (1968) 375–76.

24. Review of H. G. Cox, *On Not Leaving it to the Snake* in *Interpretation* 22 (1968) 122–23.

25. Review of G. Kittel, ed., *Theological Dictionary of the New Testament, Vol. 4* in *Interpretation* 22 (1968) 122.

26. Review of R. North, *Archaeo-Biblical Egypt* in *Interpretation* 22 (1968) 250.
27. Review of S. Sandmel, ed., *Old Testament Issues* in *The Presbyterian Outlook* 150 (December 2, 1968) 15.
28. Review of E. A. Speiser, *Oriental and Biblical Studies: Collected Writings of E. A. Speiser* in *Interpretation* 22 (1968) 375.
29. Review of C. Westermann, *Basic Forms of Prophetic Speech* in *Interpretation* 22 (1968) 121–22.

1969

30. "The Gift of God: The Deuteronomic Theology of the Land," *Interpretation* 23 (1969) 451–65.
31. "A Note on the *Mešaʿ* Inscription," *Orientalia* 38 (1969) 461–64.
32. Review of W. F. Albright, *Yahweh and the Gods of Canaan: A Historical Analysis of Two Contrasting Faiths* in *The Presbyterian Outlook* 151 (January 20, 1969) 15.
33. Review of E. W. Heaton, *The Hebrew Kingdoms* in *The Presbyterian Outlook* 151 (December 1, 1969) 15.
34. Review of K. Stendahl, *The School of St. Matthew and its Use of the Old Testament* in *Interpretation* 23 (1969) 347–48.
35. Review of H. B. Swete, *An Introduction to the Old Testament in Greek* in *Interpretation* 23 (1969) 238.

1970

36. "Animal Names as Designations in Ugaritic and Hebrew," *Ugarit-Forschungen* 2 (1970) 177–86. [Reprinted in no. 340]
37. "Apotropaic Imagery in Proverbs 6:30–32," *Journal of Near Eastern Studies* 29 (1970) 129–30.
38. "Ugaritic *ĠZR* and Hebrew *ʿZR II*," *Ugarit-Forschungen* 2 (1970) 159–75.
39. Review of D. Daube, *Studies in Biblical Law* in *Interpretation* 24 (1970) 403–4.
40. Review of E. E. Ellis and M. Wilcox, eds., *Neotestamentica et Semitica: Studies in Honour of Matthew Black* in *Interpretation* 24 (1970) 404–5.
41. Review of G. Friedrich, ed., *Theological Dictionary of the New Testament, Vol. 6* in *Interpretation* 24 (1970) 403.
42. Review of A. Jones, ed., *The Old Testament of the Jerusalem Bible* in *The Presbyterian Outlook* 152 (May 11, 1970) 15.
43. Review of K. Koch, *The Growth of the Biblical Tradition: The Form-Critical Method* in *Journal of Biblical Literature* 89 (1970) 242–43.
44. Review of W. G. Lambert and A. R. Millard, *Atra-Ḫasīs: The Babylonian Story of the Flood* in *Interpretation* 24 (1970) 402–3.

45. Review of B. Porten, *Archives from Elephantine: The Life of an Ancient Jewish Military Colony* in *Interpretation* 24 (1970) 384–86.
46. Review of J. B. Pritchard, ed., *The Ancient Near East: Supplementary Texts and Pictures Relating to the Old Testament* in *Journal of Biblical Literature* 89 (1970) 347–50.
47. Review of W. Whallon, *Formula, Character, and Context: Studies in Homeric, Old English, and Old Testament Poetry* in *Interpretation* 24 (1970) 391–92.

1971

48. "'Him Only Shall You Serve': Reflections on the Meaning of Old Testament Worship," *Andover-Newton Quarterly* 11 (1971) 139–49. [Reprinted in no. 49]
49. "'Him Only Shall You Serve': Reflections on the Meaning of Old Testament Worship," *The Bethany Guide* 46 (1971) 6–13. [Reprint of no. 48]
50. "The *MRZḤ* Text," in *The Claremont Ras Shamra Tablets* (ed. Loren R. Fisher; Analecta orientalia 48; Rome: Pontifical Biblical Institute, 1971) 37–48. [Reprinted in no. 340][4]
51. Review of B. Childs, *Biblical Theology in Crisis* in *Journal of Biblical Literature* 90 (1971) 209–10.
52. Review of G. Fohrer, *Studien zur alttestamentlichen Theologie und Geschichte* in *Interpretation* 25 (1971) 509.
53. Review of M. Noth, *Gesammelte Studien zum Alten Testament II* in *Interpretation* 25 (1971) 218–19.
54. Review of A. Rofé, *Israelite Belief in Angels in the Pre-Exilic Period as Evidenced by Biblical Tradition* (Hebrew) in *Interpretation* 25 (1971) 531–32.

1972

55. "Editorial," *Interpretation* 26 (1972) 210–11.
56. Review of F. F. Bruce, *The English Bible: A History of Translations* in *Interpretation* 26 (1972) 380.
57. Review of R. Caporale and A. Grumelli, ed., *The Culture of Unbelief: Studies and Proceedings from the First International Symposium on Belief Held at Rome, March 22–27, 1969* in *Interpretation* 26 (1972) 252.
58. Review of J. A. Fitzmyer, *The Genesis Apocryphon of Qumran Cave I: A Commentary* in *Interpretation* 26 (1972) 99.
59. Review of G. Friedrich, ed., *Theological Dictionary of the New Testament, Vol. 7* in *Interpretation* 26 (1972) 364–65.

---

4. The cover page of this volume reads 1971 but the copyright date is actually 1972.

60. Review of C. D. Ginsburg, *The Song of Songs and Cohelet (commonly called the Book of Ecclesiastes): Translated from the Original Hebrew, with a Commentary, Historical and Critical* in *Interpretation* 26 (1972) 381.

61. Review of R. Gordis, *Poets, Prophets, and Sages: Essays in Biblical Interpretation* in *Interpretation* 26 (1972) 250–52.

62. Review of J. Neusner, *There We Sat Down: Talmudic Judaism in the Making* in *Interpretation* 26 (1972) 253.

63. Review of M. Noth, *Aufsätze zur biblischen Landes- und Altertumskunde* in *Interpretation* 26 (1972) 357–58.

64. Review of J. M. Robinson, ed., *The Future of Our Religious Past: Essays in Honour of Rudolf Bultmann* in *Interpretation* 26 (1972) 249–50.

65. Review of C. C. Torrey, *Ezra Studies* in *Interpretation* 26 (1972) 380–81.

66. Review of C. C. Torrey, *Pseudo Ezekiel and the Original Prophecy* in *Interpretation* 26 (1972) 380–81.

1973

67. *The Divine Warrior in Early Israel* (Harvard Semitic Monographs 5; Cambridge: Harvard University Press, 1973).

68. "Editorial," *Interpretation* 27 (1973) 348–49.

69. "God and the Gods: History of Religion as an Approach and Context for Bible and Theology," *Affirmation* 1 (1973) 37–62. [Reprinted in no. 340]

70. Review of J. W. Brown, *The Rise of Biblical Criticism in America, 1800–1870: The New England Scholars* in *Journal of Presbyterian History* 51 (1973) 87–90.

71. Review of J. Efird, ed., *The Use of the Old Testament in the New and Other Essays: Studies in Honor of William Franklin Stinespring* in *Interpretation* 27 (1973) 222–23.

72. Review of S. Kubo, *A Reader's Greek English Lexicon of the New Testament* in *Interpretation* 27 (1973) 106.

1974

73. Review of P.-E. Langevin, *Biblical Bibliography 1930–1970* in *Interpretation* 28 (1974) 248–49.

74. Review of G. von Rad, *Wisdom in Israel* in *Interpretation* 28 (1974) 110.

1975

75. *Hope That Frees and Unites*, with Mary Ann Miller (Atlanta: General Executive Board, 1975).

76. "The Blessing of God: An Interpretation of Numbers 6:22–27," *Interpretation* 29 (1975) 240–51.

77. "Luke 4:16–21," *Interpretation* 29 (1975) 417–21.

78. Review of H. Bream et al., ed., *A Light Unto My Path: Old Testament Studies in Honor of Jacob M. Myers* in *Interpretation* 29 (1975) 318–19.

79. Review of J. L. Crenshaw and J. T. Willis, ed., *Essays in Old Testament Ethics: J. Philip Hyatt, In Memoriam* in *Interpretation* 29 (1975) 452.

80. Review of G. F. Hasel, *The Remnant: The History and Theology of the Remnant Idea from Genesis to Isaiah* in *Journal of Biblical Literature* 94 (1975) 120–22.

81. Review of W. E. Müller, *Die Vorstellung vom Rest im Alten Testament* in *Journal of Biblical Literature* 94 (1975) 120–22.

1976

82. Editor of *Magnalia Dei: The Mighty Acts of God: Essays on the Bible and Archaeology in Memory of G. Ernest Wright*, with Frank Moore Cross and Werner E. Lemke (Garden City: Doubleday, 1976).

83. "Faith and Ideology in the Old Testament," in *Magnalia Dei: The Mighty Acts of God: Essays on the Bible and Archaeology in Memory of G. Ernest Wright* (ed. Frank Moore Cross, Werner E. Lemke, and Patrick D. Miller, Jr.; Garden City: Doubleday, 1976) 464–79. [Reprinted in no. 340]

84. Review of S. Herrmann, *A History of Israel in Old Testament Times* in *Interpretation* 30 (1976) 201–2.

85. Review of J. C. Trever, *Scrolls from Qumrân Cave I* in *Interpretation* 30 (1976) 321.

86. Review of H. W. Wolff, *Anthropology of the Old Testament* in *Interpretation* 30 (1976) 202–3.

1977

87. *The Hand of the Lord: A Reassessment of the "Ark Narrative" of 1 Samuel*, with J. J. M. Roberts (The Johns Hopkins Near Eastern Studies; Baltimore: The Johns Hopkins University Press, 1977).

88. "[Review Article of] *A History of Israel in Old Testament Times* by Siegfried Herrmann" *Religious Studies Review* 3 (1977) 83–89.

89. Review of R. Banks, ed., *Reconciliation and Hope: New Testament Essays on Atonement and Eschatology Presented to L. L. Morris on his 60th Birthday* in *Interpretation* 31 (1977) 216–17.

90. Review of J. L. Crenshaw, ed., *Studies in Ancient Israelite Wisdom* in *Interpretation* 31 (1977) 100.

91. Review of F. M. Cross and S. Talmon, ed., *Qumran and the History of the Biblical Text* in *Interpretation* 31 (1977) 99–100.

92. Review of G. Friedrich, ed., *Theological Dictionary of the New Testament, Vol. 10* in *Interpretation* 31 (1977) 213–14.

93. Review of P. Garelli and V. Nikiprowetzky, *Le Proche-Orient asiatique: Les empires mesopotamiens, Israel* in *Journal of Biblical Literature* 96 (1977) 275–76.

94. Review of R. Hamerton-Kelly and R. Scroggs, ed., *Jews, Greeks and Christians: Religious Cultures in Late Antiquity: Essays in Honor of William David Davies* in *Interpretation* 31 (1977) 220.

95. Review of M. Hooker and C. Hickling, ed., *What About the New Testament? Essays in Honour of Christopher Evans* in *Interpretation* 31 (1977) 216.

96. Review of R. N. Longenecker and M. C. Tenney, ed., *New Dimensions in New Testament Study* in *Interpretation* 31 (1977) 217–18.

97. Review of J. Neusner, ed., *Christianity, Judaism, and Other Greco-Roman Cults: Studies for Morton Smith at Sixty* in *Interpretation* 31 (1977) 104–5.

98. Review of J. Neusner, *Early Rabbinic Judaism: Historical Studies in Religious, Literature and Art* in *Interpretation* 31 (1977) 218–20.

99. Review of G. von Rad, *Biblical Interpretations in Preaching* in *Interpretation* 31 (1977) 211.

100. Review of G. Vermes, *Post-Biblical Jewish Studies* in *Interpretation* 31 (1977) 218.

1978

101. *Genesis 1–11: Studies in Structure & Theme* (Journal for the Study of the Old Testament: Supplement Series 8; Sheffield: University of Sheffield, 1978).

102. Review of C. Westermann, *Lob und Klagen in der Psalmen* in *Catholic Biblical Quarterly* 40 (1978) 618–20.

1979

103. "Poetic Ambiguity and Balance in Psalm XV," *Vetus Testamentum* 29 (1979) 416–24. [Reprinted in nos. 340 and 352]

104. "Psalm 130," *Interpretation* 33 (1979) 176–81.

105. "Vocative *Lamed* in the Psalter: A Reconsideration," in *Ugarit-Forschungen* 11 [*Festschrift für C. F. A. Schaeffer*] (1979) 617–37.[5]

106. "*yāpîaḥ* in Psalm xii 6," *Vetus Testamentum* 29 (1979) 495–501.

107. Review of M. D. Coogan, *Stories from Ancient Canaan* in *Religious Studies Review* 5 (1979) 59.

108. Review of J. G. Gammie et al., ed., *Israelite Wisdom: Theological and Literary Essays in Honor of Samuel Terrien* in *Interpretation* 33 (1979) 418.

---

5. The annual is dated 1979, but the copyright date is actually 1980.

109. Review of O. Keel, *The Symbolism of the Biblical World: Ancient Near Eastern Iconography and the Book of Psalms* in *Interpretation* 33 (1979) 208–10.

110. Review of J. W. Rogerson and J. W. McKay, *The Cambridge Bible Commentary on the New English Bible: Psalms 1–150* in *Journal of the American Academy of Religion* 47 (1979) 310.

1980

111. "El, the Creator of Earth," *Bulletin of the American Schools of Oriental Research* 239 (1980) 43–46. [Reprinted in no. 340]

112. "Studies in Hebrew Word Patterns," *Harvard Theological Review* 73 (1980) 79–89.

113. "Synonymous-Sequential Parallelism in the Psalms," *Biblica* 61 (1980) 256–60.

114. Review of G. I. Davies, *The Way of the Wilderness: A Geographical Study of the Wilderness Itineraries in the Old Testament* in *Interpretation* 34 (1980) 90–92.

115. Review of M. Hörig, *Dea Syria: Studien zur religiösen Tradition der Fruchtbarkeitsgöttin in Vorderasien* in *Religious Studies Review* 6 (1980) 141.

116. Review of A. R. Johnson, *The Cultic Prophet and Israel's Psalmody* in *Interpretation* 34 (1980) 198–202.

117. Review of C. E. L'Heureux, *Rank Among the Canaanite Gods: El, Ba'al, and the Repha'im* in *Religious Studies Review* 6 (1980) 227–28.

118. Review of O. Loretz, *Die Psalmen: Beitrage der Ugarit-Texte zum Verständnis von Kolometrie und Textologie der Psalmen* in *Religious Studies Review* 6 (1980) 63.

119. Review of D. McCarthy, *Treaty and Covenant: A Study in Form in the Ancient Oriental Documents and in the Old Testament* in *Journal of Biblical Literature* 99 (1980) 300–301.

120. Review of K. Seybold, *Die Wallfahrtpsalmen: Studien zur Entstehungsgeschichte von Psalm 120–134* in *Catholic Biblical Quarterly* 42 (1980) 110–11.

121. Review of S. Terrien, *The Elusive Presence: Toward a New Biblical Theology* in *Theology Today* 37 (1980) 108–11.

122. Review of D. Irvin, *Mytharion: The Comparison of Tales from the Old Testament and the Ancient Near East* in *Religious Studies Review* 6 (1980) 141.

123. Review of E. C. Ulrich, Jr., *The Qumran Text of Samuel and Josephus* in *Interpretation* 34 (1980) 309–10.

1981

124. "Ugarit and the History of Religion," *Journal of the Northwest Semitic Languages* 9 (1981) 119–28.

125. "Psalms and Inscriptions," in *Congress Volume: Vienna, 1980* (ed. J. A. Emerton; Supplements to Vetus Testamentum 32; Leiden: E. J. Brill, 1981) 311–32. [Reprinted in no. 340]

126. Review of K. Aartun, *Die Partikeln des Ugaritischen* in *Religious Studies Review* 7 (1981) 156–57.

127. Review of K. Bergerhof, M. Dietrich, and O. Loretz, ed., *Ugarit-Forschungen 11* in *Religious Studies Review* 7 (1981) 156.

128. Review of W. Dietrich, *Israel und Kanaan: Vom Ringen Zweier Gesell-schaftssysteme* in *Religious Studies Review* 7 (1981) 157.

129. Review of J. Gray, *The Biblical Doctrine of the Reign of God* in *Catholic Biblical Quarterly* 43 (1981) 619–20.

130. Review of F. O. Hvidberg-Hansen, *La Déesse TNT: Une Étude sur la Re-ligion Canaanéo-Punique* in *Religious Studies Review* 7 (1981) 157.

131. Review of M. C. Lind, *Yahweh Is a Warrior: The Theology of Warfare in Ancient Israel* in *The Biblical Archaeologist* 44 (1981) 188–89.

132. Review of B. Margalit, *A Matter of "Life" and "Death": A Study of the Baal-Mot Epic (CTA 4-5-6)* in *Religious Studies Review* 7 (1981) 65.

133. Review of W. McKane, *Studies in the Patriarchal Narratives* in *Journal of Semitic Studies* 26 (1981) 294–98.

134. Review of E. T. Mullen, *The Assembly of the Gods: The Divine Council in Canaanite and Hebrew Literature* in *Religious Studies Review* 7 (1981) 254.

1982

135. *Sin and Judgment in the Prophets: A Stylistic and Theological Analysis* (Society of Biblical Literature Monograph Series 27; Chico: Scholars Press, 1982).

136. "Psalm 127—The House that Yahweh Builds," *Journal for the Study of the Old Testament* 22 (1982) 119–32.

137. "Wellhausen and the History of Israel's Religion," *Semeia* 25 (1982) 61–73. [Reprinted in no. 340]

138. Review of A. G. Auld, *Joshua, Moses and the Land: Tetrateuch-Pentateuch-Hexateuch in a Generation since 1938* in *Interpretation* 36 (1982) 305–6.

139. Review of K. Bergerhof, M. Dietrich, and O. Loretz, ed., *Ugarit-Forschungen 8* in *Bulletin of the American Schools of Oriental Research* 245 (1982) 80.

140. Review of K. Bergerhof, M. Dietrich, and O. Loretz, ed., *Ugarit-Forschungen 12* in *Religious Studies Review* 8 (1982) 280.

141. Review of W. Beyerlin, *Werden und Wesen des 107. Psalms* in *Vetus Testamentum* 32 (1982) 253–56.

142. Review of O. Keel, ed., *Monotheismus im Alten Israel und seiner Umwelt* in *Journal of Biblical Literature* 101 (1982) 144.

143. Review of J. L. Kugel, *The Idea of Biblical Poetry: Parallelism and Its History* in *Theology Today* 39 (1982) 331–34.

144. Review of J.-M. de Tarragon, *Le culte à Ugarit: D'après les textes de la pratique en cunéiformes alphabétiques* in *Journal of Biblical Literature* 101 (1982) 595–96.

145. Review of G. D. Young, *Ugarit in Retrospect: Fifty Years of Ugarit and Ugaritic* in *Religious Studies Review* 8 (1982) 280.

1983

146. "Trouble and Woe: Interpreting the Biblical Laments," *Interpretation* 37 (1983) 32–45. [Reprinted in no. 235]

147. Review of K. Bergerhof, M. Dietrich, and O. Loretz, ed., *Ugarit-Forschungen 13* in *Religious Studies Review* 9 (1983) 171.

148. Review of P. C. Craigie, *Ugarit and the Old Testament* in *Religious Studies Review* 9 (1983) 372.

149. Review of M. O'Connor, *Hebrew Verse Structure* in *Journal of Biblical Literature* 102 (1983) 628–29.

150. Review of H. Seidl, *Auf den Spuren der Beter: Einführung in die Psalmen* in *Journal of Biblical Literature* 102 (1983) 316.

151. Review of P. Xella, *I Testi Rituali di Ugarit I: Testi* in *Religious Studies Review* 9 (1983) 171–72.

1984

152. "The Inclusive Language Lectionary," *Theology Today* 41 (1984) 26–33.

153. "Meter, Parallelism, and Tropes: The Search for Poetic Style," *Journal for the Study of the Old Testament* 28 (1984) 99–106. [Reprinted in no. 340]

154. "The Most Important Word: The Yoke of the Kingdom," *The Iliff Review* 41 (Fall 1984) 17–29.

155. "Sin and Judgment in Jeremiah 34:17–22," *Journal of Biblical Literature* 103 (1984) 611–13.

156. "Syntax and Theology in Genesis XII 3a," *Vetus Testamentum* 34 (1984) 472–76. [Reprinted in no. 340]

157. "When Will the Killing Stop," *The Presbyterian Outlook* (April 30, 1984) 5–6.

158. "Jeremiah," in *The Encyclopedia Americana* (30 vols.; Danbury: Grolier, 1984) 16:19.[6]

159. "Jeremiah, Book of," in *The Encyclopedia Americana* (30 vols.; Danbury: Grolier, 1984) 16:20–21.

---

6. This encyclopedia has been republished many times since 1984. The pagination for this and the subsequent entries from this work were confirmed against the 1995 edition.

160. "Lamentations of Jeremiah," in *The Encyclopedia Americana* (30 vols.; Danbury: Grolier, 1984) 16:691.

161. "Joel, Book of," in *The Encyclopedia Americana* (30 vols.; Danbury: Grolier, 1984) 16:100.

162. "Joshua," in *The Encyclopedia Americana* (30 vols.; Danbury: Grolier, 1984) 16:180.

163. "Joshua, Book of," in *The Encyclopedia Americana* (30 vols.; Danbury: Grolier, 1984) 16:180–81.

164. "Judges, Book of," in *The Encyclopedia Americana* (30 vols.; Danbury: Grolier, 1984) 16:206–7.

165. "Kings, Books of," in *The Encyclopedia Americana* (30 vols.; Danbury: Grolier, 1984) 16:465–66.

166. "Pentateuch," in *The Encyclopedia Americana* (30 vols.; Danbury: Grolier, 1984) 21:676.

167. Review of n.a., *Materiali Lessicale ed Epigrafici, I* in *Religious Studies Review* 10 (1984) 285.

168. Review of R. Adamiak, *Justice and History in the Old Testament: The Evolution of Divine Retribution in the Historiographies of the Wilderness Generation* in *Interpretation* 38 (1984) 310–12.

169. Review of M. L. Barré, *The God-List in the Treaty Between Hannibal and Philip V of Macedonia: A Study in Light of the Ancient Near Eastern Treaty Tradition* in *Religious Studies Review* 10 (1984) 174.

170. Review of K. Bergerhof, M. Dietrich, and O. Loretz, ed., *Ugarit-Forschungen 14* in *Religious Studies Review* 10 (1984) 66.

171. Review of W. Beyerlin, *We Are Like Dreamers: Studies in Psalm 126* in *Catholic Biblical Quarterly* 46 (1984) 108–9.

172. Review of P. Casetti, *Gibt es ein Leben vor dem Tod?: Eine Auslegung von Psalm 49* in *Journal of Biblical Literature* 103 (1984) 445–46.

173. Review of W. C. Delsman et al., ed., *Von Kanaan bis Kerala: Festschrift für Prof. Mag. Dr. Dr. J. P. M. van der Ploeg O. P. zur Vollendung des siebzigsten Lebensjahres am 4. Juli 1979: Überreicht von Kollegen, Freunden, und Schülern* in *Religious Studies Review* 10 (1984) 386.

174. Review of G. Garbini, *I Fenici: Storia e Religione* in *Religious Studies Review* 10 (1984) 285.

175. Review of M. D. Goulder, *The Psalms of the Sons of Korah* in *Interpretation* 38 (1984) 426–30.

176. Review of D. Kinet, *Ugarit: Geschichte und Kultur einer Stadt in der Umwelt des Alten Testaments* in *Religious Studies Review* 10 (1984) 390.

177. Review of H. D. Preuss, *Deuteronomium* in *Journal of Biblical Literature* 103 (1984) 272.

1985

178. Editor, *Theology Today* 42 (October 1985).

179. "Bible—Theology—Church," *Theology Today* 42 (1985) 275–79.

180. "Current Issues in Psalms Studies," *Word and World* 5 (1985) 132–43. [Reprinted in no. 212]

181. "Enthroned on the Praises of Israel: The Praise of God in Old Testament Theology," *Interpretation* 39 (1985) 5–19.

182. "Eridu, Dunnu, and Babel: A Study in Comparative Mythology," *Hebrew Annual Review* 9 (1985) 227–51. [Reprinted in nos. 277 and 340]

183. "The Human Sabbath: A Study in Deuteronomic Theology," *The Princeton Seminary Bulletin* 6 (1985) 81–97.

184. "Theses on the Gender of God," *Haelan* 6 (1985) 4–8.

185. "Israelite Religion," in *The Hebrew Bible and Its Modern Interpreters* (ed. Douglas Knight and Gene Tucker; Chico: Scholars Press and Philadelphia: Fortress, 1985) 201–37. [Reprinted in no. 340]

186. Review of Y. Aharoni, *Arad Inscriptions* in *Catholic Biblical Quarterly* 47 (1985) 503–5.

187. Review of L. C. Allen, *Psalms 101–150* in *Interpretation* 39 (1985) 83–84.

188. Review of B. W. Anderson, ed., *Creation in the Old Testament* in *Theology Today* 42 (1985) 267.

189. Review of K. Bergerhof, M. Dietrich, and O. Loretz, ed., *Ugarit-Forschungen 15* in *Religious Studies Review* 11 (1985) 280.

190. Review of P. C. Craigie, *Psalms 1–50* in *Interpretation* 39 (1985) 83–84.

191. Review of O. Loretz, *Der Prolog des Jesaja Buches (1,1–2,5): Ugaritologische und Kolometrische Studien zum Jesaja-Buch* in *Religious Studies Review* 11 (1985) 286.

192. Review of G. del Olmo Lete, *Mitos y leyendas de Canaan: Según la tradición de Ugarit* in *Religious Studies Review* 11 (1985) 280.

1986

193. *Interpreting the Psalms* (Philadelphia: Fortress, 1986). [Pp. 14–17 reprinted in no. 236]

194. "The Absence of the Goddess in Israelite Religion," *Hebrew Annual Review* 10 (1986) 239–48. [Reprinted in no. 340]

195. "Power, Justice, and Peace: An Exegesis of Psalm 72," *Faith and Mission* 4 (1986) 65–70.

196. "The Prophetic Critique of Kings," *Ex Auditu* 2 (1986) 82–95. [Reprinted in no. 340]

197. "When the Gods Meet: Psalm 82 and the Issue of Justice," *Journal for Preachers* 9 (Pentecost 1986) 2–5.

198. "Moabite Stone," in *International Standard Bible Encyclopedia* (4 vols.; ed. G. W. Bromiley; Grand Rapids: Eerdmans, 1979–1988; vol. 3 = 1986) 3:396–98.

199. "The Sovereignty of God," in *The Hermeneutical Quest: Essays in Honor of James Luther Mays on his Sixty-Fifth Birthday* (ed. D. G. Miller; Pittsburgh: Pickwick, 1986) 129–44. [Reprinted in no. 340]

200. Review of S. E. Balentine, *The Hidden God: The Hiding of the Face of God in the Old Testament* in *Journal of Biblical Literature* 105 (1986) 312–15.

201. Review of C. Stuhlmueller, *Psalms 1 (Psalms 1–72)* and *Psalms 2 (Psalms 73–150)* in *Journal of Biblical Literature* 105 (1986) 318.

202. Review of C. Westermann, *Genesis 12–36: A Commentary* in *Theology Today* 43 (1986) 303–4.

1987

203. *Pentecost 2* (Proclamation 3, Series A; ed. Elizabeth Achtemeier; Philadelphia: Fortress, 1987).

204. Editor of *Ancient Israelite Religion: Essays in Honor of Frank Moore Cross*, with Paul D. Hanson and S. Dean McBride (Philadelphia: Fortress, 1987).

205. "Aspects of the Religion of Ugarit," in *Ancient Israelite Religion: Essays in Honor of Frank Moore Cross* (ed. Patrick D. Miller, Jr., Paul D. Hanson, and S. Dean McBride; Philadelphia: Fortress, 1987) 53–66. [Reprinted in no. 340]

206. "Introduction," in *Ancient Israelite Religion: Essays in Honor of Frank Moore Cross* (ed. Patrick D. Miller, Jr., Paul D. Hanson, and S. Dean McBride (Philadelphia: Fortress, 1987) xv–xix.

207. "Cosmology and World Order in the Old Testament: The Divine Council as Cosmic-Political Symbol," *Horizons in Biblical Theology* 9 (1987) 53–78. [Reprinted in no. 340]

208. "The Glory of God and Human Glory," *The Princeton Seminary Bulletin* 8 (1987) 66–72.

209. "'Moses My Servant': The Deuteronomic Portrait of Moses," *Interpretation* 41 (1987) 245–55. [Reprinted in nos. 218 and 265]

210. "The Translation Task," *Theology Today* 43 (1987) 540–45.

211. "The Way of Torah," *The Princeton Seminary Bulletin* 8 (1987) 17–27. [Reprinted in no. 340]

212. "Current Issues in Psalms Studies," in *The Best in Theology* (ed. J. I. Packer; Carol Stream, Illinois: Christianity Today, Inc., 1987) 1:31–43. [Reprint of no. 180]

213. "Foreword," in *Inclusive Language in the Church*, by Nancy Hardesty (Atlanta: John Knox, 1987) iii–iv.

214. Review of R. Alter, *The Art of Biblical Poetry* in *Theology Today* 43 (1987) 609–10.

215. Review of E. K. Kim, *The Rapid Change of Mood in the Lament Psalms: A Matrix for the Establishment of a Psalm Theology* in *Interpretation* 41 (1987) 88–89.

1988

216. "In Praise and Thanksgiving," *Theology Today* 45 (1988) 180–88.

217. "Der Kanon in der gegenwartigen amerikanischen Diskussion," *Jahrbuch für Biblische Theologie* 3 (Zum Problem des biblischen Kanons; ed. P. D. Hanson, U. Mauser, and M. Sæbø) (1988) 217–39. [Reprinted, in English translation, in nos. 340, 348]

218. "The Many Faces of Moses: A Deuteronomic Portrait," *Bible Review* 4 (October, 1988) 30–35. [Reprint of no. 209; also reprinted in no. 265]

219. "Israel as Host to Strangers," in *Today's Immigrants and Refugees: A Christian Understanding* (Washington, D.C.: United States Catholic Conference, 1988) 1–19. [Reprinted in no. 340]

220. "Prayer and Sacrifice in Ugarit and Israel," in *Text and Context: Old Testament and Semitic Studies for F. C. Fensham* (ed. W. Classen; Journal for the Study of the Old Testament: Supplement Series 48; Sheffield: JSOT Press, 1988) 139–55. [Reprinted in no. 340]

221. Review of K. Bergerhof, M. Dietrich, and O. Loretz, ed., *Ugarit-Bibliographie 1967–1971* in *Religious Studies Review* 14 (1988) 65.

222. Review of K. Bergerhof, M. Dietrich, and O. Loretz, ed., *Ugarit-Forschungen 16* in *Religious Studies Review* 14 (1988) 65–66.

223. Review of K. Bergerhof, M. Dietrich, and O. Loretz, ed., *Ugarit-Forschungen 17* in *Religious Studies Review* 14 (1988) 66.

224. Review of A. Berlin, *The Dynamics of Biblical Parallelism* in *Journal of Biblical Literature* 107 (1988) 734–36.

225. Review of M. Metzger, *Königsthron und Gottesthron: Thronformen und Throndarstellungen in Ägypten und in Vorderen Orient im dritten und zweiten Jahrtausend vor Christus und deren Bedeutung für das Verständnis von Aussagen über der Thron im Alten Testament* in *Religious Studies Review* 14 (1988) 151.

226. Review of D. Pardee, *Les textes hippiatriques* (Ras Shamra-Ougarit 2) in *Religious Studies Review* 14 (1988) 66.

1989

227. *Beyond Fear: Peacemaking in the Psalms* (Louisville: Presbyterian Peacemaking Program, 1989).

228. "The Place of the Decalogue in the Old Testament and Its Law," *Interpretation* 43 (1989) 229–42.

229. "The Psalms as Praise and Poetry," *The Hymn* 40 (1989) 12–16.

230. "Psalms," in *The Books of the Bible* (2 vols.; ed. Bernhard W. Anderson; New York: Charles Scribner's Sons, 1989) 1:203–21.

231. Review of B. A. Levine, *Leviticus: The Traditional Hebrew Text with the New JPS Translation* in *Theology Today* 46 (1989) 356, 358.

232. Review of N. M. Sarna, *Genesis: The Traditional Hebrew Text with the New JPS Translation* in *Theology Today* 46 (1989) 356, 358.

1990

233. *Deuteronomy* (Interpretation: A Bible Commentary for Teaching and Preaching; Louisville: John Knox, 1990). [Translated into Japanese and Korean in nos. 327 and 339, respectively]

234. "Musings of a Translator," *Theology Today* 47 (1990) 233–36.

235. "Patrick D. Miller, Jr. (essay date 1983)," *Classical and Medieval Literature Criticism* 4 (1990) 430–34. [Reprint of no. 146]

236. "Patrick D. Miller, Jr. (essay date 1986)," *Classical and Medieval Literature Criticism* 4 (1990) 448–51. [Reprint of no. 193, pp. 14–17]

237. "The Psalms and Pastoral Care," *Reformed Liturgy and Music* 24 (1990) 131–35.

238. "When Christ Calls," *The Princeton Seminary Bulletin* 11 (1990) 143–48.

239. Review of H. Fisch, *Poetry with a Purpose: Biblical Poetics and Interpretation* in *Theology Today* 47 (1990) 107–9.

240. Review of C. Kloos, *Yhwh's Combat with the Sea: A Canaanite Tradition in the Religion of Ancient Israel* in *Religious Studies Review* 16 (1990) 252.

241. Review of W. A. Maier, III, *'AŠERAH: Extrabiblical Evidence* in *Religious Studies Review* 16 (1990) 250–51.

242. Review of J. C. de Moor and K. Spronk, *A Cuneiform Anthology of Religious Texts from Ugarit: Autographed Texts and Glossaries* in *Religious Studies Review* 16 (1990) 250.

243. Review of J. C. de Moor, *An Anthology of Religious Texts from Ugarit* in *Religious Studies Review* 16 (1990) 250.

244. Review of S. Olyan, *Asherah and the Cult of Yahweh in Israel* in *Religious Studies Review* 16 (1990) 251.

245. Review of M. Yon, *Le centre de la ville* (Ras Shamra-Ougarit 3) in *Religious Studies Review* 16 (1990) 250.

1991

246. Review of C. Broyles, *The Conflict of Faith and Experience in the Psalms: A Form-Critical and Theological Study* in *Catholic Biblical Quarterly* 53 (1991) 459–60.

247. Review of B. Janowski, *Rettungsgewissheit und Epiphanie des Heils: Das Motiv der Hilfe Gottes "am Morgen" im Alten Orient und im Alten Testament* in *Theologische Literaturzeitung* 116 (1991) 172–74.

248. Review of D. Pardee, *Les textes para-mythologiques de la 24ᵉ Campagne (1961)* (Ras Shamra-Ougarit 4) in *Religious Studies Review* 17 (1991) 345.

1992

249. Editor of *Old Testament Theology: Essays on Structure, Theme and Text* by Walter Brueggemann (Minneapolis: Fortress, 1992).

250. "Introduction," in *Old Testament Theology: Essays on Structure, Theme, and Text* by Walter Brueggemann (ed. Patrick D. Miller; Minneapolis: Fortress, 1992) xiii–xviii.

251. "*In Memoriam*: Hugh Thompson Kerr, 1909–1992," with Thomas G. Long, *Theology Today* 49 (1992) 147–51.

252. "Toward a Theology of Leadership: Some Clues from the Prophets," *The Asbury Theological Journal* 47 (1992) 43–50. [Reprinted in no. 340]

253. "Biblical Theology," in *A New Handbook of Christian Theology* (ed. Donald W. Musser and Joseph L. Price; Nashville: Abingdon, 1992) 63–69.

254. Review of B. C. Birch, *Let Justice Roll Down: The Old Testament, Ethics, and Christian Life* in *The Princeton Seminary Bulletin* 13 (1992) 341–42.

255. Review of M. Z. Brettler, *God Is King: Understanding an Israelite Metaphor* in *Journal of Biblical Literature* 111 (1992) 120–22.

256. Review of S.-M. Kang, *Divine War in the Old Testament and in the Ancient Near East* in *Bibliotheca Orientalis* 49 (1992) 473–76.

257. Review of W. Soll, *Psalm 119: Matrix, Form, and Setting* in *Theologische Literaturzeitung* 117 (1992) 743–45.

1993

258. "The Death and Birth of Theological Journals," *Theology Today* 50 (1993) 341–44.

259. "The Old Testament and Christian Faith," *Currents in Theology and Mission* 20 (1993) 245–52. [Reprinted in no. 340]

260. "Prayer as Persuasion: The Rhetoric and Intention of Prayer," *Word and World* 13 (1993) 356–62. [Reprinted in no. 340]

261. "What You Need to Know," *The Princeton Seminary Bulletin* 14 (1993) 236–39.

262. "The W/Right Space," *Theology Today* 50 (1993) 1–3.

263. "The Beginning of the Psalter," in *The Shape and Shaping of the Psalter* (ed. J. Clinton McCann; Journal for the Study of the Old Testament: Supplement Series 159; Sheffield: JSOT Press, 1993) 83–92. [Reprinted in no. 340]

264. "Introduction and Notes to the Psalms," in *The HarperCollins Study Bible* (ed. W. A. Meeks et al.; San Francisco: Harper Collins, 1993) 797–937.

265. "'Moses My Servant': The Deuteronomic Portrait of Moses," in *A Song of Power and the Power of Song: Essays on the Book of Deuteronomy* (ed. Duane L. Christensen; Sources for Biblical and Theological Study 3; Winona Lake: Eisenbrauns, 1993) 301–12. [Reprint of nos. 209 and 218]

266. "Things Too Wonderful: Prayers of Women in the Old Testament," in *Biblische Theologie und gesellschaftlicher Wandel: Für Norbert Lohfink S.J.* (ed. Georg Braulik, Walter Gross, and Sean McEvenue; Freiburg: Herder, 1993) 237–51.

267. Review of A. Caquot, J.-M. de Tarragon, and J.-L. Cunchillos, *Textes ougaritiques II: Textes Religieux, Rituels, Correspondance* in *Religious Studies Review* 19 (1993) 248.

268. Review of B. Margalit, *The Ugaritic Poem of Aqht: Text, Translation, Commentary* in *Religious Studies Review* 19 (1993) 248.

269. Review of M. A. Taylor, *The Old Testament in the Old Princeton School* in *The Princeton Seminary Bulletin* 14 (1993) 288–90.

270. Review of M. Weinfeld, *Deuteronomy 1–11: A New Translation with Introduction and Commentary* in *Catholic Biblical Quarterly* 55 (1993) 787–89.

1994

271. *They Cried to the Lord: The Form and Theology of Biblical Prayer* (Minneapolis: Fortress, 1994).

272. Editor of *A Social Reading of the Old Testament: Prophetic Approaches to Israel's Communal Life* by Walter Brueggemann (Minneapolis: Fortress, 1994).

273. "Introduction," in *A Social Reading of the Old Testament: Prophetic Approaches to Israel's Communal Life* by Walter Bruggemann (ed. Patrick D. Miller; Minneapolis: Fortress, 1994) 1–9.

274. "Dietrich Bonhoeffer and the Psalms," *The Princeton Seminary Bulletin* 15 (1994) 274–82. [Reprinted in no. 340]

275. "Imagining God," *Theology Today* 51 (1994) 341–44.

276. "Whatever Happened to the Soul?," *Theology Today* 50 (1994) 507–10.

277. "Eridu, Dunnu, and Babel: A Study in Comparative Mythology," in *"I Studied Inscriptions from before the Flood": Ancient Near Eastern, Literary, and Linguistic Approaches to Genesis 1–11* (ed. Richard S. Hess and David Toshio Tsumura; Sources for Biblical and Theological Study 4; Winona Lake: Eisenbrauns, 1994) 143–68. [Reprint of no. 182; also reprinted in no. 340]

278. "Kingship, Torah Obedience, and Prayer: The Theology of Psalms 15–24," in *Neue Wege der Psalmenforschung: Festschrift für W. Beyerlin zum 65. Geburtstag* (ed. Klaus Seybold and Erich Zenger; Herders Biblische Studien 1; Freiburg: Herder, 1994) 127–42. [Reprinted in no. 340]

279. "The Theological Significance of Biblical Poetry," in *Language, Theology, and the Bible: Essays in Honor of James Barr* (ed. John Barton and Samuel E. Balentine; Oxford: Oxford University Press, 1994) 213–30. [Reprinted in no. 340]

280. Review of H. C. Brichto, *Toward a Grammar of Biblical Poetics: Tales of the Prophets* in *Interpretation* 48 (1994) 194–95.

281. Review of Toni Craven, *The Book of Psalms*, in *Catholic Biblical Quarterly* 56 (1994) 327–28.

282. Review of Othmar Keel and Christoph Uehlinger, *Göttinnen, Götter und Gottessymbole: Neue Erkenntnisse zur Religionsgeschichte Kanaans und Israels Aufgrund bislang unerschlossener ikonographischer Quellen* in *Journal of Biblical Literature* 113 (1994) 503–5.

1995

283. Editor of *The Psalms and the Life of Faith* by Walter Brueggemann (Minneapolis, Fortress, 1995).

284. "Introduction," in *The Psalms and the Life of Faith* by Walter Brueggemann (ed. Patrick D. Miller; Minneapolis: Fortress, 1995) xi–xviii.

285. "Can Two Walk Together Without an Appointment?," *Theology Today* 52 (1995) 169–72.

286. "Much Ado about the Bible: A Review of *The Anchor Bible Dictionary*," *Hebrew Studies* 36 (1995) 101–9.

287. "Poetry and Theology," *Theology Today* 52 (1995) 309–12.

288. "Psalm 136:1–9, 23–26," *Interpretation* 49 (1995) 390–93.

289. "A Theocentric Theologian of Hope: J. Christiaan Beker as Biblical Theologian," *The Princeton Seminary Bulletin* 16 (1995) 22–35.

290. "Creation and Covenant," in *Biblical Theology: Problems and Perspectives: In Honor of J. Christiaan Beker* (ed. Steven J. Kraftchick, Charles D. Myers, Jr., and Ben C. Ollenburger; Nashville: Abingdon, 1995) 155–68. [Reprinted in no. 340]

291. "Elyon," with Eric E. Elnes, in *Dictionary of Deities and Demons in the Bible* (ed. K. van der Toorn, B. Becking, and P. W. van der Horst; Leiden: E. J. Brill, 1995) cols. 560–71. [Reprinted in no. 334]

292. "Olden Gods," with Eric E. Elnes, in *Dictionary of Deities and Demons in the Bible* (ed. K. van der Toorn, B. Becking, and P. W. van der Horst; Leiden: E. J. Brill, 1995) cols. 1209–18. [Reprinted in no. 335]

293. "The World and Message of the Prophets: Biblical Prophecy in Its Context," in *Old Testament Interpretation: Past, Present, and Future: Essays in Honor of Gene M. Tucker* (ed. James L. Mays, David L. Petersen, and Kent H. Richards; Nashville: Abingdon, 1995) 97–112. [Reprinted in no. 340]

294. Review of N. M. Sarna, *Songs of the Heart: An Introduction to the Book of Psalms* in *Journal of Religion* 75 (1995) 257–59.

295. Review of J. L. Thompson, *John Calvin and the Daughters of Sarah: Women in Regular and Exceptional Roles in the Exegesis of Calvin, his Predecessors, and his Contemporaries* in *The Princeton Seminary Bulletin* 16 (1995) 90–92.

296. Review of J. W. H. Van Wijk-Bos, *Reimagining God: The Case for Scriptural Diversity* in *The Presbyterian Outlook* 177 (1995) 10–11.

1996

297. "Hallelujah! The Lord God Omnipotent Reigns," *Theology Today* 53 (1996) 1–4.

298. "Precious in the Sight of the Lord," *Journal for Preachers* 19 (1996) 28–31.

299. "Psalm 73 as a Canonical Marker," with Walter Brueggemann, *Journal for the Study of the Old Testament* 72 (1996) 45–56. [Reprinted in no. 340]

300. "Remembering Our Theological Past," *Theology Today* 53 (1996) 285–88.

301. "Teaching the Faith," *Theology Today* 53 (1996) 143–47.

302. "Whither the Church?," *Theology Today* 52 (1996) 445–48.

303. "What the Scriptures Principally Teach," in *Homosexuality and Christian Community* (ed. Choon-Leong Seow; Louisville: Westminster John Knox, 1996) 53–63.

304. Review of Y. Avishur, *Studies in Hebrew and Ugaritic Psalms* in *Catholic Biblical Quarterly* 58 (1996) 698–700.

305. Review of F. E. Greenspahn, *When Brothers Dwell Together: The Preeminence of Younger Siblings in the Hebrew Bible* in *The Princeton Seminary Bulletin* 17 (1996) 93–95.

306. Review of J. G. Taylor, *Yahweh and the Sun: Biblical and Archaeological Evidence for Sun Worship in Ancient Israel* in *Toronto Journal of Theology* 12 (1996) 90–92.

307. Review of M. Weinfeld, *Social Justice in Ancient Israel and in the Ancient Near East* in *Theology Today* 53 (1996) 136.

1997

308. "Life, Death, and the Hale-Bopp Comet," *Theology Today* 54 (1997) 147–49.
309. "Popularizing the Bible," *Theology Today* 53 (1997) 435–38.
310. "Revisiting the God Who Acts," *Theology Today* 54 (1997) 1–5.
311. "A Strange Kind of Monotheism," *Theology Today* 54 (1997) 293–97.
312. "The Wilderness Journey in Deuteronomy: Style, Structure, and Theology in Deuteronomy 1–3," *Covenant Quarterly* 55 (May–August 1997) 50–68. [= no. 315 and reprinted in no. 340]
313. "Closing Remarks: An Oral Response Presented to the Plenary Attending the 1994 Conference," in *Power, Powerlessness, and the Divine: New Inquiries in Bible and Theology* (ed. C. Rigby; Atlanta: Scholars Press, 1997) 291–301.
314. "Imagining God," in *Women, Gender, and Christian Community* (ed. Jane Dempsey Douglass and James F. Kay; Louisville: Westminster John Knox, 1997) 3–12.
315. "The Wilderness Journey in Deuteronomy: Style, Structure, and Theology in Deuteronomy 1–3," in *To Hear and Obey: Essays in Honor of Fredrick Carlson Holmgren* (ed. Paul Koptak and Bradley J. Bergfalk; Chicago: Covenant Publications, 1997) 50–68. [= no. 312 and reprinted in no. 340]
316. Review of M. R. Hauge, *Between Sheol and Temple: Motif Structure and Function in the I-Psalms* in *Theologische Literaturzeitung* 122 (1997) cols. 243–45.
317. Review of M. Millard, *Die Komposition des Psalters: Ein formgeschichtlicher Ansatz* in *Journal of Biblical Literature* 116 (1997) 539–41.

1998

318. "A is for Augustine, Aquinas . . . ," *Theology Today* 55 (1998) 1–4.
319. "The End of the Psalter: A Response to Erich Zenger," *Journal for the Study of the Old Testament* 80 (1998) 103–10. [Reprinted in no. 340]
320. "Good-bye Seinfeld," *Theology Today* 55 (1998) 147–51.
321. "Preaching Repentance in a Narcissistic Age: Psalm 51," *Journal for Preachers* 21 (1998) 3–8.
322. "Theology and Science in Conversation," *Theology Today* 55 (1998) 301–4.
323. "Böse, das, II. Altes Testament," in *Religion in Geschichte und Gegenwart* (4th ed.; ed. H. D. Betz et al.; Tübingen: J. C. B. Mohr [Paul Siebeck], 1998) 1:cols. 1704–5.
324. "Prayer and Divine Action," in *God in the Fray: A Tribute to Walter Brueggemann* (ed. Tod Linafelt and Timothy K. Beal; Minneapolis: Fortress, 1998) 211–32. [Reprinted in no. 340]

325. Review of J. T. Bretzke, *Bibliography on Scripture and Christian Ethics* in *Theology Today* 55 (1998) 486–87.
326. Review of T. Veijola, ed., *Das Deuteronomium und seine Querbeziehungen* in *Catholic Biblical Quarterly* 60 (1998) 190–91.

1999

327. [*Deuteronomy*] (1999; Japanese translation of no. 233).
328. Editor of *The Covenanted Self: Explorations in Law and Covenant* by Walter Brueggemann (Minneapolis, Fortress, 1999).
329. "Editor's Foreword," in *The Covenanted Self: Explorations in Law and Covenant* by Walter Brueggemann (ed. Patrick D. Miller; Minneapolis: Fortress, 1999) vii–viii.
330. "The Church's First Theologian," *Theology Today* 56 (1999) 293–96.
331. "Deuteronomy and Psalms: Evoking a Biblical Conversation," *Journal of Biblical Literature* 118 (1999) 3–18. [Reprinted in no. 340]
332. "The Millennium Bug," *Theology Today* 55 (1999) 491–95.
333. "The State of the World," *Theology Today* 56 (1999) 147–51.
334. "Elyon," with Eric E. Elnes, in *Dictionary of Deities and Demons in the Bible* (2d rev. ed.; ed. Karel van der Toorn, Bob Becking, and Pieter W. van der Horst; Leiden: E. J. Brill and Grand Rapids: Eerdmans, 1999) 293–99. [Reprint of no. 291]
335. "Olden Gods," with Eric E. Elnes, in *Dictionary of Deities and Demons in the Bible* (2d rev. ed.; ed. Karel van der Toorn, Bob Becking, and Pieter W. van der Horst; Leiden: E. J. Brill and Grand Rapids: Eerdmans, 1999) 641–45. [Reprint of no. 292]
336. "God's Other Stories: On the Margins of Deuteronomic Theology," in *Realia Dei: Essays in Archaeology and Biblical Interpretation in Honor of Edward F. Campbell, Jr. at his Retirement* (ed. Prescott Williams Jr. and Theodore Hiebert; Atlanta: Scholars Press, 1999) 185–94. [Reprinted in no. 340]
337. Review of E. Jenni and C. Westermann, ed., *Theological Lexicon of the Old Testament* in *Theology Today* 56 (1999) 290.
338. Review of E. Nielsen, *Deuteronomium* in *Journal of Biblical Literature* 118 (1999) 342–44.

2000

339. [*Deuteronomy*] (2000; Korean translation of no. 233).
340. *Israelite Religion and Biblical Theology: Collected Essays* (Journal for the Study of the Old Testament: Supplement Series 267; Sheffield: Sheffield Academic Press, 2000). [Reprints of nos. 4, 5, 14, 21, 36, 50, 69, 83, 103 (= 352), 111, 125, 137, 153, 156, 182 (= 277), 185, 194, 196, 199, 205, 207, 211, 217 (= 348 [in English translation]), 219, 220, 252, 259, 260, 263,

274, 277 (= 182), 278, 279, 290, 293, 299, 312 (= 315), 315 (= 312), 319, 324, 331, 336, 348 (= [English translation of] 217), 351, 352 (= 103)][7]

341. *The Religion of Ancient Israel* (Library of Ancient Israel; Louisville: Westminster John Knox, 2000).

342. Editor of *Deep Memory, Exuberant Hope: Contested Truth in a Post-Christian World* by Walter Brueggemann (Minneapolis, Fortress, 2000).

343. "Editor's Foreword," in *Deep Memory, Exuberant Hope: Contested Truth in a Post-Christian World* by Walter Brueggemann (ed. Patrick D. Miller; Minneapolis: Fortress, 2000) vii–x.

344. Editor of *Texts That Linger, Words That Explode: Listening to Prophetic Voices* by Walter Brueggemann (Minneapolis: Fortress, 2000).

345. "Editor's Foreword," in *Texts That Linger, Words That Explode: Listening to Prophetic Voices* by Walter Brueggemann (ed. Patrick D. Miller; Minneapolis: Fortress, 2000) vii–ix.

346. "*http://theologytoday.ptsem.edu*," *Theology Today* 57 (2000) 1–4.

347. ". . . who hast made of one genome . . . ," *Theology Today* 57 (2000) 291–96.

348. "The Canon in Contemporary American Discussion," in *Israelite Religion and Biblical Theology: Collected Essays* (Journal for the Study of the Old Testament: Supplement Series 267; Sheffield: Sheffield Academic Press, 2000) 603–28. [Reprint, in English translation, of no. 217; see no. 340]

349. "The Hermeneutics of Imprecation," in *Theology in the Service of the Church: Essays in Honor of Thomas W. Gillespie* (ed. Wallace M. Alston, Jr.; Grand Rapids, Eerdmans, 2000) 153–63.

350. "Introduction: Reading the Bible with 'the End' in View," with Donald H. Juel, in *The End of the World and the Ends of God: Science and Theology on Eschatology* (ed. John Polkinghorne and Michael Welker; Harrisburg: Trinity Press International, 2000) 141–42.

351. "Judgment and Joy," in *The End of the World and the Ends of God: Science and Theology on Eschatology* (ed. John Polkinghorne and Michael Welker; Harrisburg: Trinity Press International, 2000) 155–70. [Reprinted in no. 340]

352. "Poetic Ambiguity and Balance in Psalm XV," in *Poetry in the Bible: Selected Studies from Vetus Testamentum* (ed. David Norton; Brill's Readers in Biblical Studies 6; Leiden: Brill, 2000) 139–47. [Reprint of no. 103; also reprinted in no. 340]

---

7. Note the Preface (pp. 7–11, esp. 7 n. 1) for the revisions (bibliographical, typographical, and otherwise) that accompany the reprints contained in this volume.

353. "The Poetry of Creation: Psalm 104," in *God Who Creates: Essays in Honor of W. Sibley Towner* (ed. William P. Brown and S. Dean McBride, Jr.; Grand Rapids: Eerdmans, 2000) 87–103.

354. Review of T. B. Dozemann, *God at War: A Study of Power in the Exodus Tradition* in *Journal of Biblical Literature* 119 (2000) 114–16.

355. Review of P. W. Flint, *The Dead Sea Psalms Scrolls and the Book of Psalms* in *The Catholic Biblical Quarterly* 62 (2000) 118–20.

356. Review of K. Seybold, *Die Psalmen* in *The Catholic Biblical Quarterly* 62 (2000) 337–39.

2001

357. "The Book of Jeremiah: Introduction, Commentary, and Reflections," in *The New Interpreter's Bible* (ed. Leander Keck; 12 vols.; Nashville: Abingdon, 1994–; vol. 6 = 2001) 6:553–926.

358. "Prayer and Worship," *Calvin Theological Journal* 36 (2001) 53–62.

359. "The Prophets' Sons and Daughters," *The Princeton Seminary Bulletin* 22 (2001) 279–84.

360. "What Sense Do We Make of the Ending?" *Theology Today* 52 (2001) 140–43.

361. Review of S. E. Balentine, *The Torah's Vision of Worship* in *The Princeton Seminary Bulletin* 22 (2001) 372–74.

In Press

362. "Preaching the Ten Commandments," *Journal for Preachers*.

363. "Terror All Around," *Theology Today*.

364. "Constitution or Instruction?: The Purpose of Deuteronomy."

365. "The Economics of the Straying Ox: Property and Possession in Light of the Commandments."

366. "The Good Neighborhood: Identity and Community through the Commandments."

367. "The Psalter as a Book of Theology."

368. "The Ruler in Zion and the Hope of the Poor: Psalms 9–10 in the Context of the Psalter."

369. "'Slow to Anger': The God of the Prophets."

370. "Theology from Below: The Theological Interpretation of Scripture."

371. Review of D. E. Callender, Jr., *Adam in Myth and History: Ancient Israelite Perspectives on the Primal Human* in *Journal of Near Eastern Studies*.

372. Review of N. Lohfink and E. Zenger, *The God of Israel and the Nations: Studies in Isaiah and the Psalms* in *Journal of Biblical Literature*.

Index of Authors

Index of Scripture

All Scripture references are indexed according to the versification found in English Bibles.

Old Testament

New Testament